THE
EXECUTIVE
IN
ACTION

BOOKS BY PETER F. DRUCKER

MANAGEMENT

Managing the Non-Profit Organization
Innovation and Entrepreneurship
Managing in Turbulent Times
Management: Tasks, Responsibilities, Practices
The Effective Executive
Managing for Results
The Practice of Management
Concept of the Corporation

ECONOMICS, POLITICS, SOCIETY

Post-Capitalist Society
The New Realities
The Unseen Revolution
The Age of Discontinuity
Landmarks of Tomorrow
America's Next Twenty Years
The New Society
The Future of Industrial Man
The End of Economic Man

FICTION

The Temptation to Do Good
The Last of All Possible Worlds

AUTOBIOGRAPHY

Adventures of a Bystander

THE
EXECUTIVE
IN
ACTION

MANAGING FOR RESULTS
INNOVATION AND ENTREPRENEURSHIP
THE EFFECTIVE EXECUTIVE

Three Books on Management by

PETER F. DRUCKER

HarperBusiness
A Division of HarperCollins*Publishers*

Managing for Results:
Copyright © 1964, 1986 by Peter F. Drucker

Innovation and Entrepreneurship:
Copyright © 1985 by Peter F. Drucker

The Effective Executive:
Copyright © 1966, 1967, 1985, by Peter F. Drucker

HarperCollins books may be purchased for educational, business, or sales promotional use. For information please write: Special Markets Department, HarperCollins Publishers, Inc., 10 East 53rd Street, New York, NY 10022.

FIRST EDITION

Library of Congress Cataloging-in-Publication Data

Drucker, Peter Ferdinand, 1909–
    [Selections.   1996]
    The Executive in action : 3 classic works on management / by Peter F. Drucker.
       p. cm.
    Includes index.
    Contents: Managing for results—The effective executive—Innovation and entrepreneurship.
    ISBN 0-88730-828-7
    1. Industrial management. 2. Small business—Management. 3. Executive ability. 4. Creative ability in business. I. Title.
    HD31.D76825   1996
    658—dc20   96-6380

06 07 08 09 RRD 20 19 18 17 16 15 14 13 12

CONTENTS

PREFACE

There are many "How-to-Do-It" management books; few, however, tell the executive what to do, let alone why. There are equally a great many "What-to-Do" management books; but few of them tell the executive how to do it. Yet treatment without diagnosis is as useless as diagnosis without treatment. In any practice the two go together—and *Management is a Practice.*

The three books of mine, here brought together in one volume, embrace the three dimensions of the successful practice of management:

Managing the Existing Business—*Managing for Results*

Changing Tomorrow's Business—*Innovation and Entrepreneurship*

Managing Oneself—*The Effective Executive*

Each of these three books is distinct and self-contained. Yet in the executive's work the three are always joined. Managing the Existing Business is the first day-to-day task no matter how clear the executive's vision; no matter how brilliantly he or she plans for the future and innovates, today's business has to be managed for results now or there will be no tomorrow. What knowledge is needed for that job? What actions have to be taken? What pitfalls to be avoided? *And what results should—perhaps must—be attained?*

Conversely, the seemingly most successful business of today is a sham and a failure if it does not create its own and different tomorrow. It must innovate and re-create its products or services but equally the enterprise itself. Business is society's change agent. All other major institutions of society are designed to *conserve* if not to prevent change. *Business alone is designed to innovate.* No business will long survive, let alone prosper, unless it innovates successfully. And neither innovation nor entrepreneurship are "inspiration," let alone "flash of genius." They are disciplines and require concepts, tools, and organized, systematic work.

Finally, no matter how brilliant individual executives are or how hard they work, they will be failures and their efforts will be futile unless they are *effective*. It is not so terribly difficult to be an effective executive. All it requires are a few *habits*—that is, doing a few things day in and day out and not doing a few other things. Yet few of the many executives with whom I have worked over more than fifty years were truly effective. They were mostly very bright, worked mostly very hard, yet had little to show for their ability, their knowledge, their hard work. The reason is simply that the modern organization—and with it executives in significant numbers—only emerged a little over a century ago and the human race is a slow learner.

To be sure, there have been "naturals" throughout human history. The most effective executive on record of whom we have any information was surely that minister of an ancient Egyptian pharaoh who, all of 4250 years ago, conceived the first pyramid (without any precedent whatever for such an edifice) designed it and built it—and it still stands today without once having to be "re-engineered." And he did so without any management books to help him and surely without having an MBA. But we need far too many effective executives to depend on geniuses. And then there is need for a discipline—the discipline for being an effective executive.

Together these three books should enable executives—whether high up in the organization or just beginning on their career—but also those men and women who are studying today to become executives tomorrow:

> —to know the right things to do;
>
> —to know how to do them; and
>
> —to do them effectively.

Together these three books provide *The Tool Kit for Executive Action.*

Claremont, Easter 1996   Peter F. Drucker

MANAGING FOR RESULTS

Economic Tasks and
Risk-taking Decisions

Contents

PART III:
A PROGRAM FOR PERFORMANCE

Preface

Managing for Results was the first book to address itself to what is now called "business strategy." It is still the most widely used book on the subject. When I wrote it, more than twenty years ago, my original title was, in fact, *Business Strategies*. But "strategy" in those days was not a term in common usage. Indeed, when my publisher and I tested the title with acquaintances who were business executives, consultants, management teachers, and booksellers, we were strongly advised to drop it. "Strategy," we were told again and again, "belongs to military or perhaps to political campaigns but not to business."

By now, of course, "business strategy" has become an "in" term. Yet in retrospect I am glad we changed the title. To be sure, *Managing for Results* may be less "sexy." But it is far more descriptive of what this book tries to do. Above all, it expresses the book's premise: businesses exist to produce results on the outside, in the market and the economy. On the inside there are only costs. Indeed, what are commonly called "profit centers" are as a rule really "cost centers." *Managing for Results* therefore begins with an analysis of what the book calls "business realities"—the fundamentals and constants of the outside environment, the things the business executive has to consider as "givens," as constraints, as challenges. And it proceeds to discuss how a business positions itself in respect to these "realities" to convert them into opportunities for performance and results.

This explains, I believe, why this book, after twenty years, is still far more comprehensive than books on "strategy" alone. It pioneered practically everything to be found in these books: the analysis of markets and products (it contains the first classification of products—"today's breadwinner," for instance); the organized abandonment of the old, the obsolete, the no-longer productive; the rewards for leadership; and the objectives of innovation. But it also—and in this it still stands alone—showed how to analyze the environment and how to position a business in it. It was the first—and by and large it still is the only—book to try to balance managing today's business with making the business of tomorrow. And it concludes by linking business as an economic institution measured by economic results and business as a human organization. The last chapter deals with building performance into the organization. The book thus was the first to attempt an organized presentation of the economic tasks of the business executive managing a business organization.

Above all, as the introduction states, this book took the first step toward a *discipline* of economic performance in business enterprise. Never has such a discipline been needed more than it is today, when the economic, social, technological, and political environments in which businesses live and operate are changing faster than ever before, and when every business therefore needs to ask the questions which this book raises and answers: What are the realities of *this* business? What are its result areas? How are we doing? and What is this business and what should it be?

Claremont, California
Thanksgiving Day, 1985

Acknowledgment

This book owes much to the editorial assistance given by my wife, Doris, and by my friend, Hermine Popper. Each read the manuscript several times and at several stages—for sense and sequence as well as for style, diction, and sentence structure. Their sensitivity to a misplaced thought and their intolerance of a misplaced word are in large measure responsible for whatever clarity, conceptual or textual, this book possesses. I am all the more grateful for their help as both interrupted urgent and important work of their own to read and edit *Managing for Results*.

New Year's Day 1964   PETER F. DRUCKER
Montclair, New Jersey

Introduction:
The Task

This is a "what to do" book. It deals with the economic tasks that any business has to discharge for economic performance and economic results. It attempts to organize these tasks so that executives can perform them systematically, purposefully, with understanding, and with reasonable probability of accomplishment. It tries to develop a point of view, concepts and approaches for finding what should be done and how to go about doing it.

This book draws on practical experience as a consultant to businesses of all kinds and sizes for a good many years. Everything in it has been tested and is being used today effectively in real businesses. There are illustrations of, and references to, concrete situations on almost every page—drawn mostly from the United States (simply because most of my experience has been here) but also from Europe, Japan, and Latin America.*

Though practical rather than theoretical, the book has a thesis. Economic performance, it asserts, is the specific function and contribution of business enterprise, and the reason for its existence. It is work to obtain economic performance and results. And work, to yield results, has to be thought through and done

* Wherever a company is mentioned by name the illustration is taken from published material, primarily company statements. Where no company name appears the example comes out of my own practice or observation and has been carefully disguised as to kind of business, size, location, products, and so on.

with direction, method, and purpose. There is however, so far, no discipline of economic performance, no organization of our knowledge, no systematic analysis, no purposeful approach. Even the sorting out and classification of the tasks have yet to be done. The foundation for systematic, purposeful performance of the specific task and function of business enterprise is thus still missing.

There are a good many successful businesses and effective executives—as there are many with at best mediocre results. One searches in vain, however, for an analysis that identifies what the successful are doing to give them results. Nowhere is there a description even of the economic tasks that confront a business, let alone how one goes about tackling them. To every executive's desk come dozens of problems every morning, all clamoring for his attention. But there is little to tell him which are important and which merely noisy.

This book lays little claim to originality or profundity. But it is, to my knowledge, the first attempt at an organized presentation of the economic tasks of the business executive and the first halting step toward a discipline of economic performance in business enterprise.

II

The book is divided into three parts. The first—and longest—stresses analysis and understanding. Chapter 1 deals with the "Business Realities"—the situation most likely to be found in any business at any given time. The next three chapters (chapters 2, 3, 4) develop the analysis of the result areas of the entire business and relate them to resources and efforts on the one hand and to opportunities and expectations on the other. Chapter 5 projects a similar analysis on the cost stream and cost structure—both of the individual business and of the economic process of which it is part.

Chapters 6 and 7 deal with the understanding of a business from the "outside" where both the results and the resources are. These chapters ask, "What do we get paid for?" and "What do we earn our keep with?" In Chapter 8 all analyses are pulled together into an understanding of the existing business, its fundamental economic characteristics, its performance capacity, its opportunities, and its needs.

Part II focuses on opportunities and leads to decisions. It discusses the opportunities and needs in each of the major economic dimensions of a business: making the present business effective (Chapter 9); finding and realizing business potential (Chapter 10); making the future of the business today (Chapter 11).

The last—and shortest—part presents the conversion of insights and decisions into purposeful performance. This requires that key decisions be made regarding the idea and objectives of the business, the excellences it needs, and the priorities on which it will concentrate (Chapter 12). It requires a number of strategic choices: what opportunities to pursue and what risks to assume; how to specialize and how to diversify; whether to build or to acquire; and what organization is most appropriate to the economics of the business and to its opportunities (Chapter 13). Chapter 14 finally embeds the entrepreneurial decisions for performance in the managerial structure of the organization—in work, in business practices, and in the spirit of the organization and its decisions on people.

The Conclusion projects the book and its thesis on the individual executive and his commitment—and especially on the commitment of top management.

Any first attempt at converting folklore into knowledge, and a guessing game into a discipline, is liable to be misread as a downgrading of individual ability and its replacement by a rule book. Any such attempt would be nonsense, of course. No book will ever make a wise man out of a donkey or a genius out of an incompetent. The foundation in a discipline, however, gives to today's competent physician a capacity to perform well beyond that of the ablest doctor of a century ago, and enables the outstanding physician of today to do what the medical genius of yesterday could hardly have dreamt of. No discipline can lengthen a man's arm. But it can lengthen his reach by hoisting him on the shoulders of his predecessors. Knowledge organized in a discipline does a good deal for the merely competent; it endows him with some effectivenes. It does infinitely more for the truly able; it endows him with excellence.

Executives have the economic job anyhow. Most work at it hard—too hard in many cases. This book poses no additional work. On the contrary, it aims to help them do their job with less effort and in less time, and yet with greater impact. It does not tell them how to do things right. It attempts to help them find the right things to do.

PART I

UNDERSTANDING

THE BUSINESS

1 Business Realities

That executives give neither sufficient time nor sufficient thought to the future is a universal complaint. Every executive voices it when he talks about his own working day and when he talks or writes to his associates. It is a recurrent theme in the articles and in the books on management.

It is a valid complaint. Executives should spend more time and thought on the future of their business. They also should spend more time and thought on a good many other things, their social and community responsibilities for instance. Both they and their businesses pay a stiff penalty for these neglects. And yet, to complain that executives spend so little time on the work of tomorrow is futile. The neglect of the future is only a symptom; the executive slights tomorrow because he cannot get ahead of today. That too is a symptom. The real disease is the absence of any foundation of knowledge and system for tackling the economic tasks in business.

Today's job takes all the executive's time, as a rule; yet it is seldom done well. Few managers are greatly impressed with their own performance in the immediate tasks. They feel themselves caught in a "rat race," and managed by whatever the mailboy dumps into their "in" tray. They know that crash programs which attempt to "solve" this or that particular "urgent" problem rarely achieve right and lasting results. And yet, they rush from one crash program to the next. Worse still, they known that the same problems recur again and again, no matter how many times they are "solved."

Before an executive can think of tackling the future, he must be able therefore to dispose of the challenges of today in less time and with greater impact and permanence. For this he needs a systematic approach to today's job.

There are three different dimensions to the economic task: (1) The present business must be made effective; (2) its potential must be identified and realized; (3) it must be made into a different business for a different future. Each task requires a distinct approach. Each asks different questions. Each comes out with different conclusions. Yet they are inseparable. All three have to be done at the same time: today. All three have to be carried out with the same organization, the same resources of men, knowledge, and money, and in the same entrepreneurial process. The future is not going to be made tomorrow; it is being made today, and largely by the decisions and actions taken with respect to the tasks of today. Conversely, what is being done to bring about the future directly affects the present. The tasks overlap. They require one unified strategy. Otherwise, they cannot really get done at all.

To tackle any one of these jobs, let alone all three together, requires an understanding of the true realities of the business as an economic system, of its capacity for economic performance, and of the relationship between available resources and possible results. Otherwise, there is no alternative to the "rat race." This understanding never comes ready-made; it has to be developed separately for each business. Yet the assumptions and expectations that underlie it are largely common. Businesses are different, but business is much the same, regardless of size and structure, of products, technology and markets, of culture and managerial competence. There is a common business reality.

There are actually two sets of generalizations that apply to most businesses most of the time: one with respect to the results and resources of a business, one with respect to its efforts. Together they lead to a number of conclusions regarding the nature and direction of the entrepreneurial job.

Most of these assumptions will sound plausible, perhaps even familiar, to most businessmen, but few businessmen ever pull them together into a coherent whole. Few draw action conclusions from them, no matter how much each individual statement agrees with their experience and knowledge. As a result, few executives base their actions on these, their own assumptions and expectations.

1. *Neither results nor resources exist inside the business. Both exist outside.* There are no profit centers within the business; there are only cost centers. The only thing one can say with certainty about any business activity, whether engineering or selling, manufacturing or accounting, is that it consumes efforts and thereby incurs costs. Whether it contributes to results remains to be seen.

Results depend not on anybody within the business nor on anything within the control of the business. They depend on somebody outside—the customer in a market economy, the political authorities in a controlled economy. It is always somebody outside who decides whether the efforts of a business become economic results or whether they become so much waste and scrap.

The same is true of the one and only distinct resource of any business: knowledge. Other resources, money or physical equipment, for instance, do not confer any distinction. What does make a business distinct and what is its peculiar resource is its ability to use knowledge of all kinds—from scientific and technical knowledge to social, economic, and managerial knowledge. It is only in respect to knowledge that a business can be distinct, can therefore produce something that has a value in the market place.

Yet knowledge is not a business resource. It is a universal social resource. It cannot be kept a secret for any length of time. "What one man has done, another man can always do again" is old and profound wisdom. The one decisive resource of business, therefore, is as much outside of the business as are business results.

Indeed, business can be defined as a process that converts an outside resource, namely knowledge, into outside results, namely economic values.

2. *Results are obtained by exploiting opportunities, not by solving problems.* All one can hope to get by solving a problem is to restore normality. All one can hope, at best, is to eliminate

a restriction on the capacity of the business to obtain results. The results themselves must come from the exploitation of opportunities.

3. *Resources, to produce results, must be allocated to opportunities* rather than to problems. Needless to say, one cannot shrug off all problems, but they can and should be minimized.

Economists talk a great deal about the maximization of profit in business. This, as countless critics have pointed out, is so vague a concept as to be meaningless. But "maximization of opportunities" is a meaningful, indeed a precise, definition of the entrepreneurial job. It implies that effectiveness rather than efficiency is essential in business. The pertinent question is not how to do things right but how to find the right things to do, and to concentrate resources and efforts on them.

4. *Economic results are earned only by leadership,* not by mere competence. Profits are the rewards for making a unique, or at least a distinct, contribution in a meaningful area; and what is meaningful is decided by market and customer. Profit can only be earned by providing something the market accepts as value and is willing to pay for as such. And value always implies the differentiation of leadership. The genuine monopoly, which is as mythical a beast as the unicorn (save for politically enforced, that is, governmental monopolies), is the one exception.

This does not mean that a business has to be the giant of its industry nor that it has to be first in every single product line, market, or technology in which it is engaged. To be big is not identical with leadership. In many industries the largest company is by no means the most profitable one, since it has to carry product lines, supply markets, or apply technologies where it cannot do a distinct, let alone a unique job. The second spot, or even the third spot is often preferable, for it may make possible that concentration on one segment of the market, on one class of customer, on one application of the technology, in which genuine leadership often lies. In fact, the belief of so many companies that they could—or should—have leadership in everything within their market or industry is a major obstacle to achieving it.

But a company which wants economic results has to have

leadership in *something* of real value to a customer or market. It may be in one narrow but important aspect of the product line, it may be in its service, it may be in its distribution, or it may be in its ability to convert ideas into salable products on the market speedily and at low cost.

Unless it has such leadership position, a business, a product, a service, becomes marginal. It may seem to be a leader, may supply a large share of the market, may have the full weight of momentum, history, and tradition behind it. But the marginal is incapable of survival in the long run, let alone of producing profits. It lives on borrowed time. It exists on sufferance and through the inertia of others. Sooner or later, whenever boom conditions abate, it will be squeezed out.

The leadership requirement has serious implications for business strategy. It makes most questionable, for instance, the common practice of trying to catch up with a competitor who has brought out a new or improved product. All one can hope to achieve thereby is to become a little less marginal. It also makes questionable "defensive research" which throws scarce and expensive resources of knowledge into the usually futile task of slowing down the decline of a product that is already obsolete.

5. *Any leadership position is transitory and likely to be short-lived.* No business is ever secure in its leadership position. The market in which the results exist, and the knowledge which is the resource, are both generally accessible. No leadership position is more than a temporary advantage.* In business (as in a physical system) energy always tends toward diffusion. Business tends to drift from leadership to mediocrity. And the mediocre is three-quarters down the road to being marginal. Results always drift from earning a profit toward earning, at best, a fee which is all competence is worth.

It is, then, the executive's job to reverse the normal drift. It is his job to focus the business on opportunity and away from prob-

* This is nothing but a restatement of Schumpeter's famous theorem that profits result only from the innovator's advantage and therefore disappear as soon as the innovation has become routine.

lems, to re-create leadership and counteract the trend toward mediocrity, to replace inertia and its momentum by new energy and new direction.

The second set of assumptions deals with the *efforts within the business and their cost.*

6. *What exists is getting old.* To say that most executives spend most of their time tackling the problems of today is euphemism. They spend most of their time on the problems of yesterday. Executives spend more of their time trying to unmake the past than on anything else.

This, to a large extent, is inevitable. What exists today is of necessity the product of yesterday. The business itself—its present resources, its efforts and their allocation, its organization as well as its products, its markets and its customers—expresses necessarily decisions and actions taken in the past. Its people, in the great majority, grew up in the business of yesterday. Their attitudes, expectations, and values were formed at an earlier time; and they tend to apply the lessons of the past to the present. Indeed, every business regards what happened in the past as normal, with a strong inclination to reject as abnormal whatever does not fit the pattern.

No matter how wise, forward-looking, or courageous the decisions and actions were when first made, they will have been overtaken by events by the time they become normal behavior and the routine of a business. No matter how appropriate the attitudes were when formed, by the time their holders have moved into senior, policy-making positions, the world that made them no longer exists. Events never happen as anticipated; the future is always different. Just as generals tend to prepare for the last war, businessmen always tend to react in terms of the last boom or of the last depression. What exists is therefore always aging. Any human decision or action starts to get old the moment it has been made.

It is always futile to restore normality; "normality" is only the reality of yesterday. The job is not to impose yesterday's normal on a changed today; but to change the business, its behavior, its attitudes, its expectations—as well as its products, its markets, and its distributive channels—to fit the new realities.

7. *What exists is likely to be misallocated.* Business enterprise is not a phenomenon of nature but one of society. In a social situation, however, events are not distributed according to the "normal distribution" of a natural universe (that is, they are not distributed according to the bell-shaped Gaussian curve). In a social situation a very small number of events *at one extreme—* the first 10 per cent to 20 per cent at most—account for 90 per cent of all results; whereas the great majority of events accounts for 10 per cent or so of the results. This is true in the market place: a handful of large customers out of many thousands produce the bulk of orders; a handful of products out of hundreds of items in the line produce the bulk of the volume; and so on. It is true of sales efforts: a few salesmen out of several hundred always produce two-thirds of all new business. It is true in the plant: a handful of production runs account for most of the tonnage. It is true of research: the same few men in the laboratory are apt to produce nearly all the important innovations.

It also holds true for practically all personnel problems: the bulk of the grievances always comes from a few places or from one group of employees (for example, from the older unmarried women or from the clean-up men on the night shift), as does the great bulk of absenteeism, of turnover, of suggestions under a suggestion system, of accidents. As studies at the New York Telephone Company have shown, this is true even in respect to sickness.

The implications of this simple statement about normal distribution are broad.

It means, first: while 90 per cent of the results are being produced by the first 10 per cent of events, 90 per cent of the costs are incurred by the remaining and resultless 90 per cent of events. In other words, results and costs stand in inverse relationship to each other. Economic results are, by and large, directly proportionate to revenue, while costs are directly proportionate to the number of transactions. (The only exceptions are the purchased materials and parts that go directly into the final product.)

A second implication is that resources and efforts will normally allocate themselves to the 90 per cent of events that produce practically no results. They will allocate themselves to the number of events rather than to the results. In fact, the most expensive and potentially most productive resources (i.e., highly trained people) will misallocate themselves the worst. For the pressure exerted by the bulk of transactions is fortified by the individual's pride in doing the difficult—whether productive or not. This has been proved by every study. Let me give some examples:

A large engineering company prided itself on the high quality and reputation of its technical service group, which contained several hundred expensive men. The men were indeed first-rate. But analysis of their allocation showed clearly that while they worked hard, they contributed little. Most of them worked on the "interesting" problems —especially those of the very small customers—problems which, even if solved, produced little business. The automobile industry was the company's major customer and accounted for almost one-third of all purchases. But few technical service people had within memory set foot in the engineering department or the plant of an automobile company. "General Motors and Ford don't need me; they have their own people" was their reaction.

Similarly, in many companies, salesmen are misallocated. The largest group of salesmen (and the most effective ones) are usually put on the products that are hard to sell, either because they are yesterday's products or because they are also-rans which managerial vanity desperately is trying to make into winners. Tomorrow's important products rarely get the sales effort required. And the product that has sensational success in the market, and which therefore ought to be pushed all out, tends to be slighted. "It is doing all right without extra effort, after all" is the common conclusion.

Research departments, design staffs, market development efforts, even advertising efforts have been shown to be allocated the same way in many companies—by transactions rather than by results, by what is difficult rather than by what is productive, by yesterday's problems rather than by today's and tomorrow's opportunities.

A third and important implication is that revenue money and cost money are rarely the same money stream. Most businessmen see in their mind's eye—and most accounting presentations assume—that the revenue stream feeds back into the cost stream, which then, in turn, feeds back into the revenue stream. But the loop is not a closed one. Revenue obviously produces the wherewithal for the costs. But unless management constantly works at directing efforts into revenue-producing activities, the costs will tend to allocate themselves by drifting into nothing-producing activities, into sheer busy-ness.

In respect then to efforts and costs as well as to resources and results the business tends to drift toward diffusion of energy.

There is thus need for constant reappraisal and redirection; and the need is greatest where it is least expected: *in making the present business effective.* It is the present in which a business first has to perform with effectiveness. It is the present where both the keenest analysis and the greatest energy are required. Yet it is dangerously tempting to keep on patching yesterday's garment rather than work on designing tomorrow's pattern.

A piecemeal approach will not suffice. To have a real understanding of the business, the executive must be able to see it in its entirety. He must be able to see its resources and efforts as a whole and to see their allocation to products and services, to markets, customers, end-uses, to distributive channels. He must be able to see which efforts go onto problems and which onto opportunities. He must be able to weigh alternatives of direction and allocation. Partial analysis is likely to misinform and misdirect. Only the over-all view of the entire business as an economic system can give real knowledge.

8. *Concentration is the key to economic results.* Economic results require that managers concentrate their efforts on the smallest number of products, product lines, services, customers, markets, distributive channels, end-uses, and so on, that will produce the largest amount of revenue. Managers must minimize the amount of attention devoted to products which produce primarily costs because, for instance, their volume is too small or too splintered.

Economic results require that staff efforts be concentrated on the few activities that are capable of producing significant business results.

Effective cost control requires a similar concentration of work and efforts on those few areas where improvement in cost performance will have significant impact on business performance and results—that is, on those areas where a relatively minor increase in efficiency will produce a major increase in economic effectiveness.

Finally, human resources must be concentrated on a few major opportunities. This is particularly true for the high-grade human resources through which knowledge becomes effective in work. And, above all it is true for the scarcest, most expensive, but also potentially most effective of all human resources in a business: managerial talent.

No other principle of effectiveness is violated as constantly today as the basic principle of concentration. This, of course, is true not only of businesses. Governments try to do a little of everything. Today's big university (especially in the United States) tries to be all things to all men, combining teaching and research, community services, consulting activities, and so on. But business —especially large business—is no less diffuse.

Only a few years ago it was fashionable to attack American industry for "planned obsolescence." And it has long been a favorite criticism of industry, especially American industry, that it imposes "deadening standardization." Unfortunately industry is being attacked for doing what it should be doing and fails to do.

Large United States corporations pride themselves on being willing and able to supply any specialty, to satisfy any demand for variety, even to stimulate such demands. Any number of businesses boast that they never of their own free will abandon a product. As a result, most large companies end up with thousands of items in their product line—and all too frequently fewer than twenty really sell. However, these twenty or fewer items have to contribute revenues to carry the costs of the 9,999 non-sellers.

Indeed, the basic problem of United States competitive strength in the world today may be product clutter. If properly costed, the main lines in most of our industries prove to be fully competitive, despite our high wage rate and our high tax burden. But we fritter away our competitive advantage in the volume products by subsidizing an enormous array of specialties, of which only a few recover their true cost. In electronics, for instance, the competition of the Japanese portable transistor radio rests on little more than the Japanese concentration on a few models in this one line—as against the uncontrolled plethora of barely differentiated models in the United States manufacturers' lines.

We are similarly profligate in this country with respect to staff activities. Our motto seems to be: "Let's do a little bit of everything"—personnel research, advanced engineering, customer analysis, international economics, operations research, public relations, and so on. As a result, we build enormous staffs, and yet do not concentrate enough effort in any one area.

Similarly, in our attempts to control costs, we scatter our efforts rather than concentrate them where the costs are. Typically the cost-reduction program aims at cutting a little bit—say, 5 or 10 per cent—off everything. This across-the-board cut is at best ineffectual; at worst, it is apt to cripple the important, result-producing efforts which usually get less money than they need to begin with. But efforts that are sheer waste are barely touched by the typical cost-reduction program; for typically they start out with a generous budget.

These are the business realities, the assumptions that are likely to be found valid by most businesses at most times, the concepts with which the approach to the entrepreneurial task has to begin. They have only been sketched here in outline; each will be discussed in detail in the course of the book.

That these are only assumptions should be stressed. They must be tested by actual analysis; and one or the other assumption may well be found not to apply to any one particular business at any one particular time. Yet they have sufficient probability to provide the foundation for the analysis the executive needs to understand his business. They are the starting points for the analysis needed for all three of the entrepreneurial tasks: making effective the present business; finding business potential; and making the future of the business.

The small and apparently simple business needs this understanding just as much as does the big and highly complex company. Understanding is needed as much for the immediate task of effectiveness today as it is for work on the future, many years hence. It is a necessary tool for any executive who takes seriously his entrepreneurial responsibility. And it is a tool which can neither be fashioned for him nor wielded for him. He must take part in making it and using it. The ability to design and develop this tool and the competence to use it should be standard equipment for the business executive.

2 The Result Areas

The basic business analysis starts with an examination of the business as it is now, the business as it has been bequeathed to us by the decisions, actions, and results of the past. We need to see the hard skeleton, the basic stuff that is the economic structure. We need to see the relationship and interactions of resources and results, of efforts and achievements, of revenues and costs.

Specifically we need first to identify and understand those areas in a business for which results can be measured. Such *result areas* are the businesses within the larger business complex; products and product lines (or services); markets (including customers and end-users); and distributive channels. This task is described in this chapter.

Chapter 3 relates result areas to the *revenue contributions* they make and to the *share of the cost burden* they generate. It analyzes the *leadership position* and the *prospects* of each *result area,* and looks at the allocation to each of *key resources* such as knowledge-people and money. Chapter 4 leads up to a *tentative diagnosis* of result areas.

Chapter 5, finally, subjects the *cost stream* to a similar analysis.

This analysis is in part a matter of "getting the facts." But even the first job, identifying result areas, requires business judgment. It requires decisions regarding the basic economic structure of the business which the "facts," no matter how copious or how accurate, do not yield. Moreover it requires decisions of considerable risk, decisions that will—and should—upset a good many people, should go against their ingrained habits, should provoke lively discussion and dissent.

These disagreements are important. They bring out searching questions about the company, its products, policies, direction, in the minds of the people who are closest to what really goes on. The questioners may, of course, misinterpret what they experience—but the experiences are nonetheless real and relevant. On matters of such importance disagreements should not be concealed or explained away. Nothing is more dangerous in questions of importance and impact than decision by acclamation. It is bound to be the wrong decision on the wrong problem.

The accent in this phase of the work should therefore be on bringing out areas of disagreement and judgment rather than on achieving technical perfection in the analysis. What needs to be brought out is not "right answers" but "right questions."

This does not mean that highly advanced tools and techniques—operations research or market analysis, advanced accounting systems or complex computer programs—may not be needed even at this first stage, if the business is complex enough to require them and experienced enough to use them. But as a rule there is in this analysis an inverse relationship between usefulness of results and sophistication of tools and techniques. One should always ask: What is the *simplest* method that will give us adequate results? And what are the simplest tools? Albert Einstein after all never used anything more complicated than a blackboard.

Altogether in any analysis in which the results are likely to be the subject of hot discussion and strong opinions the accent should be on utmost simplicity of tools and techniques. Otherwise the unwelcome result will be smothered under long, pseudo-learnéd, discussion of the techniques. Or it will be brushed aside because the audience distrusts a complicated and mysterious method and suspects it—often rightly—of being a smoke screen for ignorance and intellectual arrogance.

The people in charge of this analysis should therefore be told to bring to top management the *uncertainties,* the ambiguities, the disagreements among themselves and within the senior management group before they even start on tentative conclusions. Only top management can really decide in these matters; for none of these decisions is a decision on "facts" but on the business itself and its future courses of action.

BOX I

Such an analysis can be done in a short time and by a small crew. In a medium-sized company one member of the top management group did it in six months with the help of three or four bright young men borrowed from the main departments. The only figures used were accounting data and generally available economic and industry statistics. For everything else, especially for judgments such as the prospects for a product line, he asked the company's executives for their opinions. In some areas a small sample study was made. To test the leadership position of one product, for instance, one team member talked to some twenty salesmen and two dozen distributors, and had an outside firm run a small consumer survey. Every three weeks the whole team reported in full detail to top management and all department heads. Half a dozen questions required more time than the six months set aside originally. Two of them involved substantial outside efforts: a study of distributive-channel changes (which required bringing in a consulting firm to do an operations research job including a good deal of large-computer work); and a study of foreign markets, their trends, buying behavior, and distribution systems. These, however, did not hold up the main decisions which were all in effect within a year after the study team first went to work. The executive in charge of the study was promoted to senior vice president to work exclusively on the company's entrepreneurial development; his staff is kept small—never more than four or five young men brought in from the main departments on a rotating three- to five-year assignment.

Incidentally, this is no longer a "medium-sized" but a pretty large company.

II

DEFINING THE PRODUCT

The analysis of the result areas has to start with products (or services) and in particular with a definition of "product." Questions regarding product-definition, while not simple, are at least known and understood by every experienced executive. This alone makes product analysis the best place to start.

Practically every business has some "products" which are not truly products at all but parts of some other product, an accessory or a sales promotion. To judge these by the standards of products is misleading. They ought to be judged by their contribution to the real products—by their capacity to promote sales, for instance. Conversely, a business may consider as sales promotion or as an accessory—that is, as "part of the package"—what in reality is *the* product, if only because the rest of the package is not being bought.

The classic example of an apparent product that actually created the sales, is the Gillette safety razor, which was practically given away in large quantities so as to create a market for the very profitable razor blades. To expect a high return from the safety razor would have missed the point. The question to ask of such a product is not what it produces itself but whether it actually creates a market for the razor blades—and whether these then produce the economic results.

The experience of a manufacturer of office reproduction equipment was just the opposite. His "safety razor" was the reproduction machine itself. His "razor blades" were the supplies, the inks, the special stencils, the cleaning fluid, and so on, needed to obtain copies from the machine. The machine did well in the market. But the supply business, analysis showed, was not generated—it went to independent stationery suppliers that had better products and offered them at a lower price. The fact that the reproduction equipment did quite well was therefore irrelevant. It was not a "product." Its own success was actually failure in terms of the true products for which it was supposed to make the market. But the reproduction equipment turned out to be capable of being a very successful product indeed. Its sales went up sharply—even though the price was almost doubled—as soon as promotion for the equipment stopped harping on the need to use with it the company's own (inferior but expensive) supplies. As so often happens the customer was a better economist than the maker; for over the lifetime of such a machine much more is spent on the supplies than on the original equipment.

These are important business problems rather than questions of semantics. How management answers them determines what course of action it will choose.

Product A in a consumer-goods' manufacturer's line is defined differently by each of the three members of top management. It sells in large quantities but it is extremely seasonal. It is a distinct product in its end-uses, its composition, its brand name and promotion, its costs and its price. But most of it—perhaps four-fifths—is not bought as a separate purchase but through a combination offer in which product A and another—and far less seasonal—product (B) are made available for about three-quarters of what the two would cost if bought separately. However this over-all price is advertised as being the full price for A, plus half-price for B.

To the financial man therefore, A is not only a separate product but the company's best product. In his books it shows a very high profit margin—for there the entire price reduction of the combination offer is being charged to B. As a result he wants to push A, make more of it, spend a larger share of the promotion dollar on it, and so forth. And the company's retailers agree with him.

For the manufacturing manager, however, A is not a "product" at all. It is a premium offered to create demand for B at a time when sales otherwise would be low. To him the main result of the seasonal product A is to make possible steady year-round output and much lower cost of the standard product B (which, by the way, was the original purpose in developing A). What he wants is to produce less of A but to use it to move more of B. He therefore favors a lower list price for A to make possible combination with a larger quantity of B. And he would only promote B.

The marketing executive, finally, considers the combination to be the only "product"—but a real and highly distinct one. He wants to promote the combination as such, but he worries because he considers the combined profit margin to be quite low. And to protect the market standing of B he wants to distribute the price reduction of the combination offer equally between the two—which, for different reasons, both his colleagues oppose.

Even Solomon could not decide which of the three is right. Yet the company has to move one way or the other. Similar conundrums are presented whenever a whole host of products—each with its own end-use and market—come inexorably out of one process. Are the by-products of petroleum refining—that is, all the scores of raw materials for plastics, insecticides, pharmaceuticals, dyestuffs—all *one* product? They are being produced, by necessity almost, whenever crude oil is refined. What they are and how much of each is turned out is largely determined by what is in the crude oil rather than by what the refiners want to get. Or what about the starches, adhesives, and oils that emerge whenever corn is industrially processed?

Or, on a much simpler level, are the various sizes, shapes, colors in which an object may be sold all *one* product or many products within one product line? Marketing logic usually gives one answer, manufacturing logic another—and financial analysis often still another.

III

THE THREE DIMENSIONS OF BUSINESS RESULTS

That a business gets paid for its products is so obvious that it is never forgotten. But, though equally obvious, it is often overlooked that there has to be a market for the product. There also have to be distributive channels to get the product from the producer to the market. But many businessmen—especially makers of industrial products—are as unaware that they use distributive channels, let alone that they depend on them, as Molière's *M. Jourdain* was of the fact that he spoke prose.

Each of these three areas is only one dimension of result-producing activity, one result area. To each correspond specific revenue contributions but also a specific share of the cost burden; to each are committed specific resources; each has its own prospects; and in each a position of leadership is needed.

But the three must also be analyzed together and in their interrelationship. Indeed one of the most common causes of poor performance is imbalance between the three. A product may do poorly—to the point where it is about to be dropped. Yet it may well be as good a product as its makers thought when they first brought it out—but offered to the wrong market or through the wrong distributive channel.

One of the largest American producers of packaged foods brought out several years ago a line of gourmet foods. Whereas all its other products were distributed through mass-retailers of food, especially the supermarkets, the company decided to distribute the gourmet foods through specialty stores only. The line failed. Yet similar lines, offered a little later by much less well-known companies through the supermarkets, did well. The idea behind the gourmet foods was to offer the housewife the opportunity to produce without any cooking skill an unusual dinner once in a while. But for most housewives the food specialty store is not an available distributive channel; they hardly know of its existence and certainly do not shop there. For those few who go in for elaborate cooking and shop in the specialty stores, processed and packaged food made by a mass-producer of staples is the wrong product, no matter what it is called.

The present predicament of the mass-circulation magazine in America is also in large measure a distributive channel problem. Mass-magazines selling many millions of copies a week, do not use mass-distribution. They solicit individual subscriptions and mail individual copies. The cost of obtaining and supplying one reader is substantially higher than the price that could possibly be charged for subscription. As a result, the advertiser pays for both the value he gets and the value the reader gets—and this he is understandably not eager to do. This explains why several famous magazines of yesterday went out of business just when they broke all circulation records.

For the American mass-circulation magazine to survive, it will have to find new channels of mass-distribution which combine bulk-subscription and bulk-transportation with delivery to the home. No such system is available today. That it is, however, not altogether inconceivable is shown by the example of the telephone; the costs are largely the costs of a mass-system while the service is in and through individual units.

Both the market and the distributive channel are often more crucial than the product.

Products are within the business as the accountant defines it; they are within its legal boundaries. Economically the other two areas are as much part of the business. Indeed a product does not exist, economically speaking, except within a market, bought by a customer for an end-use, and brought to him through a distributive channel. Markets as well as distributive channels do exist.

however, independently of any one product. They are primary; the product is secondary.

The two "outside" areas are however much more difficult to control, precisely because they are outside. Management can order a product modification; it cannot order a market modification or a modification of distributive channels. These can be changed, to be sure, but only within narrow limits.

A manufacturer of branded and packaged products for application in the home firmly believed that only the specialized store—especially the furniture store—could give the service his products needed to do their job for the home owner. The products were excellent and had high consumer acceptance. They were well promoted. And the stores that carried them used well-trained sales people and were amply supplied with literature, displays, and other sales supports. Yet sales were small and did not grow. The furniture store was simply the wrong channel for a nationally advertised, packaged product designed to be used every other month or so. Such a product is for mass-consumption and must be sold where mass-buying exists—and through distributors who, unlike furniture stores, want mass-buyers and are geared to them.

The manufacturer's strenuous attempts to get furniture stores to reach for mass-customers, and to get mass-customers to come to a specialty store for his products, led nowhere. In the end he had to accept the fact that in the American market of today, mass-distribution takes place where the masses shop; in supermarket, department store, shopping center, and discount house. He had therefore to re-engineer his products by putting the needed service inside the package, that is, into the products. Only then did he get the benefit of his product quality, his customer acceptance, and his promotion—through mass-buying at the mass-distributors.

In respect to distributive channels there is one more complication which makes this a difficult as well as a crucial result area. There is no distributive channel which is not, at the same time, also a customer. As a distributive channel it must "fit" the product on the one hand, and the market, customer, and end-use on the other hand. But the product in turn must be right for the distinct and important customer who serves as its distributive channel. If it is the wrong channel for the product or for the market, there will be failure. The product will not get to its market, will not be bought, will not produce results. But if it is the wrong product—or if it uses the wrong policies—the distributive channel, acting as a customer, will not buy.

Manufacturers of branded, mass-consumer goods are usually aware of this. At least they know they have two distinct customers, housewife and retailer, with different—and often conflicting—expectations and wants. But few others seem to know it.

Consumer-goods manufacturers typically see the retailer as the distributive channel, rather than as the customer. This, by the way, explains why dealer relations problems are chronic in industries such as home appliances.

Industrial-goods manufacturers, on the other hand, often miss the point that their customer is also their distributive channel. They see the paper industry or the bakeries, for example, as their market. But the industrial user also gets the electrical motor, the adhesive for paper, or the sweetening for bakery products to a market or customer and, above all, an end-use. If I make a chemical used solely in one stage of steelmaking, my sales are ultimately dependent on the sales of steel. I can go out of business because the steel companies buy from someone else or use a different chemical; I can go out of business, in other words, because I lose the steel industry as a customer. But I shall also go out of business if the steel industry loses its market, no matter how much the steel companies like my product. If that happens I am out of business because I have lost my distributive channel.

The customer of an industrial-goods producer therefore plays a twofold role: He is genuine customer and genuine distributive channel. In either role he is crucial to the producer. And if the product does not disappear in the customers' manufacturing process (e.g., synthetic fibers used in cloth and garments), the producer had better concern himself also with what his industrial customers do for the final consumers' acceptance of his products.

Finally, in a modern economy, whether developed or developing, distributive channels change rapidly—more rapidly, as a rule, than either technology or customer expectations and values.

Indeed I have never seen a decision with respect to distributive channels that was not obsolescent five years later, and badly in need of new thinking and fundamental change.

Markets as well as distributive channels deserve a good deal of attention and study—much more than they usually receive. Their analysis is likely to turn up more new insights and more opportunities (but also more unpleasant surprises) than the analysis of the product area. But the burden of pushing through the step-by-step process of analysis, of establishing its purposes and its concepts, and of proving its diagnostic power must rest on the analysis of the product as the most familiar and easiest of the result areas. *

There is only one major exception to this rule. Wherever there exist genuine businesses within a larger business complex, they should be the starting point. They are not only a bigger unit than a product or a product line (or a service). Their results are more nearly "real," and so are their resources—both because they are usually distinct and separate, and because the capital investment in such a business is usually known within a fairly narrow range; while capital invested in one of many products within a business cannot generally even be surmised. Responsibility for a business within a business can be established and goals can be set. These are of course all arguments in favor of decentralization, and when it comes to analysis of a business, they are telling arguments indeed. But after the analysis of a whole such business, its main result areas have to be analyzed one by one—and then together. And this starts us off again on an analysis of the products, though on a higher level of insight and understanding.

* This is not necessarily true for a department store where typical customer purchase may be a better starting point; at least the customary analysis by the usual departments and their products is not too revealing. And an American commercial bank may also find the customer a better foundation for analysis than the various services of different departments; our commercial banks are, after all, financial supermarkets.

3 Revenues, Resources, and Prospects

What are the essentials, the few but fundamental facts on which to base a diagnosis of a business and its result areas? Every executive today is inundated with figures. And more and more data pour out every day. Which ones really have something to say? And how do they have to be presented to convey meaning rapidly, effectively, reliably?

What one might call a "Business X-Ray" is the subject of this and the following chapters. These chapters deal with concepts. They present ideas, however, through a concrete illustration: a presentation—though grossly simplified—of an actual analysis of an existing business (which I shall call Universal Products). It is a middle-sized, reasonably prosperous manufacturing company, differing from many others of the same kind only in having been for decades equally active in the American and European markets, with plants, sales forces, and managements on both sides of the Atlantic.

Only one result area is actually presented in the analysis: products. But the same concepts apply to the analyses of the other result areas—customers, markets, end-uses, and distributive channels. Nor does it make much difference whether a business makes a physical product or renders a service.

This form of analysis examines the *entire product range of a business* rather than one product at a time. All the data relate the performance, costs, resources, and prospects of an individual product to over-all business results and over-all business resources and efforts.

TABLE I. UNIVERSAL PRODUCTS COMPANY:

A SCHEMATIC EXAMPLE OF PRODUCT ANALYSIS

(dollars in millions)

Total company sales	$145		
Purchased raw materials	50		
Fixed charges	15	Net profit before taxes	$14.5
Available product revenues	$ 80	Costs assignable to products	65.5

Prod-uct	Revenue		Share in Cost Burden		Net Revenue Contribution		Contribution Coefficient [a]
	Value	*Percentage of Company Total*	*Value*	*Percentage of Company Total*	*Value*	*Percentage of Net Profit*	
A	$19.0	24.0%	$18.2	28.0%	$0.72	5.0%	0.26%
B	14.0	17.5	16.7	25.5	−2.7	−12.0	Loss
C	14.0	17.5	7.2	11.0	6.8	47.0	3.3
D	11.0	14.0	5.2	7.5	5.8	40.0	3.8
E	7.0	9.0	5.4	8.0	1.6	11.0	1.5
F	4.0	5.0	3.4	5.0	0.6	4.0	1.0
G	4.0	5.0	3.6	5.5	0.45	3.0	0.75
H	3.5	4.5	3.3	5.0	0.2	1.5	0.5
I	2.0	2.5	1.85	2.5	0.15	1.0	0.5
J	Under 1.0	1.0	1.5	2.0	−0.5	−0.5	Loss

[a] Obtained by dividing the net revenue contribution as a percentage of net profit before taxes (preceding column) by the value of the product revenue (first column).

The analysis uses mostly normal accounting data—except, for the concept of "transactions" which is explained on page 32. The form in which these data are presented (see Table I) may however seem unfamiliar (though executives who have used break-even point analyses and financial analyses will recognize old acquaintances*).

The starting point of our analysis is the "Business Realities" described in Chapter 1.

- Revenue money and cost money are not necessarily one stream.
- Business phenomena follow the normal distribution of social events in which 90 per cent of effects follow from the first 10 per cent of the causes and vice versa.
- Revenues are therefore proportionate to volume, with the bulk of the volume and of the corresponding revenues produced by a small fraction of the product numbers (markets, customers, etc.).
- Costs are therefore proportionate to transactions, with the bulk of the costs attributable to the large number—90 per cent perhaps— of the transactions that produce only a small fraction of revenues.

WHY NOT USE COST ACCOUNTING?

That costs are, on the whole, directly proportionate to transactions should occasion little surprise. For example:

- To get a $50,000 order costs no more, as a rule, than to get a $500 order; certainly it does not cost 100 times as much.
- To design a new product that does not sell is as expensive as to design a winner.
- It costs just as much to do the paper work for a small order as for a large one—the same order entry, production order, scheduling, billing, collecting, and so on.

---

* Of the large and growing literature on these two analytical techniques the American books I have found of greatest value—both in explaining concepts and in developing techniques for the businessman—are Rautenstrauch & Villiers *The Economics of Industrial Management*, 2nd ed. (New York 1957)— especially on break-even points; and Joel Dean, *Managerial Economics* (New York 1951)—especially for financial analysis. Many of the newer publications use far more advanced techniques, especially of a mathematical nature. There are situations where the advanced techniques are of material help, e.g., for the analysis of product-mix and product-time problems in a continuous materials stream such as that of a petroleum refinery, Much more advanced methods are also required for systems analysis, for instance in a major space vehicle development program. But in most business situations cruder, less complex methods are good enough; the refinements now available may improve results in these situations but do not fundamentally change them.

• It even costs almost as many dollars to turn out the product for a small order as for a large one, to manufacture it, package it, store and ship it. For the only thing that may take less time in the small order is the actual manufacturing; and that is, as a rule, a subordinate cost factor in today's industry. Everything else takes as much time and handling.

Still, many businessmen will ask, why not base our analysis on cost accounting? It tells us, doesn't it, what the precise costs are? The answer is that it is misuse of cost accounting to derive from it figures for a particular product's share of total business costs.

Cost accounting has to find a place for every penny spent. Where the cost accountant cannot document what costs are directly incurred in making this or that product, he must therefore allocate. He can only do so by assuming that all non-direct costs are distributed either in proportion to direct costs or in proportion to the sales price of a product. This is all right as long as allocation is confined to a small margin of all costs—say, 10 or 20 per cent. In the production situation of fifty years ago this was the case. Today, however, the large majority of all costs are not direct; that is, are not incurred when and only when one unit of a certain product is being made. Only raw materials and supplies bought on the outside can still be considered truly direct costs. Even so-called "direct labor" does not today fluctuate with unit volume of output. It remains pretty much unchanged whatever mix of products goes through a plant. Most of it even remains unchanged regardless of total output. Labor in most manufacturing, and in all service, industries is a charge related to time rather than to volume of output or to units of a product. Altogether less than a quarter of all costs, other than purchased raw materials, can in modern business be treated as truly direct; that is, as truly varying with, and dependent on, a given unit of a given product or process.

For the cost accountant's purposes this may matter little. Allocating costs in fixed proportion to the volume or price of a product may not materially distort the relationship between the various cost elements that make up the total unit cost of a product, for instance the relation between its fabricating costs and its finishing costs. Cost figures, in other words, still show, with reliability, where cost relations are out of line. But for the purpose of knowing what it costs a business to carry this or that product, figures that allocate the great bulk of the cost are useless. They prejudge what they are meant to document—namely, how the cost burden is distributed. Moreover they make the one assumption least likely to be correct: that costs are distributed in a "normal" Gaussian bell-shaped curve, that is, in proportion to results.

There are exceptions: for instance a business that has, essentially, only one product.

General Motors, with the bulk of its output in one product family—automobiles—has been using for forty years a cost concept which assumes that each car bears a share of the cost burden equal to the total costs of the plant when running at 80 per cent of capacity, divided by the number of cars it would produce at 80 per cent capacity. This too is generalization and has only probability; but it is a simpler generalization than ours though it expresses a similar cost definition.

And where there are very large and distinct individual cost centers, such as ships in the fleet of a steamship line or jet planes of an airline, actual costs can be known and used. But otherwise actual costs cannot, as a rule, be extracted. Their behavior has to be assumed.

Distribution according to transactions is the only close approximation to the behavior of the costs of work not focused on, and carried by, an identifiable unit of production. The bulk of all costs in business today is of this kind.

The single major cost category that is usually clearly identifiable with respect to a specific product is irrelevant both to the revenue contribution and to the share of the cost burden. This is the cost for purchased raw materials and parts. A simple example—taken from a company making small electrical household appliances such as toasters, coffee makers, and flat irons—will illustrate this:

Purchased materials and parts account for 60 per cent of the manufacturer's price in the case of product A, for 30 per cent in the case of product B. Both sell the same volume. Profit margin is 10 per cent of manufacturer's price for both products. Both therefore are believed to do equally well. But actually the manufacturer makes one dollar in profits for any three dollars worth of his own resources and efforts invested in product A; he has to spend six dollars worth of his own resources and efforts to make one dollar on product B. If both products had a ready market for a larger output at the same price, though the manufacturer had resources to expand only one,

• He would get twice as much additional output by putting his resources into product A rather than into product B. An additional unit of product A requires only thirty dollars worth of resources against a requirement of sixty dollars for product B.

• He would therefore get twice as much profit through expanding product A rather than product B.

Both revenue contribution and cost burden share therefore should use a "value-added" figure* in which purchased materials and parts have been subtracted from the totals of sales and costs.

The conventional profit margin is also only one factor in the profit stream, which is profit margin multiplied by turnover. Two products, each selling for $10.00, may have the same raw-materials content and the same profit margin of $1.50 per unit. But if five units of one are made and sold while only one unit of the other is sold, the first will yield five times the profit dollars of the other. This is elementary; but businessmen tend to forget it, unless the figures they use include both factors (as for instance, in the well-publicized return-on-investment figures of the DuPont Company). All concepts and figures used in the analysis here are therefore profit-stream figures, including both profit margins and turnover.

Those costs which are *independent* of any given volume of work and production should also be excluded from the basic calculation. These are the *truly* fixed costs—rent and property taxes, insurance, maintenance, and above all the costs of servicing capi-

---

* "Value added in manufacturing" is the commonly used term. It would be much better to speak of "cost added," whether in manufacturing or in distribution. In the first place only the customer adds value. All manufacturer and distributor can do is to add costs. Secondly, what one wants to find out is what part of this added cost is being turned into value and how much is friction and waste. But the term "value added" is so generally accepted that it would be pedantry to change it.

tal that has already been invested and has therefore to be paid for whatever the volume of sales or of profits (the costs commonly called "sunk costs" by accountants and economists).* When fixed costs are very high they require a separate cost allocation—an illustration is given on page 37 where the cost burden of freight on a steamship is being analyzed.

We thus arrive at the following definitions:

• *Net sales* are simply sales of the company less purchased raw materials.

• *Total company revenues* are net sales minus fixed costs (some people call them *"disposable revenues"*).

• *Revenue* of a product is the percentage of *total company revenues* that corresponds to the percentage which sales of the product (minus the purchased raw materials and supplies directly and uniquely attributable to the product) constitute of company net sales.

• *Share of the cost burden* of a product is the percentage of *total company cost* (less purchased raw materials and fixed costs) that corresponds to the percentage share of the *transactions* attributable to the product in the total volume of such transactions in the business.

• *Net revenue contribution* is, of course, nothing but the difference between *revenues* of a product and its *share of the cost burden*.†

• *Contribution coefficient*—i.e., the ability of a product to generate revenue as its volume goes up or down—is the *net revenue contribution* of the product for each million dollars of sales. It can be expressed, of course, as a percentage of *total company revenues* per million dollar of sales of the product or as a dollar amount of additional sales needed to increase

---

* Whether "profit," insofar as it corresponds to the minimum rate that has to be paid for capital on the market, is a "sunk cost" need not concern us here —though it is an important question in business economics. As Box II on page 34 shows, it is taken out of the figures anyhow.

† *Net revenue contribution* approximates, as the illustration in Box II on page 34 points out, profit or loss on a product only where fixed costs are a relatively small part of the total—below 20 per cent of total costs or so.

total *revenues* by a given percentage or by a given amount.*
This is a measure of the results to be expected if volume of one
product is substituted for volume of another product. In other
words, *contribution coefficient* assumes that total volume remains the same. Even with this qualification it is only a rough
approximation. It is close enough to serve as guide to the impact
on over-all results that might ensue from attempts to push sales
of any one of the products.

But What Is a Transaction?

The terms used so far may sound strange; but the concepts
they express are surely familiar.

There is one exception here, however, one new concept requiring data rarely produced by the accounting system: the
transaction.

What is a transaction? Above all, how does one decide which
of the many transactions within a business is the transaction
that is representative of the actual cost structure?

There is no set answer. The nature of the business determines
this rather than accounting practices or economic theorems.

In many businesses the number of invoices sent out is the
simplest and most easily obtainable unit of transaction. Where
paper work with its heavy cost is organized around it, the individual invoice can be used with reasonable reliability as an index
of the actual cost share of a product. Sometimes shipments are
a more convenient unit, especially where there are many different products on one invoice.

In department stores, purchase per customer has long been known
as a good indicator of cost structure. The larger the purchase per
customer, the greater the effectiveness of the retail operation. The
number of customers that have to come into the store to move a
certain quantity of a certain item of merchandise may well be a

---

* Any business using such techniques as the multiple-product break-even
analysis (see Rautenstrauch & Villiers, *op. cit.*), would of course take the
figure for *contribution coefficient* from there. However, this is not a commonly
used technique—though businessmen should understand it even if its complexity prevents their using it.

more reliable unit of transactions for department stores than any other.

A medium-sized company that makes computers for scientific work uses, as unit of transactions, the number of proposals that have to be made to obtain one order. The proposal, with all the enormous technical and clerical work that accompanies it, is the true cost center—and also the maw into which the scarcest and most expensive resources, the best technical talents of the company, disappear.

In an aluminum rolling mill, the proper unit of transactions was found to be the number of production runs through the hot-rolling stage. In the extrusion plant of the same company, however (which makes products such as radiator grilles for automobiles or door handles for refrigerators), the appropriate unit of transaction was found to be the number of skilled diemakers'-hours needed to prepare the presses for any one specific shape.

For a commercial airline the most meaningful cost unit is the number of seat-miles available but not sold on a given route or a given flight, that is, a "cost of not doing." But for a consumer-goods company making goods distributed through many independent retailers, the right transaction unit may well be the number of calls on dealers for each million dollars sales of a product. It may even be the number of dealers needed to sell its volume. To service any dealer on the books costs pretty much the same—and it comes high. If there is any difference, it is in favor of the larger dealer who usually requires fewer sales calls and less service—apart from being usually a better credit risk and paying more promptly.

For process industries with high capital investment, papermaking for instance or petrochemicals, the most meaningful unit for cost calculation may be time: the time it takes to get out the same sales value (minus purchased materials, of course) of different products. In such industries costs tend to be a function of the hours run.

To determine which transaction is appropriate for a given business is part of the analysis of the business. By itself it is a big step towards understanding a business and its economics. It is also a genuine business decision of great impact—and of high risk. Analysts or technicians might point out the available choices and their consequences. The final decision is management's responsibility.

BOX II

A sample calculation might help to show how these concepts can be used. It shows three different products—three different kinds of metal containers made in one can-making plant.

Total company sales amounted to $150 millions. *Raw materials* purchased came to $50 millions, leaving *net sales* of $100 millions. *Total* fixed charges amounted to $30 millions a year, leaving *total product revenues* of $70 millions. Product X had sales of $40 millions; its purchased raw-material content—somewhat lower than average—was $10 millions, leaving *revenues* of $30 millions or 30 per cent of *total company revenues*. Its *revenue*—30 per cent of company sales minus raw materials, minus fixed charges—was thus figured at $21 millions (30 per cent of $70 millions).

Total company costs were $135 millions. Minus *purchased raw materials* and minus *fixed charges*, this left $55 millions as *total costs attributable to products*. The unit of *transaction* found to be most nearly representative was shipments—with a total of 250,000 a year. Of these product X accounted—as established by a sample study—for 60,000 or 24 per cent. This left it with a *share of the cost burden* of $13.2 millions (24 per cent of $55 millions), and with a *net revenue contribution* of $7.8 millions (which, as will be seen, was more than half of the total company profit of $15 millions ($150 millions of sales less $135 millions of costs). Its *contribution coefficient* would thus be $195,000 for each additional $1 million of sales.

Continued next page

The power of the transactional analysis of business costs was recently demonstrated in a study of profits and costs of the grocery business conducted in 1963 by the New York management consulting firm

McKinsey & Co. for the General Foods Corporation, America's largest producer of processed foods. Traditionally, the grocer—like most retailers—has charged an "average" cost figure against a "gross

BOX II (*continued*)

Product Y accounted similarly for 22 per cent of *total product revenues*— with a *revenue* of $15.4 millions. But it accounted for 30 per cent of the transactions—or for a *share of the cost burden* of $16.5 millions; and a *negative revenue contribution* of $1.1 millions. Product Z likewise showed a *negative revenue contribution*—$3.4 millions—with 18 per cent of *total revenue* ($12.6 millions) but with a 29 per cent *share in the total cost burden* ($16 millions).

Fixed costs in this business are, however rather high. And the figures shown here are figures *after fixed-cost absorption*. This means that each of the three products had already made its contribution to fixed costs before the *net revenue contribution* calculated here. Not producing products Y and Z would therefore be more costly than producing them without recovering their total cost—which is, of course, what a *negative contribution* means: if (a) their *negative contributions* are smaller than their share of the *fixed costs;* and if (b) no other, better-yielding product could be substituted for them in total production and sales. (The latter is the crucial assumption. It is always implied but is rarely tested. Therefore the fixed cost absorption argument tends to become uncritical alibi in many cases.) As to the proportion of *fixed costs* chargeable to a product, one can use either an amount proportionate to its *revenues* or one proportionate to its *cost share*. I prefer the latter—not because it has a stronger logical case, but because it is a more stringent test of the weaker products. Under either method products Y and Z would be found to have absorbed enough *fixed charges* to have added to the *net profit* available to the company—though product Z is marginal even by this test.

profit margin." He has therefore considered that item to be the most profitable that gave the largest gross profit margin—though well-managed supermarket chains have increasingly taken speed of turn-over into account as well. The McKinsey study showed, however, that actual costs depend on the transactions each commodity needs, and that the share of the cost burden of different commodities varies greatly. The profit margin of a case of dry cereal, for instance, is almost exactly the same as that of a case of canned soup: $1.26 for the cereal and $1.21 for the soup. The grocer therefore always considered the two commodities as producing the same profit for him. But the transactional study showed that the actual profit on the cereal is only 25 cents per case as against a profit of 71 cents for the soup. And even though baby foods both have a high gross margin and move fast, they require so much handling that they actually lose money for the grocer.

Managers may never have thought of their business as a "transactional system." But once they grasp the idea (especially if conveyed by examples rather than by learned dissertation), they can usually apply it to the business they know. At least the managers' intuition will point to the right answers.

Differences of opinion among experienced managers in a company are revealing and valuable. In a given business there may well be different transactions that could serve as the unit of cost. I know one large chemical company where invoices, number of service calls to help customers use a product, and product modifications for specific uses might each be claimed to be the representative unit of transactions and the true measurement of cost. If the cost picture of a product differs sharply as different yardsticks are used, this in itself is relevant information. At least it explains to the people in the business why there have been clashes of opinion regarding the merits and performance of the product in question.

In businesses where distinct and separate operations can be isolated, the cost for each operation, based on its typical transactions, can—and usually should—be determined. The costs of all operations added together give total cost burden.

This is the right procedure where operating costs are both high and virtually fixed. One cannot sail part of a ship; hence the total costs of sailing the entire ship are always incurred whether the ship is full or empty. Similarly, the pulp mill of a paper plant can either be run or it can be shut down; it cannot run at half-speed. Its operating costs are fixed, incurred in full whenever any pulp is being made, and also high.

To illustrate: Three distinct operations can be identified in any freight shipment by sea. There is a clerical operation which is geared to the number of separate shipments. Whether the shipment is large or small, valuable or low-cost, bulky or compact, twenty-five items on one invoice or one, the clerical cost is the same. It is fixed by law; the legally prescribed documents must be issued and handled. The clerical cost burden of any shipment is therefore the share of the total clerical costs divided by the total number of shipments for the shipping route served. Then there is the loading operation. Here the cost unit is the hour of loading and unloading time. The loading net can only make so many trips per hour, whether it carries a big load or a small one. And there always has to be a full loading crew in the ship's hold and on the pier. Time is the unit of cost. The loading-cost share is the total loading cost divided by a shipment's share of total loading time. This means, of course, that a large package is much more economical for the shipping line than a small one.

Finally, there are the costs of ship operations which are practically fixed whatever the ship carries. Capital costs, maintenance, crew wages, insurance—even fuel—are just as high when a ship sails empty as when it sails full. The ship-operations burden of a shipment is therefore that share of total ship-operations cost that corresponds to the percentage of the ship's loading space occupied by revenue freight on the typical voyage which a shipment occupies.

Total cost share of a shipment is the sum of these three separate cost shares.

The analysis so far will already have yielded important results. It will have brought out new facts and will have shed light on matters that had been troubling people in the business for a long time. It will have raised many new—and often disturbing—questions (especially when the result areas other than products are being analyzed). In two places at least, important management decisions will have come to the surface: in the definition of a product and in defining the appropriate transaction unit.

We still, however, know too little about a product until its

leadership position and its prospects—the outside and the future
—have been looked at. Table II gives a sample.

II

WHAT MAKES FOR LEADERSHIP?

Experienced businessmen know that the seemingly simple
statements regarding position and prospects of each product in
Table II represent the final summation of a great deal of hard
work and prolonged discussion. In these areas even calm men
will get angry, and reasonable men will refuse to listen to facts
with a curt: "I don't believe it." Here, in other words, is need
for thorough, painstaking work. But the work itself—its tools
and techniques—from value-analysis of the product to market
research—is well known, has indeed been routine for years
even in fairly small businesses. The results, in other words, may
be controversial and hard to accept; but the work itself is
familiar.

Of course, presentation in a large and complex company will
be far more detailed than in smaller businesses. A good deal will
be quantified, and so on. But it is not my intention here to show
how complicated one can become—nor does anyone need this
lesson. I am intent only on getting across a concept—and the
concept *is* simple.

Leadership is not a quantitative term. The business with the
largest share of a market may have leadership in one segment
only. The monopolist, the single supplier of a product or of a
market, never has leadership and cannot have it.

To have leadership a product must be best fitted for one—or
more—of the genuine wants of market and customer. It must be a
genuine want. The customer must be willing to pay for it. No
matter how desirable a certain quality in a product might appear
to the manufacturer, it only gives leadership if the customer accepts the claim. His acceptance is his willingness to honor the
claim in tangible form by preferring the product to its competitors—and by being willing to pay.

TABLE II. UNIVERSAL PRODUCTS COMPANY PRODUCT ANALYSIS: LEADERSHIP

(dollars in millions)

Product	Revenue	Leadership Position	Short-term Prospects		
			Without Changes	With Changes	Static
A	$19.0	Marginal. As good as but no better than 3 or 4 other products on market. Tied for first place in sales.		Down	
B	14.0	Marginal. Is now 5 years old. Our entry in quality market. Sales should now be at least twice actual. Have made several price cuts, but orders did not increase.	Down	Down?	x
C	14.0	Leader. Success surprised us. Introduced as premium product for small segment of market. Makes heavy inroads in regular market for A. Leads all others in ease of application.	Down	Up	
D	11.0	Leader. Low-priced line with unsatisfactory profit margins. Lacks quality of B but is being bought heavily by market B was designed for. Lasts almost twice as long as competitive models and costs 20% less than cheapest competitor.	Up	Strongly up	
E	7.0	Marginal. Distinct market—medium-sized business. Little growth. Customers prefer higher-priced product of competitor; claim ours gives trouble.	Down	Up	
F	4.0	Marginal, but leads in special market. Preferred for one specific industrial application. Bought because of service we give.			x
G	4.0	Similar to F. Same comments apply.	Up (limited)		
H	3.5	Marginal. Was expected to become company's major entry in new industrial market which has not developed so far. Competitor's process technically inferior but much cheaper.			x
I	2.0	Dead. Major product 10–15 years ago. Bought now for one obsolete process used in smaller companies only.			x
J	Under 1.0	Expected to be leader. Just brought out of development. Should enable customers to run their equipment much faster and for longer periods.	Up	Strongly up	

The monopolist cannot have leadership because the customer cannot choose. Customers of a monopoly always want a second supplier and flock to him when he appears. They may have been fully satisfied with the monopolist's goods or services. But it is an exceptional business or product that, after having had a monopoly, retains customer preference.*

The monopolist is therefore always in danger of becoming marginal the moment a second supplier appears. Most businessmen know this to be true—but emotionally they find it hard to accept. Yet, in analyzing a business, one had best consider an unchallenged product as an endangered product.

The common test of leadership by "share of the market" is also deceptive. Examples abound of companies that have the largest share of the market but are far behind in their profitability compared to competitors of much smaller apparent stature. This means that they do not get paid for leadership but, in effect, have to pay for it. For while the very large company has to be active in every area, no company, as a rule, can have real distinction in everything.

In all of American industry there is only one example of a company that combines first rank in every area with first rank in profitability in every area: General Motors in the U.S. automobile market. DuPont de Nemours, while the largest and most profitable of American chem-

---

* Incidentally, the sole-source supplier has lower sales, as a rule, than he would have were there competitors in the field. Sales of a product line of any consequence do not begin to expand, let alone to reach their potential, as long as only one company supplies them. The history of the aluminum industry in the United States is an example. Though the Aluminum Company of America was the very model of the "enlightened monopolist" who constantly lowers price and seeks new uses for his product, the explosive expansion of aluminum consumption in this country started after the United States government, during World War II, had put two other companies into the aluminum business. Part of the reason for this failure of monopoly to benefit even the monopolist is certainly that one company, no matter how big, is rarely big enough to develop a new market of any size by itself; it takes at least two. There is rarely "one right way" in a new market. Yet alternatives are unlikely to be thought of or aggressively explored unless there is the challenge of competition. Another reason is probably that even the "enlightened monopolist" tends to neglect markets and customers that cannot go elsewhere. But a main reason is certainly that manufacturer, wholesaler, retailer, or consumer dislikes to be dependent on a single source of supply and therefore keeps down his purchases from a supplier in control of the market.

ical companies, works only in a few segments of industrial chemistry, especially in chemicals and fibers for the textile market. There are, to be sure, few situations comparable to that of U.S. Steel, the price and volume leader in most steel markets for many years but until a few years ago the least profitable large American steel company. Here largest share of the market seems to have been held by a producer who was marginal in the major product areas. But in most industries the largest company has leadership in only a few areas, while its very size and prominence force it to be active in a great many others.

Only an occasional very small specialty business can be the leader with all of its products or services, in all its markets and end-uses, with all its customers, and in all its distributive channels. But no company, no matter how large or how small, can afford to be marginal in all of them. Above all it cannot afford to be anything but a leader in the areas which are the mainstay of its business, produce the bulk of the sales, generate the bulk of the costs, and absorb the most important and most valuable resources. A marginal product generates inadequate returns. It is always in danger of being squeezed out altogether.

The larger the market the more dangerous is it to be marginal, the less room is there for any but products with genuine leadership position.

Contrary to what economists have been preaching for two hundred years, the alternative to monopoly in a developed, large market is not free competition—that is, an unlimited number of participants in an industry; but oligopoly—that is, competition between a fairly small number of manufacturers or suppliers. As the market gets bigger, it may take so much money to enter the industry that the attempt can be made only once in a great while—simply because one must either sell nationally or not sell at all (as in the American automobile industry). The bigger the market, the more will distributive channels concentrate on just enough well-known brands to give the customer meaningful choice, but not so many as to confuse him or as to require excessive inventories.

For this reason, for instance, concentration of the American kitchen-appliance industry (refrigerators, ranges, dishwashers, automatic laundries, etc.) on no more than half a dozen or so major brands will occur sooner or later whatever the antitrust laws may say to the contrary. Five to six major brands are all that a large appliance dealer—whether a discount house, a department store, or a shopping center—needs in order to have a full line which gives the customer all the selection he wants.

More brands, as a matter of fact, may only confuse the customer and may make him not want to buy. More brands do not increase sales, but they do increase inventory. They tie up money, floor space, and warehouse space. They make repair service difficult: the repairman has to be trained on more appliances and has to carry more spare parts. They either require additional promotion money or splinter the promotion impact, and so on. The first reaction of the appliance dealer in this situation is to put pressure for "extras" on the manufacturers of the slower-selling lines. During the last decade dealers have asked for and received lower prices, larger discounts, special financing, extra promotion allowances, and guarantees of repurchase of used appliances at a stipulated price well above the market. Each demand meant a decrease in the manufacturer's profitability.

If and when a really sharp setback in the appliance market occurs, the marginal brands will then be squeezed out altogether—simply because dealers have to curtail their inventories and therefore concentrate on the few fast-selling brands and drop the others.

The main reason why concentration increases, the larger and more highly developed the market, is that the large market makes for meaningful product differentiation. The larger the market the less room it has for products that are "just as good," the less room there is for marginal products and marginal producers.

This may be of particular importance today for Europe and for Japan where the mass-market is developing rapidly. A business or product that was a leader in the restricted German or French market of yesterday may rapidly become marginal in the mass-market of the unified European continent. This is certainly a major factor behind the rapid mergers and partnership associations between medium-sized companies—especially family-owned ones—across Common Market national boundaries. And unless they try to establish monopolies that restrict the market, such combinations of medium-sized businesses into one large group or association are healthy—are indeed needed fully to exploit the economic potential of the Common Market or of Japan's new mass-consumer economy.

The expansion of a market also creates opportunities for a host of products and services with special characteristics to attain leadership position in a distinct market-segment or end-use which, while significantly smaller than the national or mass market, is still larger than what passed for the big market only a while back.

Take for example the market for specially formulated polymer petro-chemicals. The manufacturers of the large, volume polymer products —e.g., the main plastics—are the principal customers; and the opportunities, sales, and profits for the accomplished polymer chemist are high. The Cummins Engine Company of Columbus, Indiana—a medium-sized business—has enjoyed highly profitable leadership as a maker of engines for heavy trucks. If the very large engineering companies (General Motors above all) did not offer a broad assortment of diesel engines for all uses—in buses, in ships, in locomotives —Cummins could hardly have confined itself to the specialization on one narrow line that underlies its success. Either an engine design is used widely or it becomes so difficult to install and service that it is not used at all. Some small manufacturers, each specializing in one or two special applications of low-horsepower electrical motors, have been doing proportionately better than General Electric or Westinghouse, whose dominant market share forces them to supply all kinds of motors to all customers and for all end-uses, and who therefore, of necessity, must be marginal or lose money on some lines.

A leadership position may be based on price or on reliability. Easy maintenance may be crucial in one product for one purpose; a promise that no maintenance is needed may be leadership for a similar product in some other use (e.g., for a telephone cable laid on the ocean floor or for a microwave relay station for telephone and television signals built on a mountain top in Idaho, sixty miles and two blizzards from the nearest town). Appearance, style, design—customer recognition and acceptance

—lowest cost of a finished article into which a product is being converted—small or large size—service and speedy delivery—technical counsel—these and many others can be foundations for a leadership position.

But what the manufacturer considers "quality" is not one of them; it is only too often irrelevant, if not the manufacturer's alibi for turning out a marginal product that costs more but does not contribute anything different or better. There is no leadership if the market is not willing to recognize the claim. And that always means willingness to buy and to pay. Leadership position for a product or a business is an economic term rather than a moral or an esthetic one.

Low price may be no criterion at all. (Indeed manufacturers' complaints that "the trade" buys only by price and pays no attention to quality are often unfounded; the trade has definite value preferences and is willing to pay for them—the manufacturer just does not satisfy them.) But customer willingness to pay and customer purchases in preference to competitors' products are valid criteria of economic accomplishment in a competitive market economy. If they cannot be clearly demonstrated, a product must be suspected of being—or becoming—marginal.

In analyzing products for their leadership position, the same questions should therefore always be asked: "Is the product being bought in preference to other products on the market, or at least as eagerly?" "Do we have to give anything to get the customer to buy?" (e.g., the extraordinary amount of service which, as Table III (next page) shows, products F and G require). "Do we get paid for what we deliver to him, as indicated by an at-least-average profit contribution?" "Are we getting paid for what we think is the product distinction?" "Or do we have a product with leadership position and with distinction without ourselves discerning it?" (as might well be the case with products C and D in the tables).

If the main products of a company show no signs of having such distinction and of occupying leadership position—as may be the case with Universal Products—it had better do something fast, especially if sales and profits seem to be doing well. Both sales and profits may suddenly collapse—yet no one is prepared, no one is forewarned, no one is working at restoring the leadership position of the products or developing new ones to replace what has become marginal.

TABLE III. UNIVERSAL PRODUCTS COMPANY PRODUCT ANALYSIS: PEOPLE
(*dollars in millions*)

| Product | Revenue | Quantity and Quality of Key Personnel Support | | |
		Managerial	*Technical*	*Sales and Service*
A	$19.0	Very high	Very good and plentiful	Very good and plentiful
B	14.0	Very high [a]	Very high [a]	Very high [a]
C	14.0	Good	Low	Medium in numbers and quality
D	11.0	High	Mediocre	Medium in numbers and quality
E	7.0	A nonentity	Many, but mediocre	Continuously high service demand
F	4.0 ⎫	Highly qualified	High in	Best salesmen—
G	4.0 ⎭	technically	quality	service high
H	3.5	Special task force	Our best people	High-pressure sales effort
I	2.0	Low	Low	Low in sales; high in service of old products in customer plants
J	Under 1.0	High	Quite high	Nil

[a] Two-thirds of the technically trained people appraised as "superior or better" work on this product.

Turning now to the prospects, Table II (page 39) summarized a lot of hard work—and even more internal disagreement. Judgments on prospects—on what can reasonably be expected of a product within the next few years—are of course fully as controversial as leadership position. One look at the table and every experienced executive knows that the prospect appraisal for product A will be bitterly disputed, especially by the engineering department, and that the dismal appraisal for product B is probably still too optimistic. He knows that the comptroller will challenge the high appraisal of the prospect for product D; whereas sales may want to push the estimate even higher. The expectation of continued sales for product I, even though on a very low level, is probably wishful thinking. The old-timers who made their careers designing, making, and selling it still hope it will come back.

But what the analysis tries to do—and why it should be made —hardly needs explanation.

The amazing thing is that it is done so rarely. Individual products are frequently studied and their prospects assayed. Major markets too—e.g., the market for construction materials—may be studied, especially by the larger companies. But a searching look at the prospects of *all* the products at the same time, let alone of all result areas of a business, is still uncommon—even in companies that profess to believe in long-range planning. Yet it is both an easy thing to do—though not so easy to do well— and a most revealing, question-raising approach to the business and its capacity to perform and to produce results.

III

WHERE THE RESOURCES ARE

Actually I have gotten somewhat ahead of myself. In calling this or that product "marginal," or in wondering whether another product might not have to give something "extra" (e.g., heavy technical service) in order to retain its position, I have anticipated the results of the next step in the analysis: that of the allocation of key resources.

So far, by and large, the analysis has centered on things that happen to the business and its products. Now we ask what the business does to make things happen. Business has only two kinds of key resources: knowledge resources—that is, trained people—in buying, selling and servicing, in technical work, and especially in management; and money.

What are these scarce and expensive resources being used for? In what result areas are they deployed? Are they applied to

TABLE IV. UNIVERSAL PRODUCTS COMPANY PRODUCT ANALYSIS: MONEY

(dollars in millions)

Product	Revenue	Money Allocation as Percentage of Company Totals	
		Working Capital (Inventories and Receivables)	*Promotion Expense*
A	$19.0	15% ⎫ Together account for	25%
B	14.0	45% ⎭ 80% of receivables	40%
C	14.0	5%—Mostly inventories	Under 5%
D	11.0	3%—Mostly goods in transit	Nil
E	7.0	10%—Mostly repair parts	5%
F	4.0 ⎫	Almost nil—made to order	10%—Mostly
G	4.0 ⎭	and sold for cash	technical literature
H	3.5	15%—20% of all receivables	10%—Mostly special offers
I	2.0	5%—Mostly spares for obsolete models no longer made	5% to 7.5%— Trade-in allowance
J	Under 1.0	Nil	Yet to be budgeted

opportunities or to problems? And to the important and most promising opportunities?

Tables III and IV show such an analysis of the resources allocation in Universal Products—though, of course, again in a fragmentary and grossly simplified form.

These resources have—or should have—the greatest impact. What really distinguishes a strong company from a weak one is above all its technical and professional people; its sales and service force; its managers, their knowledge, motivation, and direction.

Knowledge-people, working capital, and operating expenses such as promotion money are also the only resources of a business that can be shifted from one job to another within reasonable time. They are essentially the only "manageable" resources. Capital investments, by contrast, are more or less immovable once the original investment decision has been made.

But precisely because these resources are so eminently manageable, they must be managed, or else they will inevitably be mismanaged. Their mobility makes them particularly susceptible to pressures and urgencies, as well as to drift.

No one is likely to say: "Let's take our best plant, producing our most profitable product, and loan it for six months to a problem product; after all, the profitable product will still be there six months hence." But managements can say—indeed do say all the time: "Let's take our best design engineers working on a big new product for tomorrow, and loan them for six months to spruce up on old, obsolescent model." Or: "Let's take out some of the promotion money for the new product—it's doing well anyhow; and we need a special campaign for the old product that otherwise would be outdated fast by the new one."

The danger of misallocation also applies to working capital and to the "managed" costs, especially promotion expense of all kinds, from price discounts and technical literature to packaging and advertising.

One consumer-goods company in the United States, producing and distributing a nationally branded line for household use, found, for instance, that well over three-quarters of the advertising budget went to the four products that were at best near-failures. Four or five other products that contributed the bulk of the company's revenue, had the best market, the best growth potential and leadership had to be satisfied with an occasional mention. They should have occupied the center of the advertising effort.

Quantity is almost meaningless in respect to knowledge-people. Their quality is far more important. What working capital or promotion expenses are being used for is at least as important as their amounts. Quantitative measurements such as budget figures or manning tables therefore tell only a small part of the story. A depth analysis is needed which shows both the quality of the resources allocated and their specific use or purpose.

The most effective industrial research director I know says: "The number of competent research people grows only with the square root of the total research group, the number of people capable of sustained superior performance with the cube root of the total." To increase the number of superior research performers from three to ten, one therefore would have to increase the size of the total group from thirty to a thousand. Most experienced men would concur in the general proposition that the number of superior performers in any group—whether this be skilled mechanics, doctors in a hospital, or professors at a university—does not grow anywhere near as fast as the total group. Any sales manager, any engineering manager, any comptroller, any faculty dean knows that one has to hire and train a great many "boys" before one gets one "man."

It makes a great deal of difference what any one dollar of the manageable expenses is being spent on or invested in. A large inventory of spare parts needed because the product keeps breaking down and has to be fixed all the time may look the same on the books as a large inventory of finished products needed because demand is great. Similarly, it makes a difference in appraising performance of a piece of new equipment on the market, whether the promotion dollar goes to satisfy the demands of eager customers to have their personnel trained in using the product, or whether it goes to conceal substantial price cuts made to counteract customer-criticism and resistance.

An analysis of these resources and their allocation is therefore essential information for understanding the result areas.

The data on product E and its performance are made meaningful, for instance, by what the resources allocation analysis of Table III shows: the product is being "managed" by the service men in the field rather than by a manager. And the performance of product H would have had to be interpreted quite differently had the resources allocation analysis shown it grossly lacking in key personnel support and money allocation.

This analysis is, in other words, also an essential step towards understanding, diagnosis, and action-decision.*

There is a great deal more to knowledge and money resources than their allocation to result areas. But first one has to find out where these resources actually are and how they are related to business results.

* The analysis would, of course, be even more helpful if *total* capital employed could be related to result areas. This is possible, as a rule, only in the single-product company—or in a business which, like General Motors, has the bulk of its output in what is more or less one product in a small number of styles and sizes. However, total capital employed can usually be isolated whenever a larger business contains identifiable and separately managed smaller, decentralized businesses. There, of course, total capital allocation should be analyzed, with return on total capital as the key to business appraisal (as in the DuPont formula).

4 How Are We Doing?

There are innumerable products and services on the market, each with its distinct properties and functions. There are hundreds of distinct markets and different end-uses, all kinds of ways to group customers, and many different channels to bring a product or service to its markets and customers.

Yet practically *all* products, markets, and distributive channels can be classified under a small number of major categories. I have found eleven such categories adequate to classify all but the most exceptional cases.

The first five are fairly easy to diagnose. And the decision on their treatment is straightforward. They are:

1. Today's breadwinners
2. Tomorrow's breadwinners
3. Productive specialties
4. Development products
5. Failures

The second group of six categories contains the problem children. They are:

6. Yesterday's breadwinners
7. Repair jobs
8. Unnecessary specialties
9. Unjustified specialties
10. Investments in managerial ego
11. Cinderellas (or, sleepers)

How products might fit into these categories is shown in

Table V which continues the schematic presentation of the Business X-Ray of Universal Products.

TABLE V. UNIVERSAL PRODUCTS COMPANY PRODUCT ANALYSIS:
A TENTATIVE DIAGNOSIS
(*dollars in millions*)

Product	Revenue	Diagnosis
A	$19.0	Today's breadwinner becoming *yesterday's breadwinner*. On way down. Considerably oversupported.
B	14.0	*Investment in managerial ego.* Withdraw *all* support:
C	14.0	*Today's breadwinner.* Inadequately supported to become "tomorrow's breadwinner" and a leader.
D	11.0	Tomorrow's breadwinner. But will Prince Charming come before Cinderella gets old? Perhaps even a real "sleeper." NOT SUPPORTED.
E	7.0	*Repair job* needed on both product and management to cut out excessive service needs. Could then become a "productive specialty," perhaps even a "breadwinner." Marginal today.
F G	4.0⎱ 4.0⎰	Necessary? Have neither product, leadership nor prospects. Are either nuclei of new main product or *"unjustified specialties."*
H	3.5	Another *investment in managerial ego.*
I	2.0	The has-been. Breadwinner of the day before yesterday.
J	Under 1.0	Development. Not a product yet. Potential leader as new high-speed equipment comes into customers' plants. Do we know the market yet?

There is of course no particular magic to the number eleven (and even less to the terms chosen). Some may prefer a few more categories or get by with fewer. (Repair jobs, unnecessary specialties, and unjustified specialties might all be combined, for instance.)

But every analysis, I believe, has found that all result areas can be classified in this way and that the classification largely decides what to do with a product, a market, or a distributive channel.

These few categories, in other words, give us a tentative diagnosis for all the result areas and for the business altogether.

1. *Today's breadwinners.* Products in this category always account for substantial volume. They also make an adequate, and often a large, net revenue contribution. Their share of the cost burden should be at most no larger than their share in the revenues. Their contribution coefficient is good, though not commonly the highest. They still have some growth ahead, though usually only after considerable modification or change— in design, in pricing, in promotion, in selling methods, or in service. But even with modifications they are unlikely to grow much further. They are at their zenith or close to it.

Most company analyses turn up at least one product that is today's breadwinner. In this respect Universal Products is rather atypical in not having any one product that is clearly today's breadwinner. Product A is perilously close to becoming yesterday's breadwinner. And in its lack of adequate resources support, despite its growth potential, product C more nearly resembles tomorrow's breadwinner.

Today's breadwinner typically is amply supported by key resources. It actually should employ fewer key resources than its *present* revenue and profit contribution might seem to justify. It almost always employs more (in this respect product A is only too typical).

One reason for this common over-allocation of key resources to today's breadwinner is the belief that one can make it again into a growth product by putting a lot of effort behind it—even though everybody really knows that there is not much additional growth to be had. There is a tendency to consider a product today's breadwinner when, in reality, it has already become yesterday's breadwinner. Contribution coefficient is the best test (which product A would flunk).

2. *Tomorrow's breadwinners.* These are of course what everybody hopes all products are. And a company had better have at least one of them around. They are unfortunately not as

common as company press releases and stock market letters assume. (Indeed, that Table V shows two candidates for this category—products C and D—among only ten products is rather higher than average.)

Tomorrow's breadwinner is both sizable reality *and* promise. It already has a profitable, large market and wide acceptance. Yet its main growth is still ahead, without substantial changes in the product.

Net revenue contribution and contribution coefficient are typically high, are indeed typically higher than they should be. Because the product does so well, everybody thinks it does not need support. As a result, the key resources needed to make the most of it go elsewhere, especially to problems such as yesterday's breadwinner and above all to the investment in managerial ego. This is one of the worst ways of starving opportunities in order to feed the problems. For tomorrow's breadwinner is the product that gives the highest return on additional efforts and resources now.

Sometimes tomorrow's breadwinners are literally being starved to death. Or—all too often—there is just enough effort behind them to get them started but not enough to exploit them. The market is thus being readied for the competition to move in and reap the harvest without having done any sowing and cultivating. (This is likely to happen to product D in Table V, for instance, if it does not soon get the resources support it lacks.)

3. *Productive specialties* have both a limited and a distinct market. They should serve, however, a genuine function, should enjoy leadership in their market. Their net revenue contribution should be higher than their volume; their share in the cost burden, a good deal lower. And they should employ very limited resources, should indeed be almost by-products of the volume products.

Universal's product E might be made into a productive specialty—but it is not one yet.

4. *Development products.* Product J in Table V might serve as an example. It is not yet really a "product." It is still in process

of introduction, if not in process of development. It has still to prove itself. But potential is considered great and hopes run high.

Development products deserve the best a company has, in terms of management, in terms of technical work, in terms of sales and service. But the number of people allocated to them should be small—though it will of course be larger than the revenue generated yet justifies.

The real problem of development products is not what they are and do today. It is to make sure that they do not turn into the worst of all product categories: investments in managerial ego.

5. *Failures.* These are not likely to be a problem of diagnosis or treatment. They announce themselves and they liquidate themselves.

Indeed, healthy businesses do not succumb even to serious failures, as shown by Ford's recovery from the Edsel car in 1957–1958 (the most highly publicized product fiasco in American business history). Somehow failures are much like the pains small boys get from eating too many green apples. The pains are severe. There is danger, to be sure. But if a healthy boy survives the first thirty-six hours, he is almost certain to recover. By then the poison has liquidated itself.

II

We now come to the second—and much more difficult—group.

6. *Yesterday's breadwinners.* Like today's breadwinners, products in this group tend to have large volume sales. But they no longer make a major contribution to profit. They are being kept in the market either by price cuts, by high pressure advertising and selling, or by special services, especially to small and scattered customers. In other words, their gross revenue tends to be low in relation to their volume, while the number of transactions needed to keep them alive is constantly growing.

Product A in Table V is, as said before, likely to qualify as one of yesterday's breadwinners. And the concentration of key resources on product A which the table shows is only too typical. Everyone in the business "loves" yesterday's breadwinner; it is the "product which built this company." "There's always going to be a demand for good old A" is an article of company faith. But yesterday's breadwinners are obsolescent. Soon they will be obsolete—and shortly thereafter as senile as product I in Table V. Nothing can prevent their decline. Even to slow it takes efforts which will not pay for themselves.

7. *Repair jobs.* To qualify for this category a product must satisfy a number of stringent requirements. It must have:

- Substantial volume
- Considerable growth opportunities
- A significant leadership position
- High probability of exceptional results if successful

But it suffers from *one—and only one—*major defect, which

- Is clearly definable
- Fairly easy to correct
- Deprives the product of the full benefit of its profit and/or growth potential

Product E in Table V looks like a repair job; if the service could be built into the product instead of being given as an "extra" and as an incentive to buy, the product could become a respectable and profitable productive specialty. With some volume growth, it might even turn into a breadwinner, that is, into a profitable volume line. What it lacks is clear enough; it has no management.

Repair jobs tend to be sold to the wrong customers—or not offered to the right ones—or moved through the wrong distributive channel. More would therefore turn up if we were to analyze these other result areas.

In Universal Products, for example, a repair job identified in the market analysis revived the has-been product I. The very feature that made it obsolete in the United States market made it almost ideal for the company's Latin American businesses. They needed a product simple in application and suitable for small plants and fairly slow equipment. The company's three manufacturing subsidiaries in

Latin America were rapidly losing profitability despite market leadership; they had no cheap product with which to meet the competition of a European product designed for small plants employing a few highly skilled technicians and simple machinery.

The repair job here took the form of discontinuing domestic manufacture of product I and starting to make it in all three Latin American subsidiaries. The few United States customers who still want it have it shipped from the Mexican subsidiary; but no one tries to sell it in the United States market. In Latin America, however, this product has become today's breadwinner for all three subsidiaries, with the Mexican company exporting it all over the Caribbean, in addition. These export sales alone, a few years after the start of production in Mexico, were larger than the parent company sales of the product when it was made only in the United States.

Here is an example of a distributive channel repair job.

Having just started door-to-door selling, a producer of home maintenance equipment was pleased with the results. Compared to other companies his salesmen had an exceptionally favorable ratio of buying customers to number of calls and sold three times as much per sale. Further analysis brought out, however, that the operation produced a substantial loss. While the salesmen sold more per call than other door-to-door salesmen, they made only a fraction of the calls. Instead of completing a call in a few minutes they would have to stay hours, demonstrating their products, counseling on specific home repair or maintenance problems, and so on. And when, upon orders from the head office, they cut their calls short, sales disappeared.

The repair necessary was to give the salesmen more products to sell so as to get a much larger sale per call. The company actually made such products, including some with a fairly high unit price. But it had intentionally withheld them from door-to-door selling in the belief that only low-cost items (and few of them at a time) could be sold at the door. When it gave the door-to-door salesmen the full line (and a small truck to carry it on) sales per call went up several times in a few months.

Beware however! Not everything in trouble is a repair job—indeed, few products are. The requirements spelled out for it must be rigidly enforced. If a product fails to meet a single one, it should be rejected out of hand as a repair job. Otherwise, every yesterday's breadwinner, every unjustified specialty, above all every investment in managerial ego will claim to belong.

And under no circumstances should there be more than one repair operation on a repair job. If the repair does not work the first time, the plea "now we know what's *really* wrong here" should be most unsympathetically received. A repair job is bad enough; but an investment in managerial ego is worse. Yet this is what a "second chance" for the repair job will produce in the majority of cases.

8. *Unnecessary specialties.* But for its clumsiness, a better name would be "The specialty that needn't be one." For what is unnecessary here is the existence of specialties instead of one successful main product with enough volume to yield results.

Over the years an enormous number of special designs had been developed for fractional horsepower motors—each of them, it seemed at the time, serving a specific and slightly different need. As a result there was, in this industry, endless diversity. In reality the traditional classification of small motors had become obsolescent. But no new standardization had been attempted. When it was finally put through, during the last ten years, the apparently endless variety in the field reduced itself to five, six, or seven categories, each of them a major volume product.

One common symptom of unnecessary specialties is that half a dozen different ones are available for every customer or market requirement. Wherever a customer's need might be satisfied just as well with any of a half dozen variations—all specialties —a new "ordinary" volume product is likely to be hidden. Another sign is that advances in technology can be applied across the whole range of products, though each pretends to be a specialty for one "special" purpose.

Products F and G in Table V may be unnecessary specialties. Judged by revenue contribution they certainly are not productive specialties.

To have unsatisfactory results is not enough to make a product qualify as an unnecessary specialty, however. There must also be a real opportunity—for sales, for profits, for growth—for the

future, new main product that is to supersede the clutter of
specialties.

Otherwise we just have another unjustified specialty.

9. *Unjustified specialties.* An unjustified specialty is one which
does not really fulfill an economic function in the market place.
It is meaningless differentiation for which the customer is not
willing to pay.

The product on which a major maker of laboratory equipment prided
himself was such an unjustified specialty: a microscope which was
only a little different from standard instruments but cost much more
because it required different production and different finishing. But it
was not sufficiently different to obtain a premium price. Instead it
generated almost three-quarters of all complaints and required heavy
service support. It was just sufficiently different to need special handling and people trained in its temper tantrums. Yet because it was
expensive and difficult to make it was considered a quality product.
Only the customers did not share the illusion.

It is indeed easy to discover the unjustified specialty. Since
the customer does not pay for it, its profit performance is poor.
And since he usually does not want it either, complaints and
service calls run high. But the unjustified specialty will always
be defended with the argument, "If we didn't have it, we wouldn't
get the order for the volume products." Sometimes the plea is
valid—but in that case the specialty is not a "product" but the
promotional part of a "package." More often, however, there
is little substance to the defense. Sales-people frequently push a
customer who wants a standard product into ordering a "special"
with the argument: "Look at all the extra features you get free."

Specialties in the case of a producer of metal products in Great
Britain accounted for 20 per cent of volume but for something like
70 per cent of cost. They were stoutly defended by the entire sales
department as necessary to attract and hold the customers for the
main products. When, however, a supply of the main products from
the continent of Europe became available at a slightly lower price,
the main-product customers immediately switched over to the new
and slightly cheaper source of supply. The British company was left
with its specialties. The irony was that the British company, despite

the higher prices on its main products, was losing money because of the transactional costs of the specialties; whereas the continental supplier, despite lower prices and high capital costs, was making money fast.

Whether the buyers of main products actually buy the specialty is the best test, in other words—though it should be made before they stop buying the main grades. It is common for a specialty to have its own small, scattered customers while the volume customers shun it.

Unjustified specialties are always a drain on a company's results. They absorb a disproportionate amount of key resources. They require, as a rule, constant technical work to modify and diversify even further. For they can be kept in the market only if made to look "new" and different. Not being standard products, production runs are short and expensive, quality is not too predictable, and performance not closely controllable. As a result unjustified specialties typically produce a crop of complaints and constant service calls.

Much more dangerous, much more common, and infinitely harder to get rid of is the next category:

10. *Investments in managerial ego* (of which products B and H in Table V are examples).

This is the product that should be a success—but is not. But management has invested so much in the product by way of pride and skill that it refuses to face reality. The product, management is convinced, will succeed tomorrow—but tomorrow never comes. And the longer the product fails to live up to expectations, the more does management become addicted to it, and the more key resources are pumped into it.

I mentioned earlier Ford's Edsel venture as the most publicized American product fiasco. Actually the Edsel was the kind of failure that cannot, as a rule, be foreseen and prevented. What made it a big failure was simply that Ford is a very big company and the automobile market a very big market. And Ford dropped the Edsel fast and recovered rapidly without lasting ill-effects.

But few people outside the automobile industry realize that another automobile company was nearly destroyed by clinging for almost a quarter-century to an investment in managerial ego. This car was launched with hopes as great as those that led to the launching of the Edsel. It did not, however, fail as completely. It was a near-failure rather than a total one. For a quarter-century every survey showed that the car was the best engineered car, that it was styled and priced for the largest share of the market, and that the American public loved it.

The only thing wrong was that the American public did not buy it. Year after year this car failed in the market. But the forecasts for next year were always that it would finally take off and become the successful leader to which its qualities "entitled" it. To this end the company not only poured in more and more money. Worse, its key resources—managerial, technical, and marketing—were all sacrificed to this near failure. As soon as anybody in the company showed any ability, he was plucked out of whatever job he was doing—especially, if he worked on pushing the successful cars made by the company—and allocated to this "sick child." And six months or a year later, after he too had failed to make the car into a success, he usually became a former employee of the company.

When, after twenty-five years, the car was finally dropped, it had all but sucked dry what had been a powerful, successful, and growing company.

This example brings out the attitudes that create investments in managerial ego: the attitude that a product is "entitled" to success (or to its "proper price"); and the certainty that a product, and especially a new one, "must" succeed because "we know it is the best quality."

Both beliefs are, of course, poor economics. Moreover, they violate the most elementary probabilities. The odds against any new product's becoming even a moderate success are roughly five to one, and the odds against it becoming a smash hit are one hundred to one.

We know that out of every one hundred new products or services one, on average, becomes a real success and the foundation of a substantial and profitable business. Another nineteen or so become respectable breadwinners or productive specialties without ever becoming spectacular.

We also know that one of every hundred new products and services is as spectacular a failure as was the Edsel. One, in other words, liquidates itself immediately. Nineteen others fade before they have done serious damage.

This leaves sixty of the new products and services that, in all probability, will neither become successes to the point where they really earn their keep, nor turn into failures blatant enough to be abandoned. Sixty out of every hundred new products and services have therefore to be pruned lest they become investments in managerial ego.

The greatest self-delusion is the belief that the outlook for a product improves the more resources are poured into it.

Few popular maxims are as wide of the mark as, "If at first you don't succeed, try, try, try again." "If at first you don't succeed, try once more—and then try something else" is more realistic. Success in repetitive attempts becomes less rather than more probable with each repetition.

Every new product has to be given a limited time to come up to expectations. It should get an extension only if it has made great progress. If it still does not come through after such an extension, it should not be given another chance. Otherwise the business will become overgrown with investments in managerial ego, absorbing key resources, taking an exorbitant amount of management time—and yet never doing any better.

The only industry that seems to understand this is book publishing. If a new novel has not succeeded within a short time, publishers stop advertising and promoting it. And another six months later they sell out the remaining stock and take their loss. Contrary to popular legend no masterpiece ever suffered oblivion because of this practice.

Managerial ego is also normally involved in the next and last category:

11. *Cinderellas*—or, less poetically, *sleepers*. These products might do well if only they were given a chance. Instead they do not get the support and key resources their performance has already earned.

Product D in Table V looks like such a sleeper. The comment

on its leadership position also brings out why its opportunity is not being exploited.

One reason is the common management mistake of identifying profit margin with profit which is always profit margin multiplied by turnover. And profit margin needs adjustment to the transactions a product generates—as against the averaging of the cost burden common in accounting figures. Profit margins can also be deceptive where raw materials contents differ between products. A profit margin of $1.00 on $10-product A yields five times the profit of the $2.00 margin on $10-product B, if A sells ten times as much as B in the same time. Every businessman knows this, of course—but he remembers it only when (as in the DuPont and General Motors formulae for return on investment) turnover and margin are always associated and appear together (or are, as in the revenue figures used in our analysis, expressed together in one result figure).

The second reason why product D is disliked may be more important. It gets the sales that product B "was designed for." Its success threatens management's favorite. Other Cinderellas may encroach on today's breadwinner or speed the decline of yesterday's breadwinner. And since managers are human beings, they hope that this uncomfortable threat will go away if only one pays no attention to it. What is likely to happen instead is that a competitor—often a complete outsider to the industry—discovers Cinderella and elopes with her, leaving behind both today's breadwinner and its producer.

The developers of the transistor in the early fifties were American companies which had a large and profitable business in electronic tubes, especially in supplying replacement tubes for radio and television sets. The new transistor did the job of the electronic tube at a fraction of the cost, weighed little, and required neither energy nor space. While it was thus a definite threat to the tube, it generated no replacement business. It is only too understandable that, in this situation, the people in the large American companies felt that the transistor was "not yet ready" for general use. The Japanese, however, had no stake in the status quo. They realized that the low cost, light weight, small energy and space requirements of the transistor made possible a truly portable small radio. They took the American transistor, the same transistor that was not yet ready, and built on it their big radio business in the American market.

Not every new product that goes without support is a sleeper. But if a product does much better than expected despite lack of support, it may be one. There is a prima-facie case for increasing its key resources support, and especially for upgrading the quality of the key resources allocated to the product. At least the product has shown a greater potential than anybody had predicted.

III

Diagnosing the Changing Product

To classify products as well as the other result areas is not too difficult. But it is not enough for a valid diagnosis.

We also need to be able to anticipate a change in the character of a product, especially a degenerative one. How can we tell when tomorrow's breadwinner turns into today's breadwinner and goes on to become yesterday's breadwinner? How can we tell that yesterday's development product is on the way to becoming an investment in managerial ego, and so on?

Two simple rules apply to all classifications in all result areas (except the outright failures which take care of themselves).

1. Any significant deviation of performance from expectations is likely to signal a change in classification. At least it demands re-analysis.

2. There is a "life cycle" to every product (market, end-use, distributive channel). Analysis of the *cost of further increments of growth* shows where a product stands in its life cycle and what its life expectancy is.

The first rule requires that expectations be written down ahead of events.

The human memory is singularly elastic. Three years later nobody remembers that a product was once expected to revolutionize the industry, instead of which it just barely returns its operating expenses. What everybody is likely to remember is, "We started this as a minor addition to our product line and it is doing quite well."

Only insistence on writing out expectations for a product can therefore provide a reliable record.

By comparing the actual course of events against expectations, we can identify in particular two major problem areas: the degenerative disease of the investment in managerial ego and the missed opportunity of the sleeper. Holding performance against expectations is also the best way to find the unjustified specialty. For, almost without exception, it comes into being in the expectation that it will produce exceptionally high profits, or grow into a major product, or create a new major market, or at least that it will bring in new major customers for the volume products.

INCREMENTAL ANALYSIS

The idea of a life cycle for a product making possible incremental analysis is, unlike that of an expectations-result comparison, a new one to most businessmen. It therefore deserves some explanation.

The life-span of products is so different as to make any generalization impossible. Some products last only a few months or years. Aspirin, on the other hand, in an industry noted for its rapid change and high rate of innovation, has lasted, little changed, for seventy years now and shows few signs of getting old and tired.

Yet no product lasts forever. And the pattern of its life cycle is always the same. In its infancy, a product requires high inputs of resources without any return. This is actually the stage before it becomes a "product." It is only a "development."

When it reaches its youth, each additional dollar of new input should produce many dollars in return—whether the additional input is in the form of capital, of technical improvement, or of key resources. When the product reaches maturity and becomes today's breadwinner, the incremental acquisition to be gained by additional input goes down sharply; where the cost of incremental acquisition reaches or exceeds the additional revenue that can be acquired, a product becomes yesterday's bread-winner. The investment in managerial ego, however, goes straight from early youth into senile decline where additional efforts cost more than they return.

There exists for this a simple mathematical theorem familiar to any engineer. At one point—the engineer calls it the "knee of the curve" —the increments of output begin to decrease rapidly. Up to that point, for instance, the increment of output to be obtained by each additional unit of input has been going down in arithmetic progression, from ten, to nine, to eight, to seven, and so on. Suddenly these increments begin to go down in geometric progression. For each additional unit of input for instance one only gets one-half or less as much additional output as the preceding increment produced. At this point further inputs are actually no longer productive. Returns are diminishing too fast. At this point one, therefore, stops further inputs.*

One should actually stop further inputs before the output gain for each incremental input unit starts to go down. This, in terms of the life cycle, is the point where a product becomes today's breadwinner. It is the optimum point. It corresponds to the optimum driving speed in an automobile or the optimum flying speed of an airplane—where one gets the most performance from the fuel, the most results from the resources.

The concept of the cost of incremental acquisition does not apply only to individual products or service, markets or customers. A sharp rise in the cost of incremental acquisitions is usually the first, but also the most significant, danger signal for an entire business or industry.

That the mass-circulation magazines in the United States were headed for trouble was signaled, for instance, in the early fifties, by a sharp rise in the cost of incremental acquisition of new subscriptions. To raise their circulation further, magazines had suddenly to spend more than they got back in additional subscription fees. At that time the

---

* One application of this theorem with which many executives *are* familiar is statistical sampling. A sample is optimal when enlarging it no longer increases the reliability of the findings by a statistically significant amount.

mass-circulation magazines seemed headed for larger revenues and better business. Yet the crisis that within a few years wiped out a good many of them, and still threatens to kill more, could already be foreseen. Not being able to reverse the trend in the cost of incremental additions to circulation, the mass-magazines had to run into trouble.

Advertising, sales, and promotion expenses are particularly suited to this analysis. How much additional business does each additional million dollars of advertising generate? Actually, advertising in which the incremental yields do not go up as advertising expenditure increases is, in all probability, uneconomic advertising. It is not enough for the increments to remain steady. They must still go up. This is simply another way of saying what any advertising man knows: Advertising is either superbly effective—or it is no good at all.

Applied to the present situation in the United States, this would raise serious doubts regarding the most popular advertising medium, television. There, for the last ten years, it has only been possible to increase the money spent. But insofar as figures are available, it does not seem that any additional results have been obtainable.

The importance and applicability of the concept of the cost of incremental acquisitions go way beyond the scope of this chapter. This concept applies to a great many business tasks over and beyond that of making the present business effective. Indeed, it is one of the most important diagnostic tools at our disposal. That modern accounting is rapidly recognizing this fact and is organizing its system to provide the needed figures for incremental analysis is a major improvement in management's performance capacity. Incremental analysis converts the tentative diagnosis from an audit of the past into a tool of anticipation and prevention.

5 Cost Centers and Cost Structure

Costs—their identification, measurement, and control—are the most thoroughly worked, if not overworked, business area. In this vineyard labor the most, the busiest, and the best equipped of the business professions: accountants, industrial engineers, methods analysts, operations researchers, and so on. The Anglo-American economist in his "theory of the firm" is primarily interested in costs, their character and their control. And so is the German with his *Betriebswirtschaftslehre*. An enormous amount of work goes into cost control, an enormous amount of time goes to cost analysis. There is no lack of tools, of techniques, of books on the subject.

The annual cost-reduction drive, for instance, is as predictable in most businesses as a head cold in spring. It is about as enjoyable. But six months later costs are back where they were—and the business braces itself for the next cost-reduction drive.

The one important exception is the cost-reduction "miracle" of a new management in a sadly run-down company. The company typically has enjoyed leadership, if not monopoly position under an earlier, hard-driving management. Under weak successors it has drifted unmanaged until it found itself suddenly face-to-face with total ruin. Then costs can be slashed by one-third or by one-half by doing the obvious—by closing down, for instance, an old plant that for years has turned out neither products nor profits. But this also means that the cost-reduction miracle at best provides a breathing spell during which the new management can begin rebuilding the business.

Altogether focusing resources on results is the best and most effective cost control. Cost, after all, does not exist by itself. It is always incurred—in intent at least—for the sake of a result. What matters therefore is not the absolute cost level but the ratio between efforts and their results. No matter how cheap or efficient an effort, it is waste, rather than cost, if it is devoid of results. And if it was incapable of producing results all along, it was unjustifiable waste from the beginning. Maximizing opportunities is therefore the principal road to a high effort/result ratio and with it to cost control and low costs. It must come first; other cost-control efforts are additional rather than central.

Yet even a business that works systematically on directing its efforts and resources toward opportunities and results needs cost analysis and cost control. No business can possibly run without frittering away efforts—just as no machine on earth can be made to run without friction losses. But a business and its cost performance can be greatly improved, just as friction can be reduced.

There are several prerequisites for effective cost control:

1. Concentration must center on controlling the costs where they are. It takes approximately as much effort to cut 10 per cent off a cost item of $50,000 as it does to cut 10 per cent off a cost item of $5 millions. Costs, too, in other words are a social phenomenon, with 90 per cent or so of the costs incurred by 10 per cent or so of the activities.

2. Different costs must be treated differently. Costs vary enormously in their character—as do products.

3. The one truly effective way to cut costs is to cut out an activity altogether. To try to cut back costs is rarely effective. There is little point to trying to do cheaply what should not be done at all.

Typically, however, the cost-cutting drive starts with a declaration by management that no activity or department is to be abolished.

This condemns the whole exercise to futility. It can only result in harming essential activities—and in making sure that the unessential ones will be back at full, original cost level within a few months.

4. Effective control of costs requires that the whole business be looked at—just as all the result areas of a business have to be looked at to gain understanding.

Otherwise, costs will be reduced in one place by simply being pushed somewhere else. This looks like a great victory for cost reduction—until the final results are in a few months later, with total costs as high as ever.

There is, for example, the cost reduction in manufacturing which is achieved by pushing the burden of adjustment on the shipping room and the warehouse. There is cost reduction of inventory which pushes costs of uncontrolled fluctuation upstream onto manufacturing. There is, typically, a great cost reduction in the price of some purchased material which, however, results in longer, slower, and costlier machine work to handle the less than perfect substitute material. These examples, as every manager knows, could be continued almost ad infinitum.

5. "Cost" is a term of economics. The cost system that needs to be analyzed is therefore the entire *economic* activity which produces economic value.

"Cost" should be defined as what the customer pays to obtain certain goods or services and to derive full utility from them. It is, however, almost always defined legally rather than economically; that is, as those expenses which occur within a particular— and purely arbitrary—legal entity, the individual business. This leaves out the bulk of the true costs. Two-thirds of the cost of every single product or service lies outside any one particular business. The manufacturer accounts for at most one-quarter of the customer's cost—the rest goes for the raw material the manufacturer purchases, for the expenses of a converter or fabricator, and, of course, for the costs of distribution which normally accrue in the legally independent and different businesses of wholesaler and retailer. The retailer—the department store, for instance—is again responsible only for a small part of the total costs—the main costs are those of the goods he buys in order to sell them, and so on. What matters, however, to the customer, and what determines whether he buys or not, is total outlay. He is completely unconcerned with how the outlay is divided between a number of legally independent businesses in the economic chain from raw material to finished article. All he is concerned with is what he pays for what he gets.

"Cost control" that limits itself to the costs incurred within any of the legal entities in the economic chain can never hope to control costs. At the least, cost control demands that the entire costs be known and understood.

Indeed the definition of "costs" might go beyond customer purchases. No one buys a thing. He buys the satisfaction and utility he derives therefrom. True economic costs therefore should include everything the customer has to spend to derive the full use from his purchase—in maintenance, in repair, in running costs, and so on.

It does not follow that an article can be sold for more money if only its maintenance costs are sufficiently lowered. It may well be that the customer's own situation forces him to define "price" as initial outlay and to disregard cost of upkeep. In the United States and in England, for instance, municipalities as a rule have stringent restrictions on their borrowing powers but fairly broad taxing powers. They can therefore afford to pay higher operating costs which are defrayed out of taxes provided only that capital costs, normally provided out of borrowings, are kept low. As a result, municipalities in these two countries have been reluctant to buy aluminum poles for street lighting, which over their twenty-year life are cheaper than steel poles but cost more in terms of initial purchase. And no matter what the economic realities, they will be disregarded as long as the legal rules under which these customers operate impose on them what may be economically speaking irrational behavior.

A cost analysis therefore is not truly meaningful or reliable unless reviewed and revised against the findings of a *marketing* analysis that looks at the business from the outside. By itself it is only a partial view.

In some of the most conspicuously successful businesses the

work done on outside costs is the real key to their accomplishment.

The two retail giants who are the "distribution successes" of America and England respectively—Sears Roebuck in the United States and Marks & Spencer in England—are examples. Both owe their success above all to finding manufacturers, developing new and improved manufacturing processes for their suppliers, and specifying the costs of the manufacturers' finished products. Both have taken active responsibility for the manufacturer's costs, products and processes well beyond, and outside of, their legal control.

Similarly, the success of General Motors rests to a large extent on the company's work on the cost structure of the independent automobile dealer. IBM owes much of its success to engineering of the customer's paperwork so as to make the equipment most productive.

To be able to control costs, a business therefore needs a *cost analysis* which:

   • Identifies the *cost centers*—that is, the areas where the significant costs are, and where effective cost reduction can really produce results
   • Finds what the important *cost points* are in each major cost center
   • Looks at the entire business as one *cost stream*
   • Defines "cost" as what the customer pays rather than as what the legal or tax unit of accounting incurs
   • Classifies costs according to their basic characteristics and thus produces a *cost diagnosis*

II

TYPICAL COST CENTERS

Where are the cost centers in the business and its economic process? Where is it really worth while to work on the control of costs? Where, in other words, could a relatively minor improvement in cost have really significant results for the total costs of the business? And which are the areas where even substantial improvement would really not mean much in terms of the total costs of economic performance?

An analysis by cost centers for Universal Products is shown in Table VI. These figures are crude, to be sure. They are only intended to indicate where to look further.

TABLE VI. UNIVERSAL PRODUCTS COMPANY: TOTAL COSTS AND COST STRUCTURE [a]

THE CONSUMER'S DOLLAR			100%
I.	*Physical movement of materials and goods*		
	(a) From materials supplier to factory; from warehouse to machines and through factory	6%	
	(b) From machines as finished goods through packaging, crating, shipping, warehousing to wholesaler	6%	17%
	(c) By distributors (wholesale and retail)	5%	
II.	*Selling and sales promotion* (manufacturer, wholesaler, and retailer.)		8%
III.	*Cost of money in the manufacturer's business—including working capital, interest charges, depreciation, and maintenance of equipment* (manufacturer only)		13%
IV.	*Cost of money for distributors* (rough estimate)		6%
V.	*Manufacturing—conversion of materials into salable products*		9%
VI.	*Purchased materials and supplies*		25%
VII.	*Management, administration, and record keeping* (manufacturer, wholesaler, and retailer)		10%
VIII.	*Investment in tomorrow—research, market development, executive development, and so on*		2%
IX.	PROFITS—before taxes—of manufacturer, wholesaler, and retailer (but excluding, as unknown, profits of materials suppliers)		10%

[a] The actual analysis—here reproduced in simplified form—showed, of course, ranges rather than absolute figures; i.e., the figure for Physical Movement was 13–19 per cent rather than 17 per cent.

Money (in the manufacturer's business as well as in those of the distributors) and *physical movement of materials and goods* account together for 36 per cent of the total or for more than half of all costs after raw materials. This is quite typical. Yet these two areas tend to be overlooked as cost centers.

Cost of money in the business, a financial analyst might argue, is actually a good deal higher than shown. It probably includes most of what is shown as profits which are actually costs of capital needed to stay in business. There is merit to this position—accepting it would make the cost of money the largest of all cost centers.

Money in the business is always a major cost center. It is also the one cost area where efforts are easiest and are most likely to produce meaningful results. It is, as a rule, easier to speed up the turnover of money than to do much about unsatisfactory profit margins. Yet only in the last few years have American managements taken seriously the management of money in the business. Indeed, this job has only recently been accepted as an important function of management, for which somebody in the top group has to be responsible, and on which somebody has to work full time.

Moreover, businesses specifically fail to think through the financial structure that is most appropriate for their economics, and that gives them the best utilization of that most expensive "raw material," money. Typically, at least in the United States, businesses use equity money to finance bankable loans, though it is elementary that one cannot make an equity return on a bankable loan.

Until a few years ago, one of the major food processing companies in the United States, canning such seasonal products as tomatoes, peas, or corn, financed itself entirely through equity capital. But vegetables have to be canned when they ripen and have then to be kept on the shelves the rest of the year. Equity capital, in other words, was put into commodities and left idle for many months— where bank loans at the lowest prevailing rates of interest would have been easily obtainable. As a result this company became less profitable the more it grew—to the point where it almost succeeded in killing itself through too much success.

Similarly, it is common to find businesses using permanent indebtedness for purely seasonal demands—for instance, long-term notes for fluctuating inventories. They thus pay interest all year for money they use two to three months. It is common to find companies that are "real estate poor," having sunk tremendous amounts of equity capital into real estate of at best marginal productivity, real estate they should either not have at all or should finance through conventional mortgage or insurance-company money.

Altogether it can be said that any dogmatic financial policy is likely to be wrong. It is as wrong to say, "We do not believe in debt," as to say, "We borrow every penny we can get." The right way to manage money is to think through the economics of the business and to finance accordingly. Few things are as expensive as the wrong financial structure. Few things, however, are so completely hidden in the traditional approach to costs—and so totally beyond the reach of the conventional cost reduction drive.

But the costs of money in the business are also often inflated by economically misleading conventions, especially those of the tax regulations. The tax distinction between capital investments and operating expenses creates, for instance, hidden costs. It is a legal rather than an economic distinction. Economically, capital investment may be considered as the present value of future income expectations; while maintenance and depreciation are nothing but the installments through which capital investment is paid for. The cost center is therefore always total cost of capital, regardless whether this is shown as operating expense, e.g., maintenance, in the profit and loss statement, or as capital investment in the balance sheet, regardless, in other words, of whether this is shown as a cost or as an asset. Which costs the least amount of money (tax included) is the only appropriate criterion.

None of this can be deduced from looking at the figures of Table VI.

The one suspicion they raise immediately, however, is that the company finances its distributors heavily—though whether this is actually the case and whether it serves a purpose, cannot yet be said.

Distribution is always a major cost center—and is generally neglected. One reason is that distribution costs are spread among all the businesses in the entire economic process. And much distributive cost is incurred between two businesses in the process and is left untended by both. Another reason is that distribution costs within a business tend to be hidden in a great many places rather than shown together as the cost of a major economic activity. Moving goods and storing them are parts of the same distributive activity. Their costs may be shown in "miscellaneous" under many headings.

Inside the manufacturing plant there are, for instance, the costs incurred between finished production, i.e., the stage at which a product comes off the machine, and its shipment to a customer. These costs include cutting, labeling, packaging, storing, moving. This is usually considered "manufacturing overhead"; nobody is really accountable for the activity. But inventories outside of the plant are usually considered "working capital" and their costs a "cost of money."

The costs of physical distribution are likely to yield to cost-reduction and cost-control efforts much more readily than manufacturing costs, simply because so much less effort has been directed at them.

Warehousing, for instance, is a sizable cost point in many businesses (as well as in such distribution systems as those of the Armed Forces). In some industries it runs to 8 per cent or more of total cost to the consumer. In all but the most modern mechanized warehouse, labor accounts for the main warehousing costs. Yet in many warehouses, owned and run by companies that pride themselves on their industrial engineering in the plant, labor costs are almost twice what they need to be. They still use the traditional gang system where three or four people work together on a task that actually only one man can do; for instance, unloading a railroad car or truck. There is only room for one man in the car; all the other members of the gang stand around and wait. Forty to 60 per cent of workers' time under the gang system is normally wasted, standing and waiting. In the plant such waste would long ago have been seen and corrected.

Raw Materials in a manufacturing business are also almost always a cost center of first magnitude. They need to be treated the way an effective large retailer finds, selects, and buys the goods it resells. It is not enough to buy a certain material cheaply and in good quality. The cost-impact of raw materials is such that their selection should be part of product design. The manufacturer, in respect to a material or a part, is the distributive channel. The material must fit his product, but the product must also be designed to fit the available materials. Both must be integrated so that the best product performance is obtained from that material which, in the total process of fabrication and distribution, costs the least.

This is what people have in mind when they speak of "materials management" instead of "purchasing." There are a good many techniques for the job available now; for instance, Value Engineering, which looks at each part of a product and asks of it: "What is the simplest and least expensive way to do this particular job?" Some of the large buyers—for instance, the automobile companies—have become highly sophisticated materials managers and fully integrate design and purchasing. But most manufacturers still have to learn what some of the large retailers grasped thirty or forty years ago: Buying is as important as selling; and the best selling cannot make up for a mediocre buying specification.

By contrast, the cost of manufacturing—that is, the cost of doing something physically to change the composition, shape, configuration, or appearance of physical substances—is not a major cost center.

Manufacturing is the one area where systematic and continuing work on cost control, that of the industrial engineer, has been going on for a long time. In most industries genuine manufacturing costs have become such a small part of total costs that significant cost-cutting requires a genuine breakthrough in manufacturing technology.

Such a breakthrough might emerge from a major change in the entire manufacturing process, such as automation; that is, a much higher degree of mechanization in doing the work itself, in handling and moving material and work, and in information and control of process.

But it might also lie in going in the opposite direction toward less integration of process and greater flexibility. In a good many process industries—for instance, aluminum rolling or papermaking—real breakthroughs have been achieved by uncoupling the manufacturing from the finishing process. An aluminum rolling mill, for example, physically separated the rolling of aluminum from its cutting, coloring, and shaping. Similarly, in a large paper mill, a significant breakthrough was achieved by separating the production of paper basestock from the finishing process, coating, cutting, and so on. In both cases inventories that used to be in the form of finished goods are now kept as semifinished material between manufacturing and finishing, with great reductions in total inventory needs and yet with significant improvement in the ability to satisfy grade and delivery requirements of customers.

Sometimes the most significant breakthrough is to shut down a plant even though it is "as good as new." The plant may be the wrong size or it may be in the wrong location—or it may, altogether, be no longer appropriate.

The most important cost contribution in manufacturing may lie in organizing the process according to its economic character rather than according to tradition. A paper mill, typically, tends to be organized so as to utilize pulp optimally. But pulp is only one of the basic materials of papermaking. Temperature is expensive too. And so are the chemicals that make the paper white or opaque to light, that give it the required printing surface it needs, and so on. To organize the papermaking process around the utilization of heat and chemicals rather than as a process for converting pulp at the lowest cost and greatest speed may significantly change the economics of paper manufacturing. And the same rethinking of the materials-balance around which manufacturing is organized can be applied to other industries and processes.

Short of such a breakthrough, not much is to be gained from cost reduction in manufacturing—in any one company or in well-managed plants altogether. Yet this is where the trained force of industrial engineers is usually concentrated. And a good many managements believe that they control costs by watching day-to-day fluctuations in manufacturing cost-ratios.

III

THE COST POINTS

Cost points are simply the few activities within a cost center that are responsible for the bulk of its costs. Again the assumption is that a few activities will account for the bulk of the costs. Major cost points are of course those activities which account for the transactions on which cost-calculations in any result area analysis are based. (See chapters 2 and 3.)

Table VII shows such an analysis for major cost centers.

TABLE VII. UNIVERSAL PRODUCTS COMPANY: COST POINTS

Major Cost Center		Cost Points	Percentage of Cost Center Costs	Percentage of Customer Dollar
I. PHYSICAL MOVEMENT of materials & goods	1.	TRANSPORTATION INSIDE and between plants	15%	2.5%
	2.	TRANSPORTATION to and from OUTSIDE and plants	26	4
	3.	HANDLING in SHIPPING ROOMS & WAREHOUSES	24	4
	4.	Packaging & crating	20	3
II. SELLING (manufacturer, wholsaler, retailer)	5.	Salesmen	62	5
	6.	Promotion	25	2
III. COST OF MONEY	7.	INVENTORIES of finished goods, especially in warehouses	23	3
	8.	Receivables	20	2.5
	9.	Interest	9	1
IV. COST OF MONEY (distributors)	10.	Inventories	25	1.5
VI. MATERIALS	11.	Material A	20	5
	12.	Material B	20	5
	13.	Packaging materials	20	5
VII. ADMINISTRATION	14.	Order handling	33	3
	15.	Credit & collections	20	2
Total		Cost accounted for		48.5 [a]

[a] Fifteen activities—out of many hundreds—thus account for 50 cents of each consumer dollar.

Some of these results were expected by management. Among them were:

Item		Per Cent of Customer Dollar
4	Packaging & crating	3
7	Finished goods inventories of manufacturer	3
11	Material A	5
12	Material B	5

But most results came as a distinct surprise. Particularly upsetting—being much larger than anybody had realized—were

Item		Per Cent of Customer Dollar
3	Handling in warehouses	4
4	Warehouse inventories	3
8	Receivables	2½
10	Inventories in dealer's hands	1½
13	Packaging materials	5
14	Order handling	3
15	Credit & collections	2

Promotion—item 6—on the other hand, had been thought to run much higher; the company's dealers actually left promotion to the manufacturer when they had been expected to match his efforts. And while the size of the receivables had of course been known, their relationship to inventories confirmed the suspicion that the company was indeed not only financing the distribution of its own products but was financing the distributor himself without, apparently, getting paid. And the high cost of order handling and credit (items 14 and 15) also pointed to something basically wrong in the company's distribution system.

Packaging materials—item 13—came as a real shock. Here was a major cost element that had not been seen at all. While other materials were bought by the purchasing agent, packaging materials had been left to the package designers in marketing. And they, obviously, had not given attention to the cost of packaging, nor, as the charges for handling finished goods showed, to packages designed for cheap and easy transportation, loading, and storage.

In some important areas this analysis made possible immediate action. For example:

A transportation study was obviously in order. It reduced total transportation costs by almost one-third, and almost eliminated transportation between plants.

Warehousing and inventory costs—almost 10 per cent of the total —were drastically reduced. A small number of modern warehouses were found to be able to give faster service more cheaply than a large number of small and old-fashioned ones. Inventories in the hands of distributors were all but cut out as the warehouse could give overnight service.

Receivables were sharply cut, as were order handling and credit and collections. At the same time effectiveness of the sales effort was greatly increased. It was already known in the company—as a result of the analyses of the result areas—that while a dealer force of ten thousand individual retailers carried the company's products, the largest two thousand of these dealers accounted for something like 80 per cent of the company's sales, with the remaining eight thousand accounting for 80 per cent of the actual cost of supplying the market. Effective cost control therefore meant doing something about the three thousand retailers who, each selling at most $3,000-worth of the company's products a year, accounted for no more than 5 or 6 per cent of total company sales. But studies triggered by this analysis and focused on the major cost points such as transportation, inventories, receivables, and administration showed that these small dealers were responsible for almost 40 per cent of the costs in these areas. They accounted for the bulk of the receivables, i.e., were the ones the company had to finance. They also accounted for a disproportionate share of both transportation costs and order handling costs as they ordered only small quantities. And they, of course, *were* the credit-and-collections costs.

These small dealers were put on a cash-with-order basis. Salesmen stopped calling on them. Instead, they were solicited by mail; and only mail orders for minimum quantities were accepted from them, and shipped, with freight charged in full, from the warehouse nearest to them. Over three years this cut total costs of the delivered product by 9 per cent—as much as the total cost of manufacturing. Receivables, for instance, all but disappeared, as did the costs of credit and collection. But the purchases of the small retailers only dropped by one-third, or about 2 per cent of total sales. Total sales actually went up as the salesmen, no longer forced to spend one-third of their time calling on unproductive accounts, concentrated their energies and time where the sales opportunities were; that is, on the larger retailer.

But to treat each major cost point as a separate problem is still inadequate. An analysis of cost points will always bring out that costs constitute a system. Necessary efforts and their expenses can be taken at more than one place—though with very different results.

In Universal Products, for instance, low over-all costs may well have been achieved by keeping inventory on the high side. This might make manufacturing efficient—by enabling it, for instance, to schedule production at an even pace the year round; thus avoiding the cost of fluctuations and perhaps even the costs—fixed and operating—of a plant large enough to turn out peak demand. But higher inventories may also cost so much more than uneven production as to be sheer waste.

Only a study that looks upon the entire physical flow and storage of materials as one system (a study well within the capabilities of an operations researcher or a systems engineer) can tell whether and to what extent lower manufacturing costs compensate for higher inventory costs.

Similarly, a company might well use higher inventories, quick deliveries, and, above all, a liberal credit and collection policy for the retailer as "promotion," rather than promote its products heavily with the consumer. In respect to the small retail customer of Universal Products this was not productive, as the analysis shows. The small outlets did not produce sales commensurate to the investment in them. But what about the larger outlets? Maybe for best—and cheapest—promotion results they should be better serviced and financed.

For goods which the consumer himself picks off the shelves—packaged goods for instance—direct consumer promotion is obviously important, though not necessarily decisive. But a student going off to college and buying a portable typewriter depends heavily on the advice of the "expert," the dealer or his salesman. As long as the consumer has heard the brand name before, he will accept the dealer's decision. Promoting the dealer—through higher dealer discounts, for example, or through financing him—may be the most effective and cheapest promotion for such goods. It may, for instance, explain in large part the tremendous success of a little-advertised German typewriter in the United States these last few years.

Each major cost point has to be seen therefore as a segment of the cost stream. Each proposed course of action on one cost point must be tested against the question: What will it do to the cost of work in other areas? There is no "cheap" or "efficient" manufacturing as such. There is only manufacturing that results in a cheap or efficient product or service to the customer. The relationship of costs to each other must be understood; "sub-optimizing" which controls and reduces costs in one area at the expense of costs and effectiveness in other areas must be avoided. But it is highly desirable to make trade-offs; i.e., to be able to forego apparent cost advantages in one area (to the point even of accepting higher costs) in order to obtain larger cost advantages in other areas, and thereby significantly lower total costs for the entire processes.*

IV

THE COST CATEGORIES

Major cost points fall into four main categories:

1. *Productive costs* are the costs of efforts intended to provide the value the customer wants and is willing to pay for. True manufacturing costs belong here; and so do costs of promotion. The costs of knowledge-work and of money-work belong here, and so does the cost of selling. Packaging should be here insofar as it makes a product distinct.

---

* The much-publicized PERT and PERT/COST Systems (with PERT standing for Program Evaluation and Review Techniques) are tools to work out both visually and mathematically such relations in a very complex system such as a major new missile or a space ship, especially for trade-offs both in respect to time and to costs.

2. *Support costs* provide no value by themselves, but cannot be avoided in the process. Transportation is a typical cost of this kind. The order-handling costs in administration belong in this category, as do inspection or personnel work, accounting, and so on. In an "ideal theory" of business, these activities can be disregarded or treated as overhead. In the real world, they consume as much effort as friction consumes energy in real machines.

3. *Policing costs* are the costs of activities which do not aim at getting something done but at preventing the wrong things from happening. Any business needs early warning systems to report when a product is not selling according to expectations, for instance, or when the company's technology no longer gives it a competitive edge. And here belong also the costs of policing others, suppliers or distributors, for instance.

4. *Waste* is the cost of efforts that cannot produce results.

The costliest waste is "not-doing"; machine down-time, for instance. Everybody waits till the repairman comes or till the new production run starts. Everybody waits till the ovens, after melting one aluminum alloy, have cooled sufficiently to be cleaned and prepared for the melt of another, different alloy. Not-doing is the oil tanker running empty from the refinery on the U.S. East Coast back to the Arabian Gulf, or the equally specialized banana boat returning empty from Rotterdam to Ecuador. The 150-seat jet plane sitting in the hangar or flying with only fifteen paying customers; or the freighter spending five days in port loading or unloading—when it only earns at sea carrying cargo—all these are not-doing.

These are not moral terms but economic ones. Admittedly, they fall far short of scientific precision. But some such classification that distinguishes the major cost points by relating them to results is essential. For each classification needs different analysis and requires a different approach to controlling costs.

In analyzing *productive costs* the proper question is: What is most effective? What produces the most results with the least input of effort and expense?

The concept of the cost of incremental acquisition described in Chapter 4 therefore applies here. Productive costs should be increased up to, but not beyond, the point at which the unit of incremental acquisition for an additional unit of input falls sharply.

What this means is that productive costs are not controllable as "costs" at all. They are controlled through the concentration of resources on opportunities. They require "result control" rather can "cost control."

Their measurement is therefore always the productivity of the resources employed. Productive costs need to be measured in terms of the results obtained by the three key resources of men, time, and money. What cost control adds to the previous analysis of result areas and of the allocation of resources to them are productivity measurements: output and profit per dollar of payroll as a cost measurement of the productivity of people; output and profit per man-hour and per machine-hour as a cost measurement of the productivity of time; and output and profit per dollar of total money at work as the cost measurement of the productivity of capital.* Concentrating resources on opportunities is the only effective way to control productive costs.

Support costs always have to prove first that they are needed at all. One always asks: "How much do we stand to lose if we do nothing?" And if the answer is: "Less than the minimum cost of support," then it is better to run the risk of an occasional loss and save the support costs. One should never spend more than 99 cents to gain a dollar; and where the gain is only possible—even where it is probable—spending 99 cents for it is too much.

A good example of how *not* to handle support costs is the story, a few pages back, of the manner in which Universal Products handled its distribution costs. By putting the three thousand smallest of its retailers on a mail-order cash basis, it cut costs sharply. But it still maintained costs that were larger than any possible return. For even

---

* These should be projected on "value-added" figures of output rather than on gross sales figures. Where raw materials utilization is an important element, a raw-materials productivity figure might be added which shows sales and profits per unit of material.

on a mail-order cash basis, a small retailer is expensive; the total cost of maintaining those outlets certainly amounted to more than the possible profit from their sales. Dropping these submarginal outlets altogether would probably not even have cost any sales—bigger orders from the profitable large retailers would, in all probability, have made up the loss fast enough.

If support costs cannot be cut out altogether, one asks: "What is the least cost and effort that will get by?"

In support costs this "least-effort" principle always leads to a redesign and reorganization of activities.

The physical handling and movement of things in manufacturing and distributing businesses may be the heaviest support cost. Even where there are no physical goods to be moved—that is, in financial and service businesses—the cost of physical movement and handling, of storage, of mailing, etc., of such things as documents, policies, checks, bills, etc., is a large cost center. Yet few businesses have the remotest idea of the cost of physical handling and movement. Many do not even know their freight bill, which, after all, is a straight, out-of-pocket cash payment.

To control transportation costs, the entire flow of materials should be seen as both a physical and economic system in which the greatest amount of physical performance is to be given with the least economic effort. The entire job—from the moment things come off the machine through crating, packaging, labeling, shipping, warehousing, storage, and so on, right through to the final destination of the merchandise in the customer's home or place of business—has to be seen and analyzed as one integrated process.

It has to be accomplished at the least possible cost and give the greatest economic value to all parties—manufacturer, wholesaler, retailer and customer.

This, needless to say, cannot be done overnight. We do have, however, the tools today to do the job—in the management sciences above all—and have achieved remarkable results wherever we have really gone to work.

The best thing to do with *policing* costs is not to police. The question is again: "Are we likely to lose more than it costs us to police?" If the answer is "No," it is better not to police. If this cannot be done, the least-effort principle applies. It usually consists in policing and preventing activities by means of a small but statistically valid sample, rather than through inspecting and monitoring every single event or transaction.

Inventory controls or quality controls are already handled this way in a good many businesses. Acceptable limits of nonperformance are set. How poor can customer acceptance of the product, minimum fulfillment of delivery promises, or of manufacturing schedules be before it endangers desired business results? The control can then be carried out through a small sample—which, of course, sharply cuts work and costs.

Perhaps the most elegant way of handling policing costs through a statistical method using a small sample is to find an activity which has to be done anyhow and which yet controls and audits a great many areas that otherwise would have to be policed.

One of the major shipping lines, for instance, uses the handling of complaints as the quality control for its entire freight operation, for its piers and terminals, and for the treatment of passengers.

Claims arise when goods are damaged, delivered late, delivered to the wrong address, etc. They may also arise from injuries to passengers or from damage to their belongings. If the goal were to settle claims at lowest cost they would be put on a simple, statistical basis. Ninety-five per cent of all claims would then require no investigation.

In this shipping line, however, claims investigation is used as the quality control for all operating activities. The theory (amply confirmed by subsequent experience) was that shortcomings in the handling of freight or passengers anywhere on the line show up as claims fairly fast. Investigating every claim therefore gives 100 per cent control of all operating failures. Yet all the claims together are still a smaller sample than would be needed for statistical quality control of the entire operation.

This example also shows that truly effective control of policing costs requires study and hard, sustained work. The ordinary cost-control approach will not work here. On the contrary it may well push up these costs. The first thing management in a cost-reduction drive tends to do is to police more and to prevent more.

THE HIGH COST OF NOT-DOING

Waste rarely needs to be analyzed. It is usually quite clear that this or that cost cannot produce results; whether we can do anything about it, is another question.

But waste is often hard to find. The costs of not-doing tend to be hidden in the figures.

This is of course not true for not-doing as blatant as the tanker returning in ballast or the jet plane flying empty. But for many years the shipping companies did not realize that their main costs were costs of idle time in port rather than costs of carrying goods at sea. The port time was just "overhead." As a result the emphasis in ship design and management was on a fast trip at low operating costs at sea. But cutting down already low seagoing costs resulted in making port costs even higher, loading and unloading even slower, turn-around time in port even longer.

Such attempts to come to grips with the costs of not-doing as the "minimum economical run" for a certain model (that is, the number of pieces—or of hours—in a run required for adequate machine utilization) are on the whole inadequate. They are still figures for doing rather than for not-doing. They rarely include the often high price for interruption of work and diminution of productivity incumbent upon any shift from one model or variety to another: the cooling and cleaning of the melting ovens for aluminum alloys, for instance, during which the whole expensive rolling mill equipment and all the people employed wait idly. They also rarely include equipment-utilization differentials.

Thus one particular aluminum alloy may utilize the *rolling* equipment as well as another one, but utilize practically none of the *finishing* equipment. Because of that, accounting may set the cost of the alloy 30 per cent lower—and it will be priced accordingly. Yet, the finishing equipment has nothing to do while this particular alloy is being rolled. Though the equipment stands idle, however, its costs go on; and the finishing department is where the bulk of the people and therefore the heaviest costs are found. The normally available figures would not reveal this.

Waste runs high in any business. Man, after all, is not very efficient. Special efforts to find waste are therefore always necessary.

One indication that the costs of not-doing are high is usually furnished by the accounting figures themselves. Whenever the "allocated manufacturing expenses," or their equivalent, run to one-third or more of total manufacturing cost, I suspect high, hidden waste costs. Another warning signal is sharp discrepancy between the cost-share of a product in the accounting figures and its *share of the cost burden* as calculated on the basis of the transactions it is responsible for.

But the best way to find waste is to look for it, and especially to ask: Where are we spending time, money, and people for not-doing and on producing nonresults?

There is only one sensible thing to do with waste-creating activities: drop them.

Sometimes this requires little effort; as in the illustration above where three thousand small retailers, out of a total ten thousand or so, could be dropped, thus eliminating a high cost of doing nothing (in this case selling nothing).

But many wasteful activities are hard to get rid of. It sometimes requires a major redesign of a whole business; more often it requires basic changes in operating practices, in equipment, in policies.

To fill the empty airplane seats with paying customers might, for instance, require a redesign of routes or of tariff structures, or major promotional efforts to attract a different and new class of customers. Eliminating machine down-time might require adoption of preventive maintenance or of a new and different scheduling system and of new inventory practices. Cutting wasteful time of freighters in port might require redesign of the general-cargo freighter into a seagoing materials-handling plant, and so on.

Such efforts, however, are totally outside of the conventional approach to cost control and cost cutting. They require major, prolonged efforts; indeed, a good deal of the most expensive waste is typically found in "restraints" on a business—and as such is a major potential that needs to be converted into an opportunity.

Most cost cutting, let alone the across-the-board cut, does not even touch waste. Yet, in every business waste is a real cost center.

The management of costs requires the same kind of systematic, organized approach as has been developed in earlier chapters for the management of result areas and resources. The conclusion from the analysis of the cost streams—what to tackle, where to go to work, what to aim at—should become part of the overall understanding of the business and of the comprehensive program for making it fully effective.

6 The Customer Is the Business

The analysis of the business; its result areas, its revenues, its resources allocation and leadership position, its cost centers and cost structure, answers the question: *How* are we doing? But how do we know whether we are doing the right things? What, in other words, is our business—and what should it be? This question calls for a different analysis, an analysis that looks at the business from the outside.

Business is a process which converts a resource, distinct knowledge, into a contribution of economic value in the market place. The purpose of a business* is to create a customer. The purpose is to provide something for which an independent outsider, who can choose not to buy, is willing to exchange his purchasing power. And knowledge alone (excepting only the case of the complete monopoly) gives the products of any business that leadership position on which success and survival ultimately depend.

From the inside it is not easy to find out what a business gets paid for. Organized attempts to look at one's own business from the outside are needed.

As experienced a company as Radio Corporation of America (RCA), was convinced that the consumer would recognize and accept the

---

* To repeat something first said a decade ago, in my *Practice of Management* (New York and London 1954).

RCA trademark on refrigerators and ranges when it entered the kitchen appliance business in the forties. RCA is of course one of the best-known consumer trademarks for radios and television sets. To a manufacturer these are as much "appliances" as are kitchen ranges. For the consumer they are an entirely different category of goods, carrying different value connotations. Trademark acceptance in the market did not carry over from radios to ranges and RCA had to withdraw from the kitchen appliance business. It is quite possible—indeed, likely—that the RCA trademark would have carried customer acceptance for tape recorders and photographic cameras. To a manufacturer, however, radios and cameras are entirely different goods.

There are scores of similar examples. What to the manufacturer is one market or one category of products is to the customer often a number of unrelated markets and a number of different satisfactions and values.

People inside a business can rarely be expected to recognize their own distinct knowledge; they take it for granted. What one knows how to do, by and large, comes easy. As a result the people in the business tend to assume, unthinkingly, that there is nothing to their knowledge or special ability, indeed that everybody else must have it too. What looms large on their horizon are the things they find hard—that is, the things they are not particularly good at.

A major, highly diversified company making chemical, pharmaceutical, and cosmetic specialties has great ability in finding, developing, and holding together a group of highly individualistic, aggressive division heads. Each is a professional manager, up from the ranks. Yet each runs his division as if it were his own business. Each is jealous of any encroachment by one of the other divisions—indeed, considers some of them direct and dangerous competitors. Yet all work closely with a small but able top management group and they work with each other in a harmonious team on all matters concerning the entire company. Problems that plague every other company of this kind—where, for instance, no division head will voluntarily give up one of his good people to another division—do not exist for these men. Yet nobody has been able to convince the management group in the company that they are doing something remarkable.

Sears Roebuck is a good example here too—precisely because few companies in the United States have so carefully analyzed themselves.

To the outsider it seems obvious that Sears' most important knowledge area is buying: the design of the right merchandise; the selection of the right assortment; the selection of the source from which to buy—and if necessary, manufacturing either in a wholly-owned plant or in partnership. Not much less important is selection of store location, architecture, and design. These, however, are not the knowledge areas which Sears people themselves stress. Both inside their own group and when talking to the public, they stress selling. The outside observer is hard put, however, to see anything distinctive in Sears selling—it does not differ noticeably from every other mass-merchant's selling. But the hero of the Sears sagas is always a store manager. And far more of the top jobs seem to go to people who came up as store managers than go to people with buying or store-planning backgrounds.

I am not saying that the people inside a business are bound to be wrong in their appraisal of what the business does and what it gets paid for. But they cannot take for granted that they are right. The least they can do is to test their judgment.

II

MARKET REALITIES

All this is hardly news for businessmen any more. For a decade now the "marketing view" has been widely publicized. It has even acquired a fancy name: The Total Marketing Approach.

Not everything that goes by that name deserves it. "Marketing" has become a fashionable term. But a gravedigger remains a gravedigger even when called a "mortician"—only the cost of the burial goes up. Many a sales manager has been renamed "marketing vice president"—and all that happened was that costs and salaries went up.

A good deal of what is called "marketing" today is at best organized, systematic selling in which the major jobs—from sales forecasting to warehousing and advertising—are brought together and coordinated. This is all to the good. But its starting point is still *our* products, *our* customers, *our* technology. The starting point is still the inside.

Yet there have been enough serious efforts for us to know what we mean by the marketing analysis of a business, and how one goes about it.

Here, first, are the marketing realities that are most likely to be encountered:

1. What the people in the business think they know about customer and market is more likely to be wrong than right. There is only one person who really knows: the customer. Only by asking the customer, by watching him, by trying to understand his behavior can one find out who he is, what he does, how he buys, how he uses what he buys, what he expects, what he values, and so on.

2. The customer rarely buys what the business thinks it sells him. One reason for this is, of course, that nobody pays for a "product." What is paid for is satisfactions. But nobody can make or supply satisfactions as such—at best, only the means to attaining them can be sold and delivered.

Every few years this axiom is rediscovered by a newcomer to the advertising business who becomes an overnight sensation on Madison Avenue. For a few months he brushes aside what the company's executives tell him about the product and its virtues, and instead turns to the customer and, in effect, asks him: "And what do you look for? Maybe this product has it." The formula has never failed—not since it was used, many years ago, to promote an automobile with the slogan, "Ask the Man Who Owns One"; that is, with the promise of customer satisfaction. But it is so difficult for the people who make a product to accept that what they make and sell is the vehicle for customer satisfaction, rather than customer satisfaction itself, that the lesson is always immediately forgotten, until the next Madison Avenue sensation rediscovers it.

3. A corollary is that the goods or services which the manufacturer sees as direct competitors rarely adequately define what and whom he is really competing with. They cover both too much and too little.

Luxury cars—the Rolls Royce and the Cadillac, for instance—are obviously not in real competition with low-priced automobiles. However excellent Rolls Royce and Cadillac may be as transportation, they are mainly being bought for the prestige satisfaction they give.

Because the customer buys satisfaction, all goods and services compete intensively with goods and services that look quite different, seem to serve entirely different functions, are made, distributed, sold differently—but are alternative means for the customer to obtain the same satisfaction.

That the Cadillac competes for the customer's money with mink coats, jewelry, the skiing vacation in the luxury resort, and other prestige satisfactions, is an example—and one of the few both the general public and the businessman understand.

But the manufacturer of bowling equipment also does not, primarily, compete with the other manufacturers of bowling equipment. He makes physical equipment. But the customer buys an activity. He buys something to do rather than something to have. The competition is therefore all the other activities that compete for the rapidly growing "discretionary time" of an affluent, urban population—boating and lawn care, for instance, but also the continuing postgraduate education of already highly schooled adults (which has been the true growth industry in the United States these last twenty years). That the bowling equipment makers were first in realizing the potential and growth of the discretionary-time market, first to promote a new family activity, explains their tremendous success in the fifties. That they, apparently, defined competition as other bowling equipment makers rather than as all suppliers of activity-satisfactions is in large part responsible for the abrupt decline of their fortunes in the sixties. They apparently had not even realized that other activities were invading the discretionary-time market; and they had not given thought to developing a successor-activity to a product that, in the activities market, was clearly becoming yesterday's product.

Even the direct competitors are, however, often overlooked. The big chemical companies, for instance, despite their careful industry intelligence, are capable of acting as if there were no competitors to worry about.

When in the early fifties the first of the volume plastics, polyethylene, established itself in the market, every major chemical company in America saw its tremendous growth potential. Everyone, it seems, arrived at about the same, almost unbelievable, growth forecast. But no one, it seems, realized that what was so obvious to him might not be totally invisible to the other chemical companies. Every major chemical company seems to have based its expansion plans in polyethylene on the assumption that no one else would expand capacity. Demand for polyethylene actually grew faster than even the almost incredible forecasts of that time anticipated. But because everybody expanded on the assumption that his new plants would get the entire new business, there is such over-capacity now that the price has collapsed and the plants are half-empty.

4. Another important corollary is that what the producer or supplier thinks the most important feature of a product to be—what they mean when they speak of its "quality"—may well be relatively unimportant to the customer. It is likely to be what is hard, difficult, and expensive to make. But the customer is not moved in the least by the manufacturer's troubles. His only question is—and should be: "What does this do for *me?*"

How difficult this is for businessmen to grasp, let alone to accept, the advertisements prove. One after the other stresses how complicated, how laborious, it is to make this or that product. "Our engineers had to suspend the Laws of Nature to make this possible" is a constant theme. If this makes any impression on the customer, it is likely to be the opposite of the intended one: "If this is so hard to make right," he will say, "it probably doesn't work."

5. The customers have to be assumed to be rational. But their rationality is not necessarily that of the manufacturer; it is that of their own situation.

To assume—as has lately become fashionable—that customers are irrational is as dangerous a mistake as it is to assume that the customer's rationality is the same as that of the manufacturer or supplier—or that it should be.

A lot of pseudo-psychological nonsense has been spouted because the American housewife behaves as a different person when buying her groceries and when buying her lipstick. As the weekly food-buyer for the family, she tends to be highly price-conscious; she deserts the most familiar brand as soon as another offers a "five-cents-off" special. Of course. She buys food as a "professional," as the general home manager. But who would want to be married to a woman who buys lipstick the same way? Not to use the same criterion in what are two entirely different roles—and yet both real, rather than make-believe—is the only possible behavior for a rational person.

It is the manufacturer's or supplier's job to find out why the customer behaves in what seems to be an irrational manner. It is his job either to adapt himself to the customer's rationality or to try to change it. But he must first understand and respect it.

6. No single product or company is very important to the market. Even the most expensive and most wanted product is just a small part of a whole array of available products, services, satisfactions. It is at most of minor interest to the customer, if he thinks of it at all. And the customer cares just as little for any one company or any one industry. There is no social security in the market, no seniority, no old-age disability pensions. The market is a harsh employer who will dismiss even the most faithful servant without a penny of severance pay. The sudden disintegration of a big company would greatly upset employees and suppliers, banks, labor unions, plant-cities, and governments. But it would hardly cause a ripple in the market.

For the businessman this is hard to swallow. What one does and produces is inevitably important to oneself. The businessman must see his company and its products as the center. The customer does not, as a rule, see them at all.

How many housewives have ever discussed the whiteness of their laundry over the back fence? Of all possible topics of housewifely conversation, this surely ranks close to the bottom. Yet not only do advertisements play that theme over and over again, but soap company executives all believe that how well their soap washes is a matter of major concern, continuing interest, and constant comparison to housewives—for the simple reason that it is, of course, a matter of real concern and interest to them (and should be).

7. All the statements so far imply that we know who the customer is. However, a marketing analysis has to be based on the assumption that a business normally does not know but needs to find out.

Not "who pays" but "who determines the buying decision" is the "customer."

The customer for the pharmaceutical industry used to be the druggist who compounded medicines either according to a doctor's prescription or according to his own formula. Today the determining buying decision for prescription drugs clearly lies with the physician. But is the patient purely passive—just the man who pays the bill for whatever the physician buys for him? Or is the patient—or at least the public—a major customer, what with all the interest in, and publicity for, the wonder drugs? Has the druggist lost completely his former customer status? The drug companies clearly do not agree in their answers to these questions; yet a different answer leads to very different measures.

The minimum number of customers with decisive impact on the buying decision is always two: the ultimate buyer and the distributive channel.

A manufacturer of processed canned foods, for instance, has two main customers: the housewife and the grocery store. Unless the grocer gives his products adequate shelf space, they cannot be bought by the housewife. It is self-deception on the part of the manufacturer to believe that the housewife will be so loyal to his brand that she would rather shop elsewhere than buy another well-known brand she finds prominently displayed on the shelves.

Which of these two, ultimate buyer or distributive channel, is the more important customer is often impossible to determine. There is, for instance, a good deal of evidence that national advertising, though ostensibly directed at the consumer, is most effective with the retailer, is indeed the best way to move him to promote a brand. But there is also plenty of evidence—contrary to all that is said about "hidden persuaders"—that distributors, no matter how powerfully supported by advertising, cannot sell a product that the consumer for whatever reason does not accept.

Who is the customer tends to be more complex and more difficult to determine for industrial than for consumer goods. Who is the ultimate consumer and who is the distributive channel for the manufacturer of power equipment for machinery: the purchasing agent of the machinery manufacturer who lets the contract; or the engineer who sets the specifications? The buyer of the completed machine? While the latter is usually without power to decide from which maker the parts of the machine (e.g., the motor starter and the motor controls) should come, he almost always has power to veto any given supplier. All three—if not many more—are customers.

Each class of customers has different needs, wants, habits, expectations, value concepts, and so on. Yet each has to be sufficiently satisfied at least not to veto a purchase.

8. But what if no identifiable customer can be found for a business or an industry? A great many businesses have no one person or group of persons who could be called their customer.

Who, for example, is the customer of a major glass company which makes everything as long as it is glass? It may sell to everybody—from the buyer of automobile instrument-board lights to the collector of expensive hand-blown vases. It has no one customer, no one particular want to satisfy, no one particular value expectation to meet.

Similarly, in buying paper for a package, the printer, the packaging designer, the packaging converter, the customer's advertising agency, and the customer's sales and design people, all can—and do—decide what paper not to buy. And yet none of them makes the buying decision itself. None of these people buys paper as such. The decision is made indirectly, through deciding on shape, cost, carrying capacity of the package, graphic appearance, and so on. Who is actually the customer?

There are two large and important groups of industries in which it is difficult and sometimes impossible to identify the customer: materials industries and end-use supply (or equipment) makers.

Materials industries are organized around the exploitation of one raw material, such as petroleum or copper; or around one process, such as the glassmaker, the steel mill, or the paper mill. Their products are of necessity material-determined rather than market-determined. The end-use industries, such as a manufacturer of adhesives— starches, bonding materials, glues, and so on—have no one process or material to exploit. Adhesives can be made from vegetable matter such as corn or potatoes, from animal fats, and from synthetic polymers furnished by the petrochemical industry. But there is still no easily identifiable, no distinct customer. Adhesives are used in almost every industrial process. But to say—as one would have to say about the steel mill or the adhesives plant—that everyone is his customer, is to say that no one is an identifiable customer.

The answer is not, however, that these businesses cannot be subjected to a marketing analysis. Rather, markets or end-uses, instead of customers, are the starting point for this analysis in materials and end-use industries.

Materials businesses—steel or copper, for instance—can usually be understood best in terms of markets. It is meaningful to say, for instance, that a certain percentage of all copper products go into the construction market—though they go to such a multitude of different customers and for such a variety of end-uses that these two dimensions may well defy analysis. It is meaningful to say that the adhesives all serve one end-use: to hold together the surfaces of different materials, though neither customer analysis nor market analysis may make much sense.

The view from outside has three dimensions rather than one. It asks not only "Who buys?" but "Where it is bought?" and "What it is being bought for?" *Every business can thus be defined as serving either customers, or markets, or end-uses.* Which of the three, however, is the appropriate dimension for a given business cannot be answered without study. Every marketing analysis of a business therefore should work through all three dimensions to find the one that fits best. This, by the way, is why the phrase "customers, markets, end-uses" has appeared so often in the preceding chapters.

Again and again one finds (1) that a dimension the people in the business consider quite inappropriate—customers or end-uses in a paper company, for instance—is actually highly important; and (2) that superimposing the findings from the analysis of one of these dimensions on another one—e.g., analysis of a paper company in terms of paper end-uses, paper markets, and paper customers—yields powerful and productive insights.

Even where there is a clearly identifiable customer, one does well to examine the business also in relation to its markets or the end-uses of its products or services. This is the only way one can be sure of defining adequately what satisfaction it serves, for whom and how. It is often the only way to determine on what developments and factors its future will depend.

These market realities lead to one conclusion: the most *important* questions about a business are those that try to penetrate the real world of the consumer, the world in which the manufacturer and his products barely exist.

III

HOW TO SEE THE UNEXPECTED

All the standard questions of a market study should, of course, be asked: Who is the customer? Where is the customer? How does he buy? What does he consider value? What purposes of the customer do our products satisfy? What role in the customer's life and work does our particular product play? How important is it to him? Under what circumstances—age, for instance, or structure of the family—is this purpose most important to the customer? Under what circumstances is it least important to him? Who are the direct and the indirect competitors? What are they doing? What might they be doing tomorrow?

But the emphasis might be on different questions that are rarely asked. They are the questions that force us to see the unexpected.

1. Who is the non-customer, the man who does not buy our products even though he is (or might be) in the market? And can we find out why he is a non-customer?

One illustration is the experience of a successful manufacturer and distributor of do-it-yourself home-repair and home-maintenance supplies and equipment. A market study brought out that his main customer was the newly married family with the first home of its own. It would be an eager customer for about five years and then gradually fade out. This seemed perfectly logical to the manufacturer. After all, these were the people who were most actively interested in the home. They had the energy to do manual work. And, having small children, they normally spent most of their evenings and weekends at home.

But when non-customers—families married longer than five years —were actually looked at, they were found to be a potentially excellent market. They were non-customers primarily because the company had chosen a distributive channel, especially the neighborhood hardware store, which was not easily accessible to them except Saturday morning. Saturday morning is not a good shopping time for men, once children, though still young, are past their infancy. Putting the merchandise into shopping centers (which remain open in the evenings when, increasingly, the whole family goes shopping together), and adding mail-selling directly to the home, more than doubled the manufacturer's sales. To be sure, a smaller percentage of the older homeowners buys, and the older family buys somewhat less per year. But at any one time there are many more people who have owned a home for five years or longer than there are new owners. A smaller percentage of the older age group still yields a bigger business than a higher share of the younger market.

2. Equally important may be the question: What does the customer buy altogether? What does he do with his money and with his time?

Normally companies want to know what share of the customer's total spending—his disposable income, his discretionary income, or his discretionary time*—goes for their products, and whether the share is going up or down. This is important, of course. But to have some idea how the customer disposes of all his money and time may tell a good deal more.

Asking this question brought out, for instance, that neither price nor quality was the determinant of purchasing decisions for the products

---

* Which mean respectively: cash remaining after taxes and other compulsory deductions from the pay check; cash available after "necessities" have been paid for; time available and not needed to make a living and to get the necessary rest, i.e., time available for leisure, recreation, education, and so on.

of a major construction materials company. What determined purchase was whether it could be accounted for as capital investment or as operating expense. What made the purchase possible for one group of potential customers, especially public bodies—namely, that the purchase appeared as an operating expense in their books—made it difficult for the other group, the private businesses, for whom a capital-investment appears as an asset while operating expenses interfere with profit figures in the books. The same products had to be "packaged" differently for the two kinds of customers: Public bodies got a ten-year "rental" in which the initial investment was paid off as part of an annual rental charge; private businesses were offered a capital-asset at a price which included ten years' free maintenance.

This leads in turn to two questions that are not asked in the ordinary market survey or customer study:

3. What do customers—and non-customers—buy from others? And what value do these purchases have for them? What satisfactions do they give? Do they, indeed, actually or potentially compete with the satisfactions our products or services are offering? Or do they give satisfactions our products or services— or products or services we could render—could provide too, perhaps even better?

What this question might unearth are the value preferences of the market. How important in his life is the satisfaction the customer obtains from us? Is the importance likely to grow or to diminish? And in what areas of satisfaction does he have new or inadequately satisfied wants?

4. This is, of course, very close to the crucial question: What product or service would fufill the satisfaction areas of real importance—both those we now serve and those we might serve?

The most imaginative illustration I know is that of a South American soft drink bottler who, while doing well, noticed that he was rapidly approaching market saturation. He thereupon asked himself: "What new product would, in the present stage of our economy, most nearly resemble the satisfaction which soft drinks offered to the masses fifty years ago?" His answer was paperback books. The population, while still very poor, had become literate in the meantime. Yet books in South America are available only in a few stores in the large cities and then at prices which even the middleclass can hardly afford. Paperback books, this man concluded, are, for today's population, precisely the small luxury which soft drinks were for the barefoot Indians half a century back. And in respect to merchandising, mass-distribution, mass-display, and the need rapidly to return unsold merchandise, paperback books are almost exactly like bottled soft drinks. What the man learned about his business, in other words, is that it was not "soft drinks"; it was "mass-merchandising."

Four additional areas demand investigation.

First: What would enable the customers to do without our product or services? What would force them to do without? On what in the customer's world—economy, business, market—do we, in other words, depend? Is it economics? Is it such trends as the constant shifts from goods into services, and from low price into high convenience in an affluent society? What is the outlook? And are we geared to take advantage of the factors favorable to us?

Second: What are the meaningful aggregates in the customer's mind and in his economy? What makes them aggregates?

Two examples will explain this question:

When the automatic dishwasher was first developed, the makers went to great trouble and expense to make this new kitchen appliance look just like the clothes washer—an appliance the housewife had enthusiastically accepted and was thoroughly familiar with. Since technically the two appliances are quite different, to make them look alike—especially in outside dimensions—was no mean achievement. Yet the main reason why the dishwasher has—so far—been a disappointment to its manufacturers is the ingenuity that went into making it look exactly like its older cousin, the clothes washer. For while it looks alike, it costs twice as much. To the housewife who is no engineer—and sees no reason why she should be one—this makes no sense. If something has been made to look exactly like the automatic clothes washer, why then should it cost twice as much? In other words, the manufacturers put the automatic dishwasher into a set of aggregates in which it created price expectations it could not meet. It is likely that the dishwasher would have done much better had it looked so different from the traditional kitchen appliances as to stand out clearly as something new, as something not belonging in this familiar aggregate: kitchen appliances.

Another example is the totally different experience Sears Roebuck has had with two kinds of insurance. When it introduced, in the thirties, automobile insurance as something sold through its retail stores—like any other merchandise—it was exceedingly successful. The Sears-owned insurance company rapidly became the second largest underwriter of automobile insurance in the United States. When, twenty years later, it introduced life insurance, it met with considerable customer resistance and has not yet been able to repeat its earlier automobile insurance success. To the customer, automobile insurance is essentially a product, an automobile accessory, and as much a part of the car as brakes or steering wheel. But life insurance is something different; it is finance rather than merchandise. It simply does not belong to the same aggregate as automobile insurance—that both have the word "insurance" in their name does not make them sufficiently alike.

Another case of mistaken aggregation by the manufacturer had a happier ending.

A manufacturer of garden products introduced a line for the rose grower—a special fertilizer, pesticide, and so on. A leading supplier, he expected the new line to be rapidly accepted. Almost every home gardener has roses and wants to take care of them. As "rose products" the new line was a failure. But as products for the care of flowers and shrubs in general, they began to sell well in a few places—even though the manufacturer in all his instructions stressed their exclusive application to roses. When the manufacturer accepted the customer's verdict and offered the products for all flowers and shrubs, the line, which he was ready to give up as a failure, suddenly came to life. "Rose grower" clearly means "somebody else" to the suburban home owner.

"Aggregates," to use the terms of the psychologist, are "configurations." Their reality is in the eye of the beholder. They depend not on definition but on perception. The perceptions, and with them the aggregates of the manufacturer and of the customer, must be different; for they have different experiences and look for different things. Yet it is the customer's perception of aggregates that matters, that decides what he buys, when he buys, and whether he buys.

Another searchlight on the unexpected is the third question: Who are our non-competitors—and why?

There is nothing that changes faster than industry structures. Yet few things appear to executives so much like a law of nature as the industry structure of the moment. The present membership of the electrical industry association or of the Retail Grocers Institute is considered "the industry." Yet again and again total newcomers are suddenly the most effective competitors—especially when they offer the customer a basically different means of satisfying the same want. In no time, industry structure— yesterday seemingly so solid—is fragmented. Yet the new one, as it stabilizes after a time, is again taken for the ultimate.

Here are two examples:

The manufacturers of printing presses paid apparently no attention to the new processes for office reproduction that began to come on the market after World War II. These were not "printing"; and the equipment for the processes was not being sold to "printers." One of the large printing-press manufacturers was offered several reproduction processes by the inventors and turned them down without any study. It was not until a large part of the printer's traditional work was being done by their former customers themselves on office reproduction equipment that the printing industry woke up to the fact that a competitor had appeared who was far more dangerous than another printing-press maker could have been.

Similarly, the fertilizer industry in the United States considered itself a "chemical business." The questions—Who are the non-competitors? Are they likely to remain non-competitors?—would at once have brought out that there is no reason why the petroleum companies are not in the fertilizer business. They furnish the most important raw material: ammonia (which is a by-product of natural gas). They are experts in mass distribution and have representation in the smallest hamlet in the country. And it was increasingly clear, in the late fifties, that the petroleum companies needed additional products for their huge and expensive distribution system. Yet even when one of the big American companies went into the fertilizer field in Europe, the U.S. fertilizer companies were convinced that it couldn't happen at home—until they woke up one fine day to find that the mixed-fertilizer business in the United States was being taken over by the petroleum industry.

The question: Who is our non-competitor? logically leads to the fourth question: Whose non-competitor are we? Where are there opportunities we neither see nor exploit—because we do not consider them part of our industry at all?

I V

UNDERSTANDING THE CUSTOMER

Finally one should always ask the question: What in the customer's behavior appears to me totally irrational? And what therefore is it in *his* reality that I fail to see?

I have yet to find a consumer-goods manufacturer, for instance, who understands why every important retailer will—indeed, must—insist on having a private brand of his own. The more successful the retailer is in selling national (i.e., manufacturer's) brands, the more will he insist on carrying and promoting his own. Manufacturers ascribe this insistence to the retailer's shortsighted concern with profit margins instead of with total profit-dollars. Yet retailers usually admit that the higher profit margin of the private brand is eaten up by higher inventory costs and by the cost of goods left over which, being the retailer's own, cannot be returned. This only confirms the manufacturer in his belief that the retailer is irrational.

Actually, the retailer is perfectly rational in fearing that complete dependence on national brands will endanger him, no matter how much profit he makes on them. Why should anyone want to come to his store if all he sees and gets there are the same nationally advertised and nationally sold brands he can buy every place else for the same price and in the same quality? A store whose reputation rests exclusively on the brand names everybody else can carry has no reputation or identity at all. All it has is an address.

Attempting to understand seemingly irrational customer behavior forces the manufacturer to adopt the marketing view rather than merely talk about it. Moreover, it forces the manufacturer to take action according to the logic of the market rather than according to the logic of the supplier. He must adapt himself to the customer's behavior if he cannot turn it to his advantage. Or he has to embark on the more difficult job of changing the customer's habits and vision.

The retailer's desire for a private brand to establish his store's identity is in the retailer's own best interest. The manufacturer had therefore better adapt to it, and if possible, turn it to his own advantage. The dominant supplier in any given product range might himself become the supplier of the private brand too.

On the other hand, the buying practices of the large American electric power companies for large generating equipment—turbines, for instance—were, while rational, detrimental to the best long-term interests of manufacturers and power companies alike. They resulted in unnecessarily expensive equipment. Traditionally each generating station is designed as a completely separate project; and the power company's design engineer tries to put special features into every turbine and every generator. But the two large American turbine manufacturers—General Electric and Westinghouse—have such volume that only mass-production methods can handle it. Hence these individual touches for each turbine cause heavy additional costs. At the same time, they are unnecessary today; for practically every performance configuration can be obtained by putting standardized parts together.

In addition, power companies—rationally from their point of view —order heavy equipment not when they know they will need it, but when long-term interest rates are low. Every five years or so, there is thus a spate of rush orders. And two to three years later the turbine plants are overcrowded and run on three shifts in a desperate attempt to finish what was already overdue in most cases when it was first ordered. Few things, however, are as expensive as an overcrowded plant in which men, half-finished work, and equipment get in each other's way.

The equipment manufacturers have thus far tackled the first part of the problem. In a long educational campaign they have been trying to get across that the power company could save a great deal of money if it were to specify performance of the equipment rather than its own detailed design. Apparently, they have made considerable progress. The second part of the job—the interest-rate determination of orders—has not been tackled yet, to my knowledge. (It should be possible to solve it though. Interest rates, after all, are cyclical. If the equipment companies were to take on themselves the differential between the going rate at the time of contract and the lowest rate within the next five-year period, they would, at most, risk something like 10 per cent; for they could re-finance at the lower rate within five years. And the penalty for the feast-and-famine method of production imposed by the traditional pattern is likely to be a good deal higher.)

Wherever a manufacturer tries to impose what he considers rational on an apparent irrationality which turns out to be in the best interest of the customer, he is likely to lose the customer. At the least, the customer will resent his attempt as a gross abuse of economic power—which it is. For behavior however that is contrary to the customer's own best interests, the manufacturer in the end pays a heavy price.

The American pharmaceutical industry may soon become living proof of this. The typical doctor's preference for a branded drug over a generic one is `rational enough. Modern pharmacology and biochemistry are way beyond most doctors, especially the older ones. How to combine several modern drugs in one prescription is far too complex for a busy practitioner ever to learn. He therefore prefers to depend on the manufacturer. That the doctor does not greatly care what medicines cost is also rational. After all, health insurance pays for it in most cases—and the patient therefore is unlikely to appreciate the doctor's efforts to save him money. There is thus a strong case for the brand. It may be the only way in which the average physician can acquire the necessary competence in using the new, highly potent drugs.

But it was the pharmaceutical companies' job to make this rationality of their distributive channel redound to the benefit of the ultimate consumer, the patient. Instead, they resigned themselves to the doctor's ignorance and made the patient pay for it through pricing branded compounds way above the same compounds sold as generic drugs under their scientific names. This predictably (and it *was* predicted by more than one good friend of the drug industry) will lead to punitive measures—which, as always, will go way beyond what is necessary or desirable.

As these examples show, forcing oneself to respect what looks like irrationality on the customer's part, forcing oneself to find the realities of the customer's situation that make it rational behavior, may well be the most effective approach to seeing one's entire business from the point of view of market and customer. It is usually the quickest way to get outside one's own business and into market-focused action.

Marketing analysis is a good deal more than ordinary market research or customer research. It first tries to look at the entire business. And second, it tries to look not at our customer, our market, our products, but at the market, the customer, his purchases, his satisfactions, his values, his buying and spending patterns, his rationality.

7 Knowledge Is the Business

Knowledge is the business fully as much as the customer is the business. Physical goods or services are only the vehicle for the exchange of customer purchasing-power against business knowledge.

Business is a human organization, made or broken by the quality of its people. Labor might one day be done by machines to the point where it is fully automated. But knowledge is a specifically human resource. It is not found in books. Books contain information; whereas knowledge is the ability to apply information to specific work and performance. And that only comes with a human being, his brain or the skill of his hands.

For business success, knowledge must first be meaningful to the customer in terms of satisfaction and value. Knowledge *per se* is useless in business (and not only in business); it is only effective through the contribution it makes outside of the business —to customers, markets, and end-uses.

To be able to do something as well as others is not enough either. It does not give the leadership position without which a business is doomed. Only excellence earns a profit; the only genuine profit is that of the innovator.

Economic results are the results of differentiation. The source of this specific differentiation, and with it of business survival and growth, is a specific, distinct knowledge possessed by a group of people in the business.

But while there is always at least one such knowledge area

in every successful business, no two businesses are alike in their distinct knowledge. Here, for instance, is the specific knowledge which might seem to an outsider to characterize some well-known large businesses.

General Motors, the world's largest manufacturing company, excels in knowledge of business development, especially of businesses that produce large, highly engineered mass-produced and mass-distributed units. Having acquired this knowledge in the automobile industry, General Motors has extended it to cover diesel locomotives and heavy earth-moving equipment, as well as consumer appliances. In particular, General Motors seems to have the ability to take over a mediocre business and transform it into a successful one. There are, however, limitations; General Motors too possesses specific rather than universal knowledge. The company has not succeeded in becoming an important producer of aircraft engines. This is a different market and a different knowledge, even though the technology is close to what General Motors applies in many other areas with great success. Even within the automotive field, General Motors is not the universal management genius. Its English subsidiary Vauxhall, after forty years of General Motors ownership and management, is still a poor third in the market.

The large American commercial bank, to take another example, has to have knowledge in three areas. It has to know the management of money. It has to know the management of capital, both in its trust and its investment business. Perhaps most important is the unique knowledge of data processing which a large commercial bank has to have, since it handles figures and documents together.

IBM, as the company itself stresses, is not the leader of the office equipment industry because of its physical products, good though they are. It is the leader because it excels in the management of data and information for business needs. What it gets paid for is a service rather than a product; it earns its livelihood with its knowledge of business processes.

A large space and defense contractor—someone like the Martin Company or North American Aviation—undoubtedly has special competence in metallurgy and electronics, in aerodynamics and physics. Its really distinct knowledge, however, is systems design and systems management—in part conceptual, in part managerial—in which a great many different skills (some of them yet to be acquired) are being directed toward a job no one has ever done before. It is the ability to anticipate the unknown, to plan for the unforeseen, and to bring together productively a great many areas of ignorance that constitutes excellence in systems management.

Philips in Holland has great technical competence, to be sure. But so have two dozen or more electric-equipment makers all over. What sets Philips apart is their unique ability to build and run a truly international company. All Philips companies are fully a part of the economy, the society, the market of the country in which they operate. Yet they all have the same products; and they are all consciously and unmistakably members of a tightly knit "family" in which everyone accepts the authority of the "head of the house," the top management back home in Holland.

What a business is able to do with excellence may be quite humdrum, something which thousands of other businesses can do well but which this one does much better.

One division of a large and well-known company consistently earns higher profits than the rest. The division does nothing but stamp, cut, shape millions of pieces of metal—with processes and machines used in a hundred thousand metal-working shops all over the world. But this particular division does this common job with uncommon excellence. It is its boast that it can run off a sample of the final product before the potential customer has finished explaining what he is looking for; that its price rarely runs higher than half of what the customer would have been willing to pay; and that it can start delivering any metal part in commercial quantities before the customer has returned to his own office. What this division excels in is speed and simplicity of design. Indeed, it rarely has to go through the engineering-design stages. Its plant superintendents, mostly men with little formal schooling, can take a rough sketch and convert it into a production prototype right on the machines and in practically no time.

Sometimes the knowledge that defines the business may be purely technological.

National Distillers, for instance, one of the leading manufacturers of alcoholic beverages in the United States, defines its knowledge as fermentation chemistry. And this definition led it, shortly after World War II, into becoming a major chemical and pharmaceutical company.

But I said "knowledge," not "technology." Technology—that is, the application of the physical sciences to work—is one form of knowledge. In no business is it the only necessary knowledge. There are many successful businesses in highly technological fields that do not excel in technology. They have to be technologically competent, of course. But their specific strength lies elsewhere—for example, in marketing (as is true of at least one well-known and successful chemical company in the United States).

Thus the successful glass company that says "our business is glass" obviously has to know more than the technology of glassmaking, complex and demanding though it is. It must have knowledge in the commercial and industrial application of glassy matter. Its knowledge is as much end-use knowledge as glassmaking knowledge.

This is always true of materials industries. Yet of all businesses they are the ones most nearly definable in terms of technology and of a distinct, organized body of information that can be taught and learned.

II

WHAT CAN WE DO WELL?

The best way to come to grips with one's own business knowledge is to look at the things the business has done well, and the things it apparently does poorly. This is particularly revealing if other apparently equally well-managed and competent businesses have had the opposite experience in similar undertakings. "What have we done well—and without any sense of great strain —while somebody else has failed to do the same job?" is thus the first question. And "What do we do poorly—while someone else seems to have no difficulty with it?" is the corollary.

Take, for instance, the contrasting performances of two exceedingly successful companies, General Electric and General Motors, in the development of new businesses. General Electric has shown outstanding ability to take a new idea and build a business on it, starting from scratch. It decided apparently during World War II that the United States could not afford to depend on imports of industrial diamonds but had to be able to make its own. From there it took only five years or so until it had found a way to make synthetic diamonds commercially. And ten years later—around 1960—the synthetic diamond business of General Electric had become the world's largest industrial diamond supplier.

General Motors has an equally outstanding record in developing businesses. It buys them, as a rule, when they have already achieved a fairly substantial size and leadership position. Again and again it has taken a merely adequate business and, within a few years, made a champion out of it. This is so rare a talent that General Motors frequently is suspected of the twentieth-century version of witchcraft: some unfathomable antitrust violation.

Yet neither company appears to do well what comes so easily to the other. General Motors has never, to my knowledge, started a business. And General Electric seems to have had little luck with the businesses it acquires.

Three well-known chemical companies similarly offer an illuminating contrast.

All three companies have done well over the years. To the outsider they look much alike. They all have big research centers, big plants, sales organizations, and so on. They all work in the same lines of chemistry. They are about equal in capital investment and in sales. They all show about the same substantial returns on investment. But one company always does well if it can bring a product or product line into the consumer market. The second company is outstanding in its ability to develop new chemical specialties for the industrial user. Again and again it has tried to break into the consumer market; and it has failed in the attempt again and again. The third company is not doing particularly well in either the consumer or the industrial market. Its return on sales is quite low compared to the other two. But it has tremendous income from licensing developments, coming out of its research, to other chemical companies—developments which apparently the company itself does not know how to turn into successful products and profitable sales.

The first and the third company are obviously strong in original research. The second one says of itself—and only half in jest—"We haven't had one original idea in the last twenty years." But it has amazing ability to see the potential of commercial development in somebody else's half-formulated idea or in a laboratory curiosity; to acquire the rights to the idea; and to convert it into salable chemical specialties for industrial use.

Each of the three companies has come to understand what it can do and what it cannot do. Each sets its goals and measures its performance in terms of its specific knowledge: the first in terms of success in the consumer market; the second in terms of the new successful chemical specialties it develops; the third in terms of the ratio of license fees received to research budget.

One need not, of course, compare oneself with somebody else. One can also compare one's own failures with one's own successes, and ask: What explains our performance?

A medium-sized company, working on the instrumentation of space craft, missiles, high-speed planes, and so on, had such uneven performance that a new—and technologically rather ignorant—president was brought in to straighten it out. There seemed to be no explanation for the unevenness of the performance—there were great successes in electronics side by side with complete failures; great successes in guidance controls side by side with complete failures; great successes in optics side by side with complete failures; and so on. Nor did an analysis of the men responsible in each instance give any clue—the same men, working in the same fields, would perform quite unevenly. It was only when the projects were looked at, one by one, that the answer was found. Wherever a contract had a tight deadline, the company did well. Its specific ability was to work under pressure— then effective teams would form themselves spontaneously. Without pressure no one, it seemed, paid any attention to a contract or project. Ironically, in a well-meaning attempt to create a university atmosphere, management had worked hard to get leisurely, non-pressure contracts from the government—and had apparently succeeded only too well.

Finally, it is always a good idea to ask one's good customers, "What do we do for you that no one else does as well?" Not that the customers always know. But their answers, however confused, are likely to bring out a pattern that indicates where to look for the answer.

KNOWLEDGE REALITIES

These examples convey five fundamentals:

1. A valid definition of the specific knowledge of a business sounds simple—deceptively so. One always excels at doing something one considers so obvious that everybody else must be able to do it too. The old saying that the erudition a man is conscious of is not learning but pedantry applies also to the specific knowledge of a business.

2. It takes practice to do a knowledge analysis well.

The first analysis may come up with embarrassing generalities such as: our business is communications, or transportation, or energy. But of course every business is communications or transportation or energy. These general terms may make good slogans for a salesmen's convention; but to convert them to operational meaning—that is, to do anything with them (except to repeat them)—is impossible.

On the other extreme, one may come up with a twenty-four volume encyclopedia of the physical sciences as a knowledge-definition plus a complete set of handbooks on all business functions. It is perfectly true that everyone in a managerial job should know the fundamentals of each business function and of every business discipline. Every manager should understand the fundamentals of those areas of human inquiry—whether electrical engineering, pharmacology or, in a publishing house, the craft of the novelist—that are relevant to his business. But no one can excel at universal knowledge—one probably cannot even do moderately well at universal information.

But with repetition the attempt to define the knowledge of one's own business soon becomes easy and rewarding. Few questions force a management into as objective, as searching, as productive a look at itself as the question: What is our specific knowledge?

3. Few answers moreover are as important as the answer to this question. Knowledge is a perishable commodity. It has to be reaffirmed, relearned, repracticed all the time. One has to work constantly at regaining one's specific excellence. But how can one

work at maintaining one's excellence unless one knows what it is?

4. Every knowledge eventually becomes the wrong knowledge. It becomes obsolete. The question should always arise: What *else* do we need? Or do we need something different?

"Have our recent experiences borne out our previous conclusions that this particular ability gives us leadership?" the president of a successful Japanese chemical company asks each of his top men once every six months. He himself analyzes the performance of each product, in each market and with each important customer, to see whether actual experience is in line with the expectations and predictions of his knowledge analysis. He asks each of his top men—from research director to controller and personnel man—to do the same analysis. And he spends one of his quarterly three-day management meetings on knowledge analysis. He credits his growth—within a decade this formerly limited and fairly small company has become one of the world's leading producers in a major field—to reviewing knowledge effectiveness and knowledge needs.

5. Finally, no company can excel in many knowledge areas.

Most companies—like most people—find it hard enough to be merely competent in a single area. This, of course, means that most businesses remain marginal and just manage to hang on. The figures amply confirm this. Out of each hundred businesses started, seventy-five or so die before their fifth birthday with management failure as the leading cause of death.

A business may be able to excel in more than one area. A successful business has to be at least competent in a good many knowledge areas in addition to being excellent in one. And many businesses have to achieve beyond the ordinary in more than one area. But to have real knowledge of the kind for which the market offers economic rewards requires concentration on doing a few things superbly well.

How Good Is Our Knowledge?

The knowledge analysis, like the market analysis, leads to diagnostic questions.

1. Do we have the right knowledge? Do we concentrate where

the results are? For the answer one looks to the marketing analysis of the business. The right knowledge is the knowledge needed to exploit the market opportunities. Does the business have the knowledge needed to give it leadership position in the market, and to earn rewards where the market values excellence?

It is an unusual business that finds that its knowledge is entirely wrong for the market. Such a business is likely to have died long before it got around to analyzing itself. But it is highly probable—in any business—that the existing specific knowledge is inadequate to the need.

There is often need for learning new things. Papermakers, for instance, had to become polymer chemists of considerable skill. And when the computer came in, the old punch-card salesmen of IBM had to move into an entirely new world and learn an entirely different language.

Sometimes the balance of knowledges has to be shifted. What was the core knowledge of the business has to be subordinated.

Thus, in the steel industry, during the last twenty years, the dominant knowledge has shifted from making steel to marketing steel. With the advent of modern metallurgy, making steel has increasingly become a matter of building performance into the equipment rather than practicing a mysterious alchemy. It is not becoming less important, but it is becoming increasingly less possible to excel in production. Steel marketing, however, what with the tremendous variations in the economic and technical characteristics and results of different product mixes, is infinitely more crucial than it used to be when the main job was to sell tonnage.

Knowledge has to progress to remain knowledge.

Knowledge is indeed very much like a world record in athletics. For years it stands, apparently immovable. Then one sprinter runs the mile a little faster, one pole-vaulter jumps a little higher—and suddenly other athletes repeat the feat and have acquired a new dimension of performance. For what one man has done, another one can always do again; and this is particularly true with respect to excellence.

2. The analysis of knowledge leads to a set of questions as to how effectively the right knowledge is being used.

Are we actually getting paid for the knowledge we contribute?

This does not necessarily mean that one has to bill the customer for the knowledge. IBM bills for equipment. But both IBM and the customer know that knowledge is the essential thing, and that the customer buys service rather than product. Indeed, it is this awareness on both sides that explains why IBM, starting late and with reluctance, took the leadership in the computer field away from companies that had started earlier and that seemed to possess much greater technical competence.

3. Is our knowledge sufficiently built into our goods and services?

One example is a company that has basic knowledge in polymer chemistry—perhaps its greatest knowledge area. Yet 90 per cent of its products do not benefit from this knowledge at all, even though they are polymer chemicals. They are still made by the old "cookbook" method of trial and error without application of the scientific and technical knowledge which the company has and which the customer expects when he buys its products.

4. How can we improve? What are we missing? And how do we go about supplying it?

Most commercial banks, for instance, have not yet realized that their data-processing knowledge might lead to a profitable business. It might enable them to offer office management service to middle-sized business, business that is too small to have its own modern equipment, and too large not to use modern methods of record keeping and data processing.

Or, to give another example, the large defense and space contractor —especially with the expected leveling off of U.S. government spending in these areas—might apply his systems management knowledge to such new fields as the exploration of the ocean, or the redesign of our oldest (but totally undesigned) system, the large hospital.

The conclusions of the knowledge analysis must be fed back into the marketing analysis to bring out market opportunities that might have been missed or underrated. And the conclusions of the market analysis are projected on the knowledge analysis to bring out needs for new or changed knowledge.

8 This Is Our Business

The analyses sketched out in the preceding chapters should provide the executive with an understanding of the business adequate to the demands of his economic task. No one of the four will do the job singlehanded. But by putting together:

- The analysis of results, revenues, resources
- The analysis of cost centers and cost structure
- The marketing analysis
- The knowledge analysis

a business should be able to understand itself; to diagnose itself; and to direct itself.

There remains one essential step: to re-examine the *tentative diagnosis* in the light of the marketing and knowledge analyses. As a result—and this can be said dogmatically—it will have to be changed substantially. Even though the "facts" were recorded precisely at the tentative stage, they could not yet be truly understood.

Some of the products will require a change of classification, for example. An unjustified specialty may turn out to be a highly promising product—for a different market or in a different distributive channel. Conversely, what looked in the tentative diagnosis like a strong product, a today's breadwinner still in its prime, or maybe even a tomorrow's breadwinner, may turn out to be at or near the end of its life-span.

Some products will be found to need substantial modification.

The same holds for markets, for distributive channels, and sometimes for whole businesses.

A major aluminum company had about decided that the market for aluminum foil was saturated, and that therefore poorly selling foil products were doing as well as could be expected. But the company ran the foil business like other aluminum lines; that is, as a producer-goods business, selling to design engineers and industrial purchasing agents. A marketing analysis forced management reluctantly to accept that this was a consumer-goods business in which the retailer—especially the supermarket—was the real customer. The company separated the foil business managerially from its other businesses and entrusted it to people who had never been inside an aluminum mill but knew how to market consumer goods. The foil business, a few years later, had not only reached but exceeded the original expectations; though a comparative newcomer in aluminum foil, the company is now close to first rank in its national market.

The experience of a rather small and highly specialized chemical company illustrates reclassification of both markets and knowledge and the resulting change in the diagnosis of a product—and in the strategy of a business. For many years the family-owned and family-managed company had produced a line of intermediates for the manufacture of textile dyes, especially dyestuffs for cotton. Main customers were the big chemical companies which do not make all the intermediates for a full dyestuff line themselves. But as synthetic fibers took over more and more of the American textile industry, this company saw its market and its profits shrinking steadily. Market analysis led the management to ask: "Where is *the* market?" whereas formerly the question had always been, "Where is *our* market?" This brought out that the market for cotton textiles, and with it for cotton dyes, was far from shrinking. It was actually expanding faster than the synthetic market. Only it was expanding not in the industrially developed countries, but in Latin America, India, Pakistan, Africa, Hong Kong, and so on. In each of these countries dyes had to be imported. There was nothing wrong with the company's products; they were just in the wrong market.

The company has now gone international. It makes dyestuff intermediates in eleven industrially developing countries, ranging from Israel to Formosa, and from Nigeria to India. In every case the capital risk has been taken by somebody in the host country. The

American manufacturer supplies the technical knowledge and the management under a long-term management contract, and against a fee and a stock participation.

At home the same company also changed the business as a result of its knowledge analysis. While still making its old dyestuff intermediates, it is rapidly expanding as a designer and manufacturer of chemical engineering equipment for dyestuff manufacture. This puts to good use specific and distinct knowledge in the design and manufacturing of dyestuff-making equipment. But until the executives analyzed the company's knowledge, they did not even realize that they had this capacity, let alone that it was an asset in today's rapidly industrializing world.

Another example illustrates the consequences of redefining the customer.

The redesign of the entire line of a hospital equipment maker resulted from a study of the market. The company had always assumed that acceptance by the medical profession meant leadership and success for its products. It spent a good deal of time and money on promoting itself and its products with the doctors. And it designed its products around their concepts of value, utility, and excellence. It had the esteem of the doctors—but it did not do well in selling to hospitals.

Analysis showed that doctors do not buy hospital equipment. It is bought by administrators who, whether they have the MD degree or not, have to run a complex institution—and run it primarily with poorly paid and not particularly skilled personnel. Their concept of "excellence" is equipment that neither ties down scarce, highly skilled nurses and technicians nor requires a lot of training—equipment which relatively unskilled people can operate safely, without danger to the patient, to themselves, or to the equipment. As the company described it: "We found out that our equipment has to be end-use focused and therefore has to be 'moron-proof' rather than 'doctor focused' and sophisticated."

This, by the way, also led to a radical reclassification of costs and to a change in the deployment of scarce resources. Promotion with the medical profession had been a major cost point for this company —and the ablest people on the sales staff worked at it personally. It had been considered the most productive cost in the entire cost stream. The cost of presenting the equipment to the hospital professions, however, was considered near-waste. The promotional effort with the doctors, while not abandoned, has now been cut down—it is more or less considered support, or at best a means to prevent opposition rather than to create the market. But promotional efforts to hospital administrators and hospital employees—including, incidentally, close cooperation with the training directors of hospital employee unions—is now seen as a truly productive cost which deserves high attention.

Here are two examples from a service industry:

A major life insurance company had developed a policy especially designed for the middleclass family man in his thirties or forties, the junior executive, the younger but already established professional man, and so on. The special attraction of the policy, the company thought, was that it enabled the insured to tailor the policy to his family situation and needs and yet retain a rather low premium-base. The policy sold no better than any other policy. Analysis of the way the customer buys showed what was wrong with it; it was being sold in the evening because this was the only time the "prospect" was likely to be at home. Yet he did not want to spend a lot of time discussing an insurance policy in the evenings. After a day's hard work he wanted to be left alone. The salesman therefore rarely got a chance even to explain the policy. But the analysis also showed that the wife in these families is vitally interested in financial protection and knows at least as much as the husband about the family situation. And she has time during the day. Hence the policy is now being sold—with good results—to the wives in the morning hours and after an appointment has been set up by telephone or letter. They then "sell" the policy to their husbands.

Another company thought that it was doing quite well with a complete insurance package—automobile, fire, home and household, health and accident, life insurance, all in one master contract sold by one salesman in one call. But customer analysis showed that casualty insurance and life insurance are different aggregates in the customer's mind. They should be; they serve entirely different needs. (That both are insurance is of no conceivable importance to the customer, however relevant it may seem to the companies, to the actuaries, and to the state governments and their insurance commissioners.) Separating the two—having one casualty package and one life insurance package—helped greatly. It also brought out that a good many prospective buyers would have bought one or the other but bought neither when offered both in one package. What helped even more was adding a non-insurance to the life package, mutual investment-trust shares. For life insurance is finance to the customer; and an equity investment not only fits in with it, but makes a complete investment program out of a life insurance policy. This has been so successful that within a few years half a dozen big insurers (for instance the Sears-Roebuck-owned Allstate Insurance Company) have started imitating the new finance package.

These are, of course, examples of actions taken, rather than just of reclassification or redefinition. But every action emerged from re-examining a tentative diagnosis in the light of market and knowledge analyses.

II

WHAT IS LACKING?

Even more important than to reinterpret what the business is doing is to identify what the business should be doing but so far does not do. Market and knowledge analyses, when projected upon the earlier analyses of the business, will bring out what is lacking.

In the result areas, three gaps are so often encountered that they can almost be expected. The business may need a major *development* effort to replace what is clearly past its prime. The replacement needed may be a product. But it may also be a new area of business effort and activity, such as a new market, new end-uses, or different distributive channels. And while not "technical" in the usual sense of the term, developing a new market or a new distribution system is as much "design and development"—and requires as much knowledge, work, and money—as designing a new piece of equipment.

The second common gap is lack of *adequate support* to exploit opportunity and success.

Market analysis in an equipment making company revealed, for instance, that a major product, while highly praised in one industrial market, was not bought by it to any extent. A competitor's product, though considered both more expensive and less satisfactory, got the orders. The competitor offered a complete package consisting of the piece of machinery in question plus a power-drive which geared it into the rest of the customer's equipment. The irony was that the lagging company had such a power-drive, had indeed originally designed the machinery around it. Somehow—no one could ever figure out how—the sales department had become convinced that the drive did not suit the particular industry to which the machine was being sold.

There are similar oversights in every business. No management is blessed with omniscience; unless one's vision is systematically sharpened, one overlooks the most obvious things or misinterprets the clearest signs.

The gap may lie in the distributive channel: the business has the products and services. It promotes the goods. It may even persuade the potential customers. But when they want to buy, the product is not available where they shop. The distributive channel does not reach them, or it is clogged halfway.

Every change in a product or in the way it is presented requires a thorough review of distributive channels. And every change in distributive structure, in turn—for instance, the rush to mass retail distribution in the American economy since World War II—requires a review of product design and product line, customers, markets and end-uses in turn.

The outside analyses usually reveal a third gap in *knowledge needs* and *opportunities*. What new knowledge of real importance is needed? Where does existing core knowledge need improvement, updating, and advancement? Where does our knowledge need redefinition?

The first two needs are straightforward enough. It is the last that is generally overlooked—and yet it is often the most important. Here is an example:

Knowledge of the printing industry, ability to service a printer, understanding of a printer's business, may be the marketing knowledge of a fine-paper company. But it may need redefinition as reproduction-market knowledge or as graphic arts-market knowledge to enable the company to market to the new reproduction-paper customers, who are the owners of office-reproduction equipment. This will require learning a few new things—for businesses to whom paper is an incidental supply buy quite differently from commercial printers for whom paper is the basic and most expensive raw material. But the important new factor may well be simply a clear redefinition. Otherwise, the paper people will not use what is applicable of their old knowledge in the new market. They may even throw away their present leadership position.

Having reached the end of this self-analysis, the businessman should be able to see what the business is, what it does, and what it can do. He should be able to determine:

• The satisfactions his products or services aim to provide, the wants they should fill, and the contribution for which the business can expect to get paid

• The knowledge areas in which the business has to have excellence to make the desired contribution. It should be possible to define what the business has to do better than anybody else to earn the chance to survive and to prosper. This carries with it a decision on the human values and the human resources needed

• The customers, markets, and end-uses to whom the business contributes distinctive value; and the distributive channels that have to be developed—and satisfied as customers—to reach these customers, markets, and end-uses

• The technology, processes, product or services areas in which these objectives find implementation and through which they take physical, tangible form

• The leadership position required in each result area

Marketing analysis and knowledge-analysis, when superimposed on the analysis of results, revenues, resources, and on the analysis of cost structure and cost centers, should not only yield new facts. They should give a management the knowledge to say: "This is our business"; the vision to say: "This is what our business could be"; and the sense of direction needed to say: "And this is how we might get from where we are to where we could be."

PART II

FOCUS ON

OPPORTUNITY

9 Building on Strength

Analysis of the entire business and its basic economics always shows it to be in worse disrepair than anyone expected. The products everyone boasts of turn out to be yesterday's breadwinners or investments in managerial ego. Activities to which no one paid much attention turn out to be major cost centers and so expensive as to endanger the competitive position of the company. What everyone in the business believes to be quality turns out to have little meaning to the customer. Important and valuable knowledge either is not applied where it could produce results or produces results no one uses. I know more than one executive who fervently wished at the end of the analysis that he could forget all he had learned and go back to the old days of the "rat race" when "sufficient unto the day was the crisis thereof."

But precisely because there are so many different areas of importance, the day-by-day method of management is inadequate even in the smallest and simplest business. Because deterioration is what happens normally—that is, unless somebody counteracts it—there is need for a systematic and purposeful program. There is need to reduce the almost limitless possible tasks to a manageable number. There is need to concentrate scarce resources on the greatest opportunities and results. There is need to do the few right things and do them with excellence.

To make business effective the executive has available three well-tried and tested approaches:

1. He can start with a model of the "ideal business" which

would produce maximum results from the available markets and knowledge—or at least those results that, over a long period. are likely to be most favorable.

2. He can try to maximize opportunities by focusing the avail able resources on the most attractive possibilities and devoting them to obtaining the greatest possible results.

3. He can maximize resources so that those opportunities are found—if not created—that endow the available high-quality resources with the greatest possible impact.

The rise of every one of the truly great enterprises in economic history was based on these approaches.

THE RISE OF GENERAL MOTORS

An example of the ideal business approach is the rise of General Motors, both the world's largest automobile company and the world's largest manufacturing enterprise. Alfred P. Sloan, Jr., who first redesigned General Motors and then, as chief executive for almost thirty years, built the company, has told the story in a recent book.* General Motors was on the verge of collapse when he took over in the depression of 1921. Ford with one model had a 60 per cent share of the American automobile market. General Motors with eight models was a weak second with about 12 per cent of the market. Only two of the eight models were profitable, six were losers—and had been losing not only money but market standing as well.

Sloan began by thinking through what the ideal automobile company in the American market would look like. He came out with a design in which five models covered the market. Only two of the existing models—the Buick and the Cadillac, both at the upper end of the line—fitted into this design. Three models were completely abandoned. Three others were replaced by what amounted to a brand new car even though it retained the old name. Sloan actually practiced the total marketing approach thirty years before the term was coined.

The Sloan design changed the concept of car marketing and

* *My Years with General Motors* (New York 1964).

the approach to the customer. Each of his five models was placed in a price and performance class in which it was both the most expensive and best-performing car of a lower price range and the cheapest and simplest car of the next-higher one. For a fairly small additional sum the low-income customer could obtain a car which, in appearance as well as in performance, was well above the Ford Model T. The customer who could afford a medium-priced car could also save a little money by buying the low-priced car with most of the appearance and performance of the medium-priced line; or he could pay a little more and have a near-luxury car. Each of the five cars was a distinct entry into the market and designed to be the leader in its class. Yet each competed also with the GM car on either side of it. For Sloan rightly believed that unchallenged success was dangerous, and so provided each of his five makes with at least one strong challenger from within the family.

This design made General Motors within five years both the dominant American automobile manufacturer and by far the most profitable one. And when Ford itself hit the comeback trail after World War II, it deliberately adopted the Sloan design and imported executives from General Motors who had been reared in the Sloan concept and strategy.

For the early 1920's, Sloan's design was radical—so radical indeed that it was quite a few years before his associates at General Motors accepted it. It violated all the then "known facts." Instead of dividing the potential customers sharply into a mass-market wanting uniform automobiles at the lowest possible price, and a class-market with low volume and high prices, Sloan saw the customers as essentially homogeneous, demanding mass-production but also performance, low price and easy sale of a used car but also an annual model change, comfort, and styling.

Sloan did not try to dislodge Ford by doing just as well, nor even by doing better. He never considered doing again what Ford had done before; that is, building the cheapest, standardized, changeless car. Instead, he made the Model T obsolete through something which neither Ford (nor anyone else) could possibly produce: the one-year-old, secondhand car. It had been the new car only one year earlier. As "transportation" it could easily compete with the Model T. It had the appearance, styling, and performance of the high-priced cars, but was cheaper even than the Model T.

Till then the used-car market had been considered a nuisance by the car makers. Sloan saw that it was the real volume market; and that the manufacturer had to design, sell, and service his new car both for greatest sale this year and for easiest resale a year or two hence.

In the medium-priced car market, Sloan found price differentiation to be less important. But here the role of the car as prestige symbol was greatest. This meant deliberately creating customer identification with specific makes, expressed through distinctive styling with fair continuity. Buick, for instance, was to identify itself with the successful professional man, through its styling, its pricing, its selling, and its promotion.

For the top price range Sloan's question was: What is the highest-priced car that still can be sold in such volume as to justify mass-production? In its way this too was an original and heretical approach. It had been axiomatic that the luxury car had to be handmade and handcrafted with production small and price high. General Motors' Cadillac, before Sloan, had followed this policy with considerable success. Yet Sloan replaced the profitable handcrafted Cadillac with a volume-produced, assembly-made car, which while costing less than a handmade car, actually exceeded in performance all but the Rolls Royce. Just as Chevrolet became, within a few years, the standard of the low-priced range, so Cadillac became the standard of the high-priced range.

It should be emphasized that Sloan's design was neither flash of genius nor product of years of hard toil with mathematical models and complicated computer runs. Sloan had of course given a good deal of thought to the automobile market before he took on General Motors. But his direct concern till then had mainly been the accessory business rather than the automobile business. He did not have a big staff for his study. He worked with a small committee of company executives and had only one month for the job. He did the work primarily from observation of the market and by asking questions of his own executives and of automobile dealers.

In other words: the results of a fairly short and simple study, while crude, are good enough to serve as the foundation for major decisions and actions. The work can be done by ordinary techniques available to managers (though more sophisticated techniques should, of course, be used wherever they speed the work).

Alfred P. Sloan's grand design took a good many years to execute. Pontiac for instance really did not become the car Sloan had specified until almost fifteen years later. But from the beginning the design produced results. And this has been the experience wherever the ideal business approach, the approach that designs a business to be what the market wants, has been tried.

THE FIRST INNOVATORS

The second major approach asks: What are the opportunities for the greatest economic results?

The best illustrations of the maximization of opportunity are the two men who, independently of each other, created the electrical industry and indeed our electrified world of today: the German Werner von Siemens (1816–1892) and the American Thomas A. Edison (1847–1931). Together their impact on the world we live in has been a good deal greater than that of Henry Ford and Alfred P. Sloan.

One answer to the question: "What did Siemens invent?" is: the first practical electric generator. But one can also answer: the electric apparatus industry. To the question: "What did Edison invent?" one can answer: the electric light bulb. But one can also answer: the electric power and light industry. More than anyone else they developed methods of technological research. But there were many other men at the time working on the same inventions. One can even argue that every one of their inventions was either anticipated or perfected at the same time by someone else.* Yet only these two men designed and built major new industries.

They knew very well what they were doing. They were by no means alone in being excited by the new vistas opened up by the scientific developments in electricity, especially by the work of the great Faraday. But they alone asked: What are the major economic opportunities which this knowledge opens up? What in the way of new or additional technological invention and development is needed to realize this economic opportunity? Siemens did not develop the electric railway because he had a generator; he developed the generator because he had visualized the electric railway as a major industry, especially for travel within the city, and therefore needed an electric motor to provide traction. Similarly, Edison did not design the first light and power plant, complete with generating stations, transformers, and distribution system, because he had invented a practical light bulb. He went to work on the light bulb because it was the one thing missing in his design of an integrated citywide power and light industry.†

These men, in other words, were the first real "innovators." They systematically defined the opportunity for new knowledge and new capacity to achieve—that is, the opportunity for innovation. Then they set to work to provide the needed new knowledge, capacity, and technology. They were also, it should be said, the first genuine "systems designers."

Both lived a long productive life; but both were major figures by the time they were thirty; both had by that time already created new industries rather than merely a new piece of equipment or a new design. Both maximized economic opportunities by asking the question: In what area of application of electricity does the opportunity lie for the most successful and most profitable new industry?

Maximizing opportunity does not necessarily mean technologi-

* As does for instance the Fifth Volume (1850–1900) of the well-known *History of Technology* (edited by Charles Singer, Oxford University Press 1958) with its unconcealed British bias.
† Edison's latest biography, *Edison*, by Matthew Josephson (New York 1959) brings this out fully.

cal innovation, as shown by the development of Japan as a modern industrial nation.

In the period between 1870 and 1900 when Japan turned herself from a pre-industrial economy of rural clans into the first non-Western modern economy, Japan could not possibly have promoted technological innovation. Her problem was rather that of social innovation: to create the institutions which would enable a thoroughly non-Western country with its own culture, tradition, and social structure to accept and use Western technology and economics.

The great family businesses—the Zaibatsu—who carried forward Japan's economic development in this period, consistently maximized opportunities. They asked: Which industries, at the present stage of our development, offer the greatest economic opportunities to Japan and to our business? The answer might be: a steamship line; a life insurance company; a textile industry; and so on. This, in turn, led to the identification of needs for social innovation—for instance, the need for a factory organization that would merge Japanese traditions of personal and social relationships with the discipline of modern industrial production. It is because of the conscious focus on maximizing opportunities that Japan succeeded in doing what no other non-Western country has done so far: to develop a modern economy fairly fast and with a minimum of social dislocation and political upheaval.

Successful planning is always based on maximizing opportunities. Soviet planning rests on a theory that sees in the entrepreneur the agent who maximizes opportunities for capital investment. (See Chapter 11 for a short description of the origin of this concept; its first practical application by the Brothers Pereire in their banking venture, the *Credit Mobilier*; and its impact throughout Europe.)

But there are many smaller and no less successful examples. Sears Roebuck in the United States and Marks & Spencer in Great Britain, two leading retail businesses of today, have consistently asked themselves: Which are the opportunities where doing something new and different is likely to have the greatest economic results? Their experience shows that this is a dynamic question, which produces new answers every few years—whereas an ideal business, once designed and effective, is likely to retain its characteristics for a fairly long period.

HOW THE ROTHSCHILDS GREW

For the third approach, that of maximizing resources, there is no more instructive example than the rise of the House of Rothschild. It was anything but a foregone conclusion. In the late 1790's Meyer Amschel Rothschild, the founder of the dynasty, was still only a small-town money lender, barely known in the main centers of international finance. Less than twenty years later, at the end of the Napoleonic Wars, the House of Rothschild was the unchallenged financial great power of Europe, treating with other great powers such as France or Russia as an equal, and barely polite to minor princes and potentates. What had catapulted the Rothschilds to success in that short period was systematic maximization of the resources of the family.

The family had four first-rate resources in the four older sons, Nathan, James, Amschel and Salomon. For each their father (or more probably their mother) found and selected the major opportunity best fitted for his talent and character, the opportunity where the individual "resource" could make its greatest contribution.

Nathan was the ablest, daring and highly imaginative. But he was uncouth and arrogant. He was given London—at the time the greatest financial center in the world, but also a ruthlessly competitive market where financial and economic power was daily being fought for by aggressive business professionals who cared nothing for manners and counted only hard cash.

Napoleon's Paris went to James. Paris was then—and for a century to come—the greatest capital market on the continent. It was also the most treacherous spot in the financial universe. The financial conspiracies and plots in the novels of Balzac— James Rothschild's contemporary—were only partly fiction. Spies, paid by government or by competitors, were everywhere. Finance was a political business; yet political upheaval—revolution, terror, tyranny, and restoration—were endemic and destroyed many mightier financial powers than the Rothschilds then were or could expect to be for years to come. But this was just the spot for James—in fact he might have been misplaced anywhere else. He throve on intrigue and had been the political strategist of the family from early years.

Salomon, courteous, patient, and dignified to the point of pomposity, went to Vienna where banking still meant dealing with one client, the Hapsburg Court, with its interminable delay and indecision, its stiff ceremonial and its self-important aristocracy. Frankfurt finally, though home to the Rothschilds, was the least important of all financial centers in Europe. It became the seat of the family's "general manager," the industrious, conscientious Amschel who loved nothing better than the back office. He kept his brothers informed through voluminous handwritten letters. He built and ran the far-flung private network of information and intelligence which—before the age of daily newspaper, post office, telegraph, and telephone—gave the Rothschilds a near-monopoly on fast and dependable knowledge of world affairs. His greatest contribution was probably in the personnel field. He found, recruited, and largely trained the German-Jewish boys with a passion for anonymity who as confidential clerks and managers became the backbone of the business.

What the Rothschilds did not do is, however, even more revealing. They did not assign to Kalmann, the fifth son, any opportunity whatever. Instead they sent him to Naples—one royal court where there was no business, and where therefore no major damage could be done to the Rothschild standing or to their fortunes. There would have been plenty of important opportunities had the family wanted Kalmann to have one. Both Hamburg and Amsterdam were important enough to warrant establishing business partners and agencies there. The Rothschilds also were aware of the opportunities of the fledgling United States across the Atlantic. But Kalmann had neither superior ability nor superior industry, at least not by Rothschild standards. And it is the one absolute rule in maximizing resources that one never entrusts an opportunity to a non-resource, that is to mediocrity. It cannot turn the opportunity into advantage. But to every opportunity corresponds a risk; mediocrity is therefore bound to do harm if entrusted with opportunity. If one has a fifth son and, as a family, has to take care of him adequately, it is cheaper to support him in royal style out of harm's way than to put him in charge of opportunities.

What is important is not that General Motors, Edison, and the Rothschilds became great and strong; it is that they started near the bottom. Whether the penniless Prussian officer Siemens, or the half-deaf, almost unschooled, errand boy Edison; the provincial, awkward—not to mention Jewish—Rothschilds in a world of prejudiced, arrogant aristocrats, or the undeveloped Japanese clans of 1860; they all started with nothing, except a systematic approach. Even General Motors, while a large corporation for the America of 1920, was a poor second to Ford. One can argue, of course, that even without any such approach Siemens and Edison would have been notable inventors, the Rothschilds well-known bankers, and General Motors a sizable company. What gave them leadership, however, was the systematic approach with which they applied their ability to the opportunities time and history had put within their grasp.

All three approaches have one thing in common: they build on strength; they look for opportunities rather than for problems; they stress attainable results rather than dangers to be avoided. In fact they are complementary. Each serves a distinct function and purpose. Together they convert the insight of analysis into a *program for effective action.*

Thinking through the design of the ideal business determines the direction a company should take to attain effectiveness. It sets fundamental objectives. It establishes the theoretical optimum of economic performance against which actual results can be measured.

Maximizing opportunities shows how to move the business from yesterday to today—thereby making it ready for the new challenges of tomorrow. It shows the existing activities that should be pushed and those that should be abandoned. And it brings out the new things that might multiply results in the market or in the company's field of knowledge.

Maximizing resources, finally, is the step from insight to action. It establishes priorities. And by concentrating resources on priorities it ensures that energy and efforts go to work where performance can produce the greatest results.

II

TARGETS AND TIME

The design of the ideal business sets the direction. It also makes it possible to set targets—for efforts as well as for results.

The ideal-business design controls itself through feed-back from its results to its own validity. The closer a business approaches the design, the greater should its profitability be. When profitability ceases to go up even though the actual business is still approaching the ideal, the design needs restudy. In all probability it has become obsolete. After all, even the best design does not last forever. Mr. Sloan's proved valid for an unusually long time—thirty-five years, until the Edsel failure of 1957. For Ford in its comeback after World War II had imitated the Sloan design; and the Edsel was to be the last, major element in a Ford Motor Company reconstructed on the lines of Sloan's earlier General Motors masterpiece.

One important element in the ideal-business design is establishment of the time period which is the proper "present" for any given business; it varies greatly.

The best illustrations are the contrasting fortunes of two companies in the aircraft industry. Curtiss Wright and the Martin Company. Curtiss Wright, in the late forties, was the stronger company: the second-largest aircraft-engine builder in the United States, solidly established as a leader in both civilian and military engines, with a heavy backlog of orders and great financial resources. Martin by contrast was an ailing airframe builder without a product of distinction, deeply in debt, and altogether, it seemed, an aging "war baby" without a future. But a new management at Martin came up with a present of eight to ten years as the time needed to develop a new technology in large-scale systems work. Research of shorter duration made not much sense and could not pay off. This also meant that the business had to be something that did not exist in 1950: a space business rather than an improved aircraft business.

Curtiss Wright without an analysis of this kind stayed with the time period of World War II, when the emphasis was on production rather than on new design. Its present was one to two years. Although it spent perhaps more money than any other aircraft company on research and development, Curtiss Wright had all but disappeared as a business a decade later. Its definition of the present made management reject any project that did not promise a pay-off within twenty-four months. As a result not one of its many research projects produced anything. The Martin Company, by contrast, established a leading and successful space systems business with a relatively modest research outlay.

There is equally a present for the market, that is a period within which market results are significant.

General Motors had learned by the mid-twenties that the time-span of the present in the automobile market was five years—a complete cycle including one very good year, one poor one, and three fair ones. The logic of the secondhand car market dictated this. General Motors built this cycle into capital investments, appraisals of performance, and the planning of development work. Capital investment, according to an oft-published formula,* was judged by the expected return over the five-year cycle at an average capacity utilization of 80 per cent. If the expected return over the cycle fell below a certain figure, or if expected capacity utilization ran below 80 per cent on average, the investment proposal was not considered acceptable. Similarly, the minimum span of technical development work was set—apparently not much later—at the three years needed to make any but minor style changes in automotive design, and the maximum (except for basic research work) at the five years that were the present of the automobile market.

As these examples show, determining the time-span that is the present of a company or industry largely determines what kind of efforts will be made. Efforts that promise results in less time are likely to be a waste not only of time, but of resources and money. To set too short a time-span and ban all efforts

* Apparently first published as early as 1927.

exceeding this period (as Curtiss Wright did) is to condemn a company to sterility.

Perhaps the best way to go about designing the ideal business is to start with a broad sketch and to correct and refine as one goes along. Otherwise one may still be rewriting, polishing, and refining when the design has already become obsolete. The important thing is to get major results fast. For the largest part of the improvement in performance and results should come as soon as the business has begun to move with determination toward its vision. The first steps should be big ones.

III

From Yesterday to Today

Maximizing opportunities looks for those seven-league steps toward realizing the ideal business and obtaining rapidly the greatest benefits possible.

By projecting the ideal business design on the analysis of the existing business all the products, markets, distribution channels, cost centers, activities, and efforts of the business can be sorted out into *three categories*:

• One high-priority group where the real push has to be made, because there is a great opportunity to achieve extraordinary results.

• One high-priority group where the opportunity lies in not-doing; that is, in rapid and purposeful abandonment.

• One large and heterogeneous group of also-rans—products, markets, knowledge work, and so on—in which neither efforts to excel nor abandonment promise significant results.

To call abandonment an "opportunity" may come as a surprise. Yet planned, purposeful abandonment of the old and of the unrewarding is a prerequisite to successful pursuit of the new and highly promising. Above all, abandonment is the key to innovation—both because it frees the necessary resources and because it stimulates the search for the new that will replace the old.

Push areas and abandonment complement each other and therefore deserve equal priority.

The *push priorities* are easily identified. What should be pushed are those areas where the results, if successful, produce their costs many times over. These are invariably the products or markets that fit most closely the ideal-business design.

The General Motors' experience is characteristic. Buick and Cadillac, the two makes that were profitable in 1921 and had market leadership, were also the only two of the company's eight makes which fitted the ideal-business design.

Typical result areas which deserve priority are, for instance:

- Tomorrow's breadwinners and sleepers
- The development efforts needed to replace tomorrow's breadwinner the day after tomorrow
  - Important new knowledge and new distributive channels
  - Cutting back high support costs, high policing costs and waste in the cost structure

The areas of high potential are rarely over-supplied with resources. Hence what matters is not whether the budget for such an area is too high but whether it is high enough for results.

The *candidates for abandonment* are also usually fairly obvious.

There is first the investment in managerial ego. Unjustified specialties are also on the list. Then there are unnecessary support activities, and waste that can be eliminated without major effort.

Yesterday's breadwinner should almost always be abandoned on a fairly fast schedule. It still may produce net revenue. But it soon becomes a bar to the introduction and success of tomorrow's breadwinner. One should, therefore, abandon yesterday's breadwinner *before* one really wants to, let alone before one has to.

Altogether, whenever the cost of incremental acquisition is more than one-half of the likely return, there is a candidate for abandonment. It is not good enough that an activity does not appear to cost any money. It should produce results to be kept on.

And the hidden costs of any activity are always much greater than anybody assumes or than any accounting system shows.

To keep a man on the payroll always costs at least three times his wage or salary. He needs space to work in, heat, light, and a locker in the washroom. He needs materials to work with, supplies, a telephone, and so on. He needs a supervisor. In a hundred hidden ways he creates costs.

Every proposal for abandonment is opposed. The arguments that can be advanced to justify retention of the resultless, unpromising, and unrewarding are rarely more than excuses. Most common is the plea:

- *We must grow; we cannot afford to shrink.*

But growth, after all, is the result of success, of offering what the market wants, buys, and pays for, of using economic resources effectively, and of making the profits needed for expansion and for the risks of the future. General Motors either abandoned or completely made over six of the eight makes in the line—and the result was tremendous growth.

The argument is also sophistry: It confuses fat with muscle, and busy-ness with economic accomplishment. Activities which do not produce results waste substance. They are a burden—the way overweight is a burden on the strength of a human being.

A management in an expanding economy needs to be growth-conscious. But growth means exploiting the opportunities that the economy offers. It does not mean doing the wrong things to get volume. The volume will come soon enough if a business concentrates on doing the right things.

There are in each business products, services, activities, and efforts which are neither clear candidates for concentrated major work nor candidates for abandonment: the large number of *also-rans* which form the third category to be considered.

Among them will be today's breadwinners and frequently the productive specialties. Here also will be cost centers which, while representing a sizable cost burden, can be reduced only by efforts out of proportion to the probable results. And here will be found the repair jobs of all kinds and descriptions, the products, services, markets, and so on, which might become worth while if only some major change or modification were made.

The main rule for also-rans is that they must not absorb resources at the expense of the high opportunity areas. Only if resources are left over after the high opportunity areas have received all the support they need, should the also-rans be considered. And high-grade resources already committed to also-rans should be kept there only if they cannot make a bigger contribution in a high opportunity task.

In practice, additional resources can rarely be spared for also-rans. And only the productive specialty among them normally deserves all the resources it employs. The others will almost always be found to absorb resources that would be more productive elsewhere.

Also-rans therefore have to make do with what they have—or with less. They are put on "milking status": as long as they yield results, they will be kept—and milked. They will, however, not be "fed." And as soon as these "milk cows" go into rapid decline, they should be slaughtered.

THE FORWARD PROJECTION

Upgrading the existing business leads to doing things better. But what are the different things that ought to be done?

Here there are two distinct categories of opportunities:

• *Replacements* of present products, activities, and efforts which are almost right, by products, activities, and efforts that are completely right

• *Innovations,* the highest-opportunity group, though a small one

Replacements deserve high priority only if a very small change can convert an almost right product into one that fits the ideal business design.

What distinguishes a replacement from a development is that it represents a different idea of what the market is and what it wants, or a different exploitation of the company's knowledge. A new packaging material is a development—no matter how difficult technologically it might be to design and to produce it. A new packaging concept, shipping on pallets or in container bodies which fit on railway flatcars as well as on highway trucks, is a new idea and a replacement. In the General Motors redesign by Alfred P. Sloan, Jr., the replacements were the three cars that were revamped in everything but name: the old low-priced Chevrolet, the Oakland (later the Pontiac), and the Oldsmobile. These cars had customer acceptance and a dealer organization. They had the basic design. What they did not have was a clear idea of their function and place in the market, the right pricing policy, and management. For a downtown department store in the United States the suburban shopping centers were essentially replacements; they were ways to make the essential strengths of the department store—its reputation and its merchandising knowledge—available where the customers shopped.

A replacement should never present great technical difficulty. It should arise out of the recognition: "Now we suddenly understand what is wrong with this product, this market, this activity. Now we suddenly understand what we have done wrong, or failed to do." What changes is much less the product itself—if it is not almost right one should not waste time and effort on it—than the way the business itself sees, presents, and uses the product.

Innovation is the design and development of something new, as yet unknown and not in existence, which will establish a new economic configuration out of the old, known, existing elements. It will give these elements an entirely new economic dimension. It is the missing link between having a number of disconnected elements, each marginally effective, and an integrated system of great power.

It is this "systems" aspect of innovation that is invoked when we say that men like Siemens or Edison created a new industry. All the elements were there, except one. Adding this one new element created an entirely new economic capacity.

There are many other examples:

Sears Roebuck built its business on the innovation of a "money-back-and-no-questions-asked" guarantee to the farm customers. All the ingredients of a successful mail-order business existed. What was lacking was the simple element of confidence in the customer.

IBM similarly created the computer industry by innovating the concept of programing as a distinct function which bridged the gap between the technically highly complex machine and the technically untrained potential customers, and which yet could be learned by high school graduates in a short time.

Sloan's innovation was the idea of an automobile company supplying the entire market in a planned and organized fashion where formerly General Motors—and all the others—had seen themselves as producers of individual makes each trying to appeal to all the potential customers.

American Motors innovated the idea of the "compact," that is the smallest car that would still give adequate room and performance to people used to big cars.

Innovation is not invention or discovery. It may require either —and often does. But its focus is not knowledge but performance —and in a business this means economic performance. Its essence is conceptual rather than technical or scientific. The characteristic of the innovator is the ability to envisage as a system what to others are unrelated, separate elements. Innovation is not the better the bigger it is. On the contrary, it is the better the smaller it can be. It is, to say it again, the successful attempt to find and to provide the smallest missing part that will convert already existing elements—knowledge, products, customer demand, markets—into a new and much more productive whole.

To find the areas where innovation would create maximum opportunities, one asks: What is lacking to make effective what is already possible? What one small step would transform our economic results? What small change would alter the capacity of the whole of our resources?

To describe the need is not to satisfy it. But describing the need gives a specification for the desirable results. Whether they are likely to be obtained can then be decided. Innovation is applicable to finding business potential and to making the future.

But its first application is as a strategy for making today fully effective, and for bringing the existing business closer to the ideal business.

IV

STAFFING FOR PERFORMANCE

The crux of a program of action is the allocation of resources, and especially the staffing decisions. Until they have been made and put into effect, nothing has really been *done*.

The one principle for the deployment of the scarcest and most productive resource—high-caliber people—is maximization of resources. Few businesses have resources of a caliber comparable to that of the four older Rothschild sons. But every business should follow the Rothschild example—if it wants results.

First-class people must always be allocated to major opportunities, to the areas of greatest possible return for each unit of effort. And first-class opportunities must always be staffed with people of superior ability and performance. If there are no resources available for major opportunities one must build them. One never tries to exploit major opportunities with anything but high-grade resources. One never assigns high-grade resources to anything but major opportunities, however. And one does not create resources for secondary opportunities.

To follow these principles in practice however, is not easy. There are, first, the "Kalmann Rothschilds"—the "members of the family in good standing" whose faithful service entitles them to be taken care of even though they lack the necessary ability. It is always cheaper to give them a sinecure than to entrust them with a major opportunity. In a sinecure they cost only their salary. In charge of a major opportunity they may waste the potential return from a new big business.

Equally unpopular is the decision to leave secondary opportunities to fend for themselves. Yet unless one is ruthless, the first-rate opportunities starve to death.

But the greatest temptation is to diffuse first-rate resources rather than to concentrate them: it is so easy to avoid painful priority decisions by asking a strong man to be "available for support and advice" to a weak one. "It should after all, take only a day or two of his time, once in a while" is the standard excuse. But in no time at all the few really good men will do nothing but bolster weak men and secondary opportunities. Strength, to be effective, has to be concentrated. And any major opportunity is a challenge demanding undivided attention and dedication.

It is indeed so painful to staff for performance that managers should impose on themselves the discipline of what the psychologists call the "forced-choice method."

A list of major opportunities is drawn up, with each opportunity assigned a ranking. Here is the first forced choice—for each opportunity has to be ranked without ambiguity. The same procedure is followed with respect to first-rate people and staff groups—again ranking them by forced choice. Then to the highest-ranking opportunity is allocated all the high-ranking human resources it requires. The next-ranking opportunity comes next, then the third-ranking one, and so on. A lower-ranking opportunity is never staffed at the expense of a higher-ranking one.

The ranking of opportunities and of people becomes the real decision in this method; the rest follows.

Staffing decisions are the crucial decision. They decide whether the business has a program for effectiveness or only a scrap of paper.

10 Finding Business Potential

"Opportunity is where you find it," says an old proverb. It does not say: ". . . where it finds you." Luck, chance, and catastrophe affect business as they do all human endeavors. But luck never built a business. Prosperity and growth come only to the business that systematically finds and exploits its potential. No matter how successfully a business organizes itself for the challenges and opportunities of the present, it will still be far below its optimum performance. Its potential is always greater than its realized actuality.

Dangers and weaknesses indicate where to look for business potential. To convert them from problems into opportunities brings extraordinary returns. And sometimes all that is needed to accomplish this transformation is a change in the attitude of the executives.

Three questions will bring out the hidden potential of a business:

• What are the restraints and limitations that make the business vulnerable, impede its full effectiveness, and hold down its economic results?

• What are the imbalances of the business?

• What are we afraid of, what do we see as a threat to this business—and how can we use it as an opportunity?

Vulnerability as an Opportunity

Why is a particular business—or industry—extremely vulnerable to minor economic fluctuations? What makes its products incapable of meeting competition from new or different products? Is there a single factor that restrains the full realization of its economic capacity?

While these questions can rarely be answered offhand, most executives have a pretty good notion of the restraints, vulnerabilities, and limitations of their company and industry. The trouble is that the questions are rarely asked. Executives tend to assume that nothing can be done to change the situation. "If we knew how to overcome the limitations of our process, we would have done so long ago" is a common attitude. This process as it stands may indeed represent the best current knowledge. But it is emphatically not true that nothing can be done about it.

The development of the American steel industry in the period after World War II illustrates such a vulnerability and how it affects an industry.

Shortly after the end of World War II one of the major steel companies commissioned a group of young economists experienced in the analysis of industry structure and markets to make a forecast of steel demand in the United States. It expected the usual projection of growth trends relating steel demand to national income and production. The emphasis in the report was not on the projection, however, but on an analysis of the underlying assumptions. Much to the surprise of the steel company executives, the economists questioned the assumption that steel is of necessity the basic industrial material of a modern society. Other materials were increasingly capable of fulfilling many of the functions for which steel had been bought— and the then existing steelmaking process had such cost limitations as to make dubious its capacity to compete.

The steelmaking process, developed in the middle of the nineteenth century, requires high temperature to be created three times, only to be quenched three times. It further requires moving heavy loads over considerable distances, and handling them in a particularly difficult form; namely, as molten and very hot metal. The two most expensive things to do, however—whether one talks physics or economics—are creating temperatures and moving and handling. All the costs of a mechanical batch process were therefore built into the economic structure of the steel industry. Other materials, especially plastics, aluminum, glass, and concrete had the much more favorable economics of heat-conserving flow processes. And these other materials were reaching a state in which they could give satisfactory performance in a number of major end-uses for which steel had traditionally been the only available material—from construction work to packaging.

At the same time, the report went on, there was mounting evidence that the basic limitations of the steelmaking process were being tackled. Though until then only minor improvements and modifications, these new approaches might, within a fairly short period, result in fundamental changes in technology.

When the steel company commissioned the study it had expected recommendations for rapid expansion of its capacity. Indeed, several of the more conservative executives had opposed the study as likely to encourage wild over-expansion. But the conclusions of the study were entirely different.

The economists came up with two recommendations. One called for extreme caution in expanding capacity until such time as basic changes in the economics of the steelmaking process would become available. Till then, additional capacity should be built only for products and markets in which steel would have at least a 25 per cent price advantage compared to any potentially competitive material. The second recommendation called for an accelerated research program focused on basic process innovation.

The company executives who had ordered the study, promptly dismissed it as "typical academic nonsense." But it proved to be prophetic.

The American steel industry has pushed an expansion program in the postwar years based on the old assumptions and has built a good deal of expensive capacity applying the old processes. The demand was indeed there—but far less for steel than for its new competitors which have made sizable inroads in markets that used to be steel's very own (and they may make yet bigger inroads should fiberglass become competitive with steel sheet in automobile bodies, for instance). The European and the Soviet steel industries blithely followed the Americans, and also expanded on the assumption that the traditional relationship between steel demand and economic activity must continue. In the meantime, however, the technological changes—which steelmakers all considered "impossible" as recently as 1950—have been coming in: continuous casting, for instance, and the high-oxygen converter which materially improves heat utilization and speed and cuts down on moving costs.

As a result a good deal of the investments in steel expansion made before 1955 (that is, the bulk of the postwar investment in the United States and Russia) will probably never earn an adequate return. Even Mr. Khrushchev had to admit in 1962 that he had planned for far more steel plant than he could actually use. This capacity will either be inadequately used; or it will produce steel at a cost well above what the market will pay. But steel capacity built after 1955, when the new process technologies became available, should not only restore the competitive position of steel in a great many markets but should also be able to earn high returns both on fairly low output and on fairly low price.

This story is given here in such detail because it illustrates the essentials:

• The vulnerabilities and restraints are as a rule well-known or easily ascertained; the young economists who made the study knew little about steel or its technology and went by what the steel men themselves told them.

• Any basic change proposed to overcome the vulnerability seems to the people in an industry so unlikely as to be impossible. But it is often in train while everybody is still proclaiming that it cannot happen.

• Whenever a restraint or vulnerability of this kind can be changed, the economic results are likely to be substantial. Such a restraint therefore represents a major opportunity.

• Overcoming such a restraint almost always requires systematic innovation; that is, analysis to define the new capacity or knowledge and systematic work on its development.

There are three major areas in which restraint should be looked for: the process—as in the steel industry; the economics of the industry; and the economics of the market.

1. Any process which results in both a high break-even point in terms of volume and a high break-even point in terms of price makes a business (or industry) vulnerable. Ideally, of course, a

business should have both low volume and low price break-even points. But at the least it should not be inflexible in its volume as well as in its prices. The business that runs at a loss unless it runs at 98 per cent capacity *and* at boom-levels of price is highly vulnerable.

Wherever such a condition is found—and it is unfortunately fairly common—the process has been over-engineered to the detriment of its economics. It has been engineered for best physical performance rather than for best economic performance. Examples are, for instance, some of the "most modern" paper mills in which high-speed finishing has been integrated at great cost in ingenuity and money with the high-speed paper-forming process—with the result that the machine can indeed produce incredible quantities of finished paper, but of one kind and grade only. A minor change in demand could make it uneconomical.

Rather more complex are the process-economics of ocean shipping, discussed in Chapter 5. Ocean shipping should actually be a major growth industry, both in tonnage and in earnings. International trade is growing rapidly; and the ocean-going ship is still the main carrier. But since for generations naval architects have concentrated on the performance of a ship at sea instead of in port, they have actually made port-work (the major cost element) more difficult and time-consuming. As a result of the wrong emphasis in process-design, ocean-going shipping is not growing today. Though heavily subsidized it is threatened by the same fate that has been overtaking the railroads: replacement by another carrier as the mainstay of transportation; in this case, the air-freighter. That the ship is not inherently inferior is shown by the success of those ocean-going freighters which have been designed for loading and unloading rather than for high-speed or low-cost performance on the high seas, e.g., the specialized bulk carriers such as the petroleum tanker, the ore boat, or the banana boat.

Since prevention is easier than cure, the balance between economic and engineering performance should always be worked out in the design of a new process, particularly in automation. Automation, if properly engineered, should make the process more flexible; that is, capable of both optimum economic performance under optimum conditions—high demand for a standardized product, for instance—and optimum economic performance under less-than-optimum conditions, such as lower demand or sharply fluctuating product and order mixes. Instead a great deal of automation repeats the mistake of the paper-machine designers and sacrifices economic performance and flexibility to top speed in turning out today's product. Such equipment is actually obsolete the day it starts running; for today's product never stays the right product long. Today's automation miracle becomes tomorrow's vulnerability unless the economics of the process are engineered into it; that is, unless the inherent capacity of automation to make flexibility and diversity economical is fully utilized.

2. To illustrate restraint and vulnerability in the economics of an industry, paper again serves as an example.

Like steel, paper has been a multipurpose material, and even more than steel has tended to grow several times as fast as the total economy. As with steel, however, a host of new materials have come in, each better suited than paper for one particular purpose or application. And like steel, paper is becoming expensive in comparison to the newcomers.

The papermaking process uses no more than a quarter of the tree. Half of the wood in the tree is left behind in the forest, and another quarter is thrown away in the form of bark, leaves, small branches, and organic chemicals such as lignin. Yet the papermakers have to pay for the whole tree. As a result, pulp, the raw material of papermaking is expensive compared for instance with the raw materials from which plastics are made, which are usually by-products of petroleum refining and virtually free of cost. If the paper industry could convert into salable products the three-quarters of the tree that is today being wasted, paper would again become cheap. Otherwise, paper, now a multipurpose material, may find itself confined to a few uses, and the paper industry may shrink rather than grow with the economy.

The papermaker will immediately point out that no one knows as yet how to use the three-quarters of the tree that is thrown away. He will point out further that strenuous efforts have been made by the paper industry to develop the chemical utilization of wood, so far however with meager results. He will, in other words, point out that he is not to blame for the situation—and he is right. But that it may not yet be possible to do something about such a fundamental restraint does not alter the fact that it exists and that it may endanger the future of an industry. It does not alter the fact that removal of the restraint would have extraordinary impact on the economic potential of an industry. It does not alter the fact, in brief, that here is an area in which an industry has to keep on working, no matter how frustrating the prospect seems to be. For when the change comes, it is likely to come fast.

3. Finally, the restraint—and the vulnerability it causes—may lie in market structure and economics that are at odds with the structure and economics of the company or industry.

In Chapter 6 above, one such restraint was mentioned: the apparently irrational behavior of the customer; that is, behavior that seems contrary not only to the interest of the supplier but to that of the customer as well. But equally serious vulnerabilities can be found in technological or economic systems which prevent customer-interest from becoming a source of business and profit for the supplier.

An example is residential building. In the American residential market the price differential between a new, cheap, one-family house and a medium-priced one is only 25 per cent or so. The quality differential, however, is enormous. The cheap home deteriorates fast. In a few years—usually well before the buyers have finished paying for it—they either move on to a better one or have lost most of their investment and are condemned to living in a deteriorating home in a deteriorating neighborhood. Slums are not made by the slum dwellers. They are made when new homes are built in such a manner that they are doomed to a fast decline. The trouble is, of course, that the young couple who first buy a home have only enough money for the cheapest available building unit. This, today, means one that will deteriorate pretty fast.*

---

* I am conscious of gross oversimplification of a complex problem. Land use is at least as important a factor in real estate values and city development as is building construction. And many other factors enter the picture. I am only trying, however, to illustrate the restraint analysis, not to give an exposition of the problems of modern city planning.

The restraint here lies in the traditional way of building a house. What is needed is what might be called an add-on house. The young family, starting out life together, should be able to buy the core of a home of good quality and yet of low price, to which they can add units and features as their income grows or as they pay off the original home mortgage. Thus it would be possible for them to upgrade their home constantly and to increase its value. This would eliminate—or at least greatly lessen—the incentive for the successful families to move out of the neighborhood in which they began and thus convert it into a low-class neighborhood and eventually a slum. It would, at the same time, create the desirable "mixed" neighborhood of fair-sized homes owned and occupied by older and fairly prosperous people, and small homes for the younger and less prosperous. Yet each home would have substantial quality and would be capable of constant upgrading.

This is obviously difficult to bring about. It may be impossible. But the construction industry had better work out some such solution. It is bound to suffer if housing continues to become more expensive and yet increasingly prone to deterioration.

Such vulnerability is not confined to businesses or industries making and selling a product; it can be found in service industries as well.

The American commercial bank (like all commercial banks) derives its profits from the use of the customer's deposits. At the same time the services with which it competes for deposits are aimed at enabling the customer to operate with a minimum of cash and, therefore, with a minimum of deposits. The more value it gives its customers, the less well it is likely to do itself. The commercial banks get paid, in other words, for the exact opposite of what the customer really buys. The customer buys money management which enables him to function with the least amount of idle cash. But banks make more money the more idle cash the customer keeps on deposit. Typically, the greatest skill and virtuosity in the industry goes into managing this internal contradiction. The heroes of commercial banking are the men who can best advise customers on their money management, while at the same time persuading them to keep the largest possible deposit balance with the bank for the longest possible time.

One solution might be to get paid for what is value to the customer—that is, money management—on a fee basis.

For years any suggestion to this effect was greeted with derision by the bankers. If there was one thing they knew, it was that no bank would dream of offering such a service and no customer would dream of accepting it. Yet this is exactly the arrangement that one of the country's biggest and most conservative banks, the Morgan Guaranty Trust Company in New York, has worked out with one of the country's most conservative large corporations, Gillette Razor (as disclosed in the fall of 1963).

The most promising area of potential is the built-in restraint of a business. But to convert restraint into opportunity demands innovation.

II

TURNING WEAKNESSES INTO STRENGTHS

Perfect balance in a business exists only on the organization chart. A living business is always in a state of imbalance, growing here and shrinking there, overdoing one thing and neglecting another.

But many businesses are in chronic imbalance; they need productive resources way beyond any results they can produce. "We are just a small company with fifteen million dollars in sales; but we need a national sales force, national promotion and national distribution" is the complaint of one company. Another says: "We have to maintain a solid-state physics laboratory to match General Electric's work in the field"—and yet the field in which the company operates is narrow and highly specialized.

Such imbalance is a serious weakness; it may threaten a company's existence. The total cost structure of any business is likely to be scaled to the size of its largest resource. Support costs tend to be geared to the productive efforts that need to be supported rather than to the available results. The company with the large research force in advanced solid-state physics, for instance, provides its physicists with facilities, buildings, equipment, library services, and so on, that compare favorably with those of the General Electric Company; otherwise it risks losing its best men to the big competitor. The large national sales force for a $15-million volume will demand as much in the way of accounting, order-handling, supervision, and training as if the company handled $150 million a year of business. Total costs, in other words, tend to be proportionate to the costs of the largest needed productive effort.

But results, of course, are proportionate to the revenues; that is, to volume.

Where the imbalance in efforts is in support activities, in policing activities, or in waste, the cure is to cut out whatever causes the imbalance. The principle of least effort for support and policing costs, developed in Chapter 5, applies here, as does the rule to eliminate waste efforts altogether.

But when the imbalance lies in disproportionately large productive efforts, it often indicates a major unused potential. To exploit this potential always requires major changes in the nature and structure of the business.

Typical areas of imbalance with disproportionately large productive resources incapable of producing adequate results within the existing business are marketing and research and development.

Here is an example of an imbalance in marketing resources —together with the specific course of action taken to convert the potential into performance.

The company with the large national sales force employed to sell $15 millions worth of merchandise across the United States could not materially cut back its selling efforts without destroying its business. But the volume could also not support the 150 technically trained salesmen. An analysis showed that profitable operations required average sales per salesman of half a million a year as against the prevailing average of $100,000. The solution was a radical redefinition of the business as a distributor rather than as a manufacturer. An intensive search was made for other small manufacturers making similar goods similarly requiring national distribution. To them the company offered its services far below the sales costs of the manufacturers. Five years later the company distributed with the same sales force some $100 million worth of merchandise. Only one-fifth were its own goods; the rest were the products of seven other noncompeting manufacturers, each selling less than $20 millions worth but getting the full benefits of a sales organization geared to a $100-million volume.

Imbalance between research and development resources and the business they produce is equally costly and equally a major opportunity.

Costs of research and development skyrocketed when a medium-sized glass company began to supply glass to the electronics industry for a variety of components. The increase was so great as to threaten the profitability of the entire business—even though glass for electronic purposes was a relatively small part of the entire product line. The company at first considered withdrawing from the electronics market; but a market study showed that electronics was a major growth industry and that its use of glass was likely to grow twice as fast as the industry itself. (This was in 1952.) The company then tried to find out why its electronic industry sales required such exorbitant technological efforts and found that its research people in effect were doing the entire technical job for the electronics customer. The essential knowledge was not electronics but glass; and performance of the finished component depended primarily on the glass, its quality and design. In terms of money the glass was almost insignificant in the finished component; in terms of technological effort it dominated—but the company was not getting paid for this contribution.

The solution here was to integrate forward into electronics manufacturing. Components that are essentially electronic applications of glass technology are now being made by the company. Dollar volume and profits are several times what they would be if the company only furnished the glass. And this means more than adequate utilization of the technological effort needed.

The move was, of course, fought within the company with the old argument, "We cannot go into competition with our own customers." As often happens, the outside business with old customers has gone up—if only because the company now can give better service and design better glass than before.

Not only marketing and technological resources but every productive resource can be out of balance—a serious danger if unattended, but also an opportunity for growth.

An example is an installment finance company founded by one of the smaller American automobile companies. Financing the purchase of automobiles, it has to operate nationwide with branch offices in all big cities. But confined to the product of one of the smaller automobile manufacturers, it simply could not generate the volume of installment finance needed to carry its local administrative expenses. With a total volume of $400 million of installment finance a year, it looked like a very big company. Actually it was too small for its specific productive resources, the ability to control and manage a highly specialized installment finance business. The solution was to become the installment finance company for a fairly large number of even smaller but still nationally distributing manufacturers of durable consumer goods sold on the installment plan. With its overhead largely paid for by automobile finance, the company could offer outsiders attractive terms and soon had its volume up to $600 million or so, at which point it became profitable.

The unbalanced productive resources need not be within the legal framework of the business itself. They can be within the economic process but outside of the legal (and accounting) structure.

The shift from small, specialized retailer to mass-distributor typically creates such an imbalance. Many American manufacturers of nationally distributed goods for mass-consumption still have three-quarters of their distribution in small retail stores, whereas three-quarters of consumer purchases are in mass-distribution outlets. This inevitably creates an imbalance. On the one hand, the manufacturer has to maintain a distribution expense he can ill afford, since he has to service a large number of small stores which are at best marginally productive. On the other hand, he does not reach his market. His marketing efforts are out of balance with their possible results.

This may seem elementary. But only a cost analysis that takes the price paid by the ultimate consumer as cost basis will bring out that distribution costs are disproportionately nigh. The conventional analysis, in which costs are defined as the expenses within a given legal unit rather than as the expenses of an economic process, tends to hide such an imbalance in distribution costs and distributive channels. This imbalance itself is fairly easy to correct, but it may escape detection for many years.

In the United States this imbalance has led to the sale of a large number of businesses by frustrated and baffled owners. They could not figure out why their formerly profitable business had ceased to produce earnings. Yet the purchasers restored profitability fast by redirecting distribution into mass channels. In Europe (and increasingly in Japan) the same development is taking place now. The consumers are switching from small, specialized, low-turnover retail stores to large, fast-turnover mass-distribution. Many manufacturers, however, maintain their old distributive channels. As these cease to produce results they intensify their marketing and selling efforts which, however, only aggravates the imbalance. Ultimately they sell out to someone who understands the change and sees in it an opportunity for selling more at less cost and with greater effectiveness.

Sometimes supporting activities have to be maintained at such high level of effort and competence that they cause imbalance.

The best example I know is a large company in the processed food, hotel, and catering businesses. It requires many auxiliary services: laundry, for instance, for its hotels and restaurants, and trucking for its processed-foods distribution. Each of these services has to operate at a high level of performance. Each requires fairly substantial capital investment and has to be maintained at a level sufficient to carry the peak load. Each, therefore, is almost certain to become disproportionately large and expensive.

The company has a simple rule. Support activities that require knowledge and competence similar to the businesses they serve— the laundry service, for instance, or trucking—are developed into regular, profit-making businesses with outside customers. The laundry has become a large commercial laundry. The trucking service is a leader in its area. Both do four to five times as much work for outside customers as they do for the company's businesses. Both, as a result, have to be able to prove themselves in competitive performance.

This solution, however, requires not only a constant search for opportunities. It also requires the self-discipline not to develop businesses from support activities that can be run on the least-effort principle—let alone from those that do not fit in with the main business of the company.

In the food and catering company of the present illustration, two rules are strictly applied: support activities that need not be run at a high level of size or excellence are kept small. Even if capable of becoming profitable businesses they are not enlarged beyond the bare minimum needed for internal operations. The rule applies to the printing shop, for instance, even though it could well be made into a substantial business. And furthermore, support activities that need to be developed in size or excellence without, however, fitting in with the company's general business are developed until they are substantial, profitable concerns. Then they are sold off—and the company becomes their customer. This was done, for instance, with a department designing and building stores and restaurants; it is now one of the leading architects for commercial structures.

THE BUSINESS OF THE WRONG SIZE

The most important cases of imbalance are businesses that are the wrong size—usually too small—for the market they have to serve or for the management they need.

The European Common Market created such imbalance for many medium-sized, family-owned businesses. Perfectly adequate, perhaps, to supply their own limited national market, they found themselves short of the products, the capital, the marketing resources, or the management to compete successfully against the industrial giants in a market of 180 million people. This explains the wave of mergers in the last decade between such family companies across national boundaries in Europe, and the large number of partnership agreements, cooperative marketing agreements or research pools into which European family companies—traditionally suspicious of any outsider—have entered since the Common Market first started. A similar development is going on in Japan where small family-owned businesses find themselves unable to cope with a mass-market of almost 100 million customers. And—though on a much smaller scale—a parallel development has been taking place in California since World War II abolished the economic isolation in which high freight costs had kept the West Coast market.

Any major change in the market—and especially in its size and complexity—is likely to create an imbalance between the size of the smaller or medium-sized firm and the demands made on it. Like all imbalances this too is a hidden opportunity; but the solution is not normally to add to the existing business. It is merger, acquisition, partnership, or joint venture—that is, fundamental change of business structure and usually (though not inevitably) change of financial structure and ownership.

This is also the only solution that converts into opportunity the imbalance between the size of a business and the management it needs.

Management too is a productive resource. Serious imbalance in the size—and with it, the cost—of management, is therefore serious under-utilization of a valuable, expensive, and scarce resource. Though the company needs first-rate managers, it can neither pay them adequately nor offer enough challenge and achievement. If it succeeds in attracting the kind of man it needs —or in developing him—it soon loses him again. The business is thus stunted and may even be destroyed in the end. If, however, the imbalance is treated as an opportunity, it can become the source of rapid growth, both in volume and profitability.

Sometimes a small or medium-sized business overloads itself with expensive and unneeded management.

Typically such a business goes in for the latest management fads. When "human relations" are in season, it hires psychologists, social workers, and personnel experts and puts everybody through "leadership training." Two years later everybody talks "operations research" and attends management-science seminars. A computer big enough to handle all the paper work of the federal government is considered barely adequate for the payroll of a company employing 250 people.

In such a situation, one can scale management down to the size appropriate to the needs of the business.

But there is often genuine need for complex management in a company that lacks the business to support it.

A large engineering company maintains that a technically advanced business in the American civilian market requires a sales volume of $15 million to pay for its management and technical efforts. Most of the businesses of the company require substantial capital investment in large, highly mechanized plants, continuing research and development work, specialized selling, and a good deal of technical service. Even so, the figure is probably quite high. Independent companies in the same fields compete and prosper on a volume of no more that $10 or 12 millions. In other highly technical fields—for example, in chemical specialties—companies with a sales volume of $5 to 7 millions do well and have leadership in a market. Altogether, sales volume is probably a good deal less important than value added (that is, sales less purchased materials and parts); on that basis a chemical company with $5 million turnover using cheap raw materials (crude oil or sand, for instance) might actually be a bigger business than an engineering company of $15 million sales with 70 per cent purchased materials and parts.

The economical size for businesses varies with the industry; with the maturity of the technology (in new technologies small size may be both economical and advantageous); with the market and its structure; and so on. But the business of the wrong size pays a heavy penalty. It pays the full costs of the larger size, but gets only the benefit of the smaller size—and sometimes not even that.

In some industries a business must either be quite small and serve a distinct segment of the market or else be very big. In the American soap industry, for instance, small businesses are viable and prosperous serving one narrow geographic area in which they have leadership, or a specific class of customers—for instance, hospitals. But the next possible size in the soap industry is the giant with national brands, nationally promoted and distributed. A soap business in between cannot prosper, probably cannot even survive.

There have long been very big European automobile companies: Fiat, the British Ford, Opel and, lately, Volkswagen. But quite small companies assembling a few thousand cars a year from purchased parts could survive and prosper as long as the market was small. But with Europe going through the automotive revolution in record time, a consolidation of the industry into a fairly small number of very big companies is now clearly in the offing. Even the many medium-sized companies with well-established names and a loyal following cannot, it seems, survive; everything smaller than the giant is too small.

A recent book, *Corporations in Crisis,** mentions two companies that had to sell out to big concerns—not because they failed but because they were so successful that they grew to an untenable in-between size. Stavid Engineering, successful as a small specialty designer with a few million dollars worth of business a year, grew to a volume of $10 million and found that it had to have the management of a $20 million business—without the means to attain that volume. It is now a division of Lockheed Aircraft. Similarly, success of its V-107 helicopter forced small and prosperous Piasecki Helicopter Corporation into an uneconomical size. It sold out to big Boeing Aircraft.

Sometimes the right solution for the company that is in-between in size is to retrench to a smaller, economical, volume.

A small manufacturer of plumbers' equipment and tools did well with a volume of $8 million a year, supplying the tri-state area around Chicago (Illinois, Wisconsin, Indiana). His goods being heavy, he enjoyed a distinct freight advantage within a short radius around his plant. When he branched out into a wider territory his sales quickly went up to $20 million. But he lost so much on these additional sales—for to be competitive he had to absorb freight charges to outlying areas —that he was forced into bankruptcy. Retrenchment to his original territory restored his economic health. In this industry to be anything but a small supplier of a local market requires a multiplant operation in many locations—probably with a minimum volume close to $50 million a year.

The most important case is, however, that of the business that is below the minimum size. It is marginal, no matter how good its products. The money that should be invested in growth is needed instead to support the extra burden of management, research, sales efforts, and so on. But unless the company grows it will not be able to generate the money it needs.

*Richard Austin Smith (New York 1963).

The only solution to this vicious circle is to jump. It is a quantum jump; one cannot be between two sizes but must move in one step from one size to the next. Gradual growth from within is not possible, as a rule. Only sale of the company, acquisition of another company in the same industry, or merger will produce a business of the needed size.

III

"WHAT ARE WE AFRAID OF?"

There are hidden opportunities in developments that seem to threaten a business or an industry.

As late as 1950 the American railroads refused to accept that passenger automobile, truck, and airplane were here to stay. They considered it unthinkable that railroads could be displaced as the backbone of the country's transportation system. The new means of transportation were a threat—not only to the railroads but, they argued, to the nation, its security and prosperity.

It was not until well into the nineteen sixties that the railroads began to realize that this threat could also be seen as opportunity. With alternate means of transportation available, they could concentrate on what they do best and most profitably: long-distance hauling of bulk commodities. The car, the truck, and the bus allow the railroads to drop branch lines and unprofitable service to small communities. They ease the deeply-ingrained fear of railroad monopoly and thereby make politically acceptable mergers of competing lines and elimination of costly service duplication.

An almost immediate result of this change in attitude was the reconquest of a business the railroads had given up for lost twenty-five years earlier: long-distance hauling of new automobiles. As long as the railroads viewed the truck as "abnormal" they could not conceive of any other method of carrying automobiles than the small, closed box car—even though the trucks had all along been carrying automobiles on open double-decker trailers. To ship two cars—a normal box-car load—on the railroad cost as much as to carry six cars by truck. As soon as the railroads accepted the fact that the truck was here to stay, they saw the opportunity to carry eight or ten automobiles on one double-deck trailer—and to pull a great many of these automobile-carrying trailers behind one locomotive. Within eighteen months the railroads had recaptured the bulk of long-distance automobile haulage.

Similar developments are making grain, coal, and iron-ore shipments again profitable for the railroad—as bulk shipments, in bulk carriers, and at bulk rates. The principal lines may even again become prosperous and healthy businesses as a result of their basic change of attitude—though they waited far too long before they accepted the inevitable and attempted to cooperate with it.

Here are some further examples:

The American life insurance companies used to be the main savings channel for the community. In the years after World War II, the public, in its new affluence, began to put decreasing shares of its savings into life insurance (without, however, actually reducing the dollar amounts of life insurance bought). Most of the companies saw in this a serious threat to be fought by publicity campaigns aimed at warning the American family of the dangers of the new investment media such as common stock. Only one company— significantly enough one that had never before been prominent in the life insurance field—saw in this an opportunity. It purchased a mutual investment trust and began to sell its certificates together with its life insurance policies, thus offering the customer a balanced investment and a one-package approach to his financial planning. It soon achieved a rapid growth rate, well beyond that of the industry as a whole.

The great majority of American department stores at first fought the discount store as "unethical." When this did not work, one after the other of the major department store chains joined the parade and opened discount stores of its own. The results have mostly been poor; department stores do not know how to run a discount operation. One major store chain, however, took an entirely different tack. This chain has not opened discount stores and does not intend to do so. Instead it has upgraded its own stores. In every city in which it operates, it has become the quality store for the mass market. It concentrates on high quality lines, especially apparel of good design, fashionable though conservative. "We want our customers to buy little Susie's pajamas at the discount house in her neighborhood," an executive of the chain said. "This way the mother will have more money to spend with us when she comes to buy the one good party frock for Susie's first dance."

There is also the example of a major paper company which, for years, bemoaned the threat of plastics without doing anything about it. It finally forced itself to look upon plastics as an opportunity. As a result it expanded its investment in packaging and container manufacture to take advantage of the trend: its packaging and container subsidiaries are as willing to use plastics as any other material. To the extent to which they become major factors in the packaging market, the parent company benefits from the trend toward plastics, rather than being threatened by it.

Sometimes a business needs to ask: "What compromises with what we claim to be harmful to our business are we already making? Are they actually harmful? Or do we benefit?"

It was this question that made a leading soft-drink bottler in the United States take a new look at its market. For years the company had actively campaigned against low-calorie drinks as a fad. Management was convinced that these drinks (which are not based on a special formula or a secret ingredient) were a threat to its own branded product—which is rather high in calories. But while more and more of the company's bottlers took on low-calorie drinks, they also sold more of the old, standard beverage—the diet drinks built a market for the old product rather than cutting into it. It took management several years before it accepted the facts. Now the company itself is making, promoting, and selling low-calorie drinks of its own—and its sales of both the old and the new line have greatly increased.

What everybody in the business "knows" can never happen should be examined carefully. Is "what can never happen" actually a major opportunity for the company to make something happen? Is it perhaps even what is already happening? Quite often managements will insist that a development is impossible because they are afraid of it while convinced that it is inevitable.

Makers of heavy electrical switchgear for power houses and transformer stations maintained until the late nineteen fifties that power-switching had to be done mechanically. They even published papers proving the theoretical impossibility of electronic power-switching. The only result of this head-in-the-sand attitude was that the leading manufacturers did not work on electronic development and were in danger of losing the market when electronic switchgear was finally developed—by other companies. Their insistence that it was impossible had convinced no one but themselves.

Any threat to a business or to an industry is an indication of a change in the environment: in markets, in customers, or in knowledge. If a business continues to stick to the existing, traditional, established—or denies that anything else is possible—a change may destroy it in the end. But a change should always be an opportunity to do something different and profitable.

Many American businesses in the last ten years saw a threat to their sales in the rise of the Common Market and of Japan. The few, however, who asked: "What opportunities does this trend offer?" reaped very great benefits—both through large, new exports to the growing consumer and industrial markets of Europe and of Japan, and through building or buying profitable and rapidly growing subsidiaries abroad.

It is not always possible, of course, to convert threats into opportunities. But it is more likely that a threat can be converted into an opportunity than that it can be averted. It is more profitable to take advantage of a new trend than it is to fight it.

Finding and realizing the potential of a business is psychologically difficult. It will always be opposed from within because it means breaking with old-established habits. It often means giving up the very skill people are proudest of. To fight the threat, to manage an imbalance, and above all to make a process efficient despite its inherent weaknesses, requires great effort. It is an old observation that nothing gives people greater sense of accomplishment than the ability to do the near-impossible, if only poorly. Searching for the potential of opportunity in a company's vulnerabilities, limitations, and weaknesses is therefore likely to be resented by its most accomplished people as a direct attack on their position, pride, and power.

This is the reason why the opportunities are often not realized by the industry leaders but by people at or near the outside. The oxygen process that, for the first time in a century, changed the technology of steelmaking and affected its basic economics was, for instance, developed by people who had never made steel before: the Austrians in a new, Nazi-built plant in Linz, far away from any traditional steel center. The first electronic switchgear designs came from companies without prior switchgear business or experience, and so on.

That this area is difficult, both objectively and psychologically, only means that businesses have to work hard at it and that managements have to stress it heavily. Finding the potential and developing its opportunities are prerequisites of survival and growth.

This does not mean that every business has a hidden potential and can turn weaknesses and vulnerabilities into opportunity. But a business that has no potential cannot survive. And a business that fails to search for its potential leaves its survival to chance.

11 Making the Future Today

We know only two things about the future:
- It cannot be known.
- It will be different from what exists now and from what we now expect.

These assertions are not particularly new or particularly striking. But they have far-reaching implications.

1. Any attempt to base today's actions and commitments on *predictions* of *future events* is futile. The best we can hope to do is to anticipate *future effects of events* which have already irrevocably happened.

2. But precisely because the future is going to be different and cannot be predicted, it is possible to make the unexpected and unpredicted come to pass. To try to make the future happen is risky; but it is a rational activity. And it is less risky than coasting along on the comfortable assumption that nothing is going to change, less risky than following a prediction as to what "must" happen or what is "most probable."

Business these last ten or twenty years has accepted the need to work systematically on making the future. But long-range planning does not—and cannot—aim at the elimination of risks and uncertainties. That is not given to mortal man. The one thing he can try is to find, and occasionally to create, the right risk and to exploit uncertainty. The purpose of the work on making the future is not to decide what should be done tomorrow, but what should be done today to have a tomorrow.

The deliberate commitment of present resources to an unknown and unknowable future is the specific function of the entrepreneur in the term's original meaning. J. B. Say, the great French economist who coined the word around the year 1800, used it to describe the man who attracts capital locked up in the unproductive past (e.g., in marginal land) and commits it to the risk of making a different future. English economists such as Adam Smith with their focus on the trader saw efficiency as the central economic function. Say, however, rightly stressed the creation of risk and the exploitation of the discontinuity between today and tomorrow as the wealth-producing economic activities.

Now we are learning slowly how to do this work systematically and with direction and control. The starting point is the realization that there are two different—though complementary—approaches:

• Finding and exploiting the time lag between the appearance of a discontinuity in economy and society and its full impact—one might call this *anticipation of a future that has already happened.*

• Imposing on the as yet unborn future a new idea which tries to give direction and shape to what is to come. This one might call *making the future happen.*

THE FUTURE THAT HAS ALREADY HAPPENED

There is a time lag between a major social, economic, or cultural event and its full impact. A sharp rise or a sharp drop in the birthrate will not have an effect on the size of the available labor force for fifteen to twenty years. But the change has already happened. Only catastrophe—destructive war, famine, or pandemic—could prevent its impact tomorrow.

These are the opportunities of the future that has already happened. They might therefore be called a potential. But unlike the potential discussed in the last chapter, the future that has already happened is not within the present business; it is outside: a change in society, knowledge, culture, industry, or economic structure.

It is, moreover, a major change rather than a trend, a break in the pattern rather than a variation within it. There is, of course, considerable uncertainty and risk in committing resources to anticipation. But the risk is limited. We cannot really know how fast the impact will occur. But that it will occur we can say with a high degree of assurance; and we can, to a useful extent, describe it.

There is a lot we cannot anticipate regarding the impact of a change in birthrate on the labor force: how large a proportion of the women will be in the labor force, for instance; how many of today's young children will stay in school well beyond age fourteen or sixteen; where the future jobs will be, and how many; and so forth. But one can say with assurance: "This is the largest the labor force can be a decade or two hence—for to be in it a person has to have been born by now." One can equally say: "That Latin America in the last generation has changed from a rural to an urban society is a fact—and it is bound to have long-range impact."

Fundamental knowledge has to be available today to be able to serve us ten or fifteen years hence. In the mid-nineteenth century one could only speculate about the consequences for the economy of Michael Faraday's discoveries in electricity. A good many of the speculations were undoubtedly wide of the mark. But that this breakthrough into an entirely new field of energy would have major impact could be said with some certainty.

Major cultural changes too operate over a fairly long period. This is particularly true of the subtlest but most pervasive cultural change: a change in people's awareness. It is by no means certain that the underdeveloped countries will succeed in rapidly developing themselves. On the contrary, it is probable that only a few will succeed, and that even these few will go through difficult times and suffer severe crises. But that the peoples of Latin America, Asia, and Africa have become aware of the possibility of development and that they have committed themselves to it and to its consequences is a fact. It creates a momentum that only disaster could reverse. These countries may not succeed in industrializing themselves. But they will, for a historical period at least, give priority to industrial development—and hard times may only accentuate their new awareness of the possibility of, and need for, industrial development.

Similarly, it would take a bold man to predict how fast the Negro will gain complete equality in American society. But that, as a result of the events of 1962 and 1963, there is a new awareness of race relations in the United States on the part of Negro and white alike; above all, that the "submissive Negro" has become a thing of the past, at least as far as the young people are concerned, is a fact that already happened. It is the kind of fact that is irreversible. It will have impact; the only question is how soon.

Industry and marketing structures too are areas where the future may have already happened—but where impacts are not yet accomplished.

The Free World economy may collapse again into economic nationalism and protectionism. The tremendous scope and impact of the movement toward a truly international economy in the nineteen fifties and nineteen sixties may have created so much stress and strain (e.g., political pressure from over-protected farmers) that a severe reaction will set in. But the businessman's awareness of the existence and extent of the international economy should persist. It is unlikely, barring catastrophe, that we shall within the next generation fall back into such easy illusions of the nineteen forties as that this or that industrial region can have something like an unchallengeable economic hegemony, or that a domestic industrial economy can be sealed off from the developments in the world economy. It is unlikely that the many businesses that have gone international these last fifteen years will move back to confining themselves, their operations, and their vision to one national economy and market.

These are—intentionally—big examples. But much smaller changes may also create opportunities to anticipate the future of the business today.

One example of a rather small shift in social and cultural habits that created such an opportunity was the change in the telephone habits of the younger Americans during World War II. Till then long-distance calls were not within the normal behavior of the great mass of the population; they were for emergencies only. During the war, however, the men in uniform were encouraged to keep in touch with their families through long-distance calls. As a result the long-distance call became normal for the younger war-time generation. It would still be quite a few years before these young people of 1944 would become the heads of families and translate their new telephone behavior into the normal behavior of the population. The time could therefore be utilized by the telephone company to carry through a program of building long-distance facilities and equipment.

The changes that generate the future that has already happened can be found through systematic search. The first area to examine is always population. Population changes are the most fundamental—for the labor force, for the market, for social pressures, and economic opportunities. They are the least reversible in the normal course of events. They have a known minimum lead-time between change and impact: before a rise in the birthrate puts pressure on school facilities, at least five or six years will elapse—but then the pressure will come. And their consequences are most nearly predictable.

By the early 1960's it had become clear that the American population had undergone a drastic change in age structure, in basic cultural habits, and in expectations. While the events that brought this change about had already happened—for by 1961 everybody was already born who would be twenty by 1980—the impact had not yet begun to make itself felt. It would only begin to be felt in the late 1960's, and would reach its peak in the late 1970's.

By 1977 the American population will be the youngest it has been for 150 years, with at least two-thirds of the population under thirty-five years of age. The median age will be in the middle twenties. But unlike other countries of low average age, life expectancy in the United States is high, with an expected life-span of over seventy for both sexes. Never in history has there been such a relationship between average age and average life expectancy. Whenever in the past we had a young population, life expectancy was also short—and vice versa. What matters is, therefore, not only that people of fairly low chronological age will be the great majority in the American population of the late 1970's. They will also be people of very low relative or social age; that is, people who by the time they reach median life-span have lived no more than one-third of their life expectancy. This alone should mean tremendous changes in the behavior and expectations of the American people.

In addition, these young families will have an unprecedented degree of formal schooling. Half of them will contain at least one member, whether man or wife, who has had more than twelve years of schooling. This will mean different expectations on the part of the dominant groups in the labor force. As regards consumer behavior, we know, for instance that these couples (the young engineer employed in an electronics company and his wife, for instance) do not buy according to income. They buy according to expectations in respect to their future income and social position. Present income is a restraint on purchases rather than the motivating force.

Few changes in American economic history have been so striking or so fast as this change ahead. It is a change that has already happened.

Yet to my knowledge few if any American businesses have asked themselves: What does this change mean for us? What does it mean for employment and labor force? What does it mean in terms of new markets? How does it change the basic structure of the American market? What does it mean for our customers? Our products? Our entire business posture?

The two fastest-growing markets in the American economy are being created by this population change. But they are not yet to be found in economics books.

First there is an "activities market" which includes many goods and services hitherto not considered as belonging together: bowling, camping, and lawn care but also paperback books and adult higher education. All these activities are in competition with each other. All of them require something scarcer than money: discretionary time. The young engineer or manager who spends his evenings trying to acquire an advanced degree has no time to go bowling or to take care of his lawn. In the activities market, people do not buy to own but to do—in other words, they make no distinction between goods and services. The only distinction they can make is between time they have and time they do not have. The discretionary time market will therefore be both fast growing and rewarding and also competitive and difficult.

The other growth market ahead is the "office consumption market," i.e., the market for goods and services which, while not going to the individual family (and therefore not traditionally considered consumer goods), also are not used up in the process of production and are, therefore, not traditional producer goods—things like typewriters, computers, and all kinds of goods and services to make knowledge workers productive. Again, while rewarding, this is also likely to be a highly competitive and rapidly changing market.

Another field that always should be searched for a future that has already happened is that of knowledge. This search should not, however, be confined to the present knowledge areas of the business. We assume, in looking for the future, that the business will be different. And one of the major areas in which we may be able to anticipate a different business is that of the knowledge resource on which the specific excellence of a business is founded. We must therefore look at major knowledge areas, whether they have a direct relation to the present business or not. And wherever we find a fundamental change which has not yet had major impact, we should ask: "Are there opportunities here which we should and could anticipate?"

The behavioral sciences provide an example of a major change in a knowledge area although few businesses would consider it directly relevant to them. Learning theory is one area in psychology where really new knowledge has been developed these last thirty years. Although this may seem rather remote to businessmen, the new knowledge is likely to have impact not only on the form and content of education but on teaching and learning materials, school equipment and school design, and even on research organization and research management. A wide range of industries—from publishing to construction—might be affected significantly, with great opportunities for those who first convert the potential of the new knowledge into actual goods and services.

One also looks at other industries, other countries, other markets, with the question: Has anything happened there that might establish a pattern for our industry, our country, our market?

In the early nineteen fifties every Japanese electronics manufacturer assumed—quite rationally—that incomes in Japan were too low for television and that the Japanese farmer, in particular, could not possibly afford anything so expensive as a TV set. Most Japanese companies therefore planned for limited production of cheap sets.

Only one small and almost unknown company tried to validate the assumption by looking at what had happened in other countries such as the United States, Great Britain, or Germany. It found that a television set apparently is not considered an ordinary article by the lower-income groups, but offers a satisfaction to them out of all proportion to its cost. In all countries the poor had been the most enthusiastic television customers; they had tended to buy more expensive sets than they could possibly justify by their income status. This one Japanese manufacturer therefore brought out larger and more expensive sets than his competitors. And he aimed a concentrated sales campaign at the Japanese farmer. Ten years later, two-thirds of the low-income households in the Japanese cities and more than half of the farm homes, had television, with the larger and more expensive sets in the lead. The formerly small and almost unknown company is now one of the largest Japanese electronics concerns.

Next, one always asks: Is anything happening in the structure of an industry that indicates a major change?

Such a change—now in progress throughout the entire industrial world—is the materials revolution, which erases or blurs the lines that traditionally separated different materials streams.

Only a generation ago materials streams were separate from beginning to end. Paper was, for instance, the main manufactured material into which wood could be converted. Paper, in turn, had to be made from a tree. The same situation held for other major materials, aluminum and petroleum, steel and zinc. Most of the finished products coming out of these material streams had specific and unique end-uses. In other words, most substances determined end-uses, and most end-uses determined substances.

Today, however, almost all materials streams are open-ended, first and last. The tree can go into a good many end-products other than paper. Substances that give the same performance as paper can be made from many starting materials other than trees. In respect to end-uses, materials have also become alternatives rather than complements. Paper is on the point of becoming an important material for clothing. There is a wide area of overlap within which products derived from different starting materials can be used to do the same job. Even the process is no longer unique. The paper people increasingly incorporate into their processes techniques developed by the plastics manufacturers and converters; and the textile people increasingly adapt paper industry processes.

Every materials company is aware that its business is changing. A good many companies have done something about the change; the major American can companies have, for instance, bought container manufacturers using glass, paper, and plastics. But too few companies have, to my knowledge, realized that the fundamental change is not in their business, or even in business at all, but outside. Where we formerly saw individual substances, we now see materials. The change is so recent that no one can yet define what we mean by "materials." But it has already made obsolescent any business that defines itself in terms of one material stream.

Inside the business too there can usually be found clues to events which, while basic and irreversible, have not yet had their full impact.

One indication is often internal friction within the company. Something is being introduced—and it becomes a source of dissension. Unwittingly one has touched a sensitive spot—sensitive often, because the new activity is in anticipation of future changes and therefore in contradiction to the accepted pattern.

Wherever, in an American company, product planning is introduced as a new function and as a specific kind of work, it creates friction. Usually this manifests itself in a long wrangle as to where the new activity belongs. Does it belong in marketing? Or does it belong in research and engineering? Actually, this is much less a dispute over the new function than it is a dim first awareness that the marketing approach tends to make *all* functions secondary and that all functions are cost centers rather than producers of results. This, however, must lead to fundamental changes in organization. It is the anticipation of these changes that makes people react violently to the symptom, product planning.

Top management in the Bell Telephone System set up a new merchandising function ten years or so ago. Very few people in the telephone companies of the systems were affected by it; yet Bell Telephone managers were greatly upset. What had really happened was that the Bell System had attained its major goal of the previous seventy-five years: to equip practically every American home and business with a telephone. Its primary market, the market for the telephone installation, had become saturated. Further growth, therefore, could only be obtained by promoting the maximum use of the telephone rather than by promoting subscriptions to telephone service on a minimum basis. This change that had already happened foreshadowed a radically altered situation in respect to opportunities as well as to risks for the telephone business in the United States; the internal friction over merchandising was only a first symptom.

Any business or activity which has reached its objective is heading into a period of major change. But most people in the business or the activity will continue for a long time to try to achieve the objective that has already been gained. During that period there is a future that has already happened, an opportunity to anticipate.

In the industrially developed countries, for instance, the goal of universal general education has been substantially accomplished. But most educators still think and act on the assumption—valid for the last two hundred years—that the task is to obtain more years of compulsory education. It usually takes a complete generation-shift for the new reality to become widely accepted. But those educational institutions that understand the situation and think through what it makes possible or what it requires will have educational leadership tomorrow.

In business, too, the company that sees that an objective has been reached and acts to redirect its efforts—while its competitors still strain to get to where they already are—will emerge as tomorrow's leader.

Two additional and related questions should be asked: "What do the generally approved forecasts assert is likely to happen ten, fifteen, twenty years hence? Has it actually happened already?" Most people can imagine only what they have already seen. If, therefore, a forecast meets with widespread acceptance, it is quite likely that it does not forecast the future, but in effect, reports on the recent past.

There is in American business history one famous illustration of the productivity of this approach.

Around 1910, in the early years of Henry Ford's success, the first forecasts appeared that predicted the growth of the automobile into mass transportation. Most people at that time still considered this unlikely to happen before another thirty years or so. But William C. Durant—then a small manufacturer—asked: "Has this not already happened?" As soon as he asked the question, the answer was obvious: It *had* happened, though the main impact was yet to come. The public's awareness had changed from regarding the car as a toy of the rich to demanding a car for mass transportation. And this would require large automobile companies. On this insight Durant imagined General Motors and began to pull together a number of small automobile manufacturers and small accessory companies into the kind of business that would be able to take advantage of this new market and its opportunity.

The final question should therefore be: "What are our own assumptions regarding society and economy, market and customer, knowledge and technology? Are they still valid?"

The English middle- and lower-class housewife was well known to be inflexibly conservative in her food buying and eating habits. The two companies in Great Britain that have emerged in the last ten or fifteen years as leading food distributors, however, raised the question in the late 1940's: Is this assumption still valid? It immediately became clear that the answer was: No. As a result of the food shortages of the war and postwar periods, the formerly conservative English housewife had become used to new foods and new food distribution methods, and was willing to experiment.

Looking for the future that has already happened and anticipating its impacts introduces new perception in the beholder. The new event is easily visible as the illustrations should have made clear. The need is to make oneself see it. What then could or might be done is usually not too difficult to discover. The opportunities, in other words, are neither remote nor obscure. The pattern, however, has to be recognized first.

As the examples should also have demonstrated, this is an approach of great power. But there is also major danger: the temptation to see as a change what we believe to be happening, or worse, what we believe should happen. This is so great a danger that, as a general rule, any finding should be distrusted for which there is enthusiasm within the company. If everybody shouts, "This is what we wanted all along," it is likely that wishes rather than facts are being reported.

For the power of this approach is that it questions and ultimately overturns deeply entrenched assumptions, practices, and habits. It leads to decisions to work toward change in the entire conduct, if not in the structure, of the business. It leads to the decision to make the business different.

II

THE POWER OF AN IDEA

It is futile to try to guess what products and processes the future will want. But it is possible to make up one's mind what idea one wants to make a reality in the future, and to build a different business on such an idea.

Making the future happen also means creating a different business. But what makes the future happen is always the embodiment in a business of an idea of a different economy, a different technology, a different society. It need not be a big idea; but it must be one that differs from the norm of today.

The idea has to be an entrepreneurial one—an idea of wealth-producing potential and capacity, expressed in a going, working, producing business, and effective through business actions and behavior. It does not emerge from the question: "What should future society look like?"—the question of social reformer, revolutionary, or philosopher. Underlying the entrepreneurial idea that makes the future is always the question: "What major change in economy, market, or knowledge would enable us to conduct business the way we really would like to do it, the way we would really obtain the best economic results?"

Because this seems so limited and self-centered an approach, historians tend to overlook it and to be blind to its impact. The great philosophical idea has, of course, more profound effects. But few philosophical ideas have any effect at all. While each business idea is more limited, a large proportion of them are effective. Innovating businessmen have therefore had a good deal more impact as a group than the historians realize.

The very fact that an entrepreneurial idea does not encompass all of society or all of knowledge but just one narrow area makes it more viable. The people who have this idea may be wrong about everything else in the future economy or society. But that does not matter as long as they are approximately right in respect to their own business focus. All that they need to be successful is one small, specific development.

Thomas Watson who founded and built IBM did not see at all the development of technology. But he had the idea of data processing as a unifying concept on which to build a business. The business was, for a long time, fairly small and confined itself to such mundane work as keeping accounting ledgers and time records. But it was ready to jump when the technology came in—out of totally unrelated wartime work—which made data processing actually possible, the technology of the electronic computer. While Watson built a small and unspectacular business in the twenties, designing, selling, and installing punch-card equipment, the mathematicians and logicians of Logical Positivism (e.g., Bridgman in the United States and Carnap in Austria) talked and wrote a systematic methodology of quantification and universal measurements. It is most unlikely that they ever heard of the young, struggling IBM Company, and certain that they did not connect their ideas with it. Yet it was Watson's IBM and not their philosophical ideas that became operational when the new technology emerged in World War II.

The men who built Sears Roebuck—Richard Sears, Julius Rosenwald, Albert Loeb, and, finally, General Robert E. Wood—had active social concerns and a lively social imagination. Yet not one of them thought of remaking the economy. I doubt even that the idea of a mass market—as opposed to the traditional class markets—occurred to them until long after the event. Yet from its early beginnings, Sears Roebuck had the idea that the poor man's money could be made to have the same purchasing power as the rich man's. This was not a particularly new idea. Social reformers and economists had bandied it around for decades. The cooperative movement in Europe largely grew out of it. But Sears was the first business built on the idea in the United States. It started out with the question: "What would make the farmer a customer for a retail business?" The answer was simply: "He needs to be sure of getting goods of the same dependable quality as do city people at the same low price." At the time this was an innovating idea of considerable audacity.

Great entrepreneurial innovations have been achieved by converting an existing theoretical proposition into an effective business.

The entrepreneurial innovation that has had the greatest impact converted the theoretical proposition of the French social philosopher Saint Simon into a bank. Saint Simon starting from Say's concept of the entrepreneur, developed a philosophical system around the creative role of capital. The idea became effective, however, through a banking business: the famous Credit Mobilier, which his disciples, the Brothers Pereire, founded in Paris in the middle of the nineteenth century. The Credit Mobilier was to be the conscious developer of industry through the direction of the liquid resources of the community. It became the prototype for the entire banking system of the then underdeveloped continent of Europe—beginning with the France, Holland, and Belgium of the Pereires' day. The Pereires' imitators then founded the "business banks" of Germany, Switzerland, Austria, Scandinavia, and Italy which became the main agents for the industrial development of their countries. After the Civil War the idea crossed the Atlantic. The American bankers who developed American industry—from Jay Cooke and the American Credit Mobilier that financed the transcontinental railroad, to J. P. Morgan—were all imitators of the Pereires, whether they knew it or not. So were the Japanese Zaibatsu, the great banker-industrialists who built the economy of modern Japan.

The most faithful disciple of the Pereires, however, has been Soviet Russia. The idea of planning through the controlled allocation of capital comes directly from the Pereires; all the Russians did was to substitute the State for the individual banker. (A step taken by an Austrian, Rudolf Hilferding, who started out in Vienna as a banker in the "business bank" tradition and ended as the leading theoretician of German democratic socialism. His book, *Finance Capital* (1910) was acknowledged by Lenin to have been the source of his planning and industrialization concepts.) There is nothing of this in Marx, above all no "planning."

Every single development bank started today in an underdeveloped country is still a direct descendant of the original Credit Mobilier. Yet the Brothers Pereire did not start out to remake the economy. They started a business with the idea of making a profit.

Similarly, the modern chemical industry grew out of the conversion of an already existing idea into a business.

By all odds the modern chemical industry should have arisen in England. In the mid-nineteenth century, England with her highly developed textile industry was the major market for chemicals. It also had the scientific leadership at the time—the time of Faraday as well as of Darwin. The modern chemical industry did actually start with an English discovery: Perkin's discovery of aniline dyes (1856). Yet, twenty years after Perkin—that is, around 1875—leadership in the new industry had passed to Germany. German businessmen contributed the entrepreneurial idea that was lacking in England: the results of scientific enquiry—organic chemistry in this case—can be directly converted into marketable applications.

The idea on which a business might grow to greatness can be a much simpler one, of course.

The most powerful private business in history was probably the Japanese House of Mitsui, which before its dissolution after Japan's defeat in World War II is said to have employed a million people all over the world. (This at least was the official estimate of the American occupation authorities who decreed the dissolution of the Mitsui concern.) Its origin was the world's first department store, developed in Tokyo in the mid-seventeenth century by an early Mitsui. The entrepreneurial idea underlying this business was that of the merchant as a principal of economic life, rather than as mere middleman. This meant on the one hand fixed prices to the customer. On the other hand, Mitsui no longer acted the agent dealing with craftsman and manufacturer. He would buy for his own account and give firm orders for standardized mechandise to be made according to his specifications. In overseas trade the merchant had acted as a principal all along. Around 1650 however, overseas trade had just been suppressed in

Japan—whereupon Mitsui took the overseas-trade concepts and built a domestic merchant-business on them.

The basic entrepreneurial idea may be merely imitation of something that works well in another country or in another industry.

When Thomas Bata, the Slovak shoemaker, returned to Europe from the United States after World War I, he had the idea that everybody in Slovakia and the Balkans could have shoes to wear as everybody had in the United States. "The peasant goes barefoot," he is reported to have said, "not because he is too poor, but because there are no shoes." What was needed to make this vision of a shod peasant come true was a supply of cheap and standardized, but well-designed and durable footwear, as there was in America. On this analogy Bata built in a few years Europe's largest shoe business and one of Europe's most successful companies.

To make the future happen one need not, in other words, have a creative imagination. It is work rather than genius—and therefore accessible in some measure to everybody. The man of creative imagination will have more imaginative ideas, to be sure. But that the more imaginative idea will actually be more successful is by no means certain. Pedestrian ideas have at times been successful; Bata's idea of applying American methods to making shoes was not very original in the Europe of 1920, with its tremendous interest in Ford and his assembly line. What mattered was his courage rather than his genius.

To make the future happen one has to be willing to do something new. One has to be willing to ask: What do we really want to see happen that is quite different from today? One has to be willing to say: "This is the right thing to happen as the future of the business. We will work on making it happen."

"Creativity," which looms so large in present discussions of innovation, is not the real problem. There are more ideas in any organization, including businesses, than can possibly be put to use. What is lacking, as a rule, is the *willingness to look beyond products to ideas*. Products and processes are only the vehicle through which an idea becomes effective. And, as the illustrations should have shown, the specific future products and processes can usually not even be imagined.

When DuPont started the work on polymer chemistry out of which Nylon eventually evolved, it did not know that manmade fibers would be the end-product. DuPont acted on the assumption that any gain in man's ability to manipulate the structure of large, organic molecules —at that time in its infancy—would lead to commercially important results of some kind. Only after six or seven years of research work did manmade fibers first appear as a possible major result area.

Indeed, as the IBM experience shows, the specific products and processes that make an idea successful often come out of entirely different and unrelated work. But the willingness to think in terms of the general rather than the specific, in terms of a business, the contributions it makes, the satisfactions it supplies, the market and economy it serves, comes hard to the average businessman.

Moreover, the businessman often lacks the courage to commit resources to such an idea. The resources that should be invested in making the future happen should be small, but they must be of the best. Otherwise nothing happens.

The greatest lack of the businessman is, however, a touchstone of validity and practicality. An idea has to meet rigorous tests if it is to be capable of making the future of a business.

It has to have operational validity. Can we take action on this idea? Or can we only talk about it? Can we really do something right away to bring about the kind of future we want to make happen?

Sears Roebuck with its idea of bringing the market to the isolated American farmer could show immediate results. But DuPont with its idea of polymer chemistry could only organize research work on a small scale; all it could do was to underwrite the research of one first-rate man. Both, however, could *do* something right away.

To be able to spend money on research is not enough. It must be research directed toward the realization of the idea. The knowledge sought may be general—as was that of DuPont's project. But it must be reasonably clear at least that if available, it would be applicable knowledge.

The idea must also have economic validity. If it could be put to work right away in practice, it should be able to produce economic results. We may not be able to do what we would like to see done—not for a long time, perhaps never. But if we could do it now, the resulting products, processes, or services would find a customer, a market, an end-use; should be capable of being sold profitably, should satisfy a want and a need.

The idea itself might aim at social reform. But unless a business can be built on it, it is not a valid entrepreneurial idea. The test of the idea is not the votes it gets or the acclaim of the philosophers. It is economic performance and economic results. Even if the rationale of the business is social reform rather than business success, the touchstone must be ability to perform and to survive as a business.

Businesses started to bring about social rather than economic results are not numerous—though some of the most successful entrepreneurs were primarily reformers in their outlook and approach (Robert Owen, for instance, or the young Henry Ford). But wherever an attempt succeeds in attaining a social goal through a business, it is because the test of economic validity is applied ruthlessly.

This is being done today, for instance, by Murray Lincoln of the Nationwide Insurance Companies. Describing himself as "Vice President in Charge of Revolution," Lincoln has dedicated his life to the advancement of the cooperative movement. He has little good to say of profit-making enterprise. Yet he has tried to promote cooperation through businesses—insurance companies and financial businesses by and large—and he demands of them better business performance than their more orthodox competitors among profit-seeking companies demand of themselves.

Finally, the idea must meet the test of personal commitment. Do we really believe in the idea? Do we really want to be that kind of people, do that kind of work, run that kind of business?

To make the future demands courage. It demands work. But it also demands faith. To commit ourselves to the expedient is simply not practical. It will not suffice for the tests ahead. For no such idea is foolproof—nor should it be. The one idea regarding the future that must inevitably fail is the apparently "sure thing," the "riskless" idea, the one "that cannot fail." The idea on which tomorrow's business is to be built must be uncertain; no one can really say as yet what it will look like if and when it becomes reality. It must be risky: it has a probability of success but also of failure. If it is not both uncertain and risky, it is simply not a practical idea for the future. For the future itself is both uncertain and risky.

Unless there is personal commitment to the values of the idea and faith in them, the necessary efforts will therefore not be sustained. The businessman should not become an enthusiast, let alone a fanatic. He should realize that things do not happen just because he wants them to happen—not even if he works very hard at making them happen. Like any other effort, the work on making the future happen should be reviewed periodically to see whether continuation can still be justified both by the results of the work to date and by the prospects ahead. Ideas regarding the future can become investments in managerial ego, too, and need to be carefully tested for their capacity to perform and to give results. But the people who work on making the future also need to be able to say with conviction: "This is what we really want our business to be."

It is perhaps not absolutely necessary for every business to search for the idea that will make the future. A good many businesses and their managements do not even make their present business effective—and yet the companies somehow survive for a while. The big business, in particular, seems to be able to coast a long time on the courage, work, and vision of earlier executives.

But tomorrow always arrives. It is always different. And then even the mightiest company is in trouble if it has not worked on the future. It will have lost distinction and leadership—all that will remain is big-company overhead. It will neither control nor understand what is happening. Not having dared to take the risk of making the new happen, it perforce took the much greater risk of being surprised by what did happen. And this is a risk that even the largest and richest company cannot afford and that even the smallest business need not run.

To be more than a slothful steward of the talents given in his keeping, the executive has to accept responsibility for making the future happen. It is the willingness to tackle purposefully this, the last of the economic tasks in business enterprise, that distinguishes the great business from the merely competent one, and the business builder from the executive-suite custodian.

PART III

A PROGRAM

FOR PERFORMANCE

12 The Key Decisions

Decisions are made and actions are taken at every step in the analysis of a business and of its economic dimensions. Insights are "bled off" and converted into tasks and work assignments. At every step of the analysis there should be measurable results.

But for full effectiveness all the work needs to be integrated into a unified *program for performance*.

To make the present business effective may require one specific course of action. To make the future of the business different may require different action. Yet what is done to make the present business effective inevitably commits resources, inevitably molds the future. What is done to anticipate the future inevitably affects the present business in all its policies, expectations, products, and knowledge efforts. Major actions in every one of the economic dimensions have therefore to be consistent with one another. Conflicts between the conclusions of the various analyses have to be reconciled. There has to be balance between the efforts. Otherwise, one effort undoes what another has been trying to achieve. The hard reality of the present must not be obscured by the lure of tomorrow's promises. But the difficult and discouraging work for tomorrow must also not be smothered by the urgencies of the present.

All the work decided upon is work to be done today. It has to be done with the same presently available resources of men, knowledge, and money, whether the results are expected soon or in the distant future.

Therefore one set of key decisions must be made for the business in all of its dimensions. These decisions are

1. The idea of the business
2. The specific excellence it needs
3. The priorities

THE IDEA OF THE BUSINESS

Every company has an idea of its business: a picture of itself and of its specific capacities. Every business sees a specific contribution for which it expects to get paid. This may express itself in nothing more elaborate than the statement, "This is not our kind of business," or "This is not how we do things around here." It may also be expressed in a voluminous statement of objectives. But there is always an idea that determines how the decision-making people see the business, what course of action they are willing to pursue, and what actions seem to them alien or inconceivable.

The idea of the business always defines a satisfaction to be supplied to the market or a knowledge to be made effective in economic performance. The idea of the business thereby also defines the area in which a company has to obtain and to hold a leadership position.

As apparently simple statement such as: "We supply the office manager with the materials, supplies, and equipment the modern office needs" might define the idea of a business. It identifies the market and the contribution to be made to it. It implies that the function of the business is that of the true merchant whose knowledge of customer needs and of goods, sources, and performance characteristics enables him to buy for the customer—the office manager in this case—better value than the customer could obtain for himself. It implies further a commitment to leadership in a major segment of the market: to provide superior satisfaction today; to anticipate the needs and wants of the office of tomorrow; and to give the office manager what he considers value.

But the statement says nothing—and should say nothing—about the specific means through which this idea is realized. This might be manufacturing most of the products the office manager buys. It might be acting as a distributor who buys everything he sells. It might even be functioning as a purchasing agent who charges a commission on whatever he buys for the office manager. And what specific products and product lines should be carried at any given time is—and should be—left open. This is to be decided according to time, place, and circumstance, and will change as the office, its technology, its labor force, and the main office buyers change.

"Our business is the application of high energy physics to industrial processes" might serve as the central idea. The emphasis here is on specific knowledge. "To serve those home owners who take pride in their homes and want to take care of them" may be a perfectly adequate statement of the idea behind a home-service magazine.

Here are some concrete examples from large and well-known companies.

"Our business is public service" was the idea on which Theodore Vail built the American Telephone & Telegraph Company (the Bell System) in the early years of the present century. At the time this was near-heresy. That a business was "affected with the public interest" was a limitation and weakness. But Vail, for instance, not only accepted public regulation but insisted on it as the prerequisite for a privately owned and privately managed public service industry.

"Our business is business development" was the idea of the Brothers Pereire in their Credit Mobilier, as it has been the idea of all their imitators since.

"Our business is to build into products the work and skill of grocer and housewife" is the idea that underlies every successful processed-foods business.

To be valid such a definition should be sufficiently broad to allow the business to grow and to change. Otherwise it may become obsolete at the first change in market or technology. "Our business is television sets" is too narrow. But "our business is entertainment" is too general. The idea of the business should enforce concentration. It should make possible determination of the specific knowledges in which excellence has to be attained, and of the specific markets in which the business has to strive for leadership. A valid idea makes it possible for the people in a company to say, "This fits and should be looked at," and "This does not fit and we should not do it." In other words, it gives *direction* to the business.

An idea of the business needs to be operational. It must lead to action conclusions such as: "What we need is product development that is likely to result in both a salable piece of equipment and a constant demand for proprietary supplies to run the equipment." Or: "We look for products and processes that fit our marketing organization and distributive skill. Products and processes that do not fit easily will normally be developed only to the point where we can sell or license them to others." Or, to cite an additional example: "We are not so much interested in what specific area of technology applies to a project but whether capacity for systems design and systems management is essential to it."

One of the most important operational conclusions from the idea of the business might be a decision on size. Should the company try to become a large company? Or is it better off remaining fairly small, at least in relation to its market and its competitors. (There are no absolutely large or absolutely small businesses; size is always relative to market and to competition.) A business that aims at growth follows different policies, and requires a different management, from one that can best perform by staying small.

A company that cannot define itself in a valid idea has become amorphous and is likely to try so many things as to be unmanageable.

This applies particularly to businesses which can define themselves only in such broad generalities that they do not specify the areas of excellence needed. The "electrical industry" or the "chemical industry" are generalities which no longer serve—however meaningful they were fifty or sixty years ago. "Transportation" or "communications" are also so broad as to be meaningless. If such an all-embracing term is the only available definition, the business is doing too many things to do any one thing well.

As long as there are a few major units each of which can be set up and run as a distinct business with a specific and meaningful idea of its own, they can still be managed as one company with knowledge, direction, and purpose. When, however, a company has become a heterogeneous collection that neither serves common markets nor applies excellence in a small number of knowledge areas, it becomes unmanageable. Sooner or later it will become unmanaged. In the first serious test of economic performance and viability—that is, in the first crisis—it will find itself in trouble.

Inability to develop a valid idea of the business is therefore a danger signal. It either indicates a degree of specialization which is irrelevant to market and customer; or it indicates meaningless splintering of knowledge and effort rather than true diversification which multiplies the results of common knowledge and effort. (Specialization and diversification will be further discussed in the next chapter.)

An idea of a business which does not satisfy the requirements of validity is always the wrong definition.

But the only positive test is the test of experience.

The idea of the business sums up the answers to the questions that have been asked repeatedly in this book.

- What is our business?
- What should it be?
- What will it have to be?

It establishes *objectives*, it sets goals and direction. It determines what results are meaningful and what measurements truly appropriate.

II

WHAT IS OUR EXCELLENCE?

Closely related to the idea of the business is the determination of the excellence that characterizes it. This is always knowledge excellence, a capacity of people to do something in such a manner as to give leadership to the enterprise. Identifying the excellence of a business therefore determines what its truly important efforts are and should be.

Very different definitions of excellence can be equally valid,

as shown by the experience of many large successful companies.

As was discussed in Chapter 7, General Motors, for instance, clearly
prizes excellence in business development and business management.
At General Electric, on the other hand, people were for many years
encouraged not to concern themselves much with business, but to
excel as scientists or engineers. IBM, until recently, stressed the
ability to produce sales and customers, with the district sales manager
the key man.

There is no test except experience by which to judge a definition of excellence. There are, however, tests to identify the
invalid definitions.

The definition has to be broad enough to allow for flexibility,
growth, and change, and specific enough to allow for concentration. A company which defines its excellence in terms of a
narrow specialty—"the polymer chemist" for instance or the
"financial analyst"—inflicts anemia on itself. And a company
with excellence requirements that read like the headlines in the
classified telephone book—from "accountancy" to "zipper repair"—is unlikely even to attain mediocrity in any one area. The
only "universal" accomplishment open to a company (or to an
individual) is universal incompetence.

A valid definition of excellence must be operational and lead
to action conclusions. It has to be the basis for the decisions on
personnel: who is to be promoted and for what; who is to be
hired; what kind of people should the company try to attract and
what attractions should it hold out to them?

Excellence definitions cannot be changed very often; the definition is embodied in and expressed through people, their values
and their behavior. But no excellence definition will remain valid
forever; it must be periodically reviewed and thought through
afresh.

Both General Electric and IBM have had to add to their excellence
definitions within the last fifteen years. Changes in size, and especially
in markets, made General Electric add business management to its

central excellence areas. The computer led IBM to add stress on excellence as a professional scientist and engineer.

Any change in the idea of the business or in its structure, in the market or in the major knowledge areas, may require change in a company's definitions of its specific excellence needs.

III

The Priorities

No matter how simple and how well ordered a business, there is always a great deal more to be done than there are resources available to do it. The opportunities are always more plentiful than the means to realize them. There have to be priority decisions or nothing will get done. In these decisions a business expresses its final appraisal of all it knows about itself, its economic characteristics, its strengths and weaknesses, its opportunities and needs.

Priority decisions convert good intentions into effective commitments, and insight into action. Priority decisions bespeak the level of a management's vision and seriousness. They decide basic behavior and strategy.

Nobody seems to have much difficulty setting priorities. What people find difficult is to decide on "posteriorities"; that is, on what should not be done. It cannot be said often enough that one does not postpone; one abandons. It is almost always a serious mistake to go back to something no matter how desirable it might have appeared when, sometime back, it had to be postponed. This is, of course, why people are so reluctant to set posteriorities.

The principles of maximizing opportunities and resources (as described in Chapter 9) govern the priority decisions. Unless the few really first-rate resources are put full-time on the few outstanding opportunities, priorities have not really been set. Above all the truly big opportunities—those that realize potential and those that make the future—must receive the resources their potential deserves, even at the price of abandoning immediate, seemingly safe, but small ventures.

But the really important thing about priority decisions is that they must be made deliberately and consciously. It is better to make the wrong decision and carry it out than to shirk the job as unpleasant and painful and, as a result, to allow the accidents of the business to set priorities by default.

The key decisions on the idea of the business, its excellence and its priorities can be made systematically or haphazardly. They can be made in awareness of their impact or as an afterthought to some urgent triviality. They can be made by top management or by someone way down the line who, in disposing of a technical detail, actually determines company character and direction.

But somehow, some place, these decisions are always made in a business. Without them no action whatever could really be taken.

There is no formula to yield the "right" answers for these key decisions. But if given haphazardly and without awareness of their importance they will inevitably be the wrong answers. To have even a chance of being right, the key decisions have to be made systematically. This is one responsibility top management can neither delegate nor leave to others.

13 Business Strategies

Whatever a company's program,

- It must decide what opportunities it wants to pursue and what risks it is willing and able to accept.
- It must decide on its scope and structure, and especially on the right balance between specialization, diversification, and integration.
- It must decide between time and money, between building its own or "buying"—i.e., using sale of a business, merger, acquisition and joint venture—to attain its goals.
- It must decide on an organization structure appropriate to its economic realities, its opportunities and its program for performance.

RIGHT OPPORTUNITIES AND RIGHT RISKS

A business has to try to minimize risks. But if its behavior is governed by the attempt to escape risk, it will end up by taking the greatest and least rational risk of all: the risk of doing nothing. There are always good reasons for not doing anything if one starts out searching for the negative. Risks, however important, are not grounds of action, but restraints on action. The actions themselves should be selected so as to maximize opportunities.

What opportunities are available should emerge from the analyses of the economic dimensions of the business. Next, they must be looked at in their totality, sorted out and classified.

There are three kinds of opportunities:
- Additive
- Complementary
- Breakthrough

An *additive opportunity* more fully exploits already existing resources. It does not change the character of the business.

An extension of an existing product line into a new and growing market would be an additive opportunity. The paper manufacturer who extends his marketing from the commercial printer to the office reproduction field avails himself of an additive opportunity—even though his products and his selling methods may need considerable change.

Additive opportunities should rarely be treated as high-priority efforts. The risks should be small, for the returns are always limited. Additive opportunities should not be allowed to take resources away from complementary or breakthrough opportunities.

The *complementary opportunity* will change the structure of the business. It offers something new which, when combined with the present business, results in a new total larger than the sum of its parts.

The opportunity of establishing a paper company in the plastics field, through acquisition of a number of packaging converters who use both paper and plastics, is a complementary opportunity.

The complementary opportunity will always require at least one new knowledge area in which excellence has to be attained. A complementary opportunity, therefore, demands candid self-appraisal: Are we willing and able to change ourselves so as to acquire, support, and reward the new excellence?

A large mechanical company went into organic chemistry to exploit some rather exciting advances in the forming and shaping of plastic materials developed in its research laboratory. But it tried to run the chemical business as if it were a mechanical business, with the same kind of people and the same basic rules. Far from producing a profit its substantial investment in the plastics fields only created a market for the competitors. In the end the company liquidated its chemical venture at a considerable loss.

A complementary opportunity always carries with it considerable risk. If it appears "riskless," it is to be shunned as self-delusion. It is therefore not a big opportunity unless it promises to multiply the wealth-producing capacity of the entire business.

The breakthrough opportunity changes the fundamental economic characteristics and capacity of the business.

The typical example is the removal of restraints discussed in Chapter 10, which always requires a breakthrough but also promises extraordinary results.

A breakthrough opportunity requires great effort. It requires the employment of first-class resources, especially human resources. It often requires major spending on research and development, if not also substantial capital investment. And the risk is always great.

The minimum return, therefore, has to be correspondingly great—or else this is a small opportunity and not worth pursuing.

The story of the Xerox Corporation—one of the spectacular recent growth companies in the United States—is a breakthrough story. The process was developed to overcome a major restraint on office reproduction technology. It was first offered to a good many larger companies, all of whom turned it down as too risky and too expensive to develop. The Haloid Corporation (as Xerox was then called) was a pigmy when it picked up the process. Yet it spent some $40 millions of borrowed money until it had a process that worked. But then the rewards were extraordinary and came fast.

No company that wants to have a future can afford to slight the breakthrough opportunity. This typically is the opportunity to make the future happen. But the effort needed is so great that the breakthrough, if it is successfully realized, should always be capable of creating a new industry rather than an additional product.

Opportunities can also be classified according to their "fit" to a company.

One of the leading magazine publishers in the United States, Time Inc., has never succeeded in anything but a mass-distributed magazine for a general audience. Another publisher, McGraw-Hill, has had success only with magazines for limited audiences in particular fields or industries, e.g., chemical engineering. Time Inc. might therefore consider as highly risky, if not as inappropriate, what to McGraw-Hill might appear as fairly easy, and vice versa.

There is no obvious reason why one course of action comes easy to one company and seems to be difficult to another, equally well-managed one. It is however a fact. Opportunities therefore have to be reflected against the experience of a company and against its past successes and failures. If for any reason a company does not seem to be able to do well with a certain kind of opportunity, the odds are against success and the risk is high.

Finally one can ask: Is this the kind of opportunity that would help us to realize our idea of the business? Or would it sidetrack us?

An opportunity that runs counter to the idea of the business might yet be the right opportunity. Incongruence between the idea of the business and a major opportunity may be the first indication that a redefinition of the idea is in order. But otherwise opportunities that sidetrack the business typically carry the one risk one cannot afford to take: that of being unable to exploit success.

Risks too need to be classified. A risk is small or big according to its structure rather than according to its magnitude alone.

There are essentially four kinds of risks.

- The risk one must accept, the risk that is built into the nature of the business
- The risk one can afford to take
- The risk one cannot afford to take
- The risk one cannot afford not to take

In almost every industry there are genuine *risks that must be accepted* to stay in the business. Often they are risks that in any other business would be considered intolerable.

In developing new systemic drugs—such as a new antibiotic, tranquilizer, or vaccine—there is always the danger of bringing to the market a killer rather than a cure. The Thalidomide tragedy of 1960–1962 with its terrible legacy of malformed infants is one example. The lethal inoculations ten years earlier of the first batches of infantile paralysis vaccine is another. In neither case could the tragedy have been prevented. We know far too little about the behavior of the human body to know how to test systemic drugs for all possible effects.

To have brought out a drug of this kind is near-catastrophe for the manufacturer. It causes deep anguish and wounds his self-respect and self-confidence. For pharmaceutical manufacturers must believe in their mission to help cure or at least alleviate, if they are to be at all successful. Yet this risk has to be taken if one wants to be in today's pharmaceutical industry.

No other business, to my knowledge, would be willing to accept this risk.

Yet other risks—though usually less dramatic ones—are inherent in every business.

To lose money and effort spent in pursuit of an opportunity should always be a *risk one can afford to take*. If the money required is more than a company can lose and survive, it cannot afford the opportunity. With every new venture, one should ask: What is the worst that can happen to us if this should fail entirely? Would it destroy us? Would it cripple us and leave us permanently handicapped? Is this, in other words, a risk we can or cannot afford?

The *risk one cannot afford to take* is, therefore, in part the opposite of the risk one can afford. But there are other risks one cannot afford which are of a different nature. Here belongs, above all, the risk of being unable to exploit success.

The initial request for capital for a new venture is sufficient only if the venture fails completely. If it succeeds at all, it will inevitably require further investment. To be unable to exploit such success because capital is not available is a risk one cannot afford to take. Equally serious—and even more common—is inability to exploit a success because knowledge and market are lacking.

In starting any new venture, one therefore always asks: Could we exploit its success? Can we raise the capital to build a small success into a sizable business? Do we have the technical and marketing skills to realize the opportunity success would open up? Or will we only create an opportunity for somebody else?

The breakthrough opportunity is the *risk one cannot afford not to take.*

The classical example is the often-told story of General Electric's entry into the atomic energy field shortly after World War II. The company's scientists and engineers were apparently unanimous in rating very low the chances of making atomic energy an economical source of electric power. Nevertheless, General Electric decided that a major producer of energy sources could not take the risk of being left out should atomic power generation develop after all. It invested substantial amounts of money and allocated productive and high-quality human resources to the "long shot."

But a risk one cannot afford not to take can only be justified by very high rewards should the effort, after all, pay off.

There is no way to make sure that the right opportunities are chosen. But it is certain that the right opportunities will not be selected unless:

• The focus is on maximizing opportunities rather than on minimizing risk
• All major opportunities are scrutinized jointly, systematically, and in respect to their characteristics rather than one by one and in isolation
• The attempt is made to understand which opportunities and risks fit a particular business, and which are not appropriate
• A balance is struck between the immediate and easy opportunities for improvement and the long-range and difficult opportunities for innovation and for changing the character of the business

II

SPECIALIZATION, DIVERSIFICATION, INTEGRATION

Every business needs a core—an area where it leads. Every business must therefore specialize. But every business must also try to obtain the most from its specialization. It must diversify.

The balance between these two determines the scope of a business.

Parents Magazine Enterprises had for thirty-five years been a successful publisher of magazines and books on and for children. In the fall of 1963 it acquired F. A. O. Schwarz, the best-known American toy retail chain. This did not change its specialization at all. But it diversified the fields in which the company's specialization is utilized.

Unilever also exemplifies balance between specialization and diversification. With five hundred companies operating in more than sixty countries, Unilever is so complicated that few outsiders understand its structure. Its activities range from growing oil-bearing seeds and catching fish to selling all kinds of goods to the ultimate consumer. Yet it is at the same time a highly specialized business with a major concentration in marketing grocery products, from fish and processed foods to soaps and toiletries. Any business within Unilever, whether it is a chain of grocery stores or a fleet of fishing vessels, can be understood in terms of the highly specialized knowledge and competence of a grocery-products business.

By contrast, specialization and diversification in isolation from each other are seldom productive. The business that is only a specialty is rarely much more than the practice of an individual professional or designer. It cannot grow as a rule and is likely to die with the one man. The business that is diversified without specialization or specific excellence becomes unmanageable and eventually unmanaged.

A business needs a central resource. It needs to integrate its activities into one knowledge or one market. It needs one area in terms of which business decisions can be meaningfully made. Unless there is such a core, people in the business soon cease to speak a common language. Management itself loses its touch, does not know what is relevant and cannot make the proper decisions. On the other hand, a business needs diversification of result areas to give it the flexibility needed in a world of rapidly changing markets and technologies.

A company should either be diversified in products, market, and end-uses and highly concentrated in its basic knowledge area;

or it should be diversified in its knowledge areas and highly concentrated in its products, markets, and end-uses. Anything in between is likely to be unsatisfactory.

Cummins Engine Company exemplifies either balance—and the complete shift from one to the other. For many years the company concentrated successfully on one knowledge area: diesel engines for heavy trucks. In its customers and markets, however, it was widely diversified, selling to truck manufacturers all over the world. But recently the number of independent truck manufacturers has been going down. In a complete reversal of its traditional policy, Cummins, in the fall of 1963, merged with the largest of the remaining independent U. S. manufacturers, the White Motor Company, which also has a substantial business in other equipment using engines, such as light and medium-weight trucks, earth-moving equipment, and so on. Cummins thus shifted from concentration on one type of diesel engine to concentration on one customer, and from diversification in markets and customers to diversification in knowledge and product.

The balance between specialization and diversification largely determines the productivity of a company's resources.

Imbalance between major resources (as discussed in Chapter 10) always means a wrong relationship between specialization and diversification. In every case the solution is a change in which a business either diversifies into additional activities that feed off a common core of concentration and knowledge, or redefines the specialization needed. This was the solution for instance for the small manufacturer who, in order to utilize his large and highly trained sales force, redefined his business as distribution and shifted his center of specialization from the plant and the process to marketing and selling.

But even a perfect balance is easily upset, as the Cummins Engine story shows. It always needs to be changed when market and economy change.

The best examples are the classical entrepreneurs, the developers of businesses in an underdeveloped economy. They were the business builders in Europe, the United States, and Japan in the nineteenth century. They are the business builders today in Brazil—where the Mattarazzo family, for instance, has elaborated the most diversified entrepreneurial empire—in India, and in many other developing parts of the world. Typically, these entrepreneurs start, control, and manage a host of businesses, sugar mills, textile companies, banks, cement plants, small steel fabricating plants, and so on.

They represent in the early stages of development a high degree of specialization in the very scarce knowledge of business development and management. But when an economy grows to maturity, this knowledge ceases to be scarce. Specialized technical and marketing knowledge then become crucial. The single entrepreneur with his widespread interests at first becomes unnecessary and then a burden. He gradually turns into an investor. Eventually he disappears.

The scope of a business also has to be redefined when there is a major change in knowledge. Any change, finally, in the idea of the business and in its excellence calls for a redesign of the balance of specialization and integration.

Integration is often used as a means to diversify or to concentrate. Forward integration—that is, extension of the business scope toward the market—typically adds diversification.

The paper company that acquired a number of packaging companies to convert the threat of plastics into an opportunity used integration toward the market as a means to diversify without having to go into plastics technology. There are hundreds of similar examples.

Backward integration—that is, integration from the market to manufacturing or from manufacturing into the raw materials—is often a way to concentrate.

Every major aluminum fabricator in the world has integrated backward into making the metal despite the high investment required for an aluminum smelter. The metal itself is usually available in adequate supply, except during wartime shortages. Yet excellence in aluminum fabrication is apparently not enough foundation for a major business.

An additional reason for integration, whether forward or backward, is a disparity between the costs and rewards of certain stages of the economic process.

The paper manufacturer, for instance, who acquires a chain of paper merchants aims at higher average profitability. A paper merchant needs little capital and turns it over fast. In good years a dollar invested in paper manufacturing probably earns a good deal more than a dollar invested in a paper merchant. In poor years, however, the merchant is a better risk, if only because his break-even point is quite low.

The analysis of cost structure and cost stream for the entire economic process is therefore the starting point for decisions concerning integration. That combination of stages in the economic process which gives over the long term the most favorable ratio between costs and revenues is the best integration balance for a business. For this one pays, however, the price of increased rigidity.

Every magazine publisher who integrated backward by building his own printing plant has discovered this. Such a plant is a commitment to a printing process, a circulation figure, a frequency of appearance, a page size, and so one. As long as all these factors remain unchanged, the balance is highly advantageous. But they never stay unchanged for long. And then "our efficient printing plant" soon becomes a cost center rather than a revenue center.

Specialization, diversification and integration are strategies of high impact but also of high risk. They should be subject to two tests: the test of economic results, and the test of economic risk.

The configuration and scope chosen should make the business capable of so much greater performance as to change the characteristics of the business altogether. Two plus 2 should give a configuration that equals at least 5. And the risk incurred if anything changes in market or knowledge, products or process, should be one the business can afford to take.

III

BUILD OR BUY

The main thrust of development in a business comes from within—and therefore requires time. But up to a point money can be substituted for time: a business can buy rather than build.

And in a few cases where there is neither the time nor the knowledge to build, a business has to resort to finance: sale of a subsidiary business or product line, acquisition, merger, joint venture.

Sale is always to be considered when a business or a product line has come to have more value for somebody else. The main line of business growth may have by-passed a product, for instance.

The time clock business of IBM in the United States no longer fitted a company in which the center of concentration had shifted from simple mechanical devices to the highly complex electronic technology of the computer. IBM sold the business after World War II.

The most common example of a business that should be sold is the one that has outgrown its management. Typically, this is a business that was founded by one able man and developed by him to respectable size. Its prospects are objectively good, but somehow are not being realized. The reason is always the same: the business has outgrown the philosophy, habits, and practices of the founder or his family. Unless the people in charge can change their vision and habits, the business will soon deteriorate.

This "growth" business that suddenly slows down because its management is incapable of adjusting to growth was a main reason for the New York Stock Exchange crash in the spring of 1962. Wall Street had become intoxicated with growth and searched out companies which had been rapidly expanding. In many cases, however, these companies lacked the management to grow beyond small size. As a result they did not fulfill expectations—and stock prices collapsed.

Time is running out fast on such a business. If allowed to deteriorate for more than a short period, it will go under. The radical cure of sale is usually the only salvation for a business stunted by the incapacity of its management to grow up to the demands of success.

Acquisition or merger are similarly indicated for the business that cannot grow to the right size of its own resources—a problem discussed in Chapter 10. Such a business needs all its revenue to maintain the management imposed on it by the discrepancy between its size and the size requirement of its market or its technology. Only acquisition of another business—or by another business—can bring about the rapid expansion necessary. Or there is the alternative of merger in which two such businesses, each too small, come together and form a new business of the right size.

A joint venture, in which two companies combine as partners to found another independent but jointly-owned third company is often the best way to enter a market different from that of either parent company, or to bring two separate knowledge resources to bear on a new opportunity. Again, building would take too much time.

Joint ventures are, for instance, normally the only way in which a Western company can go into business in an alien culture, such as Japan. This requires a knowledge of the Japanese market, of Japanese traditions—and above all of the Japanese language—which would take a Western company many years to acquire. It requires also technology, product and process knowledge, and technological research which it would take the Japanese a good many years to develop. Each partner, therefore, contributes something unique. The joint venture exploits a different market from that of either partner —different in culture from its Western parent, different in technology and product line from the Japanese parent.

Acquisition is sometimes the best way to change the balance between specialization and diversification. It is often the best way to bring new competence and new knowledge into the business. Merger may be the best way to convert an imbalance of resources into a source of strength. Sale may be the quickest way to put on "milking status" an old business or an old product line.

The financial tools are, however, difficult and demanding. They cannot be used as substitutes for the development of people and organization, for innovation, or for work on the economic direction and performance of a business. These require internal efforts —and time.

Furthermore, buying time is never cheap. If one buys the time which somebody else has put into knowledge, resources, products, markets, one pays a premium price. Unless the acquisition promises to add a great deal to the business, it will not justify its cost.

Finally, buying time never succeeds unless it is followed by purposeful internal efforts.

The best example is Durant's construction of General Motors entirely through financial acquisition. With the companies he bought, Durant got an array of extraordinarily capable men. But only after Durant's ouster, when Sloan built a company, defined the idea of the business, and developed a management team, did Durant's financial creation become viable. Buying good businesses in a growth industry, each run by a first-class man, by itself had only produced near-disaster.

Every company that has put its trust in financial manipulation as a substitute for purposeful management has eventually come to grief. Using financial tools makes greater demands than development from within on a management, its competence, and its willingness to face up to the hard decisions. Because the financial tools save time and telescope years of growth and development into one legal transaction, they also telescope years of problems and decisions into a very short time. Every merger creates as many problems, especially of people and their relationship, as would have been created by developing a new and larger business from within. There has never been an acquisition which really fitted, and which did not have to be reconstructed before it began to give the expected results. And every joint venture, if successful, raises problems which force the respective parents to change their own habits and expectations.

Thus financial transactions are a tool of business policy. They are not a substitute for it.

Litton Industries, the California-based "science" company, is perhaps the outstanding postwar example of "the company that stock deals built." In ten years, from 1953 to 1963 it grew from nothing to half a billion dollars in sales—all through acquisition. Yet Charles B. Thornton the man who assembled Litton, was quoted as saying: "We had to grow big and muscular in a hurry to survive the jolt of changing technology. But we have never acquired companies as such. We have bought time, a market, a product line, a plant, a research team, a sales force." (*Time,* October 4, 1963)

Only a management that truly subordinates the financial aspect of these transactions to business policy can ever use financial tools with success. Otherwise all it does is spend money without buying anything with it, least of all time.

IV

STRUCTURE AND STRATEGY

Two recent books* have documented the relationship between organizational structure and the ability of a company to produce results and to grow. Structure, Professor Chandler demonstrates, follows strategy. Miss Penrose makes it equally clear that growth demands the right structure.

The right structure does not guarantee results. But the wrong structure aborts results and smothers even the best-directed efforts. Above all structure has to be such that it highlights the results that are truly meaningful; that is, the results that are relevant to the idea of the business, its excellence, its priorities, and its opportunities.

That it spotlights business performance and business results is, of course, one of the main benefits of decentralization (the organization structure under which individual parts of a company are set up as distinct business entities). This however requires economic understanding of the business, and indeed continuing work on the economic tasks of each decentralized business and of the company as a whole, performed for the company's top management and at the central office. There is no point in setting up as "businesses" activities which do not have a distinct product or service for a distinct market and are therefore not truly businesses. Where these two requirements are met, however, decentralization as Professor Chandler's book shows, is the structure that best serves business performance and growth.

Yet no matter how well suited to the needs of today's business, organization must be reviewed as the business changes. Is division

* Edith T. Penrose, *The Theory of the Growth of the Firm* (Oxford 1959) and Alfred D. Chandler, Jr., *Strategy and Structure* (Cambridge, Massachusetts 1962). I acknowledge here the stimulation and insights found in both works.

into different components still likely to advance the economic performance of the company as a whole? Or is it likely to make the component's results look good at the expense of the over-all company? Are the efforts in which excellence should be attained organized as distinct responsibilities or are they submerged in a general, unspecified gaggle of mediocrities?

Such structural questions always need to be asked. They are actually more important in the small than the large company— simply because the small company usually pays too little attention to structure. They are particularly pertinent in the company which has undergone a period of rapid growth. Indeed to think through its structure is the best way to prevent such a company from outgrowing its management to the point where only sale of the business can save it.

One job that always needs to be organized as a distinct activity is the economic analysis of the business, its dimensions and tasks, and the program for performance. It is distinct work. It is crucially important work. And it is a great deal of work. Someone must therefore be assigned to it and must be responsible for it. And except in the smallest business he will have a full-time job on his hands.

All I have tried to do in this chapter is to show that these big areas: opportunity and risk; scope of the business; financial strategies, or organization, should be considered and thought through by management in developing the program for performance. For the strategic decisions in these four areas will largely determine whether the means chosen by a business are adequate to its aims and ambitions.

14 Building Economic Performance into a Business

To turn an entrepreneurial program into performance requires effective management:

- The program must be converted into work for which someone is responsible.
- The program must be anchored in the practices of the business.
- The focus on economic performance must be built into the job of people and into the spirit of the organization.

THE WORK PLAN

Just as there is need for a unified, company-wide program for performance, there is need for a unified, company-wide plan for the work to be done.

The foundations of such a plan are of course the decisions on the idea of the business and its objectives; on the areas of excellence; on priorities; and on strategies. From these a work plan first derives goals and targets. What results are needed? Where? When? This then leads to an assessment of the efforts required and to the selection of the resources to be committed.

Next there are work *assignments*. Performance becomes a job for which *someone* is responsible. If it is to be a real assignment, there has to be a deadline; work without deadlines is not work assigned but work toyed with.

Special attention needs to be paid to planning knowledge work, which demands more analysis, more direction, and a more

230

sharply focused plan of action than other work. What a man should be doing at a machine is usually clear and simple. But a sales manager sitting at a desk might be doing any number of things. Or he might be doing nothing, with no one the wiser for a long time. Yet only in a few businesses is knowledge work thought through and purposefully directed.

The vague generalities with which knowledge efforts are typically defined in company manuals and budgets are symptomatic. "Advice and support to the company's marketing work in all areas" is a popular phrase; "To improve utilization of human resources on all levels" is another. But why does the marketing effort need "advice and support?" And what results are expected, and when?

In particular a clear plan, directly focused on the objectives and goals of a business, is needed for the most expensive and most demanding knowledge effort of all: research, whether in technology, in markets, on customers, or in any other areas.

Increasingly businesses need pure research; that is, research aimed at acquiring new, not yet existing knowledge. Such research particularly needs to be focused on economic results. It is more productive the more directed it is in its objectives. Whether it will produce results is, of course, unknown—and the odds are against success. But if there are results, they should be economically applicable ones. The work at DuPont that produced Nylon was pure research. But it was clearly aimed at an economic result, clearly fitted in with DuPont's idea of the business and clearly supported the DuPont objectives. The same was true of the work at Bell Laboratories which led to the transistor, or the work at General Electric out of which came the synthetic diamond. The research in polymer chemistry of the two 1963 Nobel Prize winners, Karl Ziegler of Germany and Giulio Natta of Italy, while of the purest, was from the beginning focused on economic results; that is, on creating new major industries.

It is important in knowledge work not to do things that will not lead to major results, even if done successfully. It is important in knowledge work—and again especially in research—to abandon what is no longer productive and to concentrate the scarce resources where the results are. For knowledge work is productive only when done by people of extraordinary ability. Outstanding people, however, are as scarce in knowledge work as in any other area of human endeavor.

II

BUSINESS PRACTICES

All proposals for new ventures, capital investment, or new products and services, should be directed toward the company's program for performance. All such proposals should be presented together rather than piecemeal. This applies to capital investments for a given period, to new products or new services, and to all new activities and efforts, especially knowledge efforts. Only in this way is it possible to find out whether these proposals seek the best utilization of the company's resources and whether they are focused on the right opportunities and on the needed results. Only in this way can it be seen whether the proposed investments, products, or activities aim at realizing the idea of the business and support its objectives.

Each individual proposal should clearly spell out the expectations that underlie it. What is assumed will happen? How do these assumptions compare with the expectations on which the company's program has been based? What would be the consequences of not making the new investment, not starting the new activity, not turning out the new product?

What would happen to the business should this new venture not succeed? No proposal should be seriously considered unless it presents bluntly and without concealment the worst that could conceivably happen. Equally important are the consequences of success. What are we committed to should this new venture succeed? And is it a commitment we can afford?

Every proposal for a new venture should be focused on the entire company. It is not enough to know what results are expected from the venture itself. What would it add to the total economic capacity and results of the business? Some proposals promise high returns on the capital or effort expended, yet add so little to the total economy of the business as to be inconsequential. There are also proposals which, in their own terms, barely pay their own way, and yet may add substantial capacity for results. What matters most is not the return on a specific venture but its impact on the results of the entire business.

A proposal for any new venture must spell out what resources, especially what human resources, will be needed and where they are to come from. There is no point in going into anything new unless high-quality resources can actually be made available to it.

A proposal for a major new effort should therefore always spell out what old effort will be abandoned. Resources of the necessary caliber for a new effort—especially people of the right caliber—rarely lie around idle. They have to be made available by abandoning an old effort or at the least by putting it on "milking" statue.

Another necessary business practice is a systematic review of all products (or services), all activities, all major components of the business, every three years or so. This review first holds performance against expectations. It then asks: "If this product (activity or unit) were not here today, would we start it?" If the answer is: "No," then the question should be asked: "Should we continue, and why?"

If we want the new to have a chance, we must be willing to prune the old that no longer promises results. If we want the people in an organization to be "creative," we must manage the business in such a way that jobs and careers are linked to finding the new and promising rather than to perpetuating the old and outworn, to results rather than to routine.

III

PEOPLE, THEIR JOBS AND THEIR SPIRIT

Only yesterday the economic decisions even in a very big business were made by a few men at the top. The rest carried them out. Today's reality was concisely described by Frederick R. Kappel—the head of the world's largest privately-owned and privately-managed business, the American Telephone and Telegraph Company—in a talk to the XIIIth International Management Congress, held in New York in September 1963.

Years ago, when our business was started [said Mr. Kappel] it was the vision of the top managers that established the goals of the organization. [Today by contrast] the goals of the business, the visions of the future, are not imposed by top management alone. . . . Our viewpoint is not formed by the business manager alone or by the director of research alone or by the development engineer alone. . . . The responsibility for decision rests with the head of the business but the decision itself is the product of multiple judgment. . . . To enable the knowledge workers to make their contribution, a business therefore needs: (1) a clear view both of what is needed and of what is feasible; (2) a closely reasoned determination of the best course for achieving the desired results, and (3) a dependable measure of the means already available and those that must still be discovered. . . . A business can excite the scientist . . . only if it has a clear idea of what it is aiming at, only if these aims are explicitly stated.

Even the small business today consists increasingly of people who apply knowledge, rather than manual skill and muscle, to work. Every knowledge worker makes economic decisions—whether he be a research engineer deciding to continue or drop a project, an accountant deciding what cost definitions are appropriate to the business, a sales manager deciding where to put his strongest salesmen, or a market researcher defining the market in which a product competes. To make the right decision the knowledge worker must know what performance and results are needed. In turn, the knowledge worker must be "excited," to use Mr. Kappel's word. He cannot be supervised. He must direct, manage, and motivate himself. And that he will not do unless he can see how his knowledge and work contribute to the whole business.

It is therefore essential that the job of every managerial and professional member of the organization be defined in terms of the contribution it should make to the attainment of the company's economic results. To define a job in terms of work and skill is adequate for people whose contribution is only faithful effort. For people who have to have knowledge and judgment, self-direction and the "excitement" that motivates, the emphasis has to be on contribution and results.

If a company is to obtain the needed contributions, it must reward those who make them. The spirit of a company is made, in the last analysis, by the people it chooses for senior positions. Altogether, the one and only true "control" in any organization is its decisions on people and especially its promotions. They affirm what an organization really believes in, really wants, really stands for. They speak louder than words and tell a clearer story than any figures.

To infuse the spirit of a company with a desire for economic performance requires stress in the crucial promotions on ability for the economic task. Such a promotional policy is largely the "secret" of those companies—General Motors, DuPont, Sears Roebuck are examples—whose performance has been consistently high.

The crucial promotion is not a man's first—though it may be the most important one to him and to his career. Nor is it the final promotion into a top position; there a management usually must choose from a small, already preselected group.

The crucial promotion is into the group from which tomorrow's top people will have to be selected. It is the decision at the point where the pyramid in an organization narrows abruptly. Up to this point there are in a large organization usually forty to fifty men to choose from for every vacant spot. Above it the choice narrows to one out of three or four. Up to this point also, a man usually works in one area or function. Above it he works in the business.

The military has known this for many years. Up to the rank of major, promotion is generally by seniority and depends largely on survival. But of every thirty or forty majors only one can make colonel. And yet only those that get to be colonel have an opportunity to become generals later on, while future generals are selected from a small group of colonels. In the military therefore it is at the promotion to colonel that the "Promotion Board" most carefully screens candidates.

In a business these promotions still lead, as a rule, into jobs that are functional, technical, or in one specific area—head of market research, for instance, assistant chief engineer, or assistant controller. Yet they determine the top management of tomorrow. They are, moreover, the most visible and meaningful promotions for the organization itself, and the ones its people most closely scrutinize. For the men in these positions are the only senior executives with whom most of the managerial and professional men in the organization have any close working contact.

If a business is to focus on economic performance it must, therefore, in filling these critical positions, reward men for proven capacity to contribute to the company's goals and results, for demonstrated ability at the economic tasks, and for willingness to work for the business rather than only as specialists in one function or in one technical area.

Capacity for the economic tasks and willingness to work on them is by no means the only requirement for a senior executive. In many positions it is surely not even the most important one, compared, for instance, to the ability to build and lead an effective and cohesive human organization. But for a senior executive understanding of, and sympathy for, the demands of economic performance are essential requirements.

To build business performance into the human organization is difficult. But it is essential. A company, after all, does not have a program for performance. Its executives have such a program, work it out, formulate it, make it effective. Economic results are not produced by economic forces; they are a human achievement.

Conclusion:
The Commitment

The important economic decisions today are mainly made by executives—managers employed by a company who work within and through a business organization. They are no longer made by the entrepreneur—an individual operating independently, for himself and by himself.

Organized business has become the entrepreneurial center of modern economy and society. The economic decisions it makes or foregoes largely determine the level, direction, and course of industrial economy.

The traditional entrepreneur has not disappeared. Indeed, the large and expanding industrial economy gives greater scope than any earlier age to the individual who starts a new business by himself and for himself. Since World War II a large number of "new men," starting from scratch and by themselves, have built new businesses and even whole industries—in the United States, in Western Europe, in Japan, India, Latin America. But even at his most active, this individual entrepreneur is but a small—though essential—element in the economy, compared to the already established and organized businesses. Moreover, the individual entrepreneur has to organize a business and has himself to become an executive as soon as he has any success. Otherwise his entrepreneurial achievement will evaporate in no time. Even a small business in today's economy is in size and complexity so far removed from the biggest and wealthiest individual entrepreneur as to be totally different in kind.

For every business therefore, systematic, purposeful work on economic tasks and decisions has to become a way of life. What the tasks are and how they might be organized has been the concern of this book.

But if the business enterprise is the entrepreneurial center of a modern economy, every knowledge worker in it has to act the entrepreneur. In the modern business in which knowledge is the central resource, a few people at the top cannot by themselves assure success. The more business becomes a knowledge organization the more executives there will be whose decisions have impact on the whole business and its results.

Top management does not thereby become less important nor does its job become less demanding. On the contrary, it has acquired a new and challenging dimension to its task: leading, directing, motivating the knowledge-people to become effective executives.

The man of knowledge in business—whether manager or individual professional contributor—has to impose on himself the executive's threefold commitment:

• A commitment to make his knowledge and efforts *contribute* to economic results. The knowledge worker's focus has to be on contribution rather than on the work, its skills and its techniques.

• A commitment to *concentrate*. Each knowledge worker, to be an executive, needs to take responsibility for allocating to opportunities and results the one resource truly under his control: himself.

• A commitment finally, to the *systematic, purposeful,* and *organized* discharge of the economic tasks in his own job and work as well as in the total business.

There is a great deal of stress today on the social responsibilities of the manager. The knowledge workers in business enterprise—manager and individual professional contributor—have emerged as a new leadership group in industrial society. And every leadership group has indeed responsibilities well beyond its own immediate task and scope.

But the first social responsibility of the manager today is to make understandable to the laymen—the educated people who are outside of business and necessarily ignorant of it—what it is that business does, can do and should do, and what it is the manager is doing.

A good deal of what looks like "hostility to business" is in fact nothing but the bafflement of the educated layman—the professional man, the civil servant, the academician—at an activity which apparently can neither be studied nor be explained. Mr. Nehru and his generation, for instance, became "socialists" primarily because of the contempt of their intellectual masters, the English Fabians of the early 1900's, for what they saw when they looked at the business of their day: a seemingly mindless game of chance at which any donkey could win provided only that he be ruthless. But that is, of course, how *any* human activity looks to the outsider unless it can be shown to be purposeful, organized, systematic; that is, unless it can be presented as the generalized knowledge of a discipline.

Managers have become a leadership group in the last two decades largely because they have developed such a discipline for the managerial half of their job: the planning, building, and leading of the human organization of a business. But for the other, the entrepreneurial, half—the half that deals with the specific and unique economic function of business enterprise—the systematic discipline has yet to be evolved. All over the world executives have committed themselves to management as a discipline. Now they have to commit themselves to purposeful entrepreneurship. Only when entrepreneurship is presented as a discipline and practiced as the specific task that systematically directs resources to economic performance and results, will an educated layman be able to understand what business—industrial society's economic organ—is trying to do, and to respect what it is doing. Only then can society truly accept that business is a rational pursuit and that the executive in business has an important contribution to make.

For his own sake too the knowledge worker needs the commitment to contribution, concentration, and purposeful entrepreneurship. He needs it to make meaningful and satisfying his own life and work. More and more knowledge people work in business. Indeed, modern business is the biggest source of jobs that allow men to put knowledge to productive use. The knowledge worker in whom so much expensive education has been invested should be held to high demands for effort and performance. But he also should make high demands on the job for satisfaction and stimulation.

The economic task, if done purposefully, responsibly, with knowledge and forethought, can indeed be exciting and stimulating, as this book has, I hope, conveyed. It offers intellectual challenge, the reward of accomplishment, and the unique enjoyment man derives from bringing order out of chaos.

Bibliography

There is no book so far that attempts to cover the entire field of economic decisions and tasks in business enterprise. There are in fact few books that have other than narrowly technical and functional concerns. Among those few I have found the following to be stimulating and of interest:

MAJOR ECONOMIC DECISIONS

CHANDLER, ALFRED D., JR., *Strategy and Structure*. M.I.T. Press, Cambridge, Mass. 1962.

PENROSE, EDITH T., *The Theory of the Growth of the Firm*. Oxford, 1959.

IMPORTANT TOOLS OF ECONOMIC ANALYSIS

DEAN, JOEL, *Managerial Economics*. Englewood Cliffs, N.J.: Prentice-Hall, 1951.

RAUTENSTRAUCH, WALTER and VILLERS, RAYMOND, *The Economics of Industrial Management;* 2nd ed. New York: Funk & Wagnalls, 1957.

SPENCER, MILTON and SIEGELMAN, LOUIS, *Managerial Economics; Decision Making and Forward Planning*. Homewood, Ill.: Richard D. Irwin. 1962.

FINANCIAL MANAGEMENT

GARNER, FRED V., *Profit Management & Control*. New York: McGraw-Hill Book Company, 1955.

SOLOMON, EZRA (ed.), *The Management of Corporate Capital*. Glencoe, Ill.: The Free Press, 1959.

SOLOMON, EZRA, *The Theory of Financial Management*. New York: Columbia University Press, 1963.

WESTON, J. F., *Managerial Finance*. New York: Holt, Rinehart & Winston, 1962.

PLANNING

EWING, DAVID (ed.), *Long-Range Planning for Management*, rev. ed. New York: Harper & Row, 1964.

LE BRETON, PRESTON P. and HENNING, DALE A., *Planning Theory*. Englewood Cliffs, N.J.: Prentice-Hall, 1961.

PAYNE, BRUCE, *Long-Range Planning*. New York: McGraw-Hill Book Company, 1963.

INNOVATION
AND
ENTREPRENEURSHIP

PRACTICE AND PRINCIPLES

Contents

      16. "Fustest with the Mostest"   459
      17. "Hit Them Where They Ain't"   470
      18. Ecological Niches   483
      19. Changing Values and Characteristics   493

           Conclusion: The Entrepreneurial Society   503

           Suggested Readings   517

Preface

This book presents innovation and entrepreneurship as a practice and a discipline. It does not talk of the psychology and the character traits of entrepreneurs; it talks of their actions and behavior. It uses cases, but primarily to exemplify a point, a rule, or a warning, rather than as success stories. The work thus differs, in both intention and execution, from many of the books and articles on innovation and entrepreneurship that are being published today. It shares with them the belief in the importance of innovation and entrepreneurship. Indeed, it considers the emergence of a truly entrepreneurial economy in the United States during the last ten to fifteen years the most significant and hopeful event to have occurred in recent economic and social history. But whereas much of today's discussion treats entrepreneurship as something slightly mysterious, whether gift, talent, inspiration, or "flash of genius," this book represents innovation and entrepreneurship as purposeful tasks that can be organized—are in need of being organized—and as systematic work. It treats innovation and entrepreneurship, in fact, as part of the executive's job.

This is a practical book, but it is not a "how-to" book. Instead, it deals with the what, when, and why; with such tangibles as policies and decisions; opportunities and risks; structures and strategies; staffing, compensation, and rewards.

Innovation and entrepreneurship are discussed under three main headings: The Practice of Innovation; The Practice of Entrepreneurship; and Entrepreneurial Strategies. Each of these is an "aspect" of innovation and entrepreneurship rather than a stage.

Part I on the Practice of Innovation presents innovation alike as purposeful and as a discipline. It shows first where and how the entrepreneur searches for innovative opportunities. It then discusses the

Do's and Dont's of developing an innovative idea into a viable business or service.

Part II, The Practice of Entrepreneurship, focuses on the institution that is the carrier of innovation. It deals with entrepreneurial management in three areas: the existing business; the public-service institution; and the new venture. What are the policies and practices that enable an institution, whether business or public-service, to be a successful entrepreneur? How does one organize and staff for entrepreneurship? What are the obstacles, the impediments, the traps, the common mistakes? The section concludes with a discussion of individual entrepreneurs, their roles and their decisions.

Finally, Part III, Entrepreneurial Strategies, talks of bringing an innovation successfully to market. The test of an innovation, after all, lies not its novelty, its scientific content, or its cleverness. It lies in its success in the marketplace.

These three parts are flanked by an Introduction that relates innovation and entrepreneurship to the economy, and by a Conclusion that relates them to society.

Entrepreneurship is neither a science nor an art. It is a practice. It has a knowledge base, of course, which this book attempts to present in organized fashion. But as in all practices, medicine, for instance, or engineering, knowledge in entrepreneurship is a means to an end. Indeed, what constitutes knowledge in a practice is largely defined by the ends, that is, by the practice. Hence a book like this should be backed by long years of practice.

My work on innovation and entrepreneurship began thirty years ago, in the mid-fifties. For two years, then, a small group met under my leadership at the Graduate Business School of New York University every week for a long evening's seminar on Innovation and Entrepreneurship. The group included people who were just launching their own new ventures, most of them successfully. It included mid-career executives from a wide variety of established, mostly large organizations: two big hospitals; IBM and General Electric; one or two major banks; a brokerage house; magazine and book publishers; pharmaceuticals; a worldwide charitable organization; the Catholic Archdiocese of New York and the Presbyterian Church; and so on.

The concepts and ideas developed in this seminar were tested by its members week by week during those two years in their own work and their own institutions. Since then they have been tested, validated, refined, and revised in more than twenty years of my own consulting work. Again, a wide variety of institutions has been involved. Some were businesses, including high-tech ones such as pharmaceuticals and computer companies; "no-tech" ones such as casualty insurance companies; "world-class" banks, both American and European; one-man startup ventures; regional wholesalers of building products; and Japanese multinationals. But a host of "nonbusinesses" also were included: several major labor unions; major community organizations, such as the Girl Scouts of the U.S.A. or C.A.R.E., the international relief and development cooperative; quite a few hospitals; universities and research labs; and religious organizations from a diversity of denominations.

Because this book distills years of observation, study, and practice, I was able to use actual "mini-cases," examples and illustrations both of the right and the wrong policies and practices. Wherever the name of an institution is mentioned in the text, it has either never been a client of mine (e.g., IBM) and the story is in the public domain, or the institution itself has disclosed the story. Otherwise organizations with whom I have worked remain anonymous, as has been my practice in all my management books. But the cases themselves report actual events and deal with actual enterprises.

Only in the last few years have writers on management begun to pay much attention to innovation and entrepreneurship. I have been discussing aspects of both in all my management books for decades. Yet this is the first work that attempts to present the subject in its entirety and in systematic form. This is surely a first book on a major topic rather than the last word—but I do hope it will be accepted as a seminal work.

Claremont, California
Christmas 1984

Introduction:
The Entrepreneurial Economy

I

Since the mid-seventies, such slogans as "the no-growth economy," the "deindustrialization of America," and a long-term "Kondratieff stagnation of the economy" have become popular and are invoked as if axioms. Yet the facts and figures belie every one of these slogans. What is happening in the United States is something quite different: a profound shift from a "managerial" to an "entrepreneurial" economy.

In the two decades 1965 to 1985, the number of Americans over sixteen (thereby counted as being in the work force under the conventions of American statistics) grew by two-fifths, from 129 to 180 million. But the number of Americans in paid jobs grew in the same period by one-half, from 71 to 106 million. The labor force growth was fastest in the second decade of that period, the decade from 1974 to 1984, when total jobs in the American economy grew by a full 24 million.

In no other peacetime period has the United States created as many new jobs, whether measured in percentages or in absolute numbers. And yet the ten years that began with the "oil shock" in the late fall of 1973 were years of extreme turbulence, of "energy crises," of the near-collapse of the "smokestack" industries, and of two sizable recessions.

The American development is unique. Nothing like it has happened yet in any other country. Western Europe during the period 1970 to 1984 actually *lost* jobs, 3 to 4 million of them. In 1970, western Europe still had 20 million more jobs than the United States; in 1984, it had almost 10 million less. Even Japan did far less well in job creation than the United States. During the twelve years from 1970 through 1982, jobs in Japan grew by a mere 10 percent, that is, at less than half the U.S. rate.

But America's performance in creating jobs during the seventies and early eighties also ran counter to what every expert had predicted twenty-five years ago. Then most labor force analysts expected the economy, even at its most rapid growth, to be unable to provide jobs for all the boys of the "baby boom" who were going to reach working age in the seventies and early eighties—the first large cohorts of "baby boom" babies having been born in 1949 and 1950. Actually, the American economy had to absorb twice that number. For—something nobody even dreamed of in 1970—married women began to rush into the labor force in the mid-seventies. The result is that today, in the mid-eighties, every other married woman with young children holds a paid job, whereas only one out of every five did so in 1970. And the American economy found jobs for these, too, in many cases far better jobs than women had ever held before.

And yet "everyone knows" that the seventies and early eighties were periods of "no growth," of stagnation and decline, of a "deindustrializing America," because everyone still focuses on what were the growth areas in the twenty-five years after World War II, the years that came to an end around 1970.

In those earlier years, America's economic dynamics centered in institutions that were already big and were getting bigger: the Fortune 500, that is, the country's largest businesses; governments, whether federal, state, or local; the large and super-large universities; the large consolidated high school with its six thousand or more students; and the large and growing hospital. These institutions created practically all the new jobs provided in the American economy in the quarter century after World War II. And in every recession during this period, job loss and unemployment occurred predominantly in small institutions and, of course, mainly in small businesses.

But since the late 1960s, job creation and job growth in the United States have shifted to a new sector. The old job creators have actually *lost* jobs in these last twenty years. Permanent jobs (not counting recession unemployment) in the Fortune 500 have been shrinking steadily year by year since around 1970, at first slowly, but since 1977 or 1978 at a pretty fast clip. By 1984, the Fortune 500 had lost permanently at least 4 to 6 million jobs. And governments in America, too, now employ fewer people than they did ten or fifteen years ago, if only because the number of schoolteachers has been falling as school enrollment dropped in the wake of the "baby bust" of the early sixties. Universities grew until 1980; since then, employment there has been declining. And in the early eighties, even hospital employment stopped increasing. In other words, we have not in fact created 35 million new jobs; we have created 40 million or more, since we had to offset a permanent job shrinkage of at least 5 million jobs in the traditional employing institutions. And all these new jobs must have been created by small and medium-sized institutions, most of them small and medium-sized businesses, and a great many of them, if not the majority, *new* businesses that did not even exist twenty years ago. According to *The Economist,* 600,000 new businesses are being started in the United States every year now—about seven times as many as were started in each of the boom years of the fifties and sixties.

II

"Ah," everybody will say immediately, "high tech." But things are not quite that simple. Of the 40 million-plus jobs created since 1965 in the economy, high technology did not contribute more than 5 or 6 million. High tech thus contributed no more than "smokestack" lost. All the additional jobs in the economy were generated elsewhere. And only one or two out of every hundred new businesses—a total of ten thousand a year—are remotely "high-tech," even in the loosest sense of the term.

We are indeed in the early stages of a major technological transformation, one that is far more sweeping than the most ecstatic of the "futurologists" yet realize, greater even than *Megatrends* or *Future Shock.* Three hundred years of technology came to an end after World War II. During those three centuries the model for technology was a mechanical one: the events that go on inside a star such as the sun. This period began when an otherwise almost unknown French physicist, Denis Papin, envisaged the steam engine around 1680. They ended when we replicated in the nuclear explosion the events inside a star. For these three centuries advance in technology meant—as it does in mechanical processes—more speed, higher temperatures, higher pressures. Since the end of World War II, however, the model of technology has become the biological process, the events inside an organism. And in an organism, processes are not organized around energy in the physicist's meaning of the term. They are organized around information.

There is no doubt that high tech, whether in the form of computers or telecommunication, robots on the factory floor or office automation, biogenetics or bioengineering, is of immeasurable qualitative importance. High tech provides the excitement and the headlines. It creates the vision for entrepreneurship and innovation in the community, and the receptivity for them. The willingness of young, highly trained people to go to work for small and unknown employers rather than for the giant bank or the worldwide electrical equipment maker is surely rooted in the mystique of "high tech"—even though the overwhelming majority of these young people work for employers whose technology is prosaic and mundane. High tech also probably stimulated the astonishing transformation of the American capital market from near-absence of venture capital as recently as the mid-sixties to near-surplus in the mid-eighties. High tech is thus what the logicians used to call the *ratio cognoscendi,* the reason why we perceive and understand a phenomenon rather than the explanation of its emergence and the cause of its existence.

Quantitatively, as has already been said, high tech is quite small still, accounting for not much more than one-eighth of the new jobs. Nor will it become much more important in terms of new jobs within the near future. Between now and the year 2000, no more than one-sixth of the jobs we can expect to create in the American economy will be high-tech jobs in all likelihood. In fact, if high tech were, as most people think, the entrepreneurial sector of the U.S. economy, then we would indeed face a "no-growth" period and a period of long-term stagnation in the trough of a "Kondratieff wave."

The Russian economist Nikolai Kondratieff was executed on Stalin's orders in the mid-1930s because his econometric model predicted, accurately as it turned out, that collectivization of Russian agriculture would lead to a sharp decline in farm production. The "fifty-year Kondratieff cycle" was based on the inherent dynamics of technology. Every fifty years, so Kondratieff asserted, a long technological wave crests. For the last twenty years of this cycle, the growth industries of the last technological advance seem to be doing exceptionally well. But what look like record profits are actually repayments of capital which is no longer needed in industries that have ceased to grow. This situation never lasts longer than twenty years, then there is a sudden crisis, usually signaled by some sort of panic. There follow twenty years of stagnation, during which the new, emerging technologies cannot generate enough jobs to make the economy itself grow again—and no one, least of all government, can do much about this.*

The industries that fueled the long economic expansion after World War II—automobiles, steel, rubber, electrical apparatus, consumer electronics, telephone, but also petroleum†—perfectly fit the Kondratieff cycle. Technologically, all of them go back to the fourth quarter of the nineteenth century or, at the very latest, to before World War I. In none of them has there been a significant breakthrough since the 1920s, whether in technology or in business concepts. When the economic growth began after World War II, they were all thoroughly mature industries. They could expand and create jobs with relatively little new capital investment, which explains why they could pay skyrocketing wages and workers' benefits and simultaneously show record profits. Yet, as Kondratieff had predicted, these signs of robust health were as deceptive as the flush on a consumptive's cheek. The industries were corroding from within. They did not become stagnant or decline slowly. Rather, they collapsed as soon as the "oil shocks" of 1973 and 1979 dealt them the first blows. Within a few years they went from record profits to near-bankruptcy. As soon became abundantly clear, they will not be able to return to their earlier employment levels for a long time, if ever.

The high-tech industries, too, fit Kondratieff's theory. As Kondratieff had predicted, they have so far not been able to generate more jobs than the old industries have been losing. All projections indicate that they will not do much more for long years to come, at least for the rest of the century. Despite the explosive growth of computers, for instance, data processing and information handling in all their phases (design and engineering of both hardware and software, production, sales and ser-

*Kondratieff's long-wave cycle was popularized in the West by the Austro-American economist Joseph Schumpeter, in his monumental book *Business Cycles* (1939). Kondratieff's best known, most serious, and most important disciple today—and also the most serious and most knowledgeable of the prophets of "long-term stagnation"—is the MIT scientist Jay Forrester.

†Which, contrary to common belief, was the first one to start declining. In fact, petroleum ceased to be a growth industry around 1950. Since then the incremental unit of petroleum needed for an additional unit of output, whether in manufacturing, in transportation, or in heating and air conditioning, has been falling—slowly at first but rapidly since 1973.

vice) are not expected to add as many jobs to the American economy in the late 1980s and early 1990s as the steel and automotive industries are almost certain to lose.

But the Kondratieff theory fails totally to account for the 40 million jobs which the American economy actually did create. Western Europe, to be sure, has so far been following the Kondratieff script. But not the United States, and perhaps not Japan either. Something in the United States offsets the Kondratieff "long wave of technology." Something has already happened that is incompatible with the theory of long-term stagnation.

Nor does it appear at all likely that we have simply postponed the Kondratieff cycle. For in the next twenty years the need to create new jobs in the U.S. economy will be a great deal lower than it has been in the last twenty years, so that economic growth will depend far less on job creation. The number of new entrants into the American work force will be up to one-third smaller for the rest of the century—and indeed through the year 2010—than it was in the years when the children of the "baby boom" reached adulthood, that is, 1965 until 1980 or so. Since the "baby bust" of 1960–61, the birth cohorts have been 30 percent lower than they were during the "baby boom" years. And with the labor force participation of women under fifty already equal to that of men, additions to the number of women available for paid jobs will from now on be limited to natural growth, which means that they will also be down by about 30 percent.

For the future of the traditional "smokestack" industries, the Kondratieff theory must be accepted as a serious hypothesis, if not indeed as the most plausible of the available explanations. And as far as the inability of new high-tech industries to offset the stagnation of yesterday's growth industries is concerned, Kondratieff again deserves to be taken seriously. For all their tremendous qualitative importance as vision makers and pacesetters, quantitatively the high-tech industries represent tomorrow rather than today, especially as creators of jobs. They are the makers of the future rather than the makers of the present.

But as a theory of the American economy that can explain its behavior and predict its direction, Kondratieff can be considered disproven and discredited. The 40 million new jobs created in the U.S. economy during a "Kondratieff long-term stagnation" cannot be explained in Kondratieff's terms.

I do not mean to imply that there are no economic problems or dangers. Quite the contrary. A major shift in the technological foundations of the economy such as we are experiencing in the closing quarter of the twentieth century surely presents tremendous problems, economic, social, and political. We are also in the throes of a major political crisis, the crisis of that great twentieth-century success the Welfare State, with the attendant danger of an uncontrolled and seemingly uncontrollable but highly inflationary deficit. There is surely sufficient danger in the international economy, with the world's rapidly industrializing nations, such as Brazil or Mexico, suspended between rapid economic takeoff and disastrous crash, to make possible a prolonged global depression of 1930 proportions. And then there is the frightening specter of the runaway armaments race. But at least one of the fears abroad these days, that of a Kondratieff stagnation, can be considered more a figment of the imagination than reality for the United States. There we have a new, an entrepreneurial economy.

It is still too early to say whether the entrepreneurial economy will remain primarily an American phenomenon or whether it will emerge in other industrially developed countries. In Japan, there is good reason to believe that it is emerging, albeit in its own, Japanese form. But whether the same shift to an entrepreneurial economy will occur in western Europe, no one can yet say. Demographically, western Europe lags some ten to fifteen years behind America: both the "baby boom" and the "baby bust" came later in Europe than in the United States. Equally, the shift to much longer years of schooling started in western Europe some ten years later than in the United States or in Japan; and in Great Britain it has barely started yet. If, as is quite likely, demographics has been a factor in the emergence of the entrepreneurial economy in the United States, we could well see a similar development in Europe by 1990 or 1995. But this is speculation. So far, the entrepreneurial economy is purely an American phenomenon.

III

Where did all the new jobs come from? The answer is from anywhere and nowhere; in other words, from no one single source.

The magazine *Inc.*, published in Boston, has printed each year since 1982 a list of the one hundred fastest-growing, publicly owned American companies more than five years and less than fifteen years old.

Being confined to publicly owned companies, the list is heavily biased toward high tech, which has easy access to underwriters, to stock market money, and to being traded on one of the stock exchanges or over the counter. High tech is fashionable. Other new ventures, as a rule, can go public only after long years of seasoning, and of showing profits for a good deal more than five years. Yet only one-quarter of the "*Inc.* 100" are high-tech; three-quarters remain most decidedly "low-tech," year after year.

In 1982, for instance, there were five restaurant chains, two women's wear manufacturers, and twenty health-care providers on the list, but only twenty to thirty high-tech companies. And whilst America's newspapers in 1982 ran one article after the other bemoaning the "deindustrialization of America," a full half of the *Inc.* firms were manufacturing companies; only one-third were in services. Although word had it in 1982 that the Frost Belt was dying, with the Sun Belt the only possible growth area, only one-third of the "*Inc.* 100" that year were in the Sun Belt. New York had as many of these fast-growing, young, publicly owned companies as California or Texas. And Pennsylvania, New Jersey, and Massachusetts—while supposedly dying, if not already dead—also had as many as California or Texas, and as many as New York. Snowy, Minnesota, had seven. The *Inc.* lists for 1983 and 1984 showed a very similar distribution, in respect both to industry and to geography.

In 1983, the first and second companies on another *Inc.* list— the "*Inc.* 500" list of fast-growing, young, privately held companies— were, respectively, a building contractor in the Pacific Northwest (in a year in which construction was supposedly at an all-time low) and a California manufacturer of physical exercise equipment for the home.

Any inquiry among venture capitalists yields the same pattern. Indeed, in their portfolios, high tech is usually even less prominent. The portfolio of one of the most successful venture capital investors does include several high-tech companies: a new computer software producer, a new venture in medical technology, and so on. But the most profitable investment in this portfolio, the new company that has been growing the fastest in both revenues and profitability during the three years 1981–83, is that most mundane and least high-tech of businesses, a chain of barbershops. And next to it, both in sales growth and profitability, comes a chain of dentistry offices, followed by a manufacturer of handtools and by a finance company that leases machinery to small businesses.

Among the businesses I know personally, the one that has created the most jobs during the five years 1979–84, and has also grown the fastest in revenues and profits, is a financial services firm. Within five years this firm alone has created two thousand new jobs, most of them exceedingly well paid. Though a member of the New York Stock Exchange, only about one-eighth of its business is in stocks. The rest is in annuities, tax-exempt bonds, money-market funds and mutual funds, mortgage-trust certificates, tax-shelter partnerships, and a host of similar investments for what the firm calls "the intelligent investor." Such investors are defined as the well-to-do but not rich professional, small businessman, or farmer, in small towns or in the suburbs, who makes more money than he spends and thus looks for places to put his savings, but who is also realistic enough not to expect to become rich through investment.

The most revealing source of information about the growth sectors of the U.S. economy I have been able to find is a study of the one hundred fastest-growing "mid-size" companies, that is, companies with revenues of between $25 million and $1 billion. This study was conducted during 1981–83 for the American Business Conference by two senior partners of McKinsey & Company, the consulting firm.*

These mid-sized growth companies grew at three times the rate of the Fortune 500 in sales and in profits. The Fortune 500 have been losing jobs steadily since 1970. But these mid-sized growth companies added jobs between 1970 and 1983 at three times the rate of job growth in the entire U.S. economy. Even in the depression years 1981–82 when jobs in U.S. industry declined by almost 2 percent, the hundred mid-sized growth companies increased their employment by one full percentage point. The companies span the economic spectrum. There are high-tech ones among them, to be sure. But there are also financial services companies—the New York investment and brokerage firm of Donaldson, Lufkin & Jenrette, for instance. One of the best performers in the group is a company making and selling living-room furniture; another one is making and marketing doughnuts; a third, high-quality chinaware; a fourth, writing instruments; a fifth, household paints; a

*It was published under the title "Lessons from America's Mid-sized Growth Companies," by Richard E. Cavenaugh and Donald K. Clifford, Jr., in the Autumn 1983 issue of the *McKinsey Quarterly.*

sixth has expanded from printing and publishing local newspapers into consumer marketing services; a seventh produces yarns for the textile industry; and so forth. And where "everybody knows" that growth in the American economy is exclusively in services, more than half of these "mid-sized growth" companies are in manufacturing.

To make things more confusing still, the growth sector of the U.S. economy during the last ten to fifteen years, while entirely nongovernmental, includes a fairly large and growing number of enterprises that are not normally considered businesses, though quite a few are now being organized as profit-making companies. The most visible of these are, of course, in the health-care field. The traditional American community hospital is in deep trouble these days. But there are fast-growing and flourishing hospital chains, both "profit" and (increasingly) "not-for-profit" ones. Even faster growing are the "freestanding" health facilities, such as hospices for the terminally ill, medical and diagnostic laboratories, freestanding surgery centers, freestanding maternity homes, psychiatric "walk-in" clinics, or centers for geriatric diagnosis and treatment.

The public schools are shrinking in almost every American community. But despite the decline in the total number of children of school age as a result of the "baby bust" of the 1960s, a whole new species of non-profit but private schools is flourishing. In the small California city in which I live, a neighborhood babysitting cooperative, founded around 1980 by a few mothers for their own children, had by 1984 grown into a school with two hundred students going on into the fourth grade. And a "Christian" school founded a few years ago by the local Baptists is taking over from the city of Claremont a junior high school built fifteen years ago and left standing vacant for lack of pupils for the last five years. Continuing education of all kinds, whether in the form of executive management programs for mid-career managers or refresher courses for doctors, engineers, lawyers, and physical therapists, is booming; even during the severe 1982–83 recession, such programs suffered only a short setback.

One additional area of entrepreneurship, and a very important one, is the emerging "Fourth Sector" of public-private partnerships in which government units, either states or municipalities, determine performance standards and provide the money. But then they contract out a service—fire protection, garbage collection, or bus transportation—to a private business on the basis of competitive bids, thus ensuring both better service and substantially lower costs. The city of Lincoln, Nebraska, has been a pioneer in this area since Helen Boosalis was first elected mayor in 1975—the same Lincoln, Nebraska, where a hundred years ago the Populists and William Jennings Bryan first started us on the road to municipal ownership of public services. Pioneering work in this area is also being done in Texas—in San Antonio and in Houston, for instance—and especially in Minneapolis at the Hubert Humphrey Institute of the University of Minnesota. Control Data Corporation, a leading computer manufacturer also in Minneapolis, is building public-private partnerships in education and even in the management and rehabilitation of prisoners. And if there is one action that can save the postal service in the long run—for surely there is a limit to the public's willingness to pay ever larger subsidies and ever higher rates for ever-shrinking service—it may be the contracting out of first-class service (or what's still left of it ten years hence) to the "Fourth Sector," through competitive bids.

IV

Is there anything at all that these growth enterprises have in common other than growth and defiance of the Kondratieff stagnation? Actually, they are all examples of "new technology," all new applications of knowledge to human work, which is, after all, the definition of technology. Only the "technology" is not electronics or genetics or new materials. The "new technology" is entrepreneurial management.

Once this is seen, then the astonishing job growth of the American economy during the last twenty, and especially the last ten years can be explained. It can even be reconciled with the Kondratieff theory. The United States—and to some extent also Japan—is experiencing what might be called an "atypical Kondratieff cycle."

Since Joseph Schumpeter first pointed it out in 1939, we have known that what actually happened in the United States and in Germany in the fifty years between 1873 and World War I does not fit the Kondratieff cycle. The first Kondratieff cycle, based on the railway boom, came to an end with the crash of the Vienna Stock Exchange in 1873, a crash that brought down stock exchanges worldwide and ushered in a severe depression. Great Britain and France did then enter a long period of industrial stagnation during which the new emerging technologies—steel, chemicals, electrical apparatus, telephone, and finally, automobiles—could not create enough jobs to offset the stagnation in the old industries, such as railway construction, coal mining, or textiles.

But this did not happen in the United States or in Germany, nor indeed in Austria, despite the traumatic impact of the Viennese stock market crash from which Austrian politics never quite recovered. These countries were severely jolted at first. Five years later they had pulled out of the slump and were growing again, fast. In terms of "technology," these countries were no different from stagnating Britain or France. What explains their different economic behavior was one factor, and one factor only: the entrepreneur. In Germany, for instance, the single most important economic event in the years between 1870 and 1914 was surely the creation of the Universal Bank. The first of these, the Deutsche Bank, was founded by Georg Siemens in 1870* with the specific mission of finding entrepreneurs, financing entrepreneurs, and forcing upon them organized, disciplined management. In the economic history of the United States the entrepreneurial bankers such as J. P. Morgan in New York played a similar role.

Today, something very similar seems to be happening in the United States and perhaps also to some extent in Japan.

Indeed, high tech is the one sector that is not part of this new "technology," this "entrepreneurial management." The Silicon Valley high-tech entrepreneurs still operate mainly in the nineteenth-century mold. They still believe in Benjamin Franklin's dictum: "If you invent a better mousetrap the world will beat a path to your door." It does not yet occur to them to ask what makes a mousetrap "better" or for whom?

There are, of course, plenty of exceptions, high-tech companies that know well how to manage entrepreneurship and innovation. But then there were exceptions during the nineteenth century, too. There was the German, Werner Siemens, who founded and built the company that still bears his name. There was George Westinghouse, the American, a great inventor but also a great business builder, who left behind two companies that still bear his name, one a leader in the field of transportation, the other a major force in the electrical apparatus industry.

But for the "high-tech" entrepreneur, the archetype still seems to be Thomas Edison. Edison, the nineteenth century's most successful inventor, converted invention into the discipline we now call research. His real ambition, however, was to be a business builder and to become

*On Georg Siemens and the Universal Bank, see Chapter 9.

a tycoon. Yet he so totally mismanaged the businesses he started that he had to be removed from every one of them to save it. Much, if not most high tech is still being managed, or more accurately mismanaged, Edison's way.

This explains, first, why the high-tech industries follow the traditional pattern of great excitement, rapid expansion, and then sudden shakeout and collapse, the pattern of "from rags to riches and back to rags again" in five years. Most of Silicon Valley—but most of the new biological high-tech companies as well—are still inventors rather than innovators, still speculators rather than entrepreneurs. And this, too, perhaps explains why high tech so far conforms to the Kondratieff prediction and does not generate enough jobs to make the whole economy grow again.

But the "low tech" of systematic, purposeful, managed entrepreneurship does.

V

Of all the major modern economists only Joseph Schumpeter concerned himself with the entrepreneur and his impact on the economy. Every economist knows that the entrepreneur is important and has impact. But, for economists, entrepreneurship is a "meta-economic" event, something that profoundly influences and indeed shapes the economy without itself being part of it. And so too, for economists, is technology. Economists do not, in other words, have any explanation as to why entrepreneurship emerged as it did in the late nineteenth century and as it seems to be doing again today, nor why it is limited to one country or to one culture. Indeed, the events that explain why entrepreneurship becomes effective are probably not in themselves economic events. The causes are likely to lie in changes in values, perception, and attitude, changes perhaps in demographics, in institutions (such as the creation of entrepreneurial banks in Germany and the United States around 1870), perhaps changes in education as well.

Something, surely, has happened to young Americans—and to fairly large numbers of them—to their attitudes, their values, their ambitions, in the last twenty to twenty-five years. Only it is clearly not what anyone looking at the young Americans of the late 1960s could possibly have predicted. How do we explain, for instance, that all of a sudden there are such large numbers of people willing both to work like de-

mons for long years and to choose grave risks rather than big organization security? Where are the hedonists, the status seekers, the "me-too-
ers," the conformists? Conversely, where are all the young people who,
we were told fifteen years ago, were turning their backs on material
values, on money, goods, and worldly success, and were going to restore
to America a "laid-back," if not a pastoral "greenness"? Whatever the
explanation, it does not fit in with what all the soothsayers of the last
thirty years—David Riesman in *The Lonely Crowd,* William H. Whyte
in *The Organization Man,* Charles Reich in *The Greening of America,*
or Herbert Marcuse—predicted about the younger generation. Surely
the emergence of the entrepreneurial economy is as much a cultural
and psychological as it is an economic or technological event. Yet whatever the causes, the effects are above all economic ones.

And the vehicle of this profound change in attitudes, values, and
above all in behavior is a "technology." It is called management. What
has made possible the emergence of the entrepreneurial economy in
America is new applications of management:

— to new enterprises, whether businesses or not, whereas most people until now have considered management applicable to existing
  enterprises only;
— to small enterprises, whereas most people were absolutely sure
  only a few years ago that management was for the "big boys"
  only;
— to nonbusinesses (health care, education, and so on), whereas
  most people still hear "business" when they encounter the word
  "management";
— to activities that were simply not considered to be "enterprises"
  at all, such as local restaurants;
— and above all, to systematic innovation: to the search for and the
  exploitation of new opportunities for satisfying human wants and
  human needs.

As a "useful knowledge," a *techné,* management is the same age as
the other major areas of knowledge that underlie today's high-tech
industries, whether electronics, solid-state physics, genetics, or im-
munology. Management's roots lie in the time around World War I. Its
early shoots came up in the mid-1920s. But management is a "useful
knowledge" like engineering or medicine, and as such it first had to
develop as a practice before it could become a discipline. By the late

1930s, there were a few major enterprises around—at that time mostly businesses—that practiced "management" in the United States: the DuPont Company and its half brother, General Motors, but also a large retailer, Sears, Roebuck. On the other side of the Atlantic there was Siemens in Germany, or the department store chain of Marks and Spencer in Great Britain. But management as a discipline originated during and right after World War II.*

Beginning around 1955, the entire developed world experienced a "management boom."† The social technology we call management was first presented to the general public, including managers themselves, some forty years ago. It then rapidly became a discipline rather than the hit-or-miss practice of a few isolated true believers. And in these forty years management has had as much impact as any of the "scientific breakthroughs" of the period—perhaps a good deal more. It may not be solely or even primarily responsible for the fact that society in every single developed country has become since World War II a society of organizations. It may not be solely or even primarily responsible for the fact that in every developed society today the great majority of people —and the overwhelming majority of educated people—work as employees in organizations, including of course the bosses themselves, who increasingly tend to be "professional managers," that is, hired hands, rather than owners. But surely if management had not emerged as a systematic discipline, we could not have organized what is now a social reality in every developed country: the society of organizations and the "employee society."

We still have quite a bit to learn about management, admittedly, and above all about the management of the knowledge worker. But the fundamentals are reasonably well known by now. Indeed, what was an esoteric cult only forty years ago, when most executives even in large companies did not in fact realize that they practiced management, now has become commonplace.

But by and large management until recently was seen as being

*My first two management books, *Concept of the Corporation* (1946; a study of General Motors), and *The Practice of Management* (1954) were indeed the original attempts to organize and present management as a systematic body of knowledge, that is, as a discipline.

†This by now has even reached Communist China. One of the first actions of the Chinese government after the fall of the "Gang of Four" was to establish an Enterprise Management Agency directly responsible to the prime minister, and to import a Graduate Business School from the United States.

confined to business, and within business, to "big business." In the early seventies, when the American Management Association invited the heads of small business to its "Presidents' Course" in Management, it was told again and again: "Management? That's not for me—that's only for big companies." Up to 1970 or 1975, American hospital administrators still rejected anything that was labeled "management." "We're hospital people, not business people," they said. (In the universities the faculties are still saying the same thing even though they will simultaneously complain how "badly managed" their institution is.) And indeed for a long time, from the end of World War II until 1970, "progress" meant building bigger institutions.

This twenty-five-year trend toward building bigger organizations in every social sphere—business, labor union, hospital, school, university, and so on—had many causes. But the belief that we knew how to manage bigness and did not really know how to manage small enterprises was surely a major factor. It had, for instance, a great deal to do with the rush toward the very large consolidated American high school. "Education," it was argued, "requires professional administration, and this in turn works only in large rather than small enterprises."

During the last ten or fifteen years we have reversed this trend. In fact, we might now have a trend toward "deinstitutionalizing" America rather than one toward "deindustrializing" it. For almost fifty years, ever since the 1930s, it was widely believed in the United States and in western Europe too that the hospital was the best place for anyone not quite well, let alone for anyone seriously sick. "The sooner the patient gets to the hospital, the better care we can take of him," was the prevailing belief, shared by doctors and patients alike. In the last few years, we have been reversing this trend. We now increasingly believe that the longer we can keep patients away from the hospital and the sooner we can get them out, the better. Surely this reversal has little to do with either health care or with management. It is a reaction—whether permanent or short-lived—against the worship of centralization, of "planning," of government which began in the 1920s and 1930s, and which in the United States reached its peak in the Kennedy and Johnson administrations of the 1960s. However, we could not indulge in this "deinstitutionalization" in the health-care field if we had not acquired the competence and the confidence to manage small institutions and "non-businesses," that is, health-care institutions.

All told we are learning that management may well both be more needed and have greater impact on the small entrepreneurial organization than it has in the big "managed" one. Above all, management, we are learning now, has as much to contribute to the new, the entrepreneurial enterprise, as to the existing, ongoing "managerial" one.

To take a specific example, hamburger stands have been around in the United States since the nineteenth century; after World War II they sprang up on big-city street corners. But in the McDonald's hamburger chain—one of the success stories of the last twenty-five years—management was being applied to what had always been a hit-and-miss, mom-and-pop operation. McDonald's first designed the end product; then it redesigned the entire process of making it; then it redesigned or in many cases invented the tools so that every piece of meat, every slice of onion, every bun, every piece of fried potato would be identical, turned out in a precisely timed and fully automated process. Finally, McDonald's studied what "value" meant to the customer, defined it as quality and predictability of product, speed of service, absolute cleanliness, and friendliness, then set standards for all of these, trained for them, and geared compensation to them.

All of which is management, and fairly advanced management at that.

Management is the new technology (rather than any specific new science or invention) that is making the American economy into an entrepreneurial economy. It is also about to make America into an entrepreneurial *society.* Indeed, there may be greater scope in the United States—and in developed societies generally—for social innovation in education, health care, government, and politics than there is in business and the economy. And again, entrepreneurship in society— and it is badly needed—requires above all application of the basic concepts, the basic *techné,* of management to new problems and new opportunities.

This means that the time has now come to do for entrepreneurship and innovation what we first did for management in general some thirty years ago: to develop the principles, the practice, and the discipline.

I

THE PRACTICE
OF INNOVATION

———

Innovation is the specific tool of entrepreneurs, the means by which they exploit change as an opportunity for a different business or a different service. It is capable of being presented as a discipline, capable of being learned, capable of being practiced. Entrepreneurs need to search purposefully for the sources of innovation, the changes and their symptoms that indicate opportunities for successful innovation. And they need to know and to apply the principles of successful innovation.

1

Systematic Entrepreneurship

I

"The entrepreneur," said the French economist J. B. Say around 1800, "shifts economic resources out of an area of lower and into an area of higher productivity and greater yield." But Say's definition does not tell us who this "entrepreneur" is. And since Say coined the term almost two hundred years ago, there has been total confusion over the definitions of "entrepreneur" and "entrepreneurship."

In the United States, for instance, the entrepreneur is often defined as one who starts *his own, new* and *small business.* Indeed, the courses in "Entrepreneurship" that have become popular of late in American business schools are the linear descendants of the course in starting one's own small business that was offered thirty years ago, and in many cases, not very different.

But not every new small business is entrepreneurial or represents entrepreneurship.

The husband and wife who open another delicatessen store or another Mexican restaurant in the American suburb surely take a risk. But are they entrepreneurs? All they do is what has been done many times before. They gamble on the increasing popularity of eating out in their area, but create neither a new satisfaction nor new consumer demand. Seen under this perspective they are surely not entrepreneurs even though theirs is a new venture.

McDonald's, however, was entrepreneurship. It did not invent anything, to be sure. Its final product was what any decent American restaurant had produced years ago. But by applying management concepts and management techniques (asking, What is "value" to the customer?), standardizing the "product," designing process and tools, and by basing training on the analysis of the work to be done and then setting the standards it required, McDonald's both drastically upgraded the yield from resources, and created a new market and a new customer. This is entrepreneurship.

Equally entrepreneurial is the growing foundry started by a husband and wife team a few years ago in America's Midwest, to heat-treat ferrous castings to high-performance specifications—for example, the axles for the huge bulldozers used to clear the land and dig the ditches for a natural gas pipeline across Alaska. The science needed is well known; indeed, the company does little that has not been done before. But in the first place the founders systematized the technical information: they can now punch the performance specifications into their computer and get an immediate printout of the treatment required. Secondly, the founders systematized the process. Few orders run to more than half a dozen pieces of the same dimension, the same metallic composition, the same weight, and the same performance specifications. Yet the castings are being produced in what is, in effect, a flow process rather than in batches, with computer-controlled machines and ovens adjusting themselves.

Precision castings of this kind used to have a rejection rate of 30 to 40 percent; in this new foundry, 90 percent or more are flawless when they come off the line. And the costs are less than two-thirds of those of the cheapest competitor (a Korean shipyard), even though the Midwestern foundry pays full American union wages and benefits. What is "entrepreneurial" in this business is not that it is new and still small (though growing rapidly). It is the realization that castings of this kind are distinct and separate; that demand for them has grown so big as to create a "market niche"; and that technology, especially computer technology, now makes possible the conversion of an art into a scientific process.

Admittedly, all new small businesses have many factors in common. But to be entrepreneurial, an enterprise has to have special characteristics over and above being new and small. Indeed, entrepreneurs are a minority among new businesses. They create something new, something different; they change or transmute values.

An enterprise also does not need to be small and new to be an entrepreneur. Indeed, entrepreneurship is being practiced by large and often old enterprises. The General Electric Company (G.E.), one of the world's biggest businesses and more than a hundred years old, has a long history of starting new entrepreneurial businesses from scratch and raising them into sizable industries. And G.E. has not confined itself to entrepreneurship in manufacturing. Its financing arm, G.E. Credit Corporation, in large measure triggered the upheaval that is transforming the American financial system and is now spreading rapidly to Great Britain and western Europe as well. G.E. Credit in the sixties ran around the Maginot Line of the financial world when it discovered that commercial paper could be used to finance industry. This broke the banks' traditional monopoly on commercial loans.

Marks and Spencer, the very large British retailer, has probably been more entrepreneurial and innovative than any other company in western Europe these last fifty years, and may have had greater impact on the British economy and even on British society, than any other change agent in Britain, and arguably more than government or laws.

Again, G.E. and Marks and Spencer have many things in common with large and established businesses that are totally unentrepreneurial. What makes them "entrepreneurial" are specific characteristics other than size or growth.

Finally, entrepreneurship is by no means confined solely to economic institutions.

No better text for a *History of Entrepreneurship* could be found than the creation and development of the modern university, and especially the modern American university. The modern university as we know it started out as the invention of a German diplomat and civil servant, Wilhelm von Humboldt, who in 1809 conceived and founded the University of Berlin with two clear objectives: to take intellectual and scientific leadership away from the French and give it to the Germans; and to capture the energies released by the French Revolution and turn them against the French themselves, especially Napoleon. Sixty years later, around 1870, when the German university itself had peaked, Humboldt's idea of the university as a change agent was picked up across the Atlantic, in the United States. There, by the end of the Civil War, the old "colleges" of the colonial period were dying of senility. In 1870, the United States had no more than half the college students it had had in 1830, even though the population had nearly tripled. But in the next thirty years a galaxy of American university presidents* created and built a new "American university"—both distinctly new

---

*See the section on The American University in my book *Management: Tasks, Responsibilities, Practices* (New York: Harper & Row, 1973), pages 150–152.

and distinctly American—which then, after World War I, soon gained for the United States worldwide leadership in scholarship and research, just as Humboldt's university had gained worldwide leadership in scholarship and research for Germany a century earlier.

After World War II a new generation of American academic entrepreneurs innovated once again, building new "private" and "metropolitan" universities: Pace University, Fairleigh-Dickinson, and the New York Institute of Technology in the New York area; Northeastern in Boston; Santa Clara and Golden Gate on the West Coast; and so on. They have constituted a major growth sector in American higher education in the last thirty years. Most of these new schools seem to differ little from the older institutions in their curriculum. But they were deliberately designed for a new and different "market"—for people in mid-career rather than for youngsters fresh out of high school; for big-city students commuting to the university at all hours of the day and night rather than for students living on campus and going to school full time, five days a week from nine to five; and for students of widely diversified, indeed, heterogenous backgrounds rather than for the "college kid" of the American tradition. They were a response to a major shift in the market, a shift in the status of the college degree from "upper-class" to "middle-class," and to a major shift in what "going to college" means. They represent entrepreneurship.

One could equally write a casebook on entrepreneurship based on the history of the hospital, from the first appearance of the modern hospital in the late eighteenth century in Edinburgh and Vienna, to the creation of the various forms of the "community hospital" in nineteenth-century America, to the great specialized centers of the early twentieth century, the Mayo Clinic or the Menninger Foundation, to the emergence of the hospital as health-care center in the post–World War II period. And now new entrepreneurs are busily changing the hospital again into specialized "treatment centers": ambulatory surgical clinics, freestanding maternity centers or psychiatric centers where the emphasis is not, as in the traditional hospital, on caring for the patient but on specialized "needs."

Again, not every nonbusiness service institution is entrepreneurial; far from it. And the minority that is still has all the characteristics, all the problems, all the identifying marks of the service institution.* What

*On this, see the section Performance in the Service Institution (Chapters 11–14) in

makes these service institutions entrepreneurial is something different, something specific.

Whereas English speakers identify entrepreneurship with the new, small business, the Germans identify it with power and property, which is even more misleading. The *Unternehmer*—the literal translation into German of Say's *entrepreneur*—is the person who both owns and runs a business (the English term would be "owner-manager"). And the word is used primarily to distinguish the "boss," who also owns the business, from the "professional manager" and from "hired hands" altogether.

But the first attempts to create systematic entrepreneurship—the entrepreneurial bank founded in France in 1857 by the Brothers Pereire in their Crédit Mobilier, then perfected in 1870 across the Rhine by Georg Siemens in his Deutsche Bank, and brought across the Atlantic to New York at about the same time by the young J. P. Morgan— did not aim at ownership. The task of the banker as entrepreneur was to mobilize *other people's money* for allocation to areas of higher productivity and greater yield. The earlier bankers, the Rothschilds, for example, became owners. Whenever they built a railroad, they financed it with their own money. The entrepreneurial banker, by contrast, never wanted to be an owner. He made his money by selling to the general public the shares of the enterprises he had financed in their infancy. And he got the money for his ventures by borrowing from the general public.

Nor are entrepreneurs capitalists, although of course they need capital as do all economic (and most noneconomic) activities. They are not investors, either. They take risks, of course, but so does anyone engaged in any kind of economic activity. The essence of economic activity is the commitment of present resources to future expectations, and that means to uncertainty and risk. The entrepreneur is also not an employer, but can be, and often is, an employee—or someone who works alone and entirely by himself or herself.

Entrepreneurship is thus a distinct feature whether of an individual or of an institution. It is not a personality trait; in thirty years I have seen people of the most diverse personalities and temperaments perform

---

Management: Tasks, Responsibilities, Practices, but also Chapter 14 of this book, Entrepreneurship in the Service Institution.

well in entrepreneurial challenges. To be sure, people who need certainty are unlikely to make good entrepreneurs. But such people are
unlikely to do well in a host of other activities as well—in politics, for
instance, or in command positions in a military service, or as the captain
of an ocean liner. In all such pursuits decisions have to be made, and
the essence of any decision is uncertainty.

But everyone who can face up to decision making can learn to be
an entrepreneur and to behave entrepreneurially. Entrepreneurship,
then, is behavior rather than personality trait. And its foundation lies
in concept and theory rather than in intuition.

II

Every practice rests on theory, even if the practitioners themselves are
unaware of it. Entrepreneurship rests on a theory of economy and
society..The theory sees change as normal and indeed as healthy. And
it sees the major task in society—and especially in the economy—as
doing something different rather than doing better what is already
being done. This is basically what Say, two hundred years ago, meant
when he coined the term *entrepreneur*. It was intended as a manifesto
and as a declaration of dissent: the entrepreneur upsets and disorgan-
izes. As Joseph Schumpeter formulated it, his task is "creative destruction."

Say was an admirer of Adam Smith. He translated Smith's *Wealth
of Nations* (1776) into French and tirelessly propagated throughout
his life Smith's ideas and policies. But his own contribution to economic thought, the concept of the entrepreneur and of entrepreneurship, is independent of classical economics and indeed incompatible
with it. Classical economics optimizes what already exists, as does
mainstream economic theory to this day, including the Keynesians,
the Friedmanites, and the Supply-siders. It focuses on getting the
most out of existing resources and aims at establishing equilibrium. It
cannot handle the entrepreneur but consigns him to the shadowy
realm of "external forces," together with climate and weather, government and politics, pestilence and war, but also technology. The
traditional economist, regardless of school or "ism," does not deny, of
course, that these external forces exist or that they matter. But they
are not part of his world, not accounted for in his model, his equa-
tions, or his predictions. And while Karl Marx had the keenest appre-

ciation of technology—he was the first and is still one of the best historians of technology—he could not admit the entrepreneur and entrepreneurship into either his system or his economics. *All* economic change in Marx beyond the optimization of present resources, that is, the establishment of equilibrium, is the result of changes in property and power relationships, and hence "politics," which places it outside the economic system itself.

Joseph Schumpeter was the first major economist to go back to Say. In his classic *Die Theorie der Wirtschaftlichen Entwicklung (The Theory of Economic Dynamics)*, published in 1911, Schumpeter broke with traditional economics—far more radically than John Maynard Keynes was to do twenty years later. He postulated that dynamic disequilibrium brought on by the innovating entrepreneur, rather than equilibrium and optimization, is the "norm" of a healthy economy and the central reality for economic theory and economic practice.

Say was primarily concerned with the economic sphere. But his definition only calls for the resources to be "economic." The purpose to which these resources are dedicated need not be what is traditionally thought of as economic. Education is not normally considered "economic"; and certainly economic criteria are hardly appropriate to determine the "yield" of education (though no one knows what other criteria might pertain). But the resources of education are, of course, economic. They are in fact identical with those used for the most unambiguously economic purpose such as making soap for sale. Indeed, the resources for all *social* activities of human beings are the same and are "economic" resources: capital (that is, the resources withheld from current consumption and allocated instead to future expectations), physical resources, whether land, seed corn, copper, the classroom, or the hospital bed; labor, management, and time. Hence entrepreneurship is by no means limited to the economic sphere although the term originated there. It pertains to all activities of human beings other than those one might term "existential" rather than "social." And we now know that there is little difference between entrepreneurship whatever the sphere. The entrepreneur in education and the entrepreneur in health care—both have been fertile fields—do very much the same things, use very much the same tools, and encounter very much the same problems as the entrepreneur in a business or a labor union.

Entrepreneurs see change as the norm and as healthy. Usually, they do not bring about the change themselves. But—and this defines entrepreneur and entrepreneurship—*the entrepreneur always searches for change, responds to it, and exploits it as an opportunity.*

III

Entrepreneurship, it is commonly believed, is enormously risky. And, indeed, in such highly visible areas of innovation as high tech—microcomputers, for instance, or biogenetics—the casualty rate is high and the chances of success or even of survival seem to be quite low.

But why should this be so? Entrepreneurs, by definition, shift resources from areas of low productivity and yield to areas of higher productivity and yield. Of course, there is a risk they may not succeed. But if they are even moderately successful, the returns should be more than adequate to offset whatever risk there might be. One should thus expect entrepreneurship to be considerably less risky than optimization. Indeed, nothing could be as risky as optimizing resources in areas where the proper and profitable course is innovation, that is, where the opportunities for innovation already exist. Theoretically, entrepreneurship should be the least risky rather than the most risky course.

In fact, there are plenty of entrepreneurial organizations around whose batting average is so high as to give the lie to the all but universal belief in the high risk of entrepreneurship and innovation.

In the United States, for instance, there is Bell Lab, the innovative arm of the Bell Telephone System. For more than seventy years—from the design of the first automatic switchboard around 1911 until the design of the optical fiber cable around 1980, including the invention of transistor and semiconductor, but also basic theoretical and engineering work on the computer—Bell Lab produced one winner after another. The Bell Lab record would indicate that even in the high-tech field, entrepreneurship and innovation can be low-risk.

IBM, in a fast-moving high-tech field, that of the computer, and in competition with the "old pros" in electricity and electronics, has so far not had one major failure. Nor, in a far more prosaic industry, has the most entrepreneurial of the world's major retailers, the British department store chain Marks and Spencer. The world's largest producer of branded and packaged consumer goods, Procter & Gamble, similarly has had a near-perfect record of successful innovations. And a "middle-tech" company, 3M in St. Paul, Minnesota, which has created around one hundred new businesses or new major product lines in the last sixty years, has been successful four out of every five times in its ventures. This is only a small sample of the entrepreneurs who somehow innovate at low risk. Surely there are far too many of them for low-risk entrepreneurship to be a fluke, a special dispensation of the gods, an accident, or mere chance.

There are also enough individual entrepreneurs around whose batting average in starting new ventures is so high as to disprove the popular belief of the high risk of entrepreneurship.

Entrepreneurship is "risky" mainly because so few of the so-called entrepreneurs know what they are doing. They lack the methodology. They violate elementary and well-known rules. This is particularly true of high-tech entrepreneurs. To be sure (as will be discussed in Chapter 9), high-tech entrepreneurship and innovation are intrinsically more difficult and more risky than innovation based on economics and market structure, on demographics, or even on something as seemingly nebulous and intangible as *Weltanschauung*—perceptions and moods. But even high-tech entrepreneurship need not be "high-risk," as Bell Lab and IBM prove. It does need, however, to be systematic. It needs to be managed. Above all, it needs to be based on *purposeful innovation.*

2

Purposeful Innovation and the Seven Sources for Innovative Opportunity

Entrepreneurs innovate. Innovation is the specific instrument of entrepreneurship. It is the act that endows resources with a new capacity to create wealth. Innovation, indeed, creates a resource. There is no such thing as a "resource" until man finds a use for something in nature and thus endows it with economic value. Until then, every plant is a weed and every mineral just another rock. Not much more than a century ago, neither mineral oil seeping out of the ground nor bauxite, the ore of aluminum, were resources. They were nuisances; both render the soil infertile. The penicillin mold was a pest, not a resource. Bacteriologists went to great lengths to protect their bacterial cultures against contamination by it. Then in the 1920s, a London doctor, Alexander Fleming, realized that this "pest" was exactly the bacterial killer bacteriologists had been looking for—and the penicillin mold became a valuable resource.

The same holds just as true in the social and economic spheres. There is no greater resource in an economy than "purchasing power." But purchasing power is the creation of the innovating entrepreneur.

The American farmer had virtually no purchasing power in the early nineteenth century; he therefore could not buy farm machinery. There were dozens of harvesting machines on the market, but however much he might have wanted them, the farmer could not pay for them. Then one of the many harvesting-machine inventors, Cyrus McCormick, invented installment buying. This enabled the farmer to pay for a harvesting machine out of his future earnings rather than out of past savings—and suddenly the farmer had "purchasing power" to buy farm equipment.

Equally, whatever changes the wealth-producing potential of already existing resources constitutes innovation.

There was not much new technology involved in the idea of moving a truck body off its wheels and onto a cargo vessel. This "innovation," the container, did not grow out of technology at all but out of a new perception of the "cargo vessel" as a materials-handling device rather than a "ship," which meant that what really mattered was to make the time in port as short as possible. But this humdrum innovation roughly quadrupled the productivity of the ocean-going freighter and probably saved shipping. Without it, the tremendous expansion of world trade in the last forty years—the fastest growth in any major economic activity ever recorded—could not possibly have taken place.

What really made universal schooling possible—more so than the popular commitment to the value of education, the systematic training of teachers in schools of education, or pedagogic theory—was that lowly innovation, the textbook. (The textbook was probably the invention of the great Czech educational reformer Johann Amos Comenius, who designed and used the first Latin primers in the mid-seventeenth century.) Without the textbook, even a very good teacher cannot teach more than one or two children at a time; with it, even a pretty poor teacher can get a little learning into the heads of thirty or thirty-five students.

Innovation, as these examples show, does not have to be technical, does not indeed have to be a "thing" altogether. Few technical innovations can compete in terms of impact with such social innovations as the newspaper or insurance. Installment buying literally transforms economies. Wherever introduced, it changes the economy from supply-driven to demand-driven, regardless almost of the productive level of the economy (which explains why installment buying is the first practice that any Marxist government coming to power immediately suppresses: as the Communists did in Czechoslovakia in 1948, and again in Cuba in 1959). The hospital, in its modern form a social innovation of the Enlightenment of the eighteenth century, has had greater impact on health care than many advances in medicine. Management, that is, the "useful knowledge" that enables man for the first time to render productive people of different skills and knowledge working together in an "organization," is an innovation of this century. It has converted modern society into something brand new, something, by the way, for which we have neither political nor social theory: a society of organizations.

Books on economic history mention August Borsig as the first man to build steam locomotives in Germany. But surely far more important was his innovation—against strenuous opposition from craft guilds, teachers, and government bureaucrats—of what to this day is the German system of factory organization and the foundation of Germany's industrial strength. It was Borsig who devised the idea of the *Meister* (Master), the highly skilled and highly respected senior worker who runs the shop with considerable autonomy; and the *Lehrling System* (apprenticeship system), which combines practical training *(Lehre)* on the job with schooling *(Ausbildung)* in the classroom. And the twin inventions of modern government by Machiavelli in *The Prince* (1513) and of the modern national state by his early follower, Jean Bodin, sixty years later, have surely had more lasting impacts than most technologies.

One of the most interesting examples of social innovation and its importance can be seen in modern Japan.

From the time she opened her doors to the modern world in 1867, Japan has been consistently underrated by westerners, despite her successful defeats of China and then Russia in 1894 and 1905, respectively; despite Pearl Harbor; and despite her sudden emergence as an economic superpower and the toughest competitor in the world market of the 1970s and 1980s. A major reason, perhaps the major one, is the prevailing belief that innovation has to do with things and is based on science or technology. And the Japanese, so the common belief has held (in Japan as well as in the West, by the way), are not innovators but imitators. For the Japanese have not, by and large, produced outstanding technical or scientific innovations. Their success is based on social innovation.

When the Japanese, in the Meiji Restoration of 1867, most reluctantly opened their country to the world, it was to avoid the fates of India and nineteenth-century China, both of which were conquered, colonized, and "westernized" by the West. The basic aim, in true Judo fashion, was to use the weapons of the West to hold the West at bay; and to remain Japanese.

This meant that social innovation was far more critical than steam locomotives or the telegraph. And social innovation, in terms of the development of such institutions as schools and universities, a civil service, banks and labor relations, was far more difficult to achieve than building locomotives and telegraphs. A locomotive that will pull a train from London to Liverpool will equally, without adaptation or change, pull a train from Tokyo to Osaka. But the social institutions had to be at once quintessentially "Japanese" and yet "modern." They had to be run by Japanese and yet serve an economy that was "Western" and highly technical. Technology can be imported at low cost and with a minimum of cultural risk. Institutions, by contrast, need cultural roots to grow and to prosper. The Japanese made a deliberate decision a hundred years ago to concentrate their resources on social innovations, and to imitate, import, and adapt technical innovations—with startling success. Indeed, this policy may still be the right one for them. For, as will be discussed in Chapter 17, what is sometimes half-facetiously called creative imitation is a perfectly respectable and often very successful entrepreneurial strategy.

Even if the Japanese now have to move beyond imitating, importing, and adapting other people's technology and learn to undertake genuine technical innovation of their own, it might be prudent not to underrate them. Scientific research is in itself a fairly recent "social innovation." And the Japanese, whenever they have had to do so in the past, have always shown tremendous capacity for such innovation. Above all, they have shown a superior grasp of entrepreneurial strategies.

"Innovation," then, is an economic or social rather than a technical term. It can be defined the way J. B. Say defined entrepreneurship, as changing the yield of resources. Or, as a modern economist would tend to do, it can be defined in demand terms rather than in supply terms, that is, as changing the value and satisfaction obtained from resources by the consumer.

Which of the two is more applicable depends, I would argue, on the specific case rather than on the theoretical model. The shift from the integrated steel mill to the "mini-mill," which starts with steel scrap rather than iron ore and ends with one final product (e.g., beams and rods, rather than raw steel that then has to be fabricated), is best described and analyzed in supply terms. The end product, the end uses, and the customers are the same, though the costs are substantially lower. And the same supply definition probably fits the container. But the audiocassette or the videocassette, though equally "technical," if not more so, are better described or analyzed in terms of consumer values and consumer satisfactions, as are such social innovations as the news magazines developed by Henry Luce of Time–Life–Fortune in the 1920s, or the money-market fund of the late 1970s and early 1980s.

We cannot yet develop a theory of innovation. But we already know enough to say when, where, and how one looks systematically for innovative opportunities, and how one judges the chances for their success or the risks of their failure. We know enough to develop, though still only in outline form, the practice of innovation.

It has become almost a cliché for historians of technology that one of the great achievements of the nineteenth century was the "invention of invention." Before 1880 or so, invention was mysterious; early nineteenth-century books talk incessantly of the "flash of genius." The inventor himself was a half-romantic, half-ridiculous figure, tinkering away in a lonely garret. By 1914, the time World War I broke out, "invention" had become "research," a systematic, purposeful activity, which is planned and organized with high predictability both of the results aimed at and likely to be achieved.

Something similar now has to be done with respect to innovation. Entrepreneurs will have to learn to *practice systematic innovation.*

Successful entrepreneurs do not wait until "the Muse kisses them" and gives them a "bright idea"; they go to work. Altogether, they do not look for the "biggie," the innovation that will "revolutionize the industry," create a "billion-dollar business," or "make one rich overnight." Those entrepreneurs who start out with the idea that they'll make it big—and in a hurry—can be guaranteed failure. They are almost bound to do the wrong things. An innovation that looks very big may turn out to be nothing but technical virtuosity; and innovations with modest intellectual pretensions, a McDonald's, for instance, may turn into gigantic, highly profitable businesses. The same applies to nonbusiness, public-service innovations.

Successful entrepreneurs, whatever their individual motivation—be it money, power, curiosity, or the desire for fame and recognition—try to create value and to make a contribution. Still, successful entrepreneurs aim high. They are not content simply to improve on what already exists, or to modify it. They try to create new and different values and new and different satisfactions, to convert a "material" into a "resource," or to combine existing resources in a new and more productive configuration.

And it is change that always provides the opportunity for the new and different. *Systematic innovation therefore consists in the purposeful and organized search for changes, and in the systematic analysis of the opportunities such changes might offer for economic or social innovation.*

As a rule, these are changes that have already occurred or are under way. The overwhelming majority of successful innovations *exploit* change. To be sure, there are innovations that in themselves constitute a major change; some of the major technical innovations, such as the Wright Brothers' airplane, are examples. But these are exceptions, and fairly uncommon ones. Most successful innovations are far more prosaic; they exploit change. And thus the discipline of innovation (and it is the knowledge base of entrepreneurship) is a diagnostic discipline: a systematic examination of the areas of change that typically offer entrepreneurial opportunities.

Specifically, systematic innovation means monitoring *seven sources* for innovative opportunity.

The first four sources lie within the enterprise, whether business or public-service institution, or within an industry or service sector. They are therefore visible primarily to people within that industry or service sector. They are basically symptoms. But they are highly reliable indicators of changes that have already happened or can be made to happen with little effort. These four source areas are:

- *The unexpected*—the unexpected success, the unexpected failure, the unexpected outside event;
- *The incongruity*—between reality as it actually is and reality as it is assumed to be or as it "ought to be";
- *Innovation based on process need;*
- *Changes in industry structure or market structure* that catch everyone unawares.

The second set of sources for innovative opportunity, a set of three, involves changes outside the enterprise or industry:

- *Demographics* (population changes);
- *Changes in perception, mood, and meaning;*
- *New knowledge,* both scientific and nonscientific.

The lines between these seven source areas of innovative opportunities are blurred, and there is considerable overlap between them. They can be likened to seven windows, each on a different side of the same building. Each window shows some features that can also be seen from the window on either side of it. But the view from the center of each is distinct and different.

The seven sources require separate analysis, for each has its own distinct characteristic. No area is, however, inherently more important or more productive than the other. Major innovations are as likely to come out of an analysis of symptoms of change (such as the unexpected success of what was considered an insignificant change in product or pricing) as they are to come out of the massive application of new knowledge resulting from a great scientific breakthrough.

But the order in which these sources will be discussed is not arbitrary. They are listed in descending order of reliability and predictability. For, contrary to almost universal belief, new knowledge—and especially new scientific knowledge—is not the most reliable or most predictable source of successful innovations. For all the visibility, glamour, and importance of science-based innovation, it is actually the least reliable and least predictable one. Conversely, the mundane and unglamorous analysis of such symptoms of underlying changes as the unexpected success or the unexpected failure carry fairly low risk and uncertainty. And the innovations arising therefrom have, typically, the shortest lead time between the start of a venture and its measurable results, whether success or failure.

3

Source: The Unexpected

THE UNEXPECTED SUCCESS

No other area offers richer opportunities for successful innovation than the unexpected success. In no other area are innovative opportunities less risky and their pursuit less arduous. Yet the unexpected success is almost totally neglected; worse, managements tend actively to reject it.

Here is one example.

More than thirty years ago, I was told by the chairman of New York's largest department store, R. H. Macy, "We don't know how to stop the growth of appliance sales."

"Why do you want to stop them?" I asked, quite mystified. "Are you losing money on them?"

"On the contrary," the chairman said, "profit margins are better than on fashion goods; there are no returns, and practically no pilferage."

"Do the appliance customers keep away the fashion customers?" I asked.

"Oh, no," was the answer. "Where we used to sell appliances primarily to people who came in to buy fashions, we now sell fashions very often to people who come in to buy appliances. But," the chairman continued, "in this kind of store, it is normal and healthy for fashion to produce seventy percent of sales. Appliance sales have grown so fast that they now account for three-fifths. And that's abnormal. We've tried everything we know to make fashion grow to restore the normal ratio, but nothing works. The only thing left now is to push appliance sales down to where they should be."

For almost twenty years after this episode, Macy's New York continued to drift. Any number of explanations were given for Macy's inability to exploit its dominant position in the New York retail market: the decay of the inner city, the poor economics of a store supposedly "too big," and many others. Actually, once a new management came in after 1970, reversed the emphasis, and accepted the contribution of appliances to sales, Macy's—despite inner-city decay, despite its high labor costs, and despite its enormous size—promptly began to prosper again.

At the same time that Macy's rejected the unexpected success, another New York retail store, Bloomingdale's, used the identical unexpected success to propel itself into the number two spot in the New York market. Bloomingdale's, at best a weak number four, had been even more of a fashion store than Macy's. But when appliance sales began to climb in the early 1950s, Bloomingdale's ran with the opportunity. It realized that something unexpected was happening and analyzed it. It then built a new position in the marketplace around its Housewares Department. It also refocused its fashion and apparel sales to reach a new customer: the customer of whose emergence the explosion in appliance sales was only a symptom. Macy's is still number one in New York in volume. But Bloomingdale's has become the "smart New York store." And the stores that were the contenders for this title thirty years ago—the stores that were then strong number twos, the fashion leaders of 1950 such as Best—have disappeared (for additional examples, see Chapter 15).

The Macy's story will be called extreme. But the only uncommon aspect about it is that the chairman was aware of what he was doing. Though not conscious of their folly, far too many managements act the way Macy's did. It is never easy for a management to accept the unexpected success. It takes determination, specific policies, a willingness to look at reality, and the humility to say, "We were wrong!"

One reason why it is difficult for management to accept unexpected success is that all of us tend to believe that anything that has lasted a fair amount of time must be "normal" and go on "forever." Anything that contradicts what we have come to consider a law of nature is then rejected as unsound, unhealthy, and obviously abnormal.

This explains, for instance, why one of the major U.S. steel companies, around 1970, rejected the "mini-mill."* Management knew that

*On the "mini-mill," see Chapter 4.

its steelworks were rapidly becoming obsolete and would need billions of dollars of investment to be modernized. It also knew that it could not obtain the necessary sums. A new, smaller "mini-mill" was the solution.

Almost by accident, such a "mini-mill" was acquired. It soon began to grow rapidly and to generate cash and profits. Some of the younger men within the steel company therefore proposed that the available investment funds be used to acquire additional "mini-mills" and to build new ones. Within a few years, the "mini-mills" would then give the steel company several million tons of steel capacity based on modern technology, low labor costs, and pinpointed markets. Top management indignantly vetoed the proposal; indeed, all the men who had been connected with it found themselves "ex-employees" within a few years. "The integrated steelmaking process is the only right one," top management argued. "Everything else is cheating—a fad, unhealthy, and unlikely to endure." Needless to say, ten years later the only parts of the steel industry in America that were still healthy, growing, and reasonably prosperous were "mini-mills."

To a steelmaker who has spent his entire life working to perfect the integrated steelmaking process, who is at home in the big steel mill, and who may himself be the son of a steelworker (as a great many American steel company executives have been), anything but "big steel" is strange and alien, indeed a threat. It takes an effort to perceive in the "enemy" one's own best opportunity.

Top management people in most organizations, whether small or large, public-service institution or business, have typically grown up in one function or one area. To them, this is the area in which they feel comfortable. When I sat down with the chairman of R. H. Macy, for instance, there was only one member of top management, the personnel vice-president, who had not started as a fashion buyer and made his career in the fashion end of the business. Appliances, to these men, were something that other people dealt with.

The unexpected success can be galling. Consider the company that has worked diligently on modifying and perfecting an old product, a product that has been the "flagship" of the company for years, the product that represents "quality." At the same time, most reluctantly, the company puts through what everyone in the firm knows is a perfectly meaningless modification of an old, obsolete, and "low-quality" product. It is done only because one of the company's leading salesmen lobbied for it, or because a good customer asked for it and could not be turned down. But nobody expects it to sell; in fact, nobody wants it to sell. And then this "dog" runs away with the market and even takes the sales which plans and forecasts had promised for the "prestige," "quality" line. No wonder that everybody is appalled and considers the success a "cuckoo in the nest" (a term I have heard more than once). Everybody is likely to react precisely the way the chairman of R. H. Macy reacted when he saw the unwanted and unloved appliances overtake his beloved fashions, on which he himself had spent his working life and his energy.

The unexpected success is a challenge to management's judgment. "If the mini-mills were an opportunity, we surely would have seen it ourselves," the chairman of the big steel company is quoted as saying when he turned the mini-mill proposal down. Managements are paid for their judgment, but they are not being paid to be infallible. In fact, they are being paid to realize and admit that they have been wrong—especially when their admission opens up an opportunity. But this is by no means common.

A Swiss pharmaceutical company today has world leadership in veterinary medicines, yet it has not itself developed a single veterinary drug. But the companies that developed these medicines refused to serve the veterinary market. The medicines, mostly antibiotics, were of course developed for treating human diseases. When the veterinarians discovered that they were just as effective for animals and began to send in their orders, the original manufacturers were far from pleased. In some cases they refused to supply the veterinarians; in many others, they disliked having to reformulate the drugs for animal use, to repackage them, and so on. The medical director of a leading pharmaceutical company protested around 1953 that to apply a new antibiotic to the treatment of animals was a "misuse of a noble medicine." Consequently, when the Swiss approached this manufacturer and several others, they obtained licenses for veterinary use without any difficulty and at low cost. Some of the manufacturers were only too happy to get rid of the embarrassing success.

Human medications have since come under price pressure and are carefully scrutinized by regulatory authorities. This has made veterinary medications the most profitable segment of the pharmaceutical industry. But the companies that developed the compounds in the first place are not the ones who get these profits.

Far more often, the unexpected success is simply not seen at all. Nobody pays any attention to it. Hence, nobody exploits it, with the inevitable result that the competitor runs with it and reaps the rewards.

A leading hospital supplier introduced a new line of instruments for biological and clinical tests. The new products were doing quite well. Then, suddenly, orders came in from industrial and university laboratories. Nobody was told about them, nobody noticed them; nobody realized that, by pure accident, the company had developed products with more and better customers outside the market for which those products had been developed. No salesman was being sent out to call on these new customers, no service force was being set up. Five or eight years later, another company had taken over these new markets. And because of the volume of business these markets produced, the newcomer could soon invade the hospital market offering lower prices and better services than the original market leader.

One reason for this blindness to the unexpected success is that our existing reporting systems do not as a rule report it, let alone clamor for management's attention.

Practically every company—but every public-service institution as well—has a monthly or quarterly report. The first sheet lists the areas in which performance is below expectations: it lists the problems and the shortfalls. At the monthly meetings of the management group and the board of directors, everybody therefore focuses on the problem areas. No one even looks at the areas where the company has done better than expected. And if the unexpected success is not quantitative but qualitative—as in the case of the hospital instruments mentioned above, which opened up new major markets outside the company's traditional ones—the figures will not even show the unexpected success as a rule.

To exploit the opportunity for innovation offered by unexpected success requires analysis. Unexpected success is a symptom. But a symptom of what? The underlying phenomenon may be nothing more than a limitation on our own vision, knowledge, and understanding. That the pharmaceutical companies, for instance, rejected the unexpected success of their new drugs in the animal market was a symptom of their own failure to know how big—and how important—livestock raising throughout the world is; of their blindness to the sharp increase in demand for animal proteins throughout the world after World War II, and to the tremendous changes in knowledge, sophistication, and management capacity of the world's farmers.

The unexpected success of appliances at R. H. Macy's was a symptom of a fundamental change in the behavior, expectations, and values of substantial numbers of consumers—as the people at Bloomingdale's realized. Up until World War II, department store consumers in the United States bought primarily by socioeconomic status, that is, by income group. After World War II, the market increasingly segmented itself by what we now call "lifestyles." Bloomingdale's was the first of the major department stores, especially on the East Coast, to realize this, to capitalize on it, and to innovate a new retail image.

The unexpected success of laboratory instruments designed for the hospital in industrial and university laboratories was a symptom of the disappearance of distinctions between the various users of scientific instruments, which for almost a century had created sharply different markets, with different end uses, specifications, and expectations. What it symptomized—and the company never realized this—was not just that a product line had uses that were not originally envisaged. It signaled the end of the specific market niche the company had enjoyed in the hospital market. So the company that for thirty or forty years had successfully defined itself as a designer, maker, and marketer of hospital laboratory equipment was forced eventually to redefine itself as a maker of laboratory instruments, and to develop capabilities to design, manufacture, distribute, and service way beyond its original field. By then, however, it had lost a large part of the market for good.

Thus the unexpected success is not just an opportunity for innovation; it demands innovation. It forces us to ask, What basic changes are now appropriate for this organization in the way it defines its business? Its technology? Its markets? If these questions are faced up to, then the unexpected success is likely to open up the most rewarding and least risky of all innovative opportunities.

Two of the world's biggest businesses, DuPont, the world's largest chemical company, and IBM, the giant of the computer industry, owe their preeminence to their willingness to exploit the unexpected success as an innovative opportunity.

DuPont, for 130 years, had confined itself to making munitions and explosives. In the mid-1920s it then organized its first research efforts in other areas, one of them the brand-new field of polymer chemistry, which the Germans had pioneered during World War I. For several years there were no results at all. Then, in 1928, an assistant left a burner on over the weekend. On Monday morning, Wallace H. Carothers, the chemist in charge, found that the stuff in the kettle had congealed into fibers. It took another ten years before DuPont found out how to make Nylon intentionally. The point of the story is, however, that the same accident had occurred several times in the laboratories of the big German chemical companies with the same results, and much earlier. The Germans were, of course, looking for a polymerized fiber —and they could have had it, along with world leadership in the chemical industry, ten years before DuPont had Nylon. But because they had not planned the experiment, they dismissed its results, poured out the accidentally produced fibers, and started all over again.

The history of IBM equally shows what paying attention to the unexpected success can do. For IBM is largely the result of the willingness to exploit the unexpected success not once, but twice. In the early 1930s, IBM almost went under. It had spent its available money on designing the first electro-mechanical bookkeeping machine, meant for banks. But American banks did not buy new equipment in the Depression days of the early thirties. IBM even then had a policy of not laying off people, so it continued to manufacture the machines, which it had to put in storage.

When IBM was at its lowest point—so the story goes—Thomas Watson, Sr., the founder, found himself at a dinner party sitting next to a lady. When she heard his name, she said: "Are you the Mr. Watson of IBM? Why does your sales manager refuse to demonstrate your machine to me?" What a lady would want with an accounting machine Thomas Watson could not possibly figure out, nor did it help him much when she told him she was the director of the New York Public Library; it turned out he had never been in a public library. But next morning, he appeared there as soon as its doors opened.

In those days, libraries had fair amounts of government money. Watson walked out two hours later with enough of an order to cover next month's payroll. And, as he added with a chuckle whenever he told the story, "I invented a new policy on the spot: we get cash in advance before we deliver."

Fifteen years later, IBM had one of the early computers. Like the other early American computers, the IBM computer was designed for scientific purposes only. Indeed, IBM got into computer work largely because of Watson's interest in astronomy. And when first demonstrated in IBM's show window on Madison Avenue, where it drew enormous crowds, IBM's computer was programmed to calculate all past, present, and future phases of the moon.

But then businesses began to buy this "scientific marvel" for the most mundane of purposes, such as payroll. Univac, which had the most advanced computer and the one most suitable for business uses, did not really want to "demean" its scientific miracle by supplying business. But IBM, though equally surprised by the business demand for computers, responded immediately. Indeed, it was willing to sacrifice its own computer design, which was not particularly suitable for accounting, and instead use what its rival and competitor (Univac) had developed. Within four years IBM had attained leadership in the computer market, even though for another decade its own computers were technically inferior to those produced by Univac. IBM was willing to satisfy business and to satisfy it on business' terms—to train programmers for business, for instance.

Similarly, Japan's foremost electronic company, Matsushita (better known by its brand names Panasonic and National), owes its rise to its willingness to run with unexpected success.

Matsushita was a fairly small and undistinguished company in the early 1950s, outranked on every count by such older and deeply entrenched giants as Toshiba or Hitachi. Matsushita "knew," as did every other Japanese manufacturer of the time, that "television would not grow fast in Japan." "Japan is much too poor to afford such a luxury," the chairman of Toshiba had said at a New York meeting around 1954 or 1955. Matsushita, however, was intelligent enough to accept that the Japanese farmers apparently did not know that they were too poor for television. What they knew was that television offered them, for the first time, access to a big world. They could not afford television sets, but they were prepared to buy them anyhow and pay for them. Toshiba and Hitachi made better sets at the time, only they showed them on the Ginza in Tokyo and in the big-city department stores, making it pretty clear that farmers were not particularly welcome in such elegant surroundings. Matsushita went to the farmers and sold its televisions door-to-door, something no one in Japan had ever done before for anything more expensive than cotton pants or aprons.

Of course, it is not enough to depend on accidents, nor to wait for the lady at the dinner table to express unexpected interest in one's apparently failing product. The search has to be organized.

The first thing is to ensure that the unexpected is being seen; indeed, that it clamors for attention. It must be properly featured in the information management obtains and studies. (How to do this is described in some detail in Chapter 13.)

Managements must look at every unexpected success with the questions: (1) What would it mean to us if we exploited it? (2) Where could it lead us? (3) What would we have to do to convert it into an opportunity? And (4) How do we go about it? This means, first, that managements need to set aside specific time in which to discuss unexpected successes; and second, that someone should always be designated to analyze an unexpected success and to think through how it could be exploited.

But management also needs to learn what the unexpected success demands of them. Again, this might best be explained by an example.

A major university on the eastern seaboard of the United States started, in the early 1950s, an evening program of "continuing education" for adults, in which the normal undergraduate curriculum leading to an undergraduate degree was offered to adults with a high school diploma.

Nobody on the faculty really believed in the program. The only reason it was offered at all was that a small number of returning World War II veterans had been forced to go to work before obtaining their undergraduate degrees and were clamoring for an opportunity to get the credits they still lacked. To everybody's surprise, however, the program proved immensely successful, with qualified students applying in large numbers. And the students in the program actually outperformed the regular undergraduates. This, in turn, created a dilemma. To exploit the unexpected success, the university would have had to build a fairly big first-rate faculty. But this would have weakened its main program; at the least, it would have diverted the university from what it saw as its main mission, the training of undergraduates. The alternative was to close down the new program. Either decision would have been a responsible one. Instead, the university decided to staff the program with cheap, temporary faculty, mostly teaching assistants working on their own advanced degrees. As a result, it destroyed the program within a few years; but worse, it also seriously damaged its own reputation.

The unexpected success is an opportunity, but it makes demands. It demands to be taken seriously. It demands to be staffed with the ablest people available, rather than with whoever we can spare. It demands seriousness and support on the part of management equal to the size of the opportunity. And the opportunity is considerable.

II

THE UNEXPECTED FAILURE

Failures, unlike successes, cannot be rejected and rarely go unnoticed. But they are seldom seen as symptoms of opportunity. A good many failures are, of course, nothing but mistakes, the results of greed, stupidity, thoughtless bandwagon-climbing, or incompetence whether in design or execution. Yet if something fails despite being carefully planned, carefully designed, and conscientiously executed, that failure often bespeaks underlying change and, with it, opportunity.

The assumptions on which a product or service, its design or its marketing strategy, were based may no longer fit reality. Perhaps customers have changed their values and perceptions; while they still buy the same "thing," they are actually purchasing a very different "value." Or perhaps what has always been one market or one end use is splitting itself into two or more, each demanding something quite different. Any change like this is an opportunity for innovation.

I had my first experience with an unexpected failure at the very beginning of my working life, almost sixty years ago, just out of high school. My first job was as a trainee in an old export firm, which for more than a century had been selling hardware to British India. Its best seller for years had been a cheap padlock, of which it exported whole shiploads every month. The padlock was flimsy; a pin easily opened the lock. As incomes in India went up during the 1920s, padlock sales, instead of going up, began to decline quite sharply. My employer thereupon did the obvious: he redesigned the padlock to give it a sturdier lock, that is, to make it "better quality." The added cost was minimal and the improvement in quality substantial. But the improved padlock turned out to be unsalable. Four years later, the firm went into liquidation, the decline of its Indian padlock business a major factor in its demise.

A very small competitor of this firm in the Indian export business—no more than a tenth of the size of my employer and until then barely able to survive—realized that this unexpected failure was a symptom of basic change. For the bulk of Indians, the peasants in the villages, the padlock was (and for all I know, still is) a magical symbol; no thief would have dared open a padlock. The key was never used, and usually disappeared. To get a padlock that could not easily be opened without a key —the improved padlock my employer had worked so hard to perfect without additional cost—was thus not a boon but a disaster.

A small but rapidly growing middle-class minority in the cities, however, needed a real lock. That it was not sturdy enough for their needs was the main reason why the old lock had begun to lose sales and market. But for them the redesigned product was still inadequate.

My employer's competitor broke down the padlock into two separate products: one without lock and key, with only a simple trigger release, and selling for one-third less than the old padlock but with twice its profit margin; and the other with a good sturdy lock and three keys, selling at twice the price of the old product and also with a substantially larger profit margin. Both lines immediately began to sell. Within two years, the competitor had become the largest European hardware exporter to India. He maintained this position for ten years, until World War II put an end to European exports to India altogether.

A quaint tale from horse and buggy days, some might say. Surely we have become more sophisticated in this age of computers, of market research, and of business school MBAs.

But here is another case, half a century later and from a very "sophisticated" industry. Yet it teaches exactly the same lesson.

Just at the time when the first cohorts of the "baby boom" were reaching their mid-twenties—that is, the age to form families and to buy their first house—the 1973–74 recession hit. Inflation was becoming rampant, particularly in housing prices, which rose much faster than anything else. At the same time, interest rates on home mortgages were skyrocketing. And so the mass builders in America began to design and offer what they called a "basic house," smaller, simpler, and cheaper than the house that had become standard.

But despite its being such "good value" and well within the means of the first-time homebuyer, the "basic house" was a thumping failure. The builders tried to salvage it by offering low-interest financing and long repayment terms, and by slashing prices. Still, no one bought the "basic house."

Most homebuilders did what businessmen do in an unexpected failure: they blamed that old bogeyman, the "irrational customer." But one builder, still very small, decided to look around. He found that there had been a change in what the young American couple wants in its first house. This no longer represents the family's permanent home as it had done for their grandparents, a house in which the couple expects to live the rest of its life, or at least a long time. In the 1970s, young couples were buying not one, but two separate "values" in purchasing their first home. They bought shelter for a few short years; and they also bought an option to buy—a few years later—their "real" house, a much bigger and more luxurious home, in a better neighborhood, with better schools. To make the down payment on this far more expensive permanent home, they would, however, need the equity they had built up in the first house. The young people knew very well that the "basic house" was not what they and their contemporaries really wanted, even though it was all they could afford. They feared therefore—and perfectly rationally—that they would not be able to resell the "basic house" at a decent price. So the "basic house," instead of being an option to buy the "real house" later on, would become a serious impediment to the fulfillment of their true housing needs and wants.

The young couple of 1950 had still perceived itself as "working-class," by and large. And "working-class" people in the West do not expect their incomes and their standards of living to rise materially once they are out of their apprenticeship and into a full-time job. Seniority, for working-class people (with Japan being the major exception), means greater job security rather than larger incomes. But the "middle class" traditionally can expect a steady increase in its income until the head of the household reaches age forty-five or forty-eight. Between 1950 and 1975, both the reality and the self-image of young American adults—their educations, their expectations, their jobs—had changed from "working-class" to "middle-class." And with this change had come a sharp change in what the young people's first home represented, and what "value" was connected with it.

Once this was understood—and all it took was to listen to prospective homebuyers for a few weekends—successful innovation came about easily. Almost no change was made in the physical plant itself; only the kitchen was redesigned and made somewhat roomier. Otherwise, the building remained the same "basic house" the homebuilders had not been able to sell. But instead of being offered as "your house," it was offered as "your *first* house," and as a "building block toward the house you want." Specifically, this meant that the young couple was

shown both the house as it was standing—that is, the "basic house"—
and a model of the same house in which future additions such as an
extra bathroom, one or two more bedrooms, and a basement "family
den" had been built. Indeed, the builder had already obtained the
necessary city permits for conversion of the "basic house" to a "permanent home." Furthermore, the builder guaranteed the young couple a
fixed resale price for their first house, to be credited against their purchase from his firm of a second, bigger, "permanent" home within five
to seven years. "This entailed practically no risk," he explained. "The
demographics were such, after all, as to guarantee a steady increase in
the demand for 'first houses' until the late 1980s or 1990s, during which
time the babies of the 'baby bust' of 1961 will have become twenty-five
themselves and will start forming their own families."

Before this homebuilder transformed failure into innovation, he
had operated in only one metropolitan area and was a small factor in
it. Five years later, the firm was operating in seven metropolitan areas
and was either number one or a strong number two in each of them.
Even during the building recession of 1981–82—a recession so severe
that some of the largest American builders did not sell one single new
house during an entire season—this innovative homebuilder continued to grow. "One reason," the firm's founder explained, "was
something even I had not seen when I decided to offer first-time
homebuyers a repurchase guarantee. It gave us a steady supply of
well-built and still fairly new houses that needed only a little fixing up
and could then be resold at a very decent profit to the next crop of
first-home buyers."

Faced with unexpected failure, executives, especially in large organizations, tend to call for more study and more analysis. But as both the
padlock story and the "basic house" story show, this is the wrong response. The unexpected failure demands that you go out, look around,
and listen. Failure should always be considered a symptom of an innovative opportunity, and taken seriously as such.

It is equally important to watch out for the unexpected event in a
supplier's business, and among the customers. McDonald's, for instance,
started because the company's founder, Ray Kroc, paid attention to the
unexpected success of one of his customers. At that time Kroc was
selling milkshake machines to hamburger joints. He noticed that one of
his customers, a small hamburger stand in a remote California town,
bought several times the number of milkshake machines its location

and size could justify. He investigated and found an old man who had, in effect, reinvented the fast-food business by systematizing it. Kroc bought his outfit and built it into a billion-dollar business based on the original owner's unexpected success.

A competitor's unexpected success or failure is equally important. In either case, one takes the event seriously as a possible symptom of innovative opportunity. One does not just "analyze." One goes out to investigate.

Innovation—and this is a main thesis of this book—is organized, systematic, rational work. But it is perceptual fully as much as conceptual. To be sure, what the innovator sees and learns has to be subjected to rigorous logical analysis. Intuition is not good enough; indeed, it is no good at all if by "intuition" is meant "what I feel." For that usually is another way of saying "What I like it to be" rather than "What I perceive it to be." But the analysis, with all its rigor—its requirements for testing, piloting, and evaluating—has to be based on a perception of change, of opportunity, of the new realities, of the incongruity between what most people still are quite sure is the reality and what has actually become a new reality. This requires the willingness to say: "I don't know enough to analyze, but I shall find out. I'll go out, look around, ask questions, and *listen.*"

It is precisely because the unexpected jolts us out of our preconceived notions, our assumptions, our certainties, that it is such a fertile source of innovation.

It is not in fact even necessary for the entrepreneur to understand why reality has changed. In the two cases above, it was easy to find out what had happened and why. More often, we find out what is happening without much clue as to why. And yet we can still innovate successfully.

Here is one example.

The failure of the Ford Motor Company's Edsel in 1957 has become American folklore. Even people who were not yet born when the Edsel failed have heard about it, at least in the United States. But the general belief that the Edsel was a slapdash gamble is totally mistaken.

Very few products were ever more carefully designed, more carefully introduced, more skillfully marketed. The Edsel was intended to be the final step in the most thoroughly planned strategy in American business history: a ten-year campaign during which the Ford Motor Company converted itself after World War II from near-bankruptcy into an aggressive competitor, a strong number two in the United States, and a few years later, a strong contender for the number one spot in the rapidly growing European market.

By 1957, Ford had already successfully reestablished itself as a strong competitor in three of the four main American automobile markets: the "standard" one with the Ford nameplate; the "lower-middle" one with Mercury; and the "upper" one with the Continental. The Edsel was then designed for the only remaining segment, the upper-middle one, the one for which Ford's big rival, General Motors, produced the Buick and the Oldsmobile. This "upper-middle" segment was, in the period after World War II, the fastest-growing part of the automobile market and yet the one for which the third automobile producer, Chrysler, did not have a strong entry, thereby leaving the door wide open for Ford.

Ford went to extreme lengths to plan and design the Edsel, embodying in its design the best information from market research, the best information about customer preferences in appearance and styling, and the highest standards of quality control.

Yet the Edsel became a total failure right away.

The reaction of the Ford Motor Company was very revealing. Instead of blaming the "irrational consumer," the Ford people decided there was something happening that did not jibe with the assumptions about reality everyone in the automobile industry had been making about consumer behavior—and for so long that they had become unquestioned axioms.

The result of Ford's decision to go out and investigate was the one genuine innovation in the American automobile industry since Alfred P. Sloan, in the 1920s, had defined the socioeconomic segmentation of the American market into "low," "lower-middle," "upper-middle," and "upper" segments, the insight on which he then built the General Motors Company. When the Ford people went out, they discovered that this segmentation was rapidly being replaced—or at least paralleled—by another quite different one, the one we would now call "lifestyle segmentation." The result, within a short period after the Edsel's failure, was the appearance of Ford's Thunderbird, the greatest success of any American car since Henry Ford, Sr., had introduced his Model T in 1908. The Thunderbird established Ford again as a major producer in its own right, rather than as GM's kid brother and a perennial imitator.

And yet to this day we really do not know what caused the change. It occurred well *before* any of the events by which it is usually explained, such as the shift of the center of demographic gravity to the teenagers as a result of the "baby boom," the explosive expansion of higher education, or the change in sexual mores. Nor do we really know what is meant by "lifestyle." All attempts to describe it have been futile so far. All we know is that something happened.

But that is enough to convert the unexpected, whether success or failure, into an opportunity for effective and purposeful innovation.

III

THE UNEXPECTED OUTSIDE EVENT

Unexpected successes and unexpected failure have so far been discussed as occurring within a business or an industry. But outside events, that is, events that are not recorded in the information and the figures by which a management steers its institution, are just as important. Indeed, they often are more important.

Here are some examples showing typical unexpected outside events and their exploitation as major opportunities for successful innovation.

One example concerns IBM and the personal computer.

However much executives and engineers at IBM may have disagreed with each other, there apparently was total agreement within the company on one point until well into the seventies: the future belonged to the centralized "main-frame" computer, with an ever larger memory and an ever larger calculating capacity. Everything else, every IBM engineer could prove convincingly, would be far too expensive, far too confusing, and far too limited in its performance capacity. And so IBM concentrated its efforts and resources on maintaining its leadership in the main-frame market.

And then around 1975 or 1976, to everybody's total surprise, ten- and eleven-year-old kids began to play computer games. Right away their fathers wanted their own office computer or personal computer, that is, a separate, small, freestanding machine with far less capacity than even the smallest main-frame has. All the dire things the IBM people had predicted actually did happen. The freestanding machines cost many times what a plug-in "terminal" costs, and they have far less capacity; there is such a proliferation of them and their programs, and so few of them are truly compatible with one another, that the whole field has become chaotic, with service and repairs in shambles. But this does not seem to bother the customers. On the contrary, in the U.S. market the personal computers in five short years—from 1979 to 1984 —reached the annual sales volume it had taken the "main-frames" thirty years to reach, that is, $15–$16 billion.

IBM could have been expected to dismiss this development. Instead, as early as 1977, when personal computer sales worldwide were still less than $200 million (as against main-frame sales of $7 billion for the same year), IBM set up task forces in competition with one another to develop personal computers for the company. As a result, IBM produced its own personal computer in 1980, just when the market was exploding. Three years later, in 1983, IBM had become the world's leading personal computer producer with nearly as much of a leadership position in the new field as it had in main-frames. Also in 1983 IBM then introduced its own very small "home computer," the "Peanut."

When I discuss all this with the IBM people, I always ask the same question: "What explains that IBM, of all people, saw this change as an opportunity when everybody at IBM was so totally sure that it couldn't happen and made no sense?" And I always get the same answer: "Precisely because we *knew* that this couldn't happen, and that it would make no sense at all, the development came as a profound shock to us. We realized that everything we'd assumed, everything we were so absolutely certain of, was suddenly being thrown into a cocked hat, and that we had to go out and organize ourselves to take advantage of a development we knew couldn't happen, but which then did happen."

The second example is far more mundane. But is it no less instructive despite its lack of glamour.

The United States has never been a book-*buying* country, in part because of the ubiquitous free public library. When TV appeared in the early fifties and more and more Americans began to spend more and more of their time in front of the tube—particularly people in their prime book-reading years, that is, people of high school and college age —"everyone knew" that book sales would drop drastically. Book publishers frantically began to diversify into "high-tech media": educational movies, or computer programs (in most cases, with total lack of success). But instead of collapsing, book sales in the United States have soared since TV first came in. They have grown several times as fast as every indicator had predicted, whether family incomes, total population in the "book-reading years," or even people with higher degrees.

No one knows why this happened. Indeed, no one quite knows what really happened. Books are still as rare in the typical American home as before.* Where, then, do all these books go? That we have no answer to this question does not alter the fact that books are being bought and paid for in increasing numbers.

Both the publishers and the existing bookstores knew, of course, all along that book sales were soaring. Neither, however, did anything about it. The unexpected event was exploited, instead, by a few mass retailers such as department stores in Minneapolis and Los Angeles. None of these people had ever had anything to do with books, but they knew the retail business. They started bookstore chains that are quite different from any earlier bookstore in America. Basically, these are supermarkets. They do not treat books as literature but as "mass merchandise," and they concentrate on the fast-moving items that generate the largest dollar sales per unit of shelf space. They are located in shopping centers with high rents but also with high traffic, whereas everybody in the book business had known all along that a bookstore has to be in a low-rent location, preferably near a university. Traditionally, booksellers were themselves "literary types" and tried to hire people who "love books." The managers of the new bookstores are former cosmetics salespeople. The standing joke among them is that any salesperson who wants to read anything besides the price tag on the book is hopelessly overqualified.

For ten years now, these new bookstore chains have been among the most successful and fastest-growing segments in American retailing and among the fastest-growing new businesses in this country altogether.

Each of these cases represents genuine innovation. But not one of them represents diversification.

IBM stayed in the computer business. And the chain bookstores are run by people who all along have been in retailing, in shopping centers, or managing "boutiques."

It is a condition of success in exploiting the unexpected outside event that it must fit the knowledge and expertise of one's own business. Companies, even large companies, that went into the new book market

*This is also true of Japan, the country that, *per capita,* buys more books than any other and twice as many as the United States.

or into mass merchandising without the retail expertise have uniformly come to grief.

The unexpected outside event may thus be, above all, an opportunity to apply already existing expertise to a new application, but to an application that does not change the nature of the "business we are in." It may be extension rather than diversification. Yet as the above examples show, it also demands innovation in product and often in service and distribution channels.

The second point about these cases is that they all are big-company cases. Of course, a good many of the cases in this book, as in any management book, have to be big-company cases. They are the only available ones, as a rule, the only ones that can be found in the published records, the only ones discussed on the business page of newspapers or in magazines. Small-company cases are much harder to come by and often cannot be discussed without violating confidences.

But exploiting the unexpected outside event appears to be something that particularly fits the existing enterprise, and a fairly sizable one at that. I know of few small companies that have successfully exploited the unexpected outside event; nor does any other student of entrepreneurship and innovation whom I could consult. This may be coincidence. But perhaps the existing large enterprise is more likely to see the "big picture."

It is the large retailer in the United States who is used to looking at figures that show where and how consumers spend retail dollars. The large retailer also knows about shopping-center locations and how to get the good ones. And could a small company have done what IBM did and detach four task forces of first-rate designers and engineers to work on new product lines? Smaller high-tech companies in a rapidly growing industry usually do not have enough of such people even for their existing work.

It may well be that the unexpected outside event is the innovative area that offers the large enterprise the greatest opportunity along with the lowest risk. It may be the area that is particularly suited for innovation by the large and established enterprise. It may be the area in which expertise matters the most, and in which the ability to mobilize substantial resources fast makes the greatest difference.

But as these cases also show, being big and established does not guarantee that an enterprise will perceive the unexpected event and successfully organize itself to exploit it. IBM's American competitors are all big businesses with sales in the billions. Not one of them exploited the personal computer—they were all too busy fighting IBM. And not one of the old large bookstore chains in the United States, Brentano's in New York, for instance, exploited the new book market.

The opportunity is there, in other words. It is a major opportunity, occurring frequently. And when it occurs, it holds out great promise, particularly for existing and sizable enterprises. But such opportunities require more than mere luck or intuition. They demand that the enterprise search for innovation, be organized for it, and be managed so as to exploit it.

4

Source: Incongruities

An incongruity is a discrepancy, a dissonance, between what is and what "ought" to be, or between what is and what everybody assumes it to be. We may not understand the reason for it; indeed, we often cannot figure it out. Still, an incongruity is a symptom of an opportunity to innovate. It bespeaks an underlying "fault," to use the geologist's term. Such a fault is an invitation to innovate. It creates an instability in which quite minor efforts can move large masses and bring about a restructuring of the economic or social configuration. Incongruities do not, however, usually manifest themselves in the figures or reports executives receive and pay attention to. They are qualitative rather than quantitative.

Like the unexpected event, whether success or failure, incongruity is a symptom of change, either change that has already occurred or change that can be made to happen. Like the changes that underlie the unexpected event, the changes that underlie incongruity are changes *within* an industry, a market, a process. The incongruity is thus clearly visible to the people within or close to the industry, market, or process; it is directly in front of their eyes. Yet it is often overlooked by the insiders, who tend to take it for granted—"This is the way it's always been," they say, even though "always" may be a very recent development.

There are several kinds of incongruity:

— An incongruity between the economic realities of an industry (or of a public-service area);
— An incongruity between the reality of an industry (or of a public-service area) and the assumptions about it;
— An incongruity between the efforts of an industry (or a public-

service area) and the values and expectations of its customers;
— An internal incongruity within the rhythm or the logic of a process.

I

INCONGRUOUS ECONOMIC REALITIES

If the demand for a product or a service is growing steadily, its economic performance should steadily improve, too. It should be easy to be profitable in an industry with steadily rising demand. The tide carries it. A lack of profitability and results in such an industry bespeaks an incongruity between economic realities.

Typically, these incongruities are macro-phenomena, which occur within a whole industry or a whole service sector. The major opportunities for innovation exist, however, normally for the small and highly focused new enterprise, new process, or new service. And usually the innovator who exploits this incongruity can count on being left alone for a long time before the existing businesses or suppliers wake up to the fact that they have new and dangerous competition. For they are so busy trying to bridge the gap between rising demand and lagging results that they barely even notice somebody is doing something different—something that produces results, that exploits the rising demand.

Sometimes we understand what is going on. But sometimes it is impossible to figure out why rising demand does not result in better performance. The innovator, therefore, need not always try to understand why things do not work as they should. He should ask instead: "What would exploit this incongruity? What would convert it into an opportunity? What can be done?" Incongruity between economic realities is a call to action. Sometimes the action to be taken is rather obvious, even though the problem itself is quite obscure. And sometimes we understand the problem thoroughly and yet cannot figure out what to do about it.

The steel "mini-mill" is a good example of an innovation that successfully exploited incongruity.

For more than fifty years, since the end of World War I, the large, integrated steel mill in developed countries did well only in wartime. In times of peace its results were consistently disappointing, even though the demand for steel appeared to be going up steadily, at least until 1973.

The explanation of this incongruity has long been known. The minimum incremental unit needed to satisfy additional demand in an integrated steel mill is a very big investment and adds substantially to capacity. Any expansion to an existing steel mill is thus likely to operate for a good many years at a low utilization rate, until demand—which always goes up in small, incremental steps except in wartime—reaches the new capacity level. But not to expand when demand creeps up means losing market share, and permanently. No company can afford to take that risk. The industry can therefore only be profitable for a few short years: between the time when everybody begins to build new capacity and the time when all this new capacity comes on stream.

Further, the steelmaking process invented in the 1870s is fundamentally uneconomical, as also has been known for many years. It tries to defy the laws of physics—and that means violating the laws of economics. Nothing in physics requires as much work as the creation of temperatures, whether hot or cold, unless it is working against the laws of gravity and of inertia. The integrated steel process creates very high temperatures four times, only to quench them again. And it lifts heavy masses of hot materials and then moves them over considerable distances.

It had been clear for many years that the first innovation in process that would assuage these inherent weaknesses would substantially lower costs. This is exactly what the "mini-mill" does. A mini-mill is not a "small" plant; the minimum economical size produces around $100 million of sales. But that is still about one-sixth to one-tenth the minimum economic size of an integrated steel mill. A mini-mill can thus be built to provide, economically, a fairly small additional increment of steel production for which the market already exists. The mini-mill creates heat only once, and does not quench it, but uses it for the rest of the process. It starts with steel scrap instead of iron ore, and then concentrates on one end product: sheet, for instance, or beams, or rods. And while the integrated steel mill is highly labor-intensive, the mini-mill can be automated. Its costs thus come to less than half those of the traditional steel process.

Governments, labor unions, and the integrated steel companies have been fighting the mini-mill every step of the way. But it is steadily encroaching. By the year 2000, fifty percent or more of the steel used in the United States is likely to come out of mini-mills, while the large, integrated steel mills will be in irreversible decline.

There is a catch, however, and it is an important one. A similar incongruity between the economic reality of demand and the economic reality of the process exists in the paper industry. Only in this case, we do not know how to convert it into innovation and opportunity.

Despite the constant efforts of the governments of all developed and most developing countries to increase the demand for paper—perhaps the only objective on which the governments of all countries agree— the paper industry has not been doing well. Three years of "record profits" are invariably followed by five years of "excess capacity" and losses. Yet we do not, so far, have anything like a "mini-mill" process for paper. For eighty or ninety years, it has been known that wood fiber is a monomer; and it should not be too difficult, one would say, to find a plasticizer that converts it into a polymer. This would convert paper-making from an inherently inefficient and wasteful mechanical process into an inherently efficient chemical process. Indeed, almost a hundred years ago this was achieved as far as making textile fibers out of wood pulp is concerned—in the rayon process, which dates back to the 1880s. But despite millions spent in research, nobody has so far found a technique to produce paper that way.

In an incongruity, as these cases exemplify, the innovative solution has to be clearly definable. It has to be feasible with the existing, known technology, and with easily available resources. It requires hard developmental work, of course. But if a great deal of research and new knowledge is still needed, it is not yet ready for the entrepreneur, not yet "ripe." The innovation that successfully exploits an incongruity between economic realities has to be simple rather than complicated, "obvious" rather than grandiose.

In public-service areas, too, major incongruities between economic realities can be found.

Health care in developed countries offers one example. As recently as 1929, health care represented an insignificant portion of national expenditure in all developed countries, taking up a good deal less than 1 percent of gross national product or of consumer expenditures. Now, half a century later, health care, and expecially the hospital, accounts in all developed countries for 7 to 11 percent of a much larger gross national product. Yet economic performance has been going down rather than up. Costs have risen much faster than services—perhaps three or four times as fast. The demand will continue to rise with the steady growth in the number of older people in all developed countries over the next thirty years. And so will the costs, which are closely tied to the age of the population.

We do not understand the phenomenon.* But successful innovations, simple, targeted and focused on specific objectives, have emerged in Great Britain and the United States. These innovations are quite different simply because the two countries have such radically different systems. But each exploits the specific vulnerability of its country's system and converts it into an opportunity.

In Britain, the "radical innovation" is private health insurance, which has become the fastest-growing and most popular employee benefit. All it does is to enable policyholders to be seen immediately by a specialist and to jump to the head of the queue and avoid having to wait should they need "elective surgery."† For the British system has attempted to keep health-care costs down by *"triage"* which, in effect, reserves immediate attention and treatment to routine illnesses on the one hand and to "life-threatening" ailments on the other, but puts everything else, and especially elective surgery, on hold with waiting periods now running into years (e.g., for replacing a hip destroyed by arthritis). Health insurance policyholders, however, are operated on right away.

In contrast to Great Britain, the United States has so far tried to satisfy all demands of health care regardless of cost. As a result, hospital costs in America have exploded. This created a different innovative opportunity: to "unbundle," that is, to move out of the hospital into separate locations a host of services that do not require such high-cost hospital facilities as a body scanner or cobalt X-Ray to treat cancers, the highly instrumented and automated medical laboratory, or physical rehabilitation. Each of these innovative responses is small and specific: a freestanding maternity center, which basically offers motel facilities for mother and new baby; a freestanding "ambulatory" surgical center for surgery that does not require a hospital stay and post-operative care;

*This is brought out clearly in the best discussion of the health-care problem that has appeared so far, and the only one that looks at health care across national boundaries, in all developed countries. It is given in *The Economist* of April 29, 1984.

†Surgery for complaints that yield to surgery, will not improve without it, but are not "life-threatening." Examples are cataracts, hip replacements and orthopedic surgery generally, or a prolapsed uterus.

a psychiatric diagnostic and referral center; geriatric centers of a similar nature; and so on.

These new facilities do not substitute for the hospital. What they do in effect is to push the American hospital toward the same role the British have assigned to their hospitals: as a place for emergencies, for life-threatening diseases, and for intensive and acute sickness care. But these innovations which, as in Britain, are embodied primarily in profit-making "businesses," convert the incongruity between the economic reality of rising health-care demand and the economic reality of falling health-care performance into an opportunity for innovation.

These are "big" examples, taken from major industries and public services. It is this fact, however, that makes them accessible, visible, and understandable. Above all, these examples show why the incongruity between economic realities offers such great innovative opportunities. The people who work within these industries or public services know that there are basic flaws. But they are almost forced to ignore them and to concentrate instead on patching here, improving there, fighting this fire or caulking that crack. They are thus unable to take the innovation seriously, let alone to try to compete with it. They do not, as a rule, even notice it until it has grown so big as to encroach on their industry or service, by which time it has become irreversible. In the meantime, the innovators have the field to themselves.

II

THE INCONGRUITY BETWEEN REALITY
AND THE ASSUMPTIONS ABOUT IT

Whenever the people in an industry or a service misconceive reality, whenever they therefore make erroneous assumptions about it, their efforts will be misdirected. They will concentrate on the area where results do not exist. Then there is an incongruity between reality and behavior, an incongruity that once again offers opportunity for successful innovation to whoever can perceive and exploit it.

A simple example is that old workhorse of world trade, the ocean-going general cargo vessel.

Thirty-five years ago, in the early 1950s, the ocean-going freighter was believed to be dying. The general forecast was that it would be replaced by air freight, except for bulk commodities. Costs of ocean freight were rising at a fast clip, and it took longer and longer to get merchandise delivered by freighter as one port after another became badly congested. This, in turn, increased pilferage at the docks as more and more merchandise piled up waiting to be loaded while vessels could not make it to the pier.

The basic reason was that the shipping industry had misdirected its efforts toward nonresults for many years. It had tried to design and build faster ships, and ships that required less fuel and a smaller crew. It concentrated on the economics of the ship while at sea and in transit from one port to another.

But a ship is capital equipment: and for all capital equipment the biggest cost is the cost of not working, during which interest has to be paid while the equipment does not earn. Everybody in the industry knew, of course, that the main expense of a ship is interest on the investment. Yet the industry kept on concentrating its efforts on costs that were already quite low—the costs of the ship while at sea and doing work.

The solution was simple: Uncouple loading from stowing. Do the loading on land, where there is ample space and where it can be performed before the ship is in port, so that all that has to be done is to put on and take off pre-loaded freight. Concentrate, in other words, on the costs of not working rather than on those of working. The answer was the roll-on, roll-off ship and the container ship.

The results of these simple innovations have been startling. Freighter traffic in the last thirty years has increased up to five-fold. Costs, overall, are down by 60 percent. Port time has been cut by three-quarters in many cases, and with it congestion and pilferage.

Incongruity between perceived reality and actual reality often declares itself. But whenever serious, concentrated efforts do not make things better but, on the contrary, make things worse—where faster ships only mean more port congestion and longer delivery times—it is highly probable that efforts are being misdirected. In all likelihood, refocusing on where the results are will yield substantial returns easily and fast.

Indeed, the incongruity between perceived and actual reality rarely requires "heroic" innovations. Uncoupling the loading of freight from the stowing thereof required little but adapting to the ocean-going freighter methods which, much earlier, had been developed for trucks and railroads.

The incongruity between perceived and actual reality typically characterizes a whole industry or a whole service area. The solution, however, should again be small and simple, focused and highly specific.

III

THE INCONGRUITY BETWEEN
PERCEIVED AND ACTUAL CUSTOMER
VALUES AND EXPECTATIONS

In Chapter 3, I mentioned the case of television in Japan as an example of the unexpected success. It is also a good example of the incongruity between actual and perceived customer values and customer expectations. Long before the Japanese industrialist told his American audience that the poor in his country would not buy a TV set because they could not afford it, the poor in the United States and in Europe had already shown that TV satisfies expectations which have little to do with traditional economics. But this highly intelligent Japanese simply could not conceive that for customers—and especially for poor customers—the TV set is not just a "thing." It represents access to a new world; access, perhaps, to a whole new life.

Similarly, Khrushchev could not conceive that the automobile is not a "thing" when he said on his visit to the United States in 1956 that "Russians will never want to own automobiles; cheap taxis make much more sense." Any teenager could have told him that "wheels" are not mere transportation but freedom, mobility, power, romance. And Khrushchev's misperception created one of the wildest entrepreneurial opportunities: the shortage of automobiles in Russia has brought forth the biggest and liveliest black market.

These, it will be said, are again "cosmic" examples, not much use to a businessman or to an executive in a hospital, a university, or a trade association. But they are examples of a common phenomenon. What follows is a different case, in its own way equally "cosmic" but very definitely of operational significance.

One of the fastest-growing American financial institutions for the last several years has been a securities firm located not in New York but in a suburb of a Midwestern city. It now has two thousand branch offices all over the United States. And it owes its success and growth to having exploited an incongruity.

The large financial institutions, the Merrill Lynches and Dean Witters and E. F. Huttons, assume that their customers have the same values they have. To them it is obvious, if not axiomatic, that people invest in order to get rich. This is, after all, what motivates the members of the New York Stock Exchange, and determines what they consider "success." However, this assumption holds true only for a part of the investing public, and surely not even for the majority. They are not "financial people." They know that in order to "get rich" by investing, one has to work full time at managing money and be pretty knowledgeable about it. The local professional men, the local small businessmen, the local substantial farmers, however, have neither such time nor such knowledge; they are much too busy earning their money to have time to manage it.

This is the incongruity which the Midwestern securities firm exploits. Outwardly, it looks just like any other securities firm. It is a member of the New York Stock Exchange. But only a very small portion of its business, around one-eighth, is Stock Exchange business. It stays away from the items the big trading houses on Wall Street push the hardest: options, commodity futures, and so on, appealing instead to what it calls "the intelligent investor." It does not promise—and this is a genuine innovation among American financial service institutions—that its customers will make a fortune. It does not even want customers who trade. It wants customers who earn more money than they spend, which is typical for the successful professional, the substantial farmer, or the small-town businessman, less because their incomes are high than because their spending habits are modest. And then it appeals to their psychological need to protect their money. What this firm sells is a chance to maintain one's savings—through investment in bonds and stocks, to be sure, but also in deferred annuities, tax-sheltered partnerships, real estate trust, and so on. The "product" the firm delivers is a different one and one that no Wall Street house has ever sold before: peace of mind. And this is what really represents "value" for the "intelligent investor."

The big Wall Street houses cannot even imagine that such customers exist since they defy everything the houses believe in and hold true. This successful firm has now been widely publicized. It is on every list of large and growing Stock Exchange firms. Yet the senior people in the big firms have not yet accepted that their competitor exists, let alone that it is successful.

Behind the incongruity between actual and perceived reality, there always lies an element of intellectual arrogance, of intellectual rigor and dogmatism. "It is I, not they, who know what poor people can afford," the Japanese industrialist in effect asserted. "People behave according to economic rationality, as every good Marxist knows," as Khrushchev implied. This explains why the incongruity is so easily exploited by innovators: they are left alone and undisturbed.

Of all incongruities, that between perceived and actual reality may be the most common. Producers and suppliers almost always misconceive what it is the customer actually buys. They must assume that what represents "value" to the producer and supplier is equally "value" to the customer. To succeed in doing a job, any job, one has to believe in it and take it seriously. People who make cosmetics must believe in them; otherwise, they turn out shoddy products and soon lose their customers. People who run a hospital must believe in health care as an absolute good, or the quality of medical and patient care will deteriorate fast. And yet, no customer ever perceives himself as buying what the producer or supplier delivers. Their expectations and values are always different.

The reaction of the typical producer and supplier is then to complain that customers are "irrational" or "unwilling to pay for quality." Whenever such a complaint is heard, there is reason to assume that the values and expectations the producer or supplier holds to be real are incongruous with the actual values and expectations of customers and clients. Then there is reason to look for an opportunity for innovation that is highly specific, and carries a good chance of success.

IV

INCONGRUITY WITHIN THE RHYTHM OR
LOGIC OF A PROCESS

Twenty-five years or so ago, during the late 1950s, a pharmaceutical company salesman decided that he wanted to go into business for himself. He therefore looked for an incongruity within a process in medical practice. He found one almost immediately. One of the most common surgical operations is the operation for senile cataract in the eye. Over the years the procedure had become refined, routinized and instrumented to the point where it was conducted with the rhythm of a perfectly rehearsed dance—and with total control. But there was one point in this operation that was out of character and out of rhythm: at one phase the eye surgeon had to cut a ligament, to tie blood vessels and so risk bleeding, which then endangered the eye. This procedure was done successfully in more than 99 percent of all operations; indeed, it was not very difficult. But it greatly bothered the surgeons. It forced them to change their rhythm and induced anxiety in them. Eye surgeons, no matter how often they had done the operation, dreaded this one, quick procedure.

The pharmaceutical company salesman—his name is William Connor—found out without much research that an enzyme had been isolated in the 1890s which almost instantaneously dissolves this particular ligament. Only nobody then, sixty years earlier, had been able to store this enzyme even under refrigeration for more than a few short hours. Preservation techniques have, however, made quite a bit of progress since 1890. And so Connor, within a few months, was able by trial and error to find a preservative that gives the enzyme substantial shelf life without destroying its potency. Within a few years, every eye surgeon in the world was using Connor's patented compound. Twenty years later he sold his company, Alcon Laboratories, to one of the multinationals for a very large amount.

And another telling example:

O. M. Scott & Co. is the leader among American producers of lawn-care products: grass seed, fertilizer, pesticides, and so on. Though it is now a subsidiary of a large corporation (ITT), it attained leadership while a small independent company in fierce competition with firms many times its size, ranging from Sears, Roebuck to Dow Chemicals. Its products are good but so are those of the competition. Its leadership rests on a simple, mechanical gadget called a Spreader, a small, light-weight wheelbarrow with holes that can be set to allow the proper quantities of Scott's products to pass through in an even flow. Products for the lawn all claim to be "scientific" and are compounded on the basis of extensive tests. All prescribe in meticulous detail how much of the stuff should be applied, given soil conditions and temperatures. All try to convey to the consumer that growing a lawn is "precise," "controlled," if not "scientific." But before the Scott Spreader, no supplier of lawn-care products gave the customer a tool to control the process.

And without such a tool, there was an internal incongruity in the logic of the process that upset and frustrated customers.

Does the identification of such internal incongruity within a process rest on "intuition" and on accident? Or can it be organized and systematized?

William Connor is said to have started out by asking surgeons where they felt uncomfortable about their work. O. M. Scott grew from a tiny local seed retailer into a fair-sized national company because it asked dealers and customers what they missed in available products. Then it designed its product line around the Spreader.

The incongruity within a process, its rhythm or its logic, is not a very subtle matter. Users are always aware of it. Every eye surgeon knew about the discomfort he felt when he had to cut eye muscle—and talked about it. Every hardware-store clerk knew about the frustration of his lawn customers—and talked about it. What was lacking, however, was someone willing to listen, somebody who took seriously what everybody proclaims: That the purpose of a product or a service is to satisfy the customer. If this axiom is accepted and acted upon, using incongruity as an opportunity for innovation becomes fairly easy—and highly effective.

There is, however, one serious limitation. The incongruity is usually available only to people within a given industry or service. It is not something that somebody from the outside is likely to spot, to understand, and hence is able to exploit.

5

Source: Process Need

"Opportunity is the source of innovation" has been the leitmotif of the preceding chapters. But an old proverb says, "Necessity is the mother of invention." This chapter looks at *need* as a source of innovation, and indeed as a major innovative opportunity.

The need we shall discuss as a source of innovative opportunity is a very specific one: I call it "process need." It is not vague or general but quite concrete. Like the unexpected, or the incongruities, it exists within the process of a business, an industry, or a service. Some innovations based on process need exploit incongruities, others demographics. Indeed, process need, unlike the other sources of innovation, does not start out with an event in the environment, whether internal or external. It starts out with the job to be done. It is task-focused rather than situation-focused. It perfects a process that already exists, replaces a link that is weak, redesigns an existing old process around newly available knowledge. Sometimes it makes possible a process by supplying the "missing link."

In innovations that are based on process need, everybody in the organization always knows that the need exists. Yet usually no one does anything about it. However, when the innovation appears, it is immediately accepted as "obvious" and soon becomes "standard."

One example has been mentioned earlier in Chapter 4. It is William Connor's conversion of the enzyme that dissolves a ligament in cataract surgery of the eye from a textbook curiosity into an indispensable product. The process of cataract surgery itself was a very old one. The enzyme to perfect the process had been known for decades. The innovation was the preservative to keep the enzyme fresh under refrigeration. Once that process need had been satisfied, no eye surgeon could possibly imagine doing without Connor's compound.

Very few innovations based on process need are so sharply focused as this one, in which formulating the need right away produced the required solution. But in their essentials, most, if not all, innovations based on process need have the same elements.

Here is another example of a similar process-need innovation.

Ottmar Mergenthaler designed the linotype for typesetting in 1885. During the preceding decades, printed materials of all kinds—magazines, newspapers, books—had all been growing at an exponential rate with the spread of literacy and the development of transportation and communication. All the other elements of the printing process had already changed. There were high-speed printing presses, for instance, and paper was being made on high-speed paper machines. Only typesetting had gone unchanged from the days of Gutenberg four hundred years earlier. It remained slow and expensive manual work, requiring high skill and long years of apprenticeship. Mergenthaler, like Connor, defined what was needed: a keyboard that would make possible the mechanical selection of the right letter from the typefont; a mechanism to assemble the letters and to adjust them in a line; and—the most difficult, by the way—a mechanism to return each letter to its proper receptacle for future use. Each of these required several years of hard work and considerable ingenuity. But none required new knowledge, let alone new science. Mergenthaler's linotype became the "standard" in less than five years, despite vigorous resistance from the old craftsmen-typesetters.

In both these cases—William Connor's enzyme and the linotype machine—the process need was based on an incongruity in the process. Demographics, however, are very often an equally powerful source of process need and an opportunity for process innovation.

In 1909 or thereabouts a statistician at the Bell Telephone System projected two curves fifteen years ahead: the curve for American population growth and the curve for the number of people required as central-station operators to handle the growing volume of telephone calls. These projections showed that every American woman between age seventeen and sixty would have to work as a switchboard operator by the year 1925 or 1930 if the manual system of handling calls were to be continued. Two years later, Bell engineers had designed and put into service the first automatic switchboard.

Similarly, the present rush into robotics is largely the result of a process need caused by demographics. Most of the knowledge has been around for years. But until the consequences of the "baby bust" became apparent to major manufacturers in the industrial countries, especially in Japan and the United States, the need to replace semi-skilled assembly-line labor with machines was not felt. The Japanese are not ahead in robotics because of technical superiority; their designs have mostly come from the United States. But the Japanese had their "baby bust" four or five years earlier than America and almost ten years earlier than West Germany. It took the Japanese just as long as it did the Americans or the Germans—ten years—to realize that they were facing a labor shortage. But these ten years started in Japan a good deal sooner than in the United States, and in West Germany the ten years are still not quite over as these lines are being written.

Mergenthaler's linotype was also in large measure the result of demographic pressures. With the demand for printed materials exploding, the supply of typesetters requiring an apprenticeship of six to eight years was fast becoming inadequate, and wages for typesetters were skyrocketing. As a result, printers became conscious of the "weak link" but also willing to pay good money for a machine that replaced five very expensive craftsmen with one semi-skilled machine operator.

Incongruities and demographics may be the most common causes of a process need. But there is another category, far more difficult and risky yet in many cases of even greater importance: what is now being called program research (as contrasted with the traditional "pure research" of scientists). There is a "weak link" and it is definable, indeed, clearly seen and acutely felt. But to satisfy the process need, considerable *new knowledge* has to be produced.

Very few inventions have succeeded faster than photography. Within twenty years after its invention, it had become popular worldwide. Within twenty years or so, there were great photographers in every country; Mathew Brady's photographs of the American Civil War are still unsurpassed. By 1860, every bride had to have her photograph taken. Photography was the first Western technology to invade Japan, well before the Meiji Restoration and at a time when Japan otherwise was still firmly closed to foreigners and foreign ideas.

Amateur photographers were fully established by 1870. But the available technology made things difficult for them. Photography required heavy and fragile glass plates, which had to be lugged around and treated with extreme care. It required an equally heavy camera, long preparations before a picture could be taken, elaborate settings, and so on. Everybody knew this. Indeed, the photography magazines of the time—and photography magazines were among the first specialty mass magazines—are full of complaints about the extreme difficulty of taking photographs and of suggestions what to do. But the problems could not be solved with the science and technology available in 1870.

By the mid-1880s, however, new knowledge had become available which then enabled George Eastman, the founder of Kodak, to replace the heavy glass plates with a cellulose film weighing practically nothing and impervious even to very rough handling, and to design a light-weight camera around his film. Within ten years, Eastman Kodak had taken world leadership in photography, which it still retains.

"Program research" is often needed to convert a process from potential into reality. Again, the need must be felt, and it must be possible to identify what is needed. Then the new knowledge has to be produced. The prototype innovator for this kind of process-need innovation was Edison (see also Chapter 9). For twenty-odd years, everybody had known that there was going to be an "electric power industry." For the last five or six years of that period, it had become abundantly clear what the "missing link" was: the light bulb. Without it, there could be no electric power industry. Edison defined the new knowledge needed to convert this potential electric power industry into an actual one, went to work, and had a light bulb within two years.

Program research to convert a potential into reality has become the central methodology of the first-rate industrial research laboratory and, of course, of research for defense, for agriculture, for medicine, and for environmental protection.

Program research sounds big. To many people it means "putting a man on the moon" or finding a vaccine against polio. But its most successful applications are in small and clearly defined projects—the smaller and the more sharply focused the better. Indeed, the best example—and perhaps the best single example of successful process need–based innovation—is a very small one, the highway reflector that cut the Japanese automobile accident rate by almost two-thirds.

As late as 1965, Japan had almost no paved roads outside of the big cities. But the country was rapidly shifting to the automobile, so the government frantically paved the roads. Now automobiles could—and did—travel at high speed. But the roads were the same old ones that had been laid down by the oxcarts of the tenth century—barely wide enough for two cars to pass, full of blind corners and hidden entrances, and with junctions every few kilometers at which half a dozen roads meet at every conceivable angle. Accidents began to mount at an alarming rate, especially at night. Press, radio and TV, and the opposition parties in Parliament soon began to clamor for the government to "do something." But, of course, rebuilding the roads was out of the question; it would have taken twenty years anyhow. And a massive publicity campaign to make automobilists "drive carefully" had the result such campaigns generally have, namely, none at all.

A young Japanese, Tamon Iwasa, seized on this crisis as an innovative opportunity. He redesigned the traditional highway reflector so that the little glass beads that serve as its mirrors could be adjusted to reflect the headlights of oncoming cars from any direction onto any direction. The government rushed to install Iwasa reflectors by the hundreds of thousands. And the accident rate plummeted.

To take another example.

World War I had created a public in the United States for national and international news. Everybody was aware of this. Indeed, the newspapers and magazines of those early post–World War I years are full of discussions as to how this need could be satisfied. But the local newspaper could not do the job. Several leading publishers tried, among them *The New York Times;* none of them succeeded. Then Henry Luce identified the process need and defined what was required to satisfy it. It could not be a local publication, it had to be a national one, otherwise, there would be neither enough readers nor enough advertisers. And it could not be a daily—there was not enough news of interest to a large public. The development of the editorial format was then practically dictated by these specifications. When *Time* magazine came out as the first news magazine in the world, it was an immediate success.

These examples, and especially the Iwasa story, show that successful innovations based on process needs require five basic criteria:

— A self-contained process;
— One "weak" or "missing" link;
— A clear definition of the objective;
— That the specifications for the solution can be defined clearly;
— Widespread realization that "there ought to be a better way," that is, high receptivity.

There are, however, some important caveats.

1. The need must be *understood.* It is not enough for it to be

"felt." Otherwise one cannot define the specifications for the solution.

We have known, for instance, for several hundred years that mathematics is a problem subject in school. A small minority of students, certainly no more than one-fifth, seem to have no difficulty with mathematics and learn it easily. The rest never really learn it. It is possible, of course, to drill a very much larger percentage to pass mathematics tests. The Japanese do this through heavy emphasis on the subject. But that does not mean that Japanese children learn mathematics. They learn to pass the tests and then immediately forget mathematics. Ten years later, by the time they are in their late twenties, Japanese do just as poorly on mathematics tests as do westerners. In every generation there is a mathematics teacher of genius who somehow can make even the untalented learn, or at least learn a good deal better. But nobody has ever been able, then, to replicate what this one person does. The need is acutely felt, but we do not understand the problem. Is it a lack of native ability? Is it that we are using the wrong methods? Are there psychological and emotional problems? No one knows the answer. And without understanding the problem, we have not been able to find any solution.

2. We may even understand a process and still not have the knowledge to do the job. The preceding chapter told of the clear and understood incongruity in paper making: to find a process that is less wasteful and less uneconomical than the existing one. For a century, able people have worked on the problem. We know exactly what is needed: polymerization of the lignin molecule. It should be easy—we have polymerized many molecules that are similar. But we lack the knowledge to do it, despite a hundred years of assiduous work by well-trained people. One can only say, "Let's try something else."

3. The solution must fit the way people do the work and want to do it. Amateur photographers had no psychological investment in the complicated technology of the early photographic process. All they wanted was to get a decent photograph, as easily as possible. They were receptive, therefore, to a process that took the labor and skill out of taking pictures. Similarly, eye surgeons were interested only in an elegant, logical, bloodless process. An enzyme that gave this to them therefore satisfied their expectations and values.

But here is an example of an innovation based on a clear and substantial process need that apparently does not quite fit, and therefore has not been readily accepted.

For many years the information required by a number of professionals such as lawyers, accountants, engineers, and physicians has grown much faster than the capacity to find it. Professionals have been complaining that they have to spend more and more time hunting for information in the law library, in handbooks and textbooks, in looseleaf services, and so on. One would therefore expect a "databank" to be an immediate success. It gives the professionals immediate information through a computer program and a display terminal: court decisions for the lawyers, tax rulings for the accountants, information on drugs and poisons for the physicians. Yet these services have found it very hard to gather enough subscribers to break even. In some cases, such as Lexis, a service for lawyers, it has taken more than ten years and huge sums of money to get subscribers. The reason is probably that the databanks make it *too* easy. Professionals pride themselves on their "memory," that is, on their ability either to remember the information they need or to know where to find it. "You have to remember the court decisions you need and where to find them," is still the injunction the beginning lawyer gets from the seniors. So the databank, however helpful in the work and however much time and money it saves, goes against the very values of the professional. "What would you need *me* for if it can be looked up?" an eminent physician once said when asked by one of his patients why he did not use the service that would give him the information to check and confirm his diagnosis, and then decide which alternative method of treatment might be the best in a given case.

Opportunities for innovation based on process need can be found systematically. This is what Edison did for electricity and electronics. This is what Henry Luce did while still an undergraduate at Yale. This is what William Connor did. In fact, the area lends itself to systematic search and analysis.

But once a process need has been found, it has to be tested against the five basic criteria given above. Then, finally, the process need opportunity has to be tested also against the three constraints. Do we understand what is needed? Is the knowledge available or can it be procured within the "state of the art"? And does the solution fit, or does it violate the mores and values of the intended users?

6

Source: Industry and Market Structures

Industry and market structures sometimes last for many, many years and seem completely stable. The world aluminum industry, for instance, after one century is still led by the Pittsburgh-based Aluminum Company of America which held the original patents, and by its Canadian offspring, Alcan of Montreal. There has only been one major newcomer in the world's cigarette industry since the 1920s, the South African Rembrandt group. And in an entire century only two newcomers have emerged as leading electrical apparatus manufacturers in the world: Philips in Holland and Hitachi in Japan. Similarly no major new retail chain emerged in the United States for forty years, between the early twenties when Sears, Roebuck began to move from mail order into retail stores, and the mid-sixties when an old dime-store chain, Kresge, launched the K-Mart discount stores. Indeed, industry and market structures appear so solid that the people in an industry are likely to consider them foreordained, part of the order of nature, and certain to endure forever.

Actually, market and industry structures are quite brittle. One small scratch and they disintegrate, often fast. When this happens, every member of the industry has to act. To continue to do business as before is almost a guarantee of disaster and might well condemn a company to extinction. At the very least the company will lose its leadership position; and once lost, such leadership is almost never regained. But a change in market or industry structure is also a major opportunity for innovation.

In industry structure, a change requires entrepreneurship from every member of the industry. It requires that each one ask anew: "What is our business?" And each of the members will have to give a different, but above all a new, answer to that question.

I

THE AUTOMOBILE STORY

The automobile industry in the early years of this century grew so fast that its markets changed drastically. There were four different responses to this change, all of them successful. The early industry through 1900 had basically been a provider of a luxury product for the very rich. By then, however, it was outgrowing this narrow market with a rate of growth that doubled the industry's sales volume every three years. Yet the existing companies all still concentrated on the "carriage trade."

One response to this was the British company, Rolls-Royce, founded in 1904. The founders realized that automobiles were growing so plentiful as to become "common," and set out to build and sell an automobile which, as an early Rolls-Royce prospectus put it, would have "the cachet of royalty." They deliberately went back to earlier, already obsolete, manufacturing methods in which each car was machined by a skilled mechanic and assembled individually with hand tools. And then they promised that the car would never wear out. They designed it to be driven by a professional chauffeur trained by Rolls-Royce for the job. They restricted sales to customers of whom they approved—preferably titled ones, of course. And to make sure that no "riff-raff" bought their car, they priced the Rolls-Royce as high as a small yacht, at about forty times the annual income of a skilled mechanic or prosperous tradesman.

A few years later in Detroit, the young Henry Ford also saw that the market structure was changing and that automobiles in America were no longer a rich man's toy. His response was to design a car that could be totally mass-produced, largely by semi-skilled labor, and that could be driven by the owner and repaired by him. Contrary to legend, the 1908 Model T was not "cheap": it was priced at a little over what the world's highest-priced skilled mechanic, the American one, earned in a full year. (These days, the cheapest new car on the American market costs about one-tenth of what an unskilled assembly-line worker gets in wages and benefits in a year.) But the Model T cost one-fifth of the cheapest model then on the market and was infinitely easier to drive and to maintain.

Another American, William Crapo Durant, saw the change in market structure as an opportunity to put together a professionally managed large automobile company that would satisfy all segments of what he foresaw would be a huge "universal" market. He founded General Motors in 1905, began to buy existing automobile companies, and integrated them into a large modern business.

A little earlier, in 1899, the young Italian Giovanni Agnelli had seen that the automobile would become a military necessity, especially as a staff car for officers. He founded FIAT in Turin, which within a few years became the leading supplier of staff cars to the Italian, Russian, and Austro-Hungarian armies.

Market structures in the world automobile industry changed once again between 1960 and 1980. For forty years after World War I, the automobile industry had consisted of national suppliers dominating national markets. All one saw on Italy's roads and parking lots were Fiats and a few Alfa Romeos and Lancias; outside of Italy, these makes were fairly rare. In France, there were Renaults, Peugeots, and Citroens; in Germany, Mercedes, Opels, and the German Fords; in the United States, GM cars, Fords, and Chryslers. Then around 1960 the automobile industry all of a sudden became a "global" industry.

Different companies reacted quite differently. The Japanese, who had remained the most insular and had barely exported their cars, decided to become world exporters. Their first attempt at the U.S. market in the late sixties was a fiasco. They regrouped, thought through again what their policy should be, and redefined it as offering an American-type car with American styling, American comfort, and American performance characteristics, but smaller, with better fuel consumption, much more rigorous quality control and, above all, better customer service. And when they got a second chance with the petroleum panic of 1979, they succeeded brilliantly. The Ford Motor Company, too, decided to go "global" through a "European" strategy. Ten years later, in the mid-seventies, Ford had become a strong contender for the number one spot in Europe.

Fiat decided to become a European rather than merely an Italian company, aiming to be a strong number two in every important European country while retaining its primary position in Italy. General Motors at first decided to remain American and to retain its traditional 50 percent share of the American market, but in such a way as to reap something like 70 percent of all profits from automobile sales in North

America. And it succeeded. Ten years later, in the mid-seventies, GM shifted gears and decided to contend with Ford and Fiat for leadership in Europe—and again it succeeded. In 1983–84, GM, it would seem, decided finally to become a truly global company and to link up with a number of Japanese; first with two smaller companies, and in the end with Toyota. And Mercedes in West Germany decided on yet another strategy—again a global one—where it limited itself to narrow segments of the world market, to luxury cars, taxicabs, and buses.

All these strategies worked reasonably well. Indeed, it is impossible to say which one worked better than another. But the companies that refused to make hard choices, or refused to admit that anything much was happening, fared badly. If they survive, it is only because their respective governments will not let them go under.

One example is, of course, Chrysler. The people at Chrysler knew what was happening—everybody in the industry did. But they ducked instead of deciding. Chrysler might have chosen an "American" strategy and put all its resources into strengthening its position within the United States, still the world's largest automobile market. Or it might have merged with a strong European firm and aimed at taking third place in the world's most important automobile markets, the United States and Europe. It is known that Mercedes was seriously interested —but Chrysler was not. Instead, Chrysler frittered away its resources on make-believe. It acquired defeated "also-rans" in Europe to make itself look multinational. But this, while giving Chrysler no additional strength, drained its resources and left no money for the investment needed to give Chrysler a chance in the American market. When the day of reckoning came after the petroleum shock of 1979, Chrysler had nothing in Europe and not much more in the United States. Only the U.S. government saved it.

The story is not much different for British Leyland, once Britain's largest automobile company and a strong contender for leadership in Europe; nor for the big French automobile company, Peugeot. Both refused to face up to the fact that a decision was needed. As a result, they rapidly lost both market position and profitability. Today all three —Chrysler, British Leyland, and Peugeot—have become more or less marginal.

But the most interesting and important examples are those of much smaller companies. Every one of the world's automobile manufacturers, large or small, has had to act or face permanent eclipse. However, three small and quite marginal companies saw in this a major opportunity to innovate: Volvo, BMW, and Porsche.

Around 1960, when the automobile industry market suddenly changed, the informed betting was heavily on the disappearance of these three companies during the coming "shakeout." Instead, all three have done well and have created for themselves market niches in which they are the leaders. They have done so through an innovative strategy which, in effect, has reshaped them into different businesses. Volvo in 1965 was small, struggling and barely breaking even. For a few critical years, it did lose large amounts of money. But Volvo went to work reinventing itself, so to speak. It became an aggressive worldwide marketer—especially strong in the United States— of what one might call the "sensible" car; not very luxurious, far from low-priced, not at all fashionable, but sturdy and radiating common sense and "better value." Volvo has marketed itself as the car for professionals who do not need to demonstrate how successful they are through the car they drive, but who value being known for their "good judgment."

BMW, equally marginal in 1960 if not more so, has been equally successful, especially in countries like Italy and France. It has marketed itself as the car for "young comers," for people who want to be taken as young but who already have attained substantial success in their work and profession, people who want to demonstrate that they "know the difference" and are willing to pay for it. BMW is unashamedly a luxury car for the well-to-do, but it appeals to those among the affluent who want to appear "nonestablishment." Whereas Mercedes and Cadillac are the cars for company presidents and for heads of state, BMW is *muy macho,* and bills itself as the "ultimate driving machine."

Finally Porsche (originally a Volkswagen with extra styling) repositioned itself as *the* sports car, the one and only car for those who still do not want transportation but excitement in an automobile.

But those smaller automobile manufacturers who did not innovate and present themselves differently in what is, in effect, a different business—those who continued their established ways—have become casualties. The British MG, for instance, was thirty years ago what Porsche has now become, the sports car *par excellence.* It is almost extinct by now. And where is Citroen? Thirty years ago it was the car that had the solid innovative engineering, the sturdy construction, the

middle-class reliability. Citroen would have seemed to be ideally positioned for the market niche Volvo has taken over. But Citroen failed
to think through its business and to innovate; as a result, it has neither
product nor strategy.

II

THE OPPORTUNITY

A change in industry structure offers exceptional opportunities,
highly visible and quite predictable to outsiders. But the insiders perceive these same changes primarily as threats. The outsiders who innovate can thus become a major factor in an important industry or area
quite fast, and at relatively low risk.

Here are some examples.

In the late 1950s three young men met, almost by accident, in New
York City. Each of them worked for financial institutions, mostly Wall
Street houses. They found themselves in agreement on one point: the
securities business—unchanged since the Depression twenty years earlier—was poised for rapid structural change. They decided that this
change had to offer opportunities. So they systematically studied the
financial industry and the financial markets to find an opportunity for
newcomers with limited capital resources and practically no connections. The result was a new firm: Donaldson, Lufkin & Jenrette. Five
years after it had been started in 1959, it had become a major force on
Wall Street.

What these three young men found was that a whole new group of
customers was emerging fast: the pension fund administrators. These
new customers did not need anything that was particularly difficult to
supply, but they needed something different. And no existing firm had
organized itself to give it to them. Donaldson, Lufkin & Jenrette established a brokerage firm to focus on these new customers and to give
them the "research" they needed.

About the same time, another young man in the securities business
also realized that the industry was in the throes of structural change and
that this could offer him an opportunity to build a different securities
business of his own. The opportunity he found was "the intelligent
investor" mentioned earlier. On this, he then built what is now a big
and still fast-growing firm.

During the early or mid-sixties, the structure of American health care began to change very fast. Three young people, the oldest not quite thirty, then working as junior managers in a large Midwestern hospital, decided that this offered them an opportunity to start their own innovative business. They concluded that hospitals would increasingly need expertise in running such housekeeping services as kitchen, laundry, maintenance, and so on. They systematized the work to be done. Then they offered contracts to hospitals under which their new firm would put in its own trained people to run these services, with the fee a portion of the resultant savings. Twenty years later, this company billed almost a billion dollars of services.

The final case is that of the discounters like MCI and Sprint in the American long-distance telephone market. They were total outsiders; Sprint, for instance, was started by a railroad, the Southern Pacific. These outsiders began to look for the chink in Bell System's armor. They found it in the pricing structure of long-distance services. Until World War II, long-distance calls had been a luxury confined to government and large businesses, or to emergencies such as a death in the family. After World War II, they became commonplace. Indeed, they became the growth sector of telecommunications. But under pressure from the regulatory authorities for the various states which control telephone rates, the Bell System continued to price long-distance as a luxury, way above costs, with the profits being used to subsidize local service. To sweeten the pill, however, the Bell System gave substantial discounts to large buyers of long-distance service.

By 1970, revenues from long-distance service had come to equal those from local service and were fast outgrowing them. Still, the original price structure was maintained. And this is what the newcomers exploited. They signed up for volume service at the discount and then retailed it to smaller users, splitting the discount with them. This gave them a substantial profit while also giving their subscribers long-distance service at substantially lower cost. Ten years later, in the early eighties, the long-distance discounters handled a larger volume of calls than the entire Bell System had handled when the discounters first started.

These cases would just be anecdotes except for one fact: each of the innovators concerned *knew* that there was a major innovative opportunity in the industry. Each was reasonably sure that an innovation would succeed, and succeed with minimal risk. How could they be so sure?

III

WHEN INDUSTRY STRUCTURE CHANGES

Four near-certain, highly visible indicators of impending change in industry structure can be pinpointed.

1. The most reliable and the most easily spotted of these indicators is rapid growth of an industry. This is, in effect, what each of the above examples (but also the automobile industry examples) have in common. If an industry grows significantly faster than economy or population, it can be predicted with high probability that its structure will change drastically—at the very latest by the time it has doubled in volume. Existing practices are still highly successful, so nobody is inclined to tamper with them. Yet they are becoming obsolete. Neither the people at Citroen nor those at Bell Telephone were willing to accept this, however—which explains why "newcomers," "outsiders," or former "second-raters" could beat them in their own markets.

2. By the time an industry growing rapidly has doubled in volume, the way it perceives and services its market is likely to have become inappropriate. In particular, the ways in which the traditional leaders define and segment the market no longer reflect reality, they reflect history. Yet reports and figures still represent the traditional view of the market. This is the explanation for the success of two such different innovators as Donaldson, Lufkin & Jenrette and the Midwestern "intelligent investor" brokerage house. Each found a segment that the existing financial services institutions had not perceived and therefore did not serve adequately; the pension funds because they were too new, the "intelligent investor" because he did not fit the Wall Street stereotype.

But the hospital management story is also one of traditional aggregates no longer being adequate after a period of rapid growth. What grew in the years after World War II were the "paramedics," that is, the hospital professions: X-Ray, pathology, the medical lab, therapists of all kinds, and so on. Before World War II these had barely existed. And hospital administration itself became a profession. The traditional "housekeeping" services, which had dominated hospital operations in earlier times, thus steadily became a problem for the administrator, proving increasingly difficult and costly as hospital employees, especially the low-paid ones, began to unionize.

And the case of the book chains reported earlier (in Chapter 3) is also a story of structural change because of rapid growth. What neither the publishers nor the traditional American bookstores realized was that new customers, the "shoppers," were emerging side by side with the old customers, the traditional readers. The traditional bookstore simply did not perceive these new customers and never attempted to serve them.

But there is also the tendency if an industry grows very fast to become complacent and, above all, to try to "skim the cream." This is what the Bell System did with respect to long-distance calls. The sole result is to invite competition (on this see also Chapter 17).

Yet another example is to be found in the American art field. Before World War II, museums were considered "upper-class." After World War II, going to museums became a middle-class habit; in city after city new museums were founded. Before World War II, collecting art was something a few very rich people did. After World War II, collecting all kinds of art became increasingly popular, with thousands of people getting into the act, some of them people of fairly limited means.

One young man working in a museum saw this as an opportunity for innovation. He found it in the most unexpected place—in fact, in a place he had never heard of before, insurance. He established himself as an insurance broker specializing in art and insuring both museums and collectors. Because of his art expertise, the underwriters in the major insurance companies, who had been reluctant to insure art collections, became willing to take the risk, and at premiums up to 70 percent below those charged before. This young man now has a large insurance brokerage firm.

3. Another development that will predictably lead to sudden changes in industry structure is the convergence of technologies that hitherto were seen as distinctly separate.

One example is that of the private branch exchange (PBX), that is, the switchboard for offices and other large telephone users. Basically, all the scientific and technical work on this in the United States has been done by Bell Labs, the research arm of the Bell System. But the main beneficiaries have been a few newcomers such as ROLM Corporation. In the new PBX, two different technologies converge: telephone technology and computer technology. The PBX can be seen as a telecommunications instrument that uses a computer, or as a computer that is being used in telecommunications. Technically, the Bell System would have been perfectly capable of handling this—in fact, it has all along been a computer pioneer. In its view of the market, however, and of the user, Bell System saw the computer as something totally different and far away. While it designed and actually introduced a computer-type PBX, it never pushed it. As a result, a total newcomer has become a major competitor. In fact, ROLM, started by four young engineers, was founded to build a small computer for fighter aircraft, and only stumbled by accident into the telephone business. The Bell System now has not much more than one-third of that market, despite its technical leadership.

4. An industry is ripe for basic structural change if the way in which it does business is changing rapidly.

Thirty years ago, the overwhelming majority of American physicians practiced on their own. By 1980, only 60 percent were doing so. Now, 40 percent (and 75 percent of the younger ones) practice in a group, either in a partnership or as employees of a Health Maintenance Organization or a hospital. A few people who saw what was happening early on, around 1970, realized that it offered an opportunity for innovation. A service company could design the group's office, tell the physicians what equipment they needed, and either manage their group practice for them or train their managers.

Innovations that exploit changes in industry structure are particularly effective if the industry and its markets are dominated by one very large manufacturer or supplier, or by a very few. Even if there is no true monopoly, these large, dominant producers and suppliers, having been successful and unchallenged for many years, tend to be arrogant. At first they dismiss the newcomer as insignificant and, indeed, amateurish. But even when the newcomer takes a larger and larger share of their business, they find it hard to mobilize themselves for counteraction. It took the Bell System almost ten years before it first responded to the long-distance discounters and to the challenge from the PBX manufacturers.

Equally sluggish, however, was the response of the American producers of aspirin when the "non-aspirin aspirins"—Tylenol and Datril —first appeared (on this see also Chapter 17). Again, the innovators diagnosed an opportunity because of an impending change in industry structure, based very largely on rapid growth. There was no reason whatever why the existing aspirin manufacturers, a very small number of very large companies, could not have brought out "non-aspirin aspirin" and sold it effectively. After all, the dangers and limitations of aspirin were no secret; medical literature was full of them. Yet, for the first five or eight years, the newcomers had the market to themselves.

Similarly, the United States Postal Service did not react for many years to innovators who took away larger and larger chunks of the most profitable services. First, United Parcel Service took away ordinary parcel post; then Emery Air Freight and Federal Express took away the even more profitable delivery of urgent or high-value merchandise and letters. What made the Postal Service so vulnerable was its rapid growth. Volume grew so fast that it neglected what seemed to be minor categories, and thus practically delivered an invitation to the innovators.

Again and again when market or industry structure changes, the producers or suppliers who are today's industry leaders will be found neglecting the fastest-growing market segments. They will cling to practices that are rapidly becoming dysfunctional and obsolete. The new growth opportunities rarely fit the way the industry has "always" approached the market, been organized for it, and defines it. The innovator in this area therefore has a good chance of being left alone. For some time, the old businesses or services in the field will still be doing well serving the old market the old way. They are likely to pay little attention to the new challenge, either treating it with condescension or ignoring it altogether.

But there is one important caveat. It is absolutely essential to keep the innovation in this area simple. Complicated innovations do not work. Here is one example, the most intelligent business strategy I know of and one of the most dismal failures.

Volkswagen triggered the change which converted the automobile industry around 1960 into a global market. The Volkswagen Beetle was the first car since the Model T forty years earlier that became a truly international car. It was as ubiquitous in the United States as it was in its native Germany, and as familiar in Tanganyika as it was in the Solomon Islands. And yet Volkswagen missed the opportunity it had created itself—primarily by being *too* clever.

By 1970, ten years after its breakthrough into the world market, the Beetle was becoming obsolete in Europe. In the United States, the Beetle's second-best market, it still sold moderately well. And in Brazil, the Beetle's third-largest market, it apparently still had substantial growth ahead. Obviously, new strategy was called for.

The chief executive officer of Volkswagen proposed switching the German plants entirely to the new model, the successor to the Beetle, which the German plants would also supply to the United States market. But the continuing demand for Beetles in the United States would be satisfied out of Brazil, which would then give Volkswagen do Brasil the needed capacity to enlarge its plants and to maintain for another ten years the Beetle's leadership in the growing Brazilian market. To assure the American customers of the "German quality" that was one of the Beetle's main attractions, the critical parts such as engines and transmissions for all cars sold in North America would, however, still be made in Germany, with the finished car for the North American market then assembled in the United States.

In its way, this was the first genuinely global strategy, with different parts to be made in different countries and assembled in different places according to the needs of different markets. Had it worked, it would have been the right strategy, and a highly innovative one at that. It was killed primarily by the German labor unions. "Assembling Beetles in the United States means exporting German jobs," they said, "and we won't stand for it." But the American dealers were also doubtful about a car that was "made in Brazil," even though the critical parts would still be "made in Germany." And so Volkswagen had to give up its brilliant plan.

The result has been the loss of Volkswagen's second market, the United States. Volkswagen, and not the Japanese, should have had the small car market when small cars became all the rage after the fall of the Shah of Iran triggered the second petroleum panic. Only the Germans had no product. And when, a few years later, Brazil went into a severe economic crisis and automobile sales dropped, Volkswagen do Brasil got into difficulties. There were no export customers for the capacity it had had to build there during the seventies.

The specific reasons why Volkswagen's brilliant strategy failed—to the point where the long-term future of the company may have become problematical—are secondary. The moral of the story is that a "clever" innovative strategy always fails, particularly if it is aimed at exploiting an opportunity created by a change in industry structure. Then only the very simple, specific strategy has a chance of succeeding.

7

Source: Demographics

The unexpected; incongruities; changes in market and industry structure; and process needs—the sources of innovative opportunity discussed so far in Chapters 3 through 6—manifest themselves within a business, an industry, or a market. They may actually be symptoms of changes outside, in the economy, in society, and in knowledge. But they show up internally.

The remaining sources of innovative opportunity:

— Demographics;
— Changes in perception, meaning, and mood;
— New knowledge

are external. They are changes in the social, philosophical, political, and intellectual environment.

I

Of all external changes, demographics—defined as changes in population, its size, age structure, composition, employment, educational status, and income—are the clearest. They are unambiguous. They have the most predictable consequences.

They also have known and almost certain lead times. Anyone in the American labor force in the year 2000 is alive by now (though not necessarily living in the United States; a good many of America's workers fifteen years hence may now be children in a Mexican *pueblo,* for example). All people reaching retirement age in 2030 in the developed countries are already in the labor force, and in most cases in the occupational group in which they will stay until they retire or die. And the educational attainment of the people now in their early or mid-twenties will largely determine their career paths for another forty years.

Demographics have major impact on what will be bought, by whom, and in what quantities. American teenagers, for instance, buy a good many pairs of cheap shoes a year; they buy for fashion, not durability, and their purses are limited. The same people, ten years later, will buy very few pairs of shoes a year—a sixth as many as they bought when they were seventeen—but they will buy them for comfort and durability first and for fashion second. People in their sixties and seventies in the developed countries—that is, people in their early retirement years —form the prime travel and vacation market. Ten years later the same people are customers for retirement communities, nursing homes, and extended (and expensive) medical care. Two-earner families have more money than they have time, and spend accordingly. People who have acquired extensive schooling in their younger years, especially professional or technical schooling, will, ten to twenty years later, become customers for advanced professional training.

But people with extensive schooling are also available primarily for employment as knowledge workers. Even without competition from low-wage countries with tremendous surpluses of young people trained only for unskilled or semi-skilled manual jobs—the surge of young people in the Third World countries resulting from the drop in infant mortality after 1955—the industrially developed countries of the West and of Japan would have had to automate. Demographics alone, the combined effects of the sharp drop in birth rates and of the "educational explosion"—makes it near-certain that traditional manual blue-collar employment in manufacturing in developed countries, by the year 2010, cannot be more than one-third or less than what it was in 1970. (Though manufacturing production, as a result of automation, may be three to four times what it was then.)

All this is so obvious that no one, one should think, needs to be reminded of the importance of demographics. And indeed businessmen, economists, and politicians have always acknowledged the critical importance of population trends, movements, and dynamics. But they also believed that they did not have to pay attention to demographics in their day-to-day decisions. Population changes—whether in birth rates or mortality rates, in educational attainment, in labor force composition and participation, or in the location and movement of people —were thought to occur so slowly and over such long time spans as to be of little practical concern. Great demographic catastrophes such as the Black Death in Europe in the fourteenth century were admitted to have immediate impacts on society and economy. But otherwise, demographic changes were "secular" changes, of interest to the historian and the statistician rather than to the businessman or the administrator.

This was always a dangerous error. The massive nineteenth-century migration from Europe to the Americas, both North and South, and to Australia and New Zealand, changed the economic and political geography of the world beyond recognition. It created an abundance of entrepreneurial opportunities. It made obsolete the geopolitical concepts on which European politics and military strategies had been based for several centuries. Yet it took place in a mere fifty years, from the mid-1860s to 1914. Whoever disregarded it was likely to be left behind, and fast.

Until 1860, for instance, the House of Rothschild was the world's dominant financial power. The Rothschilds failed, however, to recognize the meaning of the transatlantic migration; only "riff-raff," they thought, would leave Europe. As a result, the Rothschilds ceased to be important around 1870. They had become merely rich individuals. It was J. P. Morgan who took over. His "secret" was to spot the transatlantic migration at its very onset, to understand immediately its significance, and to exploit it as an opportunity by establishing a worldwide bank in New York rather than in Europe, and as the medium for financing the American industries that immigrant labor was making possible. It also took only thirty years, from 1830 to 1860, to transform both western Europe and the eastern United States from rural and farm-based societies into industry-dominated big-city civilizations.

Demographic changes tended to be just as fast, just as abrupt, and to have fully as much impact, in earlier times. The belief that populations changed slowly in times past is pure myth. Or rather, static populations staying in one place for long periods of time have been the exception historically rather than the rule.*

In the twentieth century it is sheer folly to disregard demographics. The basic assumption for our time must be that populations are inherently unstable and subject to sudden sharp changes—and that they are the first environmental factor that a decision maker, whether businessman or politician, analyzes and thinks through. Few issues in this century, for instance, will be as critical to both domestic and international politics as the aging of the population in the developed countries on the

---

*Here the work of the modern French historians of civilization is definitive.

one hand and the tidal wave of young adults in the Third World on the other hand. Whatever the reasons, twentieth-century societies, both developed and developing ones, have become prone to extremely rapid and radical demographic changes, which occur without advance warning.

The most prominent American population experts called together by Franklin D. Roosevelt predicted unanimously in 1938 that the U.S. population would peak at around 140 million people in 1943 or 1944, and then slowly decline. The American population—with a minimum of immigration—now stands at 240 million. For in 1949, without the slightest advance warning, the United States kicked off a "baby boom" that for twelve years produced unprecedentedly large families, only to turn just as suddenly in 1960 into a "baby bust," producing equally unprecedented small families. The demographers of 1938 were not incompetents or fools; there was just no indication then of a "baby boom."

Twenty years later another American President, John F. Kennedy, called together a group of eminent experts to work out his Latin-American aid and development program, the "Alliance for Progress." Not one of the experts paid attention in 1961 to the precipitous drop in infant mortality which, within another fifteen years, totally changed Latin America's society and economy. The experts also all assumed, without reservation, a rural Latin America. They, too, were neither incompetents nor fools. But the drop in infant mortality in Latin America and the urbanization of society had barely begun at the time.

In 1972 and 1973, the most experienced labor force analysts in the United States still accepted without question that the participation of women would continue to decline as it had done for many years. When the "baby boomers" came on the labor market in record numbers, they worried (quite unnecessarily, as it turned out) where all the jobs for the young males would be coming from. No one asked where jobs would come from for young females—they were not supposed to need any. Ten years later the labor force participation of American women under fifty stood at 64 per cent, the highest rate ever. And there is little difference in labor force participation in this group between married and unmarried women, or between women with and without children.

These shifts are not only dazzlingly sudden. They are often mysterious and defy explanation. The drop in infant mortality in the Third World can be explained in retrospect. It was caused by a convergence

of old technologies: the public-health nurse; placing the latrine below
the well; vaccination; the wire screen outside the window; and, of very
new technologies, antibiotics and pesticides such as DDT. Yet it was
totally unpredictable. And what explains the "baby boom" or the "baby
bust"? What explains the sudden rush of American women (and of
European women as well, though with a lag of a few years) into the
labor force? And what explains the rush into the slums of Latin-American cities?

Demographic shifts in this century may be inherently unpredictable, yet they do have long lead times before impact, and lead times,
moreover, which are predictable. It will be five years before newborn
babies become kindergarten pupils and need classrooms, playgrounds,
and teachers. It will be fifteen years before they become important as
customers, and nineteen to twenty years before they join the labor
force as adults. Populations in Latin America began to grow quite rapidly as soon as infant mortality began to drop. Still the babies who did
not die did not become schoolchildren for five or six years, nor adoles-
cents looking for work for fifteen or sixteen years. And it takes at least
ten years—usually fifteen—before any change in educational attain-
ments translates itself into labor force composition and available skills.

What makes demographics such a rewarding opportunity for the
entrepreneur is precisely its neglect by decision makers, whether businessmen, public-service staffs, or governmental policymakers. They still
cling to the assumption that demographics do not change—or do not
change fast. Indeed, they reject even the plainest evidence of demographic changes. Here are some fairly typical examples.

By 1970, it had become crystal clear that the number of children in
America's schools was going to be 25 to 30 percent lower than it had
been in the 1960s, for ten or fifteen years at least. After all, children
entering kindergarten in 1970 have to be alive no later than 1965, and
the "baby bust" was well established beyond possibility of rapid reversal
by that year. Yet the schools of education in American universities flatly
refused to accept this. They considered it a law of nature, it seems, that
the number of children of school age must go up year after year. And
so they stepped up their efforts to recruit students, causing substantial
unemployment for graduates a few years later, severe pressure on
teachers' salaries, and massive closings of schools of education.

And here are two examples from my own experience. In 1957, I
published a forecast that there would be ten to twelve million college

students in the United States twenty-five years later, that is, by the mid-seventies. The figure was derived simply by putting together two demographic events that had already happened: the increase in the number of births and the increase in the percentage of young adults going to college. The forecast was absolutely correct. Yet practically every established university pooh-poohed it. Twenty years later, in 1976, I looked at the age figures and predicted that retirement age in the United States would have to be raised to seventy or eliminated altogether within ten years. The change came even faster: compulsory retirement at any age was abolished in California a year later, in 1977, and retirement before seventy for the rest of the country two years later, in 1978. The demographic figures that made this prediction practically certain were well known and published. Yet most so-called experts—government economists, labor-union economists, business economists, statisticians—dismissed the forecast as utterly absurd. "It will never happen" was the all but unanimous response. The labor unions actually proposed at the time lowering the mandatory retirement age to sixty or below.

This unwillingness, or inability, of the experts to accept demographic realities which do not conform to what they take for granted gives the entrepreneur his opportunity. The lead times are known. The events themselves have already happened. But no one accepts them as reality, let alone as opportunity. Those who defy the conventional wisdom and accept the facts—indeed, those who go actively looking for them—can therefore expect to be left alone for quite a long time. The competitors will accept demographic reality, as a rule, only when it is already about to be replaced by a new demographic change and a new demographic reality.

II

Here are some examples of successful exploitation of demographic changes.

Most of the large American universities dismissed my forecast of 10 to 12 million college students by the 1970s as preposterous. But the entrepreneurial universities took it seriously: Pace University, in New York, was one, and Golden Gate University in San Francisco another. They were just as incredulous at first, but they checked the forecast and found that it was valid, and in fact the only rational prediction. They then organized themselves for the additional student enrollment; the traditional, and especially the "prestige" universities, on the other hand, did nothing. As a result, twenty years later these brash newcomers had the students, and when enrollments decreased nationwide as a result of the "baby bust," they still kept on growing.

One American retailer who accepted the "baby boom" was then a small and undistinguished shoe chain, Melville. In the early 1960s just before the first cohorts of the "baby boom" reached adolescence, Melville directed itself to this new market. It created new and different stores specifically for teenagers. It redesigned its merchandise. It advertised and promoted to the sixteen- and seventeen-year-olds. And it went beyond footwear into clothing for teenagers, both female and male. As a result, Melville became one of the fastest-growing and most profitable retailers in America. Ten years later other retailers caught on and began to cater to teenagers—just as the center of demographic gravity started to shift away from them and toward "young adults," twenty to twenty-five years old. By then Melville was already shifting its own focus to that new dominant age cohort.

The scholars on Latin America whom President Kennedy brought together to advise him on the Alliance for Progress in 1961 did not see Latin America's urbanization. But one business, the American retail chain Sears, Roebuck, had seen it several years earlier—not by poring over statistics but by going out and looking at customers in Mexico City and Lima, São Paulo and Bogotá. As a result, Sears in the mid-fifties began to build American-type department stores in major Latin-American cities, designed for a new urban middle class which, while not "rich," was part of the money economy and had middle-class aspirations. Sears became the leading retailer in Latin America within a few years.

And here are two examples of exploiting demographics to innovate in building a highly productive labor force. The expansion of New York's Citibank is largely based on its early realization of the movement of young, highly educated and highly ambitious women into the work force. Most large American employers considered these women a "problem" as late as 1980; many still do. Citibank, almost alone among large employers, saw in them an opportunity. It aggressively recruited them during the 1970s, trained them, and sent them out all over the country as lending officers. These ambitious young women very largely made Citibank into the nation's leading, and its first truly "national" bank. At the same time, a few savings and loan associations (not an industry noted for innovation or venturing) realized that older married women who had earlier dropped out of the labor force when their children were small make high-grade employees when brought back as permanent part-time workers. "Everybody knew" that part-timers are "temporary," and that women who have once left the labor force never come back into it; both were perfectly sensible rules in earlier times. But demographics made them obsolete. The willingness to accept this fact—and again such willingness stemmed not from reading statistics but from going out and looking—has given the savings and loan associations an exceptionally loyal, exceptionally productive work force, particularly in California.

The success of Club Méditerranée in the travel and resort business is squarely the result of exploiting demographic changes: the emergence of large numbers of young adults in Europe and the United States who are affluent and educated but only one generation away from working-class origins. Still quite unsure of themselves, still not self-confident as tourists, they are eager to have somebody with the know-how to organize their vacations, their travel, their fun—and yet they are not really comfortable either with their working-class parents or with older, middle-class people. Thus, they are ready-made customers for a new and "exotic" version of the old teenage hangout.

III

Analysis of demographic changes begins with population figures. But absolute population is the least significant number. Age distribution is far more important, for instance. In the 1960s, it was the rapid increase in the number of young people in most non-Communist developed countries that proved significant (the one notable exception was Great Britain, where the "baby boom" was short-lived). In the 1980s and even more in the 1990s, it will be the drop in the number of young people, the steady increase in the number of early middle-age people (up to forty) and the very rapid increase in the number of old people (seventy and over). What opportunities do these developments offer? What are the values and the expectations, the needs and wants of these various age groups?

The number of traditional college students cannot increase. The most one can hope for is that it will not fall, that the percentage of eighteen- and nineteen-year-olds who stay in school beyond secondary education will increase sufficiently to offset the decline in the total number. But with the increase in the number of people in their mid-thirties and forties who have received a college degree earlier, there are going to be large numbers of highly schooled people who want advanced professional training and retraining, whether as doctors, lawyers, architects, engineers, executives, or teachers. What do these people look for? What do they need? How can they pay? What does the traditional university have to do to attract and satisfy such very different students? And, finally, what are the wants, needs, values of the elderly? Is there indeed any one "older group," or are there rather several, each with different expectations, needs, values, satisfactions?

Particularly important in age distribution—and with the highest predictive value—are changes in the center of population gravity, that is, in the age group which at any given time constitutes both the largest and the fastest-growing age cohort in the population.

At the end of the Eisenhower presidency, in the late fifties, the center of population gravity in the United States was at its highest point in history. But a violent shift within a few years was bound to take place. As a result of the "baby boom," the center of American population gravity was going to drop so sharply by 1965 as to bring it to the lowest point since the early days of the Republic, to around sixteen or seventeen. It was predictable—and indeed predicted by anyone who took demographics seriously and looked at the figures—that there would be a drastic change in mood and values. The "youth rebellion" of the sixties was mainly a shift of the spotlight to what has always been typical adolescent behavior. In earlier days, with the center of population gravity in the late twenties or early thirties, age groups that are notoriously ultra-conservative, adolescent behavior was dismissed as "Boys will be boys" (and "Girls will be girls"). In the sixties it suddenly became the representative behavior.

But when everybody was talking of a "permanent shift in values" or of a "greening of America," the age pendulum had already swung back, and violently so. By 1969, the first effects of the "baby bust" were already discernible, and not only in the statistics. 1974 or 1975 would be the last year in which the sixteen- and seventeen-year-olds would constitute the center of population gravity. After that, the center would rapidly move up: by the early 1980s it would be in the high twenties again. And with this shift would come a change in what would be considered "representative" behavior. The teenagers would, of course, continue to behave like teenagers. But that would again be dismissed as the way teenagers behave rather than as the constitutive values and behavior of society. And so one could predict with near-certainty, for instance (and some of us did predict it), that by the mid-seventies the college campuses would cease to be "activist" and "rebellious," and college students would again be concerned with grades and jobs; but also that the overwhelming majority of the "dropouts" of 1968 would, ten years later, have become the "upward-mobile professionals" concerned with careers, advancement, tax shelters, and stock options.

Segmentation by educational attainment may be equally important; indeed, for some purposes, it may be more important (e.g., selling encyclopedias, continuing professional education, but also vacation travel). Then there is labor force participation and occupational segmentation. Finally there is income distribution, and especially distribution of disposable and discretionary income. What happens, for instance, to the propensity to save in the two-earner family?

Actually, most of the answers are available. They are the stuff of market research. All that is needed is the willingness to ask the questions.

But more than poring over statistics is involved. To be sure, statistics are the starting point. They were what got Melville to ask what opportunities the jump in teenagers offered a fashion retailer, or what got the top management at Sears, Roebuck to look upon Latin America as a potential market. But then the managements of these companies—or the administrators of metropolitan big-city universities such as Pace in New York and Golden Gate in San Francisco—went out into the field to look and listen.

This is literally how Sears, Roebuck decided to go into Latin America. Sears's chairman, Robert E. Wood, read in the early 1950s that Mexico City and São Paulo were expected to outgrow all U.S. cities by the year 1975. This so intrigued him that he went himself to look at the major cities in Latin America. He spent a week in each of them— Mexico City, Guadalajara, Bogotá, Lima, Santiago, Rio, São Paulo— walking around, looking at stores (he was appalled by what he saw), and studying traffic patterns. Then he knew what customers to aim at, what kind of stores to build, where to put the stores, and what merchandise to stock them with.

Similarly, the founders of Club Méditerranée looked at the customers of package tours, talked to them and listened to them, before they built their first vacation resort. And the two young men who turned Melville Shoe from a dowdy, undistinguished shoe chain (one among many) into the fastest-growing popular fashion retailer in America similarly spent weeks and months in shopping centers, looking at customers, listening to them, exploring their values. They studied the way young people shopped, what kind of environment they liked (do teen-age boys and girls, for instance, shop in the same place for shoes or do they want to have separate stores?), and what they considered "value" in the merchandise they bought.

Thus, for those genuinely willing to go out into the field, to look and to listen, changing demographics is both a highly productive and a highly dependable innovative opportunity.

8

Source: Changes in Perception

I

"THE GLASS IS HALF FULL"

In mathematics there is no difference between "The glass is half full" and "The glass is half empty." But the meaning of these two statements is totally different, and so are their consequences. If general perception changes from seeing the glass as "half full" to seeing it as "half empty," there are major innovative opportunities.

Here are a few examples of such changes in perception and of the innovative opportunities they opened up—in business, in politics, in education, and elsewhere.

1. All factual evidence shows that the last twenty years, the years since the early 1960s, have been years of unprecedented advance and improvement in the health of Americans. Whether we look at mortality rates for newborn babies or survival rates for the very old, at occurrence of cancers (other than lung cancer) or cure rates for cancer, and so on, all indicators of physical health and functioning have been moving upward at a good clip. And yet the nation is gripped by collective hypochondria. Never before has there been so much concern with health, and so much fear. Suddenly everything seems to cause cancer or degenerative heart disease or premature loss of memory. The glass is clearly "half empty." What we see now are not the great improvements in health and functioning, but that we are as far away from immortality as ever before and have made no progress toward it. In fact, it can be argued that if there is any real deterioration in American health during the last twenty years it lies precisely in the extreme concern with health and fitness, and the obsession with getting old, with losing fitness, with degenerating into long-term illness or senility.

Twenty-five years ago, even minor improvements in the nation's health were seen as major steps forward. Now, even major improvements are barely paid attention to.

Whatever the causes for this change in perception, it has created substantial innovative opportunities. It created, for instance, a market for new health-care magazines: one of them, *American Health,* reached a circulation of a million within two years. It created the opportunity for a substantial number of new and innovative businesses to exploit the fear of traditional foods causing irreparable damage. A firm in Boulder, Colorado, named Celestial Seasonings was started by one of the "flower children" of the late sixties picking herbs in the mountains, packaging them, and peddling them on the street. Fifteen years later, Celestial Seasonings was taking in several hundred million dollars in sales each year and was sold for more than $20 million to a very large food-processing company. And there are highly profitable chains of health-food stores. Jogging equipment has also become big business, and the fastest-growing new business in 1983 in the United States was a company making indoor exercise equipment.

2. Traditionally, the way people feed themselves was very largely a matter of income group and class. Ordinary people "ate"; the rich "dined." This perception has changed within the last twenty years. Now the same people both "eat" and "dine." One trend is toward "feeding," which means getting down the necessary means of sustenance, in the easiest and simplest possible way: convenience foods, TV dinners, McDonald's hamburgers or Kentucky Fried Chicken, and so on. But then the same consumers have also become gourmet cooks. TV programs on gourmet cooking are highly popular and achieve high ratings; gourmet cookbooks have become mass-market best-sellers; whole new chains of gourmet food stores have opened. Finally, traditional supermarkets, while doing 90 percent of their business in foods for "feeding," have opened "gourmet boutiques" which in many cases are far more profitable than their ordinary processed-food business. This new perception is by no means confined to the United States. In West Germany, a young woman physician said to me recently: "Wir essen sechs Tage in der Woche, aber einen Tag wollen wir doch richtig speisen (We feed six days, but one day a week we like to dine)." Not so long ago, "essen" was what ordinary people did seven days a week, and "speisen" what the elite, the rich and the aristocracy, did, seven days a week.

3. If anyone around 1960, in the waning days of the Eisenhower

administration and the beginning of the Kennedy presidency, had predicted the gains the American black would make in the next ten or fifteen years, he would have been dismissed as an unrealistic visionary, if not insane Even predicting half the gains that those ten or fifteen years actually registered for the American black would have been considered hopelessly optimistic. Never in recorded history has there been a greater change in the status of a social group within a shorter time. At the beginning of those years, black participation in higher education beyond high school was around one-fifth that of whites. By the early seventies, it was equal to that of whites and ahead of that of a good many white ethnic groups. The same rate of advance occurred in employment, in incomes, and especially in entrance to professional and managerial occupations. Anyone granted twelve or fifteen years ago an advance look would have considered the "negro problem" in America to be solved, or at least pretty far along the way toward solution.

But what a large part of the American black population actually sees today in the mid-eighties is not that the glass has become "half full" but that it is still "half empty." In fact, frustration, anger, and alienation have increased rather than decreased for a substantial fraction of the American blacks. They do not see the achievements of two-thirds of the blacks who have moved into the middle class, economically and socially, but the failure of the remaining one-third to advance. What they see is not how fast things have been moving, but how much still remains to be done—how slow and how difficult the going still is. The old allies of the American blacks, the white liberals—the labor unions, the Jewish community, or academia—see the advances. They see that the glass has become "half full." This then has led to a basic split between the blacks and the liberal groups which, of course, only makes the blacks feel even more certain that the glass is "half empty."

The white liberal, however, has come to feel that the blacks increasingly are no longer "deprived," no longer entitled to special treatment such as reverse discrimination, no longer in need of special allowances and priority in employment, in promotion, and so on. This became the opportunity for a new kind of black leader, the Reverend Jesse Jackson. Historically, for almost a hundred years—from Booker T. Washington around the turn of the century through Walter White in the New Deal days until Martin Luther King, Jr., during the presidencies of John Kennedy and Lyndon Johnson—a black could become leader of his community only by proving his ability to get the support of white liberals. It was the one way to obtain enough political strength to make significant gains for American blacks. Jesse Jackson saw that the change in perception that now divides American blacks from their old allies and comrades-in-arms, white liberals, is an innovative opportunity to create a totally different kind of black leadership, one based on vocal enmity to the white liberals and even all-out attack on them. In the past, to have sounded as anti-liberal, anti-union, and anti-Jewish as Jackson has done would have been political suicide. Within a few short weeks in 1984, it made Jackson the undisputed leader of the American black community.

4. American feminists today consider the 1930s and 1940s the darkest of dark ages, with women denied any role in society. Factually, nothing could be more absurd. The America of the 1930s and 1940s was dominated by female stars of the first magnitude. There was Eleanor Roosevelt, the first wife of an American President to establish for herself a major role as a conscience, and as the voice of principle and of compassion which no American male in our history has equaled. Her friend, Frances Perkins, was the first woman in an American cabinet as Secretary of Labor, and the strongest, most effective member of President Roosevelt's cabinet altogether. Anna Rosenberg was the first woman to become a senior executive of a very big corporation as personnel vice-president of R. H. Macy, then the country's biggest retailer; and later on, during the Korean War, she became Assistant Secretary of Defense for manpower and the "boss" of the generals. There were any number of prominent and strong women as university and college presidents, each a national figure. The leading playwrights, Clare Booth Luce and Lillian Hellman, were both women—and Clare Luce then became a major political figure, a member of Congress from Connecticut, and ambassador to Italy. The most publicized medical advance of the period was the work of a woman. Helen Taussig developed the first successful surgery of the living heart, the "blue baby" operation, which saved countless children all over the world and ushered in the age of cardiac surgery, leading directly to the heart transplant and the by-pass operation. And there was Marian Anderson, the black singer and the first black to enter every American living room through the radio, touching the hearts and consciences of millions of Americans as no black before her had done and none would do again until Martin Luther King, Jr., a quarter century later. The list could be continued indefinitely.

These were very proud women, conscious of their achievements, their prominence, their importance. Yet they did not see themselves as "role models." They saw themselves not as women but as individuals. They did not consider themselves as "representative" but as exceptional.

How the change occurred, and why, I leave to future historians to explain. But when it happened around 1970, these great women leaders became in effect "non-persons" for their feminist successors. Now the woman who is not in the labor force, and not working in an occupation traditionally considered "male," is seen as unrepresentative and as the exception.

This was noted as an opportunity by a few businesses, in particular, Citibank (cf. Chapter 7). It was not seen at all, however, by the very industries in which women had long been accepted as professionals and executives, such as department stores, advertising agencies, magazine or book publishers. These traditional employers of professional and managerial women actually today have fewer women in major positions than they had thirty or forty years ago. Citibank, by contrast, was exceedingly *macho*—which may be one reason why it realized there had been a change. It saw in the new perception women had of themselves a major opportunity to court exceptionally able, exceptionally ambitious, exceptionally striving women; to recruit them; and to hold them. And it could do so without competition from the traditional recruiters of career women. In exploiting a change in perception, innovators, as we have seen, can usually count on having the field to themselves for quite a long time.

5. A much older case, one from the early 1950s, shows a similar exploitation of a change in perception. Around 1950, the American population began to describe itself overwhelmingly as being "middle-class," and to do so regardless, almost, of income or occupation. Clearly, Americans had changed their perception of their own social position. But what did the change mean? One advertising executive, William Benton (later senator from Connecticut), went out and asked people what the words "middle class" meant to them. The results were unambiguous: "middle class" in contrast to "working class" means believing in the ability of one's children to rise through performance in school. Benton thereupon bought up the *Encyclopedia Britannica* company and started peddling the *Encyclopedia,* mostly through high school teachers, to parents whose children were the first generation in the family to attend high school. "If you want to be "middle-class," the

salesman said in effect, "your child has to have the *Encyclopedia Britannica* to do well in school." Within three years Benton had turned the almost-dying company around. And ten years later the company began to apply exactly the same strategy in Japan for the same reasons and with the same success.

6. Unexpected success or unexpected failure is often an indication of a change in perception and meaning. Chapter 3 told how the phoenix of the Thunderbird rose from the ashes of the Edsel. What the Ford Motor Company found when it searched for an explanation of the failure of the Edsel was a change in perception. The automobile market, which only a few short years earlier had been segmented by income groups, was now seen by the customers as segmented by "lifestyles."

When a change in perception takes place, the facts do not change. Their meaning does. The meaning changes from "The glass is half full" to "The glass is half empty." The meaning changes from seeing oneself as "working-class" and therefore born into one's "station in life," to seeing oneself as "middle-class" and therefore very much in command of one's social position and economic opportunities. This change can come very fast. It probably did not take much longer than a decade for the majority of the American population to change from considering themselves "working-class" to considering themselves "middle-class."

Economics do not necessarily dictate such changes; in fact, they may be irrelevant. In terms of income distribution, Great Britain is a more egalitarian country than the United States. And yet almost 70 percent of the British population still consider themselves "working-class," even though at least two-thirds of the British population are above "working-class" income by economic criteria alone, and close to half are above the "lower middle class" as well. What determines whether the glass is "half full" or "half empty" is mood rather than facts. It results from experiences that might be called "existential." That the American blacks feel "The glass is half empty" has as much to do with unhealed wounds of past centuries as with anything in present American society. That a majority of the English feel themselves to be "working-class" is still largely a legacy of the nineteenth-century chasm between "church" and "chapel." And the American health hypochondria expresses far more American values, such as the worship of youth, than anything in the health statistics.

Whether sociologists or economists can explain the perceptional phenomenon is irrelevant. It remains a fact. Very often it cannot be quantified; or rather, by the time it can be quantified, it is too late to serve as an opportunity for innovation. But it is not exotic or intangible. It is concrete: it can be defined, tested, and above all exploited.

II

THE PROBLEM OF TIMING

Executives and administrators admit the potency of perception-based innovation. But they tend to shy away from it as "not practical." They consider the perception-based innovator as weird or just a crackpot. But there is nothing weird about the *Encyclopedia Britannica*, about the Ford Thunderbird or Celestial Seasonings. Of course, successful innovators in any field tend to be close to the field in which they innovate. But the only thing that sets them apart is their being alert to opportunity.

One of the foremost of today's gourmet magazines was launched by a young man who started out as food editor of an airlines magazine. He became alert to the change in perception when he read in the same issue of a Sunday paper three contradictory stories. The first said that prepared meals such as frozen dinners, TV dinners, and Kentucky Fried Chicken accounted for more than half of all meals consumed in the United States and were expected to account for three-quarters within a few years. The second said that a TV program on gourmet cooking was receiving one of the highest audience ratings. And the third that a gourmet cookbook in its paperback edition, that is, an edition for the masses, had mounted to the top of the best-seller lists. These apparent contradictions made him ask, What's going on here? A year later he started a gourmet magazine quite different from any that had been on the market before.

Citibank became conscious of the opportunity offered by the moving of women into the work force when its college recruiters reported that they could no longer carry out their instructions, which were to hire the best male business school students in finance and marketing. The best students in these fields, they reported, were increasingly women. College recruiters in many other companies, including quite a few banks, told their managements the same story at that time. In response, most of them were urged, "Just try harder to get the top-flight men." At Citibank, top management saw the change as an opportunity and acted on it.

All these examples, however, also show the critical problem in perception-based innovation: timing. If Ford had waited only one year after the fiasco of the Edsel, it might have lost the "lifestyle" market to GM's Pontiac. If Citibank had not been the first one to recruit women MBAs, it would not have become the preferred employer for the best and most ambitious of the young women aiming to make a career in business.

Yet there is nothing more dangerous than to be premature in exploiting a change in perception. In the first place, a good many of what look like changes in perception turn out to be short-lived fads. They are gone within a year or two. And it is not always apparent which is fad and which is true change. The kids playing computer games were a fad. Companies which, like Atari, saw in them a change in perception lasted one or two years—and then became casualties. Their fathers going in for home computers represented a genuine change, however. It is, furthermore, almost impossible to predict what the consequences of such a change in perception will be. One good example are the consequences of the student rebellions in France, Japan, West Germany, and the United States. Everyone in the late 1960s was quite sure that these would have permanent and profound consequences. But what are they? As far as the universities are concerned, the student rebellions seem to have had absolutely no lasting impact. And who would have expected that, fifteen years later, the rebellious students of 1968 would have become the "Yuppies" to whom Senator Hart appealed in the 1984 American primaries, the young, upward-mobile professionals, ultra-materialistic, job conscious, and maneuvering for their next promotion? There are actually far fewer "dropouts" around these days than there used to be—the only difference is that the media pay attention to them. Can the emergence of homosexuals and lesbians into the limelight be explained by the student rebellion? These were certainly not the results the students themselves in 1968, nor any of the observers and pundits of those days, could possibly have predicted.

And yet, timing is of the essence. In exploiting changes in perception, "creative imitation" (described in Chapter 17) does not work. One has to be first. But precisely because it is so uncertain whether a change in perception is a fad or permanent, and what the consequences really are, perception-based innovation has to start small and be very specific.

9

Source: New Knowledge

Knowledge-based innovation is the "super-star" of entrepreneurship. It gets the publicity. It gets the money. It is what people normally mean when they talk of innovation. Of course, not all knowledge-based innovations are important. Some are truly trivial. But amongst the history-making innovations, knowledge-based innovations rank high. The knowledge, however, is not necessarily scientific or technical. Social innovations based on knowledge can have equal or even greater impact.

Knowledge-based innovation differs from all other innovations in its basic characteristics: time span, casualty rate, predictability, and in the challenges it poses to the entrepreneur. And like most "super-stars," knowledge-based innovation is temperamental, capricious, and hard to manage.

I

THE CHARACTERISTICS OF
KNOWLEDGE-BASED INNOVATION

Knowledge-based innovation has the longest lead time of all innovations. There is, first, a long time span between the emergence of new knowledge and its becoming applicable to technology. And then there is another long period before the new technology turns into products, processes, or services in the marketplace.

Between 1907 and 1910, the biochemist Paul Ehrlich developed the theory of chemotherapy, the control of bacterial microorganisms through chemical compounds. He himself developed the first antibacterial drug, Salvarsan, for the control of syphilis. The sulfa drugs which are the application of Ehrlich's chemotherapy to the control of a broad spectrum of bacterial diseases came on the market after 1936, twenty-five years later.

Rudolph Diesel designed the engine which bears his name in 1897. Everyone at once realized that it was a major innovation. Yet for many years there were few practical applications. Then in 1935 an American, Charles Kettering, totally redesigned Diesel's engine, rendering it capable of being used as the propulsion unit in a wide variety of ships, in locomotives, in trucks, buses, and passenger cars.

A number of knowledges came together to make possible the computer. The earliest was the binary theorem, a mathematical theory going back to the seventeenth century that enables all numbers to be expressed by two numbers only: one and zero. It was applied to a calculating machine by Charles Babbage in the first half of the nineteenth century. In 1890, Hermann Hollerith invented the punchcard, going back to an invention by the early nineteenth-century Frenchman J-M. Jacquard. The punchcard makes it possible to convert numbers into "instructions." In 1906 an American, Lee de Forest, invented the audion tube, and with it created electronics. Then, between 1910 and 1913, Bertrand Russell and Alfred North Whitehead, in their *Principia Mathematica,* created symbolic logic, which enables us to express all logical concepts as numbers. Finally, during World War I, the concepts of programming and feedback were developed, primarily for the purposes of antiaircraft gunnery. By 1918, in other words, all the knowledge needed to develop the computer was available. The first computer became operational in 1946.

A Ford Motor Company manufacturing executive coined the word "automation" in 1951 and described in detail the entire manufacturing process automation would require. "Robotics" and factory automation were widely talked about for twenty-five years, but nothing really happened for a long time. Nissan and Toyota in Japan did not introduce robots into their plants until 1978. In the early eighties, General Electric built an automated locomotive plant in Erie, Pennsylvania. General Motors then began to automate several of its engine and accessory plants. Early in 1985, Volkswagen began to operate its "Hall 54" as an almost completely automated manufacturing installation.

Buckminster Fuller, who called himself a geometer and who was part mathematician and part philosopher, applied the mathematics of topology to the design of what he called the "Dymaxion House," a term he chose because he liked the sound of it. The Dymaxion House com-

bines the greatest possible living space with the smallest possible surface. It therefore has optimal insulation, optimal heating and cooling,
and superb acoustics. It also can be built with lightweight materials,
requires no foundation and a minimum of suspension, and can still
withstand an earthquake or the fiercest gale. Around 1940, Fuller put
a Dymaxion House on the campus of a small New England college. And
there it stayed. Very few Dymaxion Houses have been built—Americans, it seems, do not like to live in circular homes. But around 1965,
Dymaxion structures began to be put up in the Arctic and Antarctic
where conventional buildings are impractical, expensive, and difficult
to erect. Since then they have increasingly been used for large structures such as auditoriums, concert tents, sports arenas, and so on.

Only major external crises can shorten this lead time. De Forest's
audion tube, invented in 1906, would have made radio possible almost
immediately, but it would still not have been on the market until the
late 1930s or so had not World War I forced governments, and especially the American government, to push the development of wireless
transmission of sounds. Field telephones connected by wires were
simply too unreliable, and wireless telegraphy was confined to dots
and dashes. And so, radio came on the market early in the 1920s, only
fifteen years after the emergence of the knowledge on which it is
based.

Similarly, penicillin would probably not have been developed until
the 1950s or so but for World War II. Alexander Fleming found the
bacteria-killing mold, penicillium, in the mid-twenties. Howard Florey,
an English biochemist, began to work on it ten years later. But it was
World War II that forced the early introduction of penicillin. The need
to have a potent drug to fight infections led the British government to
push Florey's research: English soldiers were made available to him as
guinea pigs wherever they fought. The computer, too, would probably
have waited for the discovery of the transistor by Bell Lab physicists in
1947 had not World War II led the American government to push
computer research and to invest large resources of men and money in
the work.

The long lead time for knowledge-based innovations is by no means
confined to science or technology. It applies equally to innovations that
are based on nonscientific and nontechnological knowledge.

The comte de Saint-Simon developed the theory of the entrepreneurial bank, the purposeful use of capital to generate economic

development, right after the Napoleonic wars. Until then bankers were moneylenders who lent against "security" (e.g., the taxing power of a prince). Saint-Simon's banker was to "invest," that is, to create new wealth-producing capacity. Saint-Simon had extraordinary influence in his time, and a popular cult developed around his memory and his ideas after his death in 1826. Yet it was not until 1852 that two disciples, the brothers Jacob and Isaac Pereire, established the first entrepreneurial bank, the Crédit Mobilier, and with it ushered in what we now call finance capitalism.

Similarly, many of the elements needed for what we now call management were available right after World War I. Indeed, in 1923, Herbert Hoover, soon to be President of the United States, and Thomas Masaryk, founder and president of Czechoslovakia, convened the first International Management Congress in Prague. At the same time a few large companies here and there, especially DuPont and General Motors in the United States, began to reorganize themselves around the new management concepts. In the next decade a few "true believers," especially an Englishman, Lyndall Urwick, the founder of the first management consulting firm which still bears his name, began to write on management. Yet it was not until my *Concept of the Corporation* (1946) and *Practice of Management* (1954) were published that management become a discipline accessible to managers all over the world. Until then each student or practitioner of "management" focused on a separate area; Urwick on organization, others on the management of people, and so on. My books codified it, organized it, systematized it. Within a few years, management became a worldwide force.

Today, we experience a similar lead time in respect to learning theory. The scientific study of learning began around 1890 with Wilhelm Wundt in Germany and William James in the United States. After World War II, two Americans—B. F. Skinner and Jerome Bruner, both at Harvard—developed and tested basic theories of learning, Skinner specializing in behavior and Bruner in cognition. Yet only now is learning theory beginning to become a factor in our schools. Perhaps the time has come for an entrepreneur to start schools based on what we know about learning, rather than on the old wives' tales about it that have been handed down through the ages.

In other words, the lead time for knowledge to become applicable technology and begin to be accepted on the market is between twenty-five and thirty-five years.

This has not changed much throughout recorded history. It is widely believed that scientific discoveries turn much faster in our day than ever before into technology, products, and processes. But this is largely illusion. Around 1250 the Englishman Roger Bacon, a Franciscan monk, showed that refraction defects of the eye could be corrected with eyeglasses. This was incompatible with what everybody then knew: the "infallible" authority of the Middle Ages Galen, the great medical scientist, had "proven conclusively" that it could not be done. Roger Bacon lived and worked on the extreme edges of the civilized world, in the wilds of northern Yorkshire. Yet a mural, painted thirty years later in the Palace of the Popes in Avignon (where it can still be seen), shows elderly cardinals wearing reading glasses; and ten years later, miniatures show elderly courtiers in the Sultan's Palace in Cairo also in glasses. The mill race, which was the first true "automation," was developed to grind grain by the Benedictine monks in northern Europe around the year 1000; within thirty years it had spread all over Europe. Gutenberg's invention of movable type and the woodcut both followed within thirty years of the West's learning of Chinese printing.

The lead time for knowledge to become knowledge-based innovation seems to be inherent in the nature of knowledge. We do not know why. But perhaps it is not pure coincidence that the same lead time applies to new scientific theory. Thomas Kuhn, in his path-breaking book *The Structure of Scientific Revolutions* (1962), showed that it takes about thirty years before a new scientific theory becomes a new paradigm—a new statement that scientists pay attention to and use in their own work.

CONVERGENCES

The second characteristic of knowledge-based innovations—and a truly unique one—is that they are almost never based on one factor but on the convergence of several different kinds of knowledge, not all of them scientific or technological.

Few knowledge-based innovations in this century have benefited humanity more than the hybridization of seeds and livestock. It enables the earth to feed a much larger population than anyone would have thought possible fifty years ago. The first successful new seed was hybrid corn. It was produced after twenty years of hard work by Henry C.

Wallace, the publisher of a farm newspaper in Iowa, and later U.S. Secretary of Agriculture under Harding and Coolidge—the only holder of this office, perhaps, who deserves to be remembered for anything other than giving away money. Hybrid corn has two knowledge roots. One was the work of the Michigan plant breeder William J. Beal, who around 1880 discovered hybrid vigor. The other was the rediscovery of Mendel's genetics by the Dutch biologist Hugo de Vries. The two men did not know of one another. Their work was totally different both in intent and content. But only by pulling it together could hybrid corn be developed.

The Wright Brothers' airplane also had two knowledge roots. One was the gasoline engine, designed in the mid-1880s to power the first automobiles built by Karl Benz and Gottfried Daimler, respectively. The other one was mathematical: aerodynamics, developed primarily in experiments with gliders. Each was developed quite independently. It was only when the two came together that the airplane became possible.

The computer, as already noted, required the convergence of no less than five different knowledges: a scientific invention, the audion tube; a major mathematical discovery, the binary theorem; a new logic; the design concept of the punchcard; and the concepts of program and feedback. Until all these were available, no computer could have been built. Charles Babbage, the English mathematician, is often called the "father of the computer." What kept Babbage from building a computer, it is argued, was only the unavailability of the proper metals and of electric power at his time. But this is a misunderstanding. Even if Babbage had had the proper materials, he could at best have built the mechanical calculator that we now call a cash register. Without the logic, the design concept of the punchcard, and the concept of program and feedback, none of which Babbage possessed, he could only imagine a computer.

The Brothers Pereire founded the first entrepreneurial bank in 1852. It failed within a few years because they had only one knowledge base and the entrepreneurial bank needs two. They had a theory of creative finance that enabled them to be brilliant venture capitalists. But they lacked the systematic knowledge of banking which was developed at exactly the same time across the Channel by the British, and codified in Walter Bagehot's classic, *Lombard Street*.

After their failure in the early 1860s, three young men independently picked up where the Brothers Pereire had left off, added the knowledge base of banking to the venture capital concept, and succeeded. The first was J. P. Morgan, who had been trained in London but had also carefully studied the Pereires' Crédit Mobilier. He founded the most successful entrepreneurial bank of the nineteenth century in New York in 1865. The second one, across the Rhine, was the young German Georg Siemens, who founded what he called the "Universal Bank," by which he meant a bank that was both a deposit bank on the British model and an entrepreneurial bank on the Pereires' model. And in remote Tokyo, another young man, Shibusawa Eichii, who had been one of the first Japanese to travel to Europe to study banking first-hand, and had spent time both in Paris and in London's Lombard Street, became one of the founders of the modern Japanese economy by establishing a Japanese version of the Universal Bank. Both Siemens's Deutsche Bank and Shibusawa's Daichi Bank are still the largest banks of their respective countries.

The first man to envisage the modern newspaper was an American, James Gordon Bennett, who founded the *New York Herald*. Bennett fully understood the problems: A newspaper had to have enough income to be editorially independent and yet be cheap enough to have mass circulation. Earlier newspapers either got their income by selling their independence and becoming the lackeys and paid propagandists of a political faction—as did most American and practically all European papers of his time. Or, like the great aristocrat of those days, *The Times* of London, they were "written by gentlemen for gentlemen," but so expensive that only a small elite could afford them.

Bennett brilliantly exploited the twin technological knowledge bases on which a modern newspaper rests: the telegraph and high-speed printing. They enabled him to produce a paper at a fraction of the traditional cost. He knew that he needed high-speed typesetting, though it was not invented until after his death. He also saw one of the two nonscientific bases, mass literacy, which made possible mass circulation for a cheap newspaper. But he failed to grasp the fifth base: mass advertising as the source of the income that makes possible editorial independence. Bennett personally enjoyed a spectacular success; he was the first of the press lords. But his newspaper achieved neither leadership nor financial security. These goals were only attained two decades later, around 1890, by three men who understood and exploited advertising: Joseph Pulitzer, first in St. Louis and then in New

York; Adolph Ochs, who took over a moribund *New York Times* and made it into America's leading paper; and William Randolph Hearst, who invented the modern newspaper chain.

The invention of plastics, beginning with Nylon, also rested on the convergence of a number of different new knowledges each emerging around 1910. Organic chemistry, pioneered by the Germans and perfected by Leo Baekeland, a Belgian working in New York, was one; X-Ray diffraction and with it an understanding of the structure of crystals was another; and high-vacuum technology. The final factor was the pressure of World War I shortages, which made the German government willing to invest heavily in polymerization research to obtain a substitute for rubber. It took a further twenty years, though, before Nylon was ready for the market.

Until all the needed knowledges can be provided, knowledge-based innovation is premature and will fail. In most cases, the innovation occurs only when these various factors are already known, already available, already in use someplace. This was the case with the Universal Bank of 1865–75. It was the case with the computer after World War II. Sometimes the innovator can identify the missing pieces and then work at producing them. Joseph Pulitzer, Adolph Ochs, and William Randolph Hearst largely created modern advertising. This then created what we today call media, that is, the merger of information and advertising in "mass communications." The Wright Brothers identified the pieces of knowledge that were missing—mostly mathematics—and then themselves developed them by building a wind tunnel and actually testing mathematical theories. But until all the knowledges needed for a given knowledge-based innovation have come together, the innovation will not take off. It will remain stillborn.

Samuel Langley, for instance, whom his contemporaries expected to become the inventor of the airplane, was a much better trained scientist than the Wright Brothers. As secretary of what was then America's leading scientific institution, the Smithsonian in Washington, he also had all the nation's scientific resources at his disposal. But even though the gasoline engine had been invented by Langley's time, he preferred to ignore it. He believed in the steam engine. As a result his airplane could fly; but because of the steam engine's weight, it could not carry any load, let alone a pilot. It needed the convergence of mathematics and the gasoline engine to produce the airplane.

Indeed, until all the knowledges converge, the lead time of a knowledge-based innovation usually does not even begin.

II

WHAT KNOWLEDGE-BASED INNOVATION REQUIRES

Its characteristics give knowledge-based innovation specific requirements. And these requirements differ from those of any other kind of innovation.

1. In the first place, knowledge-based innovation requires careful analysis of all the necessary factors, whether knowledge itself, or social, economic, or perceptual factors. The analysis must identify what factors are not yet available so that the entrepreneur can decide whether these missing factors can be produced—as the Wright Brothers decided in respect to the missing mathematics—or whether the innovation had better be postponed as not yet feasible.

The Wright Brothers exemplify the method at its best. They thought through carefully what knowledge was necessary to build an airplane for manned, motored flight. Next they set about to develop the pieces of knowledge that were needed, taking the available information, testing it first theoretically, then in the wind tunnel, and then in actual flight experiments, until they had the mathematics they needed to construct ailerons, to shape the wings, and so on.

The same analysis is needed for nontechnical knowledge-based innovation. Neither J. P. Morgan nor Georg Siemens published their papers; but Shibusawa in Japan did. And so we know that he based his decision to forsake a brilliant government career and to start a bank on a careful analysis of the knowledge available and the knowledge needed. Similarly, Joseph Pulitzer analyzed carefully the knowledge needed when he launched what became the first modern newspaper, and decided that advertising had to be invented and could be invented.

If I may inject a personal note, my own success as an innovator in the management field was based on a similar analysis in the early 1940s. Many of the required pieces of knowledge were already available: organization theory, for instance, but also quite a bit of knowledge about managing work and worker. My analysis also showed, however, that these pieces were scattered and lodged in half a dozen different disciplines. Then it found which key knowledges were missing: purpose of a business; any knowledge of the work and structure of top management; what we now term "business policy" and "strategy"; objectives; and so on. All of the missing knowledges, I decided, could be produced. But without such analysis, I could never have known what they were or that they were missing.

Failure to make such an analysis is an almost sure-fire prescription for disaster. Either the knowledge-based innovation is not achieved, which is what happened to Samuel Langley. Or the innovator loses the fruits of his innovation and only succeeds in creating an opportunity for somebody else.

Particularly instructive is the failure of the British to reap the harvest from their own knowledge-based innovations.

The British discovered and developed penicillin, but it was the Americans who took it over. The British scientists did a magnificent technical job. They came out with the right substances and the right uses. Yet they failed to identify the ability to manufacture the stuff as a critical knowledge factor. They could have developed the necessary knowledge of fermentation technology; they did not even try. As a result, a small American company, Pfizer, went to work on developing the knowledge of fermentation and became the world's foremost manufacturer of penicillin.

Similarly, the British conceived, designed, and built the first passenger jet plane. But de Havilland, the British company, did not analyze what was needed and therefore did not identify two key factors. One was configuration, that is, the right size with the right payload for the routes on which the jet would give an airline the greatest advantage. The other was equally mundane: how to finance the purchase of such an expensive plane by the airlines. As a result of de Havilland's failure to do the analysis, two American companies, Boeing and Douglas, took over the jet plane. And de Havilland has long since disappeared.

Such analysis would appear to be fairly obvious, yet it is rarely done by the scientific or technical innovator. Scientists and technologists are reluctant to make these analyses precisely because they think they already *know*. This explains why, in so many cases, the great knowledge-based innovations have had a layman rather than a scientist or a technologist for their father, or at least their godfather. The (American) General Electric Company is largely the brainchild of a financial man.

He conceived the strategy (described in Chapter 19) that made G.E. the world's leading supplier of large steam turbines and, therewith, the world's leading supplier to electric power producers. Similarly, two laymen, Thomas Watson, Sr., and his son Thomas Watson, Jr., made IBM the leader in computers. At DuPont, the analysis of what was needed to make the knowledge-based innovation of Nylon effective and successful was not done by the chemist who developed the technology, but by business people on the executive committee. And Boeing became the world's leading producer of jet planes under the leadership of marketing people who understood what the airlines and the public needed.

This is not a law of nature, however. Mostly it is a matter of will and self-discipline. There have been plenty of scientists and technologists—Edison is a good example—who forced themselves to think through what their knowledge-based innovation required.

2. The second requirement of knowledge-based innovation is a clear focus on the strategic position. It cannot be introduced tentatively. The fact that the introduction of the innovation creates excitement, and attracts a host of others, means that the innovator has to be right the first time. He is unlikely to get a second chance. In all the other innovations discussed so far, the innovator, once he has been successful with his innovation, can expect to be left alone for quite some time. This is not true of knowledge-based innovation. Here the innovators almost immediately have far more company than they want. They need only stumble once to be overrun.

There are basically only three major focuses for knowledge-based innovation. First, there is the focus Edwin Land took with Polaroid: To develop a *complete system* that would then dominate the field. This is exactly what IBM did in its early years when it chose not to sell computers but to lease them to its customers. It supplied them with such software as was available, with programming, with instruction in computer language for programmers, with instruction in computer use for a customer's executives, and with service. This was also what G.E. did when it established itself as the leader in the knowledge-based innovation of large steam turbines in the early years of this century.

The second clear focus is a *market focus*. Knowledge-based innovation can aim at creating the market for its products. This is what DuPont did with Nylon. It did not "sell" Nylon; it created a consumer market for women's hosiery and women's underwear using Nylon, a market for automobile tires using Nylon, and so on. It then delivered Nylon to the fabricators to make the articles for which DuPont had already created a demand and which, in effect, it had already sold. Similarly, aluminum from the very beginning, right after the invention of the aluminum reduction process by Charles M. Hall in 1888, began to create a market for pots and pans, for rods and other aluminum extrusions. The aluminum company actually went into making these end products and selling them. It created the market which, in turn, discouraged (if it did not keep out altogether) potential competitors.

The third focus is *to occupy a strategic position,* concentrating on a key function (the strategy is discussed in Chapter 18 under Ecological Niches). What position would enable the knowledge innovator to be largely immune to the extreme convolutions of a knowledge-based industry in its early stages? It was thinking this through and deciding to concentrate on mastering the fermentation process that gave Pfizer in the United States the early lead in penicillin it has maintained ever since. Focusing on marketing—on mastery of the requirements of airlines and of the public in respect to configuration and finance—gave Boeing the leadership in passenger planes, which it has held ever since. And despite the turbulence of the computer industry today, a few leading manufacturers of the computer's key component, semiconductors, can maintain their leadership position almost irrespective of the fate of individual computer manufacturers themselves. Intel is one example.

Within the same industry, individual knowledge-based innovators can sometimes choose between these alternatives. Where DuPont, for instance, has chosen to create markets, its closest American competitor, Dow Chemical, tries to occupy a key spot in each market segment. A hundred years ago, J. P. Morgan opted for the key function approach. He established his bank as the conduit for European investment capital in American industry, and furthermore in a capital-short country. At the same time, Georg Siemens in Germany and Shibusawa Eichii in Japan both went for the systems approach.

The power of a clear focus is demonstrated by Edison's success. Edison was not the only one who identified the inventions that had to be made to produce a light bulb. An English physicist, Joseph Swan, did so too. Swan developed his light bulb at exactly the same time as Edison. Technically, Swan's bulb was superior, to the point where Edison bought up the Swan patents and used them in his own light bulb factories. But Edison not only thought through the technical requirements;

he thought through his focus. Before he even began the technical work on the glass envelope, the vacuum, the closure, and the glowing fiber, he had already decided on a "system": his light bulb was designed to fit an electric power company for which he had lined up the financing, the rights to string wires to get the power to his light bulb customers, and the distribution system. Swan, the scientist, invented a product; Edison produced an industry. So Edison could sell and install electric power while Swan was still trying to figure out who might be interested in his technical achievement.

The knowledge-based innovator has to decide on a clear focus. Each of the three described here is admittedly very risky. But not to decide on a clear focus, let alone to try to be in between or to attempt more than one focus, is riskier by far. It is likely to prove fatal.

3. Finally, the knowledge-based innovator—and especially the one whose innovation is based on scientific or technological knowledge—needs to learn and to practice entrepreneurial management (see Chapter 15, The New Venture). In fact, entrepreneurial management is more crucial to knowledge-based innovation than to any other kind. Its risks are high, thus putting a much higher premium on foresight, both financial and managerial, and on being market-focused and market-driven. Yet knowledge-based, and especially high-tech, innovation tends to have little entrepreneurial management. In large measure the high casualty rate of knowledge-based industry is the fault of the knowledge-based, and especially the high-tech, entrepreneurs themselves. They tend to be contemptuous of anything that is not "advanced knowledge," and particularly of anyone who is not a specialist in their own area. They tend to be infatuated with their own technology, often believing that "quality" means what is technically sophisticated rather than what gives value to the user. In this respect they are still, by and large, nineteenth-century inventors rather than twentieth-century entrepreneurs.

In fact, there are enough companies around today to show that the risk in knowledge-based innovation, including high tech, can be substantially reduced if entrepreneurial management is conscientiously applied. Hoffmann-LaRoche, the Swiss pharmaceutical company, is one example; Hewlett-Packard is another, and so is Intel. Precisely because the inherent risks of knowledge-based innovation are so high, entrepreneurial management is both particularly necessary and particularly effective.

III

THE UNIQUE RISKS

Even when it is based on meticulous analysis, endowed with clear focus, and conscientiously managed, knowledge-based innovation still suffers from unique risks and, worse, an innate unpredictability.

First, by its very nature, it is turbulent.

The combination of the two characteristics of knowledge-based innovations—long lead times and convergences—gives knowledge-based innovations their peculiar rhythm. For a long time, there is awareness of an innovation about to happen—but it does not happen. Then suddenly there is a near-explosion, followed by a few short years of tremendous excitement, tremendous startup activity, tremendous publicity. Five years later comes a "shakeout," which few survive.

In 1856, Werner Siemens in Germany applied the electrical theories Michael Faraday had developed around 1830 (twenty-five years earlier) to the design of the ancestor of the first electrical motor, the first dynamo. It caused a worldwide sensation. From then on, it became certain that there would be an "electrical industry" and that it would be a major one. Dozens of scientists and inventors went to work. But nothing happened for twenty-two years. The knowledge was missing: Maxwell's development of Faraday's theories.

After it had become available, Edison invented the light bulb in 1878 and the race was on. Within the next five years all the major electrical apparatus companies in Europe and America were founded: Siemens in Germany bought up a small electrical apparatus manufacturer, Schuckert. The (German) General Electric Company, AEG, was formed on the basis of Edison's work. In the United States there arose what are now G.E. and Westinghouse; in Switzerland, there was Brown Boveri; in Sweden, ASEA was founded in 1884. But these few are the survivors of a hundred such companies—American, British, French, German, Italian, Spanish, Dutch, Belgian, Swiss, Austrian, Czech, Hungarian, and so on—all eagerly financed by the investors of their time and all expecting to be "billion-dollar companies." It was this upsurge of the electrical apparatus industry that gave rise to the first great science-fiction boom and made Jules Verne and H. G. Wells best-selling authors all over the world. But by 1895–1900, most of these companies had already disappeared, whether out of business, bankrupt, or absorbed by the few survivors.

Around 1910, there were up to two hundred automobile companies in the United States alone. By the early 1930s, their number had shrunk to twenty, and by 1960 to four.

In the 1920s, literally hundreds of companies were making radio sets and hundreds more were going into radio stations. By 1935, the control of broadcasting had moved into the hands of three "networks" and there were only a dozen manufacturers of radio sets left. Again, there was an explosion in the number of newspapers founded between 1880 and 1900. In fact, newspapers were among the major "growth industries" of the time. Since World War I, the number of newspapers in every major country has been going downhill steadily. And the same is true of banking. After the founders—the Morgans, the Siemenses, the Shibusawas—there was an almost explosive growth of new banks in the United States as well as in Europe. But around 1890, only twenty years later, consolidation set in. Banking firms began to go out of business or to merge. By the end of World War II in every major country only a handful of banks were left that had more than local importance, whether as commercial or private banks.

But each time without exception the survivor has been a company that was started during the early explosive period. After that period is over, entry into the industry is foreclosed for all practical purposes. There is a "window" of a few years during which a new venture must establish itself in any new knowledge-based industry.

It is commonly believed today that that "window" has become narrower. But this is as much a misconception as the common belief that the lead time between the emergence of new knowledge and its conversion into technology, products, and processes has become much shorter.

Within a few years after George Stephenson's "Rocket" had pulled the first train on a commercial railroad in 1830, over a hundred railroad companies were started in England. For ten years railroads were "high-tech" and railroad entrepreneurs "media events." The speculative fever of these years is bitingly satirized in one of Dickens's novels, *Little Dorrit* (published in 1855–57); it was not very different from today's speculative fever in Silicon Valley. But around 1845, the "window" slammed shut. From then on there was no money in England any more for new railroads. Fifty years later, the hundred-or-so English railroad companies of 1845 had shrunk to five or six. And the same rhythm characterized the electrical apparatus industry, the telephone industry, the automobile industry, the chemical industry, household appliances, and consumer electronics. The "window" has never been very wide nor open very long.

But there can be little doubt that today the "window" is becoming more and more crowded. The railroad boom of the 1830s was confined to England; later, every country had its own local boom quite separate from the preceding one in the neighboring country. The electrical apparatus boom already extended across national frontiers, as did the automobile boom twenty-five years later. Yet both were confined to the countries that were industrially developed at the time. The term "industrially developed" encompasses a great deal more territory today, however. It takes in Japan, for instance. It takes in Brazil. It may soon take in the non-Communist Chinese territories: Hong Kong, Taiwan, and Singapore. Communication today is practically instantaneous, travel easy and fast. And a great many countries have today what only very few small places had a hundred years ago: large cadres of trained people who can immediately go to work in any area of knowledge-based innovation, and especially of science-based or technology-based innovation.

These facts have two important implications.

1. First, science-based and technology-based innovators alike find time working against them. In all innovation based on any other source —the unexpected, incongruities, process need, changes in industry structure, demographics, or changes in perception—time is on the side of the innovator. In any other kind of innovation innovators can reasonably expect to be left alone. If they make a mistake, they are likely to have time to correct it. And there are several moments in time in which they can launch their new venture. Not so in knowledge-based innovation, and especially in those innovations based on scientific and technological knowledge. Here there is only a short time—the "window"— during which entry is possible at all. Here innovators do not get a second chance; they have to be right the first time. The environment is harsh and unforgiving. And once the "window" closes, the opportunity is gone forever.

In some knowledge-based industries, however, a second "window" does in fact open some twenty to thirty years or so after the first one has shut down. Computers are an example.

The first "window" in computers lasted from 1949 until 1955 or so. During this period, every single electrical apparatus company in the world went into computers—G.E., Westinghouse, and RCA in the United States; the British General Electric Company, Plessey, and Ferranti in Great Britain; Siemens and AEG in Germany; Philips in Holland; and so on. By 1970, every single one of the "biggies" was out of computers, ignominiously. The field was occupied by companies that had either not existed at all in 1949 or had been small and marginal: IBM, of course, and the "Seven Dwarfs," the seven smaller computer companies in the United States; ICL, the remnant of the computer businesses of the General Electric Company, of Plessey, and of Ferranti in Great Britain; some fragments sustained by heavy government subsidies in France; and a total newcomer, Nixdorf, in Germany. The Japanese companies were sustained for a long time through government support.

Then, in the late seventies, a second "window" opened with the invention of micro-chips, which led to word processors, minicomputers, personal computers, and the merging of computer and telephone switchboard.

But the companies that had failed in the first round did not come back in the second one. Even those that survived the first round stayed out of the second, or came in late and reluctantly. Neither Univac nor Control Data, nor Honeywell nor Burroughs, nor Fujitsu nor Hitachi took leadership in minicomputers or personal computers. The one exception was IBM, the undisputed champion of the first round. And this has been the pattern too in earlier knowledge-based innovations.

2. Because the "window" is much more crowded, any one knowledge-based innovator has far less chance of survival.

The number of entrants during the "window" period is likely to be much larger. But the structure of the industries, once they stabilize and mature, seems to have remained remarkably unchanged, at least for a century now. Of course there are great differences in structure between various industries, depending on technology, capital requirements, and ease of entry, on whether the product can be shipped or distributed only locally, and so on. But at any one time any given industry has a typical structure: in any given market there are so many companies altogether, so many big ones, so many medium-sized ones, so many small ones, so many specialists. And increasingly there is only one "market" for any new knowledge-based industry, whether computers or modern banking—the world market.

The number of knowledge-based innovators that will survive when an industry matures and stabilizes is therefore no larger than it has traditionally been. But largely because of the emergence of a world market and of global communications, the number of entrants during the "window" period has greatly increased. When the shakeout comes, the casualty rate is therefore much higher than it used to be. And the shakeout always comes; it is inevitable.

THE SHAKEOUT

The "shakeout" sets in as soon as the "window" closes. And the majority of ventures started during the "window" period do not survive the shakeout, as has already been shown for such high-tech industries of yesterday as railroads, electrical apparatus makers, and automobiles. As these lines are being written, the shakeout has begun among microprocessor, minicomputer, and personal computer companies—only five or six years after the "window" opened. Today, there are perhaps a hundred companies in the industry in the United States alone. Ten years hence, by 1995, there are unlikely to be more than a dozen left of any size or significance.

But which ones will survive, which ones will die, and which ones will become permanently crippled—able neither to live nor to die—is unpredictable. In fact, it is futile to speculate. Sheer size may ensure survival. But it does not guarantee success in the shakeout, otherwise Allied Chemical rather than DuPont would today be the world's biggest and most successful chemical company. In 1920, when the "window" opened for the chemical industry in the United States, Allied Chemical looked invincible, if only because it had obtained the German chemical patents which the U.S. government had confiscated during World War I. Seven years later, after the shakeout, Allied Chemical had become a weak also-ran. It has never been able to regain momentum.

No one in 1949 could have predicted that IBM would emerge as the computer giant, let alone that such big, experienced leaders as G.E. or Siemens would fail completely. No one in 1910 or 1914 when automobile stocks were the favorites of the New York Stock Exchange could have predicted that General Motors and Ford would survive and prosper and that such universal favorites as Packard or Hupmobile would disappear. No one in the 1870s and 1880s, the period in which the modern banks were born, could have predicted that Deutsche Bank would swallow up dozens of the old commercial banks of Germany and emerge as the leading bank of the country.

That a certain industry will become important is fairly easy to predict. There is no case on record where an industry that reached the explosive phase, the "window" phase, as I called it, has then failed to become a major industry. The question is, Which of the specific units in this industry will be its leaders and so survive?

This rhythm—a period of great excitement during which there is also great speculative ferment, followed by a severe "shakeout"—is particularly pronounced in the high-tech industries.

In the first place, such industries are in the limelight and thus attract far more entrants and far more capital than more mundane areas. Also the expectations are much greater. More people have probably become rich building such prosaic businesses as a shoe-polish or a watchmaking company than have become rich through high-tech businesses. Yet no one expects shoe-polish makers to build a "billion-dollar business," nor considers them a failure if all they build is a sound but modest family company. High tech, by contrast, is a "high–low game," in which a middle hand is considered worthless. And this makes high-tech innovation inherently risky.

But also, high tech is not profitable for a very long time. The world's computer industry began in 1947–48. Not until the early 1980s, more than thirty years later, did the industry as a whole reach break-even point. To be sure, a few companies (practically all of them American, by the way) began to make money much earlier. And one, IBM, the leader, began to make a great deal of money earlier still. But across the industry the profits of those few successful computer makers were more than offset by the horrendous losses of the rest; the enormous losses, for instance, which the big international electrical companies took in their abortive attempts to become computer manufacturers.

And exactly the same thing happened in every earlier "high-tech" boom—in the railroad booms of the early nineteenth century, in the electrical apparatus and the automobile booms between 1880 and 1914, in the electric appliance and the radio booms of the 1920s, and so on.

One major reason for this is the need to plow more and more money back into research, technical development, and technical services to stay in the race. High tech does indeed have to run faster and faster in order to stand still.

This is, of course, part of its fascination. But it also means that when the shakeout comes, very few businesses in the industry have the financial resources to outlast even a short storm. This is the reason why high-tech ventures need financial foresight even more than other new ventures, but also the reason why financial foresight is even scarcer among high-tech new ventures than it is among new ventures in general.

There is only one prescription for survival during the shakeout: entrepreneurial management (described in Chapters 12–15). What distinguished Deutsche Bank from the other "hot" financial institutions of its time was that Georg Siemens thought through and built the world's first top management team. What distinguished DuPont from Allied Chemical was that DuPont in the early twenties created the world's first systematic organization structure, the world's first long-range planning, and the world's first system of management information and control. Allied Chemical, by contrast, was run arbitrarily by one brilliant egomaniac. But this is not the whole story. Most of the large companies that failed to survive the more recent computer shakeout—G.E. and Siemens, for instance—are usually considered to have first-rate management. And the Ford Motor Company survived, though only by the skin of its teeth, even though it was grotesquely mismanaged during the shakeout years.

Entrepreneurial management is thus probably a precondition of survival, but not a guarantee thereof. And at the time of the shakeout, only insiders (and perhaps not even they) can really know whether a knowledge-based innovator that has grown rapidly for a few boom years is well managed, as DuPont was, or basically unmanaged, as Allied Chemical was. By the time we do know, it is likely to be too late.

THE RECEPTIVITY GAMBLE

To be successful, a knowledge-based innovation has to be "ripe"; there has to be receptivity to it. This risk is inherent in knowledge-based innovation and is indeed a function of its unique power. All other innovations exploit a change that has already occurred. They satisfy a need that already exists. But in knowledge-based innovation, the innovation brings about the change. It aims at creating a want. And no one can tell in advance whether the user is going to be receptive, indifferent, or actively resistant.

There are exceptions, to be sure. Whoever produces a cure for cancer need not worry about "receptivity." But such exceptions are few. In most knowledge-based innovations, receptivity is a gamble. And the odds are unknown, are indeed mysterious. There may be great receptivity, yet no one realizes it. And there may be no receptivity, or even heavy resistance when everyone is quite sure that society is actually eagerly waiting for the innovation.

Stories of the obtuseness of the high and mighty in the face of a knowledge-based innovation abound. Typical is the anecdote which has a king of Prussia predicting the certain failure of that new-fangled contraption, the railroad, because "No one will pay good money to get from Berlin to Potsdam in one hour when he can ride his horse in one day for free." But the king of Prussia was not alone in his misreading of the receptivity to the railroad; the majority of the "experts" of his day inclined to his opinion. And when the computer appeared there was not one single "expert" who could imagine that businesses would ever want such a contraption.

The opposite error is, however, just as common. "Everybody knows" that there is a real need, a real demand, when in reality there is total indifference or resistance. The same authorities who, in 1948, could not imagine that a business would ever want a computer, a few years later, around 1955, predicted that the computer would "revolutionize the schools" within a decade.

The Germans consider Philip Reis rather than Alexander Graham Bell to be the inventor of the telephone. Reis did indeed build an instrument in 1861 that could transmit music and was very close to transmitting speech. But then he gave up, totally discouraged. There was no receptivity for a telephone, no interest in it, no desire for it. "The telegraph is good enough for us," was the prevailing attitude. Yet when Bell, fifteen years later, patented his telephone, there was an immediate enthusiastic response. And nowhere was it greater than in Germany.

The change in receptivity in these fifteen years is not too difficult to explain. Two major wars, the American Civil War and the Franco-

Prussian War, had shown that the telegraph was by no means "good enough." But the real point is not why receptivity changed. It is that every authority in 1861 enthusiastically predicted overwhelming receptivity when Reis demonstrated his instrument at a scientific meeting. And every authority was wrong.

But, of course, the authorities can also be right, and often are. In 1876–77, for instance, they all knew that there was receptivity for both a light bulb and a telephone—and they were right. Similarly, Edison, in the 1880s, was supported by the expert opinion of his time when he embarked on the invention of the phonograph, and again the experts were right in assuming high receptivity for the new device.

But only hindsight can tell us whether the experts are right or wrong in their assessment of the receptivity for this or that knowledge-based innovation.

Nor do we necessarily perceive, even by hindsight, why a particular knowledge-based innovation has receptivity or fails to find it. No one, for instance, can explain why phonetic spelling has been so strenuously resisted. Everyone agrees that nonphonetic spelling is a major obstacle in learning to read and write, forces schools to devote inordinate time to the reading skill, and is responsible for a disproportionate number of reading disabilities and emotional traumas among children. The knowledge of phonetics is a century old at least. Means to achieve phonetic spelling are available in the two languages where the problem is most acute: any number of phonetic alphabets for English, and the much older, forty-eight-syllable Kana scripts in Japanese. For both countries there are examples next door of a successful shift to a phonetic script. The English have the successful model of German spelling reform of the mid-nineteenth century; the Japanese, the equally successful—and much earlier—phonetic reform of the Korean script. Yet in neither country is there the slightest receptivity for an innovation that, one would say, is badly needed, eminently rational, and proven by example to be safe, fairly easy, and efficacious. Why? Explanations abound, but no one really knows.

There is no way to eliminate the element of risk, no way even to reduce it. Market research does not work—one cannot do market research on something that does not exist. Opinion research is probably not just useless but likely to do damage. At least this is what the experience with "expert opinion" on the receptivity to knowledge-based innovation would indicate.

Yet there is no choice. If we want knowledge-based innovation, we must gamble on receptivity to it.

The risks are highest in innovations based on new knowledge in science and technology. They are particularly high, of course, in innovations in areas that are currently "hot"—personal computers, at the present time, or biotechnology. By contrast, areas that are not in the public eye have far lower risks, if only because there is more time. And in innovations where the knowledge base is not science or technology —social innovations, for instance—the risks are lower still. But high risk is inherent in knowledge-based innovation. It is the price we have to pay for its impact and above all for its capacity to bring about change, not only in products and services but in how we see the world, our place in it, and eventually ourselves.

Yet the risks even of high-tech innovation can be substantially reduced by integrating new knowledge as the source of innovation with one of the other sources defined earlier, the unexpected, incongruities, and especially process need. In these areas receptivity has either already been established or can be tested fairly easily and with good reliability. And in these areas, too, the knowledge or knowledges that have to be produced to complete an innovation can usually be defined with considerable precision. This is the reason why "program research" is becoming so popular. But even program research requires a great deal of system and self-discipline, and has to be organized and purposeful.

The demands on knowledge-based innovators are thus very great. They are also different from those in other areas of innovation. The risks they face are different, too; time, for instance, is not on their side. But if the risks are greater, so are the potential rewards. The other innovators may reap a fortune. The knowledge-based innovator can hope for fame as well.

10

The Bright Idea

Innovations based on a bright idea probably outnumber all other categories taken together. Seven or eight out of every ten patents belong here, for example. A very large proportion of the new businesses that are described in the books on entrepreneurs and entrepreneurships are built around "bright ideas": the zipper, the ballpoint pen, the aerosol spray can, the tab to open soft drink or beer cans, and many more. And what is called research in many businesses aims at finding and exploiting bright ideas, whether for a new flavor in breakfast cereals or soft drinks, for a better running shoe, or for yet one more nonscorching clothes iron.

Yet bright ideas are the riskiest and least successful source of innovative opportunities. The casualty rate is enormous. No more than one out of every hundred patents for an innovation of this kind earns enough to pay back development costs and patent fees. A far smaller proportion, perhaps as low as one in five hundred, makes any money above its out-of-pocket costs.

And no one knows which ideas for an innovation based on a bright idea have a chance to succeed and which ones are likely to fail. Why did the aerosol can succeed, for instance? And why did a dozen or more similar inventions for the uniform delivery of particles fail dismally? Why does one universal wrench sell and most of the many others disappear? Why did the zipper find acceptance and practically displace buttons, even though it tends to jam? (After all, a jammed zipper on a dress, jacket, or pair of trousers can be quite embarrassing.)

Attempts to improve the predictability of innovations based on bright ideas have not been particularly successful.

Equally unsuccessful have been attempts to identify the personal traits, behavior, or habits that make for a successful innovator. "Successful inventors," an old adage says, "keep on inventing. They play the odds. If they try often enough, they will succeed."

This belief that you'll win if only you keep on trying out bright ideas is, however, no more rational than the popular fallacy that to win the jackpot at Las Vegas one only has to keep on pulling the lever. Alas, the machine is rigged to have the house win 70 percent of the time. The more often you pull, the more often you lose.

There is actually no empirical evidence at all for the belief that persistence pays off in pursuing the "brilliant idea," just as there is no evidence of any "system" to beat the slot machines. Some successful inventors have had only one brilliant idea and then quit: the inventor of the zipper, for instance, or of the ballpoint pen. And there are hundreds of inventors around who have forty patents to their name, and not one winner. Innovators do, of course, improve with practice. But only if they practice the right method, that is, if they base their work on a systematic analysis of the sources of innovative opportunity.

The reasons for both the unpredictability and the high casualty rate are fairly obvious. Bright ideas are vague and elusive. I doubt that anyone except the inventor of the zipper ever thought that buttons or hooks-and-eyes were inadequate to fasten clothing, or that anyone but the inventor of the ballpoint pen could have defined what, if anything, was unsatisfactory about that nineteenth-century invention, the fountain pen. What need was satisfied by the electric toothbrush, one of the market successes of the 1960s? It still has to be hand-held, after all.

And even if the need can be defined, the solution cannot usually be specified. That people sitting in their cars in a traffic jam would like some diversion was perhaps not so difficult to figure out. But why did the small TV set which Sony developed around 1965 to satisfy this need fail in the marketplace, whereas the far more expensive car stereo succeeded? In retrospect, it is easy to answer this. But could it possibly have been answered in prospect?

The entrepreneur is therefore well advised to forgo innovations based on bright ideas, however enticing the success stories. After all, somebody wins a jackpot on the Las Vegas slot machines every week, yet the best any one slot-machine player can do is try not lose more than he or she can afford. Systematic, purposeful entrepreneurs analyze the systematic areas, the seven sources that I've discussed in Chapters 3 through 9.

There is enough in these areas to keep busy any one individual entrepreneur and any one entrepreneurial business or public-service institution. In fact, there is far more than anyone could possibly fully exploit. And in these areas we know how to look, what to look for, and what to do.

All one can do for innovators who go in for bright ideas is to tell them what to do should their innovation, against all odds, be successful. Then the rules for a new venture apply (see Chapter 15). And this is, of course, the reason why so much of the literature on entrepreneurship deals with starting and running the new venture rather than with innovation itself.

And yet an entrepreneurial economy cannot dismiss cavalierly the innovation based on a bright idea. The individual innovation of this kind is not predictable, cannot be organized, cannot be systematized, and fails in the overwhelming majority of cases. Also many, very many, are trivial from the start. There are always more patent applications for new can openers, for new wig stands, and for new belt buckles than for anything else. And in any list of new patents there is always at least one foot warmer than can double as a dish towel. Yet the volume of such bright-idea innovation is so large that the tiny percentage of successes represents a substantial source of new businesses, new jobs, and new performance capacity for the economy.

In the theory and practice of innovation and entrepreneurship, the bright-idea innovation belongs in the appendix. But it should be appreciated and rewarded. It represents qualities that society needs: initiative, ambition, and ingenuity. There is little society can do, perhaps, to promote such innovation. One cannot promote what one does not understand. But at least society should not discourage, penalize, or make difficult such innovations. Seen in this perspective, the recent trend in developed countries, and especially in the United States, to discourage the individual who tries to come up with a bright-idea innovation (by raising patent fees, for instance) and generally to discourage patents as "anticompetitive" is short-sighted and deleterious.

11

Principles of Innovation

I

All experienced physicians have seen "miracle cures." Patients suffering from terminal illnesses recover suddenly—sometimes spontaneously, sometimes by going to faith healers, by switching to some absurd diet, or by sleeping during the day and being up and about all night. Only a bigot denies that such cures happen and dismisses them as "unscientific." They are real enough. Yet no physician is going to put miracle cures into a textbook or into a course to be taught to medical students. They cannot be replicated, cannot be taught, cannot be learned. They are also extremely rare; the overwhelming majority of terminal cases do die, after all.

Similarly, there are innovations that do not proceed from the sources described in the preceding chapters, innovations that are not developed in any organized, purposeful, systematic manner. There are innovators who are "kissed by the Muses," and whose innovations are the result of a "flash of genius" rather than of hard, organized, purposeful work. But such innovations cannot be replicated. They cannot be taught and they cannot be learned. There is no known way to teach someone how to be a genius. But also, contrary to popular belief in the romance of invention and innovation, "flashes of genius" are uncommonly rare. What is worse, I know of not one such "flash of genius" that turned into an innovation. They all remained brilliant ideas.

The greatest inventive genius in recorded history was surely Leonardo da Vinci. There is a breathtaking idea—submarine or helicopter or automatic forge—on every single page of his notebooks. But not one of these could have been converted into an innovation with the technology and the materials of 1500. Indeed, for none of them would there have been any receptivity in the society and economy of the time.

Every schoolboy knows of James Watt as the "inventor" of the steam engine, which he was not. Historians of technology know that Thomas Newcomen in 1712 built the first steam engine which actually performed useful work: it pumped the water out of an English coal mine. Both men were organized, systematic, purposeful innovators. Watt's steam engine in particular is the very model of an innovation in which newly available knowledge (how to ream a smooth cylinder) and the design of a "missing link" (the condenser) were combined into a process need-based innovation, the receptivity for which had been created by Newcomen's engine (several thousand were by then in use). But the true "inventor" of the combustion engine, and with it of what we call modern technology, was neither Watt nor Newcomen. It was the great Anglo-Irish chemist Robert Boyle, who did so in a "flash of genius." Only Boyle's engine did not work and could not have worked. For Boyle used the explosion of gunpower to drive the piston, and this so fouled the cylinder that it had to be taken apart and cleaned after each stroke. Boyle's idea enabled first Denis Papin (who had been Boyle's assistant in building the gunpowder engine), then Newcomen, and finally Watt, to develop a working combustion engine. All Boyle, the genius, had was a brilliant idea. It belongs in the history of ideas and not in the history of technology or of innovation.

The purposeful innovation resulting from analysis, system, and hard work is all that can be discussed and presented as the practice of innovation. But this is all that need be presented since it surely covers at least 90 percent of all effective innovations. And the extraordinary performer in innovation, as in every other area, will be effective only if grounded in the discipline and master of it.

What, then, are the principles of innovation, representing the hard core of the discipline? There are a number of "do's"—things that have to be done. There are also a few "dont's"—things that had better not be done. And then there are what I would call "conditions."

II

THE DO'S

1. Purposeful, systematic innovation begins with the analysis of the opportunities. It begins with thinking through what I have called the sources of innovative opportunities. In different areas, different sources

will have different importance at different times. Demographics, for instance, may be of very little concern to innovators in fundamental industrial processes, to someone looking, say, for the "missing link" in a process such as papermaking, where there is a clear incongruity between economic realities. New knowledge, by the same token, may be of very little relevance to someone innovating a new social instrument to satisfy a need created by changing demographics. But all the sources of innovative opportunity should be systematically analyzed and systematically studied. It is not enough to be alerted to them. The search has to be organized, and must be done on a regular, systematic basis.

2. Innovation is both conceptual and perceptual. The second imperative of innovation is therefore to go out to look, to ask, to listen. This cannot be stressed too often. Successful innovators use both the right side and the left side of their brains. They look at figures, and they look at people. They work out analytically what the innovation has to be to satisfy an opportunity. And then they go out and look at the customers, the users, to see what their expectations, their values, their needs are.

Receptivity can be perceived, as can values. One can perceive that this or that approach will not fit in with the expectations or the habits of the people who have to use it. And then one can ask: "What does this innovation have to reflect so that the people who have to use it will *want* to use it, and see in it *their* opportunity?" Otherwise one runs the risk of having the right innovation in the wrong form—as happened to the leading producer of computer programs for learning in American schools, whose excellent and effective programs were not used by teachers scared stiff of the computer, who perceived the machine as something that, far from being helpful, threatened them.

3. An innovation, to be effective, has to be simple and it has to be focused. It should do only one thing, otherwise, it confuses. If it is not simple, it won't work. Everything new runs into trouble; if complicated, it cannot be repaired or fixed. All effective innovations are breathtakingly simple. Indeed, the greatest praise an innovation can receive is for people to say: "This is obvious. Why didn't I think of it?"

Even the innovation that creates new uses and new markets should be directed toward a specific, clear, designed application. It should be focused on a specific need that it satisfies, on a specific end result that it produces.

4. Effective innovations start small. They are not grandiose. They try to do one specific thing. It may be to enable a moving vehicle to draw electric power while it runs along rails—the innovation that made possi-

ble the electric streetcar. Or it may be as elementary as putting the same number of matches into a matchbox (it used to be fifty), which made possible the automatic filling of matchboxes and gave the Swedish originators of the idea a world monopoly on matches for almost half a century. Grandiose ideas, plans that aim at "revolutionizing an industry," are unlikely to work.

Innovations had better be capable of being started small, requiring at first little money, few people, and only a small and limited market. Otherwise, there is not enough time to make the adjustments and changes that are almost always needed for an innovation to succeed. Initially innovations rarely are more than "almost right." The necessary changes can be made only if the scale is small and the requirements for people and money fairly modest.

5. But—and this is the final "do"—a successful innovation aims at leadership. It does not aim necessarily at becoming eventually a "big business"; in fact, no one can foretell whether a given innovation will end up as a big business or a modest achievement. But if an innovation does not aim at leadership from the beginning, it is unlikely to be innovative enough, and therefore unlikely to be capable of establishing itself. Strategies (to be discussed in Chapters 16 through 19) vary greatly, from those that aim at dominance in an industry or a market to those that aim at finding and occupying a small "ecological niche" in a process or market. But all entrepreneurial strategies, that is, all strategies aimed at exploiting an innovation, must achieve leadership within a given environment. Otherwise they will simply create an opportunity for the competition.

III

THE DONT'S

And now the few important "dont's."

1. The first is simply not to try to be clever. Innovations have to be handled by ordinary human beings, and if they are to attain any size and importance at all, by morons or near-morons. Incompetence, after all, is the only thing in abundant and never-failing supply. Anything too clever, whether in design or execution, is almost bound to fail.

2. Don't diversify, don't splinter, don't try to do too many things at once. This is, of course, the corollary to the "do": be focused! Innova-

tions that stray from a core are likely to become diffuse. They remain ideas and do not become innovations. The core does not have to be technology or knowledge. In fact, market knowledge supplies a better core of unity in any enterprise, whether business or public-service institution, than knowledge or technology do. But there has to be a core of unity to innovative efforts or they are likely to fly apart. An innovation needs the concentrated energy of a unified effort behind it. It also requires that the people who put it into effect understand each other, and this, too, requires a unity, a common core. This, too, is imperiled by diversity and splintering.

3. Finally, don't try to innovate for the future. Innovate for the present! An innovation may have long-range impact; it may not reach its full maturity until twenty years later. The computer, as we have seen, did not really begin to have any sizable impact on the way business was being done until the early 1970s, twenty-five years after the first working models were introduced. But from the first day the computer had some specific current applications, whether scientific calculation, making payroll, or simulation to train pilots to fly airplanes. It is not good enough to be able to say, "In twenty-five years there will be so many very old people that they will need this." One has to be able to say, "There are enough old people around today for this to make a difference to them. Of course, time is with us—in twenty-five years there will be many more." But unless there is an immediate application in the present, an innovation is like the drawings in Leonardo da Vinci's notebook—a "brilliant idea." Very few of us have Leonardo's genius and can expect that our notebooks alone will assure immortality.

The first innovator who fully understood this third caveat was probably Edison. Every other electrical inventor of the time began to work around 1860 or 1865 on what eventually became the light bulb. Edison waited for ten years until the knowledge became available; up to that point, work on the light bulb was "of the future." But when the knowledge became available—when, in other words, a light bulb could become "the present"—Edison organized his tremendous energies and an extraordinarily capable staff and concentrated for a couple of years on that one innovative opportunity.

Innovative opportunities sometimes have long lead times. In pharmaceutical research, ten years of research and development work are by no means uncommon or particularly long. And yet no pharmaceutical company would dream of starting a research project for something which does not, if successful, have immediate application as a drug for health-care needs that already exist.

THREE CONDITIONS

Finally, there are three conditions. All three are obvious but often go disregarded.

1. *Innovation is work.* It requires knowledge. It often requires great ingenuity. There are clearly people who are more talented innovators than the rest of us. Also, innovators rarely work in more than one area. For all his tremendous innovative capacity, Edison worked only in the electrical field. And an innovator in financial areas, Citibank in New York, for instance, is unlikely to embark on innovations in retailing or health care. In innovation as in any other work there is talent, there is ingenuity, there is predisposition. But when all is said and done, innovation becomes hard, focused, purposeful work making very great demands on diligence, on persistence, and on commitment. If these are lacking, no amount of talent, ingenuity, or knowledge will avail.

2. *To succeed, innovators must build on their strengths.* Successful innovators look at opportunities over a wide range. But then they ask, "Which of these opportunities fits *me*, fits *this* company, puts to work what we (or I) are good at and have shown capacity for in performance?" In this respect, of course, innovation is no different from other work. But it may be more important in innovation to build on one's strengths because of the risks of innovation and the resulting premium on knowledge and performance capacity. And in innovation, as in any other venture, there must also be a temperamental "fit." Businesses do not do well in something they do not really respect. No pharmaceutical company—run as it has to be by scientifically minded people who see themselves as "serious"—has done well in anything so "frivolous" as lipsticks or perfumes. Innovators similarly need to be temperamentally attuned to the innovative opportunity. It must be important to them and make sense to them. Otherwise they will not be willing to put in the persistent, hard, frustrating work that successful innovation always requires.

3. And finally, *innovation is an effect in economy and society,* a change in the behavior of customers, of teachers, of farmers, of eye surgeons—of people in general. Or it is a change in a process—that is,

in how people work and produce something. Innovation therefore always has to be close to the market, focused on the market, indeed market-driven.

THE CONSERVATIVE INNOVATOR

A year or two ago I attended a university symposium on entrepreneurship at which a number of psychologists spoke. Although their papers disagreed on everything else, they all talked of an "entrepreneurial personality," which was characterized by a "propensity for risk-taking."

A well-known and successful innovator and entrepreneur who had built a process-based innovation into a substantial worldwide business in the space of twenty-five years was then asked to comment. He said: "I find myself baffled by your papers. I think I know as many successful innovators and entrepreneurs as anyone, beginning with myself. I have never come across an 'entrepreneurial personality.' The successful ones I know all have, however, one thing—and only one thing—in common: they are *not* 'risk-takers.' They try to define the risks they have to take and to minimize them as much as possible. Otherwise none of us could have succeeded. As for myself, if I had wanted to be a risk-taker, I would have gone into real estate or commodity trading, or I would have become the professional painter my mother wanted me to be."

This jibes with my own experience. I, too, know a good many successful innovators and entrepreneurs. Not one of them has a "propensity for risk-taking."

The popular picture of innovators—half pop-psychology, half Hollywood—makes them look like a cross between Superman and the Knights of the Round Table. Alas, most of them in real life are unromantic figures, and much more likely to spend hours on a cash-flow projection than to dash off looking for "risks." Of course innovation is risky. But so is stepping into the car to drive to the supermarket for a loaf of bread. All economic activity is by definition "high-risk." And defending yesterday—that is, not innovating—is far more risky than making tomorrow. The innovators I know are successful to the extent to which they define risks and confine them. They are successful to the extent to which they systematically analyze the sources of innovative opportunity, then pinpoint the opportunity and exploit it. Whether opportunities of small and clearly definable risk, such as exploiting the unexpected or a process need, or opportunities of much greater but still definable risk, as in knowledge-based innovation.

Successful innovators are conservative. They have to be. They are not "risk-focused"; they are "opportunity-focused."

II

THE PRACTICE OF
ENTREPRENEURSHIP

———

The entrepreneurial requires different management from the existing. But like the existing it requires systematic, organized, purposeful management. And while the ground rules are the same for every entrepreneurial organization, the existing business, the public-service institution, and the new venture present different challenges, have different problems, and have to guard against different degenerative tendencies. There is need also for individual entrepreneurs to face up to decisions regarding their own roles and their own commitments.

12

Entrepreneurial Management

Entrepreneurship is based on the same principles, whether the entrepreneur is an existing large institution or an individual starting his or her new venture singlehanded. It makes little or no difference whether the entrepreneur is a business or a nonbusiness public-service organization, nor even whether the entrepreneur is a governmental or nongovernmental institution. The rules are pretty much the same, the things that work and those that don't are pretty much the same, and so are the kinds of innovation and where to look for them. In every case there is a discipline we might call *Entrepreneurial Management.*

Yet the existing business faces different problems, limitations, and constraints from the solo entrepreneur, and it needs to learn different things. The existing business, to oversimplify, knows how to manage but needs to learn how to be an entrepreneur and how to innovate. The nonbusiness public-service institution, too, faces different problems, has different learning needs, and is prone to making different mistakes. And the new venture needs to learn how to be an entrepreneur and how to innovate, but above all, it needs to learn how to manage.

For each of these three:

- the existing business
- the public-service institution
- the new venture

a specific guide to the practice of entrepreneurship must be developed. What does each have to do? What does each have to watch for? And what had each better avoid doing?

Logically, the discussion might start with the new venture, just as, logically, the study of medicine might start with the embryo and newborn baby. But the medical student starts out by studying the anatomy and pathology of the adult, and the practice of entrepreneurship is

393

likewise best started by discussing the "adult," the existing business and the policies, practices and problems that are pertinent in managing it for entrepreneurship.

Today's businesses, especially the large ones, simply will not survive in this period of rapid change and innovation unless they acquire entrepreneurial competence. In this respect the late twentieth century is totally different from the last great entrepreneurial period in economic history, the fifty or sixty years that came to an end with the outbreak of World War I. There were not many big businesses around in those years, and not even many middle-sized ones. Today, it is not only in the self-interest of the many existing big businesses to learn to manage themselves for entrepreneurship; they have a social responsibility to do so. In sharp contrast to the situation a century ago, rapid destruction of the existing businesses—especially the big ones—by innovation, the "creative destruction" by the innovator, in Joseph Schumpeter's famous phrase, poses a genuine social threat today to employment, to financial stability, to social order, and to governmental responsibility.

Existing businesses will need to change, and change greatly in any event. Within twenty-five years (see Chapter 7) every industrially developed non-Communist country will see the blue-collar labor force engaged in manufacturing shrink to one-third of what it is now, while manufacturing output should go up three- or four-fold—a development that will parallel the development in agriculture in the industrialized non-Communist countries during the twenty-five years following World War II. In order to impart stability and leadership in a transition of this magnitude, existing businesses will have to learn how to survive, indeed, how to propser. And that they can only do if they learn to be successful entrepreneurs.

In many cases, the entrepreneurship needed can only come from existing businesses. Some of the giants of today may well not survive the next twenty-five years. But we now know that the medium-sized business is particularly well positioned to be a successful entrepreneur and innovator, provided only that it organize itself for entrepreneurial management. It is the existing business—and the fair-sized rather than the small one—that has the best capability for entrepreneurial leadership. It has the necessary resources, especially the human resources. It has already acquired managerial competence and built a management team. It has both the opportunity and the responsibility for effective entrepreneurial management.

The same holds true for the public-service institutions, and especially for those discharging nonpolitical functions, whether owned by
government and financed by tax money or not; for hospitals, schools,
and universities; for the public services of local governments; for community agencies and volunteer organizations such as the Red Cross, the
Boy Scouts, and the Girl Scouts; for churches and church-related organizations; but also for professional and trade associations, and many more.
A period of rapid change makes obsolete a good many of the old concerns, or at least makes ineffectual a good many of the ways in which
they have been addressed. At the same time, such a period creates
opportunities for tackling new tasks, for experimentation, and for social
innovation.

Above all, there has been a major change in perception and mood
in the public domain (cf. Chapter 8). A hundred years ago, the "panic"
of 1873 brought to an end the century of *laissez faire* that had begun
with Adam Smith's *Wealth of Nations* in 1776. For a hundred years
from 1873 on, being "modern," "progressive," or "forward-looking"
meant looking to government as the agent of social change and better-
ment. For better or worse, that period has come to an end in all non-
Communist developed countries (and probably in the developed Communist countries as well). We do not yet know what the next wave of
"progressivism" will be. But we do know that anyone who still preaches
the "liberal" or "progressive" gospel of 1930—or even of 1960, of the
Kennedy and Johnson years—is not a "progressive" but a "reactionary."
We do not know whether privatization,* that is, turning activities back
from government to nongovernmental operation (albeit not necessarily
to operation by a business enterprise, as most people have interpreted
the term) will work or will go very far. But we do know that no non-
Communist developed country will move further toward nationalization and governmental control out of hope, expectation, and belief in
the traditional promises. It will do so only out of frustration and with
a sense of failure. And this is a situation in which public-service institutions have both an opportunity and a responsibility to be entrepreneurial and to innovate.

But precisely because they are public-service institutions, they face
specific different obstacles and challenges, and are prone to making

---

*A word that I coined in 1969 in *The Age of Discontinuity* (New York: Harper & Row;
London: William Heinemann).

different mistakes. Entrepreneurship in the public-service institution thus needs to be discussed separately.

Finally, there is the new venture. This will continue to be a main vehicle for innovation, as it has been in all major entrepreneurial periods and is again today in the new entrepreneurial economy of the United States. There is indeed no lack of would-be entrepreneurs in the United States, no shortage of new ventures. But most of them, especially the high-tech ones, have a great deal to learn about entrepreneurial management and will have to learn it if they are to survive.

The gap between the performance of the average practitioner and that of the leaders in entrepreneurship and innovation is enormous in all three categories. Fortunately, there are enough examples around of the successful practice of entrepreneurship to make possible a systematic presentation of entrepreneurial management that is both practice and theory, both description and prescription.

13

The Entrepreneurial Business

I

"Big businesses don't innovate," says the conventional wisdom. This sounds plausible enough. True, the new, major innovations of this century did not come out of the old, large businesses of their time. The railroads did not spawn the automobile or the truck; they did not even try. And though the automobile companies did try (Ford and General Motors both pioneered in aviation and aerospace), all of today's large aircraft and aviation companies have evolved out of separate new ventures. Similarly, today's giants of the pharmaceutical industry are, in the main, companies that were small or nonexistent fifty years ago when the first modern drugs were developed. Every one of the giants of the electrical industry—General Electric, Westinghouse, and RCA in the United States; Siemens and Philips on the Continent; Toshiba in Japan —rushed into computers in the 1950s. Not one was successful. The field is dominated by IBM, a company that was barely middle-sized and most definitely not high-tech forty years ago.

And yet the all but universal belief that large businesses do not and cannot innovate is not even a half-truth; rather, it is a misunderstanding.

In the first place, there are plenty of exceptions, plenty of large companies that have done well as entrepreneurs and innovators. In the United States, there is Johnson & Johnson in hygiene and health care, and 3M in highly engineered products for both industrial and consumer markets. Citibank, America's and the world's largest non-governmental financial institution, well over a century old, has been a major innovator in many areas of banking and finance. In Germany, Hoechst—one of the world's largest chemical companies, and more than 125 years old by now—has become a successful innovator in the pharmaceutical industry. In Sweden, ASEA, founded in 1884 and for the last sixty or seventy years a very big company, is a true innovator in both long-distance transmission of electrical power and robotics for factory automation.

To confuse things even more there are quite a few big, older businesses that have succeeded as entrepreneurs and innovators in some fields while failing dismally in others. The (American) General Electric Company failed in computers, but has been a successful innovator in three totally different fields: aircraft engines, engineered inorganic plastics, and medical electronics. RCA also failed in computers but succeeded in color television. Surely things are not quite as simple as the conventional wisdom has it.

Secondly, it is not true that "bigness" is an obstacle to entrepreneurship and innovation. In discussions of entrepreneurship one hears a great deal about the "bureaucracy" of big organizations and of their "conservatism." Both exist, of course, and they are serious impediments to entrepreneurship and innovation—but to all other performance just as much. And yet the record shows unambiguously that among existing enterprises, whether business or public-sector institutions, the small ones are least entrepreneurial and least innovative. Among existing entrepreneurial businesses there are a great many very big ones; the list above could have been enlarged without difficulty to one hundred companies from all over the world, and a list of innovative public-service institutions would also include a good many large ones.

And perhaps the most entrepreneurial business of them all is the large middle-sized one, such as the American company with $500 million in sales in the mid-1980s.* But *small* existing enterprises would be conspicuously absent from any list of entrepreneurial businesses.

It is not size that is an impediment to entrepreneurship and innovation; it is the existing operation itself, and especially the existing *successful* operation. And it is easier for a big or at least a fair-sized company to surmount this obstacle than it is for a small one. Operating anything—a manufacturing plant, a technology, a product line, a distribution system—requires constant effort and unremitting atten-

*This has long been suspected. Now, however, conclusive evidence is available in the study of one hundred medium-sized "growth" companies by Richard E. Cavenaugh and Donald K. Clifford, Jr., "Lessons from America's Mid-Sized Growth Companies," *McKinsey Quarterly* (Autumn 1983).

tion. The one thing that can be guaranteed in any kind of operation is the daily crisis. The daily crisis cannot be postponed, it has to be dealt with right away. And the existing operation demands high priority and deserves it.

The new always looks so small, so puny, so unpromising next to the size and performance of maturity. Anything truly new that looks big is indeed to be distrusted. The odds are heavily against its succeeding. And yet successful innovators, as was argued earlier, start small and, above all, simple.

The claim of so many businesses, "Ten years from now, ninety percent of our revenues will come from products that do not even exist today," is largely boasting. Modifications of existing products, yes; variations, yes; even extensions of existing products into new markets and new end uses—with or without modifications. But the truly new venture tends to have a longer lead time. Successful businesses, businesses that are today in the right markets with the right products or services, are likely ten years hence to get three-quarters of their revenues from products and services that exist today, or from their linear descendants. In fact, if today's products or services do not generate a continuing and large revenue stream, the enterprise will not be able to make the substantial investment in tomorrow that innovation requires.

It thus takes special effort for the existing business to become entrepreneurial and innovative. The "normal" reaction is to allocate productive resources to the existing business, to the daily crisis, and to getting a little more out of what we already have. The temptation in the existing business is always to feed yesterday and to starve tomorrow.

It is, of course, a deadly temptation. The enterprise that does not innovate inevitably ages and declines. And in a period of rapid change such as the present, an entrepreneurial period, the decline will be fast. Once an enterprise or an industry has started to look back, turning it around is exceedingly difficult, if it can be done at all. But the obstacle to entrepreneurship and innovation which the success of the present business constitutes is a real one. The problem is precisely that the enterprise is so successful, that it is "healthy" rather than degeneratively diseased by bureaucracy, red tape, or complacency.

This is what makes the examples of existing businesses that do manage successfully to innovate so important, and especially the examples

of existing large and fair-sized businesses that are also successful entrepreneurs and innovators. These businesses show that the obstacle of
success, the obstacle of the existing, *can* be overcome. And it can be
overcome in such a way that both the existing and the new, the mature
and the infant, benefit and prosper. The large companies that are successful entrepreneurs and innovators—Johnson & Johnson, Hoechst,
ASEA, 3M, or the one hundred middle-sized "growth" companies—
clearly know how to do it.

Where the conventional wisdom goes wrong is in its assumption that
entrepreneurship and innovation are natural, creative, or spontaneous.
If entrepreneurship and innovation do not well up in an organization,
something must be stifling them. That only a minority of existing successful businesses are entrepreneurial and innovative is thus seen as
conclusive evidence that existing businesses quench the entrepreneurial spirit.

But entrepreneurship is not "natural"; it is not "creative." It is work.
Hence, the correct conclusion from the evidence is the opposite of the
one commonly reached. That a substantial number of existing businesses, and among them a goodly number of fair-sized, big, and very big
ones, succeed as entrepreneurs and innovators indicates that entrepreneurship and innovation can be achieved by any business. But they
must be consciously striven for. They can be learned, but it requires
effort. Entrepreneurial businesses treat entrepreneurship as a duty.
They are disciplined about it . . . they work at it . . . they practice it.

Specifically, entrepreneurial management requires *policies and
practices* in four major areas.

First, the organization must be made receptive to innovation and
willing to perceive change as an opportunity rather than a threat. It
must be organized to do the hard work of the entrepreneur. Policies
and practices are needed to create the entrepreneurial climate.

Second, systematic measurement or at least appraisal of a company's
performance as entrepreneur and innovator is mandatory, as well as
built-in learning to improve performance.

Third, entrepreneurial management requires specific practices per-
taining to organizational structure, to staffing and managing, and to
compensation, incentives, and rewards.

Fourth, there are some "dont's": things *not to do* in entrepreneurial
management.

II

ENTREPRENEURIAL POLICIES

A Latin poet called the human being *"rerum novarum cupidus* (greedy for new things)." Entrepreneurial management must make each manager of the existing business *"rerum novarum cupidus."*

"How can we overcome the resistance to innovation in the existing organization?" is a question commonly asked by executives. Even if we knew the answer, it would still be the wrong question. The right one is: "How can we make the organization receptive to innovation, want innovation, reach for it, work for it?" When innovation is perceived by the organization as something that goes against the grain, as swimming against the current, if not as a heroic achievement, there will be no innovation. Innovation must be part and parcel of the ordinary, the norm, if not routine.

This requires specific policies. First, innovation, rather than holding on to what already exists, must be made attractive and beneficial to managers. There must be clear understanding throughout the organization that innovation is the best means to preserve and perpetuate that organization, and that it is the foundation for the individual manager's job security and success.

Second, the importance of the need for innovation and the dimensions of its time frame must be both defined and spelled out.

And finally, there needs to be an innovation plan, with specific objectives laid out.

1. There is only one way to make innovation attractive to managers: a systematic policy of abandoning whatever is outworn, obsolete, no longer productive, as well as the mistakes, failures, and misdirections of effort. Every three years or so, the enterprise must put every single product, process, technology, market, distributive channel, not to mention every single internal staff activity, on trial for its life. It must ask: Would we *now* go into this product, this market, this distributive channel, this technology *today?* If the answer is "No," one does not respond with, "Let's make another study." One asks, "What do we have to do to stop wasting resources on this product, this market, this distributive channel, this staff activity?"

Sometimes abandonment is not the answer, and may not even be possible. But then at least one limits further efforts and makes sure that productive resources of men and money are no longer devoured by yesterday. This is the right thing to do in any event to maintain the health of the organization: every organism needs to eliminate its waste products or else it poisons itself. It is, however, an absolute necessity, if an enterprise is to be capable of innovation and is to be receptive to it. "Nothing so powerfully concentrates a man's mind as to know that he will be hung on the morning," Dr. Johnson was fond of saying. Nothing so powerfully concentrates a manager's mind on innovation as the knowledge that the present product or service will be abandoned within the foreseeable future.

Innovation requires major effort. It requires hard work on the part of performing, capable people—the scarcest resource in any organization. "Nothing requires more heroic efforts than to keep a corpse from stinking, and yet nothing is quite so futile," is an old medical proverb. In almost any organization I have come across, the best people are engaged in this futile effort; yet all they can hope to accomplish is to delay acceptance of the inevitable a little longer and at great cost.

But if it is known throughout the organization that the dead will be left to bury their dead, then the living will be willing—indeed, eager —to go to work on innovation.

To allow it to innovate, a business has to be able to free its best performers for the challenges of innovation. Equally it has to be able to devote financial resources to innovation. It will not be able to do either unless it organizes itself to slough off alike the successes of the past, the failures, and especially the "near-misses," the things that "should have worked" but didn't. If executives know that it is company policy to abandon, then they will be motivated to look for the new, to encourage entrepreneurship, and will accept the need to become entrepreneurial themselves. This is the first step—a form of organizational hygiene.

2. The second step, the second policy needed to make an existing business "greedy for new things," is to face up to the fact that all existing products, services, markets, distributive channels, processes, technologies, have limited—and usually short—health and life expectancies.

An analysis of the life cycle of existing products, services, and so on has become popular since the 1970s. Some examples are the strategy concepts advocated by the Boston Consulting group; the books on strategy by the Harvard Business School professor Michael Porter; and so-called portfolio management.*

In the strategies that have been widely advertised these last ten years, especially portfolio management, the findings of such analysis constitute an action program by themselves. This is a misunderstanding and bound to lead to disappointing results, as a good many companies found out when they rushed into such strategies in the late 1970s and early 1980s. The findings should lead to a *diagnosis.* This in turn requires judgment. It requires knowledge of the business, of its products, its markets, its customers, its technologies. It requires experience rather than analysis alone. The idea that bright young people straight from business school and equipped only with sharp analytical tools could crunch out of their computer life-and-death decisions about businesses, products, and markets is pure quackery, to be blunt.

This analysis (in *Managing for Results,* I called it a "Business X-Ray") is intended as a tool to find the right questions rather than a way automatically to come up with the right answers. It is a challenge to all the knowledge that can be found in a given company, and all the experience. It will—and should—provoke dissent. The action that follows from classifying this or that product as "today's breadwinner" is a *risk-taking decision.* And so is what to do with the product that is on the point of becoming "yesterday's breadwinner," or with an "unjustified specialty," or with an "investment in managerial ego."†

3. The Business X-Ray furnishes the information needed to define how much innovation a given business requires, in what areas, and within what time frame. The best and simplest approach to this was developed by Michael J. Kami as a member of the Entrepreneurship Seminar at the New York University Graduate Business School in the 1950s. Kami first applied his approach to IBM, where he served as head of business planning; and then, in the early 1960s, to Xerox, where he served for several years in a similar capacity.

In this approach a company lists each of its products or services, but

---

*All these approaches have their origin in a book of mine published twenty years ago, *Managing for Results* (New York: Harper & Row, 1964), the first systematic work on business strategy, to my knowledge. This in turn grew out of the Entrepreneurship Seminar I ran in the late fifties at New York University. The analysis presented in *Managing for Results* (Chapters 1–5), with its ranking of all products and services into a small number of categories according to their performance, characteristics, and life expectancies, is still a useful tool for the analysis of product-life and product-health.

†For a definition of these terms, see *Managing for Results,* especially Chapter 4, How Are We Doing?

also the markets each serves and the distributive channels it uses, in order to estimate their position on the product life cycle. How much longer will this product still grow? How much longer will it still maintain itself in the marketplace? How soon can it be expected to age and decline—and how fast? When will it become obsolescent? This enables the company to estimate where it would be if it confined itself to managing to the best of its ability what already exists. And this then shows the gap between what can be expected realistically, and what a company still needs to do to achieve its objectives, whether in sales, in market standing, or in profitability.

The gap is the minimum that must be filled if the company is not to go downhill. In fact, the gap has to be filled or the company will soon start to die. The entrepreneurial achievement must be large enough to fill the gap, and timely enough to fill it before the old becomes obsolescent.

But innovative efforts do not carry certainty; they have a high probability of failure and an even higher one of delay. A company therefore should have under way at least three times the innovative efforts which, if successful, would fill the gap.

Most executives consider this excessively high. Yet experience has proved that it errs on the low side, if it errs at all. To be sure, some innovative efforts will do better than anyone expects, but others will do much less well. And everything takes longer than we hope or estimate; everything also requires more effort. Finally, the one thing certain about any major innovative effort is that there are going to be last-minute hitches and last-minute delays. To demand innovative efforts which, if everything goes according to plan, yield three times the minimum results needed is only elementary precaution.

4. Systematic abandonment; the Business X-Ray of the existing business, its products, its services, its markets, its technologies; and the definition of innovation gap and innovation need—these together enable a company to formulate an *entrepreneurial plan* with objectives for innovation and deadlines.

Such a plan ensures that the innovation budget is adequate. And—the most important result of all—it determines how many people are needed, with what abilities and capacities. Only when people with proven performance capacity have been assigned to a project, supplied with the tools, the money, and the information they need to do the work, and given clear and unambiguous deadlines—only then do we have a plan. Until then, we have "good intentions," and what those are good for, everybody knows.

These are the fundamental policies needed to endow a business with entrepreneurial management; to make a business and its management greedy for new things; to make it perceive innovation as the healthy, normal, necessary course of action. Because it is based on a "Business X-Ray"—that is, on an analysis and diagnosis of the current business, its products, services, and markets—this approach also ensures that the existing business will not be neglected in the search for the new, and that the opportunities inherent in the existing products, services, and markets will not be sacrificed to the fascination with novelty.

The Business X-Ray is a tool for decision making. It enables us, indeed forces us, to allocate resources to results in the existing business. But it also makes it possible for us to determine how much is needed to create the business of tomorrow and its new products, new services, and new markets. It enables us to turn innovative intentions into innovative performance.

To render an existing business entrepreneurial, management must take the lead in making obsolete its own products and services rather than waiting for a competitor to do so. The business must be managed so as to perceive in the new an opportunity rather than a threat. It must be managed to work *today* on the products, services, processes, and technologies that will make a different tomorrow.

III

ENTREPRENEURIAL PRACTICES

Entrepreneurship in the existing business also requires managerial practices.

1. First among these, and the simplest, is focusing managerial vision on opportunity. People see what is presented to them; what is not presented tends to be overlooked. And what is presented to most managers are "problems"—especially in the areas where performance falls below expectations—which means that managers tend not to see the opportunities. They are simply not being presented with them.

Management, even in small companies, usually get a report on operating performance once a month. The first page of this report always lists the areas in which performance has fallen below budget, in which there is a "shortfall," in which there is a "problem." At the monthly management meeting, everyone then goes to work on the so-called problems. By the time the meeting adjourns for lunch, the whole morning has been taken up with the discussion of those problems.

Of course, problems have to be paid attention to, taken seriously, and tackled. But if they are the only thing that is being discussed, opportunities will die of neglect. In businesses that want to create receptivity to entrepreneurship, special care is therefore taken that the opportunities are also attended to (cf. Chapter 3 on the unexpected success).

In these companies, the operating report has *two* "first pages": the traditional one lists the problems; the other one lists all the areas in which performance is better than expected, budgeted, or planned for. For, as was stressed earlier, the unexpected success in one's own business is an important symptom of innovative opportunity. If it is not seen as such, the business is altogether unlikely to be entrepreneurial. In fact the business and its managers, in focusing on the "problems," are likely to brush aside the unexpected success as an intrusion on their time and attention. They will say, "Why should we do anything about it? It's going well without our messing around with it." But this only creates an opening for the competitor who is a little more alert and a little less arrogant.

Typically, in companies that are managed for entrepreneurship, there are therefore two meetings on operating results: one to focus on the problems and one to focus on the opportunities.

One medium-sized supplier of health-care products to physicians and hospitals, a company that has gained leadership in a number of new and promising fields, holds an "operations meeting" the second and the last Monday of each month. The first meeting is devoted to problems —to all the things which, in the last month, have done less well than expected or are still doing less well than expected six months later. This meeting does not differ one whit from any other operating meeting. But the second meeting—the one on the last Monday—discusses the areas where the company is doing better than expected: the sales of a given product that have grown faster than projected, or the orders for a new product that are coming in from markets for which it was not designed. The top management of the company (which has grown ten-fold in twenty years) believes that its success is primarily the result of building this opportunity focus into its monthly management meetings. "The opportunities we spot in there," the chief executive officer has said many times, "are not nearly as important as the entrepreneurial attitude which the habit of looking for opportunities creates throughout the entire management group."

2. This company follows a second practice to generate an entrepreneurial spirit throughout its entire management group. Every six months it holds a two-day management meeting for all executives in charge of divisions, markets, and major product lines—a group of about forty or fifty people. The first morning is set aside for reports to the entire group from three or four executives whose units have done exceptionally well as entrepreneurs and innovators during the past year. They are expected to report on what explains their success: "What did we do that turned out to be successful?" "How did we find the opportunity?" "What have we learned, and what entrepreneurial and innovative plans do we have in hand now?"

Again, what actually is reported in these sessions is less important than the impact on attitudes and values. But the operating managers in the company also stress how much they learn in each of these sessions, how many new ideas they get, and how they return back home from these sessions full of plans and eager to try them.

Entrepreneurial companies always look for the people and units that do better and do differently. They single them out, feature them, and constantly ask them: "What are you doing that explains your success?" "What are you doing that the rest of us aren't doing, and what are you *not* doing that the rest of us are?"

3. A third practice, and one that is particularly important in the large company, is a session—informal but scheduled and well prepared—in which a member of the top management group sits down with the junior people from research, engineering, manufacturing, marketing, accounting and so on. The senior opens the session by saying: "I'm not here to make a speech or to tell you anything, I'm here to listen. I want to hear from you what your aspirations are, but above all, where you see opportunities for this company and where you see threats. And what are your ideas for us to try to do new things, develop new products, design new ways of reaching the market? What questions do you have about the company, its policies, its direction . . . its position in the industry, in technology, in the marketplace?"

These sessions should not be held too often; they are a substantial time-burden on senior people. No senior executive should therefore be expected to sit down more than three times a year for a long afternoon or evening with a group of perhaps twenty-five or thirty juniors. But the sessions should be maintained systematically. They are an excellent vehicle for upward communications, the best means to enable juniors, and especially professionals, to look up from their narrow specialties and see the whole enterprise. They enable juniors to understand what top management is concerned with, and why. In turn, they give the seniors badly needed insight into the values, vision, and concerns of their younger colleagues. Above all, these sessions are one of the most effective ways to instill entrepreneurial vision throughout the company.

This practice has one built-in requirement. Those who suggest anything new, or even a change in the way things are being done, whether in respect to product or process, to market or service, should be expected to *go to work.* They should be asked to submit, within a reasonable period, a working paper to the presiding senior and to their colleagues in the session, in which they try to develop their idea. What would it look like if converted into reality? What in turn does reality have to look like for the idea to make sense? What are the assumptions regarding customers and markets, and so on. How much work is needed . . . how much money and how many people . . . and how much time? And what results might be expected?

Again, the yield of entrepreneurial ideas from all this may not be its most important product—though in many organizations the yield has been consistently high. The most valuable achievement may well be entrepreneurial vision, receptivity to innovation, and "greed for new things" throughout the entire organization.

IV

MEASURING INNOVATIVE PERFORMANCE

For a business to be receptive to entrepreneurship, innovative performance must be included among the measures by which that business controls itself. Only if we assess the entrepreneurial performance of a business will entrepreneurship become action. Human beings tend to behave as they are expected to.

In the normal assessments of a business, innovative performance is conspicuous by its absence. Yet it is not particularly difficult to build measurement, or at least judgment, of entrepreneurial and innovative performance into the controls of the business.

1. The first step builds into each innovative project feedback from results to expectations. This indicates the quality and reliability of both our innovative plans and our innovative efforts.

Research managers long ago learned to ask at the beginning of any research project: "What results do we expect from this project? When do we expect those results? When do we appraise the progress of the project so that we have control?" They have also learned to check whether their expectations are borne out by the actual course of events. This shows them whether they are tending to be too optimistic or too pessimistic, whether they expect results too soon or are willing to wait too long, whether they are inclined either to overestimate the impact of a successfully concluded research project or to underestimate it. And this in turn enables them to correct said tendencies, and to identify both the areas in which they do well and the ones in which they tend to do poorly. Such feedback is, of course, needed for all innovative efforts, not merely for technical research and development.

The first aim is to find out what we are doing well, for one can always go ahead and do more of the same, even if we usually do not have the slightest idea why we are doing well in a given area. Next, one finds out the limitations on one's strengths: for instance, a tendency either to underestimate the amount of time needed or to overestimate it; or a tendency to overestimate the amount of research required in a given area while underestimating the resources required for developing the results of research into a product or a process. Or one finds a tendency, very common and very damaging, to slow down marketing or promotion efforts for the new venture just when it is about to take off.

One of the most successful of the world's major banks attributes its achievements to the feedback it builds into all new efforts, whether it is going into a new market such as South Korea, into equipment leasing, or into issuing credit cards. By building feedback frcm results to expectations for all new endeavors, the bank and its top management have also learned what they can expect from new ventures: How soon a new effort can be expected to produce results and when it should be supported by greater efforts and greater resources.

Such feedback is needed for all innovative efforts, the development and introduction of a new safety program, say, or a new compensation plan. What are the first indications that the new effort is likely to get

into trouble and needs to be reconsidered? And what are the indications that enable us to say that this effort, even though it looks as if it
were headed for trouble, is actually doing all right, but also that it may
take more time than we originally anticipated?

2. The next step is to develop a systematic review of innovative
efforts all together. Every few years an entrepreneurial management
looks at all the innovative efforts of the business. Which ones should
receive more support at this stage and should be pushed? Which ones
have opened up new opportunities? Which ones, on the other hand, are
not doing what we expected them to do, and what action should we
take? Has the time come to abandon them, or, on the contrary, has the
time come to redouble our efforts—but with what expectations and
what deadline?

The top management people at one of the world's largest and most
successful pharmaceutical companies sit down once a year to review its
innovative efforts. First, they review every new drug development,
asking: "Is this development going in the right direction and at the right
speed? Is it leading to something we want to put into our own line, or
is it going to be something that won't fit our markets so we'd better
license it to another pharmaceutical manufacturer? Or ought we perhaps abandon it?" And then the same people look at all the other
innovative efforts, especially in marketing, asking exactly the same
questions. Finally, they review, equally carefully, the innovative performance of their major competitors. In terms of its research budget
and its total expenditures for innovation, this company ranks only in the
middle level. Its record as an innovator and entrepreneur is, however,
outstanding.

3. Finally, entrepreneurial management entails judging the company's total innovative performance against the company's innovative
objectives, against its performance and standing in the market, and
against its performance as a business all together.

Every five years, perhaps, top management sits down with its associates in each major area and asks: "What have you contributed to this
company in the past five years that really made a difference? And what
do you plan to contribute in the next five years?"

But are not innovative efforts by their nature intangible? How can
one measure them?

It is indeed true that there are some areas in which no one can, or
should, decide the degree of relative importance. Which is more signifi-

cant, a breakthrough in basic research, which years later may lead to an effective cure for certain cancers, or a new formulation that enables patients to administer an old but effective medication themselves instead of having to visit a physician or a hospital three times a week? It is impossible to decide. Equally, a company must choose between a new way to service customers, which enables the company to retain an important account it would otherwise have lost, and a new product, which gives the company leadership in markets that, while still small, may within a few years become big and important ones. These are judgments rather than measurements. But they are not arbitrary; they are not even subjective. And they are quite rigorous even though not capable of quantification. Above all, they do what a "measurement" is meant to enable us to do: to take purposeful action based on knowledge rather than on opinion or guesswork.

The most important question for the typical business in this review is probably: Have we gained innovative leadership, or at least maintained it? Leadership does not necessarily equate with size. It means to be accepted as the leader, recognized as the standard-setter; above all, it means having the freedom to lead rather than being obliged to follow. This is the acid test of successful entrepreneurship in the existing business.

V

STRUCTURES

Policies, practices, and measurements make possible entrepreneurship and innovation. They remove or reduce possible impediments. They create the proper attitude and provide the proper tools. But innovation is done by people. And people work within a structure.

For the existing business to be capable of innovation, it has to create a structure that allows people to be entrepreneurial. It has to devise relationships that center on entrepreneurship. It has to make sure that its rewards and incentives, its compensation, personnel decisions, and policies, all reward the right entrepreneurial behavior and do not penalize it.

1. This means, first, that the entrepreneurial, the new, has to be organized separately from the old and existing. Whenever we have tried to make an existing unit the carrier of the entrepreneurial project,

we have failed. This is particularly true, of course, in the large business, but it is true in medium-sized businesses as well, and even in small businesses.

One reason is that (as said earlier) the existing business always requires time and effort on the part of the people responsible for it, and deserves the priority they give it. The new always looks so puny—so unpromising—next to the reality of the massive, ongoing business. The existing business, after all, has to nourish the struggling innovation. But the "crisis" in today's business has to be attended to as well. The people responsible for an existing business will therefore always be tempted to postpone action on anything new, entrepreneurial, or innovative until it is too late. No matter what has been tried—and we have now been trying every conceivable mechanism for thirty or forty years—existing units have been found to be capable mainly of extending, modifying, and adapting what already is in existence. The new belongs elsewhere.

2. This means also that there has to be a special locus for the new venture within the organization, and it has to be pretty high up. Even though the new project, by virtue of its current size, revenues, and markets, does not rank with existing products, somebody in top management must have the specific assignment to work on tomorrow as an entrepreneur and innovator.

This need not be a full-time job; in the smaller business, it very often cannot be a full-time job. But it needs to be a clearly defined job and one for which somebody with authority and prestige is fully accountable. These people will normally also be responsible for the policies necessary to build entrepreneurship into the existing business, for the abandonment analysis, for the Business X-Ray, and for developing the innovation objectives to plug the gap between what can be expected of the existing products and services and what is needed for survival and growth of the company. They are also normally charged with the systematic analysis of innovative opportunities—the analysis of the innovative opportunities presented in the preceding section of this book, the Practice of Innovation. They should be further charged with responsibility for the analysis of the innovative and entrepreneurial ideas that come up from the organization, for example, in the recommended "informal" session with the juniors.

And innovative efforts, especially those aimed at developing new businesses, products, or services, should normally report directly to this "executive in charge of innovation" rather than to managers further down the hierarchy. They should never report to line managers charged with responsibility for ongoing operations.

This will be considered heresy in most companies, particularly "well-managed" ones. But the new project is an infant and will remain one for the foreseeable future, and infants belong in the nursery. The "adults," that is, the executives in charge of existing businesses or products, will have neither time nor understanding for the infant project. They cannot afford to be bothered.

Disregard of this rule cost a major machine-tool manufacturer its leadership in robotics.

The company had the basic patents on machine tools for automated mass production. It had excellent engineering, an excellent reputation, and first-rate manufacturing. Everyone in the early years of factory automation—around 1975—expected it to emerge as the leader. Ten years later it had dropped out of the race entirely. The company had placed the unit charged with the development of machine tools for automated production three or four levels down in the organization, and had it report to people charged with designing, making, and selling the company's traditional machine-tool lines. These people were supportive; in fact, the work on robotics had been mainly their idea. But they were far too busy defending their traditional lines against a lot of new competitors such as the Japanese, redesigning them to fit new specifications, demonstrating, marketing, financing, and servicing them. Whenever the people in charge of the "infant" went to their bosses for a decision, they were told, "I have no time now, come back next week." Robotics were, after all, only a promise; the existing machine-tool lines produced millions of dollars each year.

Unfortunately, this is a common error.

The best, and perhaps the only, way to avoid killing off the new by sheer neglect is to set up the innovative project from the start as a separate business.

The best known practitioners of this approach are three American companies: Procter & Gamble, the soap, detergent, edible oil, and food producer—a very large and aggressively entrepreneurial company; Johnson & Johnson, the hygiene and health-care supplier; and 3M, a major manufacturer of industrial and consumer products. These three companies differ in the details of practice but essentially all three have the same policy. They set up the new venture as a separate business from the beginning and put a project manager in charge. The project manager remains in charge until the project is either abandoned or has achieved its objective and become a full-fledged business. And until then, the project manager can mobilize all the skills as they are needed—research, manufacturing, finance, marketing—and put them to work on the project team.

A company that engages in more than one innovative effort at a time (and bigger companies usually do) might have all the "infants" report directly to the same member of the top management group. It does not greatly matter that the ventures have different technologies, markets, or product characteristics. They all are new, small, and entrepreneurial. They are all exposed to the same "childhood diseases." The problems from which the entrepreneurial venture suffers, and the decisions it requires, tend to be pretty much the same regardless of technology, of market, or of product line. Somebody has to have time for them, to give them the attention they need, to take the trouble to understand what the problems are, the crucial decisions, the things that really matter in a given innovative effort. And this person has to have sufficient stature in the business to be able to represent the infant project—and to make the decision to stop an effort if it is going nowhere.

3. There is another reason why a new, innovative effort is best set up separately: to keep away from it the burdens it cannot yet carry. Both the investment in a new product line and its returns should, for instance, not be included in the traditional return-on-investment analysis until the product line has been on the market for a number of years. To ask the fledgling development to shoulder the full burdens an existing business imposes on its units is like asking a six-year-old to go on a long hike carrying a sixty-pound pack; neither will get very far. And yet the existing business has requirements with respect to accounting, to personnel policy, to reporting of all kinds, which it cannot easily waive.

The innovative effort and the unit that carries it require different policies, rules, and measurements in many areas. How about the company's pension plan, for instance? Often it makes sense to give people in the innovative unit a participation in future profits rather than to put them into a pension plan when they are producing, as yet, no earnings to supply a pension fund contribution.

The area in which separation of the new, innovative unit from the ongoing business is most important is compensation and rewards of key people. What works best in a going, established business would kill the "infant"—and yet not be adequate compensation for its key people.

Indeed, the compensation scheme that is most popular in large businesses, one based on return on assets or on investment, is a near-complete bar to innovation.

I learned this many years ago in a major chemical company. Everybody knew that one of its central divisions had to produce new materials to stay in business. The plans for these materials were there, the scientific work had been done . . . but nothing happened. Year after year there was another excuse. Finally, the division's general manager spoke up at a review meeting, "My management group and I are compensated primarily on the basis of return-on-investment. The moment we spend money on developing the new materials, our return will go down by half for at least four years. Even if I am still here in four years time when we should show the first returns on these investments—and I doubt that the company will put up with me that long if profits are that much lower—I'm taking bread out of the mouths of all my associates in the meantime. Is it reasonable to expect us to do this?" The formula was changed and the developmental expenses for the new project were taken out of the return-on-investment figures. Within eighteen months the new materials were on the market. Two years later they had given the division leadership in its field which it has retained to this day. Four years later the division doubled its profits.

In terms of compensation and rewards for innovative efforts, however, it is far easier to define what should not be done than it is to spell out what should. The requirements are conflicting: the new project must not be burdened with a compensation load it cannot carry, yet the people involved must be adequately motivated by rewards appropriate to their efforts.

Specifically, this means that the people in charge of the new project should be kept at a moderate salary. It is, however, quite unrealistic to ask them to work for less money than they received in their old jobs. People put in charge of a new area within an existing business are likely to make good money. They are also the people who could easily move to other jobs, either within or outside the company, in which they would make more money. One therefore has to start out with their existing compensation and benefits.

One method that both 3M and Johnson & Johnson use effectively is to promise that the person who successfully develops a new product, a new market, or a new service and then builds a business on it will become the head of that business: general manager, vice-president, or division president, with the rank, compensation, bonuses, and stock options appropriate to the level. This can be a sizable reward, and yet it does not commit the company to anything except in case of success.

Another method—and which one is preferable will depend largely on the tax laws at the time—is to give the people who take on the new development a share in future profits. The venture might, for instance, be treated as if it were a separate company in which the entrepreneurial managers in charge have a stake, say 25 percent. When the venture reaches maturity, they are bought out at a pre-set formula based on sales and profits.

One thing more is needed: the people who take on the innovating task in an existing business also "venture." It is only fair that their employer share the risk. They should have the option of returning to their old job at their old compensation rate if the innovation fails. They should not be rewarded for failure, but they should certainly not be penalized for trying.

4. As implied in discussing individual compensation, the returns on innovation will be quite different from those of the existing business and will have to be measured differently. To say, "We expect all our businesses to show at least a fifteen percent pre-tax return each year and ten percent annual growth" may make sense for existing businesses and existing products. It makes absolutely no sense for the new project, being at once much too high and much too low.

For a long time (years, in many cases) the new endeavor shows neither profits nor growth. It absorbs resources. But then it should grow very fast for quite a long time and return the money invested in its development at least fifty-fold—if not at a much higher rate—or else the innovation is a failure. An innovation starts small but it should end big. It should result in a new major business rather than in just another "specialty" or a "respectable" addition to the product line.

Only by analyzing a company's own innovative experience, the feedback from its performance on its expectations, can the company determine what the appropriate expectations are for innovations in its industry and its markets. What are the appropriate time spans? And what is the optimal distribution of effort? Should there be a heavy investment of men and money at the beginning, or should the effort at the start be confined to one person, with a helper or two, working alone? When should the effort then be scaled up? And when should "development" become "business," producing large but conventional returns?

These are key questions. The answers to them are not to be found in books. Yet they cannot be answered arbitrarily, by hunch, or by fighting it out. Entrepreneurial companies do know what patterns, rhythms, and time spans pertain to innovations in their specific industry, technology, and market.

The innovative major bank mentioned earlier knows, for instance, that a new subsidiary established in a new country will require investment for at least three years. It should break even in the fourth year, and should have repaid the total investment by the middle of the sixth year. If it still requires investment by the end of the sixth year, it is a disappointment and should probably be shut down.

A new major service—leasing, for example—has a similar though somewhat shorter cycle. Procter & Gamble—or so it looks from the outside—knows that its new products should be on the market and selling two to three years after work on them has begun. They should have established themselves as market leaders eighteen months later. IBM, it seems, figures on a five-year lead time for a new major product before market introduction. Within another year the new product should then start to grow fast. It should attain market leadership and profitability fairly early in its second year on the market, have repaid the full investment by the early months of the third year, and peak and level out in its fifth year on the market. By then, a new IBM product should already have begun to make it obsolescent.

The only way, however, to know these things is through the systematic analysis of the performance of the company and of its competitors, that is, by systematic feedback from innovation results to innovation expectations and by regular appraisal of the company's performance as entrepreneur.

And once a company understands what results should and could be expected from its innovative efforts, it can then design the appropriate controls. These will both measure how well units and their managers perform in innovation and determine which innovative efforts to push, which to reconsider, and which to abandon.

5. The final structural requirement for entrepreneurship in the existing business is that a person or a component group should be held clearly accountable.

In the "middle-sized growth companies" mentioned earlier, this is usually the primary responsibility of the chief executive officer (CEO). In large companies, it probably is more likely a designated and very senior member of the top management group. In smaller businesses, this executive in charge of entrepreneurship and innovation may well carry other responsibilities as well.

The cleanest organizational structure for entrepreneurship, though suitable only in the very large company, is a totally separate innovating operation or development company.

The earliest example of this was set up more than one hundred years ago, in 1872, by Hefner-Alteneck, the first college-trained engineer hired by a manufacturing company anywhere, the German Siemens Company. Hefner started the first "research lab" in industry. Its members were charged with inventing new and different products and processes. But they were also responsible for identifying new and different end uses and new and different markets. And they not only did the technical work; they were responsible for development of the manufacturing process, for the introduction of the new product into the marketplace, and for its profitability.

Fifty years later, in the 1920s, the American DuPont Company independently set up a similar unit and called it a Development Department. This department gathers innovative ideas from all over the company, studies them, thinks them through, analyzes them. Then it proposes to top management which ones should be tackled as major innovative projects. From the beginning, it brings to bear on the innovation all the resources needed: research, development, manufacturing, marketing, finance, and so on. It is in charge until the new product or service has been on the market for a few years.

Whether the responsibility for innovation rests with the chief executive officer, with another member of top management, or with a separate component, whether it is a full-time assignment or part of an executive's responsibilities, it should always be set up and recognized both as a separate responsibility and as a responsibility of top management. And it should always include the systematic and purposeful search for innovative opportunities.

It might be asked, Are all these policies and practices necessary? Don't they interfere with the entrepreneurial spirit and stifle creativity? And cannot a business be entrepreneurial without such policies and practices? The answer is, Perhaps, but neither very successfully nor for very long.

Discussions of entrepreneurship tend to focus on the personalities and attitudes of top management people, and especially of the chief executive.* Of course, any top management can damage and stifle entrepreneurship within its company. It's easy enough. All it takes is to say "No" to every new idea and to keep on saying it for a few years— and then make sure that those who came up with the new ideas never get a reward or a promotion and become ex-employees fairly swiftly. It is far less certain, however, that top management personalities and attitudes can by themselves—without the proper policies and practices —create an entrepreneurial business, which is what most of the books on entrepreneurship assert, at least by implication. In the few short-lived cases I know of, the companies were built and still run by the founder. Even then, when it gets to be successful the company soon ceases to be entrepreneurial unless it adopts the policies and practices of entrepreneurial management. The reason why top management personalities and attitudes do not suffice in any but the very young or very small business is, of course, that even a medium-sized enterprise is a pretty large organization. It requires a good many people who know what they are supposed to do, want to do it, are motivated toward doing it, and are supplied with both the tools and continuous reaffirmation. Otherwise there is only lip service; entrepreneurship soon becomes confined to the CEO's speeches.

And I know of no business that continued to remain entrepreneurial beyond the founder's departure, unless the founder had built into the organization the policies and practices of entrepreneurial management. If these are lacking, the business becomes timid and backward-looking within a few years at the very latest. And these companies do not even realize, as a rule, that they have lost their essential quality, the one element that had made them stand out, until it is perhaps too late. For this realization one needs a measurement of entrepreneurial performance.

Two companies that were entrepreneurial businesses *par excellence* under their founders' management are good examples: Walt Disney Productions and McDonald's. The respective founders, Walt Disney and Ray Kroc, were men of tremendous imagination and drive, each the very embodiment of creative, entrepreneurial, and innovative thinking. Both built into their companies strong operating day-to-day

---

*The best presentation of this viewpoint is in Rosabeth M. Kanter's *The Change Masters* (New York: Simon & Schuster, 1983).

management. But both kept to themselves the entrepreneurial responsibility within their companies. Both depended on the "entrepreneurial
personality" and did not embed the entrepreneurial spirit in specific
policies and practices. Within a few years after the death of these men,
their companies had become stodgy, backward-looking, timid, and defensive.

Companies that have built entrepreneurial management into their
structure—Procter & Gamble, Johnson & Johnson, Marks and Spencer
—continue to be innovators and entrepreneurial leaders decade after
decade, irrespective of changes in chief executives or economic conditions.

VI

STAFFING

How should the existing business staff for entrepreneurship and
innovation? Are there such people as "entrepreneurs"? Are they a
special breed?

The literature is full of discussions of these questions; full of stories
of the "entrepreneurial personality" and of people who will never do
anything but innovate. In the light of our experience—and it is considerable—these discussions are pointless. By and large, people who do not
feel comfortable as innovators or as entrepreneurs will not volunteer
for such jobs; the gross misfits eliminate themselves. The others can
learn the practice of innovation. Our experience shows that an executive who has performed in other assignments will do a decent job as an
entrepreneur. In successful entrepreneurial businesses, nobody seems
to worry whether a given person is likely to do a good job of development or not. People of all kinds of temperaments and backgrounds
apparently do equally well. Any young engineer in 3M who comes to
top management with an idea that makes sense is expected to take on
its development.

Equally, there is no reason to worry where the successful entrepreneur will end up. To be sure, there are some people who only want to
work on new projects and never want to run anything. When most
English families still had nannies, many did not want to stay after
"their" baby got to the stage when it began to walk and talk—in other
words, when it was no longer a baby. But many were perfectly content

to stay on and did not find it difficult to look after a much older child. The people who do not want to be anything but entrepreneurs are unlikely to be in the employ of an existing business to begin with, and even more unlikely to have been successful in it. And the people who do well as entrepreneurs in an existing business have, as a rule, proved themselves earlier as managers in the same organization. It is thus reasonable to assume that they can both innovate and manage what already exists. There are some people at Procter & Gamble and at 3M who make a career of being project managers and who take on a new project as soon as they have successfully finished an old one. But most people at the higher levels of these companies have made their careers out of "project management," into "product management," into "market management," and finally into a senior company-wide position. And the same is true of Johnson & Johnson and of Citibank.

The best proof that entrepreneurship is a question of behavior, policies, and practices rather than personality is the growing number of older large-company people in the United States who make entrepreneurship their second career. Increasingly, middle- and upper-level executives and senior professionals who have spent their entire working lives in large companies—more often than not with the same employer —take early retirement after twenty-five or thirty years of service when they have reached what they realize is their terminal job. At fifty or fifty-five, these middle-aged people then become entrepreneurs. Some start their own business. Some, especially technical specialists, set up shop as consultants to new and small ventures. Some join a new small company in a senior position. And the great majority are both successful and happy in their new assignment.

Modern Maturity, the magazine of the American Association of Retired Persons, is full of stories of such people, and of advertisements by new small companies looking for them. In a management seminar for chief executive officers that I ran in 1983, there were fifteen such second-career entrepreneurs (fourteen men and one woman) among the forty-eight participants. During a special session for these people, I asked them whether they had been frustrated or stifled while working all those years for big companies, as "entrepreneurial personalities" are supposed to be. They thought the question totally absurd. I then asked whether they had much difficulty changing their roles; they thought this equally absurd. As one of them said—and all the others nodded assent—"Good management is good management, whether you run a

$180 million department at General Electric, with its billions of sales as I used to do, or a new, growing diagnostic-instrument innovator with $6 million in sales, as I do now. Of course I do different things and do things differently. But I apply the concepts I learned at G.E. and do exactly the same analysis. The transition was easier, in fact, than when I moved, ten years earlier, from being a bench engineer into my first management job."

Public-service institutions teach the same lesson. Among the most successful innovators in recent American history are two men in higher education, Alexander Schure and Ernest Boyer. Schure started out as a successful inventor in the electronics field, with a good many patents to his name. But in 1955, when he was in his early thirties, he founded the New York Institute of Technology as a private university without support from government, foundation, or big company, and with brand-new ideas regarding the kind of students to be recruited and what they were to be taught as well as how. Thirty years later, his institute has become a leading technical university with four campuses, one of them a medical school, and almost twelve thousand students. Schure still works as a successful electronics inventor. But he has also been for these thirty years the full-time chancellor of his university, and has, by all accounts, built up a professional and effective management team.

In contrast to Schure, Boyer started out as an administrator, first in the University of California system, then in the State University of New York, which with 350,000 student and 64 campuses is the biggest and most bureaucratic of American university systems. By 1970, Boyer, at forty-two, had worked his way to the top and was appointed chancellor. He immediately founded the Empire State College—actually not a college at all but an unconventional solution to one of the oldest and most frustrating failures of American higher education, the degree program for adults who do not have full academic credentials.

Although tried many times, this had never worked before. If these adults were admitted to college programs together with the "regular" younger students, no attention was usually paid to their aims, their needs, and least of all to their experience. They were treated as if they were eighteen years old, got discouraged, and soon dropped out. But if, as was tried repeatedly, they were put into special "continuing education programs," they were likely to be considered a nuisance and shoved aside, with programs staffed by whatever faculty the university could most easily spare. In Boyer's Empire State College, the adults attend regular university courses in one of the colleges or universities of the state university. But first the adult students are assigned a "mentor," usually a member of a nearby state university faculty. The mentor helps them work out their programs and decide whether they need special preparation, and where, conversely, their experience qualifies them for advanced standing and work. And then the mentor acts as broker, negotiating admission, standing, and program for each applicant with the appropriate institution.

All this may sound like common sense—and so it is. Yet it was quite a break with the habits and mores of American academia and was fought hard by the state university establishment. But Boyer persisted. His Empire State College program has now become the first successful program of this kind in American higher education, with more than six thousand students, a negligible dropout rate, and a master's program. Boyer, the arch-innovator, did not cease to be an "administrator." From chancellor of the State University of New York he went on to become, first, President Carter's Commissioner of Education, and then president of the Carnegie Foundation for the Advancement of Teaching—respectively, the most "bureaucratic" and the most "establishment" job in American academia.

These examples do not prove that anyone can excel at being both a bureaucrat and an innovator. Schure and Boyer are surely exceptional people. But their experiences do show that there is no specific "personality" for either task. What is needed is willingness to learn, willingness to work hard and persistently, willingness to exercise self-discipline, willingness to adapt and to apply the right policies and practices. Which is exactly what any enterprise that adopted entrepreneurial management has found out with respect to people and staffing.

To enable the entrepreneurial project to be run successfully, as something new, the structure and organization have to be right; relationships have to be appropriate; and compensation and rewards have to fit. But when all this has been done, the question of who is to run the unit, and what should be done with them when they have succeeded in building up the new project, must be decided on an individual basis for this person or that person, rather than according to this or that psychological theory for none of which there is much empirical evidence.

Staffing decisions in the entrepreneurial business are made like any other decision about people and jobs. Of course, they are risk-taking decisions: decisions about people always are. Of course, they have to be made carefully and conscientiously. And they have to be made the correct way. First, the assignment must be thought through; then one considers a number of people; then one checks carefully their performance records; and finally one checks out each of the candidates with a few people for whom he or she has worked. But all this applies to every decision that puts a person into a job. And in the entrepreneurial company, the batting average in people-decisions is the same for entrepreneurs as it is for other managerial and professional people.

VII

THE DONT'S

There are some things the entrepreneurial management of an existing business should not do.

1. The most important caveat is not to mix managerial units and entrepreneurial ones. Do not ever put the entrepreneurial into the existing managerial component. Do not make innovation an objective for people charged with running, exploiting, optimizing what already exists.

But it is also inadvisable—in fact, almost a guarantee of failure—for a business to try to become entrepreneurial without changing its basic policies and practices. To be an entrepreneur on the side rarely works.

In the last ten or fifteen years a great many large American companies have tried to go into joint ventures with entrepreneurs. Not one of these attempts has succeeded; the entrepreneurs found themselves stymied by policies by basic rules, by a "climate" they felt was bureaucratic, stodgy, reactionary. But at the same time their partners, the people from the big company, could not figure out what the entrepreneurs were trying to do and thought them undisciplined, wild, visionary.

By and large, big companies have been successful as entrepreneurs only if they use their own people to build the venture. They have been successful only when they use people whom they understand and who understand them, people whom they trust and who in turn know how to get things done in the existing business; people, in other words, with whom one can work as partners. But this presupposes that the entire company is imbued with the entrepreneurial spirit, that it wants innovation and is reaching out for it, considering it both a necessity and an opportunity. It presupposes that the entire organization has been made "greedy for new things."

2. Innovative efforts that take the existing business out of its own field are rarely successful. Innovation had better not be "diversification." Whatever the benefits of diversification, it does not mix with entrepreneurship and innovation. The new is always sufficiently difficult not to attempt it in an area one does not understand. An existing business innovates where it has expertise, whether knowledge of market or knowledge of technology. Anything new will predictably get into trouble, and then one has to know the business. Diversification itself rarely works unless it, too, is built on commonality with the existing business, whether commonality of the market or commonality of the technology. Even then, as I have discussed elsewhere,* diversification has its problems. But if one adds to the difficulties and demands of diversification the difficulties and demands of entrepreneurship, the result is predictable disaster. So one innovates only where one understands.

3. Finally, it is almost always futile to avoid making one's own business entrepreneurial by "buying in," that is, by acquiring small entrepreneurial ventures. Acquisitions rarely work unless the company that does the acquiring is willing and able within a fairly short time to furnish management to the acquisition. The managers that have come with the acquired company rarely stay around very long. If they were owners, they have now become wealthy; if they were professional managers, they are likely to stay around only if given much bigger opportunities in the new, acquiring company. So, within a year or two, the acquirer has to furnish management to run the business that has been bought. This is particularly true when a non-entrepreneurial company buys an entrepreneurial one. The management people in the new acquired venture soon find that they cannot work with the people in their new parent company, and vice versa. I myself know of no case where "buying in" has worked.

A business that wants to be able to innovate, wants to have a chance to succeed and prosper in a time of rapid change, has to build entre-

*In *Management: Tasks, Responsibilities, Practices,* especially Chapters 56 and 57.

preneurial management into its own system. It has to adopt policies that
create throughout the entire organization the desire to innovate and
the habits of entrepreneurship and innovation. To be a successful entrepreneur, the existing business, large or small, has to be managed as an
entrepreneurial business.

14

Entrepreneurship in
the Service Institution

I

Public-service institutions such as government agencies, labor unions, churches, universities, and schools, hospitals, community and charitable organizations, professional and trade associations and the like, need to be entrepreneurial and innovative fully as much as any business does. Indeed, they may need it more. The rapid changes in today's society, technology, and economy are simultaneously an even greater threat to them and an even greater opportunity.

Yet public-service institutions find it far more difficult to innovate than even the most "bureaucratic" company. The "existing" seems to be even more of an obstacle. To be sure, every service institution likes to get bigger. In the absence of a profit test, size is the one criterion of success for a service institution, and growth a goal in itself. And then, of course, there is always so much more that needs to be done. But stopping what has "always been done" and doing something new are equally anathema to service institutions, or at least excruciatingly painful to them.

Most innovations in public-service institutions are imposed on them either by outsiders or by catastrophe. The modern university, for instance, was created by a total outsider, the Prussian diplomat Wilhelm von Humboldt. He founded the University of Berlin in 1809 when the traditional university of the seventeenth and eighteenth century had been all but completely destroyed by the French Revolution and the Napoleonic wars. Sixty years later, the modern American university came into being when the country's traditional colleges and universities were dying and could no longer attract students.

Similarly, all basic innovations in the military in this century, whether in structure or in strategy, have followed on ignominious malfunction or crushing defeat: the organization of the American Army and of its strategy by a New York lawyer, Elihu Root, Teddy Roosevelt's Secretary of War, after its disgraceful performance in the Spanish-American War; the reorganization, a few years later, of the British Army and its strategy by Secretary of War Lord Haldane, another civilian, after the equally disgraceful performance of the British in the Boer War; and the rethinking of the German Army's structure and strategy after the defeat of World War I.

And in government, the greatest innovative thinking in recent political history, America's New Deal of 1933–36, was triggered by a Depression so severe as almost to unravel the country's social fabric.

Critics of bureaucracy blame the resistance of public-service institutions to entrepreneurship and innovation on "timid bureaucrats," on time-servers who "have never met a payroll," or on "power-hungry politicians." It is a very old litany—in fact, it was already hoary when Machiavelli chanted it almost five hundred years ago. The only thing that changes is who intones it. At the beginning of this century, it was the slogan of the so-called liberals and now it is the slogan of the so-called neo-conservatives. Alas, things are not that simple, and "better people"—that perennial panacea of reformists—are a mirage. The most entrepreneurial, innovative people behave like the worst time-serving bureaucrat or power-hungry politician six months after they have taken over the management of a public-service institution, particularly if it is a government agency.

The forces that impede entrepreneurship and innovation in a public-service institution are inherent in it, integral to it, inseparable from it.* The best proof of this are the internal staff services in businesses, which are, in effect, the "public-service institutions" within business corporations. These are typically headed by people who have come out of operations and have proven their capacity to perform in competitive markets. And yet the internal staff services are not notorious as innovators. They are good at building empires—and they always want to do more of the same. They resist abandoning anything they are doing. But they rarely innovate once they have been established.

*On the public-service institution and its characteristics, see the section on Performance in the Service Institution, Chapters 11–14, in *Management: Tasks, Responsibilities, Practices.*

There are three main reasons why the existing enterprise presents so much more of an obstacle to innovation in the public-service institution than it does in the typical business enterprise.

1. First, the public-service institution is based on a "budget" rather than being paid out of its results. It is paid for its efforts and out of funds somebody else has earned, whether the taxpayer, the donors of a charitable organization, or the company for which a personnel department or the marketing services staff work. The more efforts the public service institution engages in, the greater its budget will be. And "success" in the public-service institution is defined by getting a larger budget rather than obtaining results. Any attempt to slough off activities and efforts therefore diminishes the public-service institution. It causes it to lose stature and prestige. Failure cannot be acknowledged. Worse still, the fact that an objective has been attained cannot be admitted.

2. Second, a service institution is dependent on a multitude of constituents. In a business that sells its products on the market, one constituent, the consumer, eventually overrides all the others. A business needs only a very small share of a small market to be successful. Then it can satisfy the other constituents, whether shareholders, workers, the community, and so on. But precisely because public-service institutions —and that includes the staff activities within a business corporation— have no "results" out of which they are being paid, any constituent, no matter how marginal, has in effect a veto power. A public-service institution has to satisfy everyone; certainly, it cannot afford to alienate anyone.

The moment a service institution starts an activity, it acquires a "constituency," which then refuses to have the program abolished or even significantly modified. But anything new is always controversial. This means that it is opposed by existing constituencies without having formed, as yet, a constituency of its own to support it.

3. The most important reason, however, is that public-service institutions exist after all to "do good." This means that they tend to see their mission as a moral absolute rather than as economic and subject to a cost/benefit calculus. Economics always seeks a different allocation of the same resources to obtain a higher yield. Everything economic is therefore relative. In the public-service institution, there is no such thing as a higher yield. If one is "doing good," then there is no "better."

Indeed, failure to attain objectives in the quest for a "good" only means that efforts need to be redoubled. The forces of evil must be far more powerful than expected and need to be fought even harder.

For thousands of years the preachers of all sorts of religions have held forth against the "sins of the flesh." Their success has been limited, to say the least. But this is no argument as far as the preachers are concerned. It does not persuade them to devote their considerable talents to pursuits in which results may be more easily attainable. On the contrary, it only proves that their efforts need to be redoubled. Avoiding the "sins of the flesh" is clearly a "moral good," and thus an absolute, which does not admit of any cost/benefit calculation.

Few public-service institutions define their objectives in such absolute terms. But even company personnel departments and manufacturing service staffs tend to see their mission as "doing good," and therefore as being moral and absolute instead of being economic and relative.

This means that public-service institutions are out to maximize rather than to optimize. "Our mission will not be completed," asserts the head of the Crusade Against Hunger, "as long as there is one child on the earth going to bed hungry." If he were to say, "Our mission will be completed if the largest possible number of children that can be reached through existing distribution channels get enough to eat not to be stunted," he would be booted out of office. But if the goal is maximization, it can never be attained. Indeed, the closer one comes toward attaining one's objective, the more efforts are called for. For, once optimization has been reached (and the optimum in most efforts lies between 75 and 80 percent of theoretical maximum), additional costs go up exponentially while additional results fall off exponentially. The closer a public-service institution comes to attaining its objectives, therefore, the more frustrated it will be and the harder it will work on what it is already doing.

It will, however, behave exactly the same way the less it achieves. Whether it succeeds or fails, the demand to innovate and to do something else will be resented as an attack on its basic commitment, on the very reason for its existence, and on its beliefs and values.

These are serious obstacles to innovation. They explain why, by and large, innovation in public services tends to come from new ventures rather than from existing institutions.

The most extreme example around these days may well be the labor risk-taking leadership and rapid growth, even though it has a monopoly in a vital area and has achieved saturation of its original market.

The explanation is not luck, or "American conservatism." The explanation lies in four strategic decisions Vail made in the course of almost twenty years.

Vail saw early that a telephone system had to do something distinct and different to remain in private ownership and under autonomous management. All over Europe governments were running the telephone without much trouble or risk. To attempt to keep Bell private by defending it against government take-overs would be a delaying action only. Moreover, a purely defensive posture could only be self-defeating. It would paralyze management's imagination and energies. A policy was needed which would make Bell, as a private company, stand for the interest of the public more forcefully than any government agency could. This led to Vail's early decision that the business of the Bell Telephone Company must be anticipation and satisfaction of the service requirements of the public.

"Our business is service" became the Bell commitment as soon as Vail took over. At the time, shortly after the turn of the century, this was heresy. But Vail was not content to preach that it was the business of the company to give service, and that it was the job of management to make service possible and profitable. He saw to it that the yardsticks throughout the system by which managers and their operations were judged, measured service fulfillment rather than profit performance. Managers are responsible for service results. It is then the job of top management to organize and finance the company so as to make the best service also result in optimal financial rewards.

Vail, at about the same time, realized that a nationwide communications monopoly could not be a free enterprise in the traditional sense—that is, unfettered private business. He recognized public regulation as the only alternative to government ownership. Effective, honest, and principled public regulation was, therefore, in the interest of the Bell System and vital to its preservation.

Public regulation, while by no means unknown in the United States, was by and large impotent when Vail reached this conclusion. Business opposition, powerfully aided by the courts, had drawn the teeth of the laws on the statute books. The commissions themselves were understaffed and underfinanced and had become sinecures for third-rate and often venal political hacks.

Vail set the Bell Telephone Sytem the objective of making regulation effective. He gave this as their main task to the heads of each of the affiliated regional telephone companies. It was their job to rejuvenate the regulatory bodies and to innovate concepts of regulation and of rate-making that would be fair and equitable and would protect the public, while at the same time permitting the Bell System to do its job. The affiliated company presidents were the group from which Bell's top management was recruited. This ensured that positive attitudes toward regulation permeated the entire company.

Vail's third decision led to the establishment of one of the most successful scientific laboratories in industry, the Bell Laboratories. Again, Vail started out with the need to make a private monopoly viable. Only this time he asked: "How can one make such a monopoly truly competitive?" Obviously it was not subject to the normal competition from another supplier who offers the purchaser the same product or one supplying the same want. And yet without competition such a monopoly would rapidly become rigid and incapable of growth and change.

But even in a monopoly, Vail concluded, one can organize the future to compete with the present. In a technical industry such as telecommunications, the future lies in better and different technologies. The Bell Laboratories which grew out of this insight were by no means the first industrial laboratory, not even in the United States. But it was the first industrial research institution that was deliberately designed to make the present obsolete, no matter how profitable and efficient.

When Bell Labs took its final form, during the World War I period, this was a breath-taking innovation in industry. Even today few businessmen understand that research, to be productive, has to be the "disorganizer," the creator of a different future and the enemy of today. In most industrial laboratories, "defensive research" aimed at perpetuating today, predominates. But from the very beginning, the Bell Labs shunned defensive research.

■ The last ten or fifteen years have proven how sound Vail's concept was. Bell Labs first extended telephone technology so that the entire North American continent became one automated switchboard. It then extended the Bell System's reach into areas never dreamed of by Vail and his generation, e.g., the transmission of television programs, the transmission of computer data—in the last few years the most rapidly growing communications area—and the communications satellites. The scientific and technical developments that make possible these new transmission systems originated largely in the Bell Labs, whether they were scientific theory such as mathematical information theory, new products and processes such as the transistor, or computer logic and design.

Finally, toward the end of his career, in the early twenties, Vail invented the mass capital market—again to ensure survival of the Bell System as a private business.

■ Industries are more commonly taken over by government because they fail to attract the capital they need than because of socialism. Failure to attract the needed capital was a main reason why the European railroads were taken over by government between 1860 and 1920. Inability to attract the needed capital to modernize certainly played a big part in the nationalization of the coal mines and of the elec-

tric power industry in Great Britain. It was one of the major
reasons for the nationalization of the electric power industry on the European continent in the inflationary period
after World War I. The electric power companies, unable
to raise their rates to offset currency depreciation, could no
longer attract capital for modernization and expansion.

Whether Vail saw the problem in its full breadth, the record does not show. But he clearly saw that the Bell Telephone
System needed tremendous sums of capital in a dependable,
steady supply which could not be obtained from the then existing capital markets. The other public utilities, especially the
electric power companies, tried to make investment in their
securities attractive to the one and only mass participant visible in the twenties: the speculator. They built holding companies that gave the common shares of the parent company
speculative leverage and appeal, while the needs of the operating businesses were satisfied primarily by debt money raised
from traditional sources such as insurance companies. Vail
realized that this was not a sound capital foundation.

The AT&T common stock, which he designed to solve his
problem in the early twenties, had nothing in common with
the speculative shares except legal form. It was to be a security for the general public, the "Aunt Sally's" of the emerging
middle class, who could put something aside for investment,
but had not enough capital to take much risk. Vail's AT&T
common, with its almost-guaranteed dividend, was close
enough to a fixed interest-bearing obligation for widows and
orphans to buy it. At the same time, it was a common share
so that it held out the promise of capital appreciation and of
protection in inflation.

■ When Vail designed this financial instrument, the "Aunt
   Sally" type of investor did not, in effect, exist. The middle
   class that had enough money to buy any kind of common
   share had only recently emerged. It was still following older
   habits of investment in savings banks, insurance policies,

and mortgages. Those who ventured further went into the speculative stock market of the twenties—where they had no business to be at all. Vail did not, of course, invent the "Aunt Sally's." But he made them into investors and mobilized their savings for their benefit as well as for that of the Bell System. This alone has enabled the Bell System to raise the hundreds of billions of dollars it has had to invest over the last half-century. All this time AT&T common has remained the foundation of investment planning for the middle classes in the United States and Canada.

Vail again provided this idea with its own means of execution. Rather than depend on Wall Street, the Bell System has all these years been its own banker and underwriter. And Vail's principal assistant on financial design, Walter Gifford, was made chief officer of the Bell System and became Vail's successor.

The decisions Vail reached were, of course, peculiar to his problems and those of his company. But the basic thinking behind them characterizes the truly effective decision.

The example of Alfred P. Sloan, Jr., shows this clearly.* Sloan, who in General Motors designed and built the world's largest manufacturing enterprise, took over as head of a big business in 1922, when Vail's career was drawing to its close. He was a very different man, as his was a very different time. And yet the decision for which Sloan is best remembered, the decentralized organization structure of General Motors, is of the same kind as the major decisions Theodore Vail had made somewhat earlier for the Bell Telephone System.

As Sloan has recounted in his recent book, *My Years with*

---

* Business examples are chosen here because they are still taken in a small enough compass to be easily comprehended—whereas most decisions in government policy require far too much explanation of background, history, and politics. At the same time, these are large enough examples to show structure. But decisions in government, the military, the hospital, or the university exemplify the same concepts as the next sections in this and the following chapter will demonstrate.

General Motors,* the company he took over in 1922 was a loose federation of almost independent chieftains. Each of these men ran a unit which a few short years before had still been his own company—and each ran it as if it were still his own company.

■ There were two traditional ways of handling such a situation. One was to get rid of the strong independent men after they had sold out their business. This was the way in which John D. Rockefeller had put together the Standard Oil Trust, and J. P. Morgan, only a few years before Sloan, had put together U.S. Steel. The alternative was to leave the former owners in their commands with a minimum of interference from the new central office. It was "anarchy tempered by stock options" in which, it was hoped, their own financial interest would make the chieftains act for the best interests of the entire business. Durant, the founder of General Motors, and Sloan's predecessor, Pierre du Pont, had followed this route. When Sloan took over, however, the refusal of these strong and self-willed men to work together had all but destroyed the company.

Sloan realized that this was not the peculiar and short-term problem of the company just created through merger, but a generic problem of big business. The big business, Sloan saw, needs unity of direction and central control. It needs its own top management with real powers. But it equally needs energy, enthusiasm, and strength in operations. The operating managers have to have the freedom to do things their own way. They have to have responsibility and the authority that goes with it. They have to have scope to show what they can do, and they have to get recognition for performance. This, Sloan apparently saw right away, becomes even more important as a company gets older and as it has to depend on developing strong, independent performing executives from within.

Everyone before Sloan had seen the problem as one of per-

* New York, Doubleday, 1964.

sonalities, to be solved through a struggle for power from which one man would emerge victorious. Sloan saw it as a constitutional problem to be solved through a new structure; decentralization which balances local autonomy in operations with central control of direction and policy.

- How effective this solution has been shows perhaps best by contrast; that is, in the one area where General Motors has not had extraordinary results. General Motors, at least since the mid-thirties, has done poorly in anticipating and understanding the political temper of the American people and the direction and policies of American government. This is the one area, however, where there has been no "decentralization" in General Motors. Since 1935 or so it has been practically unthinkable for any senior GM executive to be anything but a conservative Republican.

These specific decisions—Vail's as well as Sloan's—have major features in common, even though they dealt with entirely different problems and led to highly specific solutions. They all tackled a problem at the highest conceptual level of understanding. They tried to think through what the decision was all about, and then tried to develop a principle for dealing with it. Their decisions were, in other words, strategic, rather than adaptations to the apparent needs of the moment. They all innovated. They were all highly controversial. Indeed, all five decisions went directly counter to what "everybody knew" at the time.

- Vail had actually been fired earlier by the board of the Bell System when he first was president. His concept of service as the business of the company seemed almost insane to people who "knew" that the only purpose of a business is to make a profit. His belief that regulation was in the best interest of the company, was indeed a necessity for survival, appeared harebrained if not immoral to people who "knew" that regulation was "creeping socialism" to be fought tooth and nail. It was only years later, after 1900,

when they had become alarmed—and with good reason—
by the rising tide of demand for the nationalization of the
telephone, that the board called Vail back. But his decision
to spend money on obsoleting current processes and techniques just when they made the greatest profits for the company and to build a large research laboratory designed to
this end, as well as his refusal to follow the fashion in finance
and build a speculative capital structure, were equally resisted by his board as worse than eccentricity.

Similarly, Alfred Sloan's decentralization was completely
unacceptable at the time and seemed to fly in the face of
everything everybody "knew."

The acknowledged radical among American business leaders of those days was Henry Ford. But Vail's and Sloan's decisions were much too "wild" for Ford. He was certain that
the Model T, once it had been designed, was the right car for
all time to come. Vail's insistence on organized self-obsoles-
cence would have struck him as lunacy. He was equally convinced that only the tightest centralized control could produce
efficiency and results. Sloan's decentralization appeared to him
self-destructive weakness.

THE ELEMENTS OF THE DECISION PROCESS

The truly important features of the decisions Vail and Sloan
made are neither their novelty nor their controversial nature.
They are:

1. The clear realization that the problem was generic and
   could only be solved through a decision which established a rule, a principle;
2. The definition of the specifications which the answer to
   the problem had to satisfy, that is, of the "boundary conditions";
3. The thinking through what is "right," that is, the solution which will fully satisfy the specifications *before* at-

tention is given to the compromises, adaptations, and concessions needed to make the decision acceptable;

4. The building into the decision of the action to carry it out;

5. The "feedback" which tests the validity and effectiveness of the decision against the actual course of events.

These are the *elements* of the effective decision process.

1. The first question the effective decision-maker asks is: "Is this a generic situation or an exception?" "Is this something that underlies a great many occurrences? Or is the occurrence a unique event that needs to be dealt with as such?" The generic always has to be answered through a rule, a principle. The exceptional can only be handled as such and as it comes.

Strictly speaking, one might distinguish between four, rather than between two, different types of occurrences.

There is first the truly generic of which the individual occurrence is only a symptom.

■ Most of the problems that come up in the course of the executive's work are of this nature. Inventory decisions in a business, for instance, are not "decisions." They are adaptations. The problem is generic. This is even more likely to be true of events within production.

Typically, a product control and engineering group will handle many hundreds of problems in the course of a month. Yet, whenever these are analyzed, the great majority prove to be just symptoms—that is, manifestations of underlying basic situations. The individual process control engineer or production engineer who works in one part of the plant usually cannot see this. He might have a few problems each month with the couplings in the pipes that carry steam or hot liquids. But only when the total workload of the group over several months is analyzed does the generic problem appear. Then one sees that temperatures or pressures have become too great for the existing equipment and that the couplings, holding different lines together, need to be redesigned for greater loads. Until this is done, process control will spend a tremendous amount of time fixing leaks without ever getting control of the situation.

Then there is the problem which, while a unique event for the individual institution, is actually generic.

- The company that receives an offer to merge from another, larger one, will never receive such an offer again if it accepts. This is a nonrecurrent situation as far as the individual company, its board of directors, and its management are concerned. But it is, of course, a generic situation which occurs all the time. To think through whether to accept or to reject the offer requires some general rules. For these, however, one has to look to the experience of others.

Next there is the truly exceptional, the truly unique event.

- The power failure that plunged into darkness the whole of northeastern North America from the St. Lawrence to Washington in November 1965 was, according to the first explanations, a truly exceptional situation. So was the thalidomide tragedy which led to the birth of so many deformed babies in the early sixties. The probability of these events, we were told, was one in ten million or one in a hundred million. Such concatenation of malfunctions is as unlikely ever to recur again as it is unlikely, for instance, for the chair on which I sit to disintegrate into its constituent atoms.

Truly unique events are rare, however. Whenever one appears, one has to ask: Is this a true exception or only the first manifestation of a new genus?

And this, the early manifestation of a new generic problem, is the fourth and last category of events with which the decision process deals.

- We know now, for instance, that both the northeastern power failure and the thalidomide tragedy were only the first occurrences of what, under conditions of modern power technology or of modern pharmacology, are likely to become fairly frequent malfunctions unless generic solutions are found.

All events but the truly unique require a generic solution. They require a rule, a policy, a principle. Once the right principle has been developed all manifestations of the same generic situation can be handled pragmatically; that is, by adaptation of the rule to the concrete circumstances of the case. Truly unique events, however, must be treated individually. One cannot develop rules for the exceptional.

The effective decision-maker spends time to determine with which of these four situations he is dealing. He knows that he will make the wrong decision if he classifies the situation wrongly.

By far the most common mistake is to treat a generic situation as if it were a series of unique events; that is, to be pragmatic when one lacks the generic understanding and principle. This inevitably leads to frustration and futility.

■ This was clearly shown, I think, by the failure of most of the policies, whether domestic or foreign, of the Kennedy administration. For all the brilliance of its members, the administration achieved fundamentally only one success, in the Cuban missile crisis. Otherwise, it achieved practically nothing. The main reason was surely what its members called "pragmatism"; that is, its refusal to develop rules and principles, and its insistence on treating everything "on its merits." Yet it was clear to everyone, including the members of the administration, that the basic assumptions on which its policies rested, the basic assumptions of the postwar years, had become increasingly unrealistic in international as well as in domestic affairs.

Equally common is the mistake of treating a new event as if it were just another example of the old problem to which, therefore, the old rules should be applied.

■ This was the error that snowballed a local power failure on the New York-Ontario border into the great northeastern blackout. The power engineers, especially in New York City, applied the right rule for a normal overload. Yet their own instruments had signaled that something quite extraordinary was going on which called for exceptional, rather than for standard, countermeasures.

By contrast, the one great triumph of President Kennedy, in the Cuban missile crisis, rested on acceptance of the challenge to think through an extraordinary, exceptional occurrence. As soon as Mr. Kennedy accepted this, his own tremendous resources of intelligence and courage effectively came into play.

Almost as common is the plausible but erroneous definition of the fundamental problem. Here is one example.

■ Since the end of World War II the American military services have been plagued by their inability to keep highly trained medical people in uniform. There have been dozens of studies and dozens of proposed remedies. However, all of the studies start out with the plausible hypothesis that pay is the problem—whereas the real problem lies in the traditional structure of military medicine. With its emphasis on the general practitioner, it is out of alignment with today's medical profession, which stresses the specialist. The career ladder in military medicine leads from specialization to medical and hospital administration and away from research and specialized practice. Today's young, well-trained physicians, therefore, feel that they waste their time and skill in the military service where they either have to work as general practitioners or become chairbound administrators. They want the opportunity to develop the skills and apply the practice of today's highly scientific, specialized doctor.

So far the military has not faced up to the basic decision. Are the armed services willing to settle for a second-rate medical organization staffed with people who cannot make the grade in the highly scientific, research-oriented, and highly specialized civilian profession of medicine? Or are they willing and able to organize the practice of medicine within the services in ways that differ fundamentally from the organization and structure of a military service? Until the military accepts this as the real decision, its young doctors will keep on leaving as soon as they can.

Or the definition of the problem may be incomplete.

■ This largely explains why the American automobile industry found itself in 1966 suddenly under sharp attack for its unsafe cars—and also why the industry itself was so totally bewildered by the attack. It is simply not true that the industry has paid no attention to safety. On the contrary, it has worked hard at safer highway engineering and at driver training. That accidents are caused by unsafe roads and unsafe drivers is plausible enough. Indeed, all other agencies concerned with automotive safety, from the highway patrol to the schools, picked the same targets for their campaigns. These campaigns have produced results. Highways built for safety have many fewer accidents; and so have safety-trained drivers. But though the ratio of accidents per thousand cars or per thousand miles driven has been going down, the total number of accidents and their severity has kept creeping up.

Long ago it should have been clear that a small percentage of drivers—drunken drivers, for instance, or the 5 per cent who are "accident-prone" and cause three quarters or so of all accidents—are beyond the reach of driver training and can cause accidents on the safest road. Long ago it should have become clear that we have to do something about a small but significant probability of accidents that will occur despite safety laws and safety training. And this means that safe-highway and safe-driving campaigns have to be supplemented by engineering to make accidents themselves less dangerous. Where we engineered to make cars safe when used right, we also have to engineer to make cars safe when used wrong. This, however, the automobile industry failed to see.

This example shows why the incomplete explanation is often more dangerous than the totally wrong explanation. Everyone connected with safe-driving campaigns—the automobile industry, but also state highway commissioners, automobile clubs, and insurance companies—felt that to accept a probability of accidents was to condone, if not to encourage, dangerous driving—just as my grandmother's generation believed that the doctor who treated venereal diseases abetted immorality. It is this common human tendency to confuse plausibility with morality which makes the incomplete hypothesis so dangerous a mistake and so hard to correct.

The effective decision-maker, therefore, always assumes initially that the problem is generic.

He always assumes that the event that clamors for his attention is in reality a symptom. He looks for the true problem. He is not content with doctoring the symptom alone.

And if the event is truly unique, the experienced decision-maker suspects that this heralds a new underlying problem and that what appears as unique will turn out to have been simply the first manifestation of a new generic situation.

This also explains why the effective decision-maker always tries to put his solution on the highest possible conceptual level. He does not solve the immediate financing problem by issuing whatever security would be easiest to sell at the best price for the next few years. If he expects to need the capital market for the foreseeable future, he invents a new kind of investor and designs the appropriate security for a mass-capital market that does not yet exist. If he has to bring into line a flock of undisciplined but capable divisional presidents, he does not get rid of the most obstreperous ones and buy off the rest. He develops a constitutional concept of large-scale organization. If he sees his industry as necessarily monopolistic, he does not content himself with fulminating against socialism. He builds the public regulatory agency into a deliberate "third way" between the Scylla of irresponsible private enterprise unchecked by competition and the Charybdis of equally irresponsible, indeed essentially uncontrollable, government monopoly.

One of the most obvious facts of social and political life is the longevity of the temporary. British licensing hours for taverns, for instance, French rent controls, or Washington "temporary" government buildings, all three hastily developed in World War I to last "a few months of temporary emergency" are still with us fifty years later. The effective decision-maker knows this. He too improvises, of course. But he asks himself every time, "If I had to live with this for a long time, would I be willing to?" And if the answer is "No," he keeps on working to find a more general, a more conceptual, a more comprehensive solution—one which establishes the right principle.

As a result, the effective executive does not make many decisions. But the reason is not that he takes too long in making one—in fact, a decision on principle does not, as a rule, take longer than a decision on symptoms and expediency. The effective executive does not need to make many decisions. Because he solves generic situations through a rule and policy, he can handle most events as cases under the rule; that is, by adaptation. "A country with many laws is a country of incompetent lawyers," says an old legal proverb. It is a country which attempts to solve every problem as a unique phenomenon, rather than as a special case under general rules of law. Similarly, an executive who makes many decisions is both lazy and ineffectual.

The decision-maker also always tests for signs that something atypical, something unusual, is happening; he always asks: "Does the explanation explain the observed events and does it explain all of them?; he always writes out what the solution is expected to make happen—make automobile accidents disappear, for instance—and then tests regularly to see if this really happens; and finally, he goes back and thinks the problem through again when he sees something atypical, when he finds phenomena his explanation does not really explain, or when the course of events deviates, even in details, from his expectations.

These are in essence the rules Hippocrates laid down for medical diagnosis well over 2,000 years ago. They are the rules for scientific observation first formulated by Aristotle and then reaffirmed by Galileo three hundred years ago. These, in other words, are old, well-known, time-tested rules, rules one can learn and can systematically apply.

2. The second major element in the decision process is clear specifications as to what the decision has to accomplish. What are the objectives the decision has to reach? What are the minimum goals it has to attain? What are the conditions it has to satisfy? In science these are known as "boundary conditions." A decision, to be effective, needs to satisfy the boundary conditions. It needs to be adequate to its purpose.

The more concisely and clearly boundary conditions are stated, the greater the likelihood that the decision will indeed be an effective one and will accomplish what it set out to do. Conversely, any serious shortfall in defining these boundary conditions is almost certain to make a decision ineffectual, no matter how brilliant it may seem.

"What is the minimum needed to resolve this problem?" is the form in which the boundary conditions are usually probed. "Can our needs be satisfied," Alfred P. Sloan presumably asked himself when he took command of General Motors in 1922, "by removing the autonomy of the division heads?" His answer was clearly in the negative. The boundary conditions of his problem demanded strength and responsibility in the chief operating positions. This was needed as much as unity and control at the center. The boundary conditions demanded a solution to a problem of structure, rather than an accommodation among personalities. And this in turn made his solution last.

It is not always easy to find the appropriate boundary conditions. And intelligent people do not necessarily agree on them.

■ On the morning after the power blackout one New York newspaper managed to appear: *The New York Times*. It had shifted its printing operations immediately across the Hudson to Newark, New Jersey, where the power plants were functioning and where a local paper, *The Newark Evening News*, had a substantial printing plant. But instead of the million copies the *Times* management had ordered, fewer than half this number actually reached the readers. Just as the *Times* went to press (so at least goes a widely told anecdote) the executive editor and three of his assistants started arguing how to hyphenate *one* word. This took them forty-eight minutes (so it is said)—or half of the available press time. The *Times*, the editor argued, sets a standard for written English in the United States and therefore cannot afford a grammatical mistake.

Assuming the tale to be true—and I do not vouch for it —one wonders what the management thought about the decision. But there is no doubt that, given the fundamental assumptions and objectives of the executive editor, it was the right decision. His boundary conditions quite clearly were not the number of copies sold at any one morning, but the infallibility of the *Times* as a grammarian and as *Magister Americae*.

The effective executive knows that a decision that does not satisfy the boundary conditions is ineffectual and inappropriate. It may be worse indeed than a decision that satisfies the wrong boundary conditions. Both will be wrong, of course. But one can salvage the appropriate decision for the incorrect boundary conditions. It is still an effective decision. One cannot get anything but trouble from the decision that is inadequate to its specifications.

In fact, clear thinking about the boundary conditions is needed so that one knows when a decision has to be abandoned. There are two famous illustrations for this—one of a decision where the boundary conditions had become confused and one of a decision where they were kept so clear as to make possible immediate replacement of the outflanked decision by a new and appropriate policy.

■ The first example is the famous Schlieffen Plan of the German General Staff at the outbreak of World War I. This plan was meant to enable Germany to fight a war on both the eastern and the western fronts simultaneously without having to splinter her forces between East and West. To accomplish this, the Schlieffen Plan proposed to offer only token opposition to the weaker enemy, that is, to Russia, and to concentrate all forces first on a quick knockout blow against France, after which Russia would be dealt with. This, of course, implied willingness to let the Russian armies move fairly deeply into German territory at the outbreak of the war and until the decisive victory over France. But in August 1914, it became clear that the speed of the Russian armies had been underrated. The Junkers in East Prussia whose estates were overrun by the Russians set up a howl for protection.

Schlieffen himself had kept the boundary conditions clearly in his mind. But his successors were technicians rather than decision-makers and strategists. They jettisoned the basic commitment underlying the Schlieffen Plan, the commitment not to splinter the German forces. They should have dropped the plan. Instead they kept it but made its attainment impossible. They weakened the armies in the West sufficiently to deprive their initial victories of full impact, yet did not strengthen the armies in the East sufficiently to knock out the Russians. They thereby brought about the one thing the Schlieffen Plan had been designed to prevent: a stalemate with its ensuing war of attrition in which superiority of manpower, rather than superiority of strategy, eventually had to win. Instead of a strategy, all they had from there on was confused improvisation, impassioned rhetoric, and hopes for miracles.

■ Contrast with this the second example: the action of Franklin D. Roosevelt when becoming president in 1933. All through his campaign Roosevelt had worked on a plan for *economic recovery*. Such a plan, in 1933, could only be built on financial conservatism and a balanced budget. Then, immediately before FDR's inauguration, the economy collapsed in the Bank Holiday. Economic policy might still have done the work economically. But it had become clear that the patient would not survive politically.

Roosevelt immediately substituted a political objective for his former economic one. He switched from recovery to reform. The new specifications called for political dynamics. This, almost automatically, meant a complete change of economic policy from one of conservatism to one of radical innovation. The boundary conditions had changed—and Roosevelt was enough of a decision-maker to know almost intuitively that this meant abandoning his original plan altogether if he wanted to have any effectiveness.

But clear thinking about the boundary conditions is needed also to identify the most dangerous of all possible decisions: the one that might—just might—work if nothing whatever goes wrong. These decisions always seem to make sense. But when one thinks through the specifications they have to satisfy, one always finds that they are essentially incompatible with each other. That such a decision might succeed is not impossible—it is merely grossly improbable. The trouble with miracles is not, after all, that they happen rarely; it is that one cannot rely on them.

■ A perfect example was President Kennedy's Bay of Pigs decision in 1961. One specification was clearly Castro's overthrow. But at the same time, there was another specification: not to make it appear that U.S. forces were intervening in one of the American republics. That the second specification was rather absurd, and that no one in the whole world would have believed for one moment that the invasion was a spontaneous uprising of the Cubans, is beside the point. To the American policy-makers at the time, the appearance of nonintervention seemed a legitimate and indeed a necessary condition. But these two specifications would have been compatible with each other only if an immediate islandwide uprising against Castro would have completely paralyzed the Cuban army. And this, while not impossible, was clearly not highly probable in a police state. Either the whole idea should have been dropped or American full-scale support should have been provided to ensure success of the invasion.

It is not disrespect for President Kennedy to say that his mistake was not, as he explained, that he had "listened to the experts." The mistake was failure to think through clearly the boundary conditions that the decision had to satisfy, and refusal to face up to the unpleasant reality that a decision that has to satisfy two different and at bottom incompatible specifications is not a decision but a prayer for a miracle.

Yet, defining the specifications and setting the boundary conditions cannot be done on the "facts" in any decision of importance. It always has to be done on interpretation. It is risk-taking judgment.

Everyone can make the wrong decision—in fact, everyone will sometimes make a wrong decision. But no one needs to make a decision which, on its face, falls short of satisfying the boundary conditions.

3. One has to start out with what is right rather than what is acceptable (let alone who is right) precisely because one always has to compromise in the end. But if one does not know what is right to satisfy the specifications and boundary conditions, one cannot distinguish between the right compromise and the wrong compromise—and will end up by making the wrong compromise.

- I was taught this when I started in 1944 on my first big consulting assignment, a study of the management structure and management policies of the General Motors Corporation. Alfred P. Sloan, Jr., who was then chairman and chief executive officer of the company, called me to his office at the start of my study and said: "I shall not tell you what to study, what to write, or what conclusions to come to. This is your task. My only instruction to you is to put down what you think is right as you see it. Don't you worry about our reaction. Don't you worry about whether we will like this or dislike that. And don't you, above all, concern yourself with the compromises that might be needed to make your recommendations acceptable. There is not one executive in this company who does not know how to make every single conceivable compromise without any help from you. But he can't make the *right* compromise unless you first tell him what 'right' is." The executive thinking through a decision might put this in front of himself in neon lights.

President Kennedy learned this lesson from the Bay of Pigs fiasco. It largely explains his triumph in the Cuban missile crisis two years later. His ruthless insistence then on thinking through what boundary conditions the decision had to satisfy gave him the knowledge of what compromise to accept (namely, tacitly to abandon the U.S. demand for on-the-ground inspection after air reconnaissance had shown such inspection to be no longer necessary) and what to insist on (namely, the physical dismantling and return to Russia of the Soviet missiles themselves).

For there are two different kinds of compromise. One kind is expressed in the old proverb: "Half a loaf is better than no bread." The other kind is expressed in the story of the Judgment of Solomon, which was clearly based on the realization that "half a baby is worse than no baby at all." In the first instance, the boundary conditions are still being satisfied. The purpose of bread is to provide food, and half a loaf is still food. Half a baby, however, does not satisfy the boundary conditions. For half a baby is not half of a living and growing child. It is a corpse in two pieces.

It is fruitless and a waste of time to worry about what is acceptable and what one had better not say so as not to evoke resistance. The things one worries about never happen. And objections and difficulties no one thought about suddenly turn out to be almost insurmountable obstacles. One gains nothing in other words by starting out with the question: "What is acceptable?" And in the process of answering it, one gives away the important things, as a rule, and loses any chance to come up with an effective, let alone with the right, answer.

4. Converting the decision into action is the fourth major element in the decision process. While thinking through the boundary conditions is the most difficult step in decision-making, converting the decision into effective action is usually the most time-consuming one. Yet a decision will not become effective unless the action commitments have been built into the decision from the start.

In fact, no decision has been made unless carrying it out in specific steps has become someone's work assignment and responsibility. Until then, there are only good intentions.

- This is the trouble with so many policy statements, especially of business: They contain no action commitment. To carry them out is no one's specific work and responsibility. No wonder that the people in the organization tend to view these statements cynically if not as declarations of what top management is really not going to do.

Converting a decision into action requires answering several distinct questions: Who has to know of this decision? What action has to be taken? Who is to take it? And what does the action have to be so that the people who have to do it *can* do it? The first and the last of these are too often overlooked—with dire results.

- A story that has become a legend among operations researchers illustrates the importance of the question "Who has to know?" A major manufacturer of industrial equipment decided several years ago to discontinue one model. For years it had been standard equipment on a line of machine tools, many of which were still in use. It was decided, therefore, to sell the model to present owners of the old equipment for another three years as a replacement, and then to stop making and selling it. Orders for this particular model had been going down for a good many years. But they shot up as former customers reordered against the day when the model would no longer be available. No one had, however, asked, "Who needs to know of this decision?" Therefore nobody informed the clerk in the purchasing department who was in charge of buying the parts from which the model itself was being assembled. His instructions were to buy parts in a given ratio to current sales—and the instructions remained unchanged. When the time came to discontinue further production of the model, the company had in its warehouse enough parts for another eight to ten years of production, parts that had to be written off at a considerable loss.

The action must also be appropriate to the capacities of the people who have to carry it out.

■ A chemical company found itself, in recent years, with fairly large amounts of blocked currency in two West African countries. It decided that to protect this money, it had to invest it locally in businesses which would contribute to the local economy, would not require imports from abroad, and would, if successful, be the kind that could be sold to local investors if and when currency remittances became possible again. To establish these businesses, the company developed a simple chemical process to preserve a tropical fruit which is a staple crop in both countries and which, up until then, had suffered serious spoilage in transit to its Western markets.

The business was a success in both countries. But in one country the local manager set the business up in such a manner that it required highly skilled and, above all, technically trained management of the kind not easily available in West Africa. In the other country the local manager thought through the capacities of the people who would eventually have to run the business and worked hard at making both process and business simple and at staffing from the start with nationals of the country right up to the top.

A few years later it became possible again to transfer currency from these two countries. But though the business flourished, no buyer could be found for it in the first country. No one available locally had the necessary managerial and technical skills. The business had to be liquidated at a loss. In the other country so many local entrepreneurs were eager to buy the business that the company repatriated its original investment with a substantial profit.

The process and the business built on it were essentially the same in both places. But in the first country no one had asked: "What kind of people do we have available to make this decision effective? And what can they do?" As a result, the decision itself became frustrated.

All this becomes doubly important when people have to change behavior, habits, or attitudes if a decision is to become effective action. Here one has to make sure not only that responsibility for the action is clearly assigned and that the people responsible are capable of doing the needful. One has to make sure that their measurements, their standards for accomplishment, and their incentives are changed simultaneously. Otherwise, the people will get caught in a paralyzing internal emotional conflict.

■ Theodore Vail's decision that the business of the Bell System was service might have remained dead letter but for the yardsticks of service performance which he designed to measure managerial performance. Bell managers were used to being measured by the profitability of their units, or at the least, by cost. The new yardsticks made them accept rapidly the new objectives.

■ In sharp contrast is the recent failure of a brilliant chairman and chief executive to make effective a new organization structure and new objectives in an old, large, and proud

American company. Everyone agreed that the changes were needed. The company, after many years as leader of its industry, showed definite signs of aging; in almost all major fields newer, smaller, and more aggressive competitors were outflanking it. But to gain acceptance for the new ideas, the chairman promoted the most prominent spokesmen of the old school into the most visible and best-paid positions—especially into three new executive vice-presidencies. This meant only one thing to the people in the company: "They don't really mean it."

If the greatest rewards are given for behavior contrary to that which the new course of action requires, then everyone will conclude that this contrary behavior is what the people at the top really want and are going to reward.

Not everyone can do what Vail did and build the execution of his decisions into the decision itself. But everyone can think what action commitments a specific decision requires, what work assignments follow from it, and what people are available to carry it out.

5. Finally, a feedback has to be built into the decision to provide a continuous testing, against actual events, of the expectations that underlie the decision.

Decisions are made by men. Men are fallible; at their best their works do not last long. Even the best decision has a high probability of being wrong. Even the most effective one eventually becomes obsolete.

■ If this needs documentation, the Vail and Sloan decisions supply it. Despite their imagination and daring, only one of Vail's decisions, the decision that service was the business of the Bell System, is still valid today and applicable in the form in which he worked it out. The investment character of the AT&T common share had to be drastically changed in the nineteen-fifties in response to the emergence of the institutional investors—pension trusts and mutual funds—as the new channels through which the middle class invests.

While Bell Labs has maintained its dominant position, the new scientific and technological developments—especially in space technology and in such devices as the laser—have made it reasonably clear that no communications company, no matter how large, can any longer hope to provide by its own means all its own technological and scientific needs. At the same time, the development of technology has made it probable—for the first time in seventy-five years—that new processes of telecommunications will seriously compete with the telephone, and that in major communications fields, for example, information and data communication, no single communications medium can maintain dominance, let alone the monopoly which Bell has had for oral communications over distance. And while regulation remains a necessity for the existence of a privately owned telecommunications company, the regulation Vail worked so hard to make effective—that is, regulation by the individual states—is becoming increasingly inappropriate to the realities of a nationwide and indeed international system. But the inevitable—and necessary—regulation by the federal government has not been worked out by the Bell System and has instead been fought by it through the kind of delaying action Vail was so careful not to engage in.

As to Sloan's decentralization of General Motors, it still stands—but it is becoming clear that it will have to be thought through again soon. Not only have basic principles of his design been changed and revised so often that they have become fuzzy beyond recognition—the autonomous automotive divisions, for instance, increasingly are not in full control of their manufacturing and assembly operations and therefore not fully responsible for the results. The individual makes of car, from Chevrolet to Cadillac, have also long ceased to represent major price classes the way Sloan originally designed them. Above all, Sloan designed a U.S. company; and though it soon acquired foreign subsidiaries, it remained a U.S. company in its organization and management structure. But General Motors is clearly an international company today. Its great growth and major opportunities are increasingly outside the United States and especially in Europe. It will survive and prosper only if it finds the right principles and the right organization for the multinational company. The job Sloan did in 1922 will have to be done over again soon—it will predictably become pressing as soon as the industry runs into a period of economic difficulties. And if not done over fairly drastically, Sloan's solution is likely to become a millstone around GM's neck and increasingly a bar to its success.

When General Eisenhower was elected president, his predecessor, Harry S. Truman, said: "Poor Ike; when he was a general, he gave an order and it was carried out. Now he is going to sit in that big office and he'll give an order and not a damn thing is going to happen."

The reason why "not a damn thing is going to happen" is, however, not that generals have more authority than presidents. It is that military organizations learned long ago that futility is the lot of most orders and organized the feedback to check on the execution of the order. They learned long ago that to go oneself and look is the only reliable feedback.* Reports—all a president is normally able to mobilize—are not much help. All military services have long ago learned that the officer who has given an order goes out and sees for himself whether it has been carried out. At the least he sends one of his own aides— he never relies on what he is told by the subordinate to whom the order was given. Not that he distrusts the subordinate; he has learned from experience to distrust communications.

- This is the reason why a battalion commander is expected to go out and taste the food served his men. He could, of course, read the menus and order this or that item to be brought in to him. But no; he is expected to go into the mess

---

* This was certainly established military practice in very ancient times— Thucydides and Xenophon both take it for granted, as do the earliest Chinese texts on war we have—and so did Caesar.

hall and take his sample of the food from the same kettle that serves the enlisted men.

With the coming of the computer this will become even more important, for the decision-maker will, in all likelihood, be even further removed from the scene of action. Unless he accepts, as a matter of course, that he had better go out and look at the scene of action, he will be increasingly divorced from reality. All a computer can handle are abstractions. And abstractions can be relied on only if they are constantly checked against the concrete. Otherwise, they are certain to mislead us.

To go and look for oneself is also the best, if not the only, way to test whether the assumptions on which a decision had been made are still valid or whether they are becoming obsolete and need to be thought through again. And one always has to expect the assumptions to become obsolete sooner or later. Reality never stands still very long.

Failure to go out and look is the typical reason for persisting in a course of action long after it has ceased to be appropriate or even rational. This is true for business decisions as well as for governmental policies. It explains in large measure the failure of Stalin's postwar policy in Europe but also the inability of the United States to adjust its policies to the realities of de Gaulle's Europe or the failure of the British to accept, until too late, the reality of the European Common Market.

One needs organized information for the feedback. One needs reports and figures. But unless one builds one's feedback around direct exposure to reality—unless one disciplines oneself to go out and look—one condemns oneself to a sterile dogmatism and with it to ineffectiveness.

These are the elements of the decision process. But what about the decision itself?

7: Effective Decisions

A decision is a judgment. It is a choice between alternatives. It is rarely a choice between right and wrong. It is at best a choice between "almost right" and "probably wrong"—but much more often a choice between two courses of action neither of which is provably more nearly right than the other.

Most books on decision-making tell the reader: "First find the facts." But executives who make effective decisions know that one does not start with facts. One starts with opinions. These are, of course, nothing but untested hypotheses and, as such, worthless unless tested against reality. To determine what is a fact requires first a decision on the criteria of relevance, especially on the appropriate measurement. This is the hinge of the effective decision, and usually its most controversial aspect.

Finally, the effective decision does not, as so many texts on decision-making proclaim, flow from a consensus on the facts. The understanding that underlies the right decision grows out of the clash and conflict of divergent opinions and out of the serious consideration of competing alternatives.

To get the facts first is impossible. There are no facts unless one has a criterion of relevance. Events by themselves are not facts.

- In physics the taste of a substance is not a fact. Nor, until fairly recently, was its color. In cooking, the taste is a fact of supreme importance, and in painting, the color matters. Physics, cooking, and painting consider different things as relevant and therefore consider different things to be facts.

But the effective executive also knows that people do not start out with the search for facts. They start out with an opinion. There is nothing wrong with this. People experienced in an area should be expected to have an opinion. Not to have an opinion after having been exposed to an area for a good long time would argue an unobservant eye and a sluggish mind.

People inevitably start out with an opinion; to ask them to search for the facts first is even undesirable. They will simply do what everyone is far too prone to do anyhow: look for the facts that fit the conclusion they have already reached. And no one has ever failed to find the facts he is looking for. The good statistician knows this and distrusts all figures—he either knows the fellow who found them or he does not know him; in either case he is suspicious.

The only rigorous method, the only one that enables us to test an opinion against reality, is based on the clear recognition that opinions come first—and that this is the way it should be. Then no one can fail to see that we start out with untested hypotheses—in decision-making as in science the only starting point. We know what to do with hypotheses—one does not argue them; one tests them. One finds out which hypotheses are tenable, and therefore worthy of serious consideration, and which are eliminated by the first test against observable experience.

The effective executive encourages opinions. But he insists that the people who voice them also think through what it is that the "experiment"—that is, the testing of the opinion against

reality—would have to show. The effective executive, therefore, asks: "What do we have to know to test the validity of this
hypothesis?" "What would the facts have to be to make this
opinion tenable?" And he makes it a habit—in himself and in
the people with whom he works—to think through and spell
out what needs to be looked at, studied, and tested. He insists
that people who voice an opinion also take responsibility for
defining what factual findings can be expected and should be
looked for.

Perhaps the crucial question here is: "What is the criterion
of relevance?" This, more often than not, turns on the measurement appropriate to the matter under discussion and to the
decision to be reached. Whenever one analyzes the way a truly
effective, a truly right, decision has been reached, one finds that
a great deal of work and thought went into finding the appropriate measurement.

■ This, of course, is what made Theodore Vail's conclusion
   that service was the business of the Bell System such an effective decision.

The effective decision-maker assumes that the traditional
measurement is not the right measurement. Otherwise, there
would generally be no need for a decision; a simple adjustment
would do. The traditional measurement reflects yesterday's
decision. That there is need for a new one normally indicates
that the measurement is no longer relevant.

■ That the procurement and inventory policies of the U.S.
   armed services were in bad shape had been known ever since
   the Korean War. There had been countless studies—but
   things got worse, rather than better. When Robert Mc-
   Namara was appointed Secretary of Defense by President
   Kennedy, however, he challenged the traditional measurements of military inventory—measurements in total dollars
   and in total number of items in procurement and inventory.
   Instead, Mr. McNamara identified and separated the very

few items—maybe 4 per cent of the items by number—
which together account for 90 per cent or more of the total
procurement dollars. He similarly identified the very few
items—perhaps again 4 per cent—which account for 90
per cent of combat readiness. Since some items belong in
both categories, the list of crucial items came to 5 or 6 per
cent of the total, whether measured by number or by dollars.
Each of these, McNamara insisted, had to be managed
separately and with attention to minute detail. The rest, the
95 per cent or so of all items which account neither for the
bulk of the dollars nor for essential combat readiness, he
changed to management by exception, that is, to management by probability and averages. The new measurement
immediately made possible highly effective decisions on procurement and inventory-keeping and on logistics.

The best way to find the appropriate measurement is again
to go out and look for the "feedback" discussed earlier—only
this is "feedback" before the decision.

■ In most personnel matters, for instance, events are measured
in "averages," such as the average number of lost-time accidents per hundred employees, the average percentage of
absenteeism in the whole work force, or the average illness
rate per hundred. But the executive who goes out and looks
for himself will soon find that he needs a different measurement. The averages serve the purposes of the insurance company, but they are meaningless, indeed misleading, for per-
sonel management decisions.

The great majority of all accidents occur in one or two
places in the plant. The great bulk of absenteeism is in one
department. Even illness resulting in absence from work, we
now know, is not distributed as an average, but is concentrated in a very small part of the work force, e.g., young
unmarried women. The personnel actions to which dependence on the averages will lead—for instance, the typical
plantwide safety campaign—will not produce the desired
results, may indeed make things worse.

Similarly, failure to go and look was a major factor in the failure of the automobile industry to realize in time the need for safety engineering of the car. The automobile companies measured only by the conventional averages of number of accidents per passenger mile or per car. Had they gone out and looked, they would have seen the need to measure also the severity of bodily injuries resulting from accidents. And this would soon have highlighted the need to supplement their safety campaigns by measures aimed at making the accident less dangerous; that is, by automotive design.

Finding the appropriate measurement is thus not a mathematical exercise. It is a risk-taking judgment.

Whenever one has to judge, one must have alternatives among which one can choose. A judgment in which one can only say "yes" or "no" is no judgment at all. Only if there are alternatives can one hope to get insight into what is truly at stake.

Effective executives therefore insist on alternatives of measurement—so that they can choose the one appropriate one.

■ There are a number of measurements for a proposal on a capital investment. One of these focuses on the length of time it will take before the original investment has been earned back. Another one focuses on the rate of profitability expected from the investment. A third one focuses on the present value of the returns expected to result from the investment, and so on. The effective executive will not be content with any one of these conventional yardsticks, no matter how fervently his accounting department assures him that only one of them is "scientific." He knows, if only from experience, that each of these analyses brings out a different aspect of the same capital investment decision. Until he has looked at each possible dimension of the decision, he cannot really know which of these ways of analyzing and measuring is appropriate to the specific capital decision before him. Much as it annoys the accountants, the effective executive will insist on having the same investment decision calculated in all three ways—so as to be able to say at the end: "This measurement is appropriate to this decision."

Unless one has considered alternatives, one has a closed mind.

This, above all, explains why effective decision-makers deliberately disregard the second major command of the textbooks on decision-making and create dissension and disagreement, rather than consensus.

Decisions of the kind the executive has to make are not made well by acclamation. They are made well only if based on the clash of conflicting views, the dialogue between different points of view, the choice between different judgments. The first rule in decision-making is that one does not make a decision unless there is disagreement.

■ Alfred P. Sloan is reported to have said at a meeting of one of his top committees: "Gentlemen, I take it we are all in complete agreement on the decision here." Everyone around the table nodded assent. "Then," continued Mr. Sloan, "I propose we postpone further discussion of this matter until our next meeting to give ourselves time to develop disagreement and perhaps gain some understanding of what the decision is all about."

Sloan was anything but an "intuitive" decision-maker. He always emphasized the need to test opinions against facts and the need to make absolutely sure that one did not start out with the conclusion and then look for the facts that would support it. But he knew that the right decision demands adequate disagreement.

Every one of the effective Presidents in American history had his own method of producing the disagreement he needed in order to make an effective decision. Lincoln, Theodore Roosevelt, Franklin D. Roosevelt, Harry Truman—each had his own ways. But each created the disagreement he needed for "some understanding of what the decision is all about." Washington, we know, hated conflicts and quarrels and wanted a united Cabinet. Yet he made quite sure of the necessary differences of opinion on important matters by asking both Hamilton and Jefferson for their opinions.

■ The President who understood best the need for organized disagreement was probably Franklin D. Roosevelt. Whenever anything of importance came up, he would take aside one of his aides and say to him, "I want you to work on this for me—but keep it a secret." (This made sure, as Roosevelt knew perfectly well, that everybody in Washington heard about it immediately.) Then Roosevelt would take aside a few other men, known to differ from the first and would give them the same assignment, again "in the strictest confidence." As a result, he could be reasonably certain that all important aspects of every matter were being thought through and presented to him. He could be certain that he would not become the prisoner of somebody's preconceived conclusions.

This practice was severely criticized as execrable administration by the one "professional manager" in Roosevelt's Cabinet, his secretary of the Interior, Harold Ickes, whose diaries are full of diatribes against the President's "sloppiness," "indiscretions," and "treachery." But Roosevelt knew that the main task of an American President is not administration. It is the making of policy, the making of the right decisions. And these are made best on the basis of "adversary proceedings" to use the term of the lawyers for their method of getting at the true facts in a dispute, and of making sure that all relevant aspects of a case are presented to the court.

There are three main reasons for the insistence on disagreement.

It is, first, the only safeguard against the decision-maker's becoming the prisoner of the organization. Everybody always wants something from the decision-maker. Everybody is a special pleader, trying—often in perfectly good faith—to obtain the decision he favors. This is true whether the decision-maker is the President of the United States or the most junior engineer working on a design modification.

The only way to break out of the prison of special pleading and preconceived notions is to make sure of argued, documented, thought-through disagreements.

Second, disagreement alone can provide alternatives to a decision. And a decision without an alternative is a desperate gambler's throw, no matter how carefully thought through it might be. There is always a high possibility that the decision will prove wrong—either because it was wrong to begin with or because a change in circumstances makes it wrong. If one has thought through alternatives during the decision-making process, one has something to fall back on, something that has already been thought through, that has been studied, that is understood. Without such an alternative, one is likely to flounder dismally when reality proves a decision to be inoperative.

- In the last chapter, I referred to both the Schlieffen Plan of the German army in 1914 and President Franklin D. Roosevelt's original economic program. Both were disproven by events at the very moment when they should have taken effect.

  The German army never recovered. It never formulated another strategic concept. It went from one ill-conceived improvisation to the next. But this was inevitable. For twenty-five years no alternatives to the Schlieffen Plan had been considered by the General Staff. All its skills had gone into working out the details of this master plan. When the plan fell to pieces, no one had an alternative to fall back on.

  Despite all their careful training in strategic planning, the generals could only improvise; that is, dash off first in one direction and then in another, without any real understanding why they dashed off in the first place.

- Another 1914 event also shows the danger of having no alternative. After the Russians had ordered mobilization, the Tsar had second thoughts. He called in his Chief of Staff and asked him to halt the mobilization. "Your Majesty," the general answered, "this is impossible; there is no plan for calling off the mobilization once it has started." I do not believe that World War I would necessarily have been averted had the Russians been able to stop their military machine at the last moment. But there would have been one last chance for sanity.

- By contrast, President Roosevelt, who, in the months before he took office, had based his whole campaign on the slogan of economic orthodoxy, had a team of able people, the later "Brains Trust," working on an alternative —a radical policy based on the proposals of the old-time "Progressives," and aimed at economic and social reform on a grand scale. When the collapse of the banking system made it clear that economic orthodoxy had become political suicide, Roosevelt had his alternative ready. He therefore had a policy.

Yet without a prepared alternative, Roosevelt was as totally lost as the German General Staff or the Tsar of the Russians. When he assumed the Presidency, Roosevelt was committed to conventional nineteenth-century theory for the international economy. Between his election in November 1932, however, and his taking office the following March, the bottom fell out of the international economy just as much as it had fallen out of the domestic economy. Roosevelt clearly saw this but, without alternatives, he was reduced to impotent improvisation. And even as able and agile a man as President Roosevelt could only grope around in what suddenly had become total fog, could only swing wildly from one extreme to another—as he did when he torpedoed the London Economic Conference—could only become the prisoner of the economic snake-oil salesmen with their patent nostrums such as dollar devaluation or the remonetization of silver—both totally irrelevant to any of the real problems.

An even clearer example was Roosevelt's plan to "pack" the Supreme Court after his landslide victory in 1936. When this plan ran into strong opposition in a Congress which he thought he controlled completely, Roosevelt had no alternative. As a result, he not only lost his plan for court reform. He lost control of domestic politics—despite his towering popularity and his massive majorities.

Above all, disagreement is needed to stimulate the imagination. One does not, to be sure, need imagination to find the right solution to a problem. But then this is of value only in mathematics. In all matters of true uncertainty such as the executive deals with—whether his sphere is political, economic, social, or military—one needs "creative" solutions which create a new situation. And this means that one needs imagination—a new and different way of perceiving and understanding.

Imagination of the first order is, I admit, not in abundant supply. But neither is it as scarce as is commonly believed. Imagination needs to be challenged and stimulated, however, or else it remains latent and unused. Disagreement, especially if forced to be reasoned, thought through, documented, is the most effective stimulus we know.

■ Few people have Humpty-Dumpty's ability to imagine a great many impossible things before breakfast. And still fewer have the imagination of Humpty-Dumpty's creator, Lewis Carroll, the author of *Alice in Wonderland*. But even very small children have the imagination to enjoy *Alice*. And as Jerome S. Bruner points out, even an eight-year-old sees in a flash that while "4×6 equals 6×4, 'a blind Venetian' isn't the same thing as 'a Venetian blind.' "* This is imaginative sight of a high order. Far too many adult decisions are

* See his perceptive book, *Toward a Theory of Instruction* (Cambridge, Harvard, 1966), p. 64.

made on the assumption that a "blind Venetian" must indeed be the same as a "Venetian blind."

An old story tells of a South Sea Islander of Victorian times who, after his return from a visit to the West, told his fellow islanders that the Westerners had no water in their houses and buildings. On his native island water flowed through hollowed logs and was clearly visible. In the Western city it was conducted in pipes and, therefore, flowed only when someone turned a tap. But no one had explained the tap to the visitor.

Whenever I hear this story, I think of imagination. Unless we turn the "tap," imagination will not flow. The tap is argued, disciplined disagreement.

The effective decision-maker, therefore, organizes disagreement. This protects him against being taken in by the plausible but false or incomplete. It gives him the alternatives so that he can choose and make a decision, but also so that he is not lost in the fog when his decision proves deficient or wrong in execution. And it forces the imagination—his own and that of his associates. Disagreement converts the plausible into the right and the right into the good decision.

The effective decision-maker does not start out with the assumption that one proposed course of action is right and that all others must be wrong. Nor does he start out with the assumption, "I am right and he is wrong." He starts out with the commitment to find out why people disagree.

Effective executives know, of course, that there are fools around and that there are mischief-makers. But they do not assume that the man who disagrees with what they themselves see as clear and obvious is, therefore, either a fool or a knave. They know that unless proven otherwise, the dissenter has to be assumed to be reasonably intelligent and reasonably fair-minded. Therefore, it has to be assumed that he has reached his so obviously wrong conclusion because he sees a different reality and is concerned with a different problem. The effective executive, therefore, always asks: "What does this fellow have to see if his position were, after all, tenable, rational, intelligent?" The effective executive is concerned first with *understanding*. Only then does he even think about who is right and who is wrong.*

■ In a good law office, the beginner, fresh out of law school, is first assigned to drafting the strongest possible case for the other lawyer's client. This is not only the intelligent thing to do before one sits down to work out the case for one's own client. (One has to assume, after all, that the opposition's lawyer knows his business too.) It is also the right training for a young lawyer. It trains him not to start out with, "I know why my case is right," but with thinking through what it is that the other side must know, see, or take as probable to believe that it has a case at all. It tells him to see the two cases as alternatives. And only then is he likely to understand what his own case is all about. Only then can he make out a strong case in court that his alternative is to be preferred over that of the other side.

Needless to say, this is not done by a great many people, whether executives or not. Most people start out with the certainty that what they see is the only way to see at all.

■ The American steel executives have never missed the question: "Why do these union people get so terribly exercised every time we mention the word 'featherbedding'?" The union people in turn have never asked themselves why steel managements make such a fuss over featherbedding when every single instance thereof they have ever produced has proved to be petty, and irrelevant to boot. Instead, both sides have worked mightily to prove each other wrong. If either side had tried to understand what the other one sees and

* This, of course, is nothing new. It is indeed only a rephrasing of Mary Parker Follet (see her *Dynamic Administration*, ed. by Henry C. Metcalf and L. Urwick [New York, Harper & Row, 1942]), who in turn only extended Plato's arguments in his great dialogue on rhetoric, the *Phaedrus*.

why, both would be a great deal stronger, and labor relations in the steel industry, if not in U.S. industry, would be a good deal better and healthier.

No matter how high his emotions run, no matter how certain he is that the other side is completely wrong and has no case at all, the executive who wants to make the right decision forces himself to see opposition as *his* means to think through the alternatives. He uses conflict of opinion as his tool to make sure all major aspects of an important matter are looked at carefully.

There is one final question the effective decision-maker asks: "Is a decision really necessary?" *One* alternative is always the alternative of doing nothing.

Every decision is like surgery. It is an intervention into a system and therefore carries with it the risk of shock. One does not make unnecessary decisions any more than a good surgeon does unnecessary surgery. Individual decision-makers, like individual surgeons, differ in their styles. Some are more radical or more conservative than others. But by and large, they agree on the rules.

One has to make a decision when a condition is likely to degenerate if nothing is done. This also applies with respect to opportunity. If the opportunity is important and is likely to vanish unless one acts with dispatch, one acts—and one makes a radical change.

- Theodore Vail's contemporaries agreed with him as to the degenerative danger of government ownership: But they wanted to fight it by fighting symptoms—fighting this or that bill in the legislature, opposing this or that candidate and supporting another, and so on. Vail alone understood that this is the ineffectual way to fight a degenerative condition. Even if one wins every battle, one can never win the war.

He saw that drastic action was needed to create a new situation. He alone saw that private business had to make public regulation into an effective alternative to nationalization.

At the opposite end there are those conditions in respect to which one can, without being unduly optimistic, expect that they will take care of themselves even if nothing is done. If the answer to the question "What will happen if we do nothing?" is "It will take care of itself," one does not interfere. Nor does one interfere if the condition, while annoying, is of no importance and unlikely to make any difference anyhow.

■ It is a rare executive who understands this. The controller who in a desperate financial crisis preaches cost reduction is seldom capable of leaving alone minor blemishes, elimination of which will achieve nothing. He may know, for instance, that the significant costs that are out of control are in the sales organization and in physical distribution. And he will work hard and brilliantly at getting them under control. But then he will discredit himself and the whole effort by making a big fuss about the "unnecessary" employment of two or three old employees in an otherwise efficient and well-run plant. And he will dismiss as immoral the argument that eliminating these few semipensioners will not make any difference anyhow. "Other pople are making sacrifices," he will argue, "Why should the plant people get away with inefficiency?"

When it is all over, the organization will forget fast that he saved the business. They will remember, though, his vendetta against the two or three poor devils in the plant— and rightly so. *"De minimis non curat praetor"* [The magistrate does not consider trifles] said the Roman law almost two thousand years ago—but many decision-makers still need to learn it.

The great majority of decisions will lie between these extremes. The problem is not going to take care of itself; but it is unlikely to turn into degenerative malignancy either. The opportunity is only for improvement rather than for real change and innovation; but it is still quite considerable. If we do not act, in other words, we will in all probability survive. But if we do act, we may be better off.

In this situation the effective decision-maker compares effort and risk of action to risk of inaction. There is no formula for the right decision here. But the guidelines are so clear that decision in the concrete case is rarely difficult. They are:

- Act if on balance the benefits greatly outweigh cost and risk; and
- Act or do not act; but do not "hedge" or compromise.

The surgeon who only takes out half the tonsils or half the appendix risks as much infection or shock as if he did the whole job. And he has not cured the condition, has indeed made it worse. He either operates or he doesn't. Similarly, the effective decision-maker either acts or he doesn't act. He does not take half-action. This is the one thing that is always wrong, and the one sure way not to satisfy the minimum specifications, the minimum boundary conditions.

The decision is now ready to be made. The specifications have been thought through, the alternatives explored, the risks and gains weighed. Everything is known. Indeed, it is always reasonably clear by now what course of action must be taken. At this point the decision does indeed almost "make itself."

And it is at this point that most decisions are lost. It becomes suddenly quite obvious that the decision is not going to be pleasant, is not going to be popular, is not going to be easy. It becomes clear that a decision requires courage as much as it requires judgment. There is no inherent reason why medicines should taste horrible—but effective ones usually do. Similarly, there is no inherent reason why decisions should be distasteful—but most effective ones are.

One thing the effective executive will not do at this point. He will not give in to the cry, "Let's make another study." This is the coward's way—and all the coward achieves is to die a thousand deaths where the brave man dies but one. When confronted with the demand for "another study" the effective executive asks: "Is there any reason to believe that additional study will produce anything new? And is there reason to believe that the new is likely to be relevant?" And if the answer is "no"—as it usually is—the effective executive does not permit another study. He does not waste the time of good people to cover up his own indecision.

But at the same time he will not rush into a decision unless he is sure he understands it. Like any reasonably experienced adult, he has learned to pay attention to what Socrates called his "daemon": the inner voice, somewhere in the bowels, that whispers, "Take care." Just because something is difficult, disagreeable, or frightening is no reason for not doing it if it is right. But one holds back—if only for a moment—if one finds oneself uneasy, perturbed, bothered without quite knowing why. "I always stop when things seem out of focus," is the way one of the best decision-makers of my acquaintance puts it.

Nine times out of ten the uneasiness turns out to be over some silly detail. But the tenth time one suddenly realizes that one has overlooked the most important fact in the problem, has made an elementary blunder, or has misjudged altogether. The tenth time one suddenly wakes up at night and realizes —as Sherlock Holmes did in the famous story—that the "most significant thing is that the hound of Baskerville didn't bark."

But the effective decision-maker does not wait long—a few days, at the most a few weeks. If the "daemon" has not spoken by then, he acts with speed and energy whether he likes to or not.

Executives are not paid for doing things they like to do. They are paid for getting the right things done—most of all in their specific task, the making of effective decisions.

Decision-making and the Computer

Does all this still apply today when we have the computer? The computer, we are being told, will replace the decision-maker, at least in middle management. It will make, in a few years, all the operating decisions—and fairly soon thereafter it will take over the strategic decisions too.

Actually the computer will force executives to make, as true decisions, what are today mostly made as on-the-spot adaptations. It will convert a great many people who traditionally have reacted rather than acted into genuine executives and decision-makers.

The computer is a potent tool of the executive. Like hammer or pliers—but unlike wheel or saw—it cannot do anything man cannot do. But it can do one human job—addition and subtraction—infinitely faster than man can do it. And, being a tool, it does not get bored, does not get tired, does not charge overtime. Like all tools that do better something man can do, the computer multiplies man's capacity (the other tools, such as the wheel, the airplane, or the television set that do something man cannot do at all, add a new dimension to man, i.e., extend his nature). But like all tools the computer can only do one or two things. It has narrow limitations. And it is the limitations of the computer that will force us to do as genuine decision what now is largely done as *ad hoc* adaptation.

The strength of the computer lies in its being a logic machine. It does precisely what it is programed to do. This makes it fast and precise. It also makes it a total moron; for logic is essentially stupid. It is doing the simple and obvious. The human being, by contrast, is not logical; he is perceptual. This means that he is slow and sloppy. But he is also bright and has insight. The human being can adapt; that is, he can infer from scanty information or from no information at all what the total picture might be like. He can remember a great many things nobody has programed.

- A simple and a common area where the typical traditional manager acts by way of on-the-spot adaptation is the commonplace inventory and shipping decision. The typical district sales manager knows, albeit most inaccurately, that customer A usually runs his plant on a tight schedule and would be in real trouble if a promised delivery did not arrive on time. He knows also that customer B usually has adequate inventories of materials and supplies and can presumably manage to get by for a few days even if a delivery were late. He knows that customer C is already annoyed at his company and is only waiting for a pretext to shift his purchases to another supplier. He knows that he can get additional supplies of one item by asking for them as a special favor from this or that man in the plant back home, and so on. And on the basis of these experiences, the typical district sales manager adapts and adjusts as he goes along.

The computer knows none of these things. At least it does not know them unless it has been specifically told that these are the facts that determine company policy toward consumer A or in respect to product B. All it can do is react the way it has been instructed and programed. It no more makes "decisions" than the slide rule or the cash register. All it can do is compute.

The moment a company tries to put inventory control on the computer, it realizes that it has to develop rules. It has to develop an inventory *policy*. As soon as it tackles this, it finds that the basic decisions in respect to inventory are not inventory decisions at all. They are highly risky business decisions. Inventory emerges as a means of balancing different risks: the risk of disappointing customer expectations in respect to delivery and service; the risk and cost of turbulence and instability in manufacturing schedules; and the risk and cost of locking up money in merchandise which might spoil, become obsolete, or otherwise deteriorate.

■ The traditional clichés do not greatly help. "It is our aim to give 90 per cent of our customers 90 per cent fulfillment of delivery promises" sounds precise. It is actually meaningless, as one finds out when one tries to convert it into the step-by-step moron logic of the computer. Does it mean that all our customers are expected to get nine out of ten orders when we promised them? Does it mean that our really good customers should get fulfillment all the time on all their orders —and how do we define a "really good customer" anyhow? Does it mean that we aim to give fulfillment of these promises on all our products? or only on the major ones which together account for the bulk of our production? And what policy, if any, do we have with respect to the many hundreds of products which are not major for us, though they might well be major for the customer who orders one of them?

Each of these questions requires a risk-taking decision and, above all, a decision on principle. Until all these decisions have been made, the computer cannot control inventory. They are decisions of uncertainty—and what is relevant to them could not even be defined clearly enough to be conveyed to the computer.

To the extent, therefore, to which the computer—or any similar tool—is expected to keep operations on an even keel or to carry out predetermined reactions to expected events (whether the appearance of hostile nuclear missiles on the far horizon or the appearance of a crude oil with an unusual sulfur content in the petroleum refinery) the decision has to be anticipated and thought through. It can no longer be improvised. It can no longer be groped for in a series of small adaptations, each specific, each approximate, each, to use the physicist's terminology, a "virtual" rather than a real decision. It has to be a decision in *principle*.

- The computer is not the cause of this. The computer, being a tool, is probably not the cause of anything. It only brings out in sharp relief what has been happening all along. For this shift from the small adaptation to the decision in principle has been going on for a long time. It became particularly apparent during World War II and after, in the military. Precisely because military operations became so large and interdependent, requiring, for instance, logistics systems embracing whole theaters of operations and all branches of the armed services, middle-level commanders increasingly had to know the framework of strategic decisions within which they were operating. They increasingly had to make real decisions, rather than adapt their orders to local events. The second-level generals who emerged as the great men of World War II—a Rommel, a Bradley, a Zhukov—were all "middle managers" who thought through genuine decisions, rather than the dashing cavalry generals, the *"beaux sabreurs"* of earlier wars.

As a result, decision-making can no longer be confined to the very small group at the top. In one way or another almost every knowledge worker in an organization will either have to become a decision-maker himself or will at least have to be able to play an active, an intelligent, and an autonomous part in the decision-making process. What in the past had been a highly specialized function, discharged by a small and usually clearly defined organ—with the rest adapting within a mold of custom and usage—is rapidly becoming a normal if not an everyday task of every single unit in this new social institution, the large-scale knowledge organization. The ability to make effective decisions increasingly determines the ability of every knowledge worker, at least of those in responsible positions, to be effective altogether.

- A good example of the shift to decision which the new techniques impose on us is the much discussed PERT (Program Evaluation and Review Technique) which aims at providing a road map for the critical tasks in a highly complex program such as the development and construction of a new space vehicle. PERT aims at giving control of such a program by advance planning of each part of the work, of its sequence, and of the deadlines each part has to meet for the whole program to be ready on time. This sharply curtails *ad hoc* adaptation. In its place there are high-risk decisions. The first few times operating men have to work out a PERT schedule, they are invariably wrong in almost every one of their judgments. They are still trying to do, through *ad hoc* adaptations, what can only be done through systematic risk-taking decision-making.

The computer has the same impact on strategic decisions. It cannot make them, of course. All it can do—and even that is potential rather than actual so far—is to work through what conclusions follow from certain assumptions made regarding an uncertain future, or conversely, what assumptions underlie certain proposed courses of action. Again, all it can do is compute. For this reason it demands clear analysis, especially of the boundary conditions the decision has to satisfy. And that requires risk-taking judgment of a high order.

There are additional implications of the computer for decision-making. If properly used, for instance, it should free senior executives from much of the preoccupation with events inside the organization to which they are now being condemned by the absence or tardiness of reliable information. It should make it much easier for the executive to go and look for himself on the outside; that is, in the area where alone an organization can have results.

The computer might also change one of the typical mistakes in decision-making. Traditionally we have tended to err toward treating generic situations as a series of unique events. Traditionally we have tended to doctor symptoms. The computer, however, can only handle generic situations—this is all logic is ever concerned with. Hence we may well in the future tend to err by handling the exceptional, the unique, as if it were a symptom of the generic.

- This tendency underlies the complaints that we are trying to substitute the computer for the proven and tested judgment of the military man. This should not be lightly dismissed as the grumbling of brass-hats. The most cogent attack on the attempt to standardize military decisions was made by an outstanding civilian "management scientist," Sir Solly Zuckerman, the eminent British biologist, who as scientific adviser to the British Ministry of Defense has played a leading part in the development of computer analysis and operations research.

The greatest impact of the computer lies in its limitations, which will force us increasingly to make decisions, and above all, force middle managers to change from operators into executives and decision-makers.

This should have happened anyhow. One of the great strengths of such organizations as, for instance, General Motors among business firms, or the German General Staff among military groups, was precisely that these organizations long ago organized operating events as true decisions.

The sooner operating managers learn to make decisions as genuine judgments on risk and uncertainty, the sooner we will overcome one of the basic weaknesses of large organization—the absence of any training and testing for the decision-making top positions. As long as we can handle the events on the operating level by adaptation rather than by thinking, by "feel" rather than by knowledge and analysis, operating people—in government, in the military, or in business—will be untrained, untried, and untested when, as top executives, they are first confronted with strategic decisions.

The computer will, of course, no more make decision-makers out of clerks than the slide rule makes a mathematician out of a high school student. But the computer will force us to make an early distinction between the clerk and the potential decision-maker. And it will permit the latter—may indeed force him—to learn purposeful, effective decision-making. For unless someone does this, and does it well, the computer cannot compute.

There is indeed ample reason why the appearance of the computer has sparked interest in decision-making. But the reason is not that the computer will "take over" the decision. The reason is that with the computer's taking over computation, people all the way down the line in the organization will have to learn to be executives and to make effective decisions.

Conclusion:
Effectiveness Must Be Learned

This book rests on two premises:
- The executive's job is to be effective; and
- Effectiveness can be learned.

The executive is paid for being effective. He owes effectiveness to the organization for which he works. What then does the executive have to learn and have to do to deserve being an executive? In trying to answer this question, this book has, on the whole, taken organizational performance and executive performance to be goals in and by themselves.

Effectiveness can be learned is the second premise. The book has therefore tried to present the various dimensions of executive performance in such sequence as to stimulate readers to learn for themselves how to become effective executives. This is not a textbook, of course—if only because effectiveness, while capable of being learned, surely cannot be taught. Effectiveness is, after all, not a "subject," but a self-discipline. But throughout this book, and implicit in its structure and in the way it treats its subject matter, is always the question: "What makes for effectiveness in an organization and in any of the major areas of an executive's day and work?" Only rarely is the question asked: "Why should there be effectiveness?" The goal of effectiveness is taken for granted.

In looking back on the arguments and flow of these chapters and on their findings, another and quite different aspect of executive effectiveness emerges, however. Effectiveness reveals itself as crucial to a man's self-development; to organization development; and to the fulfillment and viability of modern society.

1. The first step toward effectiveness is a procedure: *recording where the time goes.* This is mechanical if not mechanistic. The executive need not even do this himself; it is better done by a secretary or assistant. Yet if this is all the executive ever does, he will reap a substantial improvement. The results should be fast, if not immediate. If done with any continuity, recording one's time will also prod and nudge a man toward the next steps for greater effectiveness.

The analysis of the executive's time, the elimination of the unnecessary time-wasters, already requires some action. It requires some elementary decisions. It requires some changes in a man's behavior, his relationships, and his concerns. It raises searching questions regarding the relative importance of different uses of time, of different activities and of their goals. It should affect the level and the quality of a good deal of work done. Yet this can perhaps still be done by going down a checklist every few months, that is, by following a form. It still concerns itself only with efficiency in the utilization of a scarce resource—namely, time.

2. The next step, however, in which the executive is asked to *focus his vision on contribution* advances from the procedural to the conceptual, from mechanics to analysis, and from efficiencies to concern with results. In this step the executive disciplines himself to think through the reason why he is

on the payroll and the contribution he ought to make. There is nothing very complicated about this. The questions the executive asks himself about his contribution are still straightforward and more or less schematic. But the answers to these questions should lead to high demands on himself, to thinking about his own goals and those of the organization, and to concern with values. They should lead to demands on himself for high standards. Above all, these questions ask the executive to assume responsibility, rather than to act the subordinate, satisfied if he only "pleases the boss." In focusing himself and his vision on contribution the executive, in other words, has to think through purpose and ends rather than means alone.

3. *Making strengths productive* is fundamentally an attitude expressed in behavior. It is fundamentally respect for the person—one's own as well as others. It is a value system in action. But it is again "learning through doing" and self-development through practice. In making strengths productive, the executive integrates individual purpose and organization needs, individual capacity and organization results, individual achievement and organization opportunity.

4. Chapter 5, "First Things First," serves as antiphon to the earlier chapter, "Know Thy Time." These two chapters might be called the twin pillars between which executive effectiveness is suspended and on which it rests. But the procedure here no longer deals with a resource, time, but with the end product, the performance of organization and executive. What is being recorded and analyzed is no longer what happens to us but what we should try to make happen in the environment around us. And what is being developed here is not information, but character: foresight, self-reliance, courage. What is being developed here, in other words, is leadership—not the leadership of brilliance and genius, to be sure, but the

much more modest yet more enduring leadership of dedication, determination, and serious purpose.

5. The *effective decision*, which the final chapters discuss, is concerned with rational action. There is no longer a broad and clearly marked path which the executive only has to walk down to gain effectiveness. But there are still clear surveyor's benchmarks to give orientation and guidance how to get from one to the next. How the executive, for instance, is to move from identifying a pattern of events as constituting a generic problem to the setting of the boundary conditions which the decision has to satisfy, is not spelled out. This has to be done according to the specific situation encountered. But what needs to be done and in what sequence should be clear enough. In following these benchmarks, the executive, it is expected, will develop and train himself in responsible judgment. Effective decision-making requires both procedure and analysis, but its essence is an ethics of action.

There is much more to the self-development of an executive than his training in effectiveness. He has to acquire knowledges and skills. He has to learn a good many new work habits as he proceeds along his career, and he will occasionally have to unlearn some old work habits. But knowledges, skills, and habits, no matter how accomplished, will avail the executive little unless he first develops himself in effectiveness.

There is nothing exalted about being an effective executive. It is simply doing one's job like thousands of others. There is little danger that anyone will compare this essay on training oneself to be an effective executive with, say, Kierkegaard's great self-development tract, *Training in Christianity*. There are surely higher goals for a man's life than to become an effective executive. But only because the goal is so modest can we hope at all to achieve it; that is, to have the large number of effective executives modern society and its organizations need.

If we required saints, poets, or even first-rate scholars to staff our knowledge positions, the large-scale organization would simply be absurd and impossible. The needs of large-scale organization have to be satisfied by common people achieving uncommon performance. This is what the effective executive has to make himself able to do. Though this goal is a modest one, one that everyone should be able to reach if he works at it, the self-development of an effective executive is true development of the person. It goes from mechanics to attitudes, values and character, from procedure to commitment.

Self-development of the effective executive is central to the development of the organization, whether it be a business, a government agency, a research laboratory, a hospital, or a military service. It is the way toward performance of the organization. As executives work toward becoming effective, they raise the performance level of the whole organization. They raise the sights of people—their own as well as others.

As a result, the organization not only becomes capable of doing better. It becomes capable of doing different things and of aspiring to different goals. Developing executive effectiveness challenges directions, goals, and purposes of the organization. It raises the eyes of its people from preoccupation with problems to a vision of opportunity, from concern with weakness to exploitation of strengths. This, in turn, wherever it happens, makes an organization attractive to people of high ability and aspiration, and motivates people to higher performance and higher dedication. Organizations are not more effective because they have better people. They have better people because they motivate to self-development through their standards, through their habits, through their climate. And these, in turn, result from systematic, focused, purposeful self-training of the individuals in becoming effective executives.

Modern society depends for its functioning, if not for its

survival, on the effectiveness of large-scale organizations, on their performance and results, on their values, standards, and self-demands.

Organization performance has become decisive well beyond the economic sphere or even the social sphere, for instance, in education, in health care, and in the advancement of knowledge. Increasingly, the large-scale organization that counts is the knowledge-organization, employing knowledge workers and staffed heavily with men and women who have to perform as executives, men and women who have in their own work to assume responsibility for the results of the whole, and who, by the nature of their knowledge and work, make decisions with impact upon the results and performance of the whole.

Effective organizations are not common. They are even rarer than effective executives. There are shining examples here and there. But on the whole, organization performance is still primitive. Enormous resources are brought together in the modern large business, in the modern large government agency, in the modern large hospital, or in the university; yet far too much of the result is mediocrity, far too much is splintering of efforts, far too much is devoted to yesterday or to avoiding decision and action. Organizations as well as executives need to work systematically on effectiveness and need to acquire the habit of effectiveness. They need to learn to feed their opportunities and to starve their problems. They need to work on making strength productive. They need to concentrate and to set priorities instead of trying to do a little bit of everything.

But executive effectiveness is surely one of the basic requirements of effective organization and in itself a most important contribution toward organization development.

Executive effectiveness is our one best hope to make modern society productive economically and viable socially.

The knowledge worker, as has been said again and again in

this book, is rapidly becoming the major resource of the developed countries. He is becoming the major investment; for education is the most expensive investment of them all. He is becoming the major cost center. To make the knowledge worker productive is the specific economic need of an industrially developed society. In such a society, the manual worker is not competitive in his costs with manual workers in underdeveloped or developing countries. Only productivity of the knowledge worker can make it possible for developed countries to maintain their high standard of living against the competition of low-wage, developing economies.

So far, only a superoptimist would be reassured as to the productivity of the knowledge worker in the industrially developed countries. The tremendous shift of the center of gravity in the work force from manual to knowledge work that has taken place since World War II has not, I submit, shown extraordinary results. By and large, neither the increase in productivity nor the increase in profitability—the two yardsticks that measure economic results—has shown marked acceleration. No matter how well the industrially developed countries have done since World War II—and their record has been impressive—the job of making the knowledge worker productive is still ahead. The key to it is surely the effectiveness of the executive. For the executive is himself the decisive knowledge worker. His level, his standards, his demands on himself determine to a large extent the motivation, the direction, the dedication of the other knowledge workers around him.

Even more important is the social need for executive effectiveness. The cohesion and strength of our society depend increasingly on the integration of the psychological and social needs of the knowledge worker with the goals of organization and of industrial society.

The knowledge worker normally is not an economic problem. He tends to be affluent. He has high job security and his very knowledge gives him freedom to move. But his psychological needs and personal values need to be satisfied in and through his work and position in the organization. He is considered—and considers himself—a professional. Yet he is an employee and under orders. He is beholden to a knowledge area, yet he has to subordinate the authority of knowledge to organizational objectives and goals. In a knowledge area there are no superiors or subordinates, there are only older and younger men. Yet organization requires a hierarchy. These are not entirely new problems, to be sure. Officer corps and civil service have known them for a long time, and have known how to resolve them. But they are real problems. The knowledge worker is not poverty-prone. He is in danger of alienation, to use the fashionable word for boredom, frustration, and silent despair.

Just as the economic conflict between the needs of the manual worker and the role of an expanding economy was *the* social question of the nineteenth century in the developing countries, so the position, function and fulfillment of the knowledge worker is the social question of the twentieth century in these countries now that they are developed.

It is not a question that will go away if we deny its existence. To assert (as do in their own way both orthodox economists and Marxists) that only the "objective reality" of economic and social performance exists will not make the problem go away. Nor, however, will the new romanticism of the social psychologists (e.g., Professor Chris Argyris at Yale) who quite rightly point out that organizational goals are not automatically individual fulfillment and therefrom conclude that we had better sweep them aside. We will have to satisfy *both* the objective needs of society for performance by the organization, and the needs of the person for achievement and fulfillment.

Self-development of the executive toward effectiveness is the only available answer. It is the only way in which organization goals and individual needs can come together. The executive who works at making strengths productive—his own as well as those of others—works at making organizational performance compatible with personal achievement. He works at making his knowledge area become organizational opportunity. And by focusing on contribution, he makes his own values become organization results.

The manual worker, so at least the nineteenth century believed, had only economic goals and was content with economic rewards. That, as the "human relations" school demonstrated, was far from the whole truth. It certainly ceased to be true the moment pay went above the subsistence level. The knowledge worker demands economic rewards too. Their absence is a deterrent. But their presence is not enough. He needs opportunity, he needs achievement, he needs fulfillment, he needs values. Only by making himself an effective executive can the knowledge worker obtain these satisfactions. Only executive effectiveness can enable this society to harmonize its two needs: the needs of organization to obtain from the individual the contribution it needs, and the need of the individual to have organization serve as his tool for the accomplishment of his purposes. Effectiveness *must* be learned.

INDEX

HarperBusiness

union. It is probably the most successful institution of the century in the developed countries. It has clearly attained its original objectives. There can be no more "more" when the labor share of gross national product in Western developed countries is around 90 percent—and in some countries, such as Holland, close to 100 percent. Yet the labor union is incapable of even thinking about new challenges, new objectives, new contributions. All it can do is repeat the old slogans and fight the old battles. For the "cause of labor" is an absolute good. Clearly, it must not be questioned, let alone redefined.

The university, however, may not be too different from the labor union, and in part for the same reason—a level of growth and success second in this century only to that of the labor union.

Still there are enough exceptions among public-service institutions (although, I have to admit, not many among government agencies) to show that public-service institutions, even old and big ones, can innovate.

One Roman Catholic archdiocese in the United States, for instance, has brought in lay people to run the diocese, including a married lay woman, the former personnel vice-president of a department store chain, as the general manager. Everything that does not involve dispensing sacraments and ministering to congregations is done by lay professionals and managers. Although there is a shortage of priests throughout the American Catholic Church, this archdiocese has priests to spare and has been able to move forward aggressively to build congregations and expand religious services.

One of the oldest of scientific societies, the American Association for the Advancement of Science, redirected itself between 1960 and 1980 to become a "mass organization" without losing its character as a leader. It totally changed its weekly magazine, *Science*, to become the spokesman for science to public and government, and to be the authoritative reporter on science policy. And it created a scientifically solid yet popular mass circulation magazine for lay readers.

A large hospital on the West Coast recognized, as early as 1965 or so, that health care was changing as a result of its success. Where other large city hospitals tried to fight such trends as those toward hospital chains or freestanding ambulatory treatment centers, this institution has been an innovator and a leader in these developments. Indeed, it was the first to build a freestanding maternity center in which the expectant mother is given a motel room at fairly low cost, yet with all the medical services available should they be needed. It was the first to go into freestanding surgical centers for ambulatory care. But it also started to build its own voluntary hospital chain, in which it offers management contracts to smaller hospitals throughout the region.

Beginning around 1975, the Girl Scouts of the U.S.A., a large organization dating back to the early years of the century with several million young women enrolled, introduced innovations affecting membership, programs, and volunteers—the three basic dimensions of the organization. It began actively to recruit girls from the new urban middle classes, that is, blacks, Asians, Latins; these minorities now account for one-fifth of the members. It recognized that with the movement of women into professions and managerial positions, girls need new programs and role models that stress professional and business careers rather than the traditional careers as homemaker or nurse. The Girl Scouts management people realized that the traditional sources for volunteers to run local activities were drying up because young mothers no longer were sitting at home searching for things to do. But they recognized, too, that the new professional, the new working mother represents an opportunity and that the Girl Scouts have something to offer her; and for any community organization, volunteers are the critical constraint. They therefore set out to make work as a volunteer for the Girl Scouts attractive to the working mother as a good way to have time and fun with her child while also contributing to her child's development. Finally, the Girl Scouts realized that the working mother who does not have enough time for her child represents another opportunity: they started Girl Scouting for preschool children. Thus, the Girl Scouts reversed the downward trend in enrollment of both children and volunteers, while the Boy Scouts—a bigger, older, and infinitely richer organization—is still adrift.

II

ENTREPRENEURIAL POLICIES

These are all American examples, I fully realize. Doubtless, similar examples are to be found in Europe or Japan. But I hope that these cases, despite their limitations, will suffice to demonstrate the entrepreneurial policies needed in the public-service institution to make it capable of innovation.

1. First, the public-service institution needs a clear definition of its mission. What is it trying to do? Why does it exist? It needs to focus on objectives rather than on programs and projects. Programs and projects are means to an end. They should always be considered as temporary and, in fact, short-lived.

2. The public-service institution needs a realistic statement of goals. It should say, "Our job is to assuage famine," rather than, "Our job is to eliminate hunger." It needs something that is genuinely attainable and therefore a commitment to a realistic goal, so that it can say eventually, "Our job is finished."

There are, of course, objectives that can never be attained. To administer justice in any human society is clearly an unending task, one that can never be fully accomplished even to modest standards. But most objectives can and should be phrased in optimal rather than in maximal terms. Then it is possible to say: "We have attained what we were trying to do."

Surely, this should be said with respect to the traditional goals of the schoolmaster: to get everyone to sit in school for long years. This goal has long been attained in developed countries. What does education have to do now, that is, what is the meaning of "education" as against mere schooling?

3. Failure to achieve objectives should be considered an indication that the objective is wrong, or at least defined wrongly. The assumption has then to be that the objective should be economic rather than moral. If an objective has not been attained after repeated tries, one has to assume that it is the wrong one. It is not rational to consider failure a good reason for trying again and again. The probability of success, as mathematicians have known for three hundred years, diminishes with each successive try; in fact, the probability of success in any succeeding try is never more than one-half the probability of the preceding one. Thus, failure to attain objectives is a *prima facie* reason to question the validity of the objective—the exact opposite of what most public-service institutions believe.

4. Finally, public-service institutions need to build into their policies and practices the constant search for innovative opportunity. They need to view change as an opportunity rather than a threat.

The innovating public-service institutions mentioned in the preceding pages succeeded because they applied these basic rules.

In the years after World War II, the Roman Catholic Church in the

United States was confronted for the first time with the rapid emergence of a well-educated Catholic laity. Most Catholic dioceses, and indeed most institutions of the Roman Catholic Church, perceived in this a threat, or at least a problem. With an educated Catholic laity, unquestioned acceptance of bishop and priest could no longer be taken for granted. And yet there was no place for Catholic lay people in the structure and governance of the Church. Similarly, all Roman Catholic dioceses in the United States, beginning around 1965 or 1970, faced a sharp drop in the number of young men entering the priesthood—and perceived this as a major threat. Only one Catholic archdiocese saw both as opportunities. (As a result, it has a different problem. Young priests from all over the United States want to enter it; for in this one archdiocese, the priest gets to do the things he trained for, the things which he entered the priesthood to do.)

All American hospitals, beginning in 1970 or 1975, saw changes coming in the delivery of health care. Most of them organized themselves to fight these changes. Most of them told everybody that "these changes will be catastrophic." Only the one hospital saw in them opportunities.

The American Association for the Advancement of Science saw in the expansion of people with scientific backgrounds and working in scientific pursuits a tremendous opportunity to establish itself as a leader, both within the scientific community and outside.

And the Girl Scouts looked at demographics and said: "How can we convert population trends into new opportunities for us?"

Even in government, innovation is possible if simple rules are obeyed. Here is one example.

Lincoln, Nebraska, 120 years ago, was the first city in the Western world to take into municipal ownership public services such as public transportation, electric power, gas, water, and so on. In the last ten years, under a woman mayor, Helen Boosalis, it has begun to privatize such services as garbage pickup, school transportation, and a host of others. The city provides the money, with private businesses bidding for the contracts; there are substantial savings in cost and even greater improvements in service.

What Helen Boosalis has seen in Lincoln is the opportunity to separate the "provider" of public services, that is, government, and the "supplier." This makes possible both high service standards and the efficiency, reliability, and low cost which competition can provide.

The four rules outlined above constitute the *specific* policies and practices the public-service institution requires if it is to make itself entrepreneurial and capable of innovation. In addition, however, it also needs to adopt those policies and practices that any existing organization requires in order to be entrepreneurial, the policies and practices discussed in the preceding chapter, The Entrepreneurial Business.

III

THE NEED TO INNOVATE

Why is innovation in the public-service institution so important? Why cannot we leave existing public-service institutions the way they are, and depend for the innovations we need in the public-service sector on new institutions, as historically we have always done?

The answer is that public-service institutions have become too important in developed countries, and too big. The public-service sector, both the governmental one and the nongovernmental but not-for-profit one, has grown faster during this century than the private sector— maybe three to five times as fast. The growth has been especially fast since World War II.

To some extent, this growth has been excessive. Wherever public-service activities can be converted into profit-making enterprises, they should be so converted. This applies not only to the kind of municipal services the city of Lincoln, Nebraska, now "privatizes." The move from non-profit to profit has already gone very far in the American hospital. I expect it to become a stampede in professional and graduate education. To subsidize the highest earners in developed society, the holders of advanced professional degrees, can hardly be justified.

A central economic problem of developed societies during the next twenty or thirty years is surely going to be capital formation; only in Japan is it still adequate for the economy's needs. We therefore can ill afford to have activities conducted as "non-profit," that is, as activities that devour capital rather than form it, if they can be organized as activities that form capital, as activities that make a profit.

But still the great bulk of the activities that are being discharged in and by public-service institutions will remain public-service activities, and will neither disappear nor be transformed. Consequently, they have to be made producing and productive. Public-service institutions will have to learn to be innovators, to manage themselves entrepreneurially. To achieve this, public-service institutions will have to learn to look upon social, technological, economic, and demographic shifts as opportunities in a period of rapid change in all these areas. Otherwise, they will become obstacles. The public-service institutions will increasingly become unable to discharge their mission as they adhere to programs and projects that cannot work in a changed environment, and yet they will not be able or willing to abandon the missions they can no longer discharge. Increasingly, they will come to look the way the feudal barons came to look after they had lost all social function around 1300: as parasites, functionless, with nothing left but the power to obstruct and to exploit. They will become self-righteous while increasingly losing their legitimacy. Clearly, this is already happening to the apparently most powerful among them, the labor union. Yet a society in rapid change, with new challenges, new requirements and opportunities, needs public-service institutions.

The public school in the United States exemplifies both the opportunity and the dangers. Unless it takes the lead in innovation it is unlikely to survive this century, except as a school for the minorities in the slums. For the first time in its history, the United States faces the threat of a class structure in education in which all but the very poor remain outside of the public school system—at least in the cities and suburbs where most of the population lives. And this will squarely be the fault of the public school itself because what is needed to reform the public school is already known (see Chapter 9).

Many other public-service institutions face a similar situation. The knowledge is there. The need to innovate is clear. They now have to learn how to build entrepreneurship and innovation into their own system. Otherwise, they will find themselves superseded by outsiders who will create competing entrepreneurial public-service institutions and so render the existing ones obsolete.

The late nineteenth century and early twentieth century was a period of tremendous creativity and innovation in the public-service field. Social innovation during the seventy-five years until the 1930s was surely as much alive, as productive, and as rapid as technological innovation if not more so. But in these periods the innovation took the form of creating new public-service institutions. Most of the ones we have around now go back no more than sixty or seventy years in their present form and with their present mission. The next twenty or thirty years will be very different. The need for social innovation may be even greater, but it will very largely have to be social innovation within the existing public-service institution. To build entrepreneurial management into the existing public-service institution may thus be the foremost political task of this generation.

15

The New Venture

For the existing enterprise, whether business or public-service institution, the controlling word in thé term "entrepreneurial management" is "entrepreneurial." For the new venture, it is "management." In the existing business, it is the existing that is the main obstacle to entrepreneurship. In the new venture, it is its absence.

The new venture has an idea. It may have a product or a service. It may even have sales, and sometimes quite a substantial volume of them. It surely has costs. And it may have revenues and even profits. What it does not have is a "business," a viable, operating, organized "present" in which people know where they are going, what they are supposed to do, and what the results are or should be. But unless a new venture develops into a new business and makes sure of being "managed," it will not survive no matter how brilliant the entrepreneurial idea, how much money it attracts, how good its products, nor even how great the demand for them.

Refusal to accept these facts destroyed every single venture started by the nineteenth century's greatest inventor, Thomas Edison. Edison's ambition was to be a successful businessman and the head of a big company. He should have succeeded, for he was a superb business planner. He knew exactly how an electric power company had to be set up to exploit his invention of the light bulb. He knew exactly how to get all the money he could possibly need for his ventures. His products were immediate successes and the demand for them practically insatiable. But Edison remained an entrepreneur; or rather, he thought that "managing" meant being the boss. He refused to build a management team. And so every one of his four or five companies collapsed ignominiously once it got to middle size, and was saved only by booting Edison himself out and replacing him with professional management.

438

Entrepreneurial management in the new venture has four requirements:

It requires, first, a focus on the market.

It requires, second, financial foresight, and especially planning for cash flow and capital needs ahead.

It requires, third, building a top management team long before the new venture actually needs one and long before it can actually afford one.

And finally, it requires of the founding entrepreneur a decision in respect to his or her own role, area of work, and relationships.

I

THE NEED FOR MARKET FOCUS

A common explanation for the failure of a new venture to live up to its promise or even to survive at all is: "We were doing fine until these other people came and took our market away from us. We don't really understand it. What they offered wasn't so very different from what we had." Or one hears: "We were doing all right, but these other people started selling to customers we'd never even heard of and all of a sudden they had the market."

When a new venture does succeed, more often than not it is in a market other than the one it was originally intended to serve, with products or services not quite those with which it had set out, bought in large part by customers it did not even think of when it started, and used for a host of purposes besides the ones for which the products were first designed. If a new venture does not anticipate this, organizing itself to take advantage of the unexpected and unseen markets; if it is not totally market-focused, if not market-driven, then it will succeed only in creating an opportunity for a competitor.

There are exceptions, to be sure. A product designed for one specific use, especially if scientific or technical, often stays with the market and the end use for which it was designed. But not always. Even a prescription drug designed for a specific ailment and tested for it sometimes ends up being used for some other quite different ailment. One example is a compound that is effectively used in the treatment of stomach ulcers. Or a drug designed primarily for the treatment of human beings may find its major market in veterinary medicine.

Anything genuinely new creates markets that nobody before even imagined. No one knew that he needed an office copier before the first Xerox machine came out around 1960; five years later no business could imagine doing without a copier. When the first jet planes started to fly, the best market research pointed out that there were not even enough passengers for all the transatlantic liners then in service or being built. Five years later the transatlantic jets were carrying fifty to one hundred times as many passengers each year as had ever before crossed the Atlantic.

The innovator has limited vision, in fact, he has tunnel-vision. He sees the area with which he is familiar—to the exclusion of all other areas.

An example is DDT. Designed during World War II to protect American soldiers against tropical insects and parasites, it eventually found its greatest application in agriculture to protect livestock and crops against insects—to the point where it had to be banned for being too effective. Yet not one of the distinguished scientists who designed DDT during World War II envisaged these uses of DDT. Of course they knew that babies die from fly-borne "summer" diarrhea. Of course they knew that livestock and crops are infested by insect parasites. But these things they knew as laymen. As experts, they were concerned with the tropical diseases of humans. It was the ordinary American soldier who then applied DDT to the areas in which he was the "expert," that is, to his home, his cows, his cotton patch.

Similarly, the 3M Company did not see that an adhesive tape it had developed for industry would find myriad uses in the household and in the office—becoming Scotch Tape. 3M had for many years been a supplier of abrasives and adhesives to industry, and moderately successful in industrial markets. It had never even thought of consumer markets. It was pure accident which led the engineer who had designed an industrial product no industrial user wanted to the realization that the stuff might be salable in the consumer market. As the story goes, he took some samples home when the company had already decided to abandon the product. To his surprise, his teenage daughters began to use it to hold their curls overnight. The only unusual thing about this story is that he and his bosses at 3M recognized that they had stumbled upon a new market.

A German chemist developed Novocain as the first local anesthetic in 1905. But he could not get the doctors to use it; they preferred total anesthesia (they only accepted Novocain during World War I). But totally unexpectedly, dentists began to use the stuff. Whereupon—or so the story goes—the chemist began to travel up and down Germany making speeches against Novocain's use in dentistry. He had not designed it for that purpose!

That reaction was somewhat extreme, I admit. Still, entrepreneurs *know* what their innovation is meant to do. And if some other use for it appears, they tend to resent it. They may not actually refuse to serve customers they have not "planned" for, but they are likely to make it clear that these customers are not welcome.

This is what happened with the computer. The company that had the first computer, Univac, knew that its magnificent machine was designed for scientific work. And so it did not even send a salesman out when a business showed interest in it; surely, it argued, these people could not possibly know what a computer was all about. IBM was equally convinced that the computer was an instrument for scientific work: their own computer had been designed specifically for astronomical calculations. But IBM was willing to take orders from businesses and to serve them. Ten years later, around 1960, Univac still had by far the most advanced and best machine. IBM had the computer market.

The textbook prescription for this problem is "market research." But it is the wrong prescription.

One cannot do market research for something genuinely new. One cannot do market research for something that is not yet on the market. Around 1950, Univac's market research concluded that, by the year 2000, about one thousand computers would be sold; the actual figure in 1984 was about one million. And yet this was the most "scientific," careful, rigorous market research ever done. There was only one thing wrong with it: it started out with the assumption, then shared by everyone, that computers were going to be used for advanced scientific work —and for that use, the number is indeed quite limited. Similarly, several companies who turned down the Xerox patents did so on the basis of thorough market research which showed that printers had no use at all for a copier. Nobody had any inkling that businesses, schools, universities, colleges, and a host of private individuals would want to buy a copier.

The new venture therefore needs to start out with the assumption that its product or service may find customers in markets no one thought of, for uses no one envisaged when the product or service was designed, and that it will be bought by customers outside its field of vision and even unknown to the new venture.

If the new venture does not have such a market focus from the very beginning, all it is likely to create is the market for a competitor. A few years later "those people" will come in and take away "our market," or "those other people" who started "selling to customers we'd never even heard of" all of a sudden will indeed have preempted the market.

To build market focus into a new venture is not in fact particularly difficult. But what is required runs counter to the inclinations of the typical entrepreneur. It requires, first, that the new venture systematically hunt out both the unexpected success and the unexpected failure (cf. Chapter 3). Rather than dismiss the unexpected as an "exception," as entrepreneurs are inclined to do, they need to go out and look at it carefully and as a distinct opportunity.

Shortly after World War II, a small Indian engineering firm bought the license to produce a European-designed bicycle with an auxiliary light engine. It looked like an ideal product for India; yet it never did well. The owner of this small firm noticed, however, that substantial orders came in for the engines alone. At first he wanted to turn down those orders; what could anyone possibly do with such a small engine? It was curiosity alone that made him go to the actual area the orders came from. There he found farmers were taking the engines off the bicycles and using them to power irrigation pumps that hitherto had been hand-operated. This manufacturer is now the world's largest maker of small irrigation pumps, selling them by the millions. His pumps have revolutionized farming all over Southeast Asia.

To be market-driven also requires that the new venture be willing to experiment. If there is any interest in the new venture's product or service on the part of consumers or markets that were not in the original plan, one tries to find somebody in that new and unexpected area who might be willing to test the new product or service and find out what, if any, application it might have. One provides free samples to people in the "improbable" market to see what they can do with it, whether they can use the stuff at all, or what it would have to be like for them to become customers for it. One advertises in the trade papers of the industry whence indications of interest came, and so on.

The DuPont Company never thought of automobile tires as a major application for the new Nylon fiber it had developed. But when one of the Akron tire manufacturers showed interest in trying out Nylon,

DuPont set up a plant. A few years later, tires had become Nylon's biggest and most profitable market.

It does not require a great deal of money to find out whether an unexpected interest from an unexpected market is an indication of genuine potential or a fluke. It requires sensitivity and a little systematic work.

Above all, the people who are running a new venture need to spend time outside: in the marketplace, with customers and with their own salesmen, looking and listening. The new venture needs to build in systematic practices to remind itself that a "product" or a "service" is defined by the customer, not by the producer. It needs to work continuously on challenging itself in respect to the utility and value that its products or services contribute to customers.

The greatest danger for the new venture is to "know better" than the customer what the product or service is or should be, how it should be bought, and what it should be used for. Above all, the new venture needs willingness to see the unexpected success as an opportunity rather than as an affront to its expertise. And it needs to accept that elementary axiom of marketing: Businesses are not paid to reform customers. They are paid to satisfy customers.

II

FINANCIAL FORESIGHT

Lack of market focus is typically a disease of the "neo-natal," the infant new venture. It is the most serious affliction of the new venture in its early stages—and one that can permanently stunt even those that survive.

The lack of adequate financial focus and of the right financial policies is, by contrast, the greatest threat to the new venture in the next stage of its growth. It is, above all, a threat to the rapidly growing new venture. The more successful a new venture is, the more dangerous the lack of financial foresight.

Suppose that a new venture has successfully launched its product or service and is growing fast. It reports "rapidly increasing profits" and issues rosy forecasts. The stock market then "discovers" the new venture, especially if it is high-tech or in a field otherwise currently fashionable. Predictions abound that the new venture's sales will reach a billion dollars within five years. Eighteen months later, the new venture collapses. It may not go out of existence or go bankrupt. But it is suddenly awash in red ink, lays off 180 of its 275 employees, fires the president, or is sold at a bargain price to a big company. The causes are always the same: lack of cash; inability to raise the capital needed for expansion; and loss of control, with expenses, inventories, and receivables in disarray. These three financial afflictions often hit together at the same time. Yet any one of them by itself endangers the health, if not the life, of the new venture.

Once this financial crisis has erupted, it can be cured only with great difficulty and considerable suffering. But it is eminently preventable.

Entrepreneurs starting new ventures are rarely unmindful of money; on the contrary, they tend to be greedy. They therefore focus on profits. But this is the wrong focus for a new venture, or rather, it comes last rather than first. Cash flow, capital, and controls come much earlier. Without them, the profit figures are fiction—good for twelve to eighteen months, perhaps, after which they evaporate.

Growth has to be fed. In financial terms this means that growth in a new venture demands adding financial resources rather than taking them out. Growth needs more cash and more capital. If the growing new venture shows a "profit" it is a fiction: a bookkeeping entry put in only to balance the accounts. And since taxes are payable on this fiction in most countries, it creates a liability and a cash drain rather than "surplus." The healthier a new venture and the faster it grows, the more financial feeding it requires. The new ventures that are the darlings of the newspapers and the stock market letters, the new ventures that show rapid profit growth and "record profits," are those most likely to run into desperate trouble a couple of years later.

The new venture needs cash flow analysis, cash flow forecasts, and cash management. The fact that America's new ventures of the last few years (with the significant exception of high-tech companies) have been doing so much better than new ventures used to do is largely because the new entrepreneurs in the United States have learned that entrepreneurship demands financial management.

Cash management is fairly easy if there are reliable cash flow forecasts, with "reliable" meaning "worst case" assumptions rather than hopes. There is an old banker's rule of thumb, according to which in forecasting cash income and cash outlays one assumes that bills will have to be paid sixty days earlier than expected and receivables will come in sixty days later. If the forecast is overly conservative, the worst that can happen—it rarely does in a growing new venture—is a temporary cash surplus.

A growing new venture should know twelve months ahead of time how much cash it will need, when, and for what purposes. With a year's lead time, it is almost always possible to finance cash needs. But even if a new venture is doing well, raising cash in a hurry and in a "crisis" is never easy and always prohibitively expensive. Above all, it always sidetracks the key people in the company at the most critical time. For several months they then spend their time and energy running from one financial institution to another and cranking out one set of questionable financial projections after another. In the end, they usually have to mortgage the long-range future of the business to get through a ninety-day cash bind. When they finally are able again to devote time and thought to the business, they have irrevocably missed the major opportunities. For the new venture, almost by definition, is under cash pressure when the opportunities are greatest.

The successful new venture will also outgrow its capital structure. A rule of thumb with a good deal of empirical evidence to support it says that a new venture outgrows its capital base with every increase in sales (or billings) of the order of 40 to 50 percent. After such growth, a new venture also needs a new and different capital structure, as a rule. As the venture grows, private sources of funds, whether from the owners and their families or from outsiders, become inadequate. The company has to find access to much larger pools of money by going "public," by finding a partner or partners among established companies, or by raising money from insurance companies and pension funds. A new venture that had been financed by equity money now needs to shift to long-term debt, or vice versa. As the venture grows, the existing capital structure always becomes the wrong structure and an obstacle.

In some new ventures, capital planning is comparatively easy. When the business consists of uniform and entirely local units—restaurants in a chain, freestanding surgical centers or individual hospitals in different cities, homebuilders with separate operations in a number of different metropolitan areas, specialty stores and the like—each unit can be financed as a separate business. One solution is franchising (which is, in essence, a way to finance rapid expansion). Another is setting up each local unit as a company, with separate and often local investors as "limited" partners. The capital needed for growth and expansion can thus be raised step by step, and the success of the preceding unit furnishes documentation and the incentive for the investors in the succeeding ones. But it only works when: (a) each unit breaks even fairly soon, at most perhaps within two or three years; (b) when the operation can be made routine, so that people of limited managerial competence —the typical franchise holder, or the business manager of a local free-standing surgical center—can do a decent job without much supervision; and (c) when the individual unit itself reaches fairly swiftly the optimum size beyond which it does not require further capital but produces cash surplus to help finance the startup of additional units.

For new ventures other than those capable of being financed as separate units, capital planning is a survival necessity. If a growing new venture plans realistically—and that again means assuming the maximum rather than the minimum need—for its capital requirement and its capital structure three years ahead, it should normally have little difficulty in obtaining the kind of money it needs, when it needs it, and in the form in which it needs it. If it waits until it outgrows its capital base and its capital structure, it is putting its survival—and most assuredly its independence—on the block. At the very least, the founders will find that they have taken all the entrepreneurial risk and worked hard only to make other people the rich owners. From being owners, they will have become employees, with the new investors taking control.

Finally, the new venture needs to plan the financial system it requires to manage growth. Again and again, a growing new venture starts off with an excellent product, excellent standing in its market, and excellent growth prospects. Then suddenly everything goes out of control: receivables, inventory, manufacturing costs, administrative costs, service, distribution, everything. Once one area gets out of control, all of them do. The enterprise has outgrown its control structure. By the time control has been reestablished, markets have been lost, customers have become disgruntled if not hostile, distributors have lost their confidence in the company. Worst of all, employees have lost trust in management, and with good reason.

Fast growth always makes obsolete the existing controls. Again, a growth of 40 to 50 percent in volume seems to be the critical figure.

Once control has been lost, it is hard to recapture. Yet the loss of control can be prevented quite easily. What is needed is first to think through the critical areas in a given enterprise. In one, it may be product quality; in another, service; in a third, receivables and inventory; in a fourth, manufacturing costs. Rarely are there more than four or five critical areas in any given enterprise. (Managerial and administrative overhead should, however, always be included. A disproportionate and fast increase in the percentage of revenues absorbed by managerial and administrative overhead, which means that the enterprise hires managerial and administrative people faster than it actually grows, is usually the first sign that a business is getting out of control, that its management structure and practices are no longer adequate to the task.)

To live up to its growth expectations, a new venture must establish today the controls in these critical areas it will need three years hence. Elaborate controls are not necessary nor does it matter that the figures are only approximate. What matters is that the management of the new venture is aware of these critical areas, is being reminded of them, and can thus act fast if the need arises. Disarray normally does not appear if there is adequate attention to the key areas. Then the new venture will have the controls it needs when it needs them.

Financial foresight does not require a great deal of time. It does require a good deal of thought, however. The technical tools to do the job are easily available; they are spelled out in most texts on managerial accounting. But the work will have to be done by the enterprise itself.

III

BUILDING A TOP MANAGEMENT TEAM

The new venture has successfully established itself in the right market and has then successfully found the financial structure and the financial system it needs. Nonetheless, a few years later it is still prone to run into a serious crisis. Just when it appears to be on the threshold of becoming an "adult"—a successful, established, going concern—it gets into trouble nobody seems to understand. The products are first-rate, the prospects are excellent, and yet the business simply cannot grow. Neither profitability nor quality, nor any of the other major areas performs.

The reason is always the same: a lack of top management. The business has outgrown being managed by one person, or even two people, and it now needs a management team at the top. If it does not have one already in place at the time, it is very late—in fact, usually too late. The best one can then hope is that the business will survive. But it is likely to be permanently crippled or to suffer scars that will bleed for many years to come. Morale has been shattered and employees throughout the company are disillusioned and cynical. And the people who founded the business and built it almost always end up on the outside, embittered and disenchanted.

The remedy is simple: To build a top management team *before* the venture reaches the point where it must have one. Teams cannot be formed overnight. They require long periods before they can function. Teams are based on mutual trust and mutual understanding, and this takes years to build up. In my experience, three years is about the minimum.

But the small and growing new venture cannot afford a top management team; it cannot sustain half a dozen people with big titles and corresponding salaries. In fact, in the small and growing business, a very small number of people do everything as it comes along. How, then, can one square this circle?

Again, the remedy is relatively simple. But it does require the will on the part of the founders to build a team rather than to keep on running everything themselves. If one or two people at the top believe that they, and they alone, must do everything, then a management crisis a few months, or at the latest, a few years down the road becomes inevitable.

Whenever the objective economic indicators of a new venture— market surveys, for instance, or demographic analysis—indicate that the business may double within three or five years, then it is the duty of the founder or founders to build the management team the new venture will very soon require. This is preventive medicine, so to speak.

First of all the founders, together with other key people in the firm, will have to think through the key activities of their business. What are the specific areas upon which the survival and success of this particular business depend? Most of the areas will be on everyone's list. But if there are divergencies and dissents—and there should be on a question as important as this—they should be taken seriously. Every activity which any member of the group thinks belongs there should go down on the list.

The key activities are not to be found in books. They emerge from analysis of the specific enterprise. Two enterprises that to an outsider appear to be in an identical line of business may well end up defining their key activities quite differently. One, for instance, may put production in the center; the other, customer service. Only two key activities are always present in any organization: there is always the management of people and there is always the management of money. The rest has to be determined by the people within looking at the enterprise and at their own jobs, values, and goals.

The next step is, then, for each member of the group, beginning with the founder, to ask: "What are the activities that *I* am doing well? And what are the activities that each of my key associates in this business is actually doing well?" Again, there is going to be agreement on most of the people and on most of their strengths. But, again, any disagreement should be taken seriously.

Next, one asks: "Which of the key activities should each of us, therefore, take on as his or her first and major responsibility because they fit the individual's strengths? Which individual fits which key activity?"

Then the work on building a team can begin. The founder starts to discipline himself (or herself) not to handle people and their problems, if this is not the key activity that fits him best. Perhaps this individual's key strength is new products and new technology. Perhaps this individual's key activity is operations, manufacturing, physical distribution, service. Or perhaps it is money and finance and someone else had better handle people. But all key activities need to be covered by someone who has proven ability in performance.

There is no rule that says "A chief executive has to be in charge of this or that." Of course a chief executive is the court of last resort and has ultimate accountability. And the chief executive also has to make sure of getting the information necessary to discharge this ultimate accountability. The chief executive's own *work*, however, depends on what the enterprise requires and on who the individual is. As long as the CEO's work program consists of key activities, he or she does a CEO's job. But the CEO also is responsible for making sure that all the other key activities are adequately covered.

Finally, goals and objectives for each area need to be set. Everyone who takes on the primary responsibility for a key activity, whether product development or people, or money, must be asked: "What can this enterprise expect of *you?* What should we hold *you* accountable for? What are *you* trying to accomplish and by what time?" But this is elementary management, of course.

It is prudent to establish the top management team informally at first. There is no need to give people titles in a new and growing venture, nor to make announcements, nor even to pay extra. All this can wait a year or so, until it is clear that the new setup works, and how. In the meantime, all the members of the team have much to learn: their job; how they work together; and what they have to do to enable the CEO and their colleagues to do their jobs. Two or three years later, when the growing venture needs a top management, it has one.

However, should it fail to provide for a top management before it actually needs one, it will lose the capacity to manage itself long before it actually needs a top management team. The founder will have become so overloaded that important tasks will not get done. At this point the company can go one of two ways. The first possibility is that the founder concentrates on the one or two areas that fit his or her abilities and interests. These are key areas indeed, but they are not the only crucial ones, and no one is then left to look after the others. Two years later, important areas have been slighted and the business is in dire straits. The other, worse, possibility is that the founder is conscientious. He knows that people and money are key activities and need to be taken care of. His own abilities and interests, which actually built the business, are in the design and development of new products. But being conscientious, the founder forces himself to take care of people and finance. Since he is not very gifted in either area, he does poorly in both. It also takes him forever to reach decisions or to do any work in these areas, so that he is forced, by lack of time, to neglect what he is really good at and what the company depends on him for, the development of new technology and new products. Three years later the company will have become an empty shell without the products it needs, but also without the management of people and the management of money it needs.

In the first example, it may be possible to save the company. After all, it has the products. But the founder will inevitably be removed by whoever comes in to salvage the company. In the second case, the company usually cannot be saved at all and has to be sold or liquidated.

Long before it has reached the point where it needs the balance of a top management team, the new venture has to create one. Long before the time has come at which management by one person no longer works and becomes mismanagement, that one person also has to start learning how to work with colleagues, has to learn to trust people, yet also how to hold them accountable. The founder has to learn to become the leader of a team rather than a "star" with "helpers."

IV

"WHERE CAN I CONTRIBUTE?"

Building a top management team may be the single most important step toward entrepreneurial management in the new venture. It is only the first step, however, for the founders themselves, who then have to think through what their own future is to be.

As a new venture develops and grows, the roles and relationships of the original entrepreneurs inexorably change. If the founders refuse to accept this, they will stunt the business and may even destroy it.

Every founder-entrepreneur nods to this and says, "Amen." Everyone has horror stories of other founder-entrepreneurs who did not change as the venture changed, and who then destroyed both the business and themselves. But even among the founders who can accept that they themselves need to do something, few know how to tackle changing their own roles and relationships. They tend to begin by asking: "What do I like to do?" Or at best, "Where do I fit in?" The right question to start with is: "What will the venture need *objectively* by way of management from here on out?" And in a growing new venture, the founder has to ask this question whenever the business (or the public-service institution) grows significantly or changes direction or character, that is, changes its products, services, markets, or the kind of people it needs.

The next question the founder must ask is: "What am I good at? What, of all these needs of the venture, could I supply, and supply with distinction?" Only after having thought through these two questions should a founder then ask: "What do I really want to do, and believe in doing? What am I willing to spend years on, if not the rest of my life? Is this something the venture really needs? Is it a major, essential, indispensable contribution?"

One example is that of the successful American post–World War II metropolitan university, Pace, in New York City. Dr. Edward Mortola built up the institution from nothing in 1947 into New York City's third-largest and fastest-growing university, with 25,000 students and well-regarded graduate schools. In the university's early years he was a radical innovator. But when Pace was still very small (around 1950), Mortola built a strong top management team. All members were given a major, clearly defined responsibility, for which they were expected to take full accountability and give leadership. A few years later, Mortola then decided what his own role was to be and converted himself into a traditional university president, while at the same time building a strong independent board of trustees to advise and support him.

But the questions of what a venture needs, what the strengths of the founder-entrepreneur are, and what he or she wants to do, might be answered quite differently.

Edwin Land, for instance, the man who invented Polaroid glass and the Polaroid camera, ran the company during the first twelve or fifteen years of its life, until the early 1950s. Then it began to grow fast. Land thereupon designed a top management team and put it in place. As for himself, he decided that he was not the right man for the top management job in the company: what he and he alone could contribute was scientific innovation. Accordingly, Land built himself a laboratory and established himself as the company's consulting director for basic research. The company itself, in its day-to-day operations, he left to others to run.

Ray Kroc, the man who conceived and built McDonald's, reached a similar conclusion. He remained president until he died well past age eighty. But he put a top management team in place to run the company and appointed himself the company's "marketing conscience." Until shortly before his death, he visited two or three McDonald's restaurants each week, checking their quality carefully, the level of cleanliness and friendliness. Above all, he looked at the customers, talked to them and listened to them. This enabled the company to make the necessary changes to retain its leadership in the fast-food industry.

Similarly, in a much smaller new venture, a building supply company in the Pacific Northwest of the United States, the young man who built the company decided that his role was not to run the company but to develop its critical resource, the managers who are responsible for its two hundred branches in small towns and suburbs. These managers are in effect running their own local business. They are supported by strong services in headquarters: central buying, quality control, control of credit and receivables, and so on. But the selling is done by each manager, locally and with very little help—maybe one salesman and a couple of truck drivers.

The business depends on the motivation, drive, ability, and enthusiasm of these isolated, fairly unsophisticated individuals. None of them has a college degree and few have even finished high school. So the founder of this company makes it his business to spend twelve to fifteen days each month in the field visiting branch managers, spending half a day with them, discussing their business, their plans, their aspirations. This may well be the only distinction the company has—otherwise, every other building materials wholesaler does the same things. But this performance of the one key activity by the chief executive has enabled the company to grow three to four times as fast as any competitor, even in recession times.

Yet another quite different answer to the same question was given by the three scientists who, together, founded what has become one of the largest and most successful companies in the semiconductor industry. When they asked themselves, "What are the needs of the business?" the answer was that there were three: "One for basic business strategy, one for scientific research and development, and one for the development of people—especially scientific and technical people." They decided which of the three was most suited for each of these assignments, and then divided them according to their strengths. The person who took the human relations and human development job had actually been a prolific scientific innovator and had high standing in scientific circles. But he decided, and his colleagues concurred, that he was superbly-fitted for the managerial, the people task, so he took it. "It was not," he once said in a speech, "what I really wanted to do, but it was where I could make the greatest contribution."

These questions may not always lead to such happy endings. They may even lead to the decision to leave the company.

In one of the most successful new financial services ventures in the United States, this is what the founder concluded. He did establish a top management team. He asked what the company needed. He looked at himself and his strengths; and he found no match between the needs of the company and his own abilities, let alone between the needs of the company and the things he wanted to do. "I trained my own successor for about eighteen months, then turned the company over to him and resigned," he said. Since then he has started three new businesses, not one of them in finance, has developed them successfully to medium size, and then quit again. He wants to develop new businesses but does not enjoy running them. He accepts that both the businesses and he are better off divorced from one another.

Other entrepreneurs in this same situation might reach different conclusions. The founder of a well-known medical clinic, a leader in its particular field, faced a similar dilemma. The needs of the institution were for an administrator and money-raiser. His own inclinations were to be a researcher and a clinician. But he realized that he was good at raising money and capable of learning to be the chief executive officer of a fairly large health-care organization. "And so," he says, "I felt it my duty to the venture I had created, and to my associates in it, to suppress my own desires and to take on the job of chief administrator and money-raiser. But I would never have done so had I not known that I had the abilities to do the job, and if my advisors and my board had not all assured me that I had these abilities."

The question, "Where do I belong?" needs to be faced up to and thought through by the founder-entrepreneur as soon as the venture shows the first signs of success. But the question can be faced up to much earlier. Indeed, it might be best thought through before the new venture is even started.

This is what Soichiro Honda, the founder and builder of Honda Motor Company in Japan, did when he decided to open a small business in the darkest days after Japan's defeat in World War II. He did not start his venture until he had found the right man to be his partner and to run administration, finance, distribution, marketing, sales, and personnel. For Honda had decided from the outset that he belonged in engineering and production and would not run anything else. This decision made the Honda Motor Company.

There is an earlier and even more instructive example, that of Henry Ford. When Ford decided in 1903 to go into business for himself, he did exactly what Honda did forty years later: before starting, he found the right man to be his partner and to run the areas where Ford knew he did not belong—administration, finance, distribution, marketing, sales, and personnel. Like Honda, Henry Ford knew that he belonged in engineering and manufacturing and was going to confine himself to these two areas. The man he found, James Couzens,* contributed as much as Ford to the success of the company. Many of the

---

*Who later became mayor of Detroit and senator from Michigan, and might well have become President of the United States had he not been born in Canada.

best known policies and practices of the Ford Motor Company for which Henry Ford is often given credit—the famous $5-a-day wage of 1913, or the pioneering distribution and service policies, for example —were Couzens's ideas and at first resisted by Ford. So effective did Couzens become that Ford grew increasingly jealous of him and forced him out in 1917. The last straw was Couzens's insistence that the Model T was obsolescent and his proposal to use some of the huge profits of the company to start work on a successor.

The Ford Motor Company grew and prospered to the very day of Couzens's resignation. Within a few short months thereafter, as soon as Henry Ford had taken every single top management function into his own hands, forgetting that he had known earlier where he belonged, the Ford Motor Company began its long decline. Henry Ford clung to the Model T for a full ten years, until it had become literally unsalable. And the company's decline was not reversed for thirty years after Couzens's dismissal until, with his grandfather dying, a very young Henry Ford II took over the practically bankrupt business.

THE NEED FOR OUTSIDE ADVICE

These last cases point up an important factor for the entrepreneur in the new and growing venture, the need for independent, objective outside advice.

The growing new venture may not need a formal board of directors. Moreover, the typical board of directors very often does not provide the advice and counsel the founder needs. But the founder does need people with whom he can discuss basic decisions and to whom he listens. Such people are rarely to be found within the enterprise. Somebody has to challenge the founder's appraisal of the needs of the venture, and of his own personal strengths. Someone who is not a part of the problem has to ask questions, to review decisions and, above all, to push constantly to have the long-term survival needs of the new venture satisfied by building in the market focus, supplying financial foresight, and creating a functioning top management team. This is the final requirement of entrepreneurial management in the new venture.

The new venture that builds such entrepreneurial management into its policies and practices will become a flourishing large business.*

*A fine description of this process is to be found in *High-Output Management* (New

In so many new ventures, especially high-tech ventures, the techniques discussed in this chapter are spurned and even despised. The argument is that they constitute "management" and "We are entrepreneurs." But this is not informality; it is irresponsibility. It confuses manners and substance. It is old wisdom that there is no freedom except under the law. Freedom without law is license, which soon degenerates into anarchy, and shortly thereafter into tyranny. It is precisely because the new venture has to maintain and strengthen the entrepreneurial spirit that it needs foresight and discipline. It needs to prepare itself for the demands its own success will make of it. Above all, it needs responsibility—and this, in the last analysis, is what entrepreneurial management supplies to the new venture.

There is much more that could be said about managing the new venture, about financing, staffing, marketing its products, and so on. But these specifics are adequately covered in a number of publications.* What this chapter has tried to do is to identify and discuss the few fairly simple policies that are crucial to the survival and success of any new venture, whether a business or a public-service institution, whether "high-tech," "low-tech," or "no-tech," whether started by one man or woman or by a group, and whether intended to remain a small business or to become "another IBM."

York: Random House, 1983), by Andrew S. Grove, co-founder and president of Intel, one of the largest manufacturers of semiconductors.

*For some of these, see the Suggested Readings at the back of this book.

III

ENTREPRENEURIAL
STRATEGIES

———

Just as entrepreneurship requires entrepreneurial management, that is, practices and policies within the enterprise, so it requires practices and policies outside, in the marketplace. It requires entrepreneurial strategies.

16

"Fustest with the Mostest"

Of late, "strategy in business"* has become the "in" word, with any
number of books written about it.† However, I have not come across
any discussion of entrepreneurial strategies. Yet they are important;
they are distinct; and they are different.

There are four specifically entrepreneurial strategies:

1. Being "Fustest with the Mostest";
2. "Hitting Them Where They Ain't";
3. Finding and occupying a specialized "ecological niche";
4. Changing the economic characteristics of a product, a market, or
an industry.

These four strategies are not mutually exclusive. One and the same
entrepreneur often combines two, sometimes even elements of three,
in one strategy. They are also not always sharply differentiated; the
same strategy might, for instance, be classified as "Hitting Them Where
They Ain't" or as "Finding and occupying a specialized 'ecological
niche.' " Still, each of these four has its prerequisites. Each fits certain
kinds of innovation and does not fit others. Each requires specific behavior on the part of the entrepreneur. Finally, each has its own limitations and carries its own risks.

*The 1952 edition of the *Concise Oxford Dictionary* still defined strategy as: "Gener-
alship; the art of war; management of an army or armies in a campaign." Alfred D.
Chandler, Jr., first applied the term to the conduct of a business in 1962 in his pioneering
Strategy and Structure (Cambridge, Mass.: M.I.T. Press), which studied the evolution of
management in the big corporation. But shortly thereafter, in 1963, when I wrote the first
analysis of business strategy, the publisher and I found that the word could not be used
in the title without risk of serious misunderstanding. Booksellers, magazine editors, and
senior business executives all assured us that "strategy" for them meant the conduct of
military or election campaigns. The book discussed most that is now considered "strategy." It uses the word in the text. But the title we chose was *Managing for Results.*
†Of which I have found Michael Porter's *Competitive Strategies* (New York: Free
Press, 1980) the most useful.

459

I

BEING "FUSTEST WITH THE MOSTEST"

Being "Fustest with the Mostest" was how a Confederate cavalry general in America's Civil War explained consistently winning his battles. In this strategy the entrepreneur aims at leadership, if not at dominance of a new market or a new industry. Being "Fustest with the Mostest" does not necessarily aim at creating a big business right away, though often this is indeed the aim. But it aims from the start at a permanent leadership position.

Being "Fustest with the Mostest" is the approach that many people consider the entrepreneurial strategy *par excellence.* Indeed, if one were to go by the popular books on entrepreneurs,* one would conclude that being "Fustest with the Mostest" is the only entrepreneurial strategy—and a good many entrepreneurs, especially the high-tech ones, seem to be of the same opinion.

They are wrong, however. To be sure, a good many entrepreneurs have indeed chosen this strategy. Yet being "Fustest with the Mostest" is not even the dominant entrepreneurial strategy, let alone the one with the lowest risk or the highest success ratio. On the contrary, of all entrepreneurial strategies it is the greatest gamble. And it is unforgiving, making no allowances for mistakes and permitting no second chance.

But if successful, being "Fustest with the Mostest" is highly rewarding.

Here are some examples to show what this strategy consists of and what it requires.

Hoffmann-LaRoche of Basel, Switzerland, has for many years been the world's largest and in all probability its most profitable pharmaceutical company. But its origins were quite humble: until the mid-1920s, Hoffmann-LaRoche was a small and struggling manufacturing chemist, making a few textile dyes. It was totally overshadowed by the huge German dye-stuff makers and two or three much bigger chemical firms in its own country. Then it gambled on the newly discovered vitamins at a time when the scientific world still could not quite accept

*E.g., George Gilder's *The Spirit of Enterprise* (New York: Simon & Schuster, 1984), perhaps the most readable recent example of the genre.

that such substances existed. It acquired the vitamin patents—nobody else wanted them. It hired the discoverers away from Zürich University at several times the salaries they could hope to get as professors, salaries even industry had never paid before. And it invested all the money it had and all it could borrow in manufacturing and marketing these new substances.

Sixty years later, long after all vitamin patents have expired, Hoffmann-LaRoche has nearly half the world's vitamin market, now amounting to billions of dollars a year. The company followed the same strategy twice more: in the 1930s, when it went into the new sulfa drugs even though most scientists of the time "knew" that systemic drugs could not be effective against infections; and twenty years later, in the mid-fifties, when it went into the muscle-relaxing tranquilizers, Librium and Valium—at that time considered equally heretical and incompatible with what "every scientist knew."

DuPont followed the same strategy. When it came up with Nylon, the first truly synthetic fiber, after fifteen years of hard, frustrating research, DuPont at once mounted massive efforts, built huge plants, went into mass advertising—the company had never before had consumer products to advertise—and created the industry we now call plastics.

These are "big-company" stories, it will be said. But Hoffmann-LaRoche was not a big company when it started. And here are some more recent examples of companies that started from nothing with a strategy of getting there "Fustest with the Mostest."

The word processor is not much of a "scientific" invention. It hooks up three existing instruments: a typewriter, a display screen, and a fairly elementary computer. But this combination of existing elements has resulted in a genuine innovation that is radically changing office work. Dr. An Wang was a lone entrepreneur when he conceived of the combination some time in the mid-fifties. He had no track record as an entrepreneur and a minimum of financial backing. Yet he clearly aimed from the beginning at creating a new industry and at changing office work—and Wang Laboratories has, of course, become a very big company.

Similarly, the two young engineers who started the Apple computer in the proverbial garage, without financial backers or previous business experience, aimed from the beginning at creating an industry and dominating it.

Not every "Fustest with the Mostest" strategy needs to aim at creating a big business, though it must always aim at creating a business that dominates its market. The 3M Company in St. Paul, Minnesota, does not —as a matter of deliberate policy, it seems—attempt an innovation that might result in a big business by itself. Nor does Johnson & Johnson, the health-care and hygiene producer. Both companies are among the most fertile and most successful innovators. Both look for innovations that will lead to medium-sized rather than to giant enterprises, which are, however, dominant in their markets.

Being "Fustest with the Mostest" is not confined to businesses. It is also available to public-service institutions. When Wilhelm von Humboldt founded the University of Berlin in 1809—an event mentioned before in this book—he clearly aimed at being "Fustest with the Mostest." Prussia had just been defeated by Napoleon and had barely escaped total dismemberment. It was bankrupt, politically, militarily, and, above all, financially. It looked very much the way Germany was to look after Hitler's defeat in 1945. Yet Humboldt went out to build the largest university the Western world had ever seen or heard of— three to four times as large as anything then in existence. He went out to hire the leading scholars in every single discipline, beginning with the foremost philosopher of the time, Georg W. F. Hegel. And he paid his professors up to ten times as much as professors had ever been paid before, at a period when first-class scholars were going begging since the Napoleonic wars had forced many old and famous universities to disband.

A hundred years later, in the early years of this century, two surgeons in Rochester, an obscure Minnesota town far from population centers or medical schools, decided to establish a medical center based on totally new—and totally heretical—concepts of medical practice, and especially on building teams in which outstanding specialists would work together under a coordinating team leader. Frederick William Taylor, the so-called father of scientific management, had never met the Mayo Brothers. But in his well-known testimony before the Congress in 1911, he called the Mayo Clinic the "only complete and successful scientific management" he knew. These unknown provincial surgeons aimed from the beginning at dominance of the field, at attracting outstanding practitioners in every branch of medicine and the most gifted of the younger men, and at attracting also patients able and willing to pay what were then outrageous fees.

And twenty-five years later, the strategy of being "Fustest with the Mostest" was used by the March of Dimes to organize research into infantile paralysis (polio). Instead of aiming at gathering new knowledge step by step, as all earlier medical research had done, the March of Dimes aimed from the beginning at total victory over a completely mysterious disease. No one before had ever organized a "research lab without walls," in which a large number of scientists in a multitude of research institutions were commissioned to work on specific stages of a planned and managed research program. The March of Dimes established the pattern on which the United States, a little later, organized the first great research projects of World War II: the atom bomb, the radar lab, the proximity fuse, and then another fifteen years later, "Putting a Man on the Moon"—all innovative efforts using the "Fustest with the Mostest" strategy.

These examples show, first, that being "Fustest with the Mostest" requires an ambitious aim; otherwise it is bound to fail. It always aims at creating a new industry or a new market. At the least, as in the case of the Mayo Clinic or the March of Dimes, being "Fustest with the Mostest" aims at creating a quite different and highly unconventional process. The DuPonts surely did not say to themselves in the mid-twenties when they brought in Carothers: "We will establish the plastics industry" (indeed, the term was rarely used until the 1950s). But enough of the internal DuPont documents of the time have been published to show that the top management people did aim at creating a new industry. They were far from convinced that Carothers and his research would succeed. But they knew that they would have founded something big and brand new in the event of success, and something that would go far beyond a single product or even beyond a single major product line. Dr. Wang did not coin the term "the Office of the Future," as far as I know. But in his first advertisements, he announced a new office environment and new concepts of office work. Both the DuPonts and Wang from the beginning clearly aimed at dominating the industry they hoped they would succeed in creating.

The best example of what is implied in the strategy of being "Fustest with the Mostest" is not a business case but Humboldt's University of Berlin. Humboldt was actually not a bit interested in a university, as such. It was for him the means to create a new and different *political* order, which would be neither the absolute monarchy of the eighteenth century nor the democracy of the French Revolution in which the bourgeoisie ruled. Rather, it would be a balanced system, in which a totally apolitical professional civil service and an equally apolitical professional officer corps, recruited and promoted strictly by merit, would be autonomous in their very narrow spheres. These people—today we would call them technocrats—would have limited tasks and would be under the strict supervision of an independent professional judiciary. But within these limits they would be the masters. There would then be two spheres of individual freedom for the bourgeoisie, a moral and cultural one, and an economic one.

Humboldt had presented this concept earlier in book form.* After the total defeat of the Prussian monarchy by Napoleon in 1806, the collapse paralyzed all the forces that would otherwise have stopped Humboldt—the king, the aristocracy, the military. He ran with the opportunity and founded the University of Berlin as the main carrier of his political concepts, with brilliant success. The University of Berlin did indeed create the peculiar political structure the Germans in the nineteenth century called the *"Rechtsstaat"* (the Lawful State), in which an autonomous and self-governing elite of civil servants and general staff officers was in full control of the political and military sphere; an autonomous and self-governing elite of educated people *("die Gebildeten Staende")* organized around self-governing universities provided a "liberal" cultural sphere; and in which there was an autonomous and largely unrestricted economy. This structure first gave Prussia the moral and cultural, and soon thereafter the political and economic ascendancy in Germany. Both leadership in Europe and admiration outside of it followed in short order, especially on the part of the British and the Americans for whom the Germans, until 1890 or so, were the cultural and intellectual models. All this was exactly what Humboldt in the hour of darkest defeat and total despair had envisaged and aimed at. Indeed, he spelled out his aims clearly in the prospectus and the charter of his university.

Perhaps because "Fustest with the Mostest" must aim at creating something truly new, something truly different, nonexperts and outsiders seem to do as well as the experts, in fact, often better. Hoffmann-LaRoche, for instance, did not owe its strategy to chemists, but to a musician who had married the granddaughter of the company's foun-

---

*Under the title *The Limits on the Effectiveness of Government (Die Grenzen der Wirksamkeit des Staates)*, one of the very few original books on political philosophy ever written by a German.

der and needed more money to support his orchestra than the company then provided through its meager dividends. To this day the company has never been managed by chemists, but always by financial men who have made their career in a major Swiss bank. Wilhelm von Humboldt himself was a diplomat with no earlier ties to academia or experience in it. The DuPont top management people were businessmen rather than chemists and researchers. And while the Brothers Mayo were well-trained surgeons, they were totally outside the medical establishment of the time and isolated from it.

Of course, there are also the true "insiders," Dr. Wang or the people at 3M or the young computer engineers who designed the Apple computer. But when it comes to being "Fustest with the Mostest," the outsider may have an advantage. He does not know what everybody within the field knows, and therefore does not know what cannot be done.

II

The strategy of being "Fustest with the Mostest" has to hit right on target or it misses altogether. Or, to vary the metaphor, being "Fustest with the Mostest" is very much like a moon shot: a deviation of a fraction of a minute of the arc and the missile disappears into outer space. And once launched, the "Fustest with the Mostest" strategy is difficult to adjust or to correct.

To use this strategy, in other words, requires thought and careful analysis. The entrepreneur of so much of the popular literature or of Hollywood movies, the person who suddenly has a "brilliant idea" and rushes off to put it into effect, is not going to succeed with it. In fact, for this strategy to succeed at all, the innovation must be based on a careful and deliberate attempt to exploit one of the major opportunities for innovation that were discussed in Chapters 3 to 9.

There is, for instance, no better example of exploiting a *change in perception* than Humboldt's University of Berlin. The French Revolution with its Terror, followed by Napoleon's ruthless wars of conquest, had left the educated bourgeoisie disillusioned with politics; and yet they also quite clearly would have rejected any attempt to move the clock back and return to the absolute monarchy of the eighteenth century, let alone to feudalism. They needed a "liberal" but apolitical sphere, coupled with an apolitical government based on the same principles of law and education in which they themselves believed. And all of them at the time were followers of Adam Smith, whose *Wealth of Nations* was probably the most widely read and most highly respected political book of the period. It was this which Humboldt's political structure exploited and which his plan for the University of Berlin translated into institutional reality.

Wang's word processor brilliantly exploited a process need. By the 1970s the fear of the computer that had been rampant in offices only a little while earlier was beginning to be replaced by the question, "And what will the computer do for *me?*" By that time, office workers had become familiar with the computer in such activities as making payroll or controlling inventories; they also by that time had acquired office copiers so that the paperload in every office was going up very sharply. Wang's word processor then addressed itself to the one remaining nonautomated chore, a chore every office worker hated: rewriting letters, speeches, reports, manuscripts to embody minor changes, and having to do so again and again.

Hoffmann-LaRoche, in picking the vitamins in the early twenties, exploited new knowledge. The musician who laid down its strategy understood the "structure of scientific revolutions" a full thirty years before a philosopher, Thomas Kuhn, wrote the celebrated book by that title. He understood that a new basic theorem in science, even though buttressed by enough evidence to make it impossible to reject, will still not be accepted by a majority of scientists should it conflict with basic theorems they have grown up with and hold as articles of faith. They pay no attention to it for a long time, until the old "paradigm," the old basic theory, becomes totally untenable. And during that time those who accept the new theorem and run with it have the field all to themselves.

Only with such a base in careful analysis can the strategy of being "Fustest with the Mostest" possibly succeed.

Even then, it requires extreme concentration of effort. There has to be one clear-cut goal and all efforts have to be focused on it. And when this effort begins to produce results, the innovator has to be ready to mobilize resources massively. As soon as DuPont had a usable synthetic fiber—long before the market had begun to respond to it—the company built large factories and bombarded both textile manufacturers and the general public with advertisements, trial presentations, and samples.

Then, after the innovation has become a successful business, the work really begins. Then the strategy of "Fustest with the Mostest" demands substantial and continuing efforts to retain a leadership position; otherwise, all one has done is create a market for a competitor. The innovator has to run even harder now that he has leadership than he ran before and to continue his innovative efforts on a very large scale. The research budget must be higher *after* the innovation has successfully been accomplished than it was before. New uses have to be found; new customers must be identified, and persuaded to try the new materials. Above all, the entrepreneur who has succeeded in being "Fustest with the Mostest" has to make his product or his process obsolete before a competitor can do it. Work on the successor to the successful product or process has to start immediately, with the same concentration of effort and the same investment of resources that led to the initial success.

Finally, the entrepreneur who has attained leadership by being "Fustest with the Mostest" has to be the one who systematically cuts the price of his own product or process. To keep prices high simply holds an umbrella over potential competitors and encourages them (on this, see the next chapter, "Hit Them Where They Ain't").

This was established by the longest-lived private monopoly in economic history, the Dynamite Cartel, founded by Alfred Nobel after his invention of dynamite. The Dynamite Cartel maintained a worldwide monopoly until World War I and even beyond, long after the Nobel patents had expired. It did this by cutting price every time demand rose by 10 to 20 percent. By that time, the companies in the cartel had fully depreciated the investment they had had to make to get the additional production. This made it unattractive for any potential competitor to build new dynamite factories, while the cartel itself maintained its profitability. It is no accident that DuPont has consistently followed this policy in the United States, for the DuPont Company was the American member of the Dynamite Cartel. But Wang has done the same with respect to the word processor, Apple with respect to its computers, and 3M with respect to all its products.

III

These are all success stories. They do *not* show how risky the strategy of being "Fustest with the Mostest" actually is. The failures disappeared. Yet we know that for everyone who succeeds with this strategy, many more fail. There is only one chance with the "Fustest with the Mostest" strategy. If it does not work right away, it is a total failure.

Everyone knows the old Swiss story of Wilhelm Tell the archer, whom the tyrant promised to pardon if he succeeded in shooting an apple off his son's head on the first try. If he failed, he would either kill the child or be killed himself. This is exactly the situation of the entrepreneur in the "Fustest with the Mostest" strategy. There can be no "almost-success" or "near-miss." There is only success or failure.

Even the successes may be perceived only by hindsight. At least we know that in two of the examples failure was very close; a combination of luck and chance saved them.

Nylon only succeeded because of a fluke. There was no market for a synthetic fiber in the mid-thirties. It was far too expensive to compete with cotton and rayon, the cheap fibers of the time, and was actually even more expensive than silk, the luxury fiber which the Japanese in the severe depression of the late thirties had to sell for whatever price they could get. What saved Nylon was the outbreak of World War II, which stopped Japanese silk exports. By the time the Japanese could start up their silk industry again, around 1950 or so, Nylon was firmly entrenched, with its cost and price down to a fraction of what both had been in the late thirties. The story of 3M's best known product, Scotch Tape, was told earlier. Again, but for pure accident, Scotch Tape would have been a failure.

The strategy of being "Fustest with the Mostest" is indeed so risky that an entire major strategy—the one that will be discussed in the next chapter under the heading Creative Imitation—is based on the assumption that being "Fustest with the Mostest" will fail far more often than it can possibly succeed. It will fail because the will is lacking. It will fail because efforts are inadequate. It will fail because, despite successful innovation, not enough resources are deployed, are available, or are being put to work to exploit success, and so on. While the strategy is indeed highly rewarding when successful, it is much too risky and much too difficult to be used for anything but major innovations, for creating a new political order as Humboldt successfully did, or a whole new field of therapy as Hoffmann-LaRoche did with the vitamins, or a new approach to medical diagnosis and practice as the Mayo Brothers set out to do. In effect, it fits a fairly small minority of innovations. It requires profound analysis and a genuine understanding of the sources of innovation and of their dynamics. It requires an extreme concentration of effort and substantial resources. In most cases alternative strategies are available and preferable—not primarily because they carry less risk, but because for most innovations the opportunity is not great enough to justify the cost, the effort, and the investment of resources required for the "Fustest with the Mostest" strategy.

17

"Hit Them Where They Ain't"

Two completely different entrepreneurial strategies were summed up by another battle-winning Confederate general in America's Civil War, who said: "Hit Them Where They Ain't." They might be called creative imitation and entrepreneurial judo, respectively.

I

CREATIVE IMITATION

Creative imitation* is clearly a contradiction in terms. What is creative must surely be original. And if there is one thing imitation is not, it is "original." Yet the term fits. It describes a strategy that is "imitation" in its substance. What the entrepreneur does is something somebody else has already done. But it is "creative" because the entrepreneur applying the strategy of "creative imitation" understands what the innovation represents better than the people who made it and who innovated.

The foremost practitioner of this strategy and the most brilliant one is IBM. But it is also very largely the strategy that Procter & Gamble has been using to obtain and maintain leadership in the soap, detergent, and toiletries markets. And the Japanese Hattori Company, whose Seiko watches have become the world's leader, also owes its domination of the market to creative imitation.

In the early thirties IBM built a high-speed calculating machine to do calculations for the astronomers at New York's Columbia University. A few years later it built a machine that was already designed as a computer—again, to do astronomical calculations, this time at Harvard. And by the end of World War II, IBM had built a real computer

---

*The term was coined by Theodore Levitt of the Harvard Business School.

470

—the first one, by the way, that had the features of the true computer: a "memory" and the capacity to be "programmed." And yet there are good reasons why the history books pay scant attention to IBM as a computer innovator. For as soon as it had finished its advanced 1945 computer—the first computer to be shown to a lay public in its showroom in midtown New York, where it drew immense crowds—IBM abandoned its own design and switched to the design of its rival, the ENIAC developed at the University of Pennsylvania. The ENIAC was far better suited to business applications such as payroll, only its designers did not see this. IBM structured the ENIAC so that it could be manufactured and serviced and could do mundane "numbers crunching." When IBM's version of the ENIAC came out in 1953, it at once set the standard for commercial, multipurpose, mainframe computers.

This is the strategy of "creative imitation." It waits until somebody else has established the new, but only "approximately." Then it goes to work. And within a short time it comes out with what the new really should be to satisfy the customer, to do the work customers want and pay for. The creative imitation has then set the standard and takes over the market.

IBM practiced creative imitation again with the personal computer. The idea was Apple's. As described earlier (in Chapter 3), everybody at IBM "knew" that a small, freestanding computer was a mistake—uneconomical, far from optimal, and expensive. And yet it succeeded. IBM immediately went to work to design a machine that would become the standard in the personal computer field and dominate or at least lead the entire field. The result was the PC. Within two years it had taken over from Apple leadership in the personal computer field, becoming the fastest-selling brand and the standard in the field.

Procter & Gamble acts very much the same way in the market for detergents, soaps, toiletries, and processed foods.

When semiconductors became available, everyone in the watch industry knew that they could be used to power a watch much more accurately, much more reliably, and much more cheaply than traditional watch movements. The Swiss soon brought out a quartz-powered digital watch. But they had so much investment in traditional watchmaking that they decided on a gradual introduction of quartz-powered digital watches over a long period of time, during which these new timepieces would remain expensive luxuries.

Meanwhile, the Hattori Company in Japan had long been making conventional watches for the Japanese market. It saw the opportunity and went in for creative imitation, developing the quartz-powered digital watch as the standard timepiece. By the time the Swiss had woken up, it was too late. Seiko watches had become the world's best-sellers, with the Swiss almost pushed out of the market.

Like being "Fastest with the Mostest," creative imitation is a strategy aimed at market or industry leadership, if not at market or industry dominance. But it is much less risky. By the time the creative imitator moves, the market has been established and the new venture has been accepted. Indeed, there is usually more demand for it than the original innovator can easily supply. The market segmentations are known or at least knowable. By then, too, market research can find out what customers buy, how they buy, what constitutes value for them, and so on. Most of the uncertainties that abound when the first innovator appears have been dispelled or can at least be analyzed and studied. No one has to explain any more what a personal computer or a digital watch are and what they can do.

Of course, the original innovator may do it right the first time, thus closing the door to creative imitation. There is the risk of an innovator bringing out and doing the right job with vitamins as Hoffmann-LaRoche did, or with Nylon as did DuPont, or as Wang did with the word processor. But the number of entrepreneurs engaging in creative imitation, and their substantial success, indicates that perhaps the risk of the first innovator's preempting the market by getting it right is not an overwhelming one.

Another good example of creative imitation is Tylenol, the "non-aspirin aspirin." This case shows more clearly than any other I know what the strategy consists of, what its requirements are, and how it works.

Acetaminophen (the substance that is sold under the Tylenol brand name in the U.S.) had been used for many years as a painkiller, but until recently it was available in the United States only by prescription. Until recently also, aspirin, the much older pain-killing substance, was considered perfectly safe and had the pain-relief market to itself. Acetaminophen is a less potent drug than aspirin. It is effective as a painkiller but has no anti-inflammatory effect and also no effect on blood coagulation. Because of this it is free from the side effects, especially gastric upsets and stomach bleeding, which aspirin can cause, particularly if used in large doses and over long periods of time for an illness like arthritis.

When acetaminophen became available without prescription, the first brand on the market was presented and promoted as a drug for those who suffered side effects from aspirin. It was eminently successful, indeed, far more successful than its makers had anticipated. But it was this very success that created the opportunity for creative imitation. Johnson & Johnson realized that there was a market for a drug that *replaced* aspirin as the painkiller of choice, with aspirin confined to the fairly small market where anti-inflammatory and blood coagulation effects were needed. From the start Tylenol was promoted as the safe, *universal* painkiller. Within a year or two it had the market.

Creative imitation, these cases show, does not exploit the failure of the pioneers as failure is commonly understood. On the contrary, the pioneer must be successful. The Apple computer was a great success story, and so was the acetaminophen brand that Tylenol ultimately pushed out of market leadership. But the original innovators failed to understand their success. The makers of the Apple were product-focused rather than user-focused, and therefore offered additional hardware where the user needed programs and software. In the Tylenol case, the original innovators failed to realize what their own success meant.

The creative innovator exploits the success of others. Creative imitation is not "innovation" in the sense in which the term is most commonly understood. The creative imitator does not invent a product or service; he perfects and positions it. In the form in which it has been introduced, it lacks something. It may be additional product features. It may be segmentation of product or services so that slightly different versions fit slightly different markets. It might be proper positioning of the product in the market. Or creative imitation supplies something that is still lacking.

The creative imitator looks at products or services from the viewpoint of the customer. IBM's personal computer is practically indistinguishable from the Apple in its technical features, but IBM from the beginning offered the customer programs and software. Apple maintained traditional computer distribution through specialty stores. IBM —in a radical break with its own traditions—developed all kinds of distribution channels, specialty stores, major retailers like Sears, Roebuck, its own retail stores, and so on. It made it easy for the consumer to buy and it made it easy for the consumer to use the product. These, rather than hardware features, were the "innovations" that gave IBM the personal computer market.

All told, creative imitation starts out with markets rather than with products, and with customers rather than with producers. It is both market-focused and market-driven.

These cases show what the strategy of creative imitation requires:

It requires a rapidly growing market. Creative imitators do not succeed by taking away customers from the pioneers who have first introduced a new product or service; they serve markets the pioneers have created but do not adequately service. Creative imitation satisfies a demand that already exists rather than creating one.

The strategy has its own risks, and they are considerable. Creative imitators are easily tempted to splinter their efforts in the attempt to hedge their bets. Another danger is to misread the trend and imitate creatively what then turns out not to be the winning development in the marketplace.

IBM, the world's foremost creative imitator, exemplifies these dangers. It has successfully imitated every major development in the office-automation field. As a result, it has the leading product in every single area. But because they originated in imitation, the products are so diverse and so little compatible with one another that it is all but impossible to build an integrated, automated office out of IBM building blocks. It is thus still doubtful that IBM can maintain leadership in the automated office and provide the integrated system for it. Yet this is where the main market of the future is going to be in all probability. And this risk, *the risk of being too clever,* is inherent in the creative imitation strategy.

Creative imitation is likely to work most effectively in high-tech areas for one simple reason: high-tech innovators are least likely to be market-focused, and most likely to be technology- and product-focused. They therefore tend to misunderstand their own success and to fail to exploit and supply the demand they have created. But as acetaminophen and the Seiko watch show, they are by no means the only ones to do so.

Because creative imitation aims at market dominance, it is best suited to a major product, process, or service: the personal computer, the worldwide watch market, or a market as large as that for pain relief. But the strategy requires less of a market than being "Fustest with the Mostest." It carries less risk. By the time creative imitators go to work, the market has already been identified and the demand has already been created. What it lacks in risk, however, creative imitation makes up for in its requirements for alertness, for flexibility, for willingness to accept the verdict of the market, and above all, for hard work and massive efforts.

II

ENTREPRENEURIAL JUDO

In 1947, Bell Laboratories invented the transistor. It was at once realized that the transistor was going to replace the vacuum tube, especially in consumer electronics such as the radio and the brand-new television set. Everybody knew this; but nobody did anything about it. The leading manufacturers—at that time they were all Americans— began to study the transistor and to make plans for conversion to the transistor "sometime around 1970." Till then, they proclaimed, the transistor "would not be ready." Sony was practically unknown outside of Japan and was not even in consumer electronics at the time. But Akio Morita, Sony's president, read about the transistor in the newspapers. As a result, he went to the United States and bought a license for the new transistor from Bell Labs for a ridiculous sum, all of $25,000. Two years later, Sony brought out the first portable transistor radio, which weighed less than one-fifth of comparable vacuum tube radios on the market, and cost less than one-third. Three years later, Sony had the market for cheap radios in the United States; and five years later, the Japanese had captured the radio market all over the world.

Of course, this is a classic case of the rejection of the unexpected success. The Americans rejected the transistor because it was "not invented here," that is, not invented by the electrical and electronic leaders, RCA and G.E. It is a typical example of pride in doing things the hard way. The Americans were so proud of the wonderful radios of those days, the great Super Heterodyne sets that were such marvels of craftsmanship. Compared to them, they thought silicon chips low grade, if not indeed beneath their dignity.

But Sony's success is not the real story. How do we explain that the Japanese repeated this same strategy again and again, and always with success, always surprising the Americans? They repeated it with television sets and digital watches and hand-held calculators. They repeated it with copiers when they moved in and took away a large share of the market from the original inventor, the Xerox Company. The Japanese, in other words, have been successful again and again in practicing "entrepreneurial judo" against the Americans.

But so did MCI and Sprint when they used the Bell Telephone System's (AT&T) own pricing to take away from the Bell System a very large part of the long-distance business (see Chapter 6). So did ROLM when it used Bell System's policies against it to take away a large part of the private branch exchange (PBX) market. And so did Citibank when it started a consumer bank in Germany, the *"Familienbank"* (Family Bank), which within a few short years came to dominate German consumer finance.

The German banks knew that ordinary consumers had obtained purchasing power and had become desirable clients. They went through the motions of offering consumers banking services. But they really did not want them. Consumers, they felt, were beneath the dignity of a major bank, with its business customers and its rich investment clients. If consumers needed an account at all, they should have it with the postal savings bank. Whatever their advertisements said to the contrary, the banks made it abundantly clear when consumers came into the august offices of the local branch that they had little use for them.

This was the opening Citibank exploited when it founded its German *Familienbank,* which catered to none but individual consumers, designed the services consumers needed, and made it easy for consumers to do business with a bank. Despite the tremendous strength of the German banks and their pervasive presence in a country where there is a branch of a major bank on the corner of every downtown street, Citibank's *Familienbank* attained dominance in the German consumer banking business within five years or so.

All these newcomers—the Japanese, MCI, ROLM, Citibank—practiced "entrepreneurial judo." Of the entrepreneurial strategies, especially the strategies aimed at obtaining leadership and dominance in an industry or a market, entrepreneurial judo is by all odds the least risky and the most likely to succeed.

Every policeman knows that a habitual criminal will always commit his crime the same way—whether it is cracking a safe or entering a building he wants to loot. He leaves behind a "signature," which is as individual and as distinct as a fingerprint. And he will not change that signature even though it leads to his being caught time and again.

But it is not only the criminal who is set in his habits. All of us are. And so are businesses and industries. The habit will be persisted in even though it leads again and again to loss of leadership and loss of market. The American manufacturers persisted in the habits that enabled the Japanese to take over their market again and again.

If the criminal is caught, he rarely accepts that his habit has betrayed him. On the contrary, he will find all kinds of excuses—and continue the habit that led to his being captured. Similarly, businesses that are being betrayed by their habits will not admit it and will find all kinds of excuses. The American electronics manufacturers, for instance, attribute the Japanese successes to "low labor costs" in Japan. Yet the few American manufacturers that have faced up to reality, for example, RCA and Magnavox in television sets, are able to turn out in the United States products at prices competitive with those of the Japanese, and competitive also in quality, despite their paying American wages and union benefits. The German banks uniformly explain the success of Citibank's *Familienbank* by its taking risks they themselves would not touch. But *Familienbank* has lower credit losses with consumer loans than the German banks, and its lending requirements are as strict as those of the Germans. The German banks know this, of course. Yet they keep on explaining away their failure and *Familienbank*'s success. This is typical. And it explains why the same strategy—the same entrepreneurial judo—can be used over and over again.

There are in particular five fairly common bad habits that enable newcomers to use entrepreneurial judo and to catapult themselves into a leadership position in an industry against the entrenched, established companies.

1. The first is what American slang calls "NIH" ("Not Invented Here"), the arrogance that leads a company or an industry to believe that something new cannot be any good unless they themselves thought of it. And so the new invention is spurned, as was the transistor by the American electronics manufacturers.

2. The second is the tendency to "cream" a market, that is, to get the high-profit part of it.

This is basically what Xerox did and what made it an easy target for the Japanese imitators of its copying machines. Xerox focused its strategy on the big users, the buyers of large numbers of machines or of expensive, high-performance machines. It did not reject the others; but it did not go after them. In particular, it did not see fit to give them service. In the end it was dissatisfaction with the service—or rather, with the lack of service—Xerox provided for its smaller customers that made them receptive to competitors' machines.

"Creaming" is a violation of elementary managerial and economic precepts. It is always punished by loss of market.

Xerox was resting on its laurels. They were indeed substantial and well earned, but no business ever gets paid for what it did in the past. "Creaming" attempts to get paid for past contributions. Once a business gets into that habit, it is likely to continue in it and thus continue to be vulnerable to entrepreneurial judo.

3. Even more debilitating is the third bad habit: the belief in "quality." "Quality" in a product or service is not what the supplier puts in. It is what the customer gets out and is willing to pay for. A product is not "quality" because it is hard to make and costs a lot of money, as manufacturers typically believe. That is incompetence. Customers pay only for what is of use to them and gives them value. Nothing else constitutes "quality."

The American electronics manufacturers in the 1950s believed that their products with all those wonderful vacuum tubes were "quality" because they had put in thirty years of effort making radio sets more complicated, bigger, and more expensive. They considered the product to be "quality" because it needed a great deal of skill to turn out, whereas a transistor radio is simple and can be made by unskilled labor on the assembly line. But in consumer terms, the transistor radio is clearly far superior "quality." It weighs much less so that it can be taken on a trip to the beach or to a picnic. It rarely goes wrong; there are no tubes to replace. It costs a great deal less. And in range and fidelity it very soon surpassed even the most magnificent Super Heterodyne with sixteen vacuum tubes, one of which always burned out just when needed.

4. Closely related to both "creaming" and "quality" is the fourth bad habit, the delusion of the "premium" price. A "premium" price is always an invitation to the competitor.

For two hundred years, since the time of J. B. Say in France and of David Ricardo in England in the early years of the nineteenth century, economists have known that the only way to get a higher profit margin, except through a monopoly, is through lower costs. The attempt to achieve a higher profit margin through a higher price is always self-defeating. It holds an umbrella over the competitor. What looks like higher profits for the established leader is in effect a subsidy to the newcomer who, in a very few years, will unseat the leader and claim the throne for himself. "Premium" prices, instead of being an occasion for joy—and a reason for a higher stock price or a higher price/earnings multiple—should always be considered a threat and dangerous vulnerability.

Yet the delusion of higher profits to be achieved through "premium" prices is almost universal, even though it always opens the door to entrepreneurial judo.

5. Finally, there is a fifth bad habit that is typical of established businesses and leads to their downfall—Xerox is a good example. They maximize rather than optimize. As the market grows and develops, they try to satisfy every single user through the same product or service.

A new analytical instrument to test chemical reaction is being introduced, for instance. At first its market is quite limited, let's say to industrial laboratories. But then university laboratories, research institutes, and hospitals all begin to buy the instrument, but each wants something slightly different. And so the manufacturer puts in one feature to satisfy this customer, then another one to satisfy that customer, and so on, until what started out as a simple instrument has become complicated. The manufacturer has maximized what the instrument can do. As a result, the instrument no longer satisfies anyone. For, by trying to satisfy everybody, one always ends up satisfying nobody. The instrument also has become expensive, as well as being hard to use and hard to maintain. But the manufacturer is proud of the instrument; indeed, his full-page advertisement lists sixty-four different things it can do.

This manufacturer will almost certainly become the victim of entrepreneurial judo. What he thinks is his very strength will be turned against him. The newcomer will come in with an instrument designed to satisfy one of the markets, the hospital, for instance. It will not contain a single feature the hospital people do not need, and do not need every day. But everything the hospital needs will be there and with higher performance capacity than the multipurpose instrument can possibly offer. The same manufacturer will then bring out a model for the research laboratory, for the government laboratory, for industry—and in no time at all the newcomer will have taken away the markets with instruments that are specifically designed for their users, instruments that optimize rather than maximize.

Similarly, when the Japanese came in with their copiers in competition with Xerox, they designed machines that fitted specific groups of users—for example, the small office, whether that of the dentist, the doctor, or the school principal. They did not try to match the features of which the Xerox people themselves were the proudest, such as the speed of the machine or the clarity of the copy. They gave the small office what the small office needed most, a simple machine at a low cost. And once they had established themselves in that market, they then moved in on the other markets, each with a product designed to serve optimally a specific market segment.

Sony similarly first moved into the low end of the radio market, the market for cheap portables with limited range. Once it had established itself there, it moved in on the other market segments.

Entrepreneurial judo aims first at securing a beachhead, and one which the established leaders either do not defend at all or defend only halfheartedly—the way the Germans did not counterattack when Citibank established its *Familienbank*. Once that beachhead has been secured, that is, once the newcomers have an adequate market and an adequate revenue stream, they then move on to the rest of the "beach" and finally to the whole "island." In each case, they repeat the strategy. They design a product or a service which is specific to a given market segment and optimal for it. And the established leaders hardly ever beat them to this game. Hardly ever do the established leaders manage to change their own behavior before the newcomers have taken over the leadership and acquired dominance.

There are three situations in which the entrepreneurial judo strategy is likely to be particularly successful.

The first is the common situation in which the established leaders refuse to act on the unexpected, whether success or failure, and either overlook it altogether or try to brush it aside. This is what Sony exploited.

The second situation is the Xerox situation. A new technology emerges and grows fast. But the innovators who have brought to the market the new technology (or the new service) behave like the classical "monopolists": they use their leadership position to "cream" the market and to get "premium" prices. They either do not know or refuse to acknowledge what has been amply proven: that a leadership position, let alone any kind of monopoly, can only be maintained if the leader behaves as a "benevolent monopolist" (the term is Joseph Schumpeter's).

A benevolent monopolist cuts his prices before a competitor can cut them. And he makes his product obsolete and introduces new product before a competitor can do so. There are enough examples of this around to prove the validity of the thesis. It is the way in which the DuPont Company has acted for many years and in which the American Bell Telephone System (AT&T) used to act before it was overcome by the inflationary problems of the 1970s. But if the leader uses his leadership position to raise prices or to raise profit margins except by lowering his cost, he sets himself up to be knocked down by anyone who uses entrepreneurial judo against him.

Similarly, the leader in a rapidly growing new market or new technology who tries to maximize rather than to optimize will soon make himself vulnerable to entrepreneurial judo.

Finally, entrepreneurial judo works as a strategy when market or industry structure changes fast—which is the *Familienbank* story. As Germany became prosperous in the fifties and sixties, ordinary people became customers for financial services beyond the traditional savings account or the traditional mortgage. But the German banks stuck to their old markets.

Entrepreneurial judo is always market-focused and market-driven. The starting point may be technology, as it was when Akio Morita traveled to the United States from a Japan that had barely emerged from the destruction of World War II to acquire a transistor license. Morita looked at the market segment which the existing technology satisfied the least, simply because of the weight and fragility of vacuum tubes: the market for portables. He then designed the right radio for that market, a market of young people with little money but also fairly simple demands with respect to range of the instrument and to quality of sound, a market, in other words, that the old technology simply could not adequately serve.

Similarly, the long-distance discounters in the United States who saw the opportunity to buy from the Bell Telephone System wholesale and to resell retail, designed a service first for the fairly modest number of substantial businesses that were too small to build their own longdistance system but large enough to have heavy long-distance bills. Only after they had secured a substantial share of that market did they move out and try to go after both the very big and the small users.

To use the entrepreneurial judo strategy, one starts out with an analysis of the industry, the producers and the suppliers, their habits, especially their bad habits, and their policies. But then one looks at the markets and tries to pinpoint the place where an alternative strategy would meet with the greatest success and the least resistance.

Entrepreneurial judo requires some degree of genuine innovation. It is, as a rule, not good enough to offer the same product or the same service at lower cost. There has to be something that distinguishes it from what already exists. When the ROLM Company offered a private branch exchange—a switchboard for business and office users—in competition with AT&T, it built in additional features designed around a small computer. These were not high-tech, let alone new inventions. Indeed, AT&T itself had designed similar features. But AT&T did not push them—and ROLM did. Similarly, when Citibank went into Germany with the *Familienbank,* it put in some innovative services which German banks as a rule did not offer to small depositors, such as travelers checks or tax advice.

It is not enough, in other words, for the newcomer simply to do as good a job as the established leader at a lower cost or with better service. The newcomers have to make themselves distinct.

Like being "Fustest with the Mostest" and creative imitation, entrepreneurial judo aims at obtaining leadership position and eventually dominance. But it does not do so by competing with the leaders—or at least not where the leaders are aware of competitive challenge or worried about it. Entrepreneurial judo "Hits Them Where They Ain't."

18

Ecological Niches

The entrepreneurial strategies discussed so far, being "Fustest with the Mostest," creative imitation, and entrepreneurial judo, all aim at market or industry leadership, if not at dominance. The "ecological niche" strategy aims at control. The strategies discussed earlier aim at positioning an enterprise in a large market or a major industry. The ecological niche strategy aims at obtaining a practical monopoly in a small area. The first three strategies are competitive strategies. The ecological niche strategy aims at making its successful practitioners immune to competition and unlikely to be challenged. Successful practitioners of "Fustest with the Mostest," creative imitation, and entrepreneurial judo become big companies, highly visible if not household words. Successful practitioners of the ecological niche take the cash and let the credit go. They wallow in their anonymity. Indeed, in the most successful of the ecological niche strategies, the whole point is to be so inconspicuous, despite the product's being essential to a process, that no one is likely to try to compete.

There are three distinct niche strategies, each with its own requirements, its own limitations, and its own risks:

- the toll-gate strategy;
- the specialty skill strategy; and
- the specialty market strategy.

I

THE TOLL-GATE STRATEGY

Earlier, in Chapter 4, I discussed the strategy of the Alcon Company, which developed an enzyme to eliminate the one feature of the standard surgical operation for senile cataracts that went counter to the rhythm and the logic of the process. Once this enzyme had been developed and patented, it had a "toll-gate" position. No eye surgeon would do without it. No matter what Alcon charged for the teaspoonful of enzyme that was needed for each cataract operation, the cost was insignificant in relation to the total cost of the operation. I doubt that any eye surgeon or any hospital ever even inquired what the stuff cost. The total market for this particular preparation was so small—maybe $50 million dollars a year worldwide—that it clearly would not have been worth anybody's while to try to develop a competing product. There would not have been one additional cataract operation in the world just because this particular enzyme had become cheaper. All that potential competitors could possibly do, therefore, would have been to knock down the price for everybody, without deriving much benefit for themselves.

A very similar toll-gate position has been occupied for many years by a medium-sized company which, fifty or sixty years ago, developed a blowout protector for oil wells. The cost of drilling an oil well may run into many millions. One blowout will destroy the entire well and everything that has been invested in it. The blowout protector, which safeguards the well while being drilled, is thus cheap insurance, no matter what its price. Again, the total market is so limited as to make it unattractive for any would-be competitor. Lowering the price of blowout protectors, which constitute maybe 1 percent of the total cost of a deep well, could not possibly stimulate anyone to drill more wells. Competition could only degrade the price without increasing the demand.

Another example of a toll-gate strategy is Dewey & Almy—now a division of W. R. Grace. This company developed a compound to seal tin cans in the 1930s. The seal is an essential ingredient of the can: if a can goes bad, it can cause catastrophic damage. One death from one case of botulism in a can can easily destroy a food packer. A can-sealing compound that offers protection against spoilage is therefore cheap at any price. And yet the cost of sealing—a fraction of a cent at best—is so insignificant to both the cost of the total can and the risk of spoilage that nobody is much concerned about it. What matters is performance, not cost. Again, the total market, while larger than that for enzymes in cataract operations or for blowout protectors, is still a limited one. And lowering the price for can-sealing compound is quite unlikely to increase the demand by a single can.

The toll-gate position is thus in many ways the most desirable position a company can occupy. But it has stringent requirements. The product has to be essential to a process. The risk of not using it—the risk of losing an eye, losing an oil well, or spoilage in a tin can—must be infinitely greater than the cost of the product. The market must be so limited that whoever occupies it first preempts it. It must be a true "ecological niche" which one species fills completely, and which at the same time is small and discreet enough not to attract rivals.

Such toll-gate positions are not easily found. Normally they occur only in an incongruity situation (cf. Chapter 4). The incongruity, as in the case of Alcon's enzyme, might be an incongruity in the rhythm or the logic of a process. Or, as in the case of the blowout protector or the can-sealing compound, it might be an incongruity between economic realities—between the cost of malfunction and the cost of adequate protection.

The toll-gate position also has severe limitations and serious risks. It is basically a static position. Once the ecological niche has been occu-pied, there is unlikely to be much growth. There is nothing the company that occupies the toll-gate position can do to increase its business or to control it. No matter how good its product or how cheap, the demand is dependent upon the demand for the process or product to which the toll-gate product furnishes an ingredient.

This may not be too important for Alcon. Cataracts can be assumed to be impervious to economic fluctuations, whether boom or depression. But the company making blowout protectors had to invest enormous amounts of money in new plants when oil drilling skyrocketed in 1973, and again after the 1979 petroleum panic. It suspected that the boom could not last; yet it had to make the investments even though it was reasonably sure it could never earn them back. Not to have done so would have meant losing its market irretrievably. Equally, it was powerless when, a few years later, the oil boom collapsed and oil drilling shrank by 80 percent within twelve months, and with it orders for oil-drilling equipment.

Once the toll-gate strategy has attained its objective, the company is "mature." It can only grow as fast as its end users grow. But it can go down fast. It can become obsolete almost overnight if someone finds a different way of satisfying the same end use. Dewey & Almy, for instance, has no defense against the replacement of tin cans by other container materials such as glass, paper, or plastics, or by other methods of preserving food such as freezing and irradiation.

And the toll-gate strategist must never exploit his monopoly. He must not become what the Germans call a *Raubritter* (the English "robber baron" does not mean quite the same thing) who robbed and raped the hapless travelers as they passed through the mountain defiles and river gorges atop of which perched his castle. He must not abuse his monopoly to exploit, to extort, to maltreat his customers. If he does, the users will put another supplier into business, or they will switch to less effective substitutes which they can then control.

The right strategy is the one Dewey & Almy has successfully pursued for more than forty years now. It offers its users, especially those in the Third World, extensive technical service, teaches their people, and designs new and better canning and can-sealing machinery for them to use with the Dewey & Almy sealing compounds. Yet it also constantly upgrades the compounds.

The toll-gate position might be impregnable—or nearly so. But it can only control within a narrow radius. Alcon tried to overcome this limitation by diversifying into all kinds of consumer products for the eye: artificial tears, contact lens fluids, anti-allergic eyedrops, and so on. This was successful insofar as it made the company attractive to one of the leading consumer goods multinationals, the Swiss Néstlé Company, which bought out Alcon for a very substantial sum. To the best of my knowledge, Alcon is the only toll-gate company of this kind that succeeded in establishing itself in markets outside its original position and with products that were different in their economic characteristics. But whether this diversification into highly competitive consumer markets of which the company knew very little was profitable, is not known.

II

THE SPECIALTY SKILL

Everybody knows the major automobile nameplates. But few people know the names of the companies that supply the electrical and lighting systems for these cars, and yet there are far fewer such systems than there are automobile nameplates: in the United States, the Delco group of GM; in Germany, Robert Bosch; in Great Britain, Lucas; and so on. Practically no one outside of the automobile industry knows that one firm, A. O. Smith of Milwaukee, has for decades been making every single frame used in an American passenger car, nor that for decades another firm, Bendix, has made every single set of automotive brakes used by the American automobile industry.

By now these are all old and well-established firms, of course, but only because the automobile is itself an old industry. These companies established their controlling position when the industry was in its infancy, well before World War I. Robert Bosch, for instance, was a contemporary and friend of the two German auto pioneers, Carl Benz and Gottfried Daimler, and started his firm in the 1880s.

But once these companies had attained their controlling position in their specialty skill niche, they retained it. Unlike the toll-gate companies, theirs is a fairly large niche, yet it is still unique. It was obtained by developing high skill at a very early time. A. O. Smith developed what today would be called "automation" in making automobile frames during and shortly after World War I. The electrical system which Bosch in Germany designed for Mercedes staff cars around 1911 was so far advanced that it was put into general use even in luxury automobiles only after World War II. Delco in Dayton, Ohio, developed the self-starter before becoming a part of General Motors, that is, before 1914. Such specialized skills put these companies so far ahead in their field that it was hardly worth anybody's while to try to challenge them. They had become the "standard."

Specialty skill niches are by no means confined to manufacturing. Within the last ten years a few private trading firms, most of them in Vienna, Austria, have built a similar niche in what used to be called "barter" and is now called "counter-trade": taking goods from a developing importing country, Bulgarian tobacco or Brazilian-made irrigation pumps, in payment for locomotives, machinery, or pharmaceuticals exported by a company in a developed country. And much earlier, an enterprising German attained such a hold on one specialty skill niche that guidebooks for tourists are still called by his name, "Baedeker."

As these cases show, timing is of the essence in establishing a specialty skill niche. It has to be done at the very beginning of a new industry, a new custom, a new market, a new trend. Karl Baedeker published his first guidebook in 1828, as soon as the first steamships on the Rhine opened tourist travel to the middle classes. He then had the field virtually to himself until World War I made German books unacceptable in Western countries. The counter-traders of Vienna started around 1960, when such trade was still the rare exception, largely confined to the smaller countries of the Soviet Bloc (which explains why they are concentrated in Austria). Ten years later, when hard currencies had become scarce all through the Third World, they had honed their skills and become the "specialists."

To attain a specialty niche always requires something new, something added, something that is genuine innovation. There were guidebooks for travelers before Baedeker, but they confined themselves to the cultural scene—churches, sights, and so on. For practical details—the hotels, the tariff of the horse-drawn cabs, the distances, and the proper amount to tip—the traveling English milord relied on a professional, the courier. But the middle class had no courier, and that was Baedeker's opportunity. Once he had learned what information the traveler needed, how to get at it and to present it (the format he established is still the one many guidebooks follow), it would not have paid anyone to duplicate Baedeker's investment and build a competing organization.

In the early stages of a major new development, the specialty skill niche offers an exceptional opportunity. Examples abound. For many, many years there were only two companies in the United States making airplane propellers, for instance. Both had been started before World War I.

A specialty skill niche is rarely found by accident. In every single case, it results from a systematic survey of innovative opportunities. In every single case, the entrepreneur looks for the place where a specialty skill can be developed and can give a new enterprise a unique controlling position. Robert Bosch spent years studying the new automotive field to position his new company where it could immediately establish itself as the leader. Hamilton Propeller, for many years the leading airplane propeller manufacturer in the United States, was the result of a systematic search by its founder in the early days of powered flight. Baedeker made several attempts to start a service for the tourist before he decided on the guidebook that then bore his name and made him famous.

The first point, therefore, is that in the early stages of a new industry, a new market, or a new major trend, there is the opportunity to search systematically for the specialty skill opportunity—and then there is usually time to develop a unique skill.

The second point is that the specialty skill niche does require a skill that is both unique and different. The early automobile pioneers were, without exception, mechanics. They knew a great deal about machinery, about metals and about engines. But electricity was alien to them.

It required theoretical knowledge which they neither possessed nor knew how to acquire. There were other publishers in Baedeker's time, but a guidebook that required on-the-spot gathering of an enormous amount of detailed information, constant inspection, and a staff of traveling auditors was not within their purview. "Counter-trade" is neither trading nor banking.

The business that establishes itself in a specialty skill niche is therefore unlikely to be threatened by its customers or by its suppliers. Neither of them really wants to get into something that is so alien in skill and in temperament.

Thirdly, a business occupying a specialty skill niche must constantly work on improving its own skill. It has to stay ahead. Indeed, it has to make itself constantly obsolete. The automobile companies in the early days used to complain that Delco in Dayton, and Bosch in Stuttgart, were pushing them. They turned out lighting systems that were far ahead of the ordinary automobile, ahead of what the automobile manufacturers of the times thought the customer needed, wanted, or could pay for, ahead very often of what the automobile manufacturer knew how to assemble.

While the specialty skill niche has unique advantages, it also has severe limitations. One is that it inflicts tunnel-vision on its occupants. In order to maintain themselves in their controlling position, they have to learn to look neither right nor left, but directly ahead at their narrow area, their specialized field. Airplane electronics were not too different from automobile electronics in the early stages. Yet the automobile electricians—Delco, Bosch, and Lucas—are not leaders in airplane electronics. They did not even see the field and made no attempt to get into it.

A second, serious limitation is that the occupant of a specialty skill niche is usually dependent on somebody else to bring his product or service to market. It becomes a component. The strength of the automobile electrical firms is that the customer does not know that they exist. But this is of course also their weakness. If the British automobile industry goes down, so does Lucas. A. O. Smith prospered making automotive frames until the energy crisis. Then American automobile manufacturers began to switch to cars without frames. These cars are substantially more expensive than cars with frames, but they weigh less and therefore burn less fuel. A. O. Smith could do nothing to reverse the adverse trend.

Finally, the greatest danger to the specialty niche manufacturer is for the specialty to cease being a specialty and to become universal.

The niche that the Viennese counter-traders now occupy was occupied in the 1920s and 1930s by foreign exchange traders who were mostly Swiss. Bankers of those days, having grown up before World War I, still believed that currencies ought to be stable. And when currencies became unstable, when there were blocked currencies around, currencies with different exchange rates for different purposes, and other such monstrosities, the bankers did not even want to handle the business. They were only too happy to let the specialists in Switzerland do what they thought was a dirty job. So a fairly small number of Swiss foreign exchange traders occupied a highly profitable specialty skill niche. After World War II, with the tremendous expansion of world trade, foreign exchange trading became routine. By now every bank, at least in the major money centers, has its own foreign exchange traders.

The specialty skill niche, like all ecological niches, is therefore limited—in scope as well as in time. Species that occupy such a niche, biology teaches, do not easily adapt to even small changes in the external environment. And this is true, too, of the entrepreneurial skill species. But within these limitations, the specialty skill niche is a highly advantageous position. In a rapidly expanding new technology, industry, or market, it is perhaps the most advantageous strategy. Very few of the automobile makers of 1920 are still around; every single one of the electrical and lighting systems makers is. Once attained and properly maintained, the specialty skill niche protects against competition, precisely because no automobile buyer knows or cares who makes the headlights or the brakes. No automobile buyer is therefore likely to shop around for either. Once the name "Baedeker" had become synonymous with tourist guidebooks, there was little danger that anybody else would try to muscle in, at least not until the market changed drastically. In a new technology, a new industry, or a new market, the specialty skill strategy offers an optimal ratio between opportunity and risk of failure.

III

THE SPECIALTY MARKET

The major difference between the specialty skill niche and the specialty market niche is that the former is built around a product or service and the latter around specialized knowledge of a market. Otherwise, they are similar.

Two medium-sized companies, one in northern England and one in Denmark, supply the great majority of the automated baking ovens for cookies and crackers bought in the non-Communist world. For many decades, two companies—the two earliest travel agents, Thomas Cook in Europe and American Express in the United States—had a practical monopoly on travelers checks.

There is, I am told, nothing very difficult or particularly technical about baking ovens. There are literally dozens of companies around that could make them just as well as those two firms in England and Denmark. But these two know the market: they know every single major baker, and every single major baker knows them. The market is just not big enough or attractive enough to try to compete with these two, as long as they remain satisfactory. Similarly, travelers checks were a backwater until the post–World War II period of mass travel. They were highly profitable since the issuer, whether Cook or American Express, has the use of the money and keeps the interest earned on it until the purchaser cashes the check—sometimes months after the checks were purchased. But the market was not large enough to tempt anyone else. Furthermore, travelers checks required a worldwide organization, which Cook and American Express had to maintain anyhow to service their travel customers, and which nobody else in those days had any reason to build.

The specialty market is found by looking at a new development with the question, What opportunities are there in this that would give us a unique niche, and what do we have to do to fill it ahead of everybody else? The travelers check is no great "invention." It is basically nothing more than a letter of credit, and that has been around for hundreds of years. What was new was that travelers checks were offered—at first to the customers of Cook and American Express, and then to the general public—in standard denominations. And they could be cashed wherever Cook or American Express had an office or an agent. That made them uniquely attractive to the tourist who did not want to carry a great deal of cash and did not have the established banking connections to make them eligible for a letter of credit.

There was nothing particularly advanced in the early baking ovens, nor is there any high technology in the baking ovens installed today. What the two leading firms did was to realize that the act of baking cookies and crackers was moving out of the home and into the factory. They then studied what commercial bakers needed so that they could manufacture the product their own customers, grocers and supermarkets, could in turn sell and the housewife would buy. The baking ovens were not based on engineering but on market research; the engineering would have been available to anyone.

The specialty market niche has the same requirements as the specialty skill niche: systematic analysis of a new trend, industry, or market; a specific innovative contribution, if only a "twist" like the one that converted the traditional letter of credit into the modern travelers check; and continuous work to improve the product and especially the service, so that leadership, once obtained, will be retained.

And it has the same limitations. The greatest threat to the specialty market position is success. The greatest threat is when the specialty market becomes a mass market.

Travelers checks have now become a commodity and highly competitive because travel has become a mass market.

So have perfumes. A French firm, Coty, created the modern perfume industry. It realized that World War I had changed the attitude toward cosmetics. Whereas before the war only "fast women" used cosmetics—or dared admit to their use—cosmetics had become accepted and respectable. By the mid-twenties Coty had established itself in what was almost a monopoly position on both sides of the Atlantic. Until 1929 the cosmetics market was a "specialty market," a market of the upper middle class. But then during the Depression it exploded into a genuine mass market. It also split into two segments: a prestige segment, with high prices, specialty distribution, and specialty packaging; and popular-priced, mass brands sold in every outlet including the supermarket, the variety store, and the drugstore. Within a few short years, the specialty market dominated by Coty had disappeared. But Coty could not make up its mind whether to try to become one of the mass marketers in cosmetics or one of the luxury producers. It tried to stay in a market that no longer existed, and has been drifting ever since.

19

Changing Values and Characteristics

In the entrepreneurial strategies discussed so far, the aim is to introduce an innovation. In the entrepreneurial strategy discussed in this chapter, the strategy itself is the innovation. The product or service it carries may well have been around a long time—in our first example, the postal service, it was almost two thousand years old. But the strategy converts this old, established product or service into something new. It changes its utility, its value, its economic characteristics. While physically there is no change, economically there is something different and new.

All the strategies to be discussed in this chapter have one thing in common. They create a customer—and that is the ultimate purpose of a business, indeed, of economic activity.* But they do so in four different ways:

- by creating utility;
- by pricing;
- by adaptation to the customer's social and economic reality;
- by delivering what represents true value to the customer.

I

CREATING CUSTOMER UTILITY

English schoolboys used to be taught that Rowland Hill "invented" the postal service in 1836. That is nonsense, of course. The Rome of the Caesars had an excellent service, with fast couriers carrying mail on regular schedules to the furthest corners of the Empire. A thousand years later, in 1521, the German emperor Charles V, in true Renais-

---

*As was first said more than thirty years ago in my *The Practice of Management* (New York: Harper & Row, 1954).

493

sance fashion, went back to Classical Rome and gave a monopoly on carrying mail in the imperial domains to the princely family of Thurn and Taxis. Their generous campaign contributions had enabled him to bribe enough German Electors to win the imperial crown—and the princes of Thurn and Taxis still provided the postal service in many parts of Germany as late as 1866, as stamp collectors know. By the middle of the seventeenth century, every European country had organized a postal service on the German model and so had, a hundred years later, the American colonies. Indeed, all the great letter-writers of the Western tradition, from Cicero to Madame de Sévigné, Lord Chesterfield, and Voltaire, wrote and posted their letters long before Rowland Hill "invented" the postal service.

Yet Hill did indeed create what we would now call "mail." He contributed no new technology and not one new "thing," nothing that could conceivably have been patented. But mail had always been paid for by the addressee, with the fee computed according to distance and weight. This made it both expensive and slow. Every letter had to be brought to a post office to be weighed. Hill proposed that postage should be uniform within Great Britain regardless of distance; that it be prepaid; and that the fee be paid by affixing the kind of stamp that had been used for many years to pay other fees and taxes. Overnight, mail became easy and convenient; indeed, letters could now be dropped into a collection box. Immediately, also, mail became absurdly cheap. The letter that had earlier cost a shilling or more—and a shilling was as much as a craftsman earned in a day—now cost only a penny. The volume was no longer limited. In short, "mail" was born.

Hill created utility. He asked: What do the customers *need* for a postal service to be truly a service to them? This is always the first question in the entrepreneurial strategy of changing utility, values, and economic characteristics. In fact, the reduction in the cost of mailing a letter, although 80 percent or more, was secondary. The main effect was to make using the mails convenient for everybody and available to everybody. Letters no longer had to be confined to "epistles." The tailor could now use the mail to send a bill. The resulting explosion in volume, which doubled in the first four years and quadrupled again in the next ten, then brought the cost down to where mailing a letter cost practically nothing for long years.

Price is usually almost irrelevant in the strategy of creating utility. The strategy works by enabling customers to do what serves *their pur-*

pose. It works because it asks: What is truly a "service," truly a "utility" to the customer?

Every American bride wants to get one set of "good china." A whole set is, however, far too expensive a present, and the people giving her a wedding present do not know what pattern the bride wants or what pieces she already has. So they end up giving something else. The demand was there, in other words, but the utility was lacking. A medium-sized dinnerware manufacturer, the Lenox China Company, saw this as an innovative opportunity. Lenox adapted an old idea, the "bridal register," so that it only "registers" Lenox china. The bride-to-be then picks one merchant whom she tells what pattern of Lenox china she wants, and to whom she refers potential donors of wedding gifts. The merchant then asks the donor: "How much do you want to spend?" and explains: "That will get you two coffee cups with saucers." Or the merchant can say, "She already has all the coffee cups; what she needs now is dessert plates." The result is a happy bride, a happy wedding-gift donor, and a very happy Lenox China Company.

Again, there is no high technology here, nothing patentable, nothing but a focus on the needs of the customer. Yet the bridal register, for all its simplicity—or perhaps because of it—has made Lenox the favorite "good china" manufacturer and one of the most rapidly growing of medium-sized American manufacturing companies.

Creating utility enables people to satisfy their wants and their needs *in their own way.* The tailor could not send the bill to his customer through the mails if it first took three hours to get the letter accepted by a postal clerk and if the addressee then had to pay a large sum— perhaps even as much as the bill itself. Rowland Hill did not add anything to the service. It was performed by the same postal clerks using the same mail coaches and the same letter carriers. And yet Rowland Hill's postal service was a totally different "service." It served a different function.

II

PRICING

For many years, the best known American face in the world was that of King Gillette, which graced the wrapper of every Gillette razor blade sold anyplace in the world. And millions of men all over the world used a Gillette razor blade every morning.

King Gillette did not invent the safety razor; dozens of them were patented in the closing decades of the nineteenth century. Until 1860 or 1870, only a very small number of men, the aristocracy and a few professionals and merchants, had to take care of their facial hair, and they could well afford a barber. Then, suddenly, large numbers of men, tradesmen, shopkeepers, clerks, had to look "respectable." Few of them could handle a straight razor or felt comfortable with so dangerous a tool, but visits to the barber were expensive, and worse, time-consuming. Many inventors designed a "do-it-yourself" safety razor, yet none could sell it. A visit to the barber cost ten cents and the cheapest safety razor cost five dollars—an enormous sum in those days when a dollar a day was a good wage.

Gillette's safety razor was no better than many others, and it was a good deal more expensive to produce. But Gillette did not "sell" the razor. He practically gave it away by pricing it at fifty-five cents retail or twenty cents wholesale, not much more than one-fifth of its manufacturing cost. But he designed it so that it could use only his patented blades. These cost him less than one cent apiece to make: he sold them for five cents. And since the blades could be used six or seven times, they delivered a shave at less than one cent apiece—or at less than one-tenth the cost of a visit to a barber.

What Gillette did was to price what the customer buys, namely, the shave, rather than what the manufacturer sells. In the end, the captive Gillette customer may have paid more than he would have paid had he bought a competitor's safety razor for five dollars, and then bought the competitor's blades selling at one cent or two. Gillette's customers surely knew this; customers are more intelligent than either advertising agencies or Ralph Nader believe. But Gillette's pricing made sense to them. They were paying for what they bought, that is, for a shave, rather than for a "thing." And the shave they got from the Gillette razor and the Gillette razor blade was much more pleasant than any shave they could have given themselves with that dangerous weapon, the straight-edge razor, and far cheaper than they could have gotten at the neighborhood barber's.

One reason why the patents on a copying machine ended up at a small, obscure company in Rochester, New York, then known as the Haloid Company, rather than at one of the big printing-machine manufacturers, was that none of the large established manufacturers saw any possibility of selling a copying machine. Their calculations showed that such a machine would have to sell for at least $4,000. Nobody was going to pay such a sum for a copying machine when carbon paper cost practically nothing. Also, of course, to spend $4,000 on a machine meant a capital-appropriations request, which had to go all the way up to the board of directors accompanied by a calculation showing the return on investment, both of which seemed unimaginable for a gadget to help the secretary. The Haloid Company—the present Xerox—did a good deal of technical work to design the final machine. But its major contribution was in pricing. It did not sell the machine; it sold what the machine produced, copies. At five or ten cents a copy, there is no need for a capital-appropriations request. This is "petty cash," which the secretary can disburse without going upstairs. Pricing the Xerox machine at five cents a copy was the true innovation.

Most suppliers, including public-service institutions, never think of pricing as a strategy. Yet pricing enables the customer to pay for what he buys—a shave, a copy of a document—rather than for what the supplier makes. What is being paid in the end is, of course, the same amount. But how it is being paid is structured to the needs and the realities of the consumer. It is structured in accordance with what the consumer actually buys. And it charges for what represents "value" to the customer rather than what represents "cost" to the supplier.

III

THE CUSTOMER'S REALITY

The worldwide leadership of the American General Electric Company (G.E.) in large steam turbines is based on G.E.'s having thought through, in the years before World War I, what its customers' realities were. Steam turbines, unlike the piston-driven steam engines which they replaced in the generation of electric power, are complex, requiring a high degree of engineering in their design, and skill in building and fitting them. This the individual electric power company simply cannot supply. It buys a major steam turbine maybe every five or ten years when it builds a new power station. Yet the skill has to be kept in being all the time. The manufacturer, therefore, has to set up and maintain a massive consulting organization.

But, as G.E. soon found out, the customer cannot pay for consulting services. Under American law, the state public utility commissions would have to allow such an expenditure. In the opinion of the commissions, however, the companies should have been able to do this work themselves. G.E. also found that it could not add to the price of the steam turbine the cost of the consulting services which its customers needed. Again, the public utility commissions would not have accepted it. But while a steam turbine has a very long life, it needs a new set of blades fairly often, maybe every five to seven years, and these blades have to come from the maker of the original turbine. G.E. built up the world's foremost consulting engineering organization on electric power stations—though it was careful not to call this consulting engineering but "apparatus sales"—for which it did not charge. Its steam turbines were no more expensive than those of its competitors. But it put the added cost of the consulting organization plus a substantial profit into the price it charged for replacement blades. Within ten years all the other manufacturers of steam turbines had caught on and switched to the same system. But by then G.E. had world market leadership.

Much earlier, during the 1840s, a similar design of product and process to fit customer realities led to the invention of installment buying. Cyrus McCormick was one of many Americans who built a harvesting machine—the need was obvious. And he found, as had the other inventors of similar machines, that he could not sell his product. The farmer did not have the purchasing power. That the machine would earn back what it cost within two or three seasons, everybody knew and accepted, but there was no banker then who would have lent the American farmer the money to buy a machine. McCormick offered installments, to be paid out of the savings the harvester produced over the ensuing three years. The farmer could now afford to buy the machine—and he did so.

Manufacturers are wont to talk of the "irrational customer" (as do economists, psychologists, and moralists). But there are no "irrational customers." As an old saying has it, "There are only lazy manufacturers." The customer has to be assumed to be rational. His or her reality, however, is usually quite different from that of the manufacturer. The rules and regulations of public utility commissions may appear to make no sense and be purely arbitrary. For the power companies that have to operate under them, they are realities nonetheless. The American farmer may have been a better credit risk than American bankers of

1840 thought. But it was a fact that American banks of that period did not advance money to farmers to purchase equipment. The innovative strategy consists in accepting that these realities are not extraneous to the product, but *are*, in fact, the product as far as the customer is concerned. Whatever customers buy has to fit their realities, or it is of no use to them.

IV

DELIVERING VALUE TO THE CUSTOMER

The last of these innovative strategies delivers what is "value" to the customer rather than what is "product" to the manufacturer. It is actually only one step beyond the strategy of accepting the customer's reality as part of the product and part of what the customer buys and pays for.

A medium-sized company in America's Midwest supplies more than half of all the special lubricant needed for very large earth-moving and hauling machines: the bulldozers and draglines used by contractors building highways; the heavy equipment used to remove the overlay from strip mines; the heavy trucks used to haul coal out of coal mines; and so on. This company is in competition with some of the largest oil companies, which can mobilize whole battalions of lubrication specialists. It competes by not selling lubricating oil at all. Instead, it sells what is, in effect, insurance. What is "value" to the contractor is not lubrication: it is operating the equipment. Every hour the contractor loses because this or that piece of heavy equipment cannot operate costs him infinitely more than he spends on lubricants during an entire year. In all these activities there is a heavy penalty for contractors who miss their deadlines—and they can only get the contract by calculating the deadline as finely as possible and racing against the clock. What the Midwestern lubricant maker does is to offer contractors an analysis of the maintenance needs of their equipment. Then it offers them a maintenance program with an annual subscription price, and guarantees the subscribers that their heavy equipment will not be shut down for more than a given number of hours per year because of lubrication problems. Needless to say, the program always prescribes the manufacturer's lubricant. But this is not what contractors buy. They are buying trouble-free operations, which are extremely valuable to them.

The final example—one that might be called "moving from product to system"—is that of Herman Miller, the American furniture maker in Zeeland, Michigan. The company first became well known as the manufacturer of one of the early modern designs, the Eames chair. Then, when every other manufacturer began to turn out designer chairs, Herman Miller moved into making and selling whole offices and work stations for hospitals, both with considerable success. Finally, when the "office of the future" began to come in, Herman Miller founded a Facilities Management Institute that does not even sell furniture or equipment, but advises companies on office layout and equipment needed for the best work flow, high productivity, high employee morale, all at low cost. What Herman Miller is doing is *defining* "value" for the customer. It is telling the customer, "You may pay for furniture, but you are buying work, morale, productivity. And this is what you should therefore be paying for."

These examples are likely to be considered obvious. Surely, anybody applying a little intelligence would have come up with these and similar strategies? But the father of systematic economics, David Ricardo, is believed to have said once, "Profits are not made by differential cleverness, but by differential stupidity." The strategies work, not because they are clever, but because most suppliers—of goods as well as of services, businesses as well as public-service institutions—do not think. They work precisely because they are so "obvious." Why, then, are they so rare? For, as these examples show, anyone who asks the question, What does the customer really buy? will win the race. In fact, it is not even a race since nobody else is running. What explains this?

One reason is the economists and their concept of "value." Every economics book points out that customers do not buy a "product," but what the product does for them. And then, every economics book promptly drops consideration of everything except the "price" for the product, a "price" defined as what the customer pays to take possession or ownership of a thing or a service. What the product does for the customer is never mentioned again. Unfortunately, suppliers, whether of products or of services, tend to follow the economists.

It is meaningful to say that "product A costs X dollars." It is meaningful to say that "we have to get Y dollars for the product to cover our own costs of production and have enough left over to cover the cost of capital, and thereby to show an adequate profit." But it makes no sense at all to conclude, " . . . and therefore the customer has to pay the lump sum of Y dollars in cash for each piece of product A he buys." Rather, the argument should go as follows: "What the customer pays for each piece of the product has to work out as Y dollars *for us*. But how the customer pays depends on what makes the most sense to him. It depends on what the product does for the customer. It depends on what fits his reality. It depends on what the customer sees as 'value.' "

Price in itself is not "pricing," and it is not "value." It was this insight that gave King Gillette a virtual monopoly on the shaving market for almost forty years; it also enabled the tiny Haloid Company to become the multibillion-dollar Xerox Company in ten years, and it gave General Electric world leadership in steam turbines. In every single case, these companies became exceedingly profitable. But they earned their profitability. They were paid for giving their customers satisfaction, for giving their customers what the customers wanted to buy, in other words, for giving their customers their money's worth.

"But this is nothing but elementary marketing," most readers will protest, and they are right. It is *nothing* but elementary marketing. To start out with the customer's utility, with what the customer buys, with what the realities of the customer are and what the customer's values are—this is what marketing is all about. But why, after forty years of preaching Marketing, teaching Marketing, professing Marketing, so few suppliers are willing to follow, I cannot explain. The fact remains that so far, anyone who is willing to use marketing as the basis for strategy is likely to acquire leadership in an industry or a market fast and almost without risk.

Entrepreneurial strategies are as important as purposeful innovation and entrepreneurial management. Together, the three make up *innovation and entrepreneurship.*

The available strategies are reasonably clear, and there are only a few of them. But it is far less easy to be specific about entrepreneurial strategies than it is about purposeful innovation and entrepreneurial management. We know what the areas are in which innovative opportunities are to be found and how they are to be analyzed. There are correct policies and practices and wrong policies and practices to make an existing business or public-service institution capable of entrepreneurship; right things to do and wrong things to do in a new venture. But the entrepreneurial strategy that fits a certain innovation is a high-risk decision. Some entrepreneurial strategies are better fits in a given situation, for example, the strategy that I called entrepreneurial judo, which is the strategy of choice where the leading businesses in an industry persist year in and year out in the same habits of arrogance and false superiority. We can describe the typical advantages and the typical limitations of certain entrepreneurial strategies.

Above all, we know that an entrepreneurial strategy has more chance of success the more it starts out with the users—their utilities, their values, their realities. An innovation is a change in market or society. It produces a greater yield for the user, greater wealth-producing capacity for society, higher value or greater satisfaction. The test of an innovation is always what it does for the user. Hence, entrepreneurship always needs to be market-focused, indeed, market-driven.

Still, entrepreneurial strategy remains the decision-making area of entrepreneurship and therefore the risk-taking one. It is by no means hunch or gamble. But it also is not precisely science. Rather, it is judgment.

Conclusion:
The Entrepreneurial Society

I

"Every generation needs a new revolution," was Thomas Jefferson's conclusion toward the end of his long life. His contemporary, Goethe, the great German poet, though an arch-conservative, voiced the same sentiment when he sang in his old age:

> *Vernunft wird Unsinn*
> *Wohltat, Plage.* *

Both Jefferson and Goethe were expressing their generation's disenchantment with the legacy of Enlightenment and French Revolution. But they might just as well have reflected on our present-day legacy, 150 years later, of that great shining promise, the Welfare State, begun in Imperial Germany for the truly indigent and disabled, which has now become "everybody's entitlement" and an increasing burden on those who produce. Institutions, systems, policies eventually outlive themselves, as do products, processes, and services. They do it when they accomplish their objectives and they do it when they fail to accomplish their objectives. The mechanisms may still tick. But the assumptions on which they were designed have become invalid—as, for example, have the demographic assumptions on which health-care plans and retirement schemes were designed in all developed countries over the last hundred years. Then, indeed, reason becomes nonsense and boons afflictions.

Yet "revolutions," as we have learned since Jefferson's days, are not the remedy. They cannot be predicted, directed, or controlled. They

*Reason becomes nonsense, /Boons afflictions.

bring to power the wrong people. Worst of all, their results—predictably—are the exact opposite of their promises. Only a few years after
Jefferson's death in 1826, that great anatomist of government and politics, Alexis de Tocqueville, pointed out that revolutions do not demolish
the prisons of the old regime, they enlarge them. The most lasting
legacy of the French Revolution, Tocqueville proved, was the tighten-
ing of the very fetters of pre-Revolutionary France: the subjection of
the whole country to an uncontrolled and uncontrollable bureaucracy,
and the centralization in Paris of all political, intellectual, artistic, and
economic life. The main consequences of the Russian Revolution were
new serfdom for the tillers of the land, an omnipotent secret police, and
a rigid, corrupt, stifling bureaucracy—the very features of the czarist
regime against which Russian liberals and revolutionaries had protested
most loudly and with most justification. And the same must be said of
Mao's macabre "Great Cultural Revolution."

Indeed, we now know that "revolution" is a delusion, the pervasive
delusion of the nineteenth century, but today perhaps the most discredited of its myths. We now know that "revolution" is not achievement
and the new dawn. It results from senile decay, from the bankruptcy
of ideas and institutions, from failure of self-renewal.

And yet we also know that theories, values, and all the artifacts of
human minds and human hands do age and rigidify, becoming obsolete,
becoming "afflictions."

Innovation and entrepreneurship are thus needed in society as
much as in the economy, in public-service institutions as much as in
businesses. It is precisely because innovation and entrepreneurship are
not "root and branch" but "one step at a time," a product here, a policy
there, a public service yonder; because they are not planned but
focused on this opportunity and that need; because they are tentative
and will disappear if they do not produce the expected and needed
results; because, in other words, they are pragmatic rather than dogmatic and modest rather than grandiose—that they promise to keep
any society, economy, industry, public service, or business flexible and
self-renewing. They achieve what Jefferson hoped to achieve through
revolution in every generation, and they do so without bloodshed, civil
war, or concentration camps, without economic catastrophe, but with
purpose, with direction, and under control.

What we need is an entrepreneurial society in which innovation and
entrepreneurship are normal, steady, and continuous. Just as management has become the specific organ of all contemporary institutions,

and the integrating organ of our society of organizations, so innovation and entrepreneurship have to become an integral life-sustaining activity in our organizations, our economy, our society.

This requires of executives in all institutions that they make innovation and entrepreneurship a normal, ongoing, everyday activity, a practice in their own work and in that of their organization. To provide concepts and tools for this task is the purpose of this book.

II

WHAT WILL NOT WORK

The first priority in talking about the public policies and governmental measures needed in the entrepreneurial society is to define what will not work—especially as the policies that will not work are so popular today.

"Planning" as the term is commonly understood is actually incompatible with an entrepreneurial society and economy. Innovation does indeed need to be purposeful and entrepreneurship has to be managed. But innovation, almost by definition, has to be decentralized, *ad hoc*, autonomous, specific, and micro-economic. It had better start small, tentative, flexible. Indeed, the opportunities for innovation are found, on the whole, only way down and close to events. They are not to be found in the massive aggregates with which the planner deals of necessity, but in the deviations therefrom—in the unexpected, in the incongruity, in the difference between "The glass is half full" and "The glass is half empty," in the weak link in a process. By the time the deviation becomes "statistically significant" and thereby visible to the planner, it is too late. Innovative opportunities do not come with the tempest but with the rustling of the breeze.

It is popular today, especially in Europe, to believe that a country can have "high-tech entrepreneurship" by itself. France, West Germany, even England are basing national policies on this premise. But it is a delusion. Indeed, a policy that promotes high tech and high tech alone—and that otherwise is as hostile to entrepreneurship as France, West Germany, and even England still are—will not even produce high tech. All it can come up with is another expensive flop, another supersonic *Concorde*; a little *gloire*, oceans of red ink, but neither jobs nor technological leadership.

High tech in the first place—and this is, of course, one of the major premises of this book—is only one area of innovation and entrepreneurship. The great bulk of innovations lies in other areas. But also, a high-tech policy will run into political obstacles that will defeat it in short order. In terms of job creation, high tech is the maker of tomorrow rather than the maker of today. As we saw initially (in the Introduction), "high tech" in the United States created no more jobs in the period 1970–85 than "smokestack" lost: about five to six million. *All* the additional jobs in the American economy during that period—a total of 35 million—were created by new ventures that were not "high-tech" but "middle-tech," "low-tech," or "no-tech." The European countries, however, will be under increasing pressure to find additional jobs for a growing work force. And if then the focus in innovation and entrepreneurship is high-tech, the demand that governments abandon the high-tech policies which sacrifice the needs of today—the bolstering of the ailing industrial giants—to the uncertain promise of a high-tech future will become irresistible. In France this has been the issue over which the Communists pulled out of President Mitterand's cabinet in 1984, and the left wing of Mitterand's own Socialist Party is also increasingly unhappy and restless.

Above all, to have "high-tech" entrepreneurship alone without its being embedded in a broad entrepreneurial economy of "no-tech," "low-tech," and "middle-tech," is like having a mountaintop without the mountain. Even high-tech people in such a situation will not take jobs in new, risky, high-tech ventures. They will prefer the security of a job in the large, established, "safe" company or in a government agency. Of course, high-tech ventures need a great many people who are not themselves high-tech: accountants, salespeople, managers, and so on. In an economy that spurns entrepreneurship and innovation except for that tiny extravaganza, the "glamorous high-tech venture," those people will keep on looking for jobs and career opportunities where society and economy (i.e., their classmates, their parents, and their teachers) encourage them to look: in the large, "safe," established institution. Neither will distributors be willing to take on the products of the new venture, nor investors be willing to back it.

But the other innovative ventures are also needed to supply the capital that high tech requires. Knowledge-based innovation, and in particular high-tech innovation, has the longest lead time between investment and profitability. The world's computer industry did not break even until the late seventies, that is, after thirty loss years. To be sure, IBM made very good money quite early. And one after another of the "Seven Dwarfs," the smaller American computer makers, moved into the black during the late sixties. But these profits were offset several times over by the tremendous losses of all the others, and especially of the big old companies who failed totally in computers: General Electric, Westinghouse, ITT, and RCA in America; the (British) General Electric Company, Ferranti, and Plessey in Great Britain; Thomson-Houston in France; Siemens and Telefunken in Germany; Philips in Holland; and many others. History is repeating itself now in minicomputers and personal computers: it will be many years before the industry worldwide moves into the black. And the same thing is happening in biotechnology. This was also the pattern a hundred years ago in the electrical apparatus industry of the 1880s, for instance, or in the automobile industry of 1900 or 1910.

And during this long gestation period, non-high-tech ventures have to produce the profits to offset the losses of high tech and provide the needed capital.

The French are right, of course: economic and political strength these days requires a high-tech position, whether in information technology, in biology, or in automation. The French surely have the scientific and technical capacity. And yet it is most unlikely (I am tempted to say impossible) for any country to be innovative and entrepreneurial in high tech without having an entrepreneurial economy. High tech is indeed the leading edge, but there cannot be an edge without a knife. There cannot be a viable high-tech sector by itself any more than there can be a healthy brain in a dead body. There must be an economy full of innovators and entrepreneurs, with entrepreneurial vision and entrepreneurial values, with access to venture capital, and filled with entrepreneurial vigor.

III

THE SOCIAL INNOVATIONS NEEDED

There are two areas in which an entrepreneurial society requires substantial social innovation.

1. The first is a policy to take care of redundant workers. The numbers are not large. But blue-collar workers in "smokestack industries" are concentrated in a very few places; three-quarters of all American

automobile workers live in twenty counties, for instance. They are therefore highly visible, and they are highly organized. More important, they are ill equipped to place themselves, to redirect themselves, to move. They have neither education nor skill nor social competence —and above all not much self-confidence. They never applied for a job throughout their life; when they were ready to go to work, a relative already working in the automobile plant introduced them to the supervisor. Or the parish priest gave them a letter to one of his parishioners who was already working in the mill. And the "smokestack" workers in Great Britain—or the Welsh coal miners—are no different, nor are the blue-collar workers in Germany's Ruhr, in Lorraine, or in the Belgian Borinage. These workers are the one group in developed societies that have not experienced in this century a tremendous growth in education and horizon. In respect to competence, experience, skill, and schooling they are pretty much where the unskilled laborer of 1900 was. The one thing that has happened to them is an explosive rise in their incomes —on balance they are the highest-paid group in industrial society if wages and benefits are added together—and in political power as well. They therefore do not have enough capacity, whether as individuals or as a group, to help themselves, but more than enough power to oppose, to veto, to impede. Unless society takes care of placing them—if only in lower-paying jobs—they must become a purely negative force.

The problem is soluble if an economy becomes entrepreneurial. For then the new businesses of the entrepreneurial economy create new jobs, as has been happening in the United States during the last ten years (which explains why the massive unemployment in the old "smokestack industries" has caused so little political trouble so far in the United States and has not even triggered a massive protectionist reaction). But even if an entrepreneurial economy creates the new jobs, there is need for organized efforts to train and place the redundant former "smokestack" workers—they cannot do it by themselves. Otherwise redundant "smokestack" labor will increasingly oppose anything new, including even the means of their own salvation. The "mini-mill" offers jobs to redundant steel workers. The automated automobile plant is the most appropriate work place for displaced automobile workers. And yet both the "mini-mill" and automation in the car factory are bitterly fought by the present workers—even though they know that their own jobs will not last. Unless we can make innovation an opportunity for redundant workers in the "smokestack" industries their feeling of impotence, their fears, their sense of being caught will lead them to resist all innovation—as is already the case in Great Britain (or in the U.S. Postal Service). The job has been done before—by the Mitsui *Zaibatsu* of Japan in the sharp Japanese Depression after the Russo-Japanese war of 1906, by the Swedes after World War II in the deliberate policy which converted a country of subsistence farmers and forest workers into an industrialized and highly prosperous nation. And the numbers are, as already said, not very large—especially as we need not concern ourselves overmuch with the one-third of the group that is fifty-five years old and older and has available adequate early-retirement provisions, and with another third that is under thirty years of age and capable of moving and of placing themselves. But the policy to train and place the remaining one-third—a small but hard core—of displaced "smokestack" workers has yet to be worked out.

2. The other social innovation needed is both more radical and more difficult and unprecedented: to organize the systematic abandonment of outworn social policies and obsolete public-service institutions. This was not a problem in the last great entrepreneurial era; a hundred years ago there were few such policies and institutions. Now we have them in abundance. But by now we also know that few if any are for ever. Few of them even perform more than a fairly short time.

One of the fundamental changes in world view and perception of the last twenty years—a truly monumental turn—is the realization that governmental policies and agencies are of human rather than of divine origin, and that therefore the one thing certain about them is that they will become obsolete fairly fast. Yet politics is still based on the age-old assumption that whatever government does is grounded in the nature of human society and therefore "forever." As a result there is no political mechanism so far to slough off the old, the outworn, the no-longer-productive in government.

Or rather what we have is not working yet. In the United States there has lately been a rash of "sunset laws," which prescribe that a governmental agency or a public law lapse after a certain period of time unless specifically re-enacted. These laws have not worked, however— in part because there are no objective criteria as to when an agency or a law becomes dysfunctional; in part because there is so far no organized process of abandonment; but perhaps mostly because we have not yet learned to develop new or alternative methods for achieving what an ineffectual law or agency was originally supposed to achieve.

To develop both the principles and the process for making "sunset laws" meaningful and effective is one of the important social innovations ahead of us—and one that needs to be made soon. Our societies are ready for it.

IV

THE NEW TASKS

These two social policies needed are, however, only examples. Underlying them is the need for a massive reorientation in policies and attitudes, and above all, in priorities. We need to encourage habits of flexibility, of continuous learning, and of acceptance of change as normal and as opportunity—for institutions as well as for individuals.

Tax policy is one area—important both for its impact on behavior and as a symbol of society's values and priorities. In developed countries, sloughing off yesterday is at present severely penalized by the tax system. In the United States, for instance, the tax collector treats monies realized by selling or liquidating a business or a product line as income. Actually the amounts are, of course, repayments of capital. But under the present tax system the company pays corporation income tax on them. And if it distributes the proceeds to its shareholders, they pay full personal income tax on them as if they were ordinary "dividends"— that is, distribution of "profits." As a result businesses prefer not to abandon the old, the obsolescent, the no-longer-productive; they'd rather hang on to it and keep on pouring money into it. Worse still, they then assign their most capable people to "defending" the outworn in a massive misallocation of the scarcest and most valuable resource—the human resource that needs to be allocated to making tomorrow, if the company is to have a tomorrow. And when the company then finally liquidates or sells the old, obsolescent, no-longer-productive business or product line, it does not distribute the proceeds to the shareholders and does not therefore return them to the capital market where they become available for investment in innovative entrepreneurial opportunities. Rather the company keeps these funds and commonly invests them in its old, traditional, declining business or products—that is, into those parts of its operations and activities for which it could not easily raise money on the capital market—again resulting in a massive misallocation of scarce resources.

What is needed in an entrepreneurial society is a tax system that encourages moving capital from yesterday into tomorrow rather than one that, like our present one, prevents and penalizes it.

But we also should be able in and through the tax system to assuage the most pressing financial problem of the new and growing business: cash shortage. One way might be acceptance of economic reality: during the first five or six years of the life of a new, and particularly of a growing, business, "profits" are an accounting fiction. During these years the costs of staying in business are always—and almost by definition—larger for a new venture than the surplus from yesterday's operations (that is, the excess of current income over yesterday's costs). This means in effect that a new and growing venture always has to invest every penny of operating surplus to stay alive; usually, especially if growing fast, it has to invest a good deal more than it can possibly hope to produce as "current surplus" (that is, as "profit") in its current accounts. For the first few years of its life the new and growing venture —whether standing by itself or part of an existing enterprise—should therefore be exempt from income taxes, for the same reason for which we do not expect a small and rapidly growing child to produce a "surplus" that supports a grown-up. And taxes are the means by which a producer supports somebody else—namely, a nonproducer. By the way, exempting the new venture from taxation until it has "grown up" would almost certainly in the end produce a substantially higher tax yield.

If this, however, is deemed too "radical," the new venture should at least be able to postpone paying taxes on the so-called profits of its infant years. It should be able to retain the cash until it is past the period of acute cash-flow pressure, and to do so without penalty or interest charges.

All together, an entrepreneurial society and economy require tax policies that encourage the formation of capital.

Surely one "secret" of the Japanese is their officially encouraged "tax evasion" on capital formation. Legally a Japanese adult is allowed *one* medium-sized savings account the interest on which is tax-exempt. Actually Japan has five times as many such accounts as there are people in the country, children and minors included. This is, of course, a "scandal" against which newspapers and politicians rail regularly. But the Japanese are very careful not to *do* anything to "stop the abuse." As a result they have the world's highest rate of capital formation. This may be considered too circuitous a way to escape the dilemma of modern society: the conflict between the need for capital formation at a high rate and the popular condemnation of interest and dividends as "unearned income" and "capitalist," if not as sinful and wicked. But one way or another any country that wants to remain competitive in an entrepreneurial era will have to develop tax policies which do what the Japanese do by means of semi-official hypocrisy: encourage capital formation.

Just as important as tax and fiscal policies that encourage entrepreneurship—or at least do not penalize it—is protection of the new venture against the growing burden of governmental regulations, restrictions, reports, and paperwork. My own prescription, though I have no illusion of its ever being accepted, would be to allow the new venture, whether an independent enterprise or part of an existing one, to charge the government for the costs of regulations, reports, and paperwork that exceed a certain proportion (say 5 percent) of the new venture's gross revenues. This would be particularly helpful to new ventures in the public-service sector—for example, a freestanding clinic for ambulatory surgery. In developed countries public-service institutions are even more heavily burdened by governmental red tape, and even more loaded down with doing chores for the government than are businesses. And they are even less able, as a rule, to shoulder the burden whether in money or in people.

Such a policy, by the way, would be the best—perhaps the only—remedy for that dangerous and insidious disease of developed countries: the steady growth in the invisible cost of government. It is a real cost in money and, even more, in capable people, their time, and their efforts. The cost is invisible, however, since it does not show in governmental budgets but is hidden in the accounts of the physician whose nurse spends half her time filling out governmental forms and reports, in the budget of the university where sixteen high-level administrators work on "compliance" with governmental mandates and regulations, or in the profit-and-loss statement of the small business nineteen of whose 275 employees, while being paid by the company, actually work as tax collectors for the government, deducting taxes and Social Security contributions from the pay of their fellow workers, collecting tax-identification numbers of suppliers and customers and reporting them to the government, or, as in Europe, collecting value-added-tax (VAT).

And these invisible governmental overheads are totally unproductive. Does anyone, for instance, believe that tax accountants contribute to national wealth or to productivity, and altogether add to society's well-being, whether material, physical or spiritual? And yet in every developed country government mandates misallocation of a steadily growing portion of our scarcest resource, able, diligent, trained people, to such essentially sterile pursuits.

It may be too much to hope that we can arrest—let alone excise—the cancer of government's invisible costs. But at least we should be able to protect the new entrepreneurial venture against it.

We need to learn to ask in respect to any proposed new governmental policy or measure: Does it further society's ability to innovate? Does it promote social and economic flexibility? Or does it impede and penalize innovation and entrepreneurship? To be sure, impact on society's ability to innovate cannot and should not be the determining, let alone the sole criterion. But it needs to be taken into consideration before a new policy or a new measure is enacted—and today it is not taken into account in any country (except perhaps in Japan) or by any policy maker.

V

THE INDIVIDUAL IN ENTREPRENEURIAL SOCIETY

In an entrepreneurial society individuals face a tremendous challenge, a challenge they need to exploit as an opportunity: the need for continuous learning and relearning.

In traditional society it could be assumed—and was assumed—that learning came to an end with adolescence or, at the latest, with adulthood. What one had not learned by age twenty-one or so, one would never learn. But also what one had learned by age twenty-one or so one would apply, unchanged, the rest of one's life. On these assumptions traditional apprenticeship was based, traditional crafts, traditional professions, but also the traditional systems of education and the schools. Crafts, professions, systems of education, and schools are still, by and large, based on these assumptions. There were, of course, always exceptions, some groups that practiced continuous learning and relearning: the great artists and the great scholars, Zen monks, mystics, the Jesuits. But these exceptions were so few that they could safely be ignored.

In an entrepreneurial society, however, these "exceptions" become the exemplars. The correct assumption in an entrepreneurial society is that individuals will have to learn new things well after they have become adults—and maybe more than once. The correct assumption is that what individuals have learned by age twenty-one will begin to become obsolete five to ten years later and will have to be replaced—or at least refurbished—by new learning, new skills, new knowledge.

One implication of this is that individuals will increasingly have to take responsibility for their own continuous learning and relearning, for their own self-development and for their own careers. They can no longer assume that what they have learned as children and youngsters will be the "foundation" for the rest of their lives. It will be the "launching pad"—the place to take off from rather than the place to build on and to rest on. They can no longer assume that they "enter upon a career" which then proceeds along a pre-determined, well-mapped and well-lighted "career path" to a known destination—what the American military calls "progressing in grade." The assumption from now on has to be that individuals on their own will have to find, determine, and develop a number of "careers" during their working lives.

And the more highly schooled the individuals, the more entrepreneurial their careers and the more demanding their learning challenges. The carpenter can still assume, perhaps, that the skills he acquired as apprentice and journeyman will serve him forty years later. Physicians, engineers, metallurgists, chemists, accountants, lawyers, teachers, managers had better assume that the skills, knowledges, and tools they will have to master and apply fifteen years hence are going to be different and new. Indeed they better assume that fifteen years hence they will be doing new and quite different things, will have new and different goals and, indeed, in many cases, different "careers." And only they themselves can take responsibility for the necessary learning and relearning, and for directing themselves. Tradition, convention, and "corporate policy" will be a hindrance rather than a help.

This also means that an entrepreneurial society challenges habits and assumptions of schooling and learning. The educational systems the world over are in the main extensions of what Europe developed in the seventeenth-century. There have been substantial additions and modifications. But the basic architectural plan on which our schools and universities are built goes back three hundred years and more. Now new, in some cases radically new, thinking and new, in some cases radically new, approaches are required, and on all levels. Using computers in preschool may turn out to be a passing fad. But four-year-olds exposed to television expect, demand, and respond to very different pedagogy than four-year-olds did fifty years ago. Young people headed for a "profession"—that is, four-fifths of today's college students—do need a "liberal education." But that clearly means something quite different from the nineteenth-century version of the seventeenth-century curriculum that passed for a "liberal education" in the English-speaking world or for *"Allgemeine Bildung"* in Germany. If this challenge is not faced up to, we risk losing the fundamental concept of a "liberal education" altogether and will descend into the purely vocational, purely specialized, which would endanger the educational foundation of the community and, in the end, community itself. But also educators will have to accept that schooling is not for the young only and that the greatest challenge—but also the greatest opportunity—for the school is the continuing relearning of already highly schooled adults.

So far we have no educational theory for these tasks. So far we have no one who does what, in the seventeenth century, the great Czech educational reformer Johann Comenius did or what the Jesuit educators did when they developed what to this day is the "modern" school and the "modern" university. But in the United States, at least, practice is far ahead of theory. To me the most positive development in the last twenty years, and the most encouraging one, is the ferment of educational experimentation in the United States—a happy by-product of the absence of a "Ministry of Education"—in respect to the continuing learning and relearning of adults, and especially of highly schooled professionals. Without a "master plan," without "educational philosophy," and, indeed, without much support from the educational establishment, the continuing education and professional development of already highly educated and highly achieving adults has become the true "growth industry" in the United States in the last twenty years.

The emergence of the entrepreneurial society may be a major turning point in history.

A hundred years ago, the worldwide panic of 1873 terminated the Century of Laissez-Faire that had begun with the publication of Adam

Smith's *The Wealth of Nations* in 1776. In the Panic of 1873 the modern welfare state was born. A hundred years later it had run its course, almost everyone now knows. It may survive despite the demographic challenges of an aging population and a shrinking birthrate. But it will survive only if the entrepreneurial economy succeeds in greatly raising productivities. We may even still make a few minor additions to the welfare edifice, put on a room here or a new benefit there. But the welfare state is past rather than future—as even the old liberals now know.

Will its successor be the Entrepreneurial Society?

Suggested Readings

Most of the literature on entrepreneurship is anecdotal and of the "Look, Ma, no hands" variety. The best of that genre may be the book by George Gilder: *The Spirit of Enterprise* (New York: Simon & Schuster, 1984). It consists mainly of stories of individuals who have founded new businesses; there is little discussion of what one can learn from their example. The book limits itself to new small businesses and omits discussion of entrepreneurship in both the existing business and the public-service institution. But at least Gilder does not make the mistake of confining entrepreneurship to high tech.

Far more useful to the entrepreneur—and to those who want to understand entrepreneurship—are the studies by Karl H. Vesper of the University of Washington in Seattle, Washington, especially his *New Venture Strategy* (Englewood Cliffs, N.J.: Prentice-Hall, 1980), and his annual publication, *Frontiers of Entrepreneurship Research* (Babson Park, Mass.: Babson College). Vesper, too, confines himself to the new and especially to the small business. But within these limits, his stimulating works are full of insights and practical wisdom.

The Center for Entrepreneurial Management (83 Spring Street, New York, N.Y. 10012), founded and directed by Joseph R. Mancuso, focuses entirely on "How to Do It" in the small business, as does Mancuso's well-known text *How to Start, Finance and Manage Your Own Small Business* (Englewood Cliffs, N.J.: Prentice-Hall, 1978).

Entrepreneurial management in the existing and especially in the large business is the subject of two very different books that complement each other. Andrew S. Grove, one of the founders and now the president of Intel Corporation, discusses the policies and practices needed to maintain entrepreneurship in the business that has grown fast and to large size in his *High-Output Management* (New York: Random House, 1983). Rosabeth M. Canter, an organizational psycholo-

517

gist at Yale University, discusses the attitudes and behavior of corporate leaders in entrepreneurial companies in her book *The Change Masters* (New York: Simon & Schuster, 1983). By far the most penetrating discussion of entrepreneurship in existing businesses is the almost inaccessible article by two members of the consulting firm of McKinsey & Company, Richard E. Cavenaugh and Donald K. Clifford, Jr.: "Lessons from America's Mid-Sized Growth Companies," *McKinsey Quarterly* (Autumn 1983). Publication of a book by the same authors, based on the article and the study on which it reports, is expected in 1985 or 1986.

Of the many books on strategy, the most useful may be Michael Porter's *Competitive Strategies* (New York: Free Press, 1980).

In my own earlier works, entrepreneurship and entrepreneurial management are discussed in *Managing for Results* (New York: Harper & Row, 1964), especially Chapters 1–5, and in *Management: Tasks, Responsibilities, Practices* (New York: Harper & Row, 1973), Chapters 11–14 (The Service Institution) and Chapters 53–61 (Strategies and Structures).

THE EFFECTIVE
EXECUTIVE

Contents

Preface

Management books usually deal with managing other people. The subject of this book is managing oneself for effectiveness. That one can truly manage other people is by no means adequately proven. But one can always manage oneself. Indeed, executives who do not manage themselves for effectiveness cannot possibly expect to manage their associates and subordinates. Management is largely by example. Executives who do not know how to make themselves effective in their own job and work set the wrong example.

To be reasonably effective it is not enough for the individual to be intelligent, to work hard or to be knowledgeable. Effectiveness is something separate, something different. But to be effective also does not require special gifts, special aptitude, or special training. Effectiveness as an executive demands *doing* certain—and fairly simple—things. It consists of a small number of practices, the practices that are presented and discussed in this book. But these practices are not "inborn." In forty-five years of work as a consultant with a large number of executives in a wide variety of organizations—large and small; businesses, government agencies, labor unions, hospitals, universities, community services; American, European, Latin American and Japanese—I have not come across a single "natural": an executive who was born effective. All the effective ones have had to learn to be effective. And all of them then had to practice effectiveness until it became habit. But all the ones who worked on making themselves effective executives succeeded in doing so. Effectiveness can be learned—and it also *has* to be learned.

Effectiveness is what executives are being paid for, whether they work as managers who are responsible for the performance of others as well as their own, or as individual professional contributors responsible for their own performance only. Without effectiveness there is no "performance," no matter how much intelligence and knowledge goes into the work, no matter how many hours it takes. Yet it is perhaps not too surprising that we have so far paid little attention to the effective executive. Organizations—whether business enterprises, large government agencies, labor unions, large hospitals or large universities—are, after all, brand new. A century ago almost no one had even much contact with such organizations beyond an occasional trip to the local post office to mail a letter. And effectiveness as an executive means effectiveness in and through an organization. Until recently there was little reason for anyone to pay much attention to the effective executive or to worry about the low effectiveness of so many of them. Now, however, most people—especially those with even a fair amount of schooling—can expect to spend all their working lives in an organization of some kind. Society has become a society of organizations in all developed countries. Now the effectiveness of the individual depends increasingly on his or her ability to be effective in an organization, to be effective as an executive. And the effectiveness of a modern society and its ability to perform—perhaps even its ability to survive—depend increasingly on the effectiveness of the people who work as executives in the organizations. The effective executive is fast becoming a key resource for society, and effectiveness as an executive a prime requirement for individual accomplishment and achievement—for young people at the beginning of their working lives fully as much as for people in mid-career.

Claremont, California   Peter F. Drucker
New Year's Day, 1985

1: Effectiveness Can Be Learned

To be effective is the job of the executive. "To effect" and "to execute" are, after all, near-synonyms. Whether he works in a business or in a hospital, in a government agency or in a labor union, in a university or in the army, the executive is, first of all, expected to *get the right things done*. And this is simply that he is expected to be effective.

Yet men of high effectiveness are conspicuous by their absence in executive jobs. High intelligence is common enough among executives. Imagination is far from rare. The level of knowledge tends to be high. But there seems to be little correlation between a man's effectiveness and his intelligence, his imagination or his knowledge. Brilliant men are often strikingly ineffectual; they fail to realize that the brilliant insight is not by itself achievement. They never have learned that insights become effectiveness only through hard systematic work. Conversely, in every organization there are some highly effective plodders. While others rush around in the frenzy and busyness which very bright people so often confuse with "creativity," the plodder puts one foot in front of the other and gets there first, like the tortoise in the old fable.

Intelligence, imagination, and knowledge are essential resources, but only effectiveness converts them into results. By
themselves, they only set limits to what can be attained.

WHY WE NEED EFFECTIVE EXECUTIVES

All this should be obvious. But why then has so little attention been paid to effectiveness, in an age in which there are
mountains of books and articles on every other aspect of the
executive's tasks?

One reason for this neglect is that effectiveness is the specific
technology of the knowledge worker within an organization.
Until recently, there was no more than a handful of these
around.

For manual work, we need only efficiency; that is, the ability
to do things right rather than the ability to get the right things
done. The manual worker can always be judged in terms of
the quantity and quality of a definable and discrete output,
such as a pair of shoes. We have learned how to measure efficiency and how to define quality in manual work during the last
hundred years—to the point where we have been able to multiply the output of the individual worker tremendously.

Formerly, the manual worker—whether machine operator
or front-line soldier—predominated in all organizations. Few
people of effectiveness were needed: those at the top who gave
the orders that others carried out. They were so small a fraction
of the total work population that we could, rightly or wrongly,
take their effectiveness for granted. We could depend on the
supply of "naturals," the few people in any area of human
endeavor who somehow know what the rest of us have to learn
the hard way.

■ This was true not only of business and the army. It is hard to
realize today that "government" during the American Civil
War a hundred years ago meant the merest handful of
people. Lincoln's Secretary of War had fewer than fifty

civilian subordinates, most of them not "executives" and policy-makers but telegraph clerks. The entire Washington establishment of the U.S. government in Theodore Roosevelt's time, around 1900, could be comfortably housed in any one of the government buildings along the Mall today.

The hospital of yesterday did not know any of the "health-service professionals," the X-ray and lab technicians, the dieticians and therapists, the social workers, and so on, of whom it now employs as many as two hundred and fifty for every one hundred patients. Apart from a few nurses, there were only cleaning women, cooks and maids. The physician was the knowledge worker, with the nurse as his aide.

In other words, up to recent times, the major problem of organization was efficiency in the performance of the manual worker who did what he had been told to do. Knowledge workers were not predominant in organization.

In fact, only a small fraction of the knowledge workers of earlier days were part of an organization. Most of them worked by themselves as professionals, at best with a clerk. Their effectiveness or lack of effectiveness concerned only themselves and affected only themselves.

Today, however, the large knowledge organization is the central reality. Modern society is a society of large organized institutions. In every one of them, including the armed services, the center of gravity has shifted to the knowledge worker, the man who puts to work what he has between his ears rather than the brawn of his muscles or the skill of his hands. Increasingly, the majority of people who have been schooled to use knowledge, theory, and concept rather than physical force or manual skill work in an organization and are effective insofar as they can make a contribution to the organization.

Now effectiveness can no longer be taken for granted. Now it can no longer be neglected.

The imposing system of measurements and tests which we have developed for manual work—from industrial engineering to quality control—is not applicable to knowledge work. There are few things less pleasing to the Lord, and less productive, than an engineering department that rapidly turns out beautiful blueprints for the wrong product. Working on the *right* things is what makes knowledge work effective. This is not capable of being measured by any of the yardsticks for manual work.

The knowledge worker cannot be supervised closely or in detail. He can only be helped. But he must direct himself, and he must direct himself toward performance and contribution, that is, toward effectiveness.

■ A cartoon in *The New Yorker* magazine some time ago showed an office on the door of which was the legend: CHAS. SMITH, GENERAL SALES MANAGER, AJAX SOAP COMPANY. The walls were bare except for a big sign saying THINK. The man in the office had his feet propped up on his desk and was blowing smoke rings at the ceiling. Outside two older men went by, the one saying to the other: "But how can we be sure that Smith thinks soap?"

One can indeed never be sure what the knowledge worker thinks—and yet thinking is his specific work; it is his "doing."

The motivation of the knowledge worker depends on his being effective, on his being able to achieve.* If effectiveness is lacking in his work, his commitment to work and to contribution will soon wither, and he will become a time-server going through the motions from 9 to 5.

The knowledge worker does not produce something that is effective by itself. He does not produce a physical product —a ditch, a pair of shoes, a machine part. He produces knowledge, ideas, information. By themselves these "products" are useless. Somebody else, another man of knowledge, has to take them as his input and convert them into his output before

---

* This is brought out in all studies, especially in three empirical works: Frederick Herzberg (with B. Mauser and B. Snyderman), *The Motivation to Work* (New York, Wiley, 1959); David C. McClellan, *The Achieving Society* (Princeton, N.J., Van Nostrand, 1961); and Frederick Herzberg, *Work and the Nature of Man* (Cleveland, World, 1966).

they have any reality. The greatest wisdom not applied to action and behavior is meaningless data. The knowledge worker, therefore, must do something which a manual worker need not do. He must provide effectiveness. He cannot depend on the utility his output carries with it as does a well-made pair of shoes.

The knowledge worker is the one "factor of production" through which the highly developed societies and economies of today—the United States, Western Europe, Japan, and also increasingly, the Soviet Union—become and remain competitive.

■ This is particularly true of the United States. The only resource in respect to which America can possibly have a competitive advantage is education. American education may leave a good deal to be desired, but it is massive beyond anything poorer societies can afford. For education is the most expensive capital investment we have ever known. A Ph.D. in the natural sciences represents $100,000 to $200,-000 of social capital investment. Even the boy who graduates from college without any specific professional competence represents an investment of $50,000 or more. This only a very rich society can afford.

Education is the one area, therefore, in which the richest of all societies, the United States, has a genuine advantage —provided it can make the knowledge worker productive. And productivity for the knowledge worker means the ability to get the right things done. It means effectiveness.

WHO IS AN EXECUTIVE?

Every knowledge worker in modern organization is an "executive" if, by virtue of his position or knowledge, he is responsible for a contribution that materially affects the capacity of the organization to perform and to obtain results. This may be the capacity of a business to bring out a new product or to obtain a larger share of a given market. It may be the capacity of a hospital to provide bedside care to its patients, and so on. Such a man (or woman) must make decisions; he cannot just carry out orders. He must take responsibility for his contribution. And he is supposed, by virtue of his knowledge, to be better equipped to make the right decision than anyone else. He may be overridden; he may be demoted or fired. But so long as he has the job the goals, the standards, and the contribution are in his keeping.

Most managers are executives—though not all. But many nonmanagers are also becoming executives in modern society. For the knowledge organization, as we have been learning these last few years, needs *both* "managers" and "individual professional contributors" in positions of responsibility, decision-making, and authority.

This fact is perhaps best illustrated by a recent newspaper interview with a young American infantry captain in the Vietnam jungle.

- Asked by the reporter, "How in this confused situation can you retain command?" the young captain said: "Around here, I am only the guy who is responsible. If these men don't know what to do when they run into an enemy in the jungle, I'm too far away to tell them. My job is to make sure they know. What they do depends on the situation which only they can judge. The responsibility is always mine, but the decision lies with whoever is on the spot."

In a guerrilla war, every man is an "executive."

There are many managers who are not executives. Many people, in other words, are superiors of other people—and often of fairly large numbers of other people—and still do not seriously affect the ability of the organization to perform. Most foremen in a manufacturing plant belong here. They are "overseers" in the literal sense of the word. They are "managers" in that they manage the work of others. But they have neither the responsibility for, nor authority over, the direction, the content, and the quality of the work or the methods of its performance. They can still be measured and appraised very largely in terms of efficiency and quality, and by the yardsticks we have developed to measure and appraise the work and performance of the manual worker.

Conversely, whether a knowledge worker is an executive does not depend on whether he manages people or not. In one business, the market research man may have a staff of two hundred people, whereas the market research man of the closest competitor is all by himself and has only a secretary for his staff. This should make little difference in the contribution expected of the two men. It is an administrative detail. Two hundred people, of course, can do a great deal more work than one man. But it does not follow that they produce and contribute more.

Knowledge work is not defined by quantity. Neither is knowledge work defined by its costs. Knowledge work is defined by its results. And for these, the size of the group and the magnitude of the managerial job are not even symptoms.

Having many people working in market research may endow the results with that increment of insight, imagination, and quality that gives a company the potential of rapid growth and success. If so, two hundred men are cheap. But it is just as likely that the manager will be overwhelmed by all the problems two hundred men bring to their work and cause through their interactions. He may be so busy "managing" as to have no time for market research and for fundamental decisions. He may be so busy checking figures that he never asks the question: "What do we really mean when we say "our market"? And as a result, he may fail to notice significant changes in the market which eventually may cause the downfall of his company.

But the individual market researcher without a staff may be equally productive or unproductive. He may be the source of the knowledge and vision that make his company prosper. Or he may spend so much of his time hunting down details—the footnotes academicians so often mistake for research—as to see and hear nothing and to think even less.

Throughout every one of our knowledge organizations, we have people who manage no one and yet are executives. Rarely indeed do we find a situation such as that in the Vietnam jungle, where at any moment, any member of the entire group may be called upon to make decisions with life-and-death impact for the whole. But the chemist in the research laboratory who decides to follow one line of inquiry rather than another one may make the entrepreneurial decision that determines the future of his company. He may be the research director. But he also may be—and often is—a chemist with no managerial responsibilities, if not even a fairly junior man. Similarly, the decision what to consider one "product" in the account books may be made by a senior vice-president in the company.* It may also be made by a junior. And this holds true in all areas of today's large organization.

I have called "executives" those knowledge workers, managers, or individual professionals who are expected by virtue of their position or their knowledge to make decisions in the normal course of their work that have significant impact on the performance and results of the whole. They are by no means a majority of the knowledge workers. For in knowledge work too, as in all other areas, there is unskilled work and routine. But they are a much larger proportion of the total knowledge work force than any organization chart ever reveals.

This is beginning to be realized—as witness the many attempts to provide parallel ladders of recognition and reward for managers and for individual professional contributors.† What few yet realize, however, is how many people there are even in the most humdrum organization of today, whether business or government agency, research lab or hospital, who

* On this see my *Managing for Results* (New York, Harper & Row, 1964)—especially chap. 2.

† The best statement I know was made by Frederick R. Kappel, the head of the American Telephone & Telegraph Company (The Bell Telephone System) at the XIII*th* International Management Congress in New York, September 1963. Mr. Kappel's main points are quoted in chap. 14 of *Managing for Results*.

have to make decisions of significant and irreversible impact. For the authority of knowledge is surely as legitimate as the authority of position. These decisions, moreover, are of the same *kind* as the decisions of top management. (This was the main point Mr. Kappel was making in the statement referred to above.)

The most subordinate manager, we now know, may do the same kind of work as the president of the company or the administrator of the government agency; that is, plan, organize, integrate, motivate, and measure. His compass may be quite limited, but within his sphere, he is an executive.

Similarly, every decision-maker does the same kind of work as the company president or the administrator. His scope may be quite limited. But he is an executive even if his function or his name appears neither on the organization chart nor in the internal telephone directory.

And whether chief executive or beginner, he needs to be effective.

Many of the examples used in this book are taken from the work and experience of chief executives—in government, army, hospitals, business, and so on. The main reason is that these are accessible, are indeed often on the public record. Also big things are more easily analyzed and seen than small ones.

But this book itself is not a book on what people at the top do or should do. It is addressed to everyone who, as a knowledge worker, is responsible for actions and decisions which are meant to contribute to the performance capacity of his organization. It is meant for every one of the men I call "executives."

EXECUTIVE REALITIES

The realities of the executive's situation both demand effectiveness from him and make effectiveness exceedingly difficult to achieve. Indeed, unless executives work at becoming effective, the realities of their situation will push them into futility.

Take a quick look at the realities of a knowledge worker *outside* an organization to see the problem. A physician has by and large no problem of effectiveness. The patient who walks into his office brings with him everything to make the physician's knowledge effective. During the time he is with the patient, the doctor can, as a rule, devote himself to the patient. He can keep interruptions to a minimum. The contribution the physician is expected to make is clear. What is important, and what is not, is determined by whatever ails the patient. The patient's complaints establish the doctor's priorities. And the goal, the objective, is given: It is to restore the patient to health or at least to make him more comfortable. Physicians are not noted for their capacity to organize themselves and their work. But few of them have much trouble being effective.

The executive in organization is in an entirely different position. In his situation there are four major realities over which he has essentially no control. Every one of them is built into organization and into the executive's day and work. He has no choice but to "cooperate with the inevitable." But every one of these realities exerts pressure toward nonresults and nonperformance.

1. The executive's time tends to belong to everybody else. If one attempted to define an "executive" operationally (that is, through his activities) one would have to define him as a captive of the organization. Everybody can move in on his time, and everybody does. There seems to be very little any one executive can do about it. He cannot, as a rule, like the physician, stick his head out the door and say to the nurse, "I won't see anybody for the next half hour." Just at this moment, the executive's telephone rings, and he has to speak to the com-

pany's best customer or to a high official in the city administration or to his boss—and the next half hour is already gone.*

2. Executives are forced to keep on "operating" unless they take positive action to change the reality in which they live and work.

In the United States, the complaint is common that the company president—or any other senior officer—still continues to run marketing or the plant, even though he is now in charge of the whole business and should be giving his time to its direction. This is sometimes blamed on the fact that American executives graduate, as a rule, out of functional work and operations, and cannot slough off the habits of a lifetime when they get into general management. But exactly the same complaint can be heard in countries where the career ladder is quite different. In the Germanic countries, for instance, a common route into top management has been from a central secretariat, where one works all along as a "generalist." Yet in German, Swedish, or Dutch companies top management people are criticized just as much for "operating" as in the United States. Nor, when one looks at organizations, is this tendency confined to the top; it pervades the entire executive group. There must be a reason for this tendency to "operate" other than career ladders or even the general perversity of human nature.

The fundamental problem is the reality around the executive. Unless he changes it by deliberate action, the flow of events will determine what he is concerned with and what he does.

* This comes out clearly in Sune Carlson's *Executive Behavior* (Stockholm, Strombergs, 1951), the one study of top management in large corporations which actually recorded the time-use of senior executives. Even the most effective executives in Professor Carlson's study found most of their time taken up with the demands of others and for purposes which added little if anything to their effectiveness. In fact, executives might well be defined as people who normally have no time of their own, because their time is always pre-empted by matters of importance to somebody else.

Depending on the flow of events is appropriate for the physician. The doctor who looks up when a patient comes in and says: "Why are you here today?" expects the patient to tell him what is relevant. When the patient says, "Doctor, I can't sleep. I haven't been able to go to sleep the last three weeks," he is telling the doctor what the priority area is. Even if the doctor decides, upon closer examination, that the sleeplessness is a fairly minor symptom of a much more fundamental condition he will do something to help the patient to get a few good nights' rest.

But events rarely tell the executive anything, let alone the real problem. For the doctor, the patient's complaint is central because it is central to the patient. The executive is concerned with a much more complex universe. What events are important and relevant and what events are merely distractions the events themselves do not indicate. They are not even symptoms in the sense in which the patient's narrative is a clue for the physician.

If the executive lets the flow of events determine what he does, what he works on, and what he takes seriously, he will fritter himself away "operating." He may be an excellent man. But he is certain to waste his knowledge and ability and to throw away what little effectiveness he might have achieved. What the executive needs are criteria which enable him to work on the truly important, that is, on contributions and results, even though the criteria are not found in the flow of events.

3. The third reality pushing the executive toward ineffectiveness is that he is within an *organization*. This means that he is effective only if and when other people make use of what he contributes. Organization is a means of multiplying the strength of an individual. It takes his knowledge and uses it as the resource, the motivation, and the vision of other knowledge workers. Knowledge workers are rarely in phase with each other, precisely because they are knowledge workers. Each

has his own skill and his own concerns. One man may be interested in tax accounting or in bacteriology, or in training and developing tomorrow's key administrators in the city government. But the fellow next door is interested in the finer points of cost accounting, in hospital economics, or in the legalities of the city charter. Each has to be able to use what the other produces.

Usually the people who are most important to the effectiveness of an executive are not people over whom he has direct control. They are people in other areas, people who in terms of organization, are "sideways." Or they are his superiors. Unless the executive can reach these people, can make his contribution effective for them and in their work, he has no effectiveness at all.

4. Finally, the executive is *within* an organization.

Every executive, whether his organization is a business or a research laboratory, a government agency, a large university, or the air force, sees the inside—the organization—as close and immediate reality. He sees the outside only through thick and distorting lenses, if at all. What goes on outside is usually not even known firsthand. It is received through an organizational filter of reports, that is, in an already predigested and highly abstract form that imposes organizational criteria of relevance on the outside reality.

But the organization is an abstraction. Mathematically, it would have to be represented as a point—that is, as having neither size nor extension. Even the largest organization is unreal compared to the reality of the environment in which it exists.

Specifically, there are no results within the organization. All the results are on the outside. The only business results, for instance, are produced by a customer who converts the costs and efforts of the business into revenues and profits through his willingness to exchange his purchasing power for the products or services of the business. The customer may make his decisions as a consumer on the basis of market considerations of supply and demand, or as a socialist government which regulates supply and demand on the basis of essentially noneconomic value preferences. In either case the decision-maker is outside rather than inside the business.

Similarly, a hospital has results only in respect to the patient. But the patient is not a member of the hospital organization. For the patient, the hospital is "real" only while he stays there. His greatest desire is to go back to the "nonhospital" world as fast as possible.

What happens inside any organization is effort and cost. To speak of "profit centers" in a business as we are wont to do is polite euphemism. There are only effort centers. The less an organization has to do to produce results, the better it does its job. That it takes 100,000 employees to produce the automobiles or the steel the market wants is essentially a gross engineering imperfection. The fewer people, the smaller, the less activity inside, the more nearly perfect is the organization in terms of its only reason for existence: the service to the environment.

This outside, this environment which is the true reality, is well beyond effective control from the inside. At the most, results are codetermined, as for instance in warfare, where the outcome is the result of the actions and decisions of both armies. In a business, there can be attempts to mold the customers' preferences and values through promotion and advertising. Except in an extreme shortage situation such as a war economy, the customer still has the final word and the effective veto power (which explains why every Communist economy has run into trouble as soon as it moved beyond extreme shortages and long before it reached a position of adequate market supply in which the customer, rather than the political authorities, makes the real and final decisions). But it is the inside of the organization that is most visible to the executive. It is the inside that has immediacy for him. Its relations and contacts, its problems and challenges, its crosscurrents and gossip reach him and touch him at every point. Unless he makes special efforts to gain direct access to outside reality, he will become increasingly inside-focused. The higher up in the organization he goes, the more will his attention be drawn to problems and challenges of the inside rather than to events on the outside.

- An organization, a social artifact, is very different from a biological organism. Yet it stands under the law that governs the structure and size of animals and plants: The surface goes up with the square of the radius, but the mass grows with the cube. The larger the animal becomes, the more resources have to be devoted to the mass and to the internal tasks, to circulation and information, to the nervous system, and so on.

  Every part of an amoeba is in constant, direct contact with the environment. It therefore needs no special organs to perceive its environment or to hold it together. But a large and complex animal such as man needs a skeleton to hold it together. It needs all kinds of specialized organs for ingestion and digestion, for respiration and exhalation, for carrying oxygen to the tissues, for reproduction, and so on. Above all, a man needs a brain and a number of complex nervous systems. Most of the mass of the amoeba is directly concerned with survival and procreation. Most of the mass of the higher animal—its resources, its food, its energy supply, its tissues—serve to overcome and offset the complexity of the structure and the isolation from the outside.

An organization is not, like an animal, an end in itself, and successful by the mere act of perpetuating the species. An organization is an organ of society and fulfills itself by the contribution it makes to the outside environment. And yet the bigger and apparently more successful an organization gets to be, the more will inside events tend to engage the interests, the energies, and the abilities of the executive to the exclusion of his real tasks and his real effectiveness in the outside.

This danger is being aggravated today by the advent of the computer and of the new information technology. The computer, being a mechanical moron, can handle only quantifiable data. These it can handle with speed, accuracy, and precision. It will, therefore, grind out hitherto unobtainable quantified information in large volume. One can, however, by and large quantify only what goes on inside an organization—costs and production figures, patient statistics in the hospital, or training reports. The relevant outside events are rarely available in quantifiable form until it is much too late to do anything about them.

This is not because our information-gathering capacity in respect to the outside events lags behind the technical abilities of the computer. If this were the only thing to worry about, we would just have to increase statistical efforts—and the computer itself could greatly help us to overcome this mechanical limitation. The problem is rather that the important and relevant outside events are often qualitative and not capable of quantification. They are not yet "facts." For a fact, after all, is an event which somebody has defined, has classified and, above all, has endowed with relevance. To be able to quantify one has to have a concept first. One first has to abstract from the infinite welter of phenomena a specific aspect which one then can name and finally count.

■ The thalidomide tragedy which led to the birth of so many deformed babies is a case in point. By the time doctors on the European continent had enough statistics to realize that the number of deformed babies born was significantly larger than normal—so much larger that there had to be a specific and new cause—the damage had been done. In the United States, the damage was prevented because one public health physician perceived a qualitative change—a minor and by itself meaningless skin tingling caused by the drug—related it to a totally different event that had happened many years earlier, and sounded the alarm before thalidomide actually came into use.

The Ford Edsel holds a similar lesson. All the quantitative figures that could possibly be obtained were gathered before the Edsel was launched. All of them pointed to its being the right car for the right market. The qualitative change— the shifting of American consumer-buying of automobiles from income-determined to taste-determined market-segmentation—no statistical study could possibly have shown. By the time this could be captured in numbers, it was too late—the Edsel had been brought out and had failed.

The truly important events on the outside are not the trends. They are changes in the trends. These determine ultimately success or failure of an organization and its efforts. Such changes, however, have to be perceived; they cannot be counted, defined, or classified. The classifications still produce the expected figures—as they did for Edsel. But the figures no longer correspond to actual behavior.

The computer is a logic machine, and that is its strength— but also its limitation. The important events on the outside cannot be reported in the kind of form a computer (or any other logic system) could possibly handle. Man, however, while not particularly logical is perceptive—and that is his strength.

The danger is that executives will become contemptuous of information and stimulus that cannot be reduced to computer logic and computer language. Executives may become blind to everything that is perception (i.e., event) rather than fact (i.e., after the event). The tremendous amount of computer information may thus shut out access to reality.

Eventually the computer—potentially by far the most useful management tool—should make executives aware of their insulation and free them for more time on the outside. In the short run, however, there is danger of acute "computeritis." It is a serious affliction.

The computer only makes visible a condition that existed before it. Executives of necessity live and work within an organization. Unless they make conscious efforts to perceive the outside, the inside may blind them to the true reality.

These four realities the executive cannot change. They are necessary conditions of his existence. But he must therefore assume that he will be ineffectual unless he makes special efforts to learn to be effective.

THE PROMISE OF EFFECTIVENESS

Increasing effectiveness may well be the only area where we can hope significantly to raise the level of executive performance, achievement, and satisfaction.

We certainly could use people of much greater abilities in many places. We could use people of broader knowledge. I submit, however, that in these two areas, not too much can be expected from further efforts. We may be getting to the point where we are already attempting to do the inherently impossible or at least the inherently unprofitable. But we are not going to breed a new race of supermen. We will have to run our organizations with men as they are.

The books on manager development, for instance, envisage truly a "man for all seasons" in their picture of "the manager of tomorrow." A senior executive, we are told, should have extraordinary abilities as an analyst and as a decision-maker. He should be good at working with people and at understanding organization and power relations, be good at mathematics, and have artistic insights and creative imagination. What seems to be wanted is universal genius, and universal genius has always been in scarce supply. The experience of the human race indicates strongly that the only person in abundant supply is the universal incompetent. We will therefore have to staff our organizations with people who at best excel in one of these abilities. And then they are more than likely to lack any but the most modest endowment in the others.

We will have to learn to build organizations in such a manner that any man who has strength in one important area is capable of putting it to work (as will be discussed in considerable depth in Chapter 4 below). But we cannot expect to get the executive performance we need by raising our standards for abilities, let alone by hoping for the universally gifted man. We will have to extend the range of human beings through the tools they have to work with rather than through a sudden quantum jump in human ability.

The same, more or less, applies to knowledge. However badly we may need people of more and better knowledge, the effort needed to make the major improvement may well be greater than any possible, let alone any probable, return.

- Fifteen years ago when "operations research" first came in, several of the brilliant young practitioners published their prescription for the operations researcher of tomorrow. They always came out asking for a polymath knowing everything and capable of doing superior and original work in every area of human knowledge. According to one of these studies, operations researchers need to have advanced knowledge in sixty-two or so major scientific and humanistic disciplines. If such a man could be found, he would, I am afraid, be totally wasted on studies of inventory levels or on the programing of production schedules.

Much less ambitious programs for manager development call for high knowledge in such a host of divergent skills as accounting and personnel, marketing, pricing and economic analysis, the behavioral sciences such as psychology, and the natural sciences from physics to biology and geology. And we surely need men who understand the dynamics of modern technology, the complexity of the modern world economy, and the labyrinth of modern government.

Every one of these is a big area, is indeed, too big even for men who work on nothing else. The scholars tend to specialize in fairly small segments of each of these fields and do not pretend to have more than a journeyman's knowledge of the field itself.

I am not saying that one need not try to understand the fundamentals of every one of these areas.

- One of the weaknesses of young, highly educated people today—whether in business, medicine, or government—is that they are satisfied to be versed in one narrow specialty and affect a contempt for the other areas. One need not know in detail what to do with "human relations" as an accountant, or how to promote a new branded product if an engineer. But one has a responsibility to know at least what these areas are about, why they are around, and what they are trying to do. One need not know psychiatry to be a good urologist. But one had better know what psychiatry is all about. One need not be an international lawyer to do a good job in the Department of Agriculture. But one had better know enough about international politics not to do international damage through a parochial farm policy.

This, however, is something very different from the universal expert, who is as unlikely to occur as the universal genius. Instead we will have to learn how to make better use of people who are good in any one of these areas. But this means increasing effectiveness. If one cannot increase the supply of a resource, one must increase its yield. And effectiveness is the one tool to make the resources of ability and knowledge yield more and better results.

Effectiveness thus deserves high priority because of the needs of organization. It deserves even greater priority as the tool of the executive and as his access to achievement and performance.

But Can Effectiveness Be Learned?

If effectiveness were a gift people were born with, the way they are born with a gift for music or an eye for painting, we would be in bad shape. For we know that only a small minority is born with great gifts in any one of these areas. We would therefore be reduced to trying to spot people with high potential of effectiveness early and to train them as best we know to develop their talent. But we could hardly hope to find enough people for the executive tasks of modern society this way. Indeed, if effectiveness were a gift, our present civilization would be highly vulnerable, if not untenable. As a civilization of large organizations it is dependent on a large supply of people capable of being executives with a modicum of effectiveness.

If effectiveness can be learned, however, the questions arise: What does it consist in? What does one have to learn? Of what kind is the learning? Is it a knowledge—and knowledge one learns in systematic form and through concepts? Is it a skill which one learns as an apprentice? Or is it a practice which one learns through doing the same elementary things over and over again?

I have been asking these questions for a good many years. As a consultant, I work with executives in many organizations. Effectiveness is crucial to me in two ways. First, a consultant who by definition has no authority other than that of knowledge must himself be effective—or else he is nothing. Second, the most effective consultant depends on people within the client organization to get anything done. Their effectiveness therefore determines in the last analysis whether a consultant contributes and achieves results, or whether he is pure "cost center" or at best a court jester.

I soon learned that there is no "effective personality."* The

* As is asserted in an unpublished (and undated) talk which Professor Chris Argyris of Yale University made at the graduate business school of Columbia University. According to Professor Argyris, the "successful" executive (as he calls him) has ten characteristics, among them "High Frustration Tolerance," understanding of the "Laws of Competitive Warfare," or that he "Identifies with Groups." If this were indeed the executive personality we need, we would be in real trouble. There are not too many people around with such personality traits, and no one has ever known a way of

effective executives I have seen differ widely in their temperaments and their abilities, in what they do and how they do it, in
their personalities, their knowledge, their interests—in fact in
almost everything that distinguishes human beings. All they
have in common is the ability to get the right things done.

Among the effective executives I have known and worked
with, there are extroverts and aloof, retiring men, some even
morbidly shy. Some are eccentrics, others painfully correct conformists. Some are fat and some are lean. Some are worriers,
some are relaxed. Some drink quite heavily, others are total
abstainers. Some are men of great charm and warmth, some
have no more personality than a frozen mackerel. There are a
few men among them who would answer to the popular concep-
tion of a "leader." But equally there are colorless men who
would attract no attention in a crowd. Some are scholars and
serious students, others almost unlettered. Some have broad
interests, others know nothing except their own narrow area
and care for little else. Some of the men are self-centered, if not
indeed selfish. But there are also some who are generous of
heart and mind. There are men who live only for their work
and others whose main interests lie outside—in community
work, in their church, in the study of Chinese poetry, or in
modern music. Among the effective executives I have met, there
are people who use logic and analysis and others who rely
mainly on perception and intuition. There are men who make
decisions easily and men who suffer agonies every time they
have to move.

Effective executives, in other words, differ as widely as
physicians, high-school teachers, or violinists. They differ
as widely as do ineffectual ones, are indeed indistinguishable
from ineffectual executives in type, personality, and talents.

What all these effective executives have in common is the

---

acquiring them. Fortunately, I know many highly effective—and successful—
executives who lack most, if not all, of Argyris' "characteristics." I also
know quite a few who, though they answer Argyris' description, are singularly ineffectual.

practices that make effective whatever they have and whatever they are. And these practices are the same, whether the effective executive works in a business or in a government agency, as hospital administrator, or as university dean.

But whenever I have found a man, no matter how great his intelligence, his industry, his imagination, or his knowledge, who fails to observe these practices, I have also found an executive deficient in effectiveness.

Effectiveness, in other words, is a habit; that is, a complex of practices. And practices can always be learned. Practices are simple, deceptively so; even a seven-year-old has no difficulty in understanding a practice. But practices are always exceedingly hard to do well. They have to be acquired, as we all learn the multiplication table; that is, repeated *ad nauseam* until "6 x 6 = 36" has become unthinking, conditioned reflex, and firmly ingrained habit. Practices one learns by practicing and practicing and practicing again.

To every practice applies what my old piano teacher said to me in exasperation when I was a small boy. "You will never play Mozart the way Arthur Schnabel does, but there is no reason in the world why you should not play your scales the way he does." What the piano teacher forgot to add—probably because it was so obvious to her—is that even the great pianists could not play Mozart as they do unless they practiced their scales and kept on practicing them.

There is, in other words, no reason why anyone with normal endowment should not acquire competence in any practice. Mastery might well elude him; for this one might need special talents. But what is needed in effectiveness is competence. What is needed are "the scales."

These are essentially five such practices—five such habits of the mind that have to be acquired to be an effective executive:

1. Effective executives know where their time goes. They work systematically at managing the little of their time that can

be brought under their control.

2. Effective executives focus on outward contribution. They gear their efforts to results rather than to work. They start out with the question, "What results are expected of me?" rather than with the work to be done, let alone with its techniques and tools.

3. Effective executives build on strengths—their own strengths, the strengths of their superiors, colleagues, and subordinates; and on the strengths in the situation, that is, on what they can do. They do not build on weakness. They do not start out with the things they cannot do.

4. Effective executives concentrate on the few major areas where superior performance will produce outstanding results. They force themselves to set priorities and stay with their priority decisions. They know that they have no choice but to do first things first—and second things not at all. The alternative is to get nothing done.

5. Effective executives, finally, make effective decisions. They know that this is, above all, a matter of system—of the right steps in the right sequence. They know that an effective decision is always a judgment based on "dissenting opinions" rather than on "consensus on the facts." And they know that to make many decisions fast means to make the wrong decisions. What is needed are few, but fundamental, decisions. What is needed is the right strategy rather than razzle-dazzle tactics.

These are the elements of executive effectiveness—and these are the subjects of this book.

2: Know Thy Time

Most discussions of the executive's task start with the advice to plan one's work. This sounds eminently plausible. The only thing wrong with it is that it rarely works. The plans always remain on paper, always remain good intentions. They seldom turn into achievement.

Effective executives, in my observation, do not start with their tasks. They start with their time. And they do not start out with planning. They start by finding out where their time actually goes. Then they attempt to manage their time and to cut back unproductive demands on their time. Finally they consolidate their "discretionary" time into the largest possible continuing units. This three-step process:

- recording time,
- managing time, and
- consolidating time

is the foundation of executive effectiveness.

Effective executives know that time is the limiting factor. The output limits of any process are set by the scarcest resource. In the process we call "accomplishment," this is time.

Time is also a unique resource. Of the other major resources, money is actually quite plentiful. We long ago should have learned that it is the demand for capital, rather than the supply thereof, which sets the limit to economic growth and activity. People—the third limiting resource—one can hire, though one can rarely hire enough good people. But one cannot rent, hire, buy, or otherwise obtain more time.

The supply of time is totally inelastic. No matter how high the demand, the supply will not go up. There is no price for it and no marginal utility curve for it. Moreover, time is totally perishable and cannot be stored. Yesterday's time is gone forever and will never come back. Time is, therefore, always in exceedingly short supply.

Time is totally irreplaceable. Within limits we can substitute one resource for another, copper for aluminum, for instance. We can substitute capital for human labor. We can use more knowledge or more brawn. But there is no substitute for time.

Everything requires time. It is the one truly universal condition. All work takes place in time and uses up time. Yet most people take for granted this unique, irreplaceable, and necessary resource. Nothing else, perhaps, distinguishes effective executives as much as their tender loving care of time.

Man is ill-equipped to manage his time.

■ Though man, like all living beings, has a "biological clock"—as anyone discovers who crosses the Atlantic by jet—he lacks a reliable time sense, as psychological experiments have shown. People kept in a room in which they cannot see light and darkness outside rapidly lose all sense of time. Even in total darkness, most people retain their sense of space. But even with the lights on, a few hours in a sealed room make most people incapable of estimating how much time has elapsed. They are as likely to underrate grossly the time spent in the room as to overrate it grossly.

If we rely on our memory, therefore, we do not know how time has been spent.

■ I sometimes ask executives who pride themselves on their memory to put down their guess as to how they spend their own time. Then I lock these guesses away for a few weeks or months. In the meantime, the executives run an actual time record on themselves. There is never much resemblance between the way these men thought they used their time and their actual records.

One company chairman was absolutely certain that he divided his time roughly into three parts. One third he thought he was spending with his senior men. One third he thought he spent with his important customers. And one third he thought was devoted to community activities. The actual record of his activities over six weeks brought out clearly that he spent almost no time in any of these areas. These were the tasks on which he knew he *should* spend time—and therefore memory, obliging as usual, told him that these were the tasks on which he actually had spent his time. The record showed, however, that he spent most of his hours as a kind of dispatcher, keeping track of orders from customers he personally knew, and bothering the plant with telephone calls about them. Most of these orders were going through all right anyhow and his intervention could only delay them. But when his secretary first came in with the time record, he did not believe her. It took two or three more time logs to convince him that record, rather than memory, has to be trusted when it comes to the use of time.

The effective executive therefore knows that to manage his time, he first has to know where it actually goes.

The Time Demands on the Executive

There are constant pressures toward unproductive and wasteful time-use. Any executive, whether he is a manager or not, has to spend a great deal of his time on things that do not contribute at all. Much is inevitably wasted. The higher up in the organization he is, the more demands on his time will the organization make.

- The head of a large company once told me that in two years as chief executive officer he had "eaten out" every evening except on Christmas Day and New Year's Day. All the other dinners were "official" functions, each of which wasted several hours. Yet he saw no possible alternative. Whether the dinner honored an employee retiring after fifty years of service, or the governor of one of the states in which the company did business, the chief executive officer had to be there. Ceremony is one of his tasks. My friend had no illusions that these dinners contributed anything either to the company or to his own entertainment or self-development. Yet he had to be there and dine graciously.

Similar time-wasters abound in the life of every executive. When a company's best customer calls up, the sales manager cannot say "I am busy." He has to listen, even though all the customer wants to talk about may be a bridge game the preceding Saturday or the chances of his daughter's getting into the right college. The hospital administrator has to attend the meetings of every one of his staff committees, or else the physicians, the nurses, the technicians, and so on feel that they are being slighted. The government administrator had better pay attention when a congressman calls and wants some information he could, in less time, get out of the telephone book or the *World Almanac*. And so it goes all day long.

Nonmanagers are no better off. They too are bombarded with demands on their time which add little, if anything, to their productivity, and yet cannot be disregarded.

In every executive job, a large part of the time must therefore be wasted on things which, though they apparently have to be done, contribute nothing or little.

Yet most of the tasks of the executive require, for minimum

effectiveness, a fairly large quantum of time. To spend in one stretch less than this minimum is sheer waste. One accomplishes nothing and has to begin all over again.

- To write a report may, for instance, require six or eight hours, at least for the first draft. It is pointless to give seven hours to the task by spending fifteen minutes twice a day for three weeks. All one has at the end is blank paper with some doodles on it. But if one can lock the door, disconnect the telephone, and sit down to wrestle with the report for five or six hours without interruption, one has a good chance to come up with what I call a "zero draft"—the one before the first draft. From then on, one can indeed work in fairly small installments, can rewrite, correct and edit section by section, paragraph by paragraph, sentence by sentence.

  The same goes for an experiment. One simply has to have five to twelve hours in a single stretch to set up the apparatus and to do at least one completed run. Or one has to start all over again after an interruption.

To be effective, every knowledge worker, and especially every executive, therefore needs to be able to dispose of time in fairly large chunks. To have small dribs and drabs of time at his disposal will not be sufficient even if the total is an impressive number of hours.

This is particularly true with respect to time spent working with people, which is, of course, a central task in the work of the executive. People are time-consumers. And most people are time-wasters.

To spend a few minutes with people is simply not productive. If one wants to get anything across, one has to spend a fairly large minimum quantum of time. The manager who thinks that he can discuss the plans, direction, and performance of one of his subordinates in fifteen minutes—and many managers believe this—is just deceiving himself. If one wants to get to the point of having an impact, one needs probably at least an hour and usually much more. And if one has to establish a human relationship, one needs infinitely more time.

Relations with other knowledge workers are especially time-consuming. Whatever the reason—whether it is the absence of or the barrier of class and authority between superior and subordinate in knowledge work, or whether he simply takes himself more seriously—the knowledge worker makes much greater time demands than the manual worker on his superior as well as on his associates. Moreover, because knowledge work cannot be measured the way manual work can, one cannot tell a knowledge worker in a few simple words whether he is doing the right job and how well he is doing it. One can say to a manual worker, "our work standard calls for fifty pieces an hour, and you are only turning out forty-two." One has to sit down with a knowledge worker and think through with him what should be done and why, before one can even know whether he is doing a satisfactory job or not. And this is time-consuming.

Since the knowledge worker directs himself, he must understand what achievement is expected of him and why. He must also understand the work of the people who have to use his knowledge output. For this, he needs a good deal of information, discussion, instruction—all things that take time. And contrary to common belief, this time demand is made not only on his superior but equally on his colleagues.

The knowledge worker must be focused on the results and performance goals of the entire organization to have any results and performance at all. This means that he has to set aside time to direct his vision from his work to results, and from his specialty to the outside in which alone performance lies.

■ Wherever knowledge workers perform well in large organizations, senior executives take time out, on a regular schedule, to sit down with them, sometimes all the way down to green juniors, and ask: "What should we at the head of this organization know about your work? What do you want to tell me regarding this organization? Where do you see opportunities we do not exploit? Where do you see dangers to which we are still blind? And, all together, what do you want to know from me about the organization?"

This leisurely exchange is needed equally in a government agency and in a business, in a research lab and in an army staff. Without it, the knowledge people either lose enthusiasm and become time-servers, or they direct their energies toward their specialty and away from the opportunities and needs of the organization. But such a session takes a great deal of time, especially as it should be unhurried and relaxed. People must feel that "we have all the time in the world." This actually means that one gets a great deal done fast. But it means also that one has to make available a good deal of time in one chunk and without too much interruption.

Mixing personal relations and work relations is time-consuming. If hurried, it turns into friction. Yet any organization rests on this mixture. The more people are together, the more time will their sheer interaction take, the less time will be available to them for work, accomplishment, and results.

▪ Management literature has long known the theorem of "the span of control," which asserts that one man can manage only a few people if these people have to come together in their own work (that is, for instance, an accountant, a sales manager, and a manufacturing man, all three of whom have to work with each other to get any results). On the other hand, managers of chain stores in different cities do not have to work with each other, so that any number could conceivably report to one regional vice-president without violating the principle of the "span of control." Whether this theorem is valid or not, there is little doubt that the more people have to work together, the more time will be spent on "interacting" rather than on work and accomplishment. Large organization creates strength by lavishly using the executive's time.

The larger the organization, therefore, the less actual time will the executive have. The more important will it be for him to know where his time goes and to manage the little time at his disposal.

The more people there are in an organization, the more often does a decision on people arise. But fast personnel decisions are likely to be wrong decisions. The time quantum of the good personnel decision is amazingly large. What the decision involves often becomes clear only when one has gone around the same track several times.

Among the effective executives I have had occasion to observe, there have been people who make decisions fast, and people who make them rather slowly. But without exception, they make personnel decisions slowly and they make them several times before they really commit themselves.

- Alfred P. Sloan, Jr., former head of General Motors, the world's largest manufacturing company, was reported never to make a personnel decision the first time it came up. He made a tentative judgment, and even that took several hours as a rule. Then, a few days or weeks later, he tackled the question again, as if he had never worked on it before. Only when he came up with the same name two or three times in a row was he willing to go ahead. Sloan had a deserved reputation for the "winners" he picked. But when asked about his secret, he is reported to have said: "No secret— I have simply accepted that the first name I come up with is likely to be the wrong name—and I therefore retrace the whole process of thought and analysis a few times before I act." Yet Sloan was far from a patient man.

Few executives make personnel decisions of such impact. But all effective executives I have had occasion to observe have learned that they have to give several hours of continuous and uninterrupted thought to decisions on people if they hope to come up with the right answer.

- The director of a medium-sized government research institute found this out when one of his senior administrators had to be removed from his job. The man was in his fifties and had been with the institute all his working life. After years of good work, the man suddenly began to deteriorate. He clearly could no longer handle his job. But even if civil service rules had permitted it, the man could not be fired. He could of course have been demoted. But this, the director felt, would destroy the man—and the institute owed him consideration and loyalty for years of productive, loyal service. Yet he could not be kept in an administrative position; his shortcomings were much too obvious and were, indeed, weakening the whole institute.

The director and his deputy had been over this situation many times without seeing a way out. But when they sat down for a quiet evening where they could give three or four hours uninterruptedly to the problem, the "obvious" solution finally emerged. It was indeed so simple that neither could explain why he had not seen it before. It got the man out of the wrong job into a job which needed being done and which yet did not require the administrative performance he was no longer able to give.

Time in large, continuous, and uninterrupted units is needed for such decisions as whom to put on a task force set up to study a specific problem; what responsibilities to entrust to the manager of a new organizational unit or to the new manager of an old organizational unit; whether to promote into a vacancy a man who has the marketing knowledge needed for the job but lacks technical training, or whether to put in a first-rate technical man without much marketing background, and so on.

People-decisions are time-consuming, for the simple reason that the Lord did not create people as "resources" for organization. They do not come in the proper size and shape for the tasks that have to be done in organization—and they cannot be machined down or recast for these tasks. People are always "almost fits" at best. To get the work done with people (and no other resource is available) therefore requires lots of time, thought, and judgment.

The Slavic peasant of Eastern Europe used to have a proverb: "What one does not have in one's feet, one's got to have in one's head." This may be considered a fanciful version of the law of the conservation of energy. But it is above all something like a "law of the conservation of time." The more time we take out of the task of the "legs"—that is, of physical, manual work—the more will we have to spend on the work of the "head"—that is, on knowledge work. The easier we make it for rank-and-file workers, machine tenders as well as clerks, the more will have to be done by the knowledge worker. One cannot "take knowledge out of the work." It has to be put back somewhere—and in much larger and cohesive amounts.

Time demands on the knowledge workers are not going down. Machine tenders now work only forty hours a week—and soon may work only thirty-five and live better than anybody ever lived before, no matter how much he worked or how rich he was. But the machine tender's leisure is inescapably being paid for by the knowledge worker's longer hours. It is not the executives who have a problem of spending their leisure time in the industrial countries of the world today. On the contrary, they are working everywhere longer hours and have greater demands on their time to satisfy. And the executive time scarcity is bound to become worse rather than better.

One important reason for this is that a high standard of living presupposes an economy of innovation and change. But innovation and change make inordinate time demands on the executive. All one can think and do in a short time is to think what one already knows and to do as one has always done.

- There has been an enormous amount of discussion lately to explain why the British economy has lagged so badly since World War II. One of the reasons is surely that the British businessman of the older generation tried to have it as easy as his workers and to work the same short hours. But this is possible only if the business or the industry clings to the old established routine and shuns innovation and change.

For all these reasons, the demands of the organization, the demands of people, the time demands of change and innovation, it will become increasingly important for executives to be able to manage their time. But one cannot even think of managing one's time unless one first knows where it goes.

TIME-DIAGNOSIS

That one has to record time before one can know where it goes and before, in turn, one can attempt to manage it we have realized for the best part of a century. That is, we have known this in respect to manual work, skilled and unskilled, since Scientific Management around 1900 began to record the time it takes for a specific piece of manual work to be done. Hardly any country is today so far behind in industrial methods as not to time systematically the operations of manual workers.

We have applied this knowledge to the work where time does not greatly matter; that is, where the difference between time-use and time-waste is primarily efficiency and costs. But we have not applied it to the work that matters increasingly, and that particularly has to cope with time: the work of the knowledge worker and especially of the executive. Here the difference between time-use and time-waste is effectiveness and results.

The first step toward executive effectiveness is therefore to record actual time-use.

■ The specific method in which the record is put together need not concern us here. There are executives who keep such a time log themselves. Others, such as the company chairman just mentioned, have their secretaries do it for them. The important thing is that it gets done, and that the record is made in "real" time, that is at the time of the event itself, rather than later on from memory.

A good many effective executives keep such a log continuously and look at it regularly every month. At a minimum, effective executives have the log run on themselves for three to four weeks at a stretch twice a year or so, on a regular schedule. After each such sample, they rethink and rework their schedule. But six months later, they invariably find that they have "drifted" into wasting their time on trivia. Time-use does improve with practice. But only constant efforts at managing time can prevent drifting.

Systematic time management is therefore the next step. One has to find the nonproductive, time-wasting activities and get rid of them if one possibly can. This requires asking oneself a number of diagnostic questions.

1. First one tries to identify and eliminate the things that need not be done at all, the things that are purely waste of time without any results whatever. To find these time-wastes, one asks of *all* activities in the time records: "What would happen if this were not done at all?" And if the answer is, "Nothing would happen," then obviously the conclusion is to stop doing it.

It is amazing how many things busy people are doing that never will be missed. There are, for instance, the countless speeches, dinners, committee memberships, and directorships which take an unconscionable toll of the time of busy people, which are rarely enjoyed by them or done well by them, but which are endured, year in and year out, as an Egyptian plague ordained from on high. Actually, all one has to do is to learn to say "no" if an activity contributes nothing to one's own organization, to oneself, or to the organization for which it is to be performed.

- The chief executive mentioned above who had to dine out every night found, when he analyzed these dinners, that at least one third would proceed just as well without anyone from the company's senior management. In fact, he found (somewhat to his chagrin) that his acceptance of a good many of these invitations was by no means welcome to his hosts. They had invited him as a polite gesture. But they had fully expected to be turned down and did not quite know what to do with him when he accepted.

I have yet to see an executive, regardless of rank or station, who could not consign something like a quarter of the demands on his time to the wastepaper basket without anybody's noticing their disappearance.

2. The next question is: "Which of the activities on my time log could be done by somebody else just as well, if not better?"

■ The dinner-eating company chairman found that any senior executive of the company would do for another third of the formal dinners—all the occasion demanded was the company's name on the guest list.

There has been for years a great deal of talk about "delegation" in management. Every manager whatever the organization—business, government, university, or armed service—has been exhorted to be a better "delegator." In fact, most managers in large organizations have themselves given this sermon and more than once. I have yet to see any results from all this preaching. The reason why no one listens is simple: As usually presented, delegation makes little sense. If it means that somebody else ought to do part of "*my* work," it is wrong. One is paid for doing one's own work. And if it implies, as the usual sermon does, that the laziest manager is the best manager, it is not only nonsense; it is immoral.

But I have never seen an executive confronted with his time record who did not rapidly acquire the habit of pushing at other people everything that he need not do personally. The first look at the time record makes it abundantly clear that there just is not time enough to do the things the executive himself considers important, himself wants to do, and is himself committed to doing. The only way he can get to the important things is by pushing on others anything that can be done by them at all.

■ A good example is executive travel. Professor C. Northcote Parkinson has pointed out in one of his delightful satires that the quickest way to get rid of an inconvenient superior is to make a world traveler out of him. The jet plane is indeed overrated as a management tool. A great many trips have to be made; but a junior can make most of them. Travel is still a novelty for him. He is still young enough to get a good night's rest in hotel beds. The junior can take the fatigue—and he will therefore also do a better job than the more experienced, perhaps better trained, but tired superior.

There are also the meetings one attends, even though nothing is going to happen that someone else could not handle. There are the hours spent discussing a document before there is even a first draft that can be discussed. There is, in the research lab, the time spent by a senior physicist to write a "popular" news release on some of his work. Yet there are plenty of people around with enough science to understand what the physicist is trying to say, who can write readable English, where the physicist only speaks higher mathematics. Altogether, an enormous amount of the work being done by executives is work that can easily be done by others, and therefore should be done by others.

"Delegation" as the term is customarily used, is a misunderstanding—is indeed misdirection. But getting rid of anything that can be done by somebody else so that one does not have to delegate but can really get to one's own work— that is a major improvement in effectiveness.

3. A common cause of time-waste is largely under the executive's control and can be eliminated by him. That is the time of others he himself wastes.

There is no one symptom for this. But there is still a simple way to find out. That is to ask other people. Effective executives have learned to ask systematically and without coyness: "What do I do that wastes your time without contributing to your effectiveness?" To ask this question, and to ask it without being afraid of the truth, is a mark of the effective executive.

The manner in which an executive does productive work may still be a major waste of somebody's else's time.

■ The senior financial executive of a large organization knew perfectly well that the meetings in his office wasted a lot of time. This man asked all his direct subordinates to every meeting, whatever the topic. As a result the meetings were far too large. And because every participant felt that he had to show interest, everybody asked at least one question —most of them irrelevant. As a result the meetings stretched on endlessly. But the senior executive had not known, until he asked, that his subordinates too considered the meetings a waste of their time. Aware of the great importance everyone in the organization placed on status and on being "in the know," he had feared that the uninvited men would feel slighted and left out.

Now, however, he satisfies the status needs of his subordinates in a different manner. He sends out a printed form which reads: "I have asked [Messrs Smith, Jones, and Robinson] to meet with me [Wednesday at 3] in [the fourth floor conference room] to discuss [next year's capital appropriations budget]. Please come if you think that you need the information or want to take part in the discussion. But you will in any event receive right away a full summary of the discussion and of any decisions reached, together with a request for your comments."

Where formerly a dozen people came and stayed all afternoon, three men and a secretary to take the notes now get the matter over with within an hour or so. And no one feels left out.

Many executives know all about these unproductive and unnecessary time demands; yet they are afraid to prune them. They are afraid to cut out something important by mistake. But this mistake, if made, can be speedily corrected. If one prunes too harshly, one usually finds out fast enough.

Every new President of the United States accepts too many invitations at first. Then it dawns on him that he has other work to do and that most of these invitations do not add to his effectiveness. Thereupon, he usually cuts back too sharply and becomes inaccessible. A few weeks or months later, however, he is being told by the press and the radio that he is "losing touch." Then he usually finds the right balance between being exploited without effectiveness and using public appearances as his national pulpit.

In fact, there is not much risk that an executive will cut back too much. We usually tend to overrate rather than underrate our importance and to conclude that far too many things can only be done by ourselves. Even very effective executives still do a great many unnecessary, unproductive things.

But the best proof that the danger of overpruning is a bugaboo is the extraordinary effectiveness so often attained by severely ill or severely handicapped people.

- A good example was Harry Hopkins, President Roosevelt's confidential adviser in World War II. A dying, indeed almost a dead man for whom every step was torment, he could only work a few hours every other day or so. This forced him to cut out everything but truly vital matters. He did not lose effectiveness thereby; on the contrary, he became, as Churchill called him once, "Lord Heart of the Matter" and accomplished more than anyone else in wartime Washington.

This is an extreme, of course. But it illustrates both how much control one can exercise over one's time if one really tries, and how much of the time-wasters one can cut out without loss of effectiveness.

PRUNING THE TIME-WASTERS

These three diagnostic questions deal with unproductive and time-consuming activities over which every executive has some control. Every knowledge worker and every executive should ask them. Managers, however, need to be equally concerned with time-loss that results from poor management and deficient organization. Poor management wastes everybody's time—but above all, it wastes the manager's time.

1. The first task here is to identify the time-wasters which follow from lack of system or foresight. The symptom to look for is the recurrent "crisis," the crisis that comes back year after year. A crisis that recurs a second time is a crisis that must not occur again.

■ The annual inventory crisis belongs here. That with the computer we now can meet it even more "heroically" and at greater expense than we could in the past is hardly a great improvement.

A recurrent crisis should always have been foreseen. It can therefore either be prevented or reduced to a routine which clerks can manage. The definition of a "routine" is that it makes unskilled people without judgment capable of doing what it took near-genius to do before; for a routine puts down in systematic, step-by-step form what a very able man learned in surmounting yesterday's crisis.

The recurrent crisis is not confined to the lower levels of an organization. It afflicts everyone.

■ For years, a fairly large company ran into one of these crises annually around the first of December. In a highly seasonal business, with the last quarter usually the year's low, fourth-quarter sales and profits were not easily predictable. Every year, however, management made an earnings prediction when it issued its interim report at the end of the second quarter. Three months later, in the fourth quarter, there was tremendous scurrying and companywide emergency action to live up to top management's forecast. For three to five weeks, nobody in the management group got any work done. It took only one stroke of the pen to solve this crisis; instead of predicting a definite year-end figure, top management is now predicting results within a range. This fully satisfies directors, stockholders, and the financial community. And what used to be a crisis a few years ago, now is no longer even noticed in the company—yet fourth-quarter results are quite a bit better than they used to be, since executive time is no longer being wasted on making results fit the forecast.

Prior to Mr. McNamara's appointment as Secretary of Defense, a similar last-minute crisis shook the entire American defense establishment every spring, toward the end of the fiscal year on June 30. Every manager in the defense establishment, military or civilian, tried desperately in May and June to find expenditures for the money appropriated by Congress for the fiscal year. Otherwise, he was afraid he would have to give back the money. (This last-minute spending spree has also been a chronic disease in Russian planning.) And yet, this crisis was totally unnecessary as Mr. McNamara immediately saw. The law had always permitted the placing of unspent, but needed, sums into an interim account.

The recurrent crisis is simply a symptom of slovenliness and laziness.

■ Years ago when I first started out as a consultant, I had to learn how to tell a well-managed industrial plant from a poorly managed one—without any pretense to production knowledge. A well-managed plant, I soon learned, is a quiet place. A factory that is "dramatic," a factory in which the "epic of industry" is unfolded before the visitor's eyes, is poorly managed. A well-managed factory is boring. Nothing exciting happens in it because the crises have been anticipated and have been converted into routine.

Similarly a well-managed organization is a "dull" organization. The "dramatic" things in such an organization are basic decisions that make the future, rather than heroics in mopping up yesterday.

2. Time-wastes often result from overstaffing.

■ My first-grade arithmetic primer asked: "If it takes two ditch-diggers two days to dig a ditch, how long would it take four ditch-diggers?" In first grade, the correct answer is, of course, "one day." In the kind of work, however, with which executives are concerned, the right answer is probably "four days" if not "forever."

A work force may, indeed, be too small for the task. And the work then suffers, if it gets done at all. But this is not the rule. Much more common is the work force that is too big for effectiveness, the work force that spends, therefore, an increasing amount of its time "interacting" rather than working.

There is a fairly reliable symptom of overstaffing. If the senior people in the group—and of course the manager in particular—spend more than a small fraction of their time, maybe one tenth, on "problems of human relations," on feuds and frictions, on jurisdictional disputes and questions of co-operation, and so on, then the work force is almost certainly too large. People get into each other's way. People have become an impediment to performance, rather than the means thereto. In a lean organization people have room to move without colliding with one another and can do their work without having to explain it all the time.

■ The excuse for overstaffing is always "but we have to have a thermodynamicist [or a patent lawyer, or an economist] on the staff." This specialist is not being used much; he may not be used at all; but "we have to have him around just in case we need him." (And he always "has to be familiar with our problem" and "be part of the group from the start"!) One should only have on a team the knowledges and skills that are needed day in and day out for the bulk of the work. Specialists that may be needed once in a while, or that may have to be consulted on this or on that, should always remain outside. It is infinitely cheaper to go to them and consult them against a fee than to have them in the group to say nothing of the impact an underemployed but over-skilled man has on the effectiveness of the entire group. All he can do is mischief.

3. Another common time-waster is malorganization. Its symptom is an excess of meetings.

Meetings are by definition a concession to deficient organization For one either meets or one works. One cannot do both at the same time. In an ideally designed structure (which in a changing world is of course only a dream) there would be no meetings. Everybody would know what he needs to know to do his job. Everyone would have the resources available to him to do his job. We meet because people holding different jobs have to cooperate to get a specific task done. We meet because the knowledge and experience needed in a specific situation are not available in one head, but have to be pieced together out of the experience and knowledge of several people.

There will always be more than enough meetings. Organization will always require so much working together that the attempts of well-meaning behavioral scientists to create opportunities for "cooperation" may be somewhat redundant. But if executives in an organization spend more than a fairly small part of their time in meeting, it is a sure sign of malorganization.

Every meeting generates a host of little follow-up meetings —some formal, some informal, but both stretching out for hours. Meetings, therefore, need to be purposefully directed. An undirected meeting is not just a nuisance; it is a danger. But above all, meetings have to be the exception rather than the rule. An organization in which everybody meets all the time is an organization in which no one gets anything done. Wherever a time log shows the fatty degeneration of meetings —whenever, for instance, people in an organization find themselves in meetings a quarter of their time or more—there is time-wasting malorganization.

- There are exceptions, special organs whose purpose it is to meet—the boards of directors, for instance, of such companies as Du Pont and Standard Oil of New Jersey which are the final organs of deliberation and appeal but which do not operate anything. But as these two companies realized a long time ago, the people who sit on these boards cannot be permitted to do anything else; for the same reason, by the way, that judges cannot be permitted to be also advocates in their spare time.

As a rule, meetings should never be allowed to become the main demand on an executive's time. Too many meetings always bespeak poor structure of jobs and the wrong organizational components. Too many meetings signify that work that should be in one job or in one component is spread over several jobs or several components. They signify that responsibility is diffused and that information is not addressed to the people who need it.

- In one large company, the root cause of an epidemic of meetings was a traditional but obsolescent organization of the energy business. Large steam turbines, the company's traditional business since before 1900, were one division under their own management and with their own staff. During World War II, however, the company also went into aircraft engines and, as a result, had organized in another division concerned with aircraft and defense production a large jet engine capacity. Finally, there was an atomic energy division, really an offspring of the research labs and still organizationally more or less tied to them.
  But today these three power sources are no longer separate, each with its own market. Increasingly, they are becoming substitutes for, as well as complements to, each other. Each of the three is the most economical and most advantageous generating equipment for electric power under certain conditions. In this sense the three are competitive. But by putting two of them together, one can also obtain

performance capacities which no one type of equipment by itself possesses.

What the company needed, clearly, was an energy strategy. It needed a decision whether to push all three types of generating equipment, in competition with each other; whether to make one of the three the main business and consider the other two supplementary; or finally, whether to develop two of the three—and which two—as one "energy package." It needed a decision how to divide available capital among the three. Above all, however, the energy business needed an organization which expressed the reality of one energy market, producing the same end product, electric power, for the same customers. Instead there were three components, each carefully shielded from the others by layers of organization, each having its own special folkways, rituals, and its own career ladders—and each blithely confident that it would get by itself 75 per cent of the total energy business of the next decade.

As a result, the three were engaged in a nonstop meeting for years. Since each reported to a different member of management, these meetings sucked in the entire top group. Finally, the three were cut loose from their original groups and put together into one organizational component under one manager. There is still a good deal of infighting going on; and the big strategy decisions still have to be made. But at least there is understanding now as to what these decisions are. At least top management no longer has to chair and referee every meeting. And total meeting-time is a fraction of what it used to be.

4. The last major time-waster is malfunction in information.

■ The administrator of a large hospital was plagued for years by telephone calls from doctors asking him to find a bed for one of their patients who should be hospitalized. The admissions people "knew" that there was no empty bed. Yet the administrator almost invariably found a few. The admissions people simply were not informed immediately when a patient was discharged. The floor nurse knew, of course, and so did the people in the front office who presented the bill to the departing patient. The admissions people, however, got a "bed count" made every morning at 5:00 A.M.—while the great majority of patients were being sent home in mid-morning after the doctors had made the rounds. It did not take genius to put this right; all it needed was an extra carbon copy of the chit that goes from the floor nurse to the front office.

Even worse, but equally common, is information in the wrong form.

- Manufacturing businesses typically suffer from production figures that have to be "translated" before operating people can use them. They report "averages"; that is, they report what the accountants need. Operating people, however, usually need not the averages but the range and the extremes —product mix and production fluctuations, length of runs, and so on. To get what they need, they must either spend hours each day adapting the averages or build their own "secret" accounting organization. The accountant has all the information, but no one, as a rule, has thought of telling him what is needed.

Time-wasting management defects such as overstaffing, mal-organization, or malfunctioning information can sometimes be remedied fast. At other times, it takes long, patient work to correct them. The results of such work are, however, great— and especially in terms of time gained.

Consolidating "Discretionary Time"

The executive who records and analyzes his time and then attempts to manage it can determine how much he has for his important tasks. How much time is there that is "discretionary," that is, available for the big tasks that will really make a con-tribution?

It is not going to be a great deal, no matter how ruthlessly the executive prunes time-wasters.

- One of the most accomplished time managers I have ever met was the president of a big bank with whom I worked for two years on top-management structure. I saw him once a month for two years. My appointment was always for an hour and a half. The president was always prepared for the sessions—and I soon learned to do my homework too. There was never more than one item on the agenda. But when I had been in there for an hour and twenty minutes, the president would turn to me and say, "Mr. Drucker, I believe you'd better sum up now and outline what we should do next." And an hour and thirty minutes after I had been ushered into his office, he was at the door shaking my hand and saying good-by.

  After this had been going on for about one year, I finally asked him, "Why always an hour and a half?" He answered, "That's easy. I have found out that my attention span is about an hour and a half. If I work on any one topic longer than this, I begin to repeat myself. At the same time, I have learned that nothing of importance can really be tackled in much less time. One does not get to the point where one understands what one is talking about."

  During the hour and a half I was in his office every month, there was never a telephone call, and his secretary never stuck her head in the door to announce that an important man wanted to see him urgently. One day I asked him about this. He said, "My secretary has strict instructions not to put anyone through except the President of the United States and my wife. The President rarely calls—and my wife knows better. Everything else the secretary holds till I have finished. Then I have half an hour in which I return every call and make sure I get every message. I have yet to come across a crisis which could not wait ninety minutes."

  Needless to say, this president accomplished more in this one monthly session than many other and equally able executives get done in a month of meetings.

But even this disciplined man had to resign himself to having at least half his time taken up by things of minor importance and dubious value, things that nonetheless had to be done—the seeing of important customers who just "dropped in," attendance at meetings which could just as well have proceeded without him; specific decisions on daily problems that should not have reached him but invariably did.

Whenever I see a senior executive asserting that more than half his time is under his control and is really discretionary time which he invests and spends according to his own judgment, I am reasonably certain that he has no idea where his time goes. Senior executives rarely have as much as one quarter of their time truly at their disposal and available for the important matters, the matters that contribute, the matters they are being paid for. This is true in any organization—except that in the government agency the unproductive time demands on the top people tend to be even higher than they are in other large organizations.

The higher up an executive, the larger will be the proportion of time that is not under his control and yet not spent on contribution. The larger the organization, the more time will be needed just to keep the organization together and running, rather than to make it function and produce.

The effective executive therefore knows that he has to consolidate his discretionary time. He knows that he needs large chunks of time and that small driblets are no time at all. Even one quarter of the working day, if consolidated in large time units, is usually enough to get the important things done. But even three quarters of the working day are useless if they are only available as fifteen minutes here or half an hour there.

The final step in time management is therefore to consolidate the time that record and analysis show as normally available and under the executive's control.

There are a good many ways of doing this. Some people, usually senior men, work at home one day a week; this is a particularly common method of time-consolidation for editors or research scientists.

Other men schedule all the operating work—the meetings, reviews, problem-sessions, and so on—for two days a week, for example, Monday and Friday, and set aside the mornings of the remaining days for consistent, continuing work on major issues.

- This was how the bank president handled his time. Monday and Friday he had his operating meetings, saw senior executives on current matters, was available to important customers, and so on. Tuesday, Wednesday, and Thursday afternoons were left unscheduled—for whatever might come up; and something of course always did, whether urgent personnel problems, a surprise visit by one of the bank's representatives from abroad or by an important customer, or a trip to Washington. But in the mornings of these three days he scheduled the work on the major matters—in chunks of ninety minutes each.

Another fairly common method is to schedule a daily work period at home in the morning.

- One of the most effective executives in Professor Sune Carlson's study, mentioned above, spent ninety minutes each morning before going to work in a study without telephone at home. Even if this means working very early so as to get to the office on time, it is preferable to the most popular way of getting to the important work: taking it home in the evening and spending three hours after dinner on it. By that time, most executives are too tired to do a good job. Certainly those of middle age or older are better off going to bed earlier and getting up earlier. And the reason why working home nights is so popular is actually its worst feature: It enables an executive to avoid tackling his time and its management during the day.

But the method by which one consolidates one's discretionary time is far less important than the approach. Most people tackle the job by trying to push the secondary, the less productive matters together, thus clearing, so to speak, a free space between them. This does not lead very far, however. One still gives priority in one's mind and in one's schedule to the less important things, the things that have to be done even though they contribute little. As a result, any new time pressure is likely to be satisfied at the expense of the discretionary time and of the work that should be done in it. Within a few days or weeks, the entire discretionary time will then be gone again, nibbled away by new crises, new immediacies, new trivia.

Effective executives start out by estimating how much discretionary time they can realistically call their own. Then they set aside continuous time in the appropriate amount. And if they find later that other matters encroach on this reserve, they scrutinize their record again and get rid of some more time demands from less than fully productive activities. They know that, as has been said befoie, one rarely overprunes.

And all effective executives control their time management perpetually. They not only keep a continuing log and analyze it periodically. They set themselves deadlines for the important activities, based on their judgment of their discretionary time.

- One highly effective man I know keeps two such lists—one of the urgent and one of the unpleasant things that have to be done—each with a deadline. When he finds his deadlines slipping, he knows his time is again getting away from him.

Time is the scarcest resource, and unless it is managed, nothing else can be managed. The analysis of one's time, moreover, is the one easily accessible and yet systematic way to analyze one's work and to think through what really matters in it.

"Know Thyself," the old prescription for wisdom, is almost impossibly difficult for mortal men. But everyone can follow the injunction "Know Thy Time" if he wants to, and be well on the road toward contribution and effectiveness.

3: What Can I Contribute?

The effective executive focuses on contribution. He looks up from his work and outward toward goals. He asks: "What can I contribute that will significantly affect the performance and the results of the institution I serve?" His stress is on responsibility.

- The focus on contribution is the key to effectiveness: in a man's own work—its content, its level, its standards, and its impacts; in his relations with others—his superiors his associates, his subordinates; in his use of the tools of the executive such as meetings or reports.

The great majority of executives tend to focus downward. They are occupied with efforts rather than with results. They worry over what the organization and their superiors "owe" them and should do for them. And they are conscious above all of the authority they "should have." As a result, they render themselves ineffectual.

- The head of one of the large management consulting firms always starts an assignment with a new client by spending a few days visiting the senior executives of the client organization one by one. After he has chatted with them about the assignment and the client organization, its history and its people, he asks (though rarely, of course, in these words): "And what do *you* do that justifies your being on the payroll?" The great majority, he reports, answer: "I run the accounting department," or "I am in charge of the sales force." Indeed, not uncommonly the answer is, "I have 850 people working under me." Only a few say, "It's my job to give our managers the information they need to make the right decisions," or "I am responsible for finding out what products the customer will want tomorrow," or "I have to think through and prepare the decisions the president will have to face tomorrow."

The man who focuses on efforts and who stresses his downward authority is a subordinate no matter how exalted his title and rank. But the man who focuses on contribution and who takes responsibility for results, no matter how junior, is in the most literal sense of the phrase, "top management." He holds himself accountable for the performance of the whole.

THE EXECUTIVE'S OWN COMMITMENT

The focus on contribution turns the executive's attention away from his own specialty, his own narrow skills, his own department, and toward the performance of the whole. It turns his attention to the outside, the only place where there are results. He is likely to have to think through what relationships his skills, his specialty, his function, or his department have to the entire organization and *its* purpose. He therefore will also come to think in terms of the customer, the client, or the patient, who is the ultimate reason for whatever the organization produces, whether it be economic goods, governmental policies, or health services. As a result, what he does and how he does it will be materially different.

■ A large scientific agency of the U.S. government found this
out a few years ago. The old director of publications retired.
He had been with the agency since its inception in the
thirties and was neither scientist nor trained writer. The
publications which he turned out were often criticized for
lacking professional polish. He was replaced by an accomplished science writer. The publications immediately took
on a highly professional look. But the scientific community
for whom these publications were intended stopped reading
them. A highly respected university scientist, who had for
many years worked closely with the agency, finally told the
administrator: "The former director was writing *for* us; your
new man writes *at* us."

The old director had asked the question, "What can I
contribute to the results of this agency?" His answer was, "I
can interest the young scientists on the outside in our work,
can make them want to come to work for us." He therefore
stressed major problems, major decisions, and even major
controversies inside the agency. This had brought him more
than once into head-on collision with the administrator. But
the old man had stood by his guns. "The test of our publications is not whether we like them; the test is how many young
scientists apply to us for jobs and how good they are," he
said.

To ask, "What can I contribute?" is to look for the unused
potential in the job. And what is considered excellent performance in a good many positions is often but a pale shadow
of the job's full potential of contribution.

■ The Agency department in a large American commercial
bank is usually considered a profitable but humdrum activity.
This department acts, for a fee, as the registrar and stock-
transfer agent for the securities of corporations. It keeps the
names of stockholders on record, issues and mails their
dividend checks, and does a host of similar clerical chores—
all demanding precision and high efficiency but rarely great
imagination.

Or so it seemed until a new Agency vice-president in a large New York bank asked the question, "What could Agency contribute?" He then realized that the work brought him into direct contact with the senior financial executives of the bank's customers who make the "buying decisions" on all banking services—deposits, loans, investments, pension-fund management, and so on. Of course, the Agency department by itself has to be run efficiently. But as this new vice-president realized, its greatest potential was as a sales force for all the other services of the bank. Under its new head, Agency, formerly an efficient paper-pusher, became a highly successful marketing force for the entire bank.

Executives who do not ask themselves, "What can I contribute?" are not only likely to aim too low, they are likely to aim at the wrong things. Above all, they may define their contribution too narrowly.

"Contribution," as the two illustrations just given show, may mean different things. For every organization needs performance in three major areas: It needs direct results; building of values and their reaffirmation; and building and developing people for tomorrow. If deprived of performance in any one of these areas, it will decay and die. All three therefore have to be built into the contribution of every executive. But their relative importance varies greatly with the personality and the position of the executive as well as with the needs of the organization.

The direct results of an organization are clearly visible, as a rule. In a business, they are economic results such as sales and profits. In a hospital, they are patient care, and so on. But even direct results are not totally unambiguous, as the example of the Agency vice-president in the bank illustrates. And when there is confusion as to what they should be, there are no results.

■ One example is the performance (or rather lack of performance) of the nationalized airlines of Great Britain. They are supposed to be run as a business. They are also supposed to be run as an instrument of British national policy and Commonwealth cohesion. But they have been run largely to keep alive the British aircraft industry. Whipsawed between three different concepts of direct results, they have done poorly in respect to all three.

Direct results always come first. In the care and feeding of an organization, they play the role calories play in the nutrition of the human body. But any organization also needs a commitment to values and their constant reaffirmation, as a human body needs vitamins and minerals. There has to be something "this organization stands for," or else it degenerates into disorganization, confusion, and paralysis. In a business, the value commitment may be to technical leadership or (as in Sears Roebuck) to finding the right goods and services for the American family and to procuring them at the lowest price and the best quality.

Value commitments, like results, are not unambiguous.

▪ The U.S. Department of Agriculture has for many years been torn between two fundamentally incompatible value commitments—one to agricultural productivity and one to the "family farm" as the "backbone of the nation." The former has been pushing the country toward industrial agriculture, highly mechanical, highly industrialized, and essentially a large-scale commercial business. The latter has called for nostalgia supporting a nonproducing rural proletariat. But because farm policy—at least until very recently —has wavered between two different value commitments, all it has really succeeded in doing has been to spend prodigious amounts of money.

Finally, organization is, to a large extent, a means of overcoming the limitations mortality sets to what any one man can contribute. An organization that is not capable of perpetuating itself has failed. An organization therefore has to provide today the men who can run it tomorrow. It has to renew its human capital. It should steadily upgrade its human resources. The next generation should take for granted what the hard work and dedication of this generation has accomplished. They should then, standing on the shoulders of their predecessors, establish a new "high" as the baseline for the generation after them.

An organization which just perpetuates today's level of vision, excellence, and accomplishment has lost the capacity to adapt. And since the one and only thing certain in human affairs is change, it will not be capable of survival in a changed tomorrow.

An executive's focus on contribution by itself is a powerful force in developing people. People adjust to the level of the demands made on them. The executive who sets his sights on contribution, raises the sights and standards of everyone with whom he works.

■ A new hospital administrator, holding his first staff meeting, thought that a rather difficult matter had been settled to everyone's satisfaction, when one of the participants suddenly asked: "Would this have satisfied Nurse Bryan?" At once the argument started all over and did not subside until a new and much more ambitious solution to the problem had been hammered out.

Nurse Bryan, the administrator learned, had been a long-serving nurse at the hospital. She was not particularly distinguished, had not in fact ever been a supervisor. But whenever a decision on patient care came up on her floor, Nurse Bryan would ask, "Are we doing the best we can do to help this patient?" Patients on Nurse Bryan's floor did better and recovered faster. Gradually over the years, the whole hospital had learned to adopt what came to be known as "Nurse Bryan's Rule"; had learned, in other words, to ask: "Are we really making the best contribution to the purpose of this hospital?"

Though Nurse Bryan herself had retired almost ten years earlier, the standards she had set still made demands on people who in terms of training and position were her superiors.

Commitment to contribution is commitment to responsible effectiveness. Without it, a man shortchanges himself, deprives his organization, and cheats the people he works with.

The most common cause of executive failure is inability or unwillingness to change with the demands of a new position. The executive who keeps on doing what he has done successfully before he moved is almost bound to fail. Not only do the results change to which his contribution ought to direct itself. The relative importance between the three dimensions of performance changes. The executive who fails to understand this will suddenly do the wrong things the wrong way—even though he does exactly what in his old job had been the right things done the right way.

■ This was the main reason for the failure of so many able men as executives in World War II Washington. That Washington was "political" or that men who had always been on their own suddenly found themselves "cogs in a big machine" were at most contributing factors. Plenty of men proved themselves highly effective Washington executives even though they had no political sense or had never worked in anything bigger than a two-man law practice. Robert E. Sherwood, a most effective administrator in the large Office of War Information (and the author of one of the most perceptive books on effectiveness in power*) had been a playwright whose earlier "organization" had consisted of his own desk and typewriter.

The men who succeeded in wartime Washington focused on contribution. As a result, they changed both what they did and the relative weight they gave to each of the value dimensions in their work. The failures worked much harder in a good many cases. But they did not challenge themselves, and they failed to see the need for redirecting their efforts.

* *Roosevelt and Hopkins* (New York, Harper & Row, 1948).

■ An outstanding example of success was the man who, already sixty, became chief executive officer of a large nationwide chain of retail stores. This man had been in the second spot in the company for twenty years or more. He served contentedly under an outgoing and aggressive chief executive officer who was actually several years younger. He never expected to be president himself. But his boss died suddenly while still in his fifties, and the faithful lieutenant had to take over.

The new head had come up as a financial man and was at home with figures—the costing system, purchasing and inventory, the financing of new stores, traffic studies, and so on. People were by and large a shadowy abstraction to him. But when he suddenly found himself president, he asked himself: "What can I and no one else do which, if done really well, would make a real difference to this company?" The one, truly significant contribution, he concluded, would be the development of tomorrow's managers. The company had prided itself for many years on its executive development policies. "But," the new chief executive argued, "a policy does nothing by itself. My contribution is to make sure that this actually gets done."

From then on for the rest of his tenure, he walked through the personnel department three times a week on his way back from lunch and picked up at random eight or ten file folders of young men in the supervisory group. Back in his office, he opened the first man's folder, scanned it rapidly, and put through a telephone call to the man's superior. "Mr. Robertson, this is the president in New York. You have on your staff a young man, Joe Jones. Didn't you recommend six months ago that he be put in a job where he could acquire some merchandising experience? You did. Why haven't you done anything about it?" And down would go the receiver.

The next folder opened, he would call another manager in another city: "Mr. Smith, this is the president in New York. I understand that you recommended a young man on your staff, Dick Roe, for a job in which he can learn something about store accounting. I just noticed that you have followed through with this recommendation, and I want to tell you how pleased I am to see you working at the development of our young people."

This man was in the president's chair only a few years before he himself retired. But today, ten or fifteen years later, executives who never met him attribute to him, and with considerable justice, the tremendous growth and success of the company since his time.

■ That he asked himself, "What can I contribute?" also seems to explain in large part the extraordinary effectiveness of Robert McNamara as U.S. Secretary of Defense—a position for which he was completely unprepared when President Kennedy, in the fall of 1960, plucked him out of the Ford Motor Company and put him into the toughest Cabinet job.

McNamara, who at Ford had been the perfect "inside" man, was for instance totally innocent of politics and tried to leave congressional liaison to subordinates. But after a few weeks, he realized that the Secretary of Defense depends on congressional understanding and support. As a result, he forced himself to do what for so publicity-shy and non-political a man must have been both difficult and distasteful: to cultivate Congress, to get to know the influential men on the congressional committees, and to acquire a mastery of the strange art of congressional infighting. He has surely not been completely successful in his dealings with Congress, but he has done better than any earlier Secretary.

The McNamara story shows that the higher the position an executive holds, the larger will the outside loom in his contribution. No one else in the organization can as a rule move as freely on the outside.

■ Perhaps the greatest shortcoming of the present generation of university presidents in the United States is their inside focus on administration, on money-raising, and so on. Yet no other administrator in the large university is free to establish contact with the students who are the university's "customers." Alienation of the students from the administration is certainly a major factor in the student unhappiness and unrest that underlay, for instance, the Berkeley riots at the University of California in 1965.

How to Make the Specialist Effective

For the knowledge worker to focus on contribution is particularly important. This alone can enable him to contribute at all.

Knowledge workers do not produce a "thing." They produce ideas, information, concepts. The knowledge worker, moreover, is usually a specialist. In fact, he can, as a rule, be effective only if he has learned to do one thing very well; that is, if he has specialized. By itself, however, a specialty is a fragment and sterile. Its output has to be put together with the output of other specialists before it can produce results.

The task is not to breed generalists. It is to enable the specialist to make himself and his specialty effective. This means that he must think through who is to use his output and what the user needs to know and to understand to be able to make productive the fragment the specialist produces.

■ It is popular today to believe that our society is divided into "scientists" and "laymen." It is then easy to demand that the laymen learn a little bit of the scientists' knowledge, his terminology, his tools, and so on. But if society was ever divided that way, it was a hundred years ago. Today almost everybody in modern organization is an expert with a high degree of specialized knowledge, each with its own tools, its own concerns, and its own jargon. And the sciences, in turn, have all become splintered to the point where one kind of physicist finds it difficult to comprehend what another kind of physicist is concerned with.

The cost accountant is as much a "scientist" as the biochemist, in the sense that he has his own special area of knowledge with its own assumptions, its own concerns, and its own language. And so is the market researcher and the computer logician, the budget officer of the government agency and the psychiatric case worker in the hospital. Each of these has to be understood by others before he can be effective.

The man of knowledge has always been expected to take responsibility for being understood. It is barbarian arrogance to assume that the layman can or should make the effort to understand him, and that it is enough if the man of knowledge talks to a handful of fellow experts who are his peers. Even in the university or in the research laboratory, this attitude—alas, only too common today—condemns the expert to uselessness and converts his knowledge from learning into pedantry. If a man wants to be an executive—that is, if he wants to be considered responsible for his contribution—he has to concern himself with the usability of his "product"—that is, his knowledge.

Effective executives know this. For they are almost imperceptibly led by their upward orientation into finding out what the other fellow needs, what the other fellow sees, and what the other fellow understands. Effective executives find themselves asking other people in the organization, their superiors, their subordinates, but above all, their colleagues in other areas: "What contribution from me do you require to make *your* contribution to the organization? When do you need this, how do you need it, and in what form?"

■ If cost accountants, for example, asked these questions, they would soon find out which of their assumptions—obvious to them—are totally unfamiliar to the managers who are to use the figures. They would soon find out which of the figures that to them are important are irrelevant to the operating people and which figures, barely seen by them and rarely reported, are the ones the operating people really need every day.

The biochemist who asks this question in a pharmaceutical company will soon find out that the clinicians can use the findings of the biochemist only if presented in the clinicians' language rather than in biochemical terms. The clinicians, however, in making the decision whether to put a new compound into clinical testing or not decide whether the biochemist's research product will even have a chance to become a new drug.

The scientist in government who focuses on contribution soon realizes that he must explain to the policy-maker where a scientific development *might* lead to; he must do something forbidden to scientists as a rule—that is, speculate about the outcome of a line of scientific inquiry.

The only meaningful definition of a "generalist" is a specialist who can relate his own small area to the universe of knowledge. Maybe a few people have knowledge in more than a few small areas. But that does not make them generalists; it makes them specialists in several areas. And one can be just as bigoted in three areas as in one. The man, however, who takes responsibility for his contribution will relate his narrow area to a genuine whole. He may never himself be able to integrate a number of knowledge areas into one. But he soon realizes that he has to learn enough of the needs, the directions, the limitations, and the perceptions of others to enable them to use his own work. Even if this does not make him appreciate the richness and the excitement of diversity, it will give him immunity against the arrogance of the learned—that degenerative disease which destroys knowledge and deprives it of beauty and effectiveness.

THE RIGHT HUMAN RELATIONS

Executives in an organization do not have good human relations because they have a "talent for people." They have good human relations because they focus on contribution in their own work and in their relationships with others. As a result, their relationships are productive—and this is the only valid definition of "good human relations." Warm feelings and pleasant words are meaningless, are indeed a false front for wretched attitudes, if there is no achievement in what is, after all, a work-focused and task-focused relationship. On the other hand, an occasional rough word will not disturb a relationship that produces results and accomplishments for all concerned.

■ If I were asked to name the men who, in my own experience, had the best human relations, I would name three: General George C. Marshall, Chief of Staff of the U.S. Army in World War II; Alfred P. Sloan, Jr., the head of General Motors from the early nineteen-twenties into the mid-fifties; and one of Sloan's senior associates, Nicholas Dreystadt, the man who built Cadillac into the successful luxury car in the midst of the depression (and might well have been chief executive of General Motors sometime in the nineteen-fifties but for his early death right after World War II).

These men were as different as men can be: Marshall, the "professional soldier," sparse, austere, dedicated, but with great, shy charm; Sloan, the "administrator," reserved, polite and very distant; and Dreystadt, warm, bubbling and, superficially, a typical German craftman of the "Old Heidelberg" tradition. Every one of them inspired deep devotion, indeed, true affection in all who worked for them. All three, in their different ways, built their relationship to people—their superiors, their colleagues, and their subordinates—around contribution. All three men, of necessity, worked closely with people and thought a good deal about people. All three had to make crucial "people" decisions. But not one of the three worried about "human relations." They took them for granted.

The focus on contribution by itself supplies the four basic requirements of effective human relations:
- communications;
- teamwork;

- self-development; and,
- development of others.

1. Communications have been in the center of managerial attention these last twenty years or more. In business, in public administration, in armed services, in hospitals, in other words in all the major institutions of modern society, there has been great concern with communications.

Results to date have been meager. Communications are by and large just as poor today as they were twenty or thirty years ago when we first became aware of the need for, and lack of, adequate communications in the modern organization. But we are beginning to understand why this massive communications effort cannot produce results.

We have been working at communications downward from management to the employees, from the superior to the subordinate. But communications are practically impossible if they are based on the downward relationship. This much we have learned from our work in perception and communications theory. The harder the superior tries to say something to his subordinate, the more likely is it that the subordinate will *mishear*. He will hear what he expects to hear rather than what is being said.

But executives who take responsibility for contribution in their own work will as a rule demand that their subordinates take responsibility too. They will tend to ask their men: "What are the contributions for which this organization and I, your superior, should hold you accountable? What should we expect of you? What is the best utilization of your knowledge and your ability?" And then communication becomes possible, becomes indeed easy.

Once the subordinate has thought through what contribution should be expected of him, the superior has, of course, both the right and the responsibility to judge the validity of the proposed contribution.

- According to all our experience, the objectives set by subordinates for themselves are almost never what the superior thought they should be. The subordinates or juniors, in other words, do see reality quite differently. And the more capable they are, the more willing to take responsibility, the more will their perception of reality and of its objective opportunities and needs differ from the view of their superior or of the organization. But any discrepancy between their conclusions and what their superior expected will stand out strongly.

Who is right in such a difference is not as a rule important. For effective communication in meaningful terms has already been established.

2. The focus on contribution leads to communications sideways and thereby makes teamwork possible.

The question, "Who has to use my output for it to become effective?" immediately shows up the importance of people who are not in line of authority, either upward or downward, from and to the individual executive. It underlines what is the reality of a knowledge organization: The effective work is actually done in and by teams of people of diverse knowledges and skills. These people have to work together voluntarily and according to the logic of the situation and the demands of the task, rather than according to a formal jurisdictional structure.

- In a hospital, for instance—perhaps the most complex of the modern knowledge organizations—nurses, dieticians, physical therapists, medical and X-ray technicians, pharmacologists, pathologists, and a host of other health-service professionals, have to work on and with the same patient, with a minimum of conscious command or control by anyone. And yet, they have to work together for a common end and in line with a general plan of action: the doctor's prescription for treatment. In terms of organizational structure, each of these health-service professionals reports to his own chief. Each operates in terms of his own highly specialized field of knowledge; that is, as a "professional." But each has to keep all the others informed according to the specific situation, the condition, and the need of an individual patient. Otherwise, their efforts are more likely to do harm than good.

In a hospital in which the focus on contribution has become ingrained habit, there is almost no difficulty in achieving such team work. In other hospitals this sideways communication, this spontaneous self-organization into the right task-focused teams, does not occur despite frantic efforts to obtain communications and coordination through all kinds of committees, staff conferences, bulletins, sermons, and the like.

The typical institution of today has an organization problem for which traditional concepts and theories are totally inadequate. Knowledge workers must be professionals in their attitude toward their own field of knowledge. They must consider themselves responsible for their own competence and for the standards of their work. In terms of formal organization, they will see themselves as "belonging" to a functional specialty—whether this is biochemistry or, as in the hospitals, nursing, for example. In terms of their personnel management—their training, their records, but also their appraisal and promotion—they will be governed by this knowledge-oriented function. But in their work they increasingly have to act as responsible members of a team with people from entirely different knowledge areas, organized around the specific task on hand.

Focus on upward contribution will not, by itself, provide the organizational solution. It will, however, contribute understanding of the task and communications to make imperfect organization perform.

■ Communications within the knowledge work force is becoming critical as a result of the computer revolution in information. Throughout the ages the problem has always been how to get "communication" out of "information." Because information had to be handled and transmitted by people, it was always distorted by communications; that is, by opinion, impression, comment, judgment, bias, and so on. Now suddenly we are in a situation in which information is largely impersonal and, therefore, without any communications content. It is pure information.

But now we have the problem of establishing the necessary minimum of communications so that we understand each other and can know each other's needs, goals, perceptions, and ways of doing things. Information does not supply this. Only direct contact, whether by voice or by written word, can communicate.

The more we automate information-handling, the more we will have to create opportunities for effective communication.

3. Individual self-development in large measure depends on the focus on contributions.

The man who asks of himself, "What is the most important contribution I can make to the performance of this organization?" asks in effect, "What self-development do I need? What knowledge and skill do I have to acquire to make the contribution I should be making? What strengths do I have to put to work? What standards do I have to set myself?"

4. The executive who focuses on contribution also stimulates others to develop themselves, whether they are subordinates, colleagues, or superiors. He sets standards which are not personal but grounded in the requirements of the task. At the same time, they are demands for excellence. For they are demands for high aspiration, for ambitious goals, and for work of great impact.

We know very little about self-development. But we do know one thing: People in general, and knowledge workers in particular, grow according to the demands they make on themselves. They grow according to what they consider to be

achievement and attainment. If they demand little of themselves, they will remain stunted. If they demand a good deal of
themselves, they will grow to giant stature—without any more
effort than is expended by the nonachievers.

THE EFFECTIVE MEETING

The meeting, the report, or the presentation are the typical
work situation of the executive. They are his specific, everyday
tools. They also make great demands on his time—even if he
succeeds in analyzing his time and in controlling whatever can
be controlled.

Effective executives know what they expect to get out of a
meeting, a report, or a presentation and what the purpose of the
occasion is or should be. They ask themselves: "Why are we
having this meeting? Do we want a decision, do we want to
inform, or do we want to make clear to ourselves what we
should be doing?" They insist that the purpose be thought
through and spelled out before a meeting is called, a report
asked for, or a presentation organized. They insist that the
meeting serve the contribution to which they have committed
themselves.

■ The effective man always states at the outset of a meeting the
  specific purpose and contribution it is to achieve. He makes
  sure that the meeting addresses itself to this purpose. He does
  not allow a meeting called to inform to degenerate into a
  "bull session" in which everyone has bright ideas. But a
  meeting called by him to stimulate thinking and ideas also
  does not become simply a presentation on the part of one
  of the members, but is run to challenge and stimulate everybody in the room. He always, at the end of his meetings,
  goes back to the opening statement and relates the final
  conclusions to the original intent.

There are other rules for making a meeting productive (for
instance, the obvious but usually disregarded rule that one

can either direct a meeting and listen for the important things being said, or one can take part and talk; one cannot do both). But the cardinal rule is to focus it from the start on contribution.

The focus on contribution counteracts one of the basic problems of the executive: the confusion and chaos of events and their failure to indicate by themselves which is meaningful and which is merely "noise." The focus on contribution imposes an organizing principle. It imposes relevance on events.

Focusing on contribution turns one of the inherent weaknesses of the executive's situation—his dependence on other people, his being within the organization—into a source of strength. It creates a team.

Finally, focusing on contribution fights the temptation to stay within the organization. It leads the executive—especially the top-level man—to lift his eyes from the inside of efforts, work, and relationships, to the outside; that is, to the results of the organization. It makes him try hard to have direct contact with the outside—whether markets and customers, patients in a community, or the various "publics" which are the outside of a government agency.

To focus on contribution is to focus on effectiveness.

4: Making Strength Productive

The effective executive makes strength productive. He knows that one cannot build on weakness. To achieve results, one has to use all the available strengths—the strengths of associates, the strengths of the superior, and one's own strengths. These strengths are the true opportunities. To make strength productive is the unique purpose of organization. It cannot, of course, overcome the weaknesses with which each of us is abundantly endowed. But it can make them irrelevant. Its task is to use the strength of each man as a building block for joint performance.

STAFFING FROM STRENGTH

The area in which the executive first encounters the challenge of strength is in staffing. The effective executive fills positions and promotes on the basis of what a man can do. He does not make staffing decisions to minimize weaknesses but to maximize strength.

- President Lincoln when told that General Grant, his new commander-in-chief, was fond of the bottle said: "If I knew

his brand, I'd send a barrel or so to some other generals."
After a childhood on the Kentucky and Illinois frontier,
Lincoln assuredly knew all about the bottle and its dangers.
But of all the Union generals, Grant alone had proven
consistently capable of planning and leading winning campaigns. Grant's appointment was the turning point of the
Civil War. It was an effective appointment because Lincoln
chose his general for his tested ability to win battles and not
for his sobriety, that is, for the absence of a weakness.

Lincoln learned this the hard way however. Before he
chose Grant, he had appointed in succession three or four
Generals whose main qualifications were their lack of major
weaknesses. As a result, the North, despite its tremendous
superiority in men and matériel, had not made any headway
for three long years from 1861 to 1864. In sharp contrast,
Lee, in command of the Confederate forces, had staffed from
strength. Every one of Lee's generals, from Stonewall Jackson on, was a man of obvious and monumental weaknesses.
But these failings Lee considered—rightly—to be irrelevant.
Each of them had, however, one area of real strength—and
it was this strength, and only this strength, that Lee utilized
and made effective. As a result, the "well-rounded" men
Lincoln had appointed were beaten time and again by Lee's
"single-purpose tools," the men of narrow but very great
strength.

Whoever tries to place a man or staff an organization to
avoid weakness will end up at best with mediocrity. The idea
that there are "well-rounded" people, people who have only
strengths and no weaknesses (whether the term used is the
"whole man," the "mature personality," the "well-adjusted personality," or the "generalist") is a prescription for mediocrity
if not for incompetence. Strong people always have strong
weaknesses too. Where there are peaks, there are valleys. And
no one is strong in many areas. Measured against the universe
of human knowledge, experience, and abilities, even the
greatest genius would have to be rated a total failure. There is

no such thing as a "good man." Good for what? is the question.

The executive who is concerned with what a man cannot do rather than with what he can do, and who therefore tries to avoid weakness rather than make strength effective is a weak man himself. He probably sees strength in others as a threat to himself. But no executive has ever suffered because his subordinates were strong and effective. There is no prouder boast, but also no better prescription, for executive effectiveness than the words Andrew Carnegie, the father of the U.S. steel industry, chose for his own tombstone: "Here lies a man who knew how to bring into his service men better than he was himself." But of course every one of these men was "better" because Carnegie looked for his strength and put it to work. Each of these steel executives was a "better man" in one specific area and for one specific job. Carnegie, however, was the effective executive among them.

- Another story about General Robert E. Lee illustrates the meaning of making strength productive. One of his generals, the story goes, had disregarded orders and had thereby completely upset Lee's plans—and not for the first time either. Lee, who normally controlled his temper, blew up in a towering rage. When he had simmered down, one of his aides asked respectfully, "Why don't you relieve him of his command?" Lee, it is said, turned around in complete amazement, looked at the aide, and said, "What an absurd question—he performs."

Effective executives know that their subordinates are paid to perform and not to please their superiors. They know that it does not matter how many tantrums a prima donna throws as long as she brings in the customers. The opera manager is paid after all for putting up with the prima donna's tantrums if that is her way to achieve excellence in performance. It does not matter whether a first-rate teacher or a brilliant scholar is pleasant to the dean or amiable in the faculty meeting. The dean is paid for enabling the first-rate teacher or the first-rate

scholar to do his work effectively—and if this involves un-
pleasantness in the administrative routine, it is still cheap at the
price.

Effective executives never ask "How does he get along with
me?" Their question is "What does he contribute?" Their question is never "What can a man not do?" Their question is
always "What can he do uncommonly well?" In staffing they
look for excellence in one major area, and not for performance
that gets by all around.

To look for one area of strength and to attempt to put it
to work is dictated by the nature of man. In fact, all the talk
of "the whole man" or the "mature personality" hides a profound contempt for man's most specific gift: his ability to
put all his resources behind one activity, one field of endeavor,
one area of accomplishment. It is, in other words, contempt for
excellence. Human excellence can only be achieved in one
area, or at the most in very few.

People with many interests do exist—and this is usually
what we mean when we talk of a "universal genius." People
with outstanding accomplishments in many areas are unknown.
Even Leonardo performed only in the area of design despite his
manifold interests; if Goethe's poetry had been lost and all
that were known of his work were his dabblings in optics and
philosophy, he would not even rate a footnote in the most
learned encyclopedia. What is true for the giants holds doubly
for the rest of us. Unless, therefore, an executive looks for
strength and works at making strength productive, he will only
get the impact of what a man cannot do, of his lacks, his weaknesses, his impediments to performance and effectiveness. To
staff from what there is not and to focus on weakness is wasteful—a misuse, if not abuse, of the human resource.

To focus on strength is to make demands for performance.
The man who does not first ask, "What can a man do?" is
bound to accept far less than the associate can really contribute. He excuses the associate's nonperformance in advance,

He is destructive but not critical, let alone realistic. The really "demanding boss"—and one way or another all makers of men are demanding bosses—always starts out with what a man should be able to do well—and then demands that he really do it.

To try to build against weakness frustrates the purpose of organization. Organization is the specific instrument to make human strengths redound to performance while human weakness is neutralized and largely rendered harmless. The very strong neither need nor desire organization. They are much better off working on their own. The rest of us, however, the great majority, do not have so much strength that by itself it would become effective despite our limitations. "One cannot hire a hand—the whole man always comes with it," says a proverb of the human relations people. Similarly, one cannot by oneself be only strong; the weaknesses are always with us.

But we can so structure an organization that the weaknesses become a personal blemish outside of, or at least beside, the work and accomplishment. We can so structure as to make the strength relevant. A good tax accountant in private practice might be greatly hampered by his inability to get along with people. But in an organization such a man can be set up in an office of his own and shielded from direct contact with other people. In an organization one can make his strength effective and his weakness irrelevant. The small businessman who is good at finance but poor at production or marketing is likely to get into trouble. In a somewhat larger business one can easily make productive a man who has true strength in finance alone.

Effective executives are not blind to weakness. The executive who understands that it is his job to enable John Jones to do his tax accounting has no illusions about Jones's ability to get along with people. He would never appoint Jones a manager.

But there are others who get along with people. First-rate tax accountants are a good deal rarer. Therefore, what this man— and many others like him—can do is pertinent in an organization. What he cannot do is a limitation and nothing else.

All this is obvious, one might say. Why then, is it not done all the time? Why are executives rare who make strength productive—especially the strength of their associates? Why did even a Lincoln staff from weakness three times before he picked strength?

The main reason is that the immediate task of the executive is not to place a man; it is to fill a job. The tendency is therefore to start out with the job as being a part of the order of nature. Then one looks for a man to fill the job. It is only too easy to be misled this way into looking for the "least misfit" —the one man who leaves least to be desired. And this is invariably the mediocrity.

The widely advertised "cure" for this is to structure jobs to fit the personalities available. But this cure is worse than the disease—except perhaps in a very small and simple organization. Jobs have to be objective; that is, determined by task rather than by personality.

One reason for this is that every change in the definition, structure, and position of a job within an organization sets off a chain reaction of changes throughout the entire institution. Jobs in an organization are interdependent and interlocked. One cannot change everybody's work and responsibility just because one has to replace a single man in a single job. To structure a job to a person is almost certain to result in the end in greater discrepancy between the demands of the job and the available talent. It results in a dozen people being uprooted and pushed around in order to accommodate one.

- This is by no means true only of bureaucratic organizations such as a government agency or a large business corporation. Somebody has to teach the introductory course in biochemistry in the university. It had better be a good man. Such a man will be a specialist. Yet the course has to be general and has to include the foundation materials of the discipline, regardless of the interests and inclinations of the teacher.

What is to be taught is determined by what the students need —that is, by an objective requirement—which the individual instructor has to accept. When the orchestra conductor has to fill the job of first cellist, he will not even consider a poor cellist who is a first-rate oboe player, even though the oboist might be a greater musician than any of the available cellists. The conductor will not rewrite the score to accommodate a man. The opera manager who knows that he is being paid for putting up with the tantrums of the prima donna still expects her to sing "Tosca" when the playbill announces *Tosca*.

But there is a subtler reason for insistence on impersonal, objective jobs. It is the only way to provide the organization with the human diversity it needs. It is the only way to tolerate —indeed to encourage—differences in temperament and personality in an organization. To tolerate diversity, relationships must be task-focused rather than personality-focused. Achievement must be measured against objective criteria of contribution and performance. This is possible, however, only if jobs are defined and structured impersonally. Otherwise the accent will be on "Who is right?" rather than on "What is right?" In no time, personnel decisions will be made on "Do I like this fellow?" or "Will he be acceptable?" rather than by asking "Is he the man most likely to do an outstanding job?"

Structuring jobs to fit personality is almost certain to lead to favoritism and conformity. And no organization can afford either. It needs equity and impersonal fairness in its personnel decisions. Or else it will either lose its good people or destroy their incentive. And it needs diversity. Or else it will lack the ability to change and the ability for dissent which (as Chapter 7 will discuss) the right decision demands.

■ One implication is that the men who build first-class executive teams are not usually close to their immediate colleagues and subordinates. Picking people for what they can do rather than on personal likes or dislikes, they seek performance, not conformance. To insure this outcome, they keep a distance between themselves and their close colleagues.

Lincoln, it has often been remarked, only became an effective chief executive after he had changed from close personal relations—for example, with Stanton, his Secretary of War —to aloofness and distance. Franklin D. Roosevelt had no "friend" in the Cabinet—not even Henry Morgenthau, his Secretary of the Treasury, and a close friend on all nongovernmental matters. General Marshall and Alfred P. Sloan were similarly remote. These were all warm men, in need of close human relationships, endowed with the gift of making and keeping friends. They knew however that their friendships had to be "off the job." They knew that whether they liked a man or approved of him was irrelevant, if not a distraction. And by staying aloof they were able to build teams of great diversity but also of strength.

Of course there are always exceptions where the job should be fitted to the man. Even Sloan, despite his insistence on impersonal structure, consciously designed the early engineering organization of General Motors around a man, Charles F. Kettering, the great inventor. Roosevelt broke every rule in the book to enable the dying Harry Hopkins to make his unique contribution. But these exceptions should be rare. And they should only be made for a man who has proven exceptional capacity to do the unusual with excellence.

How then do effective executives staff for strength without stumbling into the opposite trap of building jobs to suit personality?

By and large they follow four rules:

1. They do not start out with the assumption that jobs are created by nature or by God. They know that they have been designed by highly fallible men. And they are therefore forever on guard against the "impossible" job, the job that simply is not for normal human beings.

Such jobs are common. They usually look exceedingly logical on paper. But they cannot be filled. One man of proven performance capacity after the other is tried—and none does well. Six months or a year later, the job has defeated them.

Almost always such a job was first created to accommodate an unusual man and tailored to his idiosyncrasies. It usually calls for a mixture of temperaments that is rarely found in one person. Individuals can acquire very divergent kinds of knowledge and highly disparate skills. But they cannot change their temperaments. A job that calls for disparate temperaments becomes an "undoable" job, a man-killer.

The rule is simple: Any job that has defeated two or three men in succession, even though each had performed well in his previous assignments, must be assumed unfit for human beings. It must be redesigned.

■ Every text on marketing concludes, for instance, that sales management belongs together with advertising and promotion and under the same marketing executive. The experience of large, national manufacturers of branded and mass-marketed consumer goods has been, however, that this overall marketing job is impossible. Such a business needs both high effectiveness in field selling—that is, in moving goods —and high effectiveness in advertising and promotion—that is, in moving people. These appeal to different personalities which rarely can be found in one man.

The presidency of a large university in the United States is also such an impossible job. At least our experience has been that only a small minority of the appointments to this position work out—even though the men chosen have almost always a long history of substantial achievement in earlier assignments.

Another example is probably the international vice-president of today's large multinational business. As soon as production and sales outside the parent company's territory become significant—as soon as they exceed one fifth of the total or so—putting everything that is "not parent company" in one organizational component creates an impossible, a man-killing, job. The work either has to be reorganized by worldwide product groups (as Philips in Holland has done, for instance) or according to common social and economic characteristics of major markets. For instance, it might be split into three jobs: one managing the business in the industrialized countries (the United States, Canada, Western Europe, Japan); one the business in the developing countries (most of Latin America, Australia, India, the near East); one the business in the remaining underdeveloped ones. Several major chemical companies are going this route.

The ambassador of a major power today is in a similar predicament. His embassy has become so huge, unwieldy, and diffuse in its activities that a man who can administer it has no time for, and almost certainly no interest in, his first job: getting to know the country of his assignment, its government, its policies, its people, and to get known and trusted by them. And despite Mr. McNamara's lion-taming act at the Pentagon, I am not yet convinced that the job of Secretary of Defense of the United States is really possible (though I admit I cannot conceive of an alternative).

The effective executive therefore first makes sure that the job is well-designed. And if experience tells him otherwise, he does not hunt for genius to do the impossible. He redesigns the job. He knows that the test of organization is not genius. It is its capacity to make common people achieve uncommon performance.

2. The second rule for staffing from strength is to make each job demanding and big. It should have challenge to bring out whatever strength a man may have. It should have scope so that any strength that is relevant to the task can produce significant results.

This, however, is not the policy of most large organizations. They tend to make the job small—which would make sense only if people were designed and machined for specific performance at a given moment. Yet not only do we have to fill jobs with people as they come. The demands of any job above the simplest are also bound to change, and often abruptly. The "perfect fit" then rapidly becomes the misfit. Only if the job is big and demanding to begin with, will it enable a man to rise to the new demands of a changed situation.

This rule applies to the job of the beginning knowledge worker in particular. Whatever his strength it should have a chance to find full play. In his first job the standards are set by which a knowledge worker will guide himself the rest of his career and by which he will measure himself and his contribution. Till he enters the first adult job, the knowledge worker never has had a chance to perform. All one can do in school is to show promise. Performance is possible only in real work, whether in a research lab, in a teaching job, in a business or in a government agency. Both for the beginner in knowledge work and for the rest of the organization, his colleagues and his superiors, the most important thing to find out is what he really can do.

It is equally important for him to find out as early as possible whether he is indeed in the right place, or even in the right kind of work. There are fairly reliable tests for the aptitudes and skills needed in manual work. One can test in advance whether a man is likely to do well as a carpenter or as a machinist. There is no such test appropriate to knowledge work. What is needed in knowledge work is not this or that particular skill, but a configuration, and this will be revealed only by the test of performance.

A carpenter's or a machinist's job is defined by the craft and varies little from one shop to another. But for the ability of a knowledge worker to contribute in an organization, the values and the goals of the organization are at least as important as his own professional knowledge and skills. A young man who has the right strength for one organization may be a total misfit in another, which from the outside looks just the same. The first job should, therefore, enable him to test both himself and the organization.

■ This not only holds for different kinds of organization, such as government agencies, universities, or businesses. It is equally true between organizations of the same kind. I have yet to see two large businesses which have the same values and stress the same contributions. That a man who was happy and productive as a member of the faculty of one university may find himself lost, unhappy, and frustrated when he moves to another one every academic administrator has learned. And no matter how much the Civil Service Commission tries to make all government departments observe the same rules and use the same yardsticks, government agencies, once they have been in existence for a few years, have a distinct personality. Each requires a different behavior from its staff members, especially from those in the professional grades, to be effective and to make a contribution.

It is easy to move while young—at least in the Western countries where mobility is accepted. Once one has been in an organization for ten years or more, however, it becomes increasingly difficult, especially for those who have not been too effective. The young knowledge worker should, therefore, ask himself early: "Am I in the right work and in the right place for my strengths to tell?"

But he cannot ask this question, let alone answer it, if the beginning job is too small, too easy, and designed to offset his lack of experience rather than to bring out what he can do.

Every survey of young knowledge workers—physicians in the Army Medical Corps, chemists in the research lab, accountants or engineers in the plant, nurses in the hospital—produces the same results. The ones who are enthusiastic and who, in turn, have results to show for their work, are the ones whose abilities are being challenged and used. Those that are deeply frustrated all say, in one way or another: "My abilities are not being put to use."

The young knowledge worker whose job is too small to challenge and test his abilities either leaves or declines rapidly into premature middle-age, soured, cynical, unproductive. Executives everywhere complain that many young men with fire in their bellies turn so soon into burned-out sticks. They have only themselves to blame: They quenched the fire by making the young man's job too small.

3. Effective executives know that they have to start with what a man can do rather than with what a job requires. This, however, means that they do their thinking about people long before the decision on filling a job has to be made, and independently of it.

This is the reason for the wide adoption of appraisal procedures today, in which people, especially those in knowledge work, are regularly judged. The purpose is to arrive at an appraisal of a man *before* one has to decide whether he is the right person to fill a bigger position.

However, while almost every large organization has an appraisal procedure, few of them actually use it. Again and again the same executives who say that of course they appraise every one of their subordinates at least once a year, report that, to the best of their knowledge, they themselves have never been appraised by their own superiors. Again and again the appraisal forms remain in the files, and nobody looks at them when a personnel decision has to be made. Everybody dismisses them as so much useless paper. Above all, almost without exception, the "appraisal interview" in which the superior is to sit down with the subordinate and discuss the findings never takes place. Yet the appraisal interview is the crux of the whole system. One clue to what is wrong was contained in an advertisement of a new book on management which talked of the appraisal interview as "the most distasteful job" of the superior.

Appraisals, as they are now being used in the great majority of organizations, were designed originally by the clinical and abnormal psychologists for their own purposes. The clinician is a therapist trained to heal the sick. He is legitimately concerned with what is wrong, rather than with what is right with the patient. He assumes as a matter of course that nobody comes to him unless he is in trouble. The clinical psychologist or the abnormal psychologist, therefore, very properly looks upon appraisals as a process of diagnosing the weaknesses of a man.

■ I became aware of this in my first exposure to Japanese management. Running a seminar on executive development, I found to my surprise that none of the Japanese participants —all top men in large organizations—used appraisals. When I asked why not, one of them said: "Your appraisals are concerned only with bringing out a man's faults and weaknesses. Since we can neither fire a man nor deny him advancement and promotion, this is of no interest to us. On the contrary, the less we know about his weaknesses, the better. What we do need to know are the strengths of a man and what he can do. Your appraisals are not even interested in this." Western psychologists—especially those that design appraisals—might well disagree. But this is how every executive, whether Japanese, American, or German, sees the traditional appraisals.

Altogether the West might well ponder the lessons of the Japanese achievement. As everyone has heard, there is "lifetime employment" in Japan. Once a man is on the payroll, he will advance in his category—as a worker, a white-collar employee, or a professional and executive employee —according to his age and length of service, with his salary doubling about once every fifteen years. He cannot leave, neither can he be fired. Only at the top and after age forty-five is there differentiation, with a very small group selected by ability and merit into the senior executive positions. How can such a system be squared with the tremendous capacity for results and achievement Japan has shown? The answer is that their system forces the Japanese to play down weaknesses. Precisely because they cannot move people, Japanese executives always look for the man in the group who can do the job. They always look for strength.

I do not recommend the Japanese system. It is far from ideal. A very small number of people who have proven their capacity to perform do, in effect, everything of any importance whatever. The rest are carried by the organization. But if we in the West expect to get the benefit of the much greater mobility that both individual and organization enjoy in our tradition, we had better adopt the Japanese custom of looking for strength and using strength.

For a superior to focus on weakness, as our appraisals require him to do, destroys the integrity of his relationship with his subordinates. The many executives who in effect sabotage the appraisals their policy manuals impose on them follow sound instinct. It is also perfectly understandable that they consider an appraisal interview that focuses on a search for faults, defects, and weaknesses distasteful. To discuss a man's defects when he comes in as a patient seeking help is the responsibility of the healer. But, as has been known since Hippocrates, this presupposes a professional and privileged relationship between healer and patient which is incompatible with the authority relationship between superior and subordinate. It is a relationship that makes continued working together almost impossible. That so few executives use the official appraisal is thus hardly surprising. It is the wrong tool, in the wrong situation, for the wrong purpose.

Appraisals—and the philosophy behind them—are also far too much concerned with "potential." But experienced people have learned that one cannot appraise potential for any length of time ahead or for anything very different from what a man is already doing. "Potential" is simply another word for "promise." And even if the promise is there, it may well go unfulfilled, while people who have not shown such promise (if only because they may not have had the opportunity) actually produce the performance.

All one can measure is performance. And all one should measure is performance. This is another reason for making jobs big and challenging. It is also a reason for thinking through the contribution a man should make to the results and the performance of his organization. For one can measure the performance of a man only against specific performance expectations.

Still one needs some form of appraisal procedure—or else one makes the personnel evaluation at the wrong time, that is when a job has to be filled. Effective executives, therefore, usually work out their own radically different form. It starts out with a statement of the major contributions expected from a man in his past and present positions and a record of his performance against these goals. Then it asks four questions:

(a) "What has he [or she] done well?"
(b) "What, therefore, is he likely to be able to do well?"
(c) "What does he have to learn or to acquire to be able to get the full benefit from his strength?"
(d) "If I had a son or daughter, would I be willing to have him or her work under this person?"
    (i) "If yes, why?"
    (ii) "If no, why?"

This appraisal actually takes a much more critical look at a man than the usual procedure does. But it focuses on strengths. It begins with what a man can do. Weaknesses are seen as limitations to the full use of his strengths and to his own achievement, effectiveness, and accomplishment.

The last question (ii) is the only one which is not primarily concerned with strengths. Subordinates, especially bright, young, and ambitious ones, tend to mold themselves after a forceful boss. There is, therefore, nothing more corrupting and more destructive in an organization than a forceful but basically corrupt executive. Such a man might well operate effectively on his own; even within an organization, he might be tolerable if denied all power over others. But in a position of power within an organization, he destroys. Here, therefore, is the one area in which weakness in itself is of importance and relevance.

By themselves, character and integrity do not accomplish anything. But their absence faults everything else. Here, therefore, is the one area where weakness is a disqualification by itself rather than a limitation on performance capacity and strength.

4. The effective executive knows that to get strength one has to put up with weaknesses.

■ There have been few great commanders in history who were not self-centered, conceited, and full of admiration for what they saw in the mirror. (The reverse does not, of course, hold: There have been plenty of generals who were convinced of their own greatness, but who have not gone down in history as great commanders.) Similarly, the politician who does not with every fiber in his body want to be President or Prime Minister is not likely to be remembered as a statesman. He will at best be a useful—perhaps a highly useful—journeyman. To be more requires a man who is conceited enough to believe that the world—or at least the nation—really needs him and depends on his getting into power. (Again the reverse does not hold true.) If the need is for the ability to command in a perilous situation, one has to accept a Disraeli or a Franklin D. Roosevelt and not worry too much about their lack of humility. There are indeed no great men to their valets. But the laugh is on the valet. He sees, inevitably, all the traits that are not relevant, all the traits that have nothing to do with the specific task for which a man has been called on the stage of history.

The effective executive will therefore ask: "Does this man have strength in *one* major area? And is this strength relevant to the task? If he achieves excellence in this one area, will it make a significant difference?" And if the answer is "yes," he will go ahead and appoint the man.

Effective executives rarely suffer from the delusion that two mediocrities achieve as much as one good man. They have learned that, as a rule, two mediocrities achieve even less than one mediocrity—they just get in each other's way. They accept that abilities must be specific to produce performance. They never talk of a "good man" but always about a man who is "good" for some one task. But in this one task, they search for strength and staff for excellence.

This also implies that they focus on opportunity in their staffing—not on problems.

They are above all intolerant of the argument: "I can't spare this man; I'd be in trouble without him." They have learned that there are only three explanations for an "indispensable man": He is actually incompetent and can only survive if carefully shielded from demands; his strength is misused to bolster a weak superior who cannot stand on his own two feet; or his strength is misused to delay tackling a serious problem if not to conceal its existence.

In every one of these situations, the "indispensable man" should be moved anyhow—and soon. Otherwise one only destroys whatever strengths he may have.

- The chief executive who was mentioned in Chapter 3 for his unconventional methods of making effective the manager-development policies of a large retail chain also decided to move automatically anyone whose boss described him as indispensable. "This either means," he said, "that I have a weak superior or a weak subordinate—or both. Whichever of these, the sooner we find out, the better."

Altogether it must be an unbreakable rule to promote the man who by the test of performance is best qualified for the job to be filled. All arguments to the contrary—"He is indispensable" . . . "He won't be acceptable to the people there" . . . "He is too young". . . or "We never put a man in there without field experience"—should be given short shrift. Not only does the job deserve the best man. The man of proven performance has earned the opportunity. Staffing the opportunities instead of the problems not only creates the most effective organization, it also creates enthusiasm and dedication.

Conversely, it is the duty of the executive to remove ruthlessly anyone—and especially any manager—who consistently fails to perform with high distinction. To let such a man stay on corrupts the others. It is grossly unfair to the whole organization. It is grossly unfair to his subordinates who are deprived by their superior's inadequacy of opportunities for achievement and recognition. Above all, it is senseless cruelty to the man himself. He knows that he is inadequate whether he admits it to himself or not. Indeed, I have never seen anyone in a job for which he was inadequate who was not slowly being destroyed by the pressure and the strains, and who did not secretly pray for deliverance. That neither the Japanese "lifetime employment" nor the various civil service systems of the West consider proven incompetence ground for removal is a serious weakness—and an unnecessary one.

■ General Marshall during World War II insisted that a general officer be immediately relieved if found less than outstanding. To keep him in command, he reasoned, was incompatible with the responsibility the army and the nation owed the men under an officer's command. Marshall flatly refused to listen to the argument: "But we have no replacement." "All that matters," he pointed out, "is that you know that this man is not equal to the task. Where his replacement comes from is the next question."

But Marshall also insisted that to relieve a man from command was less a judgment on the man than on the commander who had appointed him. "The only thing we know is that this spot was the wrong one for the man," he argued. "This does not mean that he is not the ideal man for some other job. Appointing him was my mistake, now it's up to me to find what he can do."

Altogether General Marshall offers a good example how one makes strength productive. When he first reached a position of influence in the mid-thirties, there was no general officer in the U.S. Army still young enough for active duty. (Marshall himself only beat the deadline by four months. His sixtieth birthday when he would have been too old to take office as Chief of Staff, was on December 31, 1939. He was appointed on September 1 of the same year.) The future generals of World War II were still junior officers with few hopes for promotion when Marshall began to select and train them. Eisenhower was one of the older ones and even he, in the mid-thirties, was only a major. Yet by 1942, Marshall had developed the largest and clearly the ablest group of general officers in American history. There were almost no failures in it and not many second-raters.

This—one of the greatest educational feats in military history—was done by a man who lacked all the normal trappings of "leadership," such as the personal magnetism or the towering self-confidence of a Montgomery, a de Gaulle or a MacArthur. What Marshall had were principles. "What can this man do?" was his constant question. And if a man could do something, his lacks became secondary.

■ Marshall, for instance, again and again came to George Patton's rescue and made sure that this ambitious, vain, but powerful wartime commander would not be penalized for the absence of the qualities that make a good staff officer and a successful career soldier in peacetime. Yet Marshall himself personally loathed the dashing *beau sabreur* of Patton's type.

Marshall was only concerned with weaknesses when they limited the full development of a man's strength. These he tried to overcome through work and career opportunities.

■ The young Major Eisenhower, for instance, was quite deliberately put by Marshall into war-planning in the midthirties to help him acquire the systematic strategic understanding which he apparently lacked. Eisenhower did not himself become a strategist as a result. But he acquired respect for strategy and an understanding of its importance and thereby removed a serious limitation on his great strength as a team-builder and tactical planner.

Marshall always appointed the best qualified man no matter how badly he was needed where he was. "We owe this move to the job . . . we owe it to the man and we owe it to the troops," was his reply when someone—usually someone high up—pleaded with him not to pull out an "indispensable" man.

■ He made but one exception: When President Roosevelt pleaded that Marshall was indispensable to him, Marshall stayed in Washington, yielded supreme command in Europe to Eisenhower, and thus gave up his life's dream.

Finally Marshall knew—and everyone can learn it from him—that every people-decision is a gamble. By basing it on what a man can do, it becomes at least a rational gamble.

A superior has responsibility for the work of others. He also has power over the careers of others. Making strengths productive is therefore much more than an essential of effectiveness. It is a moral imperative, a responsibility of authority and position. To focus on weakness is not only foolish; it is irresponsible. A superior owes it to his organization to make the strength of every one of his subordinates as productive as it can be. But even more does he owe it to the human beings over whom he exercises authority to help them get the most out of whatever strength they may have. Organization must serve the individual to achieve through his strengths and regardless of his limitations and weaknesses.

This is becoming increasingly important, indeed critical. Only a short generation ago the number of knowledge jobs and the range of knowledge employments were small. To be a civil servant in the German or in the Scandinavian governments, one had to have a law degree. A mathematician need not apply. Conversely, a young man wanting to make a living by putting his knowledge to work had only three or four choices of fields and employment. Today there is a bewildering variety of knowledge work and an equally bewildering variety of employment choices for men of knowledge. Around 1900, the only knowledge fields for all practical purposes were still the traditional professions—the law, medicine, teaching, and preaching. There are now literally hundreds of different disciplines. Moreover, practically every knowledge area is being put to productive use in and by organization, especially, of course, by business and government.

On the one hand, therefore, one can today try to find the knowledge area and the kind of work to which one's abilities are best fitted. One need no longer, as one had to do even in the recent past, fit oneself to the available knowledge areas and employments. On the other hand, it is increasingly difficult for a young man to make his choice. He does not have enough information, either about himself or about the opportunities.

This makes it much more important for the individual that he be directed toward making his strengths productive. It also makes it important for the organization that its executives focus on strengths and work on making strengths productive in their own group and with their own subordinates.

Staffing for strength is thus essential to the executive's own effectiveness and to that of his organization but equally to individual and society in a world of knowledge work.

How Do I Manage My Boss?

Above all, the effective executive tries to make fully productive the strengths of his own superior.

I have yet to find a manager, whether in business, in government, or in any other institution, who did not say: "I have no great trouble managing my subordinates. But how do I manage my boss?" It is actually remarkably easy—but only effective executives know that. The secret is that effective executives make the strengths of the boss productive.

- This should be elementary prudence. Contrary to popular legend, subordinates do not, as a rule, rise to position and prominence over the prostrate bodies of incompetent bosses. If their boss is not promoted, they will tend to be bottled up behind him. And if their boss is relieved for incompetence or failure, the successor is rarely the bright, young man next in line. He usually is brought in from the outside and brings with him his own bright, young men. Conversely, there is nothing quite as conducive to success, as a successful and rapidly promoted superior.

But way beyond prudence, making the strength of the boss productive is a key to the subordinate's own effectiveness. It enables him to focus his own contribution in such a way that it finds receptivity upstairs and will be put to use. It enables him to achieve and accomplish the things he himself believes in.

One does not make the strengths of the boss productive by toadying to him. One does it by starting out with what is right and presenting it in a form which is accessible to the superior.

The effective executive accepts that the boss is human (something that intelligent young subordinates often find hard). Because the superior is human, he has his strengths; but he also has limitations. To build on his strengths, that is, to enable him to do what he can do, will make him effective—and will make the subordinate effective. To try to build on his weaknesses will be as frustrating and as stultifying as to try to build on the weaknesses of a subordinate. The effective executive, therefore, asks: "What can my boss do really well?" "What has he done really well?" "What does he need to know to use his strength?" "What does he need to get from me to perform?" He does not worry too much over what the boss cannot do.

■ Subordinates typically want to "reform" the boss. The able senior civil servant is inclined to see himself as the tutor to the newly appointed political head of his agency. He tries to get his boss to overcome his limitations. The effective ones ask instead: "What can the new boss do?" And if the answer is: "He is good at relationships with Congress, the White House, and the public," then the civil servant works at making it possible for his minister to use these abilities. For the best administration and the best policy decisions are futile unless there is also political skill in representing them. Once the politician knows that the civil servant supports him, he will soon enough listen to him on policy and on administration.

The effective executive also knows that the boss, being human, has his own ways of being effective. He looks for these ways. They may be only manners and habits, but they are facts.

It is, I submit, fairly obvious to anyone who has ever looked that people are either "readers" or "listeners" (excepting only the very small group who get their information through talking, and by watching with a form of psychic radar the reactions of the people they talk to; both President Franklin Roosevelt and President Lyndon Johnson belong in this category, as apparently did Winston Churchill). People who are both readers and listeners—trial lawyers have to be both, as a rule—are exceptions. It is generally a waste of time to talk to a reader. He only listens after he has read. It is equally a waste of time to submit a voluminous report to a listener. He can only grasp what it is all about through the spoken word.

Some people need to have things summed up for them in one page. (President Eisenhower needed this to be able to act.)

Others need to be able to follow the thought processes of the man who makes the recommendation and therefore require a big report before anything becomes meaningful to them. Some superiors want to see sixty pages of figures on everything. Some want to be in at the early stages so that they can prepare themselves for the eventual decision. Others do not want even to hear about the matter until it is "ripe," and so on.

The adaptation needed to think through the strengths of the boss and to try to make them productive always affects the "how" rather than the "what." It concerns the order in which different areas, all of them relevant, are presented, rather than what is important or right. If the superior's strength lies in his political ability in a job in which political ability is truly relevant, then one presents to him first the political aspect of a situation. This enables him to grasp what the issue is all about and to put his strength effectively behind a new policy.

All of us are "experts" on other people and see them much more clearly than they see themselves. To make the boss effective is therefore usually fairly easy. But it requires focus on his strengths and on what he can do. It requires building on strength to make weaknesses irrelevant. Few things make an executive as effective as building on the strengths of his superior.

Making Yourself Effective

Effective executives lead from strength in their own work. They make productive what they can do.

Most executives I know in government, in the hospital, in a business, know all the things they cannot do. They are only too conscious of what the boss won't let them do, of what company policy won't let them do, of what the government won't let them do. As a result, they waste their time and their strengths complaining about the things they cannot do anything about.

Effective executives are of course also concerned with limitations. But it is amazing how many things they find that can be done and are worth while doing. While the others complain about their inability to do anything, the effective executives go ahead and do. As a result, the limitations that weigh so heavily on their brethren often melt away.

- Everyone in the management of one of the major railroads knew that the government would not let the company do anything. But then a new financial vice-president came in who had not yet learned that "lesson." Instead he went to Washington, called on the Interstate Commerce Commission and asked for permission to do a few rather radical things. "Most of these things," the commissioners said, "are none of our concern to begin with. The others you have to try and test out and then we will be glad to give you the go-ahead."

The assertion that "somebody else will not let me do anything" should always be suspected as a cover-up for inertia. But even where the situation does set limitations—and everyone lives and works within rather stringent limitations—there are usually important, meaningful, pertinent things that can be done. The effective executive looks for them. If he starts out with the question: "What can I do?" he is almost certain to find that he can actually do much more than he has time and resources for.

Making strengths productive is equally important in respect to one's own abilities and work habits.

It is not very difficult to know *how* we achieve results. By the time one has reached adulthood, one has a pretty good idea as to whether one works better in the morning or at night. One usually knows whether one writes best by making a great many drafts fast, or by working meticulously on every sentence until it is right. One knows whether one speaks well in public from a prepared text, from notes, without any prop, or not at all. One knows whether one works well as a member of a committee or better alone—or whether one is altogether unproductive as a committee member.

Some people work best if they have a detailed outline in front of them; that is, if they have thought through the job before they start it. Others work best with nothing more than a few rough notes. Some work best under pressure. Others work better if they have a good deal of time and can finish the job long before the deadline. Some are "readers," others "listeners." All this one knows, about oneself—just as one knows whether one is right-handed or left-handed.

These, it will be said, are superficial. This is not necessarily correct—a good many of these traits and habits mirror fundamentals of a man's personality such as his perception of the world and of himself in it. But even if superficial, these work habits are a source of effectiveness. And most of them are compatible with any kind of work. The effective executive knows this and acts accordingly.

All in all, the effective executive tries to be himself; he does not pretend to be someone else. He looks at his own performance and at his own results and tries to discern a pattern. "What are the things," he asks, "that I seem to be able to do with relative ease, while they come rather hard to other people?" One man, for instance, finds it easy to write up the final report while many others find it a frightening chore. At the same time, however, he finds it rather difficult and unrewarding to think through the report and face up to the hard decisions. He is, in other words, more effective as a staff thinker who organizes and lays out the problems than as the decision-maker who takes command responsibility.

One can know about oneself that one usually does a good job working alone on a project from start to finish. One can know that one does, as a rule, quite well in negotiations, particularly emotional ones such as negotiating a union contract. But at the same time, one also knows whether one's predictions what the union will ask for have usually been correct or not.

These are not the things most people have in mind when they talk about the strengths or weaknesses of a man. They usually mean knowledge of a discipline or talent in an art. But temperament is also a factor in accomplishment and a big one. An adult usually knows quite a bit about his own temperament. To be effective he builds on what he knows he can do and does it the way he has found out he works best.

Unlike everything else discussed in this book so far, making strength productive is as much an attitude as it is a practice. But it can be improved with practice. If one disciplines oneself to ask about one's associates—subordinates as well as superiors—"What can this man do?" rather than "What can he not do?" one soon will acquire the attitude of looking for strength and of using strength. And eventually one will learn to ask this question of oneself.

In every area of effectiveness within an organization, *one feeds the opportunities and starves the problems.* Nowhere is this more important than in respect to people. The effective executive looks upon people including himself as an opportunity. He knows that only strength produces results. Weakness only produces headaches—and the absence of weakness produces nothing.

He knows, moreover, that the standard of any human group is set by the performance of the leaders. And he, therefore, never allows leadership performance to be based on anything but true strength.

- In sports we have long learned that the moment a new record is set every athlete all over the world acquires a new dimension of accomplishment. For years no one could run the mile in less than four minutes. Suddenly Roger Bannister broke through the old record. And soon the average sprinters in every athletic club in the world were approaching yesterday's record, while new leaders began to break through the four-minute barrier.

In human affairs, the distance between the leaders and the average is a constant. If leadership performance is high, the average will go up. The effective executive knows that it is easier to raise the performance of one leader than it is to raise the performance of a whole mass. He therefore makes sure that he puts into the leadership position, into the standard-setting, the performance-making position, the man who has the strength to do the outstanding, the pace-setting job. This always requires focus on the one strength of a man and dismissal of weaknesses as irrelevant unless they hamper the full deployment of the available strength.

The task of an executive is not to change human beings. Rather, as the Bible tells us in the parable of the Talents, the task is to multiply performance capacity of the whole by putting to use whatever strength, whatever health, whatever aspiration there is in individuals.

5: First Things First

If there is any one "secret" of effectiveness, it is concentration. Effective executives do first things first and they do one thing at a time.

The need to concentrate is grounded both in the nature of the executive job and in the nature of man. Several reasons for this should already be apparent: There are always more important contributions to be made than there is time available to make them. Any analysis of executive contributions comes up with an embarrassing richness of important tasks; any analysis of executives' time discloses an embarrassing scarcity of time available for the work that really contributes. No matter how well an executive manages his time, the greater part of it will still not be his own. Therefore, there is always a time deficit.

The more an executive focuses on upward contribution, the more will he require fairly big continuous chunks of time. The more he switches from being busy to achieving results, the more will he shift to sustained efforts—efforts which require a fairly big quantum of time to bear fruit. Yet to get even that half-day or those two weeks of really productive time requires self-discipline and an iron determination to say "No."

Similarly, the more an executive works at making strengths productive, the more will he become conscious of the need to concentrate the human strengths available to him on major opportunities. This is the only way to get results.

But concentration is dictated also by the fact that most of us find it hard enough to do well even one thing at a time, let alone two. Mankind is indeed capable of doing an amazingly wide diversity of things; humanity is a "multipurpose tool." But the way to apply productively mankind's great range is to bring to bear a large number of individual capabilities on one task. It is concentration in which all faculties are focused on one achievement.

■ We rightly consider keeping many balls in the air a circus stunt. Yet even the juggler does it only for ten minutes or so. If he were to try doing it longer, he would soon drop all the balls.

People do, of course, differ. Some do their best work when doing two tasks in parallel at the same time, thus providing a change of pace. This presupposes however that they give each of the two tasks the minimum quantum needed to get anything done. But few people, I think, can perform with excellence three major tasks simultaneously.

■ There was Mozart, of course. He could, it seems, work on several compositions at the same time, all of them master-pieces. But he is the only known exception. The other prolific composers of the first rank—Bach, for instance, Handel, or Haydn, or Verdi—composed one work at a time. They did not begin the next until they had finished the preceding one, or until they had stopped work on it for the time being and put it away in the drawer. Executives can hardly assume that they are "executive Mozarts."

Concentration is necessary precisely because the executive faces so many tasks clamoring to be done. For doing one thing at a time means doing it fast. The more one can concentrate time, effort, and resources, the greater the number and diversity of tasks one can actually perform.

■ No chief executive of any business I have ever known accomplished as much as the recently retired head of a pharmaceutical firm. When he took over, the company was small and operated in one country only. When he retired eleven years later, the company had become a worldwide leader.

This man worked for the first years exclusively on research direction, research program, and research personnel. The organization had never been a leader in research and had usually been tardy even as a follower. The new chief executive was not a scientist. But he realized that the company had to stop doing five years later what the leaders had pioneered five years before. It had to decide on its own direction. As a result, it moved within five years into a leadership position in two new important fields.

The chief executive then turned to building an international company—years after the leaders, such as the old Swiss pharmaceutical houses, had established themselves as leaders all over the world. Carefully analyzing drug consumption, he concluded that health insurance and government health services act as the main stimuli to drug demand. By timing his entry into a new country to coincide with a major expansion of its health services he managed to start big in countries where his company had never been before, and without having to take away markets from the well-entrenched international drug firms.

The last five years of his tenure he concentrated on working out the strategy appropriate to the nature of modern health care, which is fast becoming a "public utility" in which public bodies such as governments, nonprofit hospitals, and semipublic agencies (such as Blue Cross in the United States) pay the bills, although an individual, the physician, decides on the actual purchase. Whether his strategy will work out, it is too early to say—it was only perfected in 1965, shortly before he retired. But his is the only one of the major drug companies that, to my knowledge, has even thought about strategy, pricing, marketing, and the relationships of the industry worldwide.

It is unusual for any one chief executive to do one task of such magnitude during his entire tenure. Yet this man did three—in addition to building a strong, well-staffed, worldwide organization. He did this by single-minded concentration on one task at a time.

This is the "secret" of those people who "do so many things" and apparently so many difficult things. They do only one at a time. As a result, they need much less time in the end than the rest of us.

■ The people who get nothing done often work a great deal harder. In the first place, they underestimate the time for any one task. They always expect that everything will go right. Yet, as every executive knows, nothing ever goes right. The unexpected always happens—the unexpected is indeed the only thing one can confidently expect. And almost never is it a pleasant surprise. Effective executives therefore allow a fair margin of time beyond what is actually needed. In the second place, the typical (that is, the more or less ineffectual) executive tries to hurry—and that only puts him further behind. Effective executives do not race. They set an easy pace but keep going steadily. Finally, the typical executive tries to do several things at once. Therefore, he never has the minimum time quantum for any of the tasks in his program. If any one of them runs into trouble, his entire program collapses.

Effective executives know that they have to get many things done—and done effectively. Therefore, they concentrate—their own time and energy as well as that of their organization—on doing one thing at a time, and on doing first things first.

SLOUGHING OFF YESTERDAY

The first rule for the concentration of executive efforts is to slough off the past that has ceased to be productive. Effective executives periodically review their work programs—and those of their associates—and ask: "If we did not already do this, would we go into it *now*?" And unless the answer is an unconditional "Yes," they drop the activity or curtail it sharply. At the least, they make sure that no more resources are being invested in the no-longer-productive past. And those first-class resources, especially those scarce resources of human strength which are engaged in these tasks of yesterday, are immediately pulled out and put to work on the opportunities of tomorrow.

Executives, whether they like it or not, are forever bailing out the past. This is inevitable. Today is always the result of actions and decisions taken yesterday. Man, however, whatever his title or rank, cannot foresee the future. Yesterday's actions and decisions, no matter how courageous or wise they may have been, inevitably become today's problems, crises, and stupidities. Yet it is the executive's specific job—whether he works in government, in a business, or in any other institution—to commit today's resources to the future. This means that every executive forever has to spend time, energy, and ingenuity on patching up or bailing out the actions and decisions of yesterday, whether his own or those of his predecessors. In fact this always takes up more hours of his day than any other task.

But one can at least try to limit one's servitude to the past by cutting out those inherited activities and tasks that have ceased to promise results.

No one has much difficulty getting rid of the total failures. They liquidate themselves. Yesterday's successes, however, always linger on long beyond their productive life. Even more dangerous are the activities which should do well and which, for some reason or other, do not produce. These tend to become, as I have explained elsewhere "investments in managerial ego" and sacred.* Yet unless they are pruned, and pruned ruthlessly, they drain the lifeblood from an organization. It is always the most capable people who are wasted in the futile attempt to obtain for the investment in managerial ego the "success it deserves."

■ Every organization is highly susceptible to these twin diseases. But they are particularly prevalent in government. Government programs and activities age just as fast as the programs and activities of other institutions. Yet they are not only conceived as eternal; they are welded into the structure through civil service rules and immediately become vested interests, with their own spokesmen in the legislature.

This was not too dangerous when government was small and played a minor role in social life as it did up until 1914. Today's government however cannot afford the diversion of its energies and resources into yesterday. Yet, at a guess, at least half the bureaus and agencies of the federal government of the United States either regulate what no longer needs regulation—for example, the Interstate Commerce Commission whose main efforts are still directed toward protecting the public from a monopoly of the railroads that disappeared thirty years ago. Or they are directed, as is most of the farm program, toward investment in politicians' egos and toward efforts that should have had results but never achieved them.

There is serious need for a new principle of effective administration under which every act, every agency, and every program of government is conceived as temporary and as expiring automatically after a fixed number of years—maybe ten—unless specifically prolonged by new legislation following careful outside study of the program, its results and its contributions.

* See *Managing for Results.*

President Johnson in 1965-1966 ordered such a study for all government agencies and their programs, adapting the "program review" which Secretary McNamara had developed to rid the Defense department of the barnacles of obsolete and unproductive work. This is a good first step, and badly needed. But it will not produce results as long as we maintain the traditional assumption that all programs last forever unless proven to have outlived their usefulness. The assumption should rather be that all programs outlive their usefulness fast and should be scrapped unless proven productive and necessary. Otherwise, modern government, while increasingly smothering society under rules, regulations, and forms, will itself be smothered in its own fat.

But while government is particularly endangered by organizational obesity, no organization is immune to the disease. The businessman in the large corporation who complains the loudest about bureaucracy in government may encourage in his own company the growth of "controls" which do not control anything, the proliferation of studies that are only a cover-up for his own unwillingness to face up to a decision, the inflation of all kinds of staffs for all kinds of research or "relations." And he himself may waste his own time and that of his key people on the obsolescent product of yesterday while starving tomorrow's successful product. The academician who is loudest in his denunciation of the horrible wastefulness of big business may fight the hardest in the faculty meeting to prolong the life of an obsolescent subject by making it a required course.

The executive who wants to be effective and who wants his organization to be effective polices all programs, all activities, all tasks. He always asks: "Is this still worth doing?" And if it isn't, he gets rid of it so as to be able to concentrate on the few tasks that, if done with excellence, will really make a difference in the results of his own job and in the performance of his organization.

Above all, the effective executive will slough off an old activity before he starts on a new one. This is necessary in order to keep organizational "weight control." Without it, the organization soon loses shape, cohesion, and manageability. Social organizations need to stay lean and muscular as much as biological organisms.

But also, as every executive has learned, nothing new is easy. It always gets into trouble. Unless one has therefore built into the new endeavor the means for bailing it out when it runs into heavy weather, one condemns it to failure from the start. The only effective means for bailing out the new are people who have proven their capacity to perform. Such people are always already busier than they should be. Unless one relieves one of them of his present burden, one cannot expect him to take on the new task.

The alternative—to "hire in" new people for new tasks—is too risky. One hires new people to expand on already established and smoothly running activity. But one starts something new with people of tested and proven strength, that is, with veterans. Every new task is such a gamble—even if other people have done the same job many times before—that an experienced and effective executive will not, if humanly possible, add to it the additional gamble of hiring an outsider to take charge. He has learned the hard way how many men who looked like geniuses when they worked elsewhere show up as miserable failures six months after they have started working "for us."

- An organization needs to bring in fresh people with fresh points of view fairly often. If it only promotes from within it soon becomes inbred and eventually sterile. But if at all possible, one does not bring in the newcomers where the risk is exorbitant—that is, into the top executive positions or into leadership of an important new activity. One brings them in just below the top and into an activity that is already defined and reasonably well understood.

Systematic sloughing off of the old is the one and only way
to force the new. There is no lack of ideas in any organization
I know. "Creativity" is not our problem. But few organizations ever get going on their own good ideas. Everybody is
much too busy on the tasks of yesterday. Putting all programs
and activities regularly on trial for their lives and getting rid of
those that cannot prove their productivity work wonders in
stimulating creativity even in the most hidebound bureaucracy.

■ Du Pont has been doing so much better than any other of
the world's large chemical companies largely because it
abandons a product or a process *before* it begins to decline.
Du Pont does not invest scarce resources of people and
money into defending yesterday. Most other businesses,
however, inside and outside the chemical industry, are run
on different principles; namely, "There'll always be a market
for an efficient buggy-whip plant," and, "This product built
this company and it's our duty to maintain for it the market
it deserves."

It's those other companies, however, which send their
executives to seminars on creativity and which complain
about the absence of new products. Du Pont is much too
busy making and selling new products to do either.

The need to slough off the outworn old to make possible the
productive new is universal. It is reasonably certain that we
would still have stagecoaches—nationalized, to be sure,
heavily subsidized, and with a fantastic research program to
"retrain the horse"—had there been ministries of transportation around 1825.

PRIORITIES AND POSTERIORITIES

There are always more productive tasks for tomorrow than
there is time to do them and more opportunities than there
are capable people to take care of them—not to mention the
always abundant problems and crises.

A decision therefore has to be made as to which tasks deserve priority and which are of less importance. The only question is which will make the decision—the executive or the pressures. But somehow the tasks will be adjusted to the available time and the opportunities will become available only to the extent to which capable people are around to take charge of them.

If the pressures rather than the executive are allowed to make the decision, the important tasks will predictably be sacrificed. Typically, there will then be no time for the most time-consuming part of any task, the conversion of decision into action. No task is completed until it has become part of organizational action and behavior. This almost always means that no task is completed unless other people have taken it on as their own, have accepted new ways of doing old things or the necessity for doing something new, and have otherwise made the executive's "completed" project their own daily routine. If this is slighted because there is no time, then all the work and effort have been for nothing. Yet this is the invariable result of the executive's failure to concentrate and to impose priorities.

Another predictable result of leaving control of priorities to the pressures is that the work of top management does not get done at all. That is always postponable work, for it does not try to solve yesterday's crises but to make a different tomorrow. And the pressures always favor yesterday. In particular, a top group which lets itself be controlled by the pressures will slight the one job no one else can do. It will not pay attention to the outside of the organization. It will therefore lose touch with the only reality, the only area in which there are results. For the pressures always favor what goes on inside. They always favor what has happened over the future, the crisis over the opportunity, the immediate and visible over the real, and the urgent over the relevant.

The job is, however, not to set priorities. That is easy.

Everybody can do it. The reason why so few executives concentrate is the difficulty of setting "posteriorities"—that is, deciding what tasks not to tackle—and of sticking to the decision.

Most executives have learned that what one postpones, one actually abandons. A good many of them suspect that there is nothing less desirable than to take up later a project one has postponed when it first came up. The timing is almost bound to be wrong, and timing is a most important element in the success of any effort. To do five years later what it would have been smart to do five years earlier is almost a sure recipe for frustration and failure.

■ Outside of Victorian novels, happiness does not come to the marriage of two people who almost got married at age 21 and who then, at age 38, both widowed, find each other again. If married at age 21, these people might have had an opportunity to grow up together. But in seventeen years both have changed, grown apart, and developed their own ways.

The man who wanted to become a doctor as a youth but was forced to go into business instead, and who now, at age fifty and successful, goes back to his first love and enrolls in medical school is not likely to finish, let alone to become a successful physician. He may succeed if he has extraordinary motivation, such as a strong religious drive to become a medical missionary. But otherwise he will find the discipline and rote learning of medical school irksome beyond endurance, and medical practice itself humdrum and a bore.

The merger which looked so right six or seven years earlier, but had to be postponed because one company's president refused to serve under the other, is rarely still the right "marriage" for either side when the stiff-necked executive has finally retired.

That one actually abandons what one postpones makes executives, however, shy from postponing anything altogether.

They know that this or that task is not a first priority, but giving it a posteriority is risky. What one has relegated may turn out to be the competitor's triumph. There is no guarantee that the policy area a politician or an administrator has decided to slight may not explode into the hottest and most dangerous political issue.

■ Neither President Eisenhower nor President Kennedy, for instance, wanted to give high priority to civil rights. And President Johnson most definitely considered Vietnam—and foreign affairs altogether—a posteriority when he came to power. (This, in large measure, explains the violent reaction against him on the part of the liberals who had supported his original priority choice of the War on Poverty, when events forced him to change his priority schedule.)

Setting a posteriority is also unpleasant. Every posteriority is somebody else's top priority. It is much easier to draw up a nice list of top priorities and then to hedge by trying to do "just a little bit" of everything else as well. This makes everybody happy. The only drawback is, of course, that nothing whatever gets done.

A great deal could be said about the analysis of priorities. The most important thing about priorities and posteriorities is, however, not intelligent analysis but courage.

Courage rather than analysis dictates the truly important rules for identifying priorities:

- Pick the future as against the past;
- Focus on opportunity rather than on problem;
- Choose your own direction—rather than climb on the bandwagon; and
- Aim high, aim for something that will make a difference, rather than for something that is "safe" and easy to do.

A good many studies of research scientists have shown that achievement (at least below the genius level of an Einstein, a

Niels Bohr, or a Max Planck) depends less on ability in doing research than on the courage to go after opportunity. Those research scientists who pick their projects according to the greatest likelihood of quick success rather than according to the challenge of the problem are unlikely to achieve distinction. They may turn out a great many footnotes, but neither a law of physics nor a new concept is likely to be named after them. Achievement goes to the people who pick their research priorities by the opportunity and who consider other criteria only as qualifiers rather than as determinants.

Similarly, in business the successful companies are not those that work at developing new products for their existing line but those that aim at innovating new technologies or new businesses. As a rule it is just as risky, just as arduous, and just as uncertain to do something small that is new as it is to do something big that is new. It is more productive to convert an opportunity into results than to solve a problem—which only restores the equilibrium of yesterday.

■ Priorities and posteriorities always have to be reconsidered and revised in the light of realities No American president, for instance, has been allowed by events to stick to his original list of priority tasks. In fact accomplishing one's priority tasks always changes the priorities and posteriorities themselves.

The effective executive does not, in other words, truly commit himself beyond the *one* task he concentrates on right now. Then he reviews the situation and picks the next one task that now comes first.

Concentration—that is, the courage to impose on time and events his own decision as to what really matters and comes first—is the executive's only hope of becoming the master of time and events instead of their whipping boy.

6: The Elements of Decision-making

Decision-making is only one of the tasks of an executive. It usually takes but a small fraction of his time. But to make decisions is the *specific* executive task. Decision-making therefore deserves special treatment in a discussion of the effective executive.

Only executives make decisions. Indeed, to be expected—by virtue of position or knowledge—to make decisions that have significant impact on the entire organization, its performance, and results defines the executive.

Effective executives, therefore, make effective decisions.

They make these decisions as a systematic process with clearly defined elements and in a distinct sequence of steps. But this process bears amazingly little resemblance to what so many books today present as "decision-making."

Effective executives do not make a great many decisions. They concentrate on the important ones. They try to think through what is strategic and generic, rather than "solve problems." They try to make the few important decisions on the highest level of conceptual understanding. They try to find

637

the constants in a situation. They are, therefore, not overly impressed by speed in decision-making. Rather they consider virtuosity in manipulating a great many variables a symptom of sloppy thinking. They want to know what the decision is all about and what the underlying realities are which it has to satisfy. They want impact rather than technique, they want to be sound rather than clever.

Effective executives know when a decision has to be based on principle and when it should be made on the merits of the case and pragmatically. They know that the trickiest decision is that between the right and the wrong compromise and have learned to tell one from the other. They know that the most time-consuming step in the process is not making the decision but putting it into effect. Unless a decision has "degenerated into work" it is not a decision; it is at best a good intention. This means that, while the effective decision itself is based on the highest level of conceptual understanding, the action to carry it out should be as close as possible to the working level and as simple as possible.

Two Case Studies in Decision-making

The least-known of the great American business builders, Theodore Vail, was perhaps the most effective decision-maker in U.S. business history. As president of the Bell Telephone System from just before 1910 till the mid-twenties, Vail built the organization into the largest private business in the world and into one of the most prosperous growth companies.

That the telephone system is privately owned is taken for granted in the United States. But the part of the North American continent that the Bell System serves (the United States and the two most populous Canadian provinces, Quebec and Ontario) is the only developed area in the world in which telecommunications are not owned by government. The Bell System is also the only public utility that has shown itself capable of